Contemporary Sport Management

Second Edition

Janet B. Parks, DA

Bowling Green State University, Ohio

Jerome Quarterman, PhD

Florida State University, Tallahassee

Editors

Human Kinetics

Library of Congress Cataloging-in-Publication Data

Contemporary sport management / Janet B. Parks and Jerome Quarterman
editors.--2nd ed.
    p. cm.
Includes bibliographical references and index.
  ISBN 0-7360-4243-1 (Hard cover)
 1. Sports administration. 2. Physical education and
training--Administration. I. Parks, Janet B., 1942- II. Quarterman,
Jerome, 1944-
  GV713 .C66 2002
  796'.06'9--dc21

2002012905

ISBN: 0-7360-4243-1

Acquisitions Editor: Amy N. Clocksin; **Developmental Editors:** Elaine H. Mustain and Renee Thomas Pyrtel; **Assistant Editors:** Maggie Schwarzentraub and Amanda Ewing; **Copyeditor:** Patsy Fortney; **Proofreader:** Erin Cler; **Indexer:** Marie Rizzo; **Permission Manager:** Dalene Reeder; **Graphic Designer:** Nancy Rasmus; **Graphic Artist:** Kathleen Boudreau-Fuoss; **Photo Manager:** Leslie A. Woodrum; **Cover Designer:** Jack W. Davis; **Art Manager:** Kelly Hendren; **Illustrator:** Mic Greenberg; **Printer:** Phoenix

Printed in the United States of America   10 9 8 7 6 5 4 3

Human Kinetics
Web site: www.HumanKinetics.com

United States: Human Kinetics, P.O. Box 5076, Champaign, IL 61825-5076
800-747-4457
e-mail: humank@hkusa.com

Canada: Human Kinetics, 475 Devonshire Road, Unit 100, Windsor, ON N8Y 2L5
800-465-7301 (in Canada only)
e-mail: orders@hkcanada.com

Europe: Human Kinetics, 107 Bradford Road, Stanningley
Leeds LS28 6AT, United Kingdom
+44 (0) 113 255 5665
e-mail: hk@hkeurope.com

Australia: Human Kinetics, 57A Price Avenue, Lower Mitcham, South Australia 5062
08 8277 1555
e-mail: liaw@hkaustralia.com

New Zealand: Human Kinetics, Division of Sports Distributors NZ Ltd.
P.O. Box 300 226 Albany, North Shore City, Auckland
0064 9 448 1207
e-mail: blairc@hknewz.com

We gratefully dedicate the second edition
of *Contemporary Sport Management*
to the 29 contributing authors
who gave so unselfishly of their time and expertise
to make the book a reality!
To paraphrase the famous boxer, Muhammad Ali,
"*You* are the greatest!!"

Contents _____

PART I

Introduction to Sport Management

PART IV

Selected Functional Areas
of Sport Management

Contents

PART V

The Future of Sport Management

Preface: A Letter to Students _____

Contemporary Sport Management was created to introduce students to the academic and professional field of sport management. Toward that end, the book provides an overview of sport management rather than detailed instructions about how to manage sport enterprises. The distinction is important because the book must meet the needs of two types of students: those who have already decided to major in sport management as well as those who are still thinking about their choice of a major. Those of you who are currently majoring in sport management probably anticipate learning more about the field, particularly about the variety of professional opportunities that await you. Those of you who are only contemplating a major in sport management probably want to gain general knowledge about the field before making a final decision. After studying the information in this book, some of you will be even more intrigued with the idea of seeking a career in sport management, and you will pursue the remainder of your curriculum with enhanced understanding, insight, and maturity of purpose. On the other hand, others of you will discover that sport management isn't really your "cup of tea," and you will choose a different major. In either case, the book will have served a valuable purpose.

Contemporary Sport Management contains 20 chapters written by us and 29 other authors. We invited the 29 contributing authors to participate in this project not only because they are experts in their fields, but also because they are committed to sharing their knowledge with the next generation of sport managers. We believe that you will find these authors exceptionally credible and will enjoy learning from them. The authors' photographs and brief biographies are included at the back of the book. We are hopeful that seeing their faces and reading about their accomplishments will personalize the material in the chapters and will make the book more meaningful for you. We *know* you will be impressed with the authors' experience and depth of knowledge!

Scope and Organization of the Book

This edition of *Contemporary Sport Management* addresses nine of the ten content areas considered by the NASPE-NASSM Sport Management Program Review Council to be essential to the professional preparation of sport managers. These content areas include sociocultural dimensions of sport (e.g., gender, race, and disability; aggression, violence, and deviance in sport), management and leadership in sport, ethics in sport management, sport marketing, communication in sport, budget and finance in sport, legal aspects of sport, sport economics, and governance in sport. The book will provide *basic* information in these content areas; as you progress through the professional preparation curriculum at your college or university, you will study each of them in much more depth.

The chapters are organized into five separate parts of the book: Introduction to Sport Management, Social and Behavioral Foundations of Sport Management, Organizational and Managerial Foundations of Sport Management, Selected Functional Areas of Sport Management, and The Future of Sport Management. Each part begins with a brief description of its purpose, the types of information you can expect to find in the chapters it encompasses, and a "For More Information" section that identifies additional resources. After studying all of the chapters, completing selected learning activities within the chapters, and taking advantage of the "For More Information" sections, you should be able to (1) define sport management and discuss the nature and scope of opportunities the sport industry presents; (2) explain the importance of a professional perspective; (3) exhibit critical professional skills and attitudes; (4) critically evaluate major challenges confronting various segments of the industry; (5) explain the relevance of ethical, legal, historical, sociological, and psychological concepts to the management of sport; (6) demonstrate an understanding of theories associated with management, leadership, and organizational behavior and how these theories are applied in sport enterprises; (7) demonstrate an appreciation of diversity through the use of unbiased language and an inclusive approach to human relations; (8) identify research questions in sport management and demonstrate the ability to analyze and interpret published research; and (9) become a member of the profession who will have a positive impact on the way sport is managed in the future.

Features of the Book

This is the second edition of *Contemporary Sport Management*. We are pleased that so many students, faculty, and sport practitioners found the first edition helpful, and we hope the new, improved version will serve your needs even better. In order to stay current with the curricular needs of contemporary students, several new chapters have been added to this edition: Historical Sketches: The Development of the Sport Business Industry; Thinking Critically About Sport Management; Legal and Ethical Considerations in Sport Management; Psychology of Sport Consumer Behavior; Public Relations in the Sport Industry; Finance, Economics, and Budgeting in the Sport Industry; Questions, Answers, and Sport Management Research; and Understanding Sport Management Research. Of course, the addition of these chapters necessitated the deletion of other chapters, but we believe the benefits of these additions outweigh the disadvantage of having to delete the others.

Following are some other key features of *Contemporary Sport Management*:

• Each chapter reflects the inclusion of diverse populations, that is, people of different ages, genders, abilities, social classes, sexual orientations, races, ethnicities, and cultures. There are no separate chapters dedicated to select groups such as "opportunities for women," or "sport for the disabled," or "the Black athlete." We hope the inclusive nature of the text fosters a better understanding and appreciation of the wide variety of consumers that exist in the sport industry.

• The language used in the book is called "gender inclusive" language. For example, athletics teams are referred to specifically as either men's teams or women's teams, a practice that acknowledges the existence of teams for both genders. The terms *fair play* and *sporting behavior* are used in place of *sportsmanship* because the inclusive terms avoid the subtle suggestion that sport is reserved for males. This use of unbiased language is a conscious attempt to reflect and embrace the diversity that is celebrated in many other ways throughout the book.

• Although each chapter of the book addresses a particular aspect of sport management, many of the chapters share important similarities. For example, most of the chapters about careers in sport management include lists of publications, governing bodies, and professional associations. Several chapters refer to the economic impact of sport, developments in the international arena, and predictions for the future. Ethical, legal, and communication concerns are also addressed in several chapters. By including these topics in several chapters, we hope to reinforce important concepts that you will find useful as you progress in your professional preparation program.

• Each of the 20 chapters begins with learning objectives. These objectives serve as an outline for reading and studying the chapter.

• Each chapter has several learning activities that provide opportunities to "practice" with the material presented in the text. We included a wide variety of exercises throughout the book in an effort to accommodate students' different learning styles and preferences.

• The review questions at the end of each chapter are linked to the objectives at the beginning of the chapter. These questions reinforce the chapter's key points.

• Each chapter contains a reference list. Additionally, at the beginning of each of the five parts of the book you will find a "For More Information" section that provides suggestions for further reading or exploration. Both types of lists are valuable.

• Some chapters contain real-life scenarios, case studies, profiles of sport managers, or news stories that illustrate a point. We hope these features contribute to the user-friendliness of the book.

• As you would expect in a modern textbook, *Contemporary Sport Management* provides a multitude of Web sites. These sites enable you to capitalize on the vast amount of information available online. They also enable you to pursue your interests at times and locations that are most convenient for you.

Acknowledgments

Anyone who has attempted a project such as this knows that it could not have been done without the assistance of many people. We are, therefore, eager to acknowledge the individuals and groups whose collective contributions made this book a reality.

First and foremost, we express our sincere gratitude to the 29 contributing authors who wrote most of the chapters in the book. As we note in the dedication, we think you are the greatest! We are certain that the quality of the book is due to your willingness to share your energy and expertise, and we genuinely appreciate your generosity.

We owe much of the success of this project to the remarkable talent and efforts of the Human Kinetics team of editors. Amy Clocksin, our acquisitions editor, provided valuable advice and assistance as we conceptualized this edition. Without Amy's expertise, energy, and patience, the project would not have gotten off the ground, nor would it have advanced as rapidly as it did. Renee Thomas Pyrtel and Elaine Mustain, our developmental editors, and Maggie Schwarzentraub, assistant editor, actually put the book together. Dalene Reeder helped us through the process of obtaining permissions. These women made our jobs so much easier by always being there with valuable information, assistance, and direction. To Amy, Renee, Elaine, Maggie, Dalene, and all the other personnel at Human Kinetics who were associated with this project—thank you so much for a great collaborative effort!

We sincerely appreciate the valuable contributions of Beverly R.K. Zanger, our coeditor on the first edition of *Contemporary Sport Management*. Beverly has retired to Hawaii and wasn't able to join us in this venture. Even so, her ideas and perspectives continue to inform many chapters of this edition.

We are grateful to Bowling Green State University and the School of Human Movement, Sport, and Leisure Studies and to Florida State University and the Department of Sport Management, Recreation Management, and Physical Education for providing the resources that facilitated the completion of this book. We believe we are privileged to be university professors and most fortunate to work in environments that support our efforts.

Under the guidance of their instructors, Trinity Lescallett and Ted Peetz, undergraduate students in the Introduction to Sport Management course at Bowling Green State University provided us with critiques of the 1998 edition. We took these students' critiques quite seriously, and we believe their ideas, as well as Ted's and Trinity's, contributed to improvements in this edition. Thanks to all of you for sharing your perspectives with us!

We gratefully acknowledge the valuable contributions that Artemis Apostolopoulou of Bowling Green State University made to chapter 8. We also thank Beth Klocke Fox, a BGSU graduate student, for providing the arguments from the angry parents in chapter 4.

We are indebted to the anonymous reviewers of the 1998 edition for giving us many valuable ideas for improving this edition. The results of your efforts can be seen throughout the book.

We are grateful to Eric Forsyth of Bemidji State University for creating the *Instructors Guide* that accompanies the book. We know that faculty will find Dr. Forsyth's manual to be of top quality and quite useful.

As always, we extend sincere gratitude to the hundreds of students we have been privileged to teach. You inspired this project, and you motivated us to see it through. You have always been the *raison d'être* for *Contemporary Sport Management*. We thank you!

Janet B. Parks
Bowling Green State University

Jerome Quarterman
Florida State University

PART I

Introduction to Sport Management

The four chapters in the first section of this book present basic information and key concepts that form the foundation of professional preparation for *all* careers in sport management. These chapters take you through an overview of the field in general, an examination of professional considerations vital to success in the sport industry, a discussion of the history of the sport industry in the United States, and an exploration of critical thinking skills and applications. The understandings you gain from these chapters will be useful as you study the remaining chapters in the book.

In Chapter 1, Janet Parks and Jerome Quarterman introduce sport management as an academic major and a career field. After discussing several definitions of sport, the authors delineate settings in which sport occurs, examples of traditional and nontraditional sport, and different ways of segmenting the sport industry. Parks and Quarterman then discuss several characteristics of sport-related enterprises that distinguish them from other business pursuits, examine two models of organizational design, and describe competencies that will be essential for success in sport management. The chapter concludes with a discussion of personal and professional qualities expected of sport managers as well as opportunities and challenges facing sport managers of the future.

Chapter 2 contains information that will help you develop a professional perspective on your studies and your career. First, Kathryn Hoff, JoAnn Kroll, and Janet Parks provide a preview of the courses and experiences you can expect in the professional preparation program at your college or university. Next, they discuss four essential elements of a positive professional perspective—attitude, image, work transition and adjustment, and business etiquette. The final component of professional perspective is professional develop-

ment, a process that begins during your college years and continues throughout your career. The authors close the chapter with special attention to career planning and management and offer sound advice related to finding a career that is compatible with your values, interests, and skills.

Larry Fielding and Brenda Pitts delineate the history of the U.S. sport industry in chapter 3. Beginning with the 1876 opening of the A.G. Spalding sporting goods store, the authors take us from the 1870s through the 1890s, decades that were characterized variously by the commercialization of baseball, horse racing, sporting goods, and intercollegiate sport, as well as the advent of intense market competition in the sport business industry. With the 1900s came the concept of market development and segmentation, endorsement advertising, and even more intense competition, followed by a more cooperative spirit in the 1930s. Among the significant features that developed between the 1940s and the present day were the professionalization of sport, technological advances, the fitness craze, and a global expansion of sport businesses. Throughout these historical sketches, Fielding and Pitts link events of yesteryear to current events, pointing out both similarities and differences. The underlying message is clear: An understanding of the history of sport is critical because managers who know and appreciate events of the past are more likely to understand the present and more qualified to plan for the future.

The purpose of chapter 4 is to provide strategies whereby you can learn to appreciate the importance of critical thinking and apply critical thinking skills to issues in sport management. Stuart Keeley and Janet Parks present examples of contemporary issues in sport and explain why sport managers need to make principle-based decisions about these issues rather than basing their decisions on expediency. The authors then discuss the differences between learning *what* to think and learning *how* to think, describe the dispositions of critical thinkers, and incorporate the importance of values and perspective in determining personal beliefs about concerns related to sport. Keeley and Parks define eight critical thinking questions and show how they can be used in resolving a specific issue. Exercises in the chapter are designed to give you opportunities to practice critical thinking skills. Sport managers who possess the dispositions of critical thinkers and can think critically about sport-related issues will become competent, reflective professionals with the potential to become influential agents of change.

FOR MORE INFORMATION

Professional and Scholarly Associations

- Asian Association for Sport Management
- European Association for Sport Management (EASM)
- International Sport Management Alliance
- Japanese Society of Management for Physical Education and Sports
- Korean Society for Sport Management
- Sport Management Council/National Association for Sport and Physical Education (NASPE)/American Alliance for Health, Physical Education, Recreation and Dance (AAHPERD)
- North American Society for Sport History (NASSH)
- North American Society for Sport Management (NASSM)
- Sport Management Association of Australia and New Zealand (SMAANZ)

Professional and Scholarly Publications

- *Canadian Journal of Sport History*
- *Journal of Sport & Social Issues*
- *Journal of Sport History*
- *Journal of Sport Management*
- *Sociology of Sport Journal*
- *Sport History Review*

Sport Management Information

- NASSM Home Page—www.NASSM.org
- Sporting Goods Manufacturers Association International: www.sgma.com/index.html
- Sport Management Academic Programs: www.aahperd.org/NASPE/programs-smprc_list.html
- Sport Management Related Information: www.unb.ca/SportManagement/links.htm
- Global Sport Management News: www.raider.muc.edu/pe/global.html

Critical Thinking Resources

- Foundation for Critical Thinking: criticalthinking.org/
- Henderson, J.R. (2002). *ICYouSee: T is for thinking: A guide to critical thinking about what you see on the Web.* www.ithaca.edu/library/Training/hott.html
- The Reason Group. (2001). *Reason!Able: Enabling better reasoning.* www.goreason.com/
- Chaffee, J. (1998). *The thinker's way: 8 steps to a richer life.* Boston: Little, Brown.
- Damer, T.E. (2001). *Attacking faulty reasoning* (4th ed.). Belmont, CA: Wadsworth/Thomson Learning.

Sport Management Book Club Selections

- Cohen, G.L. (Ed.). (2001). *Women in sport: Issues and controversies* (2nd ed.). Oxon Hill, MD: NASPE.
- Eitzen, D.S. (1999). *Fair and foul: Beyond the myths and paradoxes of sport.* New York: Rowman and Littlefield.
- King, C.R., & Springwood, C.F. (Eds.). (2001). *Team spirits: The Native American mascots controversy.* Lincoln: University of Nebraska Press.
- Miracle, A.W., Jr., & Reese, R. (1994). *Lessons of the locker room.* New York: Prometheus Books.
- Putnam, D. (1999). *Controversies of the sports world.* Westport, CT: Greenwood Press.
- Sack, A.L., & Staurowsky, E.J. (1998). *College athletes for hire: The evolution and legacy of the NCAA's amateur myth.* Westport, CT: Praeger.

- Sperber, M. (2000). *Beer and circus: How big-time college sports is crippling undergraduate education.* New York: Holt.
- Yiannakis, A., & Melnick, M. (2001). *Contemporary issues in sociology of sport.* Champaign, IL: Human Kinetics.

The Sport Management Job Market

- www.athleticbusiness.com
- www.canada.com/sports/
- www.onlinesports.com/pages/CareerCenter.html
- www.jobsinsports.com/
- www.sportscareers.com/cbs/

- www.jobscircuit.co.uk/
- espn.go.com/special/careers/
- teamjobs.com/
- www.ucalgary.ca/library/ssportsite/
- www.sportsworkers.com/
- www.quintcareers.com/sports_jobs.html
- www.geocities.com/eureka/3638/jobs.html
- www.onlinesports.com/pages/Jobs.html
- www.womensportsjobs.com/
- www.teamworkonline.com/
- www.nassm.com/
- www.aahperd.org

Chapter 1

Sport Management: An Overview

Janet B. Parks, Bowling Green State University
Jerome Quarterman, Florida State University

In 1957 Walter O'Malley, president and chief stockholder of the Brooklyn [now Los Angeles] Dodgers Baseball Club, anticipated the future growth of organized sport and predicted the need for professionally prepared sport administrators. O'Malley wrote a letter to Dr. James Mason, a faculty member at Ohio University, stating the following:

> *I ask the question, where would one go to find a person who by virtue of education had been trained to administer a marina, race track, ski resort, auditorium, stadium, theater, convention or exhibition hall, a public camp complex, or a person to fill an executive position at a team or league level in junior athletics such as Little League baseball, football, scouting, CYO, and youth activities, etc. . . . A course that would enable a graduate to read architectural and engineering plans; or having to do with specifications and contract letting, the functions of a purchasing agent in plant operations. There would be the problems of ticket selling and accounting, concessions, sale of advertising in programs, and publications, outdoor and indoor displays and related items. . . . (Mason, Higgins, & Wilkinson, 1981, p. 44)*

As a result of that inquiry, Mason and several of his colleagues created a master's-level sport administration program at Ohio University (OU). Inaugurated in 1966, the OU program was the first recorded university-sponsored attempt to provide a graduate-level curriculum specifically designed to prepare students for jobs in a variety of sport-related industries. The idea caught on, and by the early 2000s, there were more than 200 graduate and undergraduate sport management programs in the United States and Canada (Alsop

&Fuller, 2001). Today thousands of students around the world are studying sport management, preparing to be the next generation of leaders in this exciting and fulfilling career field.

This chapter represents the first step on *your* journey toward becoming a sport manager. We hope it will provide you with valuable information, setting the stage for you to study subsequent chapters with greater insight. We have included definitions of basic terms, a discussion of the nature and scope of sport management, and explanations of unique aspects of sport management enterprises and careers. You will also learn about many of the tasks for which sport managers are responsible, personal and professional qualities successful sport managers possess, and some of the challenges and opportunities that await you as a professional sport manager.

LEARNING ACTIVITY

Visit the Web site of the North American Society for Sport Management (www.nassm.org/universities.htm). How many different countries offer sport management programs? How many programs exist in North America? Go to the Web sites of different universities and investigate their sport management curricula.

Nothing New Under the Sun

Lest we be deluded by the notion that contemporary sport management is markedly different from the ancient art of staging athletic spectacles, let us consider for a moment the following description of the games sponsored in 11 B.C. by Herod the Great, king of Judea and honorary president of the Olympics:

> The games began with a magnificent dedication ceremony. Then there were athletic and musical competitions, in which large prizes were given not only to the winners but also—an unusual feature—to those who took second and third place. Bloody spectacles were also presented, with gladiators and wild beasts fighting in various combinations, and there were also horse races. Large prizes attracted contenders from all areas and this in turn drew great numbers of spectators. Cities favored by Herod sent delegations, and these he entertained and lodged at his own expense. What comes through most clearly . . . is that gigantic sums of money were spent. (Frank, 1984, p. 158)

The success of such an extravaganza relied in all likelihood on the organizational skills of the individuals charged with planning and executing the games. Certainly there was today's equivalent of a general manager, or CEO, to whom all other personnel were responsible. Additionally, assistants who were knowledgeable in economics, accounting, and finance were indispensable if the event was to become profitable. The "business managers" were responsible for obtaining financial support, purchasing equipment (and perhaps even the requisite beasts), furnishing entertainment and lodging for the VIPs, and generally being accountable for the large sums of money that were spent. Once the financial dimension was secured, there was the challenge of attracting sufficient numbers of contestants and spectators to the games. Enter Herod's "marketing director" armed with unique and unprecedented gimmicks to assure a full complement of participants as well as a full house of onlookers. A new prize structure was devised and, in awarding prizes to musicians as well as athletes, the seeds were sown for the modern spectacle known, among other titles, as the Battle of the Bands.

The marketing directors must have enlisted the aid of assistants who were responsible for extending invitations, publicizing the games, and keeping records of the day's activities. In the years prior to the printing press, much less the electronic media, informing the public was no small task—to say nothing of offering enticements sufficient to persuade them to journey for days and endure what must have been extremely undesirable traveling conditions. The marketing and promotions people certainly had their hands full!

The parallel could continue—there was a need for crowd control, rules decisions, award ceremonies, and so forth. After all, certain tasks must be performed regardless of the venue in which the event occurs. Now, 2000 years later, we are reminded once again of Solomon's wisdom in proclaiming in Ecclesiastes 1:9 that "there is no new thing under the sun."

Reprinted, by permission, from J.B. Parks and G.A. Olafson, 1987, "Sport management and a new journal," *Journal of Sport Management* 1(1).

Getting the public's attention is easier today.

Defining Sport and Sport Management

At the outset, it might seem unnecessary to define *sport* because most people already know through experience and intuition what the word means. For most of us, sport implies having fun, but it can also be work (for a professional athlete), a means of employment (for a sport tourism director), or a business (for a sport marketing agency). Sport takes many forms. It might include many participants, as in team sports such as soccer and volleyball; two participants, as in dual sports such as tennis and badminton; or one person, as in individual sports such as golf and surfing. Sport includes a combination of these configurations when it involves team competitions, tournaments, or matches in dual sports (wrestling) or individual sports (in-line skating). What criteria qualify games or activities to be classified as sport? Is horse racing a sport? What about cycling, water skiing, pocket billiards, or chess and other table games? We know that football, basketball, ice and field hockey, tennis, golf, baseball, and softball are sports. Are they different from sailing, dog racing, marathoning, and scuba diving? If so, how are they different? If not, how are they similar?

Loy's (1968) classic definition claims that sport must have five characteristics. It must

1. be playlike in nature;
2. involve some element of competition;
3. be based on physical prowess;
4. involve elements of skill, strategy, and chance; and
5. have an uncertain outcome.

Snyder and Spreitzer (1989) defined sport as competitive human physical activity that is governed by institutional rules. VanderZwaag (1998) was more definitive: "Sport is a competitive physical activity, utilizing specialized equipment and facilities, with unique dimensions of time and space, in which the quest for records is of high significance" (p. 3). Coakley (2001) suggested that ". . . *sports are institutionalized competitive activities that involve rigorous physical exertion or the use of relatively complex physical skills by participants motivated by personal enjoyment and external rewards.*" (p. 20 [italics in original]).

Pitts, Fielding, and Miller (1994) provided the broadest definition of sport by stating that sport is any activity, experience, or business enterprise focused on fitness, recreation, athletics, or leisure. In their view, sport does not have to be competitive, nor does it always require specialized equipment or rules; in fact, sport includes activities such as working out, running, and dancing. In an effort to be as inclusive as possible, we will use

7

Pitts, Fielding, and Miller's definition of sport in this book—as a term that includes an expansive variety of physical activities and associated business endeavors.

Many of the individuals employed in business endeavors associated with sport are engaged in a career field known as *sport management*. DeSensi, Kelley, Blanton, and Beitel (1990) defined sport management as "any combination of skills related to planning, organizing, directing, controlling, budgeting, leading, and evaluating within the context of an organization or department whose primary product or service is related to sport and/or physical activity" (p. 33). Again, this is a broad definition that includes a wide variety of sport-related careers. Many chapters in this book are devoted to providing you with a greater understanding of the myriad opportunities that await you as a sport manager.

Sport management is also the name given to many university-level academic programs designed to prepare students to assume positions in the sport industry. These programs provide two additional sources of confusion regarding vocabulary. First, you might have noticed that many professional preparation programs are titled *sport* management whereas others are called *sports* management. In our view, people prefer one or the other based on their connotations of the words *sports* and *sport*. To many academics, ourselves included, *sports* implies a collection of separate activities such as golf, soccer, hockey, volleyball, softball, and gymnastics—items in a series that we can count. On the other hand, *sport* is an all-encompassing concept. It is a collective noun that includes all sporting activities, not just those that we can place on a list. We have found that students in our classes relate well to the parallel with the different connotations of the words *religions* and *religion*. The word *religions* typically connotes several specific faiths or belief systems—different denominations or sects that we can quantify. *Religion*, on the other hand, is a broad term that we can interpret as a general reverence or faith held by any number of people and churches.

A second source of confusion is the fact that many professional preparation programs are titled *sport(s) management*, and others are called *sport(s) administration*. In the past, there seemed to be a clear distinction between administration and management, with administrators working primarily in the public sector and managers working in the private sector. Currently, however, the line between administration and management has become blurred, making it counterproductive to debate which term is more appropriate. You will find excellent academic programs by either name. The quality of the curriculum is more important than the title of the program.

Nature and Scope of the Sport Industry

Just as there are several definitions of sport, there are also many ways to conceptualize the nature and scope of the sport industry. One approach involves looking at the many different *settings* in which sporting activities occur. This approach provides ideas about where to look for sites in which sport managers might be needed. VanderZwaag (1998, pp. 4-6) identified 16 settings within the sport enterprise:

School and college sports programs

Professional sport

Amateur sport organizations (e.g., Olympic committees)

Private club sport

Other commercialized sport establishments (e.g., bowling alleys, ski resorts, and public golf courses)

Arenas, coliseums, civic centers, and stadia

Community recreation sport programs

Industrial sport programs

Sport programs in social agencies (YWCA, YMCA, JCC)

Military sport programs

Sport marketing and consulting firms

Developmental programs for sport (e.g., Women's Sport Foundation, National Golf Foundation)

Corporate sponsors (e.g., LPGA Jamie Farr Kroger Classic, Volvo International Tennis Tournament)

The sporting goods industry

The sport news media (e.g., print and broadcast)

Academic programs in sport management

Another way to look at the sport industry is to examine the many different *types* of sporting activities that exist. An awareness of the wide diversity of sporting opportunities available to consumers is essential for anyone who anticipates becoming a decision maker in the world of sport. Sport marketers, in particular, must have a good understanding of both traditional and new sports so they can develop effective promotional strategies.

You are already familiar with traditional sports such as basketball, tennis, golf, football, swimming, and soccer. You might also know that in recent years, numerous new sports and physical activities have emerged. For example, Pitts and Stotlar (2002) identified the following "new" activities and sports that have appeared on the scene in the past 10 to 15 years: several varieties of aerobics, in-line skating (Rollerblading), boogie boarding, snow kayaking, parasailing, ice surfing, beach volleyball, skydive dancing, ice climbing, X-Games, and indoor soccer. Pitts and Stotlar also noted that among the other factors affecting the world of sport consumption are the increasing numbers of opportunities to engage in traditional sports and activities, an upsurge in the numbers and variety of sport-related magazines and sport-related sites on the Internet, enhanced mass media exposure of sporting activities, growth in the numbers and types of sport facilities and events, an increased interest in sport tourism and adventure travel, and the provision of sport-related goods and services for a greater variety of market segments. Moreover, new professional sports have emerged, sport opportunities are being offered to a more diverse population, endorsements and sponsorship are on the rise, sport industry education is becoming more prevalent and sophisticated, marketing and promotion orientation

is growing in the sport industry, sport managers are becoming more competent, and the globalization of the sport industry is progressing rapidly (Pitts & Stotlar, 2002).

LEARNING ACTIVITY

Investigate sport management opportunities in countries other than your own. What qualifications are required for you to be able to take advantage of these opportunities? Information in chapter 17, Sport Tourism, and chapter 18, International Sport, will be helpful to you.

A third approach to defining the nature and scope of the sport industry is to create industry models that show the interrelationships among various *segments* of the sport industries. We will present three of these models, each of which represents a different approach to conceptualizing the sport industry. All three models are useful in showing you interesting and different ways to look at the world of sport.

Product Type Model. Pitts, Fielding, and Miller (1994) developed a segmentation model of the sport industry based on the types of *products* sold or promoted by the businesses/organizations within them. These authors suggested that the industry segmentation approach is especially useful to sport *marketers*, who are typically responsible for formulating competitive strategies. Sport marketers can use their understanding of the sport product segments as they make decisions such as choosing the segments in which they wish to

The Prosperous '90s!

In 1990 sport was a $63.1 billion-a-year business, ranking 22nd among 400 plus industries in the United States (Comte & Stogel, 1990). This figure was predicted to increase to $121 billion a year by 2000 (Rosner, 1989), but its growth exceeded this expectation. Meek (1997) estimated the size of the 1995 sport industry as $152 billion, while generating an additional $259 billion in associated economic activity. In 1999 Broughton, Lee, and Nethery estimated the Gross National Sport Product (GNSP) to be $213 billion. Regardless of the measurements used, one fact is crystal clear: Sport was a booming business in the 1990s!

Will the Boom Continue?

Mahony and Howard (2001) predicted that the sport boom of the 1990s had ended. According to these analysts, successful sport managers of the future will need a higher level of sophistication than currently exists as they adopt Internet marketing and other technologies, focus on "big" competitions and stars, invent new markets, improve efforts to reach target markets, reestablish relationships with traditional consumers, employ creative financing, cut budgets, and promote efficiency.

compete, selecting the types of marketing strategies to use, and determining whether to create new industry segments.

Pitts, Fielding, and Miller (1994) proposed three product segments of the sport industry: (1) sport performance, (2) sport production, and (3) sport promotion. As shown in figure 1.1, the sport *performance* segment includes such varied products as school-sponsored athletics, fitness clubs, sport camps, professional sport, and municipal parks sport programs. Examples of products in the sport *production* segment are basketballs, fencing foils, jogging shoes, sports medicine clinics, swimming pools, and college athletics conferences. The sport *promotion* segment includes products such as T-shirts, giveaways, print and broadcast media, and celebrity endorsements. Sport marketers can use this product type model to plan marketing strategies, something you will learn more about in chapter 10. In chapter 3, Fielding and Pitts discuss the history of the sport industry in terms of these three industry segments.

Economic Impact Model. Meek (1997) took another approach to describing the sport industry. First, he proposed that the industry can be defined by describing three primary sectors:

1. *Sport entertainment and recreation such as events, teams, and individual participants; sports and related recreational activities; and [associated] spending (A. Meek, personal communication, Nov. 8, 2002)*

2. *Sport products and services such as design, testing, manufacturing, and distribution of equipment, clothing, and instruments*

3. *Sport support organizations such as leagues, law firms, and marketing organizations (p. 16)*

The three sectors of Meek's (1997) model are presented in figure 1.2. Meek proposed that his broad definition of sport enabled an analysis of the economic activity of the teams and businesses within each sector and also the economic activity *associated* with sport. **Associated economic activ-**

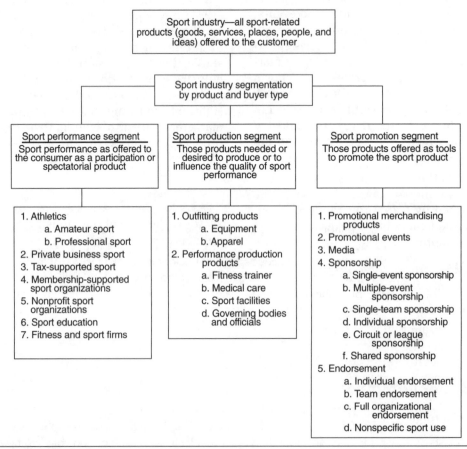

Figure 1.1 The sport industry segment model.

Reprinted, by permission, from B.G. Pitts, L.W. Fielding, and L.K. Miller, 1994, "Industry segmentation theory and the sport industry. Developing a sport industry segment model," *Sport Marketing Quarterly*, 3 (Morgantown, WV: Fitness Information Technology, Inc.)

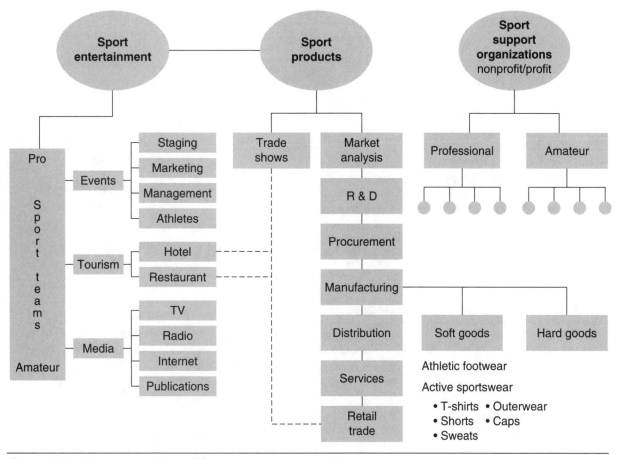

Figure 1.2 Economic impact model.

Reprinted, by permission, from A. Meek, 1997, "An estimate of the size and supported economic activity of the sports industry in the United States," *Sport Marketing Quarterly* 6(4):15-21. (Morgantown, WV: Fitness Information Technology, Inc.)

ity is the money spent by participants, spectators, and sponsors. Based on this model, Meek estimated the size of the 1995 sport industry at $152 billion, with an additional $259 billion in economic activity generated by sport. You will learn more about what these figures mean in terms of sport economics in chapter 12.

associated economic activity—Money spent by sport participants, spectators, and sponsors.

Sport Activity Model. Li, Hofacre, and Mahony (2001) proposed a model of the sport industry based on the single characteristic that differentiates sport industries from all other industries: *sport activities* (i.e., games and events). These authors proposed that the sport industry can be defined as

1. *the firms and organizations that produce sport activities,*
2. *the firms and organizations that provide products and services to support the production of sport activities, and*

3. *the firms and organizations that sell and trade products related to sport activities. (p. 6)*

As shown in figure 1.3, the sport-producing sector is the core of the industry. Six supporting subsectors surround and overlap with the activity-producing core. Organizations in these subsectors either (1) provide products and services to the core organizations or (2) sell or trade products related to sport. This model differs conceptually from the other two models in that it places sport at the center and illustrates the dependence of the subsectors on the production of sporting activities.

LEARNING ACTIVITY

Compare and contrast the three models of the sport industry, identifying specific organizations within each segment of each model.

Figure 1.3 The two-sector model of the sport industry.

Reprinted, by permission, from L. Hofacre and Mahony, 2001, An overview of the sport industry in North America. In *Economics of sport* (Morgantown, WV: Fitness Information Technology), 7.

LEARNING ACTIVITY _____

Go to one or more of the Web sites listed under "For More Information" on page 3. Make a list of the jobs you find at that site and classify them within the three sport industry segmentation models. Which jobs are most appealing to you?

Unique Aspects of Sport Management

Mullin (1980) provided insight into three unique aspects of sport management: sport marketing, sport enterprise financial structures, and sport industry career paths. These three aspects of sport management make sport different from other business enterprises and justify sport management as a distinct area of professional preparation. We would add a fourth unique aspect of sport to Mullin's list: the enormous power and influence of sport as a social institution.

Sport Marketing

Sport marketing is unique because the sport product is unlike other products purchased by consumers. For example, sport is consumed as quickly as it is produced. It is a perishable product that is not accompanied by any guarantees of customer satisfaction. Individuals providing the sport experience cannot predict the outcome due to the spontaneous nature of the activity, the inconsistency of events, and the uncertainty surrounding the results. Sport marketers, therefore, face unique challenges dictated by the nature of the enterprise. You will learn much more about sport marketing in chapter 10.

Sport Enterprise Financial Structures

Most sport businesses are financed differently from most other businesses. Typically, the sale of a product or service such as clothing, food, automobiles, or home cleaning finances the business. However, with the exception of sporting goods stores, sport enterprises earn a highly significant portion of revenue not from the sale of a service such as a game, workout, or 10K run, but from extraneous sources such as television rights, concessions, road game guarantees, parking, and merchandise. Intercollegiate athletics and municipal recreation sport programs might generate revenue from student or user fees, private donations, taxes, rentals, or licensing fees. Sport managers continually compete for the **discretionary funds** of consumers through the sale of items that may or may not be related to the apparent primary focus of the enterprise. One unique aspect of sport is that it invariably attracts consumers who spend more money outside the sporting arena than they spend on the sport itself (e.g., travel, entertainment, souvenirs, and equipment). This unique financial base requires different practices within the sport setting. Sport finance is discussed in more depth in chapter 12.

discretionary funds—Money left over after necessary expenditures (e.g., rent, food, car payment, insurance) have been made.

Sport Industry Career Paths

Career paths in sport management are not as well defined as those in other vocational areas. Traditionally, many sport management practitioners have been hired from visible groups, such as intercollegiate athletics or professional sport. An example of this phenomenon is the basketball star who becomes a basketball coach and eventually an athletics director. We can find similar career advancement patterns within municipal recreation programs, sport clubs, and professional sports teams. In some situations, sport is still a closed society in which obtaining employment might depend less on *what* the applicant knows than on *whom* the applicant knows (Clay, 1995). Additionally, the attitude that members of **underrepresented groups** do not have the requisite skills for sport management positions still exists in some organizations, and this attitude creates an obstacle for aspiring sport managers. Arthur Triche, public relations director for the Atlanta Hawks and the first African American public relations director in the NBA, credits volunteering and making contacts in the sport industry as important steps he took toward overcoming this obstacle (Clay, 1995). Most experts, both academicians and practicing sport managers, agree with Triche that volunteering and **networking** are critical to success in the sport industry.

underrepresented groups—People who traditionally have not been hired in sport management positions (e.g., women, people of color, people with disabilities).

networking—The building up or maintaining of informal relationships, especially with people who could bring advantages such as job or business opportunities (MSWord online dictionary).

LEARNING ACTIVITY

Find out what the graduates of your sport management program are doing now. Invite some of them back to speak to your class or your major student organization. Ask them how volunteering and networking affected their career development.

Growing evidence suggests that success in today's sporting enterprise depends on a good understanding of finance, marketing, and management. As a result, contemporary sport organizations are abandoning traditional employment practices and attitudes, such as hiring only those with experience as athletes or with specific enthusiasm for sport. The current level of economic competition within sport enterprises mandates that employers recognize and appreciate sound business expertise and that their hiring practices reflect these values. Jay Abraham, president of Sports Careers, states, "Companies are saying, 'What can you do for me? Can you sell? Can you do accounting?' They don't want people coming in saying, 'I want to work here because I've always liked football'" (Clay, 1995, p. 160).

In spite of some advances resulting from efforts to diversify the sport management workforce, we have a long way to go before we can claim that sport is truly an equal opportunity environment (Acosta & Carpenter, 2002; Lapchick & Matthews, 2001; Parks & Roberton, 2002; Schoenfeld, 1999). Opportunities for people of color and women continue to lag behind opportunities for white males, both in the core sport industry (e.g., pro sport senior executives, athletics directors, general managers) and in the support industries (e.g., broadcast media, sport agents, concessions). Someday soon, many of you who are currently preparing for careers as sport managers will be in positions of authority in which you can effect change in the **organizational culture** of the sport industry. If you pay careful attention to the value of having people of different ages, genders, abilities, social classes, sexual orientations, races, ethnicities, and cultures in decision-making positions, the world of sport and society at large will be well served by your efforts.

organizational culture—Workplace values, norms, and behaviors that produce patterns of behavior unique to an organization

Sport as a Social Institution

Sport is a distinctive social activity that is frequently the basis of an individual's social identity (McPherson, Curtis, & Loy, 1989). As such, it is a social institution of almost unbelievable magnitude and influence. What other social pursuit is allotted several pages in the daily newspaper, has its own slot on every television and radio news program, has its own cable channel, and creates what appears to be a national withdrawal crisis when members of its workforce go on strike? The sheer power of sport mandates that people who wish to manage it acquire a sound understanding of its historical, psychological, sociological, and philosophical dimensions. Understanding sport marketing and management is essential for prospective managers; equally important is understanding and appreciating the social and cultural implications of sporting activities. In describing the social power of sport, Parks and Roberton (2000) noted the following:

> The pervasive influence of sport on the values and attitudes of the general population demonstrates its power in American society. One example of this power is the adulation accorded many athletes, both amateur and professional, and the concomitant expectation that athletes should serve as positive role models for youth. The influence of athletes is also reflected in the sizable royalties paid for their endorsements of a multitude of products, ranging from long-distance telephone services to beer to sports bras. An additional example of the influence of sport is the amount of attention devoted to athletic contests and the sport industry by both print and broadcast media. (p. 422)

The power of sport mandates that sport managers understand social responsibility and the social implications of their actions. Contemporary sport enterprises and the larger society need well-prepared managers who have learned to make sound management decisions in the context of sport as a powerful social institution.

LEARNING ACTIVITY

In small groups, read and discuss one or more books about sport as a social and cultural phenomenon. Your instructor can direct you to books you will find interesting.

Sport Management Competencies

Bureaucratic processes and an emphasis on job specialization characterize contemporary sport organizations. In these organizations, job descriptions define the requirements of various positions, and individuals are hired to perform the jobs as described. Some scholars have predicted, however, that the organization of the future might be focused more on **competencies** of individual employees as well as the ability of those employees to learn new competencies as marketplace demands and organizational cultures change (Lawler & Ledford, 1997). With this approach, individuals would be hired "for organizational membership, not to fill a job" (p. 240), and the reward system within the organization would be based on how well employees demonstrated the required competencies. The competency approach to hiring and managing an organization will require you, as a prospective employee, to consciously develop the knowledge and skills that are valued by the organizations in your chosen field. Although the transition from the **bureaucratic model** to the competency-based model is not complete, you would be well advised to consider the competencies valued by contemporary sport organizations.

competencies—Skills and knowledge necessary for successful performance in the job.

bureaucratic model—An organizational design that stresses specialization, division of labor, hierarchy, formal rules, and standard operating procedures.

In an effort to discover competencies expected of sport organization employees, Quain and Parks (1986) conducted a survey of 368 sport managers. They asked these managers to identify competencies required in their fields and to describe specific duties and responsibilities associated with their jobs (Parks, Chopra, Quain, & Alguindigue, 1988). Quain and Parks then classified this information into the competency areas presented in figure 1.4: general sport management competencies, organization management competencies, and information management competencies. The tasks in the core of figure 1.4 are *general* sport management responsibilities, those in which all sport managers must be proficient and, to varying degrees, perform on the job. For example, regardless of whether you work in a sport club, the front office of a professional sports team, a sport governance association, or an intercollegiate athletics department, you need to be competent in areas such as marketing, sales, public speaking, and the other tasks shown in figure 1.4. These competencies are called *transferable* skills, which means that you should be able to perform these tasks in a variety of vocational settings that include, but are not limited to, sport organizations.

The competencies listed in the clusters branching out from the core cluster reflect distinctions between two types of responsibilities. As shown, leadership and management skills are necessary for performing tasks in the *organization* management cluster. Good organizational skills are needed to direct and supervise subordinates in settings such as sport clubs, municipal recreation programs, or sport associations for specific populations, such as seniors or people with differing abilities; in intercollegiate athletics and professional sport; and in the business aspect of any sport-related enterprise.

In the *information* management cluster, written and verbal communication skills are of paramount importance. Information management tasks include identifying information needs, acquiring information, categorizing and storing information, packaging and formatting information, developing information products and services, disseminating information, and analyzing and using information (McGee & Prusak, 1993). Contemporary sports information practitioners are also expected to be highly skilled in computer technology related to data storage and retrieval as well as Web-based technology. Sophisticated information management competencies are critical in areas such as sport marketing, media relations, and sport writing.

It should be noted that, while similar competencies do fall into one cluster or the other, the clusters are not mutually exclusive. For example, individuals employed in media relations (information

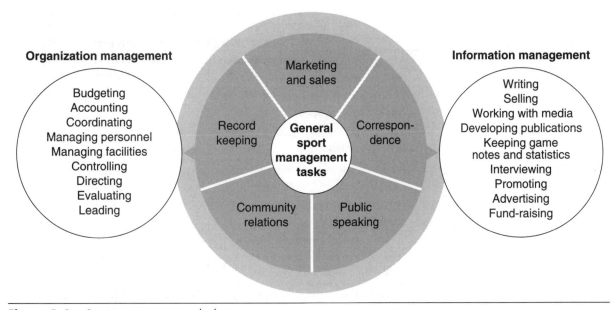

Figure 1.4 Sport management task clusters.

Communication Is the Key

"If I went back to college again, I'd concentrate on two areas: learning to write and to speak before an audience. Nothing in life is more important than the ability to communicate effectively." (Gerald R. Ford, 38th president of the United States, 1979, p. 50)

management cluster) also need to be able to manage and lead personnel (organization management cluster). Conversely, employees in organization management positions also need strong communication skills in order to be successful. In chapter 9, Managing and Leading Sport Organizations, you will learn more about the types of competencies managers are expected to possess.

LEARNING ACTIVITY

Table 1.1 presents examples of a variety of sport industry positions categorized within the segments of the Pitts, Fielding, and Miller (1994) model. Identify

the competencies you believe are required to be successful in the positions that are of interest to you.

Some of you might be planning to obtain professional positions in one of the myriad health-related industries. Sometimes, individuals preparing for careers in health-related industries are totally focused on acquiring the fundamental scientific understandings for such positions and are unaware of the need to develop proficiency in tasks associated with organization and information management. It has been our experience that health care professionals soon learn that skill in such tasks *is* required. For example, a contemporary trend is for athletic trainers to work in commercial enterprises such as sports medicine clinics, hospitals, professional sport teams, and industrial fitness programs. For athletic trainers who work in these settings, proficiency in organization and information management is as important as proficiency in athletic training (Moss & Parks, 1991). Moreover, after you have been an athletic trainer or other health care professional for a while, you might be given an opportunity to become the

Table 1.1 Examples of Job Titles in Three Product Type Segments of the Sport Industry

Sport performance segment	Sport production segment	Sport promotion segment
Collegiate sports information director; assistant director	Sales rep—sporting goods manufacturer	Sport marketing coordinator—rental car agency
Collegiate facility manager; ticket sales manager	Sales rep—sports equipment company	Writer/producer—Internet sport broadcast
Collegiate promotion/marketing director	Manager—sporting goods and apparel retail store	Financial analyst—sport sponsorship management company
Sport tourism company travel manager	Account executive—sporting goods retailer/wholesaler	Sport journalist—print
Marketing director—racetrack	Sales rep—sport surfacing manufacturer/supplier	Sales rep—sports TV channel
Campus recreation director	Assistant media director—collegiate athletics conference	Account executive—sport marketing/management agency
Media director—motor speedway	Events coordinator—pro sport facility	Legal consultant—sport business licensing company
Municipal recreation—assistant athletics supervisor; special events director; assistant general manager	Executive director—regional sports commission	Sport journalist—broadcast
Marketing director—International Special Olympics	Facilities design consultant—sport facility architectural company	Vice president—sport licensing company
Marketing manager—professional golf tournament	Legislative services assistant—governing body	Vice president, sport sponsorship and events—credit card company

director of your clinic or club. If so, competency in organization and information management functions will be a prerequisite to your success. So, although none of the chapters in this book will provide you with information regarding the scientific fundamentals of health-related careers, you will benefit from the organizational and information management knowledge that is presented.

LEARNING ACTIVITY

Conduct an informational interview with someone who has been employed in a commercial health-related setting for five years or longer. Ask about the use of management skills. See chapter 2 for suggestions about informational interviews.

The model in figure 1.4 illuminates only the technical knowledge required to manage sport. Aspiring sport managers should be aware that employers are also looking for specific personal and professional qualities in graduates of sport management programs. In addressing the common qualities and characteristics shared by *outstanding* sport management students and professionals, Cuneen and Sidwell (1998) noted that, in general, such students

> *(a) possess a good work ethic, (b) are flexible in both their personal and professional schedules, (c) are people-oriented, (d) are able to perform in committee-type work or other group projects, (e) are goal-oriented self-starters who have the ability to close-out tasks absent of supervision, (f) are creative, and (g) are intellectually curious. (p. 12)*

You will learn more about the importance of these qualities in chapter 2, Developing a Professional Perspective.

LEARNING ACTIVITY

Analyze your traits in light of Cuneen and Sidwell's advice. Do you demonstrate the qualities required to be a successful sport manager? Which characteristics are your best, and which do you need to develop further?

Future Challenges and Opportunities for Sport Managers

The future will bring sport managers many challenges and opportunities, some of which have already begun to emerge and others of which we have only dreamed. In the remaining chapters, you will learn about various challenges facing specific segments of the sport industry. For this chapter, we have chosen to address three of the opportunities and challenges that sport managers in *all* segments of the industry will face—challenges associated with technology, ethics, and social responsibility.

Technology

The technology explosion of the past several decades has been mind-boggling, and this is only the beginning! It is important to remember, however, that technology is not an end unto itself; it is a means to an end—an innovation that facilitates progress and helps us realize other accomplishments. In the future, scientific advances in computers and communication technology will play an increasingly significant role in our society and in sport management. This progress will be accompanied by acknowledging the human need for "high-touch" activities, many of which the sport experience can provide. The challenge, therefore, is to become proficient in using technology while remaining aware of the need for human interaction in people's lives and understanding how sport can facilitate such interaction.

Ethics

Sport managers are required to deal with a multitude of questions that require an understanding of ethical principles and moral psychology. Following are some examples of such questions:

How can we best achieve gender, race, and class equity in sport?

Do professional team owners owe primary allegiance to themselves or to the communities that support the team?

Should sport teams appropriate the sacred rituals and symbols of American Indians?

How can we balance academic integrity with the demands of intercollegiate competition?

Should gymnasts and wrestlers sacrifice their youth and health for victory?

Is winning really the bottom line of sport?

Is intercollegiate sport an entertainment business for public consumption or an extracurricular opportunity for student development, or both, or something else?

17

Should sport programs for men be negatively affected in the name of providing equal opportunity for women?

The list is endless, and no doubt you could add your concerns to it. Malloy and Zakus (1995) suggested that sport management students should understand the need to "challenge the assumptions, both overt and covert, of sport and society to enable themselves to make ethically sound decisions" (p. 54). Helping students develop the knowledge and skill necessary to challenge traditional assumptions and to make ethically defensible decisions requires the integration of instruction and practice into the professional preparation program. Toward that end, you will find information about crises facing sport and associated ethical choices in many chapters of this book. Now is the time to begin reflecting on these concerns because you surely will face them in the years to come. Excerpts from the code of ethics established by the North American Society for Sport Management are presented below. The principles in this code, and in ethics codes presented in other chapters of this book, should be helpful as you consider ways in which you will demonstrate ethical behavior as a sport manager.

Social Responsibility

In the future, enlightened sport managers will become more aware of their social responsibilities and will deliver their services in ways that reflect this understanding. For example, professional childcare services will become routine in sport facilities, something we have already begun to see. Sport managers will become more conscious of environmental concerns and will incorporate this understanding into their business practices. Sport managers of the future will use previously untapped and undertapped target markets, such as women and people of differing ages, abilities, and sexual orientations. They will also recognize the importance of keeping the sport experience accessible to all socioeconomic groups. The importance of socially responsible sport management is addressed in several chapters of this book.

LEARNING ACTIVITY

Go to your local library or video store and rent a copy of the 1947 movie *A Gentleman's Agreement*. Watch it either in class or at home. What lessons does this movie have for sport managers? If you like this film, watch the 1962 movie *To Kill a Mockingbird*. Discuss the social messages in this movie and explain how its messages relate to sport management.

Future of the Sport Industry

In 1989 an entire issue of a now-defunct sport magazine titled *Sports, Inc.* was devoted to predic-

---

Code of Ethics, North American Society for Sport Management

The following canons or principles, arranged according to category or dimension, shall be considered by the sport manager in the performance of professional duties:

- The sport manager should hold paramount the safety, health, and welfare of the individual in the performance of professional duties.
- The sport manager should act in accordance with the highest standards of professional integrity.
- The sport manager's primary responsibility is to students/clients.
- When setting fees for service in private or commercial settings, the sport manager should ensure that they are fair, reasonable, considerate, and commensurate with the service performed and with due respect to the students'/clients' ability to pay.
- The sport manager should adhere to any and all commitments made to the employing organization. The relationship should be characterized by fairness, non-malfeasance, and truthfulness.
- The sport manager should treat colleagues with respect, courtesy, fairness, and good faith.
- The sport manager should uphold and advance the values and ethical standards, the knowledge, and the mission of the profession.
- The sport manager should promote the general welfare of society.

North American Society for Sport Management, 1996.

tions about the nature and scope of sport in the 1990s ("Sports in the '90s," 1989). Over a decade later, in a special issue of the *Journal of Sport Management*, several authors reflected on those 1989 predictions and provided new predictions for the ensuing millennium (Cuneen & Schneider, 2001a). As shown in table 1.2, these authors' predictions encompassed sport economics, professional sport, women's sport, sport gambling, and Canadian intercollegiate sport. The information in table 1.2 raises several questions that you, as a future sport manager, will need to address. These questions include whether sport will continue to grow; how sport will be affected by North American social, political, cultural, and economic trends; how sport will be affected by global developments; and whether the global influence of North American sport will continue unabated (Cuneen & Schneider, 2001b). Of course, a major question for you is whether sport will continue to offer a vast array of job opportunities for aspiring sport managers.

Table 1.2 Summary of *Journal of Sport Management* Reflections on 1990s Sport and Forecasts for 2000-Era Sport

Topic	General points
Sport business in a new decade (Mahony & Howard, 2001)	• 1990s sports industry climbed to a new high • Abundant new venues led to greater disparity among teams • Increased need for financing affected pro sport economics • Attendance declined at most major league venues • Future economic stability depends on creativity and technology • Big events, rivalries, and marquis players will have to be exploited in order to maintain profit and interest
Managing professional teams (Gladden, Irwin, & Sutton)	• Taxpayers rejected many facility proposals • Increased ticket prices reflected financial necessity rather than supply and demand • Fan loyalty decreased due to many factors, including player mobility • Future management will focus on strategies associated with long-term franchise stability rather than short-term profit associated with winning • Relationship-building efforts will increase in an attempt to keep/build fan bases • Strategic alliances, mergers, and regional sport networks will continue to form • Consumer interaction and customer management will be paramount
Reflections on women's sport (Spencer & McClung)	• Tennis experienced a crisis in title sponsorship • Individual tennis and golf stars earned millions in product/company endorsements • Sex appeal remains a prime consideration in endorsement and marketing strategy • Summer and Winter Olympic sport stars and events grew at rapid-fire pace • Women's professional and amateur team sports such as basketball and ice hockey grew steadily • Great gender disparity remains in coaching ranks
Sport gambling (Claussen & Miller)	• Expansion or opportunities reflected expansion of public interest in gambling • "Governmental endorsement" in the form of lotteries helped to triple gambling-related games • Improved TV access generated public interest • Internet gambling is growing and prompting legal responses • Sport administrators will need to protect the integrity of sport contests
Canadian intercollegiate sport (Danylchuk & MacLean)	• CIAU implemented changes in decision making, communication, programmatic orientation, and delivery • Gender and sport equity drive many sport and financial decisions • Athletic awards (first-party scholarships) spur debates among coaches and administration • Funding crises will prompt more emphasis on marketing • Technology will change sport delivery and environments on Canadian campuses

Reprinted, by permission, from J. Cuneen and R. Schneider, 2001, "Sport in the third millennium: A retrospective and perspective on 1990 and 2000-era sport," *Journal of Sport Management* 15(4):270-271.

You Can Make a Difference!

The future will most assuredly bring change, something that can be frightening and is frequently resisted. Progressive sport managers who can anticipate and embrace change will have opportunities to be agents of change who will transform the way sport is managed. We hope you will be one of those managers!

LEARNING ACTIVITIES

Read one of the articles published in the special issue of the *Journal of Sport Management* (October 2001). Write a synopsis of the author's reflections and predictions. How will these predictions affect the sport job market? Describe your role in the sport environment of the future as described by the author. How will you cope with the challenges and opportunities they predict?

Join the sport management majors club at your university. Run for an office or volunteer to work on a project. The experience you gain through these sorts of activities will be very valuable to you when you take a position in the sport industry.

SUMMARY

In this chapter, sport is defined as any activity, experience, or business enterprise focused on fitness, recreation, athletics, or leisure. Sport management is an area of professional endeavor as well as an academic program of study. The sport industry can be conceptualized based on (1) the various settings in which it occurs, (2) the many types of sporting activities that exist, and (3) the various industry segments into which different sport businesses and organizations can be categorized. There are three models of segmentation of the sport industry: the product type model, the economic impact model, and the sport activity model. The four unique aspects of sport management are sport marketing, the sport enterprise financial structure, career paths, and the power of sport as a social institution. Sport managers are expected to possess general, transferable competencies as well as competencies specific to organization management and information management. Individuals who work in the health care industry should also possess these competencies. Three challenges facing the next generation of sport managers will be associated with technology, ethics, and social responsibility. Enlightened sport managers of the future will be competent in the technical aspects of their jobs and will also be agents of change, both in the management of sport and in the larger society.

REVIEW QUESTIONS

1. How are the definitions of sport offered by Loy; Snyder and Spreitzer; Coakley; VanderZwaag; and Pitts, Fielding, and Miller similar to one another? How are they different from one another?

2. When considering an academic program that prepares you for a career in the sport industry, what should you look for beyond the title of the program?

3. What is the difference between *sport* and *sports*?

4. List and discuss the sport business settings that might represent job opportunities for sport managers.

5. What new sports have emerged in the last few years? How has their emergence affected career opportunities in sport management?

6. Compare and contrast the three models of segmentation that have been applied to the sport industry.

7. Identify and explain four unique aspects of sport management.

8. Contrast the bureaucratic and the competency-based models of organizational design and explain the implications of each for aspiring sport managers.

9. Discuss the task clusters into which sport managers' responsibilities can be classified.

Explain how the tasks overlap those of different professional positions.

10. Identify and discuss the personal and professional characteristics of successful sport management students and professionals.

11. Explain what forecasters predict for the future of the sport industry with respect to sport economics, professional sport, women's sport, sport gambling, and Canadian intercollegiate sport.

12. Discuss opportunities and challenges in technology, ethics, and social responsibility that all sport managers will face in the future.

REFERENCES

Acosta, R.V., & Carpenter, L.J. (2002). *Women in intercollegiate sport: A longitudinal study: Twenty-five year update 1977-2002.* Unpublished manuscript, Brooklyn College.

Alsop, W.L., & Fuller, G.C. (Eds.). (2001). *Directory of academic programs in sport management.* Morgantown, WV: Fitness Information Technology.

Broughton, D., Lee, J., & Nethery, R. (1999, December 20-26). The answer: $213 billion. *Street & Smith's SportsBusiness Journal, 2,* 23, 26.

Clay, B. (1995, February). 8 great careers in the sports industry. *Black Enterprise, 25*(7), 158-160, 162, 164, 166.

Coakley, J.J. (2001). *Sport in society: Issues and controversies* (7th ed.). St. Louis: Mosby.

Comte, E., & Stogel, C. (1990). Sports: A $63.1 billion industry. *The Sporting News* (January 1), 60-61.

Cuneen, J., & Schneider, R. (Eds.). (2001a). Sport in the third millennium [Special issue]. *Journal of Sport Management, 15*(4).

Cuneen, J., & Schneider, R. (2001b). Sport in the third millennium: A retrospective and perspective on 1990s and 2000-era sport. *Journal of Sport Management, 15,* 267-274.

Cuneen, J., & Sidwell, M.J. (1998, Winter). Evaluating and selecting sport management undergraduate programs. *The Journal of College Admission,* 6-13.

DeSensi, J.T., Kelley, D.R., Blanton, M.D., & Beitel, P.A. (1990). Sport management curricular evaluation and needs assessment: A multifaceted approach. *Journal of Sport Management, 4,* 31-58.

Ford, G.R. (1979). A time to heal: *The autobiography of Gerald R. Ford.* New York: Harper & Row.

Frank, R. (1984). Olympic myths and realities. *Arete: The Journal of Sport Literature, 1*(2), 155-161.

Lapchick, R.E., & Matthews, K.J. (2001). *2001 Racial and gender report card.* Northeastern University, Boston: Center for the Study of Sport in Society.

Lawler, E.E., III, & Ledford, G.E., Jr. (1997). New approaches to organizing: Competencies, capabilities and the decline of the bureaucratic model. In C.L. Cooper & S.E. Jackson (Eds.), *Creating tomorrow's organization: A handbook for future research in organizational behavior* (pp. 231-249). New York: Wiley.

Li, M., Hofacre, S., & Mahony, D. (2001). *Economics of sport.* Morgantown, WV: Fitness Information Technology.

Loy, J.W. (1968). The nature of sport: A definitional effort. *Quest, 10,* 1-15.

Mahony, D.F., & Howard, D.R. (2001). Sport business in the next decade: A general overview of expected trends. *Journal of Sport Management, 15,* 275-296.

Malloy, D.C., & Zakus, D.H. (1995). Ethical decision making in sport administration: A theoretical inquiry into substance and form. *Journal of Sport Management, 9,* 36-58.

Mason, J.G., Higgins, C.R., & Wilkinson, O.J. (1981). Sports administration education 15 years later. *Athletic Purchasing and Facilities, 5*(1), 44-45.

McGee, J.V., & Prusak, L. (1993). *Managing information strategically.* New York: Wiley.

McPherson, B.D., Curtis, J.E., & Loy, J.W. (1989). *The social significance of sport: An introduction to the sociology of sport.* Champaign, IL: Human Kinetics.

Meek, A. (1997). An estimate of the size and supported economic activity of the sports industry in the United States. *Sport Marketing Quarterly, 6*(4), 15-21.

Moss, C.L., & Parks, J.B. (1991). Athletic training in an undergraduate sport management curriculum. *Athletic Training, 26,* 178, 180-183.

Mullin, B.J. (1980). Sport management: The nature and utility of the concept. *Arena Review, 4*(3), 1-11.

North American Society for Sport Management (1996). *The Code of Ethics. NASSM's Ethical Creed, Constitution, Operating Codes.* Houlton, ME: Author.

Parks, J.B., Chopra, P.S., Quain, R.J., & Alguindigue, I.E. (1988). ExSport 1: An expert system for sport management career counseling. *Journal of Research on Computing in Education, 21*(2), 196-209.

Parks, J.B., & Olafson, G.A. (1987). Sport management and a new journal. *Journal of Sport Management, 1*(1), 1-3.

Parks, J.B., & Roberton, M.A. (2000). Development and validation of an instrument to measure attitudes toward sexist/nonsexist language. *Sex Roles: A Journal of Research, 42,* 415-438.

Parks, J.B., & Roberton, M.A. (2002). The gender gap in student attitudes toward sexist/nonsexist language:

Implications for sport management education. *Journal of Sport Management, 16*(3), 190-208.

Pitts, B.G., & Stotlar, D.K. (2002). *Fundamentals of sport marketing* (2nd ed.). Morgantown, WV: Fitness Information Technology.

Pitts, B.G., Fielding, L.W., & Miller, L.K. (1994). Industry segmentation theory and the sport industry: Developing a sport industry segmentation model. *Sport Marketing Quarterly, 3*(1), 15-24.

Quain, R.J., & Parks, J.B. (1986). Sport management survey: Employment perspectives. *Journal of Physical Education, Recreation and Dance, 57*(4), 18-21.

Rosner, D. (1989, January 2). The world plays catch-up: Sport in the 90s. *Sports Inc.,* 6-13.

Schoenfeld, B. (1999, November 8-14). Diversity in sports isn't happening. *Street & Smith's SportsBusiness Journal, 2*(29), 3, 24-25.

Snyder, E.E., & Spreitzer, E.A. (1989). *Social aspects of sport.* Englewood Cliffs, NJ: Prentice Hall.

Sports in the '90's: The spiral goes on. (1989, January 2). *Sports, Inc.*

VanderZwaag, H.J. (1998). *Policy development in sport management* (2nd ed.). Westport, CT: Praeger.

Chapter 2

Developing a Professional Perspective

Kathryn S. Hoff, JoAnn Kroll, and Janet B. Parks
Bowling Green State University

Achieving success in most business settings requires particular knowledge, skills, values, and understanding that students are expected to begin to develop as undergraduates. The first step toward acquiring these requisites to success involves adopting the perspective that you are now more than simply a student. You are a professional. You cannot wait until four years from now to begin to accept the responsibilities of being a professional. Your professors will expect you to conduct yourself with professionalism, and you will gain more from your degree program if you consider yourself a "pro" rather than "just a student." Your perspective (viewpoint) on yourself and on your academic area of sport management will influence how you approach your course work, your extracurricular activities, and your relationships with your fellow students and instructors. Now is the time to begin to develop a professional perspective.

This chapter will present information that will be useful to you as you progress toward a career in the sport industry. It will address three elements that are necessary for a professional perspective. First, you will read about professional preparation programs—the courses and experiences you can expect in your undergraduate curriculum and their benefits. Then, you will learn about the importance of attitude—how to present a professional image, suggestions for entering the world of work and being comfortable and productive there, and the fundamentals of business etiquette. Finally, you will learn about professional development— ways in which you can continue to learn and grow after graduation. You can apply the information in this chapter to the other chapters in this book because the importance of a professional perspective extends across all business environments.

LEARNING OBJECTIVES

After studying this chapter, you will be able to do the following:

1. Discuss your perspective on professional preparation, professional attitude, and professional development as three important elements for success in sport management industries.

2. Explain the three components of an undergraduate sport management curriculum.

3. Describe the course work and content areas required by NASPE-NASSM for undergraduate sport management programs.

4. Discuss the major competencies and skills needed for successful careers in sport management in the 21st century.

5. Explain the benefits of field experiences.

6. Discuss ways in which your conduct reflects your perspective on your personal appearance, work transition and adjustment, and professional etiquette.

7. Describe the four stages involved in career planning.

Professional Preparation

Sport management preparation programs exist at the baccalaureate (undergraduate), the master's, and the doctoral levels. These programs can be found in many countries including, but not limited to, the United States, Japan, Canada, Australia, England, China, Germany, France, South Africa, the Netherlands, New Zealand, Belgium, and Spain. Baccalaureate programs prepare students for entry-level positions such as those identified in chapter 1. Master's-level education prepares students for more advanced, specialized responsibilities within the employment setting. The doctorate usually has an emphasis on research and is typically sought by those who wish to become professors or to work in some other capacity in a college or university setting.

You might be currently enrolled in an undergraduate program. You may be a high school student or a university student in another major field who wants to learn more about the opportunities that exist in sport management. In either case, you will benefit from an explanation of what to expect in a sport management curriculum at the undergraduate level. Most undergraduate sport management professional preparation programs include three components: general education courses, major courses, and field experiences.

General Education

The general education component of the undergraduate curriculum is vital because university graduates should demonstrate understanding and capabilities broader than those acquired in their major courses. As a university graduate, you will be expected to express yourself well, both in writing and in speaking. You should understand and be able to discuss—at least on a topical level—areas such as art, music, language, literature, drama, history, political science, dance, psychology, sociology, anthropology, physical sciences, and human movement. You should be able to deal with a changing society that reflects the cultural diversity of our world. You will be expected to use critical thinking skills to generate original ideas and creative solutions to a broad spectrum of societal and global concerns. Upon graduation, you should be well on your way to becoming a knowledgeable, intellectual, imaginative, socially responsible citizen who will make many positive contributions to society. Moreover, the knowledge you acquire in your general education courses will be critical as you seek upward mobility within your career field. For example, as a group sales representative for a professional baseball team, you will use your knowledge of sport marketing and enterprise to develop a promotional plan. As you advance in your career to general manager, the analytical, critical thinking, and leadership skills developed in your general education courses will become more important.

Major Courses in Sport Management

Standards for sport management academic programs have been developed through a joint effort of the National Association for Sport and Physical Education (NASPE) and the North American Society for Sport Management (NASSM). The NASPE-NASSM (2000) program approval standards require undergraduate programs to offer course content related to sport in the following 10 areas:

1. Sociocultural dimensions (e.g., sport and gender, race, disability; motivation in sport; aggression, violence, and deviance in sport)
2. Management and leadership in sport
3. Ethics in sport management
4. Sport marketing
5. Communication in sport
6. Budget and finance in sport
7. Legal aspects of sport
8. Sport economics
9. Governance in sport
10. Field experience in sport management

Sport management programs are not required to dedicate a separate course to each topical area, but the content must be covered somewhere within the curriculum. Subsequent chapters in this book will introduce you to each of these content areas.

The course work designated by NASPE-NASSM is focused on preparing you for a career in one of the many sport industries. It is important to remember, however, that as a university student, you are not being *trained* for a career in sport management; you are being *educated* for a life in which you hope to enjoy one or more positions in sport management. Your goal of entering the sport management field might not materialize. Moreover, even if you do begin your career in sport management, you might decide later to pursue some other line of work. In either case, the course content prescribed by NASPE-NASSM is sufficiently broad that you should be prepared to assume positions in a variety of other vocational fields.

Field Experiences

Sport management field experiences provide you with opportunities to learn about managerial responsibilities and the scope of the sport business while working in a sport setting. They also present opportunities for you to apply what you've learned in the classroom to a real-life situation, thus connecting theory with practice (Cuneen & Sidwell, 1994; Sutton, 1989). Typically, two terms are applied to field experience courses—practicum and internship, both of which are supervised practical experiences. The practicum is usually more abbreviated than the internship, which is typically a 40-hours-per-week, full-time, semester-long experience. After meeting the selection criteria of your university, you can obtain a practicum or internship position at one of a wide variety of organizations and agencies. You might even have the opportunity to engage in a field experience in a foreign country, either through your sport management program or through the international studies program on your campus. The following guidelines will help you in selecting a field experience:

- Choose a reputable organization so that you will increase your chances of having a good learning experience. Consult with your faculty and the staff at your career services office on campus to identify organizations providing good-quality learning/work experiences for students in sport management. At a minimum, you should be able to obtain a job description and identify learning goals with your faculty advisor and field supervisor prior to beginning a practicum or internship experience.

- Be ready to be challenged by the level of responsibility you are given.

- Maintain open communication with your on-site supervisor and faculty supervisor.

- Attempt to arrange your field experience with an agency with which you wish to be employed. If you present yourself well and do quality work, the agency *might* consider employing you after graduation. You should not, however, have your heart set on being hired by your field experience agency. Among other reasons, the agency may not have any permanent positions available for which you would be qualified.

Students, the cooperating site, universities, and faculty members—everyone involved in field experiences—benefit from them. According to the National Commission for Cooperative Education (NCCE) (2001), participating in field experiences provides *students* the following benefits:

- Enhances classroom learning by integrating academic curriculum and real-world work experience.

- Confirms or redirects career decision making through on-the-job experience in a chosen field.

- Improves job opportunities after graduation by giving students valuable work experience and contact with potential future employers.

- Teaches valuable job-search skills such as career assessment, résumé writing, and interviewing techniques.

- Encourages completion of college for all students—from top performers to traditionally non–college bound students—by linking school to work and by providing access to co-op earnings.

Casella and Brougham (1995) stated, "work experience gained while still in college is being reported as an important factor in career success, particularly in the first year after graduation" (p. 55). Casella and Brougham also noted that students benefit from work experiences before graduation by building networks, improving self-organization, establishing a greater sense of responsibility, expanding work skills, learning more about personal strengths and values, and gaining self-confidence.

Field experiences provide important benefits for the sponsoring *university* by strengthening the program's relationships with prospective employers and by keeping *faculty* up-to-date relative to the status and demands of the field. The *sport enterprise* (the cooperative site) benefits from your valuable contributions to the organization while you are completing your fieldwork. Additionally, field experiences often provide sport enterprises with motivated, career-minded workers at low or no cost.

LEARNING ACTIVITY

Go to the NCCE Web site at www.co-op.edu/benefits.html and list the benefits of field experience to students, universities, faculty, and employers.

Professional Attitude

Planning your future in sport management includes paying attention to one of the most important elements of your portfolio—your professional attitude. "Cultivating a positive, assertive outlook on life is the most crucial factor that makes the difference between those people who have a successful, satisfying life/career and those who do not" (Sukiennik, Raufman, & Bendat, 1992, p. 28). A professional attitude will enhance your opportunities for employment and advancement. It will also make you a more pleasant person for others to be around. That alone should be a worthy goal.

Attitude is reflected in many ways. Three of these ways are professional image, work transition and adjustment (including work habits), and business etiquette. These are also some of the attributes that recruiters evaluate during interviews.

Attitudes are demonstrated by behaviors, and, as noted in chapter 1, acceptable behaviors are being articulated in professional codes of ethics now being used by many professional associations, business organizations, and public and private enterprises as guidelines for professional practice. Professionals within these organizations adhere to these sets of standards or guidelines, and those in sport management are no exception. More than 29,000 Web sites can be found with a quick search of the Internet using the keywords "sport code of ethics." As an example, the code of ethics of the Institute of Sport Management (2001) states:

> The Institute of Sport Management's Code of Ethics & Professional Conduct recognizes that the objectives of the Sport Management profession are to work to the highest standards of professionalism, to attain the highest levels of performance and generally to meet the public interest requirement. These objectives require four basic needs to be met: a) Credibility, b) Professionalism, c) Quality of Services, and d) Confidence. Users of the services of professional Sport Managers should be able to feel confident that there exists a framework of professional ethics that governs the provision of those services.

The Institute of Sport Management is a company in New South Wales, Australia, that is committed to the development of the profession of sport management. For more information, go to www.ismhome.com/.

Your professional attitude is revealed in your **work behaviors** and **workplace habits**.

work behaviors—Qualities such as punctuality, attendance, appearance, and friendliness.

workplace habits—Habits such as dependability, cooperation, and honesty.

Professional Image

What kind of visual impression do you make? Upon meeting you, other people rely on your physical appearance to make judgments about you. "Studies on the overall impression that people make in the first few minutes . . . show that 7 percent of that impression is based on what a person says, 38 percent on how he or she says it, and 55 percent on what the other person SEES" (Mitchell, 1998, p. 10). Although this might seem unfair, and although initial impressions can change after someone gets to know you, remember that you can make a first impression only once—so why not make it a good one?

The impression you make through your physical presentation is related less to physical attractiveness than to other factors, all of which are within your control. Some aspects of a professional image are listed here:

• Grooming—Be aware that aromas from fragrances (e.g., cologne or perfume), smoke, or alcohol on your breath or clothing might give negative impressions to those who come into close contact with you. It may be difficult to convince an employer that you can be a role model for the healthy lifestyle expected in some sport industries if tobacco or alcohol use are detected during an interview. A true professional pays particular attention to personal hygiene.

• Posture—Your sitting, standing, and walking posture give an impression of your attitude. Again, this might seem unfair, but it is true that people will draw different conclusions about the attitude of a person who is slouching as opposed to one who is sitting erect, feet firmly planted on the floor, or leaning slightly forward to indicate good listening skills, interest, and enthusiasm.

• Attire and accessories—While in college, you have wide discretion in your choice of clothing and accessories; however, as you move into the workplace, you will be expected to conform to the norms of your employer. You may want to avoid political or religious insignia in the form of ties, pins, or rings; clothing with logos, slogans, or phrases may be seen as inappropriate. Although baseball caps are a staple of college students' wardrobes, there are certain situations in which caps are inappropriate (e.g., the classroom, meetings, mealtime, conferences with faculty or administrators, class presentations, and employment interviews) (see figure 2.1). With regard to personal taste, however, only you can decide whether conforming to the norms of a particular workplace

Peanuts

Figure 2.1   Hats off!

Peanuts © UFS. Reprinted by permission.

will compromise your values so much that you should look for a job elsewhere.

LEARNING ACTIVITY

Attitudes

You are the manager of a sport-related business. On a quarterly basis, you conduct evaluations of your employees. This quarter, you will evaluate a member of your class. Select a person in the room to be your employee. Do not reveal the person's identity. In your role as that person's supervisor, describe the person's attitude with respect to the following areas:

- Attitude toward himself or herself
- Attitude toward her or his role as a student (job)
- Attitude toward the importance of etiquette

What cues did you use to make your judgments?

1. Would you hire this person? If this person were actually your employee, how would you deal with her or his attitudes? This question applies regardless of whether you have judged the attitude as "good" or "bad."

2. If someone in the room chose *you* as their employee, what do you think he or she said about your attitude toward yourself, your attitude toward your role as a student, and your business etiquette? On what cues might these judgments have been made?

3. What did you learn from this exercise?

Work Transition and Adjustment

Are you ready to face the challenges that will present themselves in the workplace? Are you confident in your abilities and competent in your specific job skills? Are you knowledgeable about the social, political, legislative, technological, and economic trends that have influenced your field? Now is the time to begin practicing for life in the work environment. "Successful employees recognize that the workplace is really a minisociety that sends out a constant stream of information about what is expected of its members and what the rules and limits are" (Carney & Wells, 1995, p. 178). The following sections overview some tips that should help you.

Academic Preparation

Study hard and acquire the knowledge and understanding that employers expect of a college graduate. This includes both major specific courses (e.g., sport management, sport marketing, philosophy of sport) that will be instrumental in obtaining your internship, practicum, and first professional position; and general education (e.g., speech, art, history, etc.), which have been shown to assist with advancement and promotions throughout your career. Keeping up with the literature in your field is also a good idea. One way to know which periodicals are most relevant to your career goals is to pay close attention to the journals, newspapers, and magazines your instructors use for assignments. When you do the assignments, take a few minutes to look through the publication carefully. If you do this regularly, you will begin to see a pattern, and you will have a good idea of which periodicals you should be reading.

Writing

The ability to express your thoughts and ideas in writing is one of the most important competencies a good sport manager possesses. Among the many types of writing that will be expected are business correspondence (e.g., memos, e-mail messages, responses to complaints), reports, and technical manuals. Learn to organize your thoughts logically and to use grammar and punctuation correctly. Investing time and energy in learning to write well will pay huge dividends when you enter the professional world.

Electronic Communication

Although e-mail is a less formal mode of communication, adherence to the conventions of good business writing is expected in a business setting. Good judgment must be followed regarding the content of e-mail messages (e.g., avoid the use of off-color humor, slang, and profanity in all business-related electronic messages). A number of excellent Web sites address the appropriate uses of e-mail and provide tips for composing business correspondence (use the keywords "netiquette" or "e-mail etiquette"). Observe established protocols for various listservs and other communications on e-mail. For example, although it might be fun to exchange jokes of questionable taste on humor listservs or with your friends, the same jokes would be inappropriate on listservs established for professional or scholarly discussions.

Thank-You Letters

Through thank-you letters, you can express gratitude to someone who provided you with information or with his or her time. A good practice to follow is to send a thank-you letter within 24 hours of a social or business contact or event. You may send thank-you letters within an organization as well as to outsiders. Making a habit of thanking individuals who help you will go a long way toward establishing your reputation as a true professional.

Development

Commit yourself to lifelong learning, both formal and informal, so you can continue to grow professionally and personally. Participation in business and professional associations increases your knowledge and expands your network of associates throughout your career. A well-developed career network is vital to your professional advancement. Your network members can provide information, guidance, support, honest feedback, and access to career opportunities. Interaction with colleagues is stimulating and allows you to grow professionally and contribute to your field.

Dependability

Demonstrate your commitment to the organization, supervisors, and colleagues by enthusiastically completing all job assignments within the agreed-upon deadlines, keeping your word, offering assistance, and supporting others in achieving the organization's goals. Your attitude toward work is referred to as your work ethic. "Your work ethic is a set of values you work and live by. The strength of your work ethic is based on the solidarity of your values" (Curtis & Associates, 1999, p. 2). Thinking about people you admire, and the qualities and characteristics you admire in them, may help you in determining your work values. Strive to become known as a person who prepares before meetings, contributes ideas, listens to others, supports colleagues, is team oriented, and follows through on work commitments.

Learning Your Job

No one expects you to know all the answers. When you start a new job, make sure you understand the duties listed in your job description, what you are expected to do, and how to proceed. Listen carefully to directions, and ask for clarification of any instructions that you do not comprehend fully before beginning an assignment. Set up periodic meetings with your supervisor to confirm and clarify your progress on assignments to ensure that your work is accurate, thorough, and of high quality.

Teamwork

Throughout the course of your career you will be a member of many work teams (e.g., problem-solving teams, special project teams, or cross-functional teams). A work team is a group of people who work in relationship with one another to accomplish a task or solve a problem. Team members identify themselves as part of the team, are interdependent, use one another as resources to accomplish their tasks, support one another, and see team success as personal success. To be an effective team member, you will need to develop skills along several dimensions including commitment to the task, communication, collaboration, confrontation, consensus building, and caring for and demonstrating respect for other team members.

Performance Appraisals

Organizations today are incorporating goal setting and identification of professional development needs into the performance appraisal process. As a novice professional, you should appreciate the evaluation process, recognizing that the aim of constructive criticism is to improve your performance. Expect to be involved in setting goals that will challenge your learning process but not be unreachable. Also be prepared to discuss your specific needs for development and strategies to improve your job performance. Setting goals and measuring the attainment of those goals on a recurring basis will help you and your supervisor identify appropriate professional development activities so that your performance appraisals will reflect the best performance you are capable of delivering. The most important question to ask your supervisor is, What should I be doing to improve my job performance?

Conflict Resolution

Conflict is energy among groups of people or individuals; it is not about winning or losing. Conflict is an opportunity to acknowledge and appreciate our differences. Carney and Wells (1995) stated that workplace differences or conflicts are most likely to occur "when workers are under pressure, when their responsibilities are not clear, or when their personal expectations or needs are violated. . . . Conflict situations offer ideal opportunities for clarifying personal differences and for team building" (p. 179). If you disagree with a colleague, a supervisor, or a customer, try to do so without being disagreeable. Steps you can take in resolving minor workplace conflicts include the following:

Stating specific needs, concerns, and fears

Citing examples of behaviors (do not attack the individual personally)

Expressing your feelings

Inviting the other person to respond

Repeating what you heard to check for understanding (active listening)

Erasing the words *yes, but* from your vocabulary

Looking for the common ground in each of your needs

Determining next steps

When handled in this way, conflict can be healthy. Imagine that your team is brainstorming possible solutions to a marketing problem. You express your ideas, listen to the ideas of your colleague, and then look for elements of each of your ideas that could be merged to result in a solution to your problem. The idea here is to look for the best of all possible solutions, rather than shooting down the ideas of others.

Organization Culture

Each organization's culture is unique. Strive to understand and respect your work environment. Learn what behaviors are expected in your workplace. These expectations are sometimes found in the organization's policy manual, but more often are learned by observing the behaviors of others and listening to stories told about the organization at informal gatherings, during lunch conversations, and at celebrations. Pay particular attention to the links in the chain of command. Know where you fit into the organizational structure and where everyone else fits. Some of the key factors to pay particular attention to as a new employee are "the mission of the organization, guiding philosophies, basic values and norms, behavioral expectations, work ethic, what gets rewarded, social norms, management philosophies, ethical standards, sacred beliefs and events, general atmosphere, attitude of employees, communication norms, work norms, and office climate" (Nardo, 1999, p. 54). Many organizations offer formal or informal mentoring programs to assist young professionals in learning about and adapting to the culture of the organization. It is an excellent idea to take advantage of a mentoring relationship with a seasoned professional you trust and admire.

Diversity

Appreciate and celebrate diversity of gender, race, religion, sexual orientation, ability, age, and so on. Do not engage in racist, ageist, or sexist behaviors, and let it be known, tactfully, that you do not appreciate such behaviors in others. There are laws to protect people from racial and sexual harassment and discrimination—but the sensitive and educated person does not need laws to enforce kindness and inclusiveness.

Business Etiquette

The importance of correct business etiquette cannot be overstated. As Baldrige (1985) stated:

Manners are the very keystone of good human relationships. They govern how people treat each other, whether in the coalmines or in a mahogany-paneled boardroom. When people who work together in either place adhere to the rules of social behavior, their workplace becomes efficient. There is an absence of confusion and wasted time. When people treat each other with consideration, they do not run into each other; there is a minimum of stumbling about feeling awkward, groping for words, or wondering what to do next. (pp. 5-6)

As you prepare for a career in management, we encourage you to consider the following reminders of good manners:

• Telephone—Answering the telephone in a professional manner, whether at work or at home, includes clearly identifying yourself and your organization or department; giving each caller your full attention; using your listening skills and restating important information to check for understanding and accuracy; projecting a tone that is cheerful, natural, and attentive; ending the conversation with agreement on what is to happen next; and then following up appropriately. When leaving your phone number on someone's voice mail system, speak distinctly and at a reasonable speed. Remember to leave your name, phone number, and a brief message so the caller may be prepared when he or she returns your call.

• Voice mail/answering machine messages—Refrain from leaving cute or suggestive greetings on your voice mail system, especially when you are searching for an internship or professional employment. Busy callers do not appreciate long messages, cleverness, or loud music in the background, especially if they are calling long distance.

• Language—Practice using inclusive language as opposed to gender- or racially biased language. In the workplace of the 21st century, it is commonplace to interact with managers, clients, and customers who are women, people of color, or from other cultures. Demonstrating a mastery of inclusive language is a good way to demonstrate your sensitivity to such concerns and to create a more pleasant workplace (Parks, Harper, & Lopez, 1994).

• Meeting participation—You will find that certain behaviors are expected in business meetings. Some may vary by organizational culture, but general conventions exist including being prepared, arriving at least 10 minutes early, turning cell phones to the vibrate option or off, staying on task, participating openly, giving your full attention through active listening, and encouraging others to participate and offer their ideas.

• Dining etiquette—Many business meetings include a meal, and your table manners will be judged by prospective employers, customers, and other business associates. You will be more com-

fortable when you know what to expect. First, be prepared to engage in light conversation. Appropriate topics include current events, sports, and the arts. On the other hand, politics, religion, and sex are considered taboo topics. Although alcohol is never appropriate at a business lunch in the United States, know your organization's policy on alcohol at business functions, or follow your host's lead. A glass of sparkling water with a twist of lime is always a safe choice. Order foods that are easy to manage with a knife and fork. Place your napkin in your lap immediately upon being seated. Once your napkin is on your lap, if you leave the table for any reason, place the napkin on the back or arm of the chair, never on the table. The order of silverware use is from farthest from your plate to closest. If there is a spoon or fork placed at the top of your plate, it is for dessert. Once a utensil is used, it must be placed on a bread plate or other piece of tableware. One final hint: no finger licking. Many career services offices are now offering dining etiquette workshops. You might benefit from taking advantage of these opportunities.

• Travel—If you use laptop computers, cellular phones, or personal digital assistants on public transportation, be considerate of the people who are sharing the limited space with you. Do not appropriate the middle seat and tray for your papers, and be sure the sound function is muted. Ask your seatmates if they mind your typing or talking, and obey the captain when she or he directs you to put away your electronic devices.

• International experiences—Communicating with and relating to people from other cultures requires that you learn the protocols, courtesies, customs, and behaviors of other countries. To avoid embarrassment, investigate the customs of foreign countries before traveling there and before entertaining international visitors. For example, in Russia you will receive gifts and will be expected to give gifts. In Japan you present your business card with both hands, making sure the type is facing the recipient and is right side up; when receiving a business card, read and digest the information printed on the card—it is considered rude to just pocket it. Never give a Hindu anything made of cowhide or an Indian Muslim anything made of pigskin. This is insulting to their religious beliefs.

• Greeting and introductions—When you shake hands with someone, use a firm grip but do not crush the other person's hand. Grasp his or her entire hand, not just the fingers, and adjust your grip to the state of health and physical strength of the person you are greeting, regardless of gender. People with arthritis or fibromyalgia often find shaking hands to be a painful experience. It is the host's responsibility to make introductions of those who are meeting for the first time. When making an introduction, use the name of the most senior person first, and introduce everyone else to him or her. As a general rule of respect, do not use a person's first name until invited to do so. Regardless of your gender, stand when being introduced to others (e.g., supervisors, customers, guests), especially if they are older than you or outrank you.

• Office etiquette—Refrain from chewing gum and using toothpicks, tobacco, and cigarettes at work, during an interview, or while others are eating. Many organizations today are using dividers rather than walls, so you may find yourself working in a small space with a number of coworkers. Be conscious of their need for privacy and a quiet workplace. Be cautious in your use of radios, speakerphones, and other devices that can be distracting in a small, close workspace.

• Romantic relationships—The office is not an appropriate place to engage in flirting or in more overt forms of affectionate behaviors. Charges of sexual harassment are serious and can have a profoundly negative effect on your career. Moreover, people involved in these relationships often are hurt and bewildered when they end. Interns, in particular, must be aware of the dangers of falling in love with a coworker or the boss.

In summary, a positive professional attitude—as reflected in your professional image, work hab-its and behavior, and business etiquette—is essential to your future success. Look on the positive side of every situation. Optimistic people view problems as opportunities to exercise creativity, resolve difficult situations, and make things happen. The ability to stay calm and composed in stressful situations is a sign of professional maturity. Enthusiasm and a positive self-image are important parts of a professional attitude.

Professional Development

At this time in your academic journey, your attention might be focused entirely on obtaining a position with an organization in the sport industry. Another group of organizations, however, of which you should be aware are professional and scholarly associations. Participation in these organizations is an excellent way for you to learn more about your field while you are still a student. After you obtain that coveted job, these associations will help you keep up with advances in your field.

Lists of relevant associations and publications specific to various career fields are included in chapters 10 through 18. Membership in one or more of these associations will offer you opportunities to read publications, attend conferences, and perhaps present papers. Some organizations have student sections, providing you with the additional opportunity to gain experience in governance. Memberships in professional associations are an integral component of your portfolio, but sometimes it is difficult to know which ones to join. Your instructors will be able to give you advice as to which groups would be most helpful

Workforce Diversity

Workforce diversity will bring with it questions about how business people should conduct themselves. Baldrige (1993) captured the essence of the new demands created by the changing workplace when she stated the following:

There is a new informality at work in how we meet and greet, entertain, dress, and socialize with one another, and yet a new formality as we deal with a diversity of people from and in other countries, where we increasingly do business.

The needs of families, of women and men who are parents as well as respected workers, are increasingly sensitive issues in the workplace. The relations of men and women working together not only as equals, but also as new configurations of peer and superior in terms of gender and age, changes a lot of preconceived behavior codes. Also transforming life at work are the new concerns for the rights of the disabled, for more attention to ethnic equality, diversity and pluralism. (p. xxix-xxx) to you, both now and in the future. Your professional development is an ongoing process and continues long after you graduate.

As you look toward career advancement and additional responsibilities, you may choose, or be asked by your employer, to pursue a graduate degree. While it may seem too early to think about a graduate degree, it never hurts to plant the seed of advanced education early in your academic career. The first graduate degree after the baccalaureate is the master's. Programs that culminate in master's degrees typically require one or two years of additional study. Special features associated with sport management curricula and programs are the location of the program within the university, the industry focus of the program, and the experience and research interests of the faculty. Some sport management programs are located in departments of physical education or sport management, whereas others are housed within schools of business administration, departments of sport administration, or a variety of other units. The location of the program is of particular concern for advanced degree students because its location "unquestionably influences its orientation" (Parkhouse, 1987, p. 109). For example, students interested in the study of sport (e.g., sociology of sport, psychology of sport, or cultural anthropology) as well as the study of sport business will probably find relevant course work in units housed in departments of physical education or sport management and administration rather than in schools of business.

Another concern is the industry focus of the graduate program. Some programs are geared toward preparing students for positions in athletic administration within the educational structure (e.g., intercollegiate or high school athletics). Other programs focus on sport management in the private sector (e.g., professional sport), and some programs encompass both sectors. As you investigate graduate programs, you will notice that the content and requirements of each program reflect the competencies, skills, and experiences valued by the sector that serves as that unit's focus. You will also notice that graduate programs expect candidates to have high grades, involvement in extracurricular activities, experience in the sport industry, and a good work ethic. Moreover, most graduate schools require high scores on entrance exams such as the Graduate Records Exam (GRE) or Graduate Management Admission Test (GMAT).

Examining the experience and research interests of the faculty is a critical step in selecting a graduate program. Graduate faculty should be actively involved in some type of scholarship. If you consciously choose a major professor (advisor) whose research and scholarly interests are compatible with yours and who has a record of scholarly productivity, you will increase the probability of gaining valuable research experience at the master's level. This advice is especially important for students who plan to enroll in doctoral studies after earning the master's degree.

During the past several years, because of proliferating sport management curricula in colleges and universities, many sport management professorial positions have become available. Doctoral-level education, which builds on the background gained at the undergraduate and master's levels and is much more specialized in its focus, is essential for anyone who aspires to be a college professor. Currently, there is an absence of gender and racial diversity among sport management professors, with the vast majority being white, able-bodied males (Moore & Parkhouse, 1996; Parks & Bartley, 1996). Many faculty and administrators are committed to expanding diversity in the professoriate and would be receptive to applications from qualified doctoral candidates who would contribute to that objective.

In many institutions, sport management professors are expected to conduct and publish research in an effort to build the body of knowledge. Consequently, if you aspire to the professoriate, you should acquire the research skills needed to perform this aspect of your responsibilities. As you plan your doctoral studies, it will be important to find a major professor who is an established researcher in your area of interest, has experience helping students learn to conduct and publish research, and is interested in helping prospective professors learn the **pragmatics** of university life.

pragmatics—Relating to matters of fact or practical affairs often to the exclusion of intellectual or artistic matters: practical as opposed to idealistic (Merriam-Webster online dictionary).

Career Planning and Management

To thrive in the 21st century, employees will need to assume responsibility for their own career planning and management. Gone are the days when a college graduate could expect to find a job upon graduation and spend his or her entire career working for one organization. You will make multiple career and job choices throughout your life span. It is estimated that American workers will change career fields at least three to five times and switch jobs as many as 10 times throughout their working lives. While frequent job changes will become the norm, employment security can be achieved only by continuing to develop new skills through lifelong learning and by assuming personal responsibility for managing your own career.

The process of making career decisions is complex, involving self-awareness and exploration, occupational exploration, decision making, and career implementation (Hoff, 2000). Career planning can be fascinating because of the new insights you will gain about yourself as well as knowledge about the wide variety of career options available to you. The following steps will help you in your career planning. You do not have to complete them in the order presented, and you may need to repeat a step or two as you gain new information about yourself and your career options or encounter obstacles or barriers.

- *Self-awareness and exploration* entails identifying and understanding your personal and work values, interests, abilities, aptitudes, personality traits, and desired future lifestyle.

- *Occupational awareness and exploration* entails taking a broad look at career fields and researching specific occupations, work environments, and employers that may be a match with your unique career profile as identified through your self-assessment.

- *Career decision making* is the process of consciously analyzing and weighing all information you have gathered about yourself, various occupations, and career paths. At this stage you will make a tentative career decision, formulate educational and vocational goals, and develop plans to achieve them. Remember, the more you learn about yourself and the world of sport management, the better and more realistic your educational and career choices will be.

- *Career implementation* involves sharpening your job search skills. You will learn to prepare an effective résumé and cover letter, identify sources of job leads, present yourself professionally in interviews, evaluate and accept a job offer, and transition and adjust to a new position.

Career planning is not a single, once-in-a-lifetime event. You are continually developing new interests, knowledge, and skills through your course work, leisure activities, volunteer experiences, summer and part-time jobs, and internships. Throughout your career you may be motivated to reevaluate your options when changes in duties or work conditions of a job cause you to be less satisfied with it. Each time you face a career or job change, you will go through the career planning stages.

Your college career center offers services and programs to help you develop career goals, find the right academic and experiential programs to achieve those goals, and gain employment upon graduation. Career counselors can be extremely helpful in providing guidance and direction in assessing your vocational interests, identifying skills, writing résumés and cover letters, preparing for interviews, developing a professional portfolio, and conducting the job search. Be sure to take advantage of the expert assistance available at your career center. A sample résumé is presented in figure 2.2.

Values

Your values are fundamental to career planning and are indicative of what you consider most important in your life. "Values are the qualities, attitudes, beliefs, traits, and concepts that have special significance or meaning for a person" (DiMarco, 1997, p. 23). Raths, Harmin, and Simon (1966) developed seven criteria that will help you determine your values. Your actions and decisions truly reflect your values when they are (1) prized and cherished, (2) publicly affirmed, (3) chosen freely, (4) chosen from alternatives, (5) chosen after consideration of consequences, (6) acted on, and (7) acted on repeatedly and consistently to form a definite pattern. The choices that you make about your occupational life need to be in harmony with your basic values and belief systems; otherwise you will not find personal satisfaction in your job. Ultimately you should seek an occupation and job that will enhance, strengthen, and support those values that you consider important. For example, a high school coach may possess different values from those of a sport entrepreneur. While the high school coach is demonstrating his or her value of assisting with the physical, mental, and moral development of young people, the sport entrepreneur may be demonstrating his or her value of providing a high level of financial security for family members.

JUAN C. RIVERA

jcrivera@stateunet.edu

Campus Address: 2000 Main Street, University, OH 43403 • (419) 555-2112
Permanent Address: 1553 Huron Road, Somewherein, NJ 55221 • (908) 555-4489
Title: Director of Community Relations, Kansas City Royals

PROFESSIONAL BACKGROUND:

- Organized and energetic team player with background in technology, marketing, and sport management.
- Strong leadership and communication skills with a proven ability to analyze and solve problems.
- Creative, innovative thinker who enjoys learning new concepts.
- Willing to travel extensively and relocate.

EDUCATION:

Bachelor of Science in Sport Management, May 2003
The State University, University, OH

- Overall GPA: 3.1; Major GPA: 3.5
- Courses in Sport and Event Promotion, Sport and Society, Sport Facility Management, Sport Marketing, Financial Management, and Sport Law

RELEVANT EXPERIENCE:

Intern, Dallas Sports Association • May 2002–August 2002

- Created a business plan to produce and market a sports directory for the city of Dallas.
- Conducted market research to identify past and potential customers.
- Determined ways to manage an existing database of sport-related organizations and to customize it to user requests.
- Identified ways to generate revenue for the association.
- Updated the association's outdated Web site and recommended changes to improve usability.

Intern Assistant to the Director, University Athletics • January 2001–May 2001

- Completed rotational assignments in various areas of college sport management, including facilities operations, purchasing, inventory management, and concessions.
- Revised the Athletics Department Policy and Procedures Manual, a fifty-page document.
- Assisted with game operations of baseball, basketball, and ice hockey games.

Student Assistant, University Athletics • May 2000–December 2002

- Updated the Athletics Department's Web site and composed biographies of student-athletes.
- Used the Internet during home football games to assist media outlets with their broadcasts.

COMPUTER SKILLS:

- Working knowledge of HTML, MS Office, Web design software, and Adobe applications.
- Familiar with C++, Visual Basic. Extensive use of Windows and Mac OS.

ACTIVITIES:

- **Sport Management Alliance** (2000–2003), Vice President of New Member Recruitment and Treasurer
- **Wood County Special Olympics** (2001–2002), volunteer
- **University Activities Organization** (2000–2002), Member of the Sport and Promotions Committees

REFERENCES:

Available upon request

Figure 2.2   Résumé of a sport management graduate.

LEARNING ACTIVITY

Congratulations! You have just won $25 million in the lottery. You will never again have to worry about money. All of life's options are available to you. You have many choices to make about your future—where to live, how to spend your days, who will share your life, how to spend and invest your money, and so on. Write a few paragraphs outlining your new life decisions now that your financial future is secure. How are these choices a reflection of what you value in life?

Interests

Interests are those activities in which you enthusiastically engage and find most enjoyable. Interests are an integral part of your personality and are related to your values. Throughout your life, your personal experiences shape your interests. These interests often lead to competencies in the same areas. When your interests are well matched with your occupation, you experience greater job satisfaction. If you have difficulty identifying or articulating your interests, you might want to seek the assistance of a career counselor at your university career center. Using interest inventories, career counselors can help you assess your measured interests and match those interests with appropriate occupations.

LEARNING ACTIVITY

To find out more about sport management positions that are compatible with your interests, go to http://personal.bgsu.edu/~jparks/ExSport/and run ExSport II, an expert (artificial intelligence) computer program that simulates the career counseling process by asking users questions about their career interests and providing them with pertinent information about careers associated with those interests.

Skills

A skill is the developed aptitude, ability, or personal quality needed to perform a task competently. The three basic types of skills are job content skills, functional skills, and adaptive skills. Job content skills are the specialized knowledge or abilities needed to fulfill a specific job responsibility. Knowing the rules of basketball is an example of a job content skill for a basketball referee. Functional skills are general abilities that transfer to many jobs or situations. For example, a basketball referee uses functional skills to make quick, accurate decisions and to resolve player conflicts that occur on the court. Adaptive skills are personal attributes or personality traits. In our example, a basketball referee must remain calm and poised under stressful conditions.

LEARNING ACTIVITY

You have hundreds of skills and abilities. Some of your skills are more highly developed than others are. Some skills you enjoy using more than you enjoy using others. An excellent way to identify your preferred skills is to complete this four-step process:

1. Write down three to five accomplishments horizontally across the top of a blank sheet of paper (e.g., organized a softball tournament, made the dean's list, served as president of the sport management association). Your accomplishments can be related to academics, extracurricular activities, employment, or leisure pursuits.

2. Under each accomplishment, label in your own words the skills you used in that endeavor.

3. Circle the skills you used most frequently. Do you notice any patterns? Are there skills that you especially enjoyed using?

4. Rank your skills in a priority order that appeals to you. Ranking will help you identify and define the work tasks and responsibilities you would like to be involved with in your future career. Some examples of management skills that you might uncover are planning, organizing, selling, team building, writing, communicating persuasively, or strengthening interpersonal relations.

If you construct such a table using your experiences, you will have a revealing graphic description of your skills. You know you possess these skills because you have already demonstrated them!

Patterson and Allen (1996) identified the following skills needed to succeed in careers of the 21st century: "(a) computer literacy in all types of technology; (b) flexibility and adaptability to handle ever-changing roles and management styles; (c) diversity in ability to function and work with people from a broad range of ages, cultures, and learning styles; (d) language skills—especially knowledge of multiple languages for the global marketplace; (e) team players—networking and negotiating skills a must; (f) learning skills and continuous reeducation; (g) personal career planning skills (self-assessment, inner worth, current skills); (h) global awareness/orientation—knowledge of a country and region as well as the culture of the people there; (i) oral and written communications skills—become even more valuable as corporations flatten; (j) people must be self-starters; (k) self-comfort—the company no longer defines the worker; (l) strong ethical framework; (m) environmental scanning skills—knowing where your company is going, where the opportunities will be, see which direction to flex forward" (p. 61). Knowing which skills are required to be successful in today's workplace is a good starting point for assessing your level of skill attainment. Once you have identified the skills you possess and to what degree, you can develop a plan for enhancing your level of those most pertinent to your career goals.

Occupational Information

There are many opportunities for you to secure a position in an existing sport management setting. In fact, the position of sport marketing and corporate sales representative appears on a list of occupations that are expected to add a significant number of openings by 2005 (Patterson & Allen, 1996). You could also create your own opportunities by becoming an **entrepreneur.**

entrepreneur—One who organizes, manages, and assumes the risks of a business or enterprise. (Merriam-Webster online dictionary)

LEARNING ACTIVITY

Entrepreneurship

Go to the Babson College Web site (www2.babson.edu/babson/babsoneshipp.nsf/public/homepage). Select three of the eight essentials of entrepreneurship and make a list of the factors that should be considered when starting your own business related to sport. Explain why each is important.

Making solid career decisions requires you to gather extensive information about the occupations you wish to consider. By using a systematic approach, you will be able to compare occupations and make decisions that are compatible with your values, interests, skills, personality, and desired future lifestyle. For each occupation you are considering, gather the following information: the nature of the work, work setting and conditions, educational and personal qualifications required, earnings, employment outlook and competition, methods of entering the occupation, opportunities for advancement, opportunities for exploring the occupation, related occupations, and sources of additional information.

You can learn about the requirements of various jobs through several sources. These include video and print media, computer software, and informational interviews with professionals employed in the field in which you are interested. There are also many career-related publications you can find in career centers, university libraries, or large public libraries. You can also find occupational information in literature published by private companies, professional and trade associations, state employment agencies, and national magazines. A search of your university's library database as well as a Web search (keywords "sport management") will reveal numerous sources for you to explore.

Another way of collecting data regarding occupations, educational institutions, and academic programs is through a computerized career information system. Most career centers have interactive computer assisted guidance software programs, such as *System for Interactive Guidance and Information Plus (SIGI+)* (Educational Testing Service, 1996) and *ExSport II* (Parks & Sun, 2001). You can also access the Web site of the *Occupational Outlook Handbook* from the Bureau of Labor Statistics Web site at www.bls.gov/oco/home.htm.

As a college student, you have many avenues for obtaining occupational information through hands-on experience before graduation. In this way, you can test reality by engaging in such opportunities as volunteer experiences, internships, cooperative education assignments, practica, and summer and part-time jobs. Through these experiences, you can gather realistic career information while building skills and gaining confidence that will help you secure full-time employment upon graduation.

Finally, an excellent way to gain additional information about jobs and work environments is

A computerized career information system can assist in the collection of data regarding occupations.

© Human Kinetics

to interview and observe employees on site. Most sport managers are more than willing to help eager college students learn about the field. Informational interviewing is a valuable method for gathering information from an established professional about the nature of the work, entry requirements, rewards and benefits, trends in the industry, and outlook for the future. Through informational interviews you can gain an insider's view on a sport management job, obtain referrals to other professionals, and create a network of contacts. Good preparation and practice are the keys to effective informational interviewing. Select questions to ask from the list of information interview questions at www.career.fsu.edu/ccis/guides/infoint.html. Add to the list any additional questions you may have. Practice asking questions and having a conversation with a friend before you meet with the professional. Next, identify a sport manager to interview and call to arrange an appointment. In an informational interview, you are the interviewer. Ask a variety of questions about how you can prepare to enter the occupation, and remember to take notes. After the interview, send a thank-you letter within 24 hours.

SUMMARY

Three elements necessary for success in sport management are (1) professional preparation, (2) professional attitude, and (3) professional development. You can find sport management professional preparation programs at the bachelor's, master's, and doctoral levels. The typical undergraduate curriculum consists of general education courses, major courses, and field experiences. Field experiences give you opportunities to apply what you learn in the classroom in sport settings. Master's and doctoral programs will be more specific to your career goals.

Professional attitude is reflected in your personal appearance (e.g., hygiene, posture, self-confidence), your adjustment to the workplace (e.g., academic preparation, writing skills, dependability, ethics, work habits), and your business etiquette (e.g., telephone, e-mail, thank-you letters). Recruiters evaluate professional attitudes during interviews.

Professional development consists of career planning (determining your values, interests, and skills) and systematically investigating career opportunities. Your academic major does not necessarily predict your career choice. You may not progress in a direct path from college to your ultimate career objective. You are continually developing talents, abilities, and skills through your course work, leisure activities, volunteer experiences, and summer and part-time jobs. Upon graduation, you will have a broad range of skills and talents that will make you marketable in the working world. Career counselors cannot provide instant solutions, but they can provide guidance and direction. Ultimately, your long-term career success is your responsibility. Learning the skills to manage your career while you're in college will save countless hours as you progress through life and a successful career.

REVIEW QUESTIONS

1. How can solid professional preparation, a professional attitude, and lifelong professional development contribute to *your* success in sport management?

2. List the three components of your undergraduate sport management curriculum and explain which elements within each of them fulfill requirements of the NASPE-NASSM Program Approval Standards.

3. According to Patterson and Allen (1996), what skills and competencies will you need for a successful sport management career in the 21st century? Explain how you plan to acquire these skills and competencies while in college.

4. Define "field experiences" and explain how they benefit students, universities, cooperating sites, and faculty members.

5. List important elements of personal appearance, work transition and adjustment, and professional etiquette and explain what *your* conduct might reveal regarding your personal perspective on each.

6. Describe and explain the four stages involved in career planning.

REFERENCES

Baldrige, L. (1985). *Letitia Baldrige's complete guide to executive manners.* New York: Rawson Associates.

Baldrige, L. (1993). *Letitia Baldrige's new complete guide to executive manners.* New York: Simon & Schuster.

Carney, C.G., & Wells, C.F. (1995). *Discovering the career within you* (4th ed.). Pacific Grove, CA: Brooks/Cole.

Casella, D.A., & Brougham, C.E. (1995). Work works: Student jobs open front doors to careers. *Journal of Career Planning & Employment, 55*(4), 24-27, 54-55.

Cuneen, J., & Sidwell, M.J. (1994). *Sport management field experiences.* Morgantown, WV: Fitness Information Technology.

Curtis & Associates, Inc. (1999). *Work culture.* Kearney, NE: Author.

DiMarco, C. (1997). *Career transitions: A journey of survival & growth.* Scottsdale, AZ: Gorsuch Scarisbrick.

Educational Testing Service. (1996). *A computer based system of interactive guidance and information* [Computer Program]. Princeton, NJ: Author.

Hoff, K.S. (2000). *The web of personal career reality.* Academy of Human Resource Development, Conference Proceedings, Research Triangle, North Carolina.

Institute of Sport Management. (2001). *Code of ethics & professional conduct.* Retrieved January 8, 2002, from www.ismhome.com/visitor/v_ethics.htm.

Mitchell, M. (with Corr, J.) (1998). *The first five minutes: How to make a great first impression in any business situation.* New York: Wiley.

Moore, M.E., & Parkhouse, B.L. (1996, May). *An examination of diversity in sport management professional preparation programs for women, minorities, and individuals with disabilities.* Paper presented at the conference of the North American Society for Sport Management, Fredericton, New Brunswick, Canada.

Nardo, J. (1999). Helping new grads become successful new hires. *Journal of Career Planning and Employment LIX* (3), 45-56.

NASPE-NASSM. (2000). *Sport management program standards and review protocol.* Reston, VA: AAHPERD.

National Commission for Cooperative Education. (2001). *Benefits of cooperative education.* Retrieved January 8, 2002, from www.co-op.edu/benefits.html.

Parkhouse, B.L. (1987). Sport management curricula. Current status and design implications for future development. *Journal of Sport Management, 1,* 93-115.

Parks, J.B., & Bartley, M.E. (1996). Sport management scholarship: A professoriate in transition? *Journal of Sport Management, 10,* 119-130.

Parks, J.B. (Executive Producer), Harper, M.C. (Writer), & Lopez, P. G. (Director). (1994). *One person's struggle with gender-biased language: Part 1* [Videotape]. (Available from WBGU-TV, Bowling Green State University, Bowling Green, OH 43403.)

Parks, J.B., & Sun, J. (2001). *ExSport II: An artificial intelligence sport management career guidance system.* http://personal.bgsu.edu/~jparks/ExSport/

Patterson, V., & Allen, C. (1996). Occupational outlook overview: Where will the jobs be in 2005? *Journal of Career Planning and Employment, 56*(3) 32-35, 61-64.

Raths, L.E., Harmin, M., & Simon, S. (1966). *Values and teaching: Working with values in the classroom.* Columbus, OH: Merrill.

Sukiennik, D., Raufman, L., & Bendat, W. (1992). *The career fitness program: Exercising your options* (3rd ed.). Scottsdale, AZ: Gorsuch Scarisbrick.

Sutton, W.A. (1989). The role of internships in sport management curricula: A model for development. *Journal of Physical Education, Recreation and Dance, 60*(7), 20-24.

Chapter 3

Historical Sketches: The Development of the Sport Business Industry

Lawrence W. Fielding, Indiana University
Brenda G. Pitts, Georgia State University

In 1875 the Boston Red Sox baseball team won 71 out of 79 games (.898) en route to winning the championship of the National Association of Professional Baseball Players. Each victory cost the club $486 (Burk, 1994). The Boston Red Sox team of 2001 didn't do as well. The team went 82 and 79 (.509) and didn't make the play-offs. Each victory cost the club approximately $1.3 million ("By the Numbers," 2002).

In 1876 Albert Goodwill Spalding opened a retail sporting goods store, the Baseball and Sporting Goods Emporium, in Chicago a few doors down from the Chicago White Stockings Baseball Club. The Emporium sold baseball goods to professional baseball teams and department stores. Spalding, a famous pitcher and the player-coach of the White Stockings, intended to capitalize on his baseball reputation and coaching position. Ten months later his company, Spalding & Brothers, reported a profit of $1,083 ("Once Upon a Time," 1947). A century and a quarter later, Spalding & Brothers, one of the top four sporting goods companies in the United States, manufactured nearly every kind of sporting goods equipment. The firm was part of a sporting goods industry that sold more than $45 billion worth of goods. Along with the Boston Red Sox, Spalding Brothers is part of a sport business industry that produces upwards of $152 billion a year in sport products and services (Meek, 1997).

This chapter provides a basic sketch of the development of the sport business industry in the United States. We envision three broad segments within the sport business industry (Pitts, Fielding, & Miller, 1994). First is a **sport performance seg-**

LEARNING OBJECTIVES

After studying this chapter, you will be able to do the following:

1. Identify the major business and market structures that allowed people to develop different sport businesses from the 1870s to today (this information can be helpful in developing strategies in the sport business industry).

2. Explain how several people and companies affected the development and growth of the sport business industry.

3. Discuss how technologies, communication, the media, marketing, and travel have influenced the sport business industry.

4. Explain how social, cultural, economic, and legal issues influenced the sport business industry.

ment that includes opportunities for consumers to either participate or watch sport events. A second segment of the sport business industry is the **sport production segment**. This broad segment includes all products or services designed to meet consumer demand for enhanced sport performance. It includes services such as those offered by a fitness trainer. A third segment, the **sport promotion segment**, includes products or services offered as tools to promote sport products. In this segment we include sponsorship and endorsement activities (Pitts, Fielding, & Miller, 1994). This chapter provides a brief sketch of the history and development of these three segments of the sport business industry. We have divided the chapter into a series of sections corresponding to decades. For each decade we present only the most important developments.

Pitts, Fielding, and Miller sport industry segmentation model—Conceptual model that divides the sport business industry into three broad segments based on product function and market need: the sport performance segment, the sport production segment, and the sport promotion segment.

sport performance segment—One of three sport business industry segments in the Pitts, Fielding, and Miller sport industry segmentation model. Products are of a participatory or spectatorial nature.

sport production segment—One of three sport business industry segments in the Pitts, Fielding, and Miller sport industry segmentation model. Products are those that influence the quality of sport performance.

sport promotion segment—One of three sport business industry segments in the Pitts, Fielding, and Miller sport industry segmentation model. Products are those used to promote or market sport products.

1870s: Commercialization Models in Baseball

We begin our discussion with the decade of the 1870s because by then several developments were underway that made the emergence of the sport business industry possible. By 1870 the urban population had grown large enough to support a sport business industry. At the same time, changes in response to the urban populace's demand for sport made sustainable commercialization of sport possible: the urban practice of buying entertainment in general and sport entertainment in particular had become firmly entrenched by 1870 (Adelman, 1986; Somers, 1972). Several sport historians have documented the popularity of various sports during the last half of the 19th century, making sport products or services viable for sustained commercial success by 1870 (Adelman, 1986; Betts, 1974; Gorn & Goldstein, 1993; Rader, 1999; Riess, 1989; Somers, 1972). The process of modernizing sport, begun in harness racing, horse racing, and baseball before 1870, speeded up after 1870 (Adelman, 1986). The modernization process

included the specialization of athletic skill, the development of effective organizational structures to present and control sport, the standardization and routinization of the sport product, and an educated citizenry ready to learn about and follow sport in newspapers and popular magazines. The development of the sport business industry was also aided during the last quarter of the 19th century by the growth of per capita income that left consumers with discretionary funds to spend on sport and entertainment.

Technology also influenced the beginnings of a viable sport business industry after 1870. It is difficult, for example, to imagine the development of the sport business industry without the railroad to transport teams and distribute products or the telegraph to report scores and solidify business deals. By 1870 all of the major Eastern and Midwestern cities were interconnected via rail and telegraph. Technological developments in the newspaper press and in the printing industry also helped by spreading knowledge and information about sport to an increasingly interested middle class.

Finally, and perhaps most important, by the decade of the 1870s the United States had produced a group of entrepreneurs knowledgeable about the sport business industry and eager to exploit its opportunities (Fielding & Miller, 2002; Hardy, 1990). During the last quarter of the 19th century new firms organized to successfully exploit opportunities in the leisure experience market. Sport entrepreneurs concentrated on developing techniques and processes to produce products and experiences for a growing leisure market. They also invented and experimented with methods of promoting and selling sport.

In 1871 a group of professional baseball players organized the National Association of Professional Base Ball Players (NAPBBP). The act resulted from a struggle between two groups within the National Association of Amateur Base Ball Players (NAABBP), one that worked for professionalization of the players and the other that sought to keep baseball an amateur sport. The NAABBP, organized in 1858, outlawed **pay-for-play** in baseball and fought an increasingly unsuccessful fight against commercialization. Salaried players began their influx into amateur baseball in 1860, led by Jim Creighton of the Brooklyn Excelsiors and Al Reach of the Philadelphia Athletics. By 1866 paid players were common. Amateur baseball club officials looked the other way as under-the-table payments became the rule. The NAABBP was powerless to stop the growing professionalization (Burk, 1994; Seymour, 1960). The anticommercialization faction in the NAABBP took a further significant hit in 1862 when William E. Cammeyer, an enterprising Brooklyn entrepreneur, began charging admission to baseball games. Cammeyer drained a pond once used for ice skating and refilled it with dirt. He enclosed the field, graded a diamond, erected a clubhouse and saloon on the grounds, and supplied equipment sheds and benches for spectators (Seymour, 1960).

pay-for-play—Compensation to athletes for sports performance, either per game or event, or for a full season.

Amateurism was further weakened two years later when prominent New York and Brooklyn clubs began demanding a share of the gate receipts at the old Union and Capitoline Grounds in Brooklyn (Seymour, 1960). The practice of admission charges and pay for player services spread rapidly throughout the East and Midwest during the 1860s. In 1869 the Cincinnati Red Stockings, boasting a payroll of nearly $10,000, became the first all-professional team. By 1871 the desire for commercial and professional success led to the formation of an all-professional team league, the NAPBBP.

The NAPBBP, later called the players' league, proved a dismal failure and was replaced by the National League, termed the owners' league, in 1876. The formation of the players' league in 1871 marked the beginning of an effort by labor (the players) to establish a profitable baseball industry. The later creation of the National League by team owners marked the beginnings of a baseball industry run by entrepreneurs and businesspeople. The players' league permitted players to profit from baseball. The owners' league that replaced it was organized to make baseball profitable for the owners. Led by entrepreneurs and small-time robber barons such as William Hulbert, owner of the Chicago White Stockings and founder of the National League, and A.G. Spalding, player-manager of the Chicago White Sox and founder of Spalding & Brothers sporting goods firm, baseball's new proprietors appreciated the possibilities of baseball as a moneymaker as well as its connections to an ever expanding network of associated enterprises such as railroads, hotels, saloons, sport facilities, and sporting goods firms (Burk, 1994).

From the beginning, the new team owners strove to control labor costs and to increase revenues. Meager returns in 1876, 1877, and 1878 convinced franchise owners that they had not eliminated interclub financial competition for players or solved the problem of **free agency**, which increased the cost of doing business. Additional problems related to the existence of smaller cities in the league accentuated these difficulties (Burk, 1994; Seymour, 1960; Voigt, 1983).

free agency—When professional athletes are allowed, by law, to have input into their contractual agreements. For instance, an athlete can be held to a contract for a limited number of years, after which the athlete becomes free to renegotiate a contract with the same organization or with another organization.

The largest problem that owners faced in the 1870s was the rising cost of labor due to the bargaining power of players. The single most significant development in the sport business industry during the 1870s was the introduction in 1879 of the reserve clause. The reserve clause in a baseball player's contract gave the club continuous control over the services of the player. The reserve clause allowed the club owners who signed the player for a specified period of time, usually one season, to reserve his services for the next season. Because the contract perpetuated itself, the next season meant all subsequent seasons after that (Burk, 1994; Seymour, 1960; Voigt, 1983). Hence, as soon as the player signed his first contract in the National League, he was actually signing with that club for his entire career. This was true until 1975 when Marvin Miller won arbitration over the option clause in the contracts of Andy Messersmith and Dave McNally, bringing to an end the legality of the reserve clause.

1880s: Commercialization Models in Sporting Goods

Between 1880 and 1890, 79 companies began to produce sporting goods products. Some of these companies had formed much earlier, such as Draper & Maynard, which organized in 1841 to manufacture men's gloves, converted to sporting goods, and began to manufacture hunting gloves and baseball gloves during the 1880s. Other companies, such as the Weed Sewing Machine Company, changed completely. In 1878 Weed began the production of bicycles. Still others, such as B.F. Goodrich and the Narragansett Machine Company, added the manufacture of sport equipment to their other product lines. B.F. Goodrich began the production of golf balls during the 1880s, and the Narragansett Machine Company added gymnastic equipment to its production in 1885.

Some companies began with the express objective of producing sport equipment. For example, the Nelson Johnson Manufacturing Company was established in Chicago in 1883 to produce tubular skates. The John Gloy Company was established two years later in Chicago to manufacture gymnastic equipment. Some firms were transplanted to U.S. soil to produce sporting goods. Slazenger arrived from England in 1881 to produce tennis rackets. Bancroft arrived from England two years later for the same purpose. Several other firms were established to distribute and sell sporting goods. These new firms competed directly with hardware stores, which began the distribution of

sporting goods during the 1870s, and department stores and mail-order houses, which began to sell sporting goods during the 1880s. Each new entrant into the sporting goods market helped to popularize sport, thus developing and expanding the market.

A.G. Spalding & Brothers is an excellent example of the growth and success of the sporting goods industry during the 1880s. The Spalding firm is one of the first and certainly the most successful of the early sporting goods firms. The diversification of Spalding during the last quarter of the 19th century provides insight into the development of the industry. A.G. Spalding's approach toward business ("Everything is possible to him who dares") reflects the late-19th-century robber barons' attitude toward business. Spalding's ex-

A.G. Spalding (center) helped to organize the first modern sport business enterprise.

periments in marketing goods and services provide evidence of the state of the art in late-19th- and early-20th-century America. Spalding & Brothers was the first modern sport business enterprise (Fielding & Miller, 2002), and many other companies copied its techniques, methods, and attitudes.

Spalding & Brothers' success resulted from four interrelated developments within the firm: (1) vertical integration, (2) diversification, (3) the development of a modern management system, and (4) the promotional skills of A.G. Spalding himself. Although Spalding & Brothers began in 1876 as a retail store in Chicago, the firm quickly began to practice **vertical integration**. In 1877 the company began to wholesale sporting goods from the same store. By 1884 Spalding had established wholesale centers in Chicago and New York to coordinate service for Eastern and Western markets. During the 1890s Spalding added additional wholesale centers to cover the North and South. By the beginning of the 20th century, Spalding was producing sporting goods equipment in 15 plants in the United States and five plants overseas. Vertical integration meant that Spalding could benefit from economies of scale and scope, thus more effectively coordinating the manufacture and distribution of sporting goods. This directly influenced the sale of Spalding products in local stores. Vertical integration allowed the company to control resale prices (Fielding & Miller, 2002).

vertical integration—A company's expansion by moving forward or backward within an industry; expansion along a product or service value chain. The opposite of vertical integration is horizontal integration. Horizontal integration is when a company adds new products and services to its organizational structure.

Another key to Spalding & Brothers' success was **diversification**. Spalding began by selling baseball equipment. Its largest contract was with the White Stockings Baseball Club. Within two years Spalding & Brothers was selling fishing equipment, ice skates, and croquet equipment. During the 1880s Spalding expanded into football; soccer; boxing; track and field; tennis; boats; canoes; and a variety of sport clothing, uniforms, and shoes. In the early 1890s Spalding produced the first basketball for James Naismith and helped to introduce golf equipment into the U.S. market. Spalding employees were hired out to communities interested in constructing golf courses. By the mid-1890s Spalding had become a leading contender in the burgeoning bicycle market, producing and marketing bicycles and bicycle accessories. Before the end of the 19th century Spalding & Brothers manufactured nearly everything the sport enthusiast might want or require to improve sport performance or pleasure, diversifying its offerings to meet the growing demand for sport equipment by middle-class consumer-participants.

diversification—The act of adding new products to the company's product mix, thus diversifying the company's product offerings.

Spalding & Brothers also influenced market demand for sport products in a variety of ways. Spalding's Library of Sports helped to expand interest and demand for sporting equipment by providing knowledge about and training in particular sports. Spalding used popular sport figures to discuss sport rules and to provide instruction in how to develop sport skills. Spalding advertisements promoted the benefits of sport for participants, helping to popularize the motives for active involvement. Spalding promotions also motivated active participation in more direct ways. The company donated trophies for tournaments, track meets, regattas, bicycle races, baseball contests, and league championships. Spalding staff offered lessons and training for beginners as well as more advanced players and provided advice on the construction of facilities. Spalding employees taught local consumers about club organization and how to manage tournaments and contests. These services helped to expand local markets, brought goodwill to the company, and promoted Spalding products.

The purpose of Spalding & Brothers' promotions was not just to expand the market for sport equipment, but also to hawk its products. Hence, when Spalding received the contract to publish the *National League Official Rules*, the name of the rule book was changed to *Spalding's Official National League Rule Book* and advertised Spalding sporting goods equipment. When Spalding & Brothers obtained the right to produce the official baseball for the National League, the firm quickly announced to the baseball consumer that only Spalding could produce the real thing. Spalding, realizing the significance of being the official producer, tried to outdistance rivals by declaring Spalding's status as official producer of footballs and soccer balls as well as golf, tennis, and track and field equipment. Spalding pioneered the development of brand recognition in sporting goods via endorsements by professional and popular athletes. Spalding's promotional slogans, such as "First make sure it's Spalding and then go buy," further established brand identity. Spalding helped to establish the power and popularity of "reason why" advertising during the 1880s and "negative" advertising during the 1890s.

The Spalding & Brothers Company also taught other sporting goods entrepreneurs about **decentralized organization** and successful management techniques. Spalding & Brothers was the first sporting goods firm to become a multiunit enterprise. The process began almost immediately. When A.G. Spalding purchased the Wilkins Manufacturing Company in 1878, he knew little about the manufacture of baseball bats, croquet mallets, ice skates, or baseball uniforms. To overcome this problem, Spalding retained Wilkins' staff and employees. He used Wilkins employees to train Spalding staff. When Wilkins sold his interest in the company three years later, Spalding had a trained administrative staff ready to take over and run the business. Spalding used the same approach when diversifying into the manufacture of other sporting goods products. Spalding & Brothers adopted the same approach in the development of its retail and wholesale distribution networks. Instead of searching for new employees to manage newly acquired or developed retail and wholesale outlets, Spalding hired managers away from the competition. In some instances, the acquired firm was allowed to keep its own name and to continue business as it had before the merger.

decentralized organization—The act of developing separate divisions, subcompanies, or departments that focus on certain tasks or products of the company and can be run autonomously.

By 1894 Spalding had established two separate divisions, one in the East with headquarters in New York City and the other in the West with headquarters in Chicago. Each division was further subdivided into major activities: manufacturing, retail, and wholesale. These subdivisions were further subdivided into departments organized around sport categories (e.g., golf department). Departments organized and administered their own functional activities such as accounting, purchasing, and advertising. To coordinate activities across divisions and departments, Spalding developed overarching functional departments. The marketing department, for example, coordinated advertising, product promotions, and markdown sales promotions nationwide. A top-level management department observed, standardized, and

coordinated management techniques in each of Spalding's retail stores. This matrix organizational design proved to be highly effective and very efficient. It gave Spalding & Brothers a distinct advantage in management and proved to be an asset in the preparation of future top managers for the company. Both Julian Curtis and C.S. Lincoln, future presidents of Spalding & Brothers, came through this system in the last decades of the 19th century.

1880s: Commercialization Models in Intercollegiate Sport

If members of the sporting goods industry learned their trade during the 1880s from model companies such as Spalding & Brothers, entrepreneurs in the intercollegiate athletic system benefited from observing student-athletes and student organizers. Intercollegiate football is a good example. The first intercollegiate football game, really a rugby game, was played on November 6, 1869, between Rutgers and Princeton. Bernstein's (2001) account of the game is instructive. The Princeton team and its student supporters traveled to New Brunswick by train on that Saturday morning. Rutgers students met them at the station. The teams and their supporters socialized. They toured the town, played billiards, and had lunch. The game began slightly after 3 P.M. as Princeton kicked off to Rutgers. More than one hundred spectators watched the game for free. There were no seats, concession stands, or programs. The game was played until someone scored six goals. Rutgers won the game in just over three hours, 6-4 (Bernstein, 2001; Smith, 1988).

Three years later Yale played its first intercollegiate football game against Columbia. The game, played in New Haven, attracted more than 400 fans at 25 cents each. This was the first intercollegiate football game at which admission was charged. It yielded a gate of approximately $100. In 1875 Harvard met Yale on the gridiron for the first time. Each school pocketed more than $500. Commercialized intercollegiate football had begun (Bernstein, 2001; Smith, 1988).

In 1876 the student-organized and -controlled Intercollegiate Football Conference (IFC) met in a successful attempt to establish rules for football. The IFC had been trying to codify rules since its formation by students in 1873. At the 1876 meeting, students established 61 rules, 22 of which still govern football games today. The process of establishing a uniform set of rules and standardizing methods of play, prerequisites for the successful commercialization of intercollegiate football, had begun. The 1876 conference resulted in a second major accomplishment that would have a far-reaching impact on the commercialization of intercollegiate football. Students agreed to host a Thanksgiving Day game between the two best teams from the previous year. This championship game became a focal point for commercialized efforts during the 1880s and 1890s (Smith, 1988).

In 1880 the Thanksgiving Day football game was moved to New York City to accommodate the demand for seats. In 1881 10,000 fans paid 50 cents each to watch Princeton beat Yale at the Polo Grounds. Attendance grew each year during the 1880s: 15,000 in 1883; 23,000 in 1886; 30,000 in 1890; 40,000 in 1893. Paydays for the championship participant clubs grew exponentially. The 1879 Princeton–Yale game, played in Hoboken, New Jersey, netted each team $236.76 (Bernstein, 2001). In 1889 participants made almost $5,500 apiece from the Thanksgiving game. By 1893 the split had reached more than $15,000 each (Bernstein, 2001). Most other colleges and even some high schools had caught on to the Thanksgiving Day football game bonanza by the 1890s. President Warfield of Lafayette College in Pennsylvania concluded in 1894: "The Thanksgiving game in football for a big time team brings in revenue greater than the total expenditure on the trustees supporting 25 professors and educating 300 men" (Smith, 1988, p. 81). In 1895 the *Chicago Tribune* estimated that 5,000 games of football were being played on Thanksgiving involving 120,000 athletes (Smith, 1988). In Louisville, Kentucky, nearly 5,000 spectators watched Male High School beat Manual High School on Thanksgiving Day in 1896. Each customer paid 25 cents to see the game.

1890s: Intense Market Competition and the Bicycle Craze

Periodically in the history of the sport business industry **watershed events** occur that cause massive changes in the way business is conducted and lead to new ways of doing things and new strategies and techniques for achieving business success. The bicycle craze of 1893 through 1898

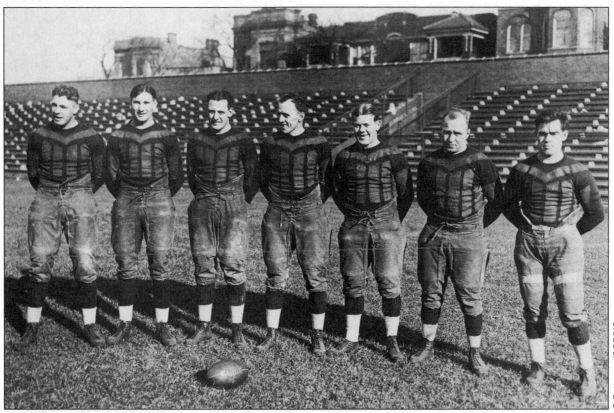

The Chicago Bears were among the teams that helped establish the Thanksgiving football game tradition.

was one of these watershed events. In 1890, 27 firms manufactured bicycles. Sales competition was relatively low. The safety bicycle, invented in England in 1887, hadn't made much of an impact on the U.S. market. The pneumatic tire invented in 1889 was just beginning to be widely used. Beginning developments in ancillary industries were under way. Dunlop, B.F. Goodrich, Goodyear, Penn Rubber Company, and a few others were beginning to manufacture bicycle tires. Bicycle sundries, such as bicycle bells, seats, and lamps were just beginning to make inroads into consumer markets. Top-grade bicycles sold for $150. Medium-grade bicycles, introduced for the first time in 1890, sold for around $100. Bicycles were sold primarily through hardware stores, although a few specialty shops and sporting goods stores sold bicycles. Distribution was targeted toward the larger cities in the East and Midwest. **"Reason why" advertisements** attempting to convince potential customers about the importance of the bicycle for fun, health, fitness, and self-development were placed predominantly in trade magazines. Promotions included trade shows (Springfield, Massachusetts, in 1883; Boston in 1886; and Philadelphia in 1891), instructional books (e.g., Pratt's *The American Bicycler*, 1879), and essay and poster contests.

watershed events—Events or developments in an industry that cause significant changes throughout the industry.

"reason why" advertisements—Advertising that tells consumers why they should buy a certain product.

All of this changed during the 1890s. By 1898, 312 companies were manufacturing bicycles and bicycle parts. Rapid technological improvements in the safety of the bicycle between 1890 and 1895 led firms to emphasize the need for consumers to purchase a new model each year. When technologies faltered after 1895 and the bicycle remained virtually the same from year to year, bicycle manufacturers resorted to stylistic changes so that consumers would think that it was necessary to purchase a new model each year. Bicycle sales skyrocketed after 1893, but so did competition among an ever expanding number of firms that produced bicycles. Competition spread quickly to ancillary industries as new entrants vied for **market share**. Bicycle sundries also experienced a boom period between 1893 and 1898, prompting the emergence of new firms

in the industry. Competition forced bicycle prices down. In 1898 top-grade bicycles could be bought for $75, middle-grade bicycles for $40, and low-grade bicycles for $20. Secondhand bicycles sold for as little as $3.

market share—Ranked position in a market determined by the percentages of a company's product sales in that market. For instance, if only three companies produce and sell basketball shoes, the company that sells the most shoes to the most consumers is considered to hold the number one market share in that product market.

The increase in competition forced bicycle firms to change the way they did business. Beginning in 1893 firms emphasized marketing and tried to meet customer needs in a variety of new ways. Firms emphasized brand equity and tried to establish entry barriers, protect against price-cutting, and move bicycles through distribution channels more quickly. To accomplish these objectives, bicycle firms advertised extensively, moving into the top 10 industries in advertising volume during the 1890s. Systematic advertising became the rule as bicycle companies planned advertising campaigns across a six- to twelve-month period. Advertising agencies became the principal planners of advertising copy. Sophisticated "reason why" advertising and **emotive advertising** became commonplace. Firms developed slogans and trademarks to help establish brand-name recognition. Advertisers trotted out the established themes of fun, health, fitness, and self-improvement that were accepted parts of sport participation ideology. They also created new advertising themes to place the bicycle in the mainstream of American social movements and perceived individual needs and wants.

emotive advertising—Advertising that attempts to appeal to consumers' emotions.

During the last years of the 19th century the bicycle became at once an engine of democracy, an escape from the bonds of technology and industrialization, a tool promoting freedom for women, a moral elevator and developer for youth, and an agent for training young men. Advertisers resorted to popular middle-class magazines and newspapers to sell bicycles. Bicycle firms resorted to the use of sales records to test advertising effectiveness. Bicycle firms employed traveling salesmen, many former athletes, and some former bicycle racing stars to visit local shops and hawk com-

Bicycles of all kinds enjoyed a boom in the 1890s.

pany products. These same traveling salesmen taught locals how to organize bicycle clubs, hold and administer bicycle races, arrange and coordinate bicycle parades and bicycle cross country runs, and establish and direct bicycle tour routes. Traveling salesmen also helped to establish training facilities. Some of these, such as Spalding's Bicycle Training School in New York City, became famous. Most were local affairs, however, unrenowned beyond city limits. These services were designed to increase participation and improve company sales. They were part of the firm's attempt to increase or protect market share.

Bicycle firms further promoted brand equity by organizing racing teams, which were quite popular and received extensive newspaper coverage during the 1890s. Bicycle firms used them to "document" the superiority of their specific bicycle models. Firms sponsored bicycle races and bicycle tours, as well as other athletic events in their

attempts to bring their company names and products before the public eye. By the end of the decade, endorsements by prominent figures who either raced or rode bicycles became commonplace techniques to sell bicycles.

The bicycle craze motivated many firms to enter the industry. New entrants were successful because the demand increased each year. Demand for bicycles and bicycle accessories amounted to a product value of $2,568,326 in 1890. Perceptive observers were well aware that demand was running well ahead of supply between 1890 and 1895. Bicycle prices remained high through 1896, with 1895 being a banner year for profits (Fielding & Miller, 1998a). However, as the decade progressed, supply caught up to and exceeded demand. By 1898 the product value had increased to $31,915,908. However, profits had dropped, and perceptive observers knew as early as 1897 that supply exceeded demand. Falling profits after 1895 were the immediate result of the intensity of competition that increased exponentially each year from 1892 through 1898. After 1898, price wars occurred frequently, replacing more solidly based marketing and promotion efforts, as firms, alarmed at shrinking profits, sold below cost to unload surplus. Despite such efforts, end-of-the-year bicycle inventories increased every year after 1897, and profits declined each year after 1895. By 1897 net earnings were less than half what they had been in 1896 (Fielding & Miller, 1998a). Bicycle prices dropped steadily after 1895. Production costs increased slightly, while selling costs skyrocketed. In the eyes of many 1899 observers, the bicycle industry was ready for a crash. The collapse happened gradually, but was in full force by 1901. By 1909 only 94 companies remained in the bicycle industry (Fielding & Miller, 1998a; Fielding, Pitts, & Miller, 1991).

The bicycle craze and the crash that followed it served as an example for members of the sport business industry. It influenced thinking about business and business strategy in three key areas. First, it raised questions about how firms coped with the uncertainty created by intense competition. Overproduction and price-cutting became watchwords in the sport industry. The need to curb intense competition for the good of the industry became a precept. Second, the impact of the bicycle advertising message, promoting sport in general, convinced sport firms of the necessity of promoting all kinds of sport. Third, the bicycle craze influenced marketing strategy. Successful bicycle companies employed a variety of marketing

49

techniques in an integrated marketing strategy. Marketing strategy emphasized brand equity. Marketing techniques integrated advertising, sponsorship, and endorsements and included organizing participation through the development of local clubs and local activities, the use of traveling salesmen, and promotion through trade shows. The sport marketing mavericks from the bicycle industry had demonstrated the importance of testing for advertising success, market segmentation and market research, and the use of specialized agencies to develop and implement advertising and promotions. Perhaps far more important, the bicycle craze taught manufacturers the necessity of helping local dealers with advertising through national advertising campaigns that linked with local advertising and promotional efforts (Fielding, Pitts, & Miller, 1991).

1900s: Market Development and Market Segmentation

Reflecting on the business of sport during the first decade of the 20th century, P.R. Robinson, president of the New York Sporting Goods Company, concluded that it had been a good decade. Robinson noted a tremendous growth in the popularity of sport. This was particularly true in baseball, tennis and golf, football, basketball, fishing and target shooting, and roller-skating. Even the business panic of 1907, remarked Robinson, hadn't hurt the sport industry. "When general trade is down," he said, "people have more time to devote to sports." Looking to the future, Robinson saw only good times for the sport business industry. As times got better, he concluded, the demand for high-priced sporting equipment would increase because people would want to perform more effectively (Robinson, 1909).

No hard data exist on sport participation or spectator interest in sport during the first decade of the 20th century. However, there are several indicators. The number of firms that manufactured sport equipment increased slightly from 217 in 1899 to 234 in 1909, an increase of only 7.8% (U.S. Bureau of the Census, 1947). The *Sporting Goods Dealer* (*SGD*), a trade journal that provided monthly marketing reports, reported that firms selling sporting goods had tripled during the decade ("Retail Sporting Goods," 1907). The *SGD* periodically reported on what it called the "golf and tennis boom" during the decade. Equipment sales for these sports

increased each year during the decade. Companies manufacturing or selling baseball equipment reported brisk business throughout the decade. Companies that made protective equipment for football, such as Rawlings Sporting Goods, reported accelerating sales each year. The roller-skating craze of 1906-1908, prompted by the building of outdoor skating facilities in several large cities, created a demand for roller skates. Equipment sales indicated that many people were participating in sport.

The growth of sport participation as evidenced by the increase in sporting goods sales during the decade was influenced by the drive to organize sport participation during the 1880s and 1890s. Sport historians have referred to these decades as the **age of organization** (Betts, 1974; Moss, 2001; Rader, 1999). YMCAs began to organize and market sport during the 1880s and 1890s, helping to create a youth sport market by the turn of the century. The United States Lawn Tennis Association (USLTA), organized in 1881, promoted tennis for both men and women by sponsoring national tournaments during the 1890s. The United States Golf Association (USGA) offered similar opportunities for men and women golfers. The National Canoe Association (1880), the National Croquet Association (1882), and the United States Skating Association (1884) all promoted participation and organized sport opportunities for men and women before 1900 (Betts, 1974). The American Bowling Congress (ABC), organized in 1895, promoted and helped organized bowling clubs for both men and women (Betts, 1974). By 1900 more than 100 commercial bowling leagues existed in New York City alone, catering to the growing interests of both sexes (Betts, 1974). Men's intercollegiate athletic organizations multiplied during the 1870s, 1880s, and 1890s, codifying rules of play and organizing and administering intercollegiate contests in such diverse sports as football, soccer, track and field, cross country, baseball, and rowing (Smith, 1988). Their efforts helped to popularize sport participation and prompted participation after college. Women's colleges offered sport opportunities during the 1880s and 1890s. Women learned the joys of participation in gymnastics, basketball, golf, tennis, field hockey, and track and field. When they left college, women took with them a desire to continue to participate in sport.

age of organization—A period of time, the 1880s and 1890s, during which companies began to formally organize and market sport to specific markets, such as youth.

By the turn of the century, perceptive observers within the sport business industry saw opportunities to make money by selling participation opportunities, charging spectators admission to watch others perform, or selling equipment for players to improve performance. Perceptive observers also saw the market for sport participants, sport audiences, and sport equipment purchasers as segmented.

The largest of these segments included the growing number of white male middle-class sport enthusiasts in U.S. cities. This was the key segment for financial success. Middle-class consumers far outnumbered spenders in other segments in the market, and they had the money to buy participation opportunities, tickets to games and matches, and high-priced equipment to perform. Other market segments could be ignored, but firms that overlooked the needs and wants of middle-class males did so at their peril. Astute observers of the sport scene were also aware of the developing youth market. Periodically, readers of the *SGD* were informed about the necessity of catering to the American boy for two important reasons. First, and most obvious, was the fact that the participation rate for boys was up and an increasing number of boys purchased sport equipment. Second, entrepreneurs realized that today's youth participant would become tomorrow's adult participant. Brand recognition and brand loyalty began in adolescence. White upper- and middle-class women constituted a third major segment in the sport market. This was particularly true for specific kinds of sport. Marketers were interested in enticing women to participate and purchase golf and tennis equipment, fishing equipment, bicycles, and athletic wear.

Promoters experimented with methods of reaching the various market segments. One of the most successful experiments was store window advertising. Window displays, it was argued, attracted consumers who were not yet aware of what they needed. Window displays informed about new developments in equipment technology, introduced new sport equipment, taught about sport, and educated about the benefits of participation. Window displays attracted attention and sold Americans on sport.

1910s: The Rise of Endorsement Advertising

In 1917 J.H. Hillerich signed George Herman Ruth, otherwise known as Babe Ruth, to a contract, allowing the sporting goods company Hillerich & Bradsby (H & B) to use Ruth's autograph on its Louisville Slugger bats. Two years later the Babe Ruth–autographed Louisville Slugger was the leading seller for H & B, outdistancing the sale of any other bat sold in America. The contract with Ruth had cost H & B $100 and a set of golf clubs. It was probably the greatest single deal in endorsement contract history.

Using an athlete's name to sell a product, particularly a sporting goods product, was not a novel idea in 1917. Hillerich had signed Honus Wagner, Hall of Fame shortstop for the Pittsburgh Pirates, to a similar deal back in 1905. Before 1910 Hillerich signed Ty Cobb and Napoleon Lajoie, both future Hall of Famers, to endorsement contracts. Wagner, Cobb, and Lajoie were chosen to endorse Louisville Slugger bats because they were expert hitters. They were excellent choices for a baseball bat company whose slogan was "the bat that gets more hits." Hillerich was using men who knew about bats, because they used them to make a living, to sell his bats. This message, endorsed by the best hitters in professional baseball, sold bats. The connection was rather obvious.

Indeed, the connection between experts and professionals and consumers had been made before. As mentioned earlier, A.G. Spalding employed the idea back in the 1880s to sell baseballs. In an attempt to increase sales, bicycle manufacturers took Spalding's endorsement ideas a step further during the 1890s. Spalding chose his experts from an existing professional league. Bicycle manufacturers had to create the professional league first and then sign experts to endorsement contracts. Successful professional bicycle racers endorsed bicycles and bicycle tires for companies willing to pay top dollar for their allegiance. The arms and ammo industry applied similar techniques at the turn of the century to attract buyers. Experts told less-skilled participants what products to use in order to improve skill, accuracy, and overall performance. Advertisers used endorsements by experts to symbolize product quality and to establish brand-name recognition. Product endorsements by experts attracted consumers who wanted to improve performance in some way. Endorsements linked participant performance to product quality.

Hillerich & Bradsby, via Babe Ruth, Ty Cobb, Honus Wagner, Nap Lajoie, and others, took the matter a step further. Ruth was more than simply an expert who informed about bats. Ruth was a personality, a hero, a human interest story, a style

51

Babe Ruth signed with H & B for $100, probably the greatest single deal in endorsement contract history.

to be copied. He was an icon, symbolizing a certain type of individuality and style. Ruth was larger than life. Indeed, vocabulary was created to describe him (e.g., people spoke of "Ruthian feats" to communicate heroic accomplishments). Consumers purchased the Babe Ruth–autographed bat not just to improve their batting average or hit more home runs. They wanted to be like the Babe. The bat was an artifact used to accomplish Ruthian feats and, more important, to copy the Ruthian style and mode. Consumers' desire to copy the Ruthian style and mode meant that Babe Ruth endorsements could be used to sell not only baseball bats but also candy bars and other products unrelated to athletics.

1920s: The Golden Age of Sports

The First World War (1914-1919) increased the attractiveness of the sporting goods industry for companies seeking long-term profitability in at least three important ways. First, military training programs that introduced and trained soldiers in sport brought a new source of revenue to the industry. The large, established companies, first on the learning curve, realized the greatest benefits, as these companies secured the majority of the lucrative military contracts. The resultant profit margins for companies that dealt with the military were high. R.J. Leacock (president of R.J. Leacock, a large St. Louis sporting goods wholesaler) reported that many companies experienced profits of 21% to 25% on military sales (Leacock, 1918). Wallace Robb, sales manager for Thomas E. Wilson & Company, reported that A.G. Spalding & Brothers, Thomas E. Wilson, and A.J. Reach each had received and filled large orders for the military (Robb, 1918). Other sporting goods companies experienced large sales and significant profit margins through military contracts ("Value of Sporting Goods," 1918). Second, the First World War had an immediate impact on the sale of sporting goods equipment at home. The demand for all kinds of athletic equipment increased ("Demand for All Kinds," 1917). High demand brought higher prices and higher profits ("War and Its Effects," 1917). Although there was only a slight increase in the number of sporting goods manufacturers between 1914 and 1919, the value of shipments sold in 1919 more than doubled the 1914 figures (U.S. Bureau of the Census, 1939). The First World War made the sporting goods industry attractive for potential sales and profits. Third, the belief that sport would nurture and develop manly traits was further solidified by the war (Lewis, 1973). Throughout the war the military urged the importance of sport for training soldiers and for developing better citizens ("Necessity of Athletics," 1917). Local and state governments recognized the benefits of sport and the resultant demand for facilities. Similarly, physical education became a mandatory part of the educational curriculum, and school and college athletic programs flourished ("Athletics as Usual," 1917). The war functioned as a catalyst for the growth of sport during the 1920s.

Established members of the sporting goods industry were confident that demand would continue to escalate after the war. Frequent editorial comments by industry leaders and market reports in the *Sporting Goods Dealer* assured manufacturers and retailers of a postwar boom period. On the eve of America's entrance into the war, R.J. Leacock predicted that when the war was over, the demand for sport equipment would be so large that manufacturers would be unable to meet it ("A Look Into the Future," 1917). Other leaders in the sporting goods industry agreed. C.S. Lincoln and Julian Curtis, vice presidents of Spalding & Brothers; Charles Tryon, president of E.K. Tryon; Harry Wilson, sales manager of Stall and Dean; and Lawrence Icely, president of Thomas E. Wilson, all believed that the postwar period would be especially advantageous for the sale of sporting goods ("Driving Dull Care Away," 1917).

The belief that the demand for sporting goods would escalate after the war and that the industry would be very profitable had three important consequences. First, it led to improved manufacturing techniques. Anticipating a huge demand for sport equipment, manufacturers worried about their ability to produce enough goods to meet the demand ("The Markets," 1919). Many scrambled to improve production facilities. A determined desire to produce at full capacity emerged (Castle, 1926). Hillerich & Bradsby is a typical example. Bradsby believed that the demand for baseball

bats would be so great that the only limit on sales would be production capacity. Before the war, H & B produced 880 bats each day (Hillerich & Bradsby, 1912-1917). In 1919 Bradsby wanted to be able to produce 10,000 bats per day. To accomplish this objective, Bradsby hired efficiency engineers and revamped the entire factory (Hillerich & Bradsby, 1920). Other sporting goods manufacturers adopted similar techniques to improve manufacturing efficiency.

The second consequence to an anticipation of postwar demand for sporting equipment was that several companies converted existing production capabilities to the manufacture of sporting goods immediately after the war. Many of these new entrants were powerful competitors. They had the capital to defend against the depression of 1920 and 1921 and the 10% luxury tax begun in 1919. They were able to make large commitments to advertising and promotions to facilitate brand identity ("Growth of Sporting Goods," 1923). Bolstered by sufficient capital and the desire to compete effectively, these new entrants became large producers of sporting goods equipment. This significantly increased the supply of sporting goods equipment. By the mid-1920s the production of sporting goods equipment was more than double what it had been in 1920 (Castle, 1926).

Winchester Repeating Arms Company is a good example of a company moving into the production of sporting goods after the war ("Got 'Em Guessing," 1922). The First World War brought financial success and expansion to Winchester's manufacture of arms and ammunition. War contracts, both foreign and American, gave the company large profit margins and funded plant growth. When the First World War ended, Winchester was faced with the prospect of either downsizing or producing new lines of products ("Winchester," 1925). Winchester decided to produce hardware and sporting goods equipment ("Winchester Accomplishments," 1921). The revenues that Winchester had retained during the First World War allowed the company to convert to peacetime production of hardware and sport equipment. Winchester began the process of conversion in 1919. By 1921 Winchester had become one of the largest manufacturers of sporting goods equipment in the United States and one of the largest postwar advertisers in the industry (Waddell, 1925).

The third result of anticipated postwar demand in the sporting goods industry was the expansion of the type of outlet in which sporting goods were distributed. The attractiveness of the sporting goods industry for investment and profit encouraged new entrants into the wholesale and retail trades (Diogenes, 1924). Sporting goods products now began to be distributed through nontraditional markets including drugstores, jewelry stores, candy stores, and clothing stores (Bradsby, 1922). This policy increased the number of stores handling sporting goods. Where there had been one store per community in 1919, there were 12 in 1922 and 17 in 1925 (Castle, 1926). During this same period, stores doing a large volume of business increased slowly but steadily. Distribution practices were further altered when many of the new jobbers and wholesalers eliminated the retailer and dealt directly with colleges, universities, high schools, industrial leagues, sport clubs, and community recreation associations (Meek, 1928). These new distributors frequently offered discounts, rebates, and gifts to generate goodwill and secure sales. Established manufacturers such as Spalding & Brothers; Goldsmith, Draper & Maynard; Stall and Dean; Thomas E. Wilson; Crawford, MacGregor and Canby; and Rawlings all turned to direct sales to remain competitive (Taylor, 1927). Traditional jobbing houses such as Dyas, Leacock, Von Lengerke & Antoine; Alex Taylor; Horace Partridge; and E.K. Tryon followed suit (Calhoun, 1924; Diogenes, 1924). The improvements in manufacturing techniques meant that the supply of sporting goods products was greatly increased. The expansion of sporting goods distribution outlets meant that sporting goods were more readily available to consumers. Increased supply and improved distribution also meant greater competition among industry members and lower prices for consumers.

The abundance of sporting goods products and distribution outlets during the 1920s meant that sport equipment was widely available to a public whose interest in sport was growing steadily. Public policies begun during the First World War and expanded during the 1920s helped to influence this growing demand in several ways. During the war, army and navy officials used sport for both training and recreation, giving thousands of young men opportunities to play and watch sport. Their extensive use of sport did much to popularize sport and to legitimate sport programs as part of public policy (Lewis, 1973). As part of the war effort, the War Camp Community Service began public recreation programs in hundreds of communities. After the war local communities continued these programs, providing opportunities for participation at public expense (Lewis, 1973). Between 1920 and 1930 the number of public recreation departments more than doubled. Community expenditures on public recreation increased sixfold during the 1920s. The notion that the provision of facilities and programs was public responsibility became firmly entrenched in the public mind. The war effort also encouraged the inclusion of sport instruction and the development of athletic programs in high schools and colleges throughout the nation. During the 1920s, 28 states passed laws requiring physical education. This process continued during the 1930s and 1940s. By 1948 only English classes had a higher enrollment in the public school system than physical education classes (Lewis, 1973).

1930s: Depression and the Age of Cooperation

Leaders in the sporting goods industry realized as early as 1927 that the industry had become highly competitive and consequently unprofitable. The supply of sporting goods products exceeded demand as early as 1925. This increased the intensity of competition as companies vied for consumer dollars. The cost of doing business increased, and profits plummeted. Manufacturers resorted to ruinous competitive practices such as price-cutting in order to survive. While the industry had been interested in curbing practices such as price-cutting as early as 1919, legislative remedies and lobbying had been ineffective (Miller & Fielding, 1995). As the end of the 1920s approached, industry leaders realized that cooperative efforts were needed in order to curb competition (Porter, 1985). Presidents and vice presidents of the large successful firms started the movement for cooperation, the primary vehicle for which was trade associations.

Trade associations served three important functions. First, they established and promoted communication among the large sporting goods firms. As competitors met to discuss trade problems and their solutions, a friendlier atmosphere developed. Intense competition could be assuaged, at least for the moment, as trade leaders got to know one another (Gilmore, 1931). Second, the discussion of similar problems promoted a better understanding of the industry and the companies within it. This better understanding led to the realization that the sporting goods market was limited and that cooperative efforts to expand the market

Knute Rockne and Brand Equity: Updating the Formula for Success

Between 1918 and 1930 Notre Dame football grew from an informal Saturday afternoon game at Cartier Field that at times drew as many as 4,000 fans to a national phenomenon that drew huge crowds in places like New York City and Los Angeles and as many as 120,000 at Soldier Field in Chicago when the team played USC in 1930. Knute Rockne, Notre Dame's head coach during this period, produced a lackluster 3-1-2 record in 1918, his first year on the job. The football team brought in revenues of approximately $17,000 against expenses of nearly $26,000. With the aid of student ticket revenues, the athletic program reported a profit of only $234 (Sperber, 1993).

Thirteen years later in 1930 Notre Dame went undefeated (9-0) and was unanimously declared the national champions. The 1930 team was considered by many contemporaries to be the greatest football team ever assembled. The team brought in revenues of $897,173 and made a profit of nearly $540,000 (Sperber, 1993). In the 12 years between 1918 and 1930, Rockne developed, built, and applied a formula for the commercial success of big-time intercollegiate football in America (Watterson, 2000). The formula (parts of it copied directly from other programs, parts of it modified from existing practices, and parts of it invented by Rockne) became the model that other programs and administrators followed to produce winning football programs that made money for their colleges and universities.

Rockne's updated formula for intercollegiate football success produced what sport marketers today call brand equity (Aaker, 1991; Gladden & Funk, 2002; Gladden & Wong, 1999). Under Rockne's guidance, Notre Dame Football became a highly recognizable and distinguished name that consumers and fans associated with value. Brand equity, a distinguished name or symbol associated with a set of values, has four main dimensions:

1. Brand loyalty—repeat customers
2. Brand awareness—the ability of football fans to recognize Notre Dame as a leader in intercollegiate matters
3. Perceived quality—the extent to which customers believe that Rockne and Notre Dame actually deliver superior quality
4. Brand associations or brand image—the connections or linkages that fans make with Notre Dame football (Aaker, 1991; Gladden & Wong, 1999).

These dimensions of brand equity translate into specific aspects of team performance such as team success, popularity of star players, popularity of the head coach, program reputation and tradition, overall entertainment package, and media coverage (Gladden & Wong, 1999). Rockne skillfully manipulated these dimensions of team performance to develop brand equity.

Rockne created brand loyalty by developing a loyal following for Notre Dame's football program. Casual customers became avid fans, purchasing tickets each year, following the team on the radio, reading about the team, talking about the team, cheering for the team, and celebrating Notre Dame's victories. This brand loyalty, defined as repeat customers and avid followers, was brought about by several interrelated developments. First, Rockne created a winning tradition. Over the course of Rockne's 13 years at Notre Dame, his teams won 86% of their games. He had five undefeated seasons and six other seasons when the team lost only one game. Under Rockne, Notre Dame was a perpetual contender for the football national championship. As mentioned earlier, the 1930 team won the national championship outright and was considered by many contemporaries to be the best team ever assembled (Oriard, 2001; Sperber, 1993; Watterson, 2000).

Star players also helped to create brand loyalty. Beginning in 1919 and 1920 with George Gipp, Notre Dame's first all-American, and continuing through "the four horsemen and the seven mules" during the early 1920s, and on to Christy Flanagan and Bucky Dahmen in the mid-1920s, and finally to Joe Savoldi and Frank Cariedo and Marty Brill and March Schwartz in 1929 and 1930, Notre Dame had star players representing the school on the football field. Perhaps more important, Notre Dame's star players both represented and drew on the school's diverse customer base. Gipp was

(continued)

(continued)

a Protestant who endeared himself to a large Midwest Protestant community. The four horsemen were of German, Irish, English, and Scottish descent. The seven mules had Irish, Italian, and Polish members. Flanagan was Irish Catholic. Savoldi and Cariedo were Italian. Brill and Schwartz were Jewish. Notre Dame football stars came from diverse backgrounds and attracted a widespread and diverse following (Oriard, 2001; Sperber, 1993). In short, Notre Dame was America's team of the 1920s (Oriard, 2001).

In addition, Rockne worked hard to develop brand loyalty by establishing an athletic culture at Notre Dame. He wanted students and faculty to feel that they were a part of Notre Dame's winning football tradition. To build this culture, Rockne introduced or supported several traditions that are now part of the fabric of collegiate football: victory marches, pep rallies, halftime shows, and halftime pep rallies. Notre Dame had cheerleaders and elected a cheer king each year. Students traveled to away games via special rented railroad cars. Students who could not spare the time were treated to special telegraph wire setups in the gym so that they could follow the team's progress play by play. These wire reports were enlivened by bands, songs, stunts, and cheers (Sperber, 1993).

The second part of the Rockne formula was brand awareness. Like brand loyalty, brand awareness relied on the school's winning tradition, its stars and their diversified backgrounds, and the school's athletic culture. In 1919 Rockne brought a young man named Archie Ward to Notre Dame to be his student press assistant. Ward got tuition in return for promoting Rockne, Notre Dame Football, and the team's stars. Ward's first major task was to promote George Gipp for all-American (Littlewood, 1990). Gipp did become an all-American in 1920 thanks in large part to Ward's promotions. Ward spent three semesters at Notre Dame promoting football and later became the sports editor of the *Chicago Tribune* (Littlewood, 1990). Francis Wallace replaced Ward. Wallace had the same assignment to promote Rockne, Notre Dame Football, and Notre Dame stars. Wallace is given primary credit for establishing the Notre Dame nickname of the Fighting Irish and is the journalist who first reported the "Win one for the Gipper" halftime speech after the Notre Dame–Army game in 1928 (Oriard, 2001; Sperber, 1993). George Strickler, the third of Rockne's student press agents, is perhaps most renowned for his lead line for the 1924 Notre Dame versus Army game, which prompted Grantland Rice to write perhaps the most famous lines in sport journalism history:

> *Outlined against a blue, gray October sky, the Four Horsemen rode again. In dramatic lore, they are known as Famine, Pestilence, Destruction, and Death. These are only aliases. Their real names are Stuhldreher, Miller, Crowley, and Layden. They formed the crest of the South Bend cyclone before which another fighting Army team was swept over the precipice at the Polo Grounds this afternoon . . . . (Sperber, 1993).*

After graduation, Strickler followed Archie Ward to the *Chicago Tribune,* where he had a long and distinguished career with the sports department (Oriard, 2001; Sperber, 1993).

A third part of the Rockne formula was the development of perceived quality. A large part of the student press agent's job was to impact consumer's perceptions of quality. Press agents such as Archie Ward, Francis Wallace, and George Strickler did this by emphasizing the Rockne system. As noted earlier, Notre Dame under Rockne was a perennial contender for the national championship. Student press releases highlighted this fact and pointed to the system that produced the players. Rockne understood the importance of self-promotion. In the early 1920s he hired Christy Walsh to promote Rockne and Notre Dame Football. Walsh, the first sport agent, helped to establish a perception of quality for Rockne and his program in a variety of ways. Walsh established a positive public image for Rockne, painting him as an intelligent and moral football coach. Walsh got Rockne several stints as journalist/coach for popular magazines and then hired ghostwriters to complete the projects. Walsh further developed Rockne's image via the after-dinner speech circuit. Rockne did radio broadcasts, had movie contracts, and received endorsement opportunities. All of these opportunities helped develop the image of Rockne as an intelligent, ethical, and entrepreneurial football coach (Sperber, 1993).

The development of brand associations was the final part of Rockne's formula for commercial football success. Brand associations relied on the aspects of brand loyalty, brand awareness, and perceived quality discussed previously. During the 1920s Notre Dame Football developed several linkages in consumer minds. Notre Dame Football players became the Fighting Irish. The Fighting Irish became synonymous with football excellence as established by the Notre Dame winning tradition. Notre Dame Football also became synonymous with Knute Rockne, the charismatic and technically brilliant leader of the Fighting Irish. While representing Catholics, Notre Dame Football also stood for the acceptance of diversity. The football program became the new melting pot for the unification of people from diverse backgrounds and heritages (Oriard, 2001; Sperber, 1993; Watterson, 2000).

Between 1918 and 1930 Knute Rockne and Notre Dame Football developed brand equity through the development of brand loyalty, brand awareness, perceived quality, and brand associations. These dimensions were developed through football success, the promotion of star players and of Rockne, the use of student press agents and a hired professional sport agent who manipulated the media for Notre Dame Football's benefit, the establishment of national schedules, and the almost yearly contention for the mythical national championship. The creation of brand equity meant that Notre Dame Football became associated with a set of values in the minds of consumers. These values translated into a solid nationwide fan base that prompted financial success for Notre Dame Football.

were necessary (Schuyler, 1929; Spink, 1928). Third, trade associations developed strategies to curb intense competition and expand the market for sporting goods. Between 1927 and 1935 trade associations concentrated on developing fair trade codes. After 1935 they concentrated on promotional efforts at local, state, and national levels to increase sport participation.

Between 1927 and 1935 all trade associations developed fair trade practice regulations to govern and restrict competition. Trade practice regulations, worked out among members of the industry, were attempts to curb ruinous competitive practices that impacted industry and firm profitability. Although some minor variations existed among the trade practice codes of the different trade organizations, nearly all trade codes were identical. One reason for this was that members of the industry faced similar problems. A second reason was that the first trade practice regulations, established by the Chamber of Commerce of Athletic Goods Manufacturers (CCAGM), became the model that others followed.

The CCAGM began in Chicago in 1905. Between 1905 and 1919 membership was largely confined to sporting goods manufacturers in Chicago and St. Louis. During this early period the organization did little besides meet twice each year ("Early Days," 1935). In 1919 Frank Bradsby, secretary-treasurer of Hillerich & Bradsby, became president of the CCAGM. Between 1919 and 1922 Bradsby increased organization membership and led the CCAGM's successful fight to eliminate the U.S. government's 10% tax on sporting goods (Levinson, 1921). In 1927 the CCAGM, led by Frank Bradsby, began a drive to establish industry-wide fair trade

practices that would eliminate price-cutting, discounts and rebates to customers, and commercial bribery. Bradsby enlisted the support of the leading sporting goods manufacturers. The efforts of the CCAGM culminated in May of 1930 when the proposed trade practice regulations were presented to the Federal Trade Commission (FTC) at an industry-wide meeting at White Sulphur Springs, Virginia ("Athletic Goods Men," 1930). A month later the FTC accepted the CCAGM's trade regulations, conferring on them the status of law. Other sporting goods trade associations followed the CCAGM example. The cooperation among firms in the industry made possible the establishment of the fair trade codes.

In the midst of cooperative trade association attempts to regulate and control competition, the depression hit the sporting goods industry in May and June of 1931 (Bradsby, 1932; Spink, 1932). The sporting goods industry was unprepared. Many leaders in the field believed that the depression would actually help the sale of sport equipment, based on the bicycle craze that took place in the middle of the 1890s depression. Well-known observers, such as Julian Curtis, president of Spalding & Brothers, pointed out that the depressions of 1907, 1913, and 1920-1921 did not adversely affect the sporting goods industry. Regardless of past experience and conventional wisdom, the depression did hit the sporting goods industry during the second quarter of 1931. When it arrived, it hit hard. Between 1931 and 1933 sporting goods sales dropped 50% (U.S. Bureau of the Census, 1939). During this same period more than 20% of sporting goods manufacturers were driven out of the business (U.S. Bureau of the Census, 1939).

The industry-wide cooperation that brought about the development of fair trade codes carried over into other cooperative efforts. The most significant of these was a concerted effort to promote sport participation. Efforts of national organizations to promote sport had been going on since 1919. National Baseball Week, National Golf Week, and National Tennis Week began in 1919. National Golf Week and National Tennis Week were dropped in 1923. They were reintroduced during the early 1930s. National Fisherman's Week, National Hunter's Week, and National Bicycle Week were added during the 1930s. These national promotions did spur some local interest. Prizes were given for window displays and advertising copy. Participation by local dealers increased each year. Some sporting goods dealers reported increased sales during promotion weeks ("A Gratifying Record," 1938).

Before 1935, national promotion campaigns were not very effective in increasing market size. They lacked local dealer support in organizing sport participation opportunities (Scudder, 1935; Tweedie, 1935). National Baseball Week is a good example. In 1930 C.T. Felker, editor of the *Sporting Goods Dealer*, alerted industry members that baseball participation had been declining since 1923. According to Felker, the popularity of baseball had not declined: local organization of amateur leagues had declined (Felker, 1930). National Baseball Week may have been "America's premier window display contest," but the sale of sport equipment depended on participation (Felker, 1930). Participation, in turn, depended on the organization of sport opportunities at the local level.

Before 1923 local dealers had been the backbone of promotional efforts to sell sports and sport equipment. They had been the organizers of teams, leagues, tournaments, and instructional schools. They expanded the market for the sport equipment they sold (Dumont, 1931; "Voice of the Trade," 1927). The changing distribution system, however, increased the number of retail competitors in the sporting goods field. The new retailers were interested in market share, not market expansion. The traditional local dealer did not want to expand the market for fear that competitors would be the beneficiaries. Local dealers might enter window and advertising contests as a way of guarding market share, but they were not interested in organizing sport participation (Spink, 1930).

This attitude changed after 1935. Exactly why it changed is unclear. The new feeling of cooperation among manufacturers, jobbers, and dealers may have been responsible. Manufacturers and jobbers pledged to help the local dealers protect their businesses. All trade codes contained regulations that favored the local dealer. Stipulations against direct selling, for example, were designed to help the local dealer. Beyond that, agreements by manufacturers not to sell to chains, department stores, or mail-order houses were welcomed by local dealers ("Large Factories," 1932; Spink, 1932). The fact that department stores began to promote local sport participation may have been a stronger incentive (Felker, 1936). Some local dealers may have been convinced by arguments presented by manufacturers and jobbers that the problem was not overproduction but rather a lack of effort to increase market size (Davis, 1937). In the opinion of manufacturers and jobbers, increasing market size was the responsibility of the local sporting goods dealer (Dumont, 1931).

Another reason for the renewed interest of local dealers in organizing sport participation was the change in the emphasis of manufacturers' and jobbers' promotional efforts. Before 1935 most manufacturers' and jobbers' promotional efforts were designed to maintain market share. Efforts at market expansion had been sporadic and uncoordinated (McMillan, 1935; Tweedie, 1935). After 1935 efforts at market expansion were increased and better coordinated.

The promotion of baseball is a good example. The Sporting Goods Manufacturers Association organized and funded the Athletic Institute in 1935. The purpose of the Institute was to promote sport. Its first objective was to promote baseball participation ("Help Institute," 1935; "Here's a Campaign to Boost Baseball," 1935). To accomplish this objective, the Institute planned to work directly with local sporting goods dealers. Two of its early promotion plans involved the creation of a "Little World Series" among cities that were natural rivals and to hire local high school baseball coaches to direct summer baseball programs. By 1937 the Institute had hooked up with the American Baseball Congress, the National Semi-Pro Baseball Congress, and the American Legion to promote baseball opportunities (Brown, 1937; Chaillaux, 1937; Dumont, 1937). The Athletic Institute published baseball instruction guides and organized baseball instructional schools. It also was involved with the National Sporting Goods Dealers Association's "It Pays to Play" drive. The Institute gave support to industrial leagues and to the National Recreation Association. It provided information and encouragement to local dealers about ways to obtain Work Projects Administration money for fields and playgrounds. The Institute became a promoter and a clearinghouse in the drive to bring back high school baseball (Bradsby, 1935). Finally, the Institute helped to promote and to coordinate National Baseball Week.

Coordinated efforts to increase participation as a strategy to increase sales were effective in some segments of the industry. The sale of golf, fishing, and tennis equipment increased every year after 1935. Fishing sales were ahead of the 1929 figure by 1937. Tennis sales in 1939 were ahead of 1929 sales. Baseball and golf sales lagged behind 1929 sales of these items as late as 1939. Baseball sales dropped throughout the 1930s, making a comeback only in 1939 even though observers claimed that baseball participation increased every year after 1935. Industry leaders shared customer credit information, discussed solutions to common problems, talked about industry profitability, shared information about demand, and in general cooperated among themselves. These practices increased the individual and collective knowledge about the sporting goods industry. Competitors gained a better understanding about the effects of competitive strategy on industry members and overall profitability. Cooperative efforts were used to increase market size and to gain a better understanding of the industry among established companies. Cutthroat competition decreased (Miller & Fielding, 1995).

1940s: World War II and Sport Policy

At a July 1939 board of directors meeting J.H. Hillerich, president of Hillerich & Bradsby, told members of the board that another world war was coming. The United States would be heavily involved in this new war in Europe, he said, and the sporting goods industry would be profoundly impacted. Hillerich suggested that the company stockpile raw materials because he believed that the world war would force shortages of materials needed for the production of baseball bats and golf clubs (Hillerich & Bradsby, 1939). Hillerich proved to be correct. World War II severely curbed the production of sporting equipment. This was especially true for goods made from rubber, leather, wood, cotton, and petroleum. H & B, like many companies, did attempt to stockpile raw materials. This proved fruitless as government policy curbed production of sport equipment regardless of material supplies. Rationing was the rule of civilian life during World War II. Many sporting and leisure activities and events were suspended, terminated, or affected in other ways. In 1942 the United States Office of Price Administration called for a stop in production of golf products because the rubber was needed to produce war products ("Two Centuries," 2000). The great Wimbledon championships were suspended from 1940 through 1945. Many male professional athletes were called into military duty, leaving many men's sports with less than top players. College and high school sport programs were cut back or eliminated altogether.

Other forms of amateur sports flourished during the war. In both military life and civilian life sport participation became a planned matter of policy. Near the end of 1940 the United States instituted the first peacetime draft in U.S. history. Inductees into the army and the navy had to be trained. Sport became part of this training as a matter of military policy (Wakefield, 1997). Highly competitive athletic sports were included for four basic reasons. First, military leaders believed that athletic team competition had a positive influence on soldier morale and helped to develop an *esprit de corps*. Second, sports kept soldiers and sailors physically and mentally fit. Third, athletic competition kept soldiers occupied during their leisure by providing spectator appeal. Finally, many military leaders believed that sport had a significant impact on the development of leadership skills. Military policy tried to coerce every soldier and every sailor into the sporting life. Military leaders advised civilian authorities to adopt similar policies as part of the war effort (Wakefield, 1997).

The military also developed sport programs to meet the needs of women. World War II brought substantial numbers of women into the army, the navy, and the coast guard. Athletic competition became part of the training program for women, which copied the men's program. Women were encouraged to participate in competitive athletic programs in volleyball, archery, basketball, bowling, tennis, table tennis, swimming, badminton, and softball (Wakefield, 1997). Women's military teams also took on civilian teams.

Women had been competing in industrial leagues since the First World War. The 1930s had witnessed a great deal of expansion in women's industrial leagues. This was particularly true of softball teams. During World War II the U.S. government encouraged women to move into the factory to aid the war effort by filling men's jobs. In certain essential industries the government prescribed that women would be paid the same wages as men. In all industries the government encouraged policies that would accommodate women's comforts and interests. Recreational sport programs for women, the outgrowth of the welfare capitalism of the First World War and the 1920s, became an important part of corporate policy (Guttman, 1991).

Some sporting and leisure activities seemed to find their niche during this time. The war brought more women into more sports. Society's views of women playing sports began to change. An example of this is the women's professional baseball league. To address the sport entertainment desires of the American public, the All-American Girls Professional Baseball League was begun (Brown, 1992; Candaele & Wilson, 1986; Johnson, 1994). Made famous today by the 1992 hit movie *A League of Their Own* starring Geena Davis, Madonna, Rosie O'Donnell, and Tom Hanks, the AAGPBL enjoyed success from 1943 to 1954 (Marshall, 1992). The league was the idea of Philip K. Wrigley, owner of the Wrigley chewing gum company and of the Chicago Cubs (Berlage, 1994,

2001), who thought that men's baseball would have to stop for the war. Although the AAGPBL is the most well-known women's baseball league, there is historical record of women playing baseball long before then: in colleges in 1866 and on professional women's teams in 1867 (Berlage, 2001). At its peak in 1948, there were 10 teams in the AAGPBL, and over one million fans watched them play. The AAGPBL, along with other societal changes in the United States, helped bring about the beginning of a positive change in thinking toward women in sport.

When the war ended in 1945, several thousand men and women returned home to the United States. The military policy to use sport as part of training and as a recreational activity had produced sport enthusiasts. Corporate business policies to organize civilian sport participants had also helped create sport enthusiasts. Postwar Americans went looking for entertainment and leisure as sport participants and as spectators. Baseball attendance, for example, grew from approximately 10 million in 1946 to 20.2 million in 1949 (Lucas & Smith, 1978). The sport industry responded to the desires of these new sport enthu-

© Bettmann/CORBIS

At its peak in 1948, the All-American Girls Professional Baseball League had 10 teams, and over one million fans watched them play.

siasts in other ways. Because of the growing popularity of men's football, a new professional football league began in 1946 and survived for three seasons before merging with the NFL for the 1950 season. In 1949 the men's Basketball Association of America merged with the National Basketball League to become the National Basketball Association (NBA). The end of the decade was a boom period for professional sports.

The late 1940s saw the color barrier broken in professional sport when Jackie Robinson signed with the Brooklyn Dodgers in 1945 (Burk, 2001; "Two Centuries," 2000). Robinson was followed by Larry Doby, who signed with Cleveland in 1946. Both would play in the major leagues during the 1947 season. Professional football saw Marion Motley and Bill Willis join the Cleveland Browns in 1946 and Kenny Washington and Woody Strode play for the Los Angeles Rams that same year. Professional basketball had to wait until 1950 before Chuck Cooper joined the Celtics and Sweetwater Clifton left the Harlem Globetrotters for the New York Knicks. The integration process was influenced by several factors. It was, at least in part, a response to the pressure for integration in

the military during World War II. Part of it was also a question of ethics and values and of changing attitudes. Part of it was economics. African Americans constituted a large untapped and inexpensive talent pool (Burk, 2001; Halberstam, 1994). During the decades that followed, team owners became aware that African American talent often meant the difference between financial success and failure (Halberstam, 1994; Voigt, 1983). This was particularly true in the 1950s and 1960s as a new breed of owners took control of professional sports (Voigt, 1983; Roberts & Olsen, 1989).

1950s: New Techniques and New Technologies

Bill Veeck, an innovator who introduced new techniques to sport managers, learned the baseball business from his father, William Veeck, Sr., president of the Chicago Cubs from 1917 to 1933. The junior Veeck continued his baseball education as owner of the Milwaukee Brewers of the minor league American Association in 1941 (Quirk & Fort, 1992). After the war, Veeck headed a syndicate that

Jackie Robinson, Brooklyn Dodgers' first baseman, broke the color barrier in professional sport in the late 1940s.

61

purchased the Cleveland Indians, a team that ranked third from the bottom in league attendance. Within two years Veeck turned the team into the hottest item in baseball (Quirk & Fort, 1992).

Veeck realized that not all baseball consumers were baseball fans. Baseball *fans* came to the park to watch baseball; they needed little else to be entertained. They came to the stadium regardless of the weather or the team's record. Veeck realized, however, that only about 20% of baseball consumers were really baseball fans. The other 80% of baseball consumers came to the park to be entertained in some fashion. When baseball was dull, they required other forms of entertainment. Baseball, thought Veeck, could be immensely exciting, but it could also be quite dull. What was needed, concluded Veeck, was activities that could excite and entertain the consumer when baseball could not (Veeck, 1965).

At Cleveland, Veeck began the process of turning baseball into popular entertainment. Veeck introduced fireworks after every game. He had midgets racing toy cars around the park. He introduced bat day to entice children to bring their parents and friends to the ballpark. As an added incentive to families, Veeck offered baby-sitting services (Burk, 2001; Quirk & Fort, 1992; Zimbalist, 1992) and a variety of other giveaways to motivate consumers into becoming fans. In 1948 Cleveland won the American League pennant and went on to become World Series champions. Led by popular stars such as Lou Boudreau, Larry Doby, Joe Gordon, and Bob Feller, and Veeck promotions, the team drew an American League record of 2,620,627 fans. The record stood for 32 years until the Yankees broke it in 1980 (Quirk and Fort, 1992). Veeck was forced to sell the Indians after the 1948 season due to poor health. He was back in baseball three years later as owner of the St. Louis Browns.

As owner of the Browns, Veeck tried other promotional efforts to attract fans and increase their involvement in and enjoyment of the game. In 1951 he sent in three-foot, six-inch Eddie Gaedel as a pinch hitter. He had Gaedel carry a kid's bat, and he put the number 1/8 on Gaedel's jersey (Quirk & Fort, 1992). The opposing manager protested and was overruled, Gaedel walked, and the fans loved it. While with the St. Louis Browns, Veeck also introduced Grand Stand Manager's Day. This provided a chance for the fans to manage the team. Fan involvement and entertainment increased as the viewers voted on strategic moves and player positioning during the game (Quirk & Fort, 1992; Zimbalist, 1992).

Near the end of the decade Veeck worked his innovative magic as owner of the Chicago White Sox. En route to winning the American League pennant in 1959, Veeck introduced the exploding scoreboard and added to consumer identification with players by putting player names on the backs of their jerseys. Also in 1959 Veeck introduced into baseball the most far-reaching of his business innovations. Veeck reasoned that players were assets for a baseball franchise in much the same way that equipment might be. Like a truck, a baseball player had a useful life span. Player skills depreciated with age in the same way that a truck depreciated as it was driven from year to year. When the useful life span was over, the truck or the player had to be replaced by the business. Replacement cost the team money. As a trained accountant, Veeck realized that since trucks could be depreciated on the company's income statement each year, why couldn't baseball players? Veeck's creative accounting technique meant that the team could get a tax break. As player skills were written off each year as an expense, the team could record a loss on the income statement, when in fact the team was making a profit (Noll, 1974; Quirk & Fort, 1992). This saved the team income tax dollars.

Advances in technology, especially in electronics and communication devices, had probably the most significant effect on the sport industry of the 20th century (Rader, 1984). Today, television is often hailed as the most influential factor in popularizing sports in America. Before television, getting information out to fans and others took the progression from word-of-mouth, to general newspaper, to sporting newspaper, to radio and telegraph, to sport magazines, and finally to television in 1936. The first sport event broadcast on radio was a boxing match: the Dempsey–Carpentier fight on RCA's WJZ in 1922 (Barnouw, 1966; Powers, 1984). The first sport event broadcast on television was the 1936 Olympic Games in Berlin. It was reported that 150,000 people were able to watch the events on television sets placed around the city at "TV locales" (Guttman, 1997). In late 1936 the BBC (British Broadcasting Company) broadcast the Oxford–Cambridge boat race. The United States started with its first sport event broadcast on television on May 17, 1939; it was a baseball game between Columbia and Princeton (Powers, 1984). Other events were added and included the National Football League championship game, an NCAA college football game between Fordham University and Waynesburg College, a boxing match

Courtesy of Celso Rodriguez, *El Tiempo*, Toledo, OH

Television's invasion into the world of sport has provided a variety of sport broadcasting jobs.

featuring Lou Nova and Max Baer, and the Eastern Grass Court Tennis Championship. These first few years of television broadcasts consisted of black-and-white fuzzy images sent to small television sets. Still, sport events on TV seemed to be popular. However, when technological progressions brought advances such as color, instant replays, slow motion, close-ups, improved picture clarity, and larger screens around the end of the 1940s, the interest in and popularity of sport events on television took off.

At first, sport executives wouldn't allow games to be televised because they were afraid that people would watch the game on TV for free as opposed to going to the game and paying admission fees. Sport executives at the time were protecting the number one revenue producer: the gate receipts. There seemed to be good reason for the worry because attendance at professional football and professional baseball games dropped as a result of television. Not yet willing to completely keep TV out, executives instituted the idea of not allowing home games to be televised in local markets (Guttman, 1997). As a result, attendance at the games increased.

It wouldn't be too many years, however, before many in the sport industry realized that the money from broadcasting rights fees would become a major revenue-producing source. At the same time, television provided the sport industry with new jobs and careers for those interested in working in this segment of the industry. Positions as journalists, camera people, commentators, managers, and many other types of sport broadcasting jobs

resulted from television's invasion into the sport world. In addition, television executives realized the moneymaking potential of sport events on TV. Companies wanted to pay for commercial time during events. Soon, broadcasting companies developed sport departments whose sole focus was to produce and broadcast sport events (Rader, 1984).

Today, TV sport is a full-grown beast with numerous events broadcast on general broadcasting stations and several sports-only broadcasting companies. Further, some sports have been created specifically for TV, such as the roller derby, ESPN's X-Games, and American Gladiators. Some would argue that the WWF (World Wrestling Federation) choreographs its events specifically for TV.

Television has been influential in other ways as well. For instance, as television companies paid their fees through the sale of commercial time to advertisers and sponsors, their desire to sell high-priced ads during the most lucrative times when the most people are watching has led to rule changes in many sports. In basketball, the rule change actually carries the word *TV* in its title: the "TV time-out." Many sport events are scheduled based on TV requirements. Major events are especially influenced. For instance, the Super Bowl is scheduled at a time of day in consideration of markets in several time zones. In another example, the Summer Olympic Games were held in Sydney, Australia, in 2000 and carried several television challenges for the U.S. viewing market. They were scheduled later in the calendar year to accommodate the warmer season in Australia for the comfort of the spectator. Events were taped and broadcast during American evening hours in order to place the events in prime-time slots so as to be aired during the time when the most Americans could watch and advertisers could be sure that their costly commercials would be seen. However, this idea backfired on NBC. They found that Americans were getting their news of the events from several other sources such as radio and the World Wide Web and therefore didn't have to watch the events on scheduled TV. Further, Americans complained that they didn't want to watch a production tape of the event because they wanted to see the event as it took place, even with the 14-hour time difference between Sydney and the United States.

Another earlier technological invention, the automobile, began to make a mark on the broadening sport industry in the 1950s in the form of car racing. Automobile racing had been part of sport

© Greg Crisp/Sports Chrome USA

Created in 1947, NASCAR has become one of the most popular spectator sports in America.

since the invention of the automobile. However, in 1947 the National Association for Stock Car Auto Racing (NASCAR) was created ("Two Centuries," 2000). Today there are several different categories of car racing, and NASCAR is one of the most popular spectator sports in the United States (Johnson, 1999). Companies compete vigorously for sponsorship and advertising space on the car and the driver, and the prices for the space reflect the competition. For instance, the space on the hood of the car can be purchased for between $4 million and $6 million (Johnson, 1999).

1960s: The Foreign Invasion

American trade policies initiated after World War II opened U.S. sporting goods markets to foreign competition during the 1960s. Foreign competitors from Japan, the European Economic Community, Britain, and the Soviet Bloc countries exploited U.S. free trade agreements and developed strategies that gave them a competitive edge in U.S. markets. Dubow Sporting Goods Corporation, a pioneer in the development and production of baseball gloves, went out of business in 1964. The company had been in the baseball glove industry

for over 70 years. Dubow survived five depressions, the intense competition that followed World War I and World War II, government luxury taxes, labor disputes, hostile buyouts, and attacks on its market share and distribution chain by mail-order houses, chain stores, and department stores. Dubow was resilient. The company grew with baseball and helped baseball to grow. But the company did not survive the Japanese invasion into the baseball glove and mitt market during the 1960s. "The Japanese have put us out of business," said Dubow. "All the people that worked for us in baseball gloves are gone" (Fielding & Miller, 1998b). Dubow cited low-cost Japanese imports as the culprit in the company's demise.

The General Agreements of Tariffs and Trade (GATT), begun in 1946 and revised periodically into the 1960s, opened U.S. markets to foreign sporting goods, but the lowering of tariffs does not by itself explain the success of these offshore invaders. The foreign competitors copied U.S. products and improved on them. They relied on research and development to produce new technologies. Mizuno, for example, copied and improved on U.S. baseball glove models and was able to offer them to consumers at lower prices. The success of foreign athletic shoe manufacturers such as Adidas and Puma was due in part to an improved vulcanizing process that made their shoes lighter and more durable. This same process permitted the mass production of molded soles, making it possible for foreign competitors to develop a greater variety of sizes and styles at less cost (Fielding & Miller, 1998b). Other strategies included penetration pricing, segmentation, and the development of new, more effective distribution channels. Mizuno, for example, used penetration pricing (low price) to introduce its high-quality products into U.S. sporting goods markets. Japanese shoe companies slipped unnoticed into the low-end sport shoe segment of the market during the early 1960s. Successful in this segment of the industry, they moved into middle and top-grade niches during the late 1960s (Fielding & Miller, 1998b).

Foreign competitors helped establish new distribution channels as well. Many Japanese firms targeted the discount stores that developed in the late 1950s and early 1960s. Other firms used the mail-order houses and department stores. Still others sold through nontraditional outlets. Japanese sporting goods, for example, could be found in grocery stores such as the A&P, 5- and 10-cent stores such as Woolworth and Newberry's, as well as hardware stores, drugstores, and variety stores (Fielding & Miller, 1998b).

Foreign competitors adopted different promotion strategies in different segments of the sporting goods industry. In baseball, golf, tennis, and fishing equipment, foreign manufacturers, principally the Japanese, offered reseller aids in the form of larger margins. This was an effective strategy in selling sporting goods to discount houses, department stores, chain stores, and mail-order retailers (Fielding & Miller, 1998b). In the athletic shoe and athletic apparel segments of the sporting goods industry, foreign competitors such as Adidas and Puma emphasized personal selling and sales promotions. Adidas sales representatives, for example, dealt directly with coaches and athletes. They outfitted track teams for free. They gave away shoes and athletic apparel at all the major track meets. Adidas sales representatives talked to college and high school track coaches about ways to improve athletic shoes and hawked Adidas equipment. By 1967, 80% of all Olympic track and field athletes wore Adidas. When Adidas became the official track and field outfitter for the 1968 Olympics, they banned other companies from the Olympic village. Direct selling and promotional giveaways made Adidas synonymous with track and field success (Fielding & Miller, 1998b).

U.S. sporting goods firms responded to the foreign invasion in a variety of ways. A.G. Spalding, a division of Questor Corporation of Toledo, led a movement toward offshore production. Spalding moved its tennis ball operation to Ireland in 1961. During the same year, it transferred the manufacture of tennis rackets to Belgium. A year later it developed manufacturing plants for tennis rackets and tennis balls in Sweden and Britain. Spalding baseballs were manufactured in the West Indies as early as 1960. The company moved its manufacturer of baseball and softball mitts and gloves to Korea in 1965. The manufacture of golf equipment was transferred overseas in 1970. In 1972 Spalding set up manufacturing plants in Spain and Italy to produce ski equipment. By early 1974 Spalding did most of its manufacturing in Canada, Australia, Japan, Korea, Europe, and the West Indies (Fielding & Miller, 1998b).

Many U.S. companies emphasized research and development. This led to the production of sport equipment using new materials and new technologies. Rawlings, Wilson, Spalding, MacGregor, Lannom, and Hillerich & Bradsby turned to the use of aluminum at least in part as a response to the increase in golf and baseball imports. Wilson and Rawlings introduced aluminum and fiberglass composition tennis rackets in the late 1960s.

U.S. sporting goods companies also responded by increasing sales promotions, personal selling efforts, and reseller support. MacGregor, for example, launched the Jack Nicklaus Golden Bear line of golf clubs and used Nicklaus-led golf clinics and other on-site promotions to sell golf equipment. Wilson introduced tennis racket models bearing the signatures of Arthur Ashe, Jimmy Connors, and Billie Jean King (Fielding & Miller 1998b). Sporting goods firms also increased the size of their sales forces in order to cover assigned territories more effectively. Many companies reinstituted sales training programs. Foreign competition also led to a reemphasis on reseller supports. U.S. sporting goods companies increased regional advertising efforts and provided local retailers with advertising copy. Sales representatives provided local firms with information about displays and effective merchandising techniques. Factory representatives spent more time explaining product features to retailers and providing sales information.

By lowering tariffs, the GATT agreements opened U.S. markets to a greater degree than ever before. Foreign competitors used this opening and the fact that sporting goods are labor intensive to gain

65

In Profile

The Roone Revolution in TV Sport and Entertainment

The Roone Revolution changed how sports were televised during the last part of the 20th century.

In July of 1960 Roone Arledge proposed to Tom Moore and Ed Sherick, ABC's directors of programming and sports, a new plan for covering football games. Arledge's plan and its application revolutionized how sports were televised during the remainder of the 20th century. Arledge wanted to bring the TV viewer to the game, to get the audiences emotionally involved. He wanted viewers at home to experience the game as though they were actually at the stadium (Rader, 1984; Roberts & Olsen, 1989). Even if they were not football fans, reasoned Arledge, they could still enjoy the game. Bringing the consumer to the game required that Arledge develop a new method for covering the game. Arledge increased the number of cameras from three to nine and then to twelve and more. He introduced instant replay to make sure the viewer hadn't missed or misunderstood a key play or the essential artistry of a particular action. To bring the action up close and personal, he used handheld and isolated cameras. Split screens and other technical devices helped the viewer experience the atmosphere of the game. To help duplicate the live atmosphere, Arledge used directional and remote microphones to capture the sounds of the game and the stadium crowd (Rader, 1984; Roberts & Olsen, 1989).

Arledge, who died in 2002, believed that televised sport was in the commercial entertainment business. Television programs survived and televised sport continued only if they could draw higher ratings, higher advertising dollars, and higher corporate profits. The success of collegiate or professional football was measured in terms of the number of viewers on any given Saturday, Sunday, or Monday. This meant that the game had to attract a wide variety of viewers. Like Veeck before him, Arledge realized that the casual viewer and the "sometimes" fan were far more important than the avid football consumer. The reason for this was simple: There were more of them. These folks required more than just football or sport to be entertained. Sport was far less important than entertainment. Arledge believed that the participants in a sport contest were the essence of entertainment. People, he thought, watched sports to be entertained by people performing. Sport viewing was experiential. By presenting, by examining, by analyzing, by making the sport performance up close and personal, Arledge believed he was extending the experience. In so doing, he was extending the entertainment value of sport beyond the game itself (Rader, 1984; Roberts & Olsen, 1989).

Arledge's lessons on improving sport entertainment were copied by other entrepreneurs. Ted Giannoulas, also known as the San Diego Chicken, began performing for baseball fans in 1974 and ushered in the age of the mascot (Rader, 1984). A decade later nearly half of professional baseball teams had mascots, and Giannoulas was making over $100,000 a year at Padres games, minor league baseball parks, professional basketball games, fairs, and other public entertainment venues (Rader, 1984). Later in the 1970s the Dallas Cowboys Cheerleaders began adding entertainment to Cowboy football games. Their success prompted other teams to add cheerleaders. By the end of the decade nearly every pro football franchise had hired cheerleaders to extend the entertainment value of the game. The idea was to tailor sports to appeal to potential viewers who were not devoted followers of the game. This meant packaging or repackaging the sport for the television media. On one hand, it meant mascots and cheerleaders. On the other hand, it meant exploding scoreboards, artificial grass, extended schedules and play-off systems, and changing the rules of the sport to make it more action packed and more exciting for less knowledgeable viewers (Rader, 1984).

a competitive advantage in U.S. markets. They built on this initial advantage by manipulating the marketing mix (see chapter 10). They created products for specific segments of the U.S. market, developed new distribution channels or relied on underused channels, manipulated pricing, and resorted to personal selling and promotional efforts to sell their goods. U.S. sporting goods firms responded with similar strategies. The result was a heightened emphasis on marketing and the concomitant manipulation of the marketing mix. Sporting goods firms also began to spend more time and energy on research and development (Fielding & Miller, 1998b).

1970s: From Woodstock to Nautilus

The people who came of age in the 1960s and 1970s (born after World War II and before 1960) are known as the baby boomers. Members of this generation received the sobriquets of "hippies" and "flower children" and were blamed for loosening the moral fiber of U.S. society. In the 1980s people in this same group were labeled "yuppies" (young, upwardly mobile professionals) and were given credit for the great wealth-building era of the 1980s. They were later held responsible for the recession in the early 1990s and then credited with bringing the country out of the recession with a revitalized commitment to consumerism, commercialism, and computers. This group has had the highest divorce rate and the highest single-parent rate, and are the parents of the Generation X-ers.

The baby boomers are the generation that challenged sport most profoundly in terms of its intellectual underpinnings during the 1960s, 1970s, and 1980s. They questioned the emphasis on winning, they didn't believe that sport developed character, they wondered whether there were any real sport heroes, and they thought sport had become too commercialized. They were interested in health and fitness and participation. They saw spectator sport as entertainment, and they demanded more for their money. They are expected to have another major impact on the industry as they reach retirement age between 2010 and 2020.

In 1968 Jim Fixx weighed 214 pounds and smoked two packs of cigarettes a day. Worried about his health (his father had died of a heart attack at age 43), Fixx gave up cigarettes and started running. He lost 60 pounds and in the process helped to popularize running as the road to health. He also helped to extol the virtues of strenuous exercise. Running and exercise, it seemed, led to long life, freedom from depression, elimination of stress caused by the worries of job and life, energy, and the "runner's high." Exercise was the yuppie panacea. Working out would make the baby boomers immune to the ravages of stress and time (Roberts & Olsen, 1989). On July 21, 1984, as Fixx began his last run, he was the picture of health. Approximately 20 minutes later he was dead, the victim of a massive heart attack. Later that day, a motorcyclist discovered his body by the side of the road (Roberts & Olsen, 1989).

Fixx's death didn't slow the "exercise as the road to health" movement, but it did change some of its particulars. Fixx's autopsy showed dangerously high levels of cholesterol. One of his coronary arteries was 98% blocked, another was 85% blocked, and a third was nearly 50% blocked (Roberts & Olsen, 1989). Fixx had been complaining for several months of chest pains while running, an obvious signal that something was wrong. Friends had urged him to seek professional advice. Fixx ignored the signs and the warnings and paid the price. For Fixx and for many other Americans, sports, exercise, and fitness had become an obsession (Roberts & Olsen, 1989). What was needed for these exercised-obsessed people was an industry dedicated to helping Americans exercise, diet, jog, run, and lift weights under expert supervision.

Beginning in the late 1960s and developing slowly in the 1970s, Americans like Jim Fixx planned their own workouts, constructed their own diets, and provided their own prognoses for pain and injury. During the 1980s the demand for such services grew exponentially, and health clubs expanded to fill the void. The number of commercial health, racquet, and sport clubs more than doubled during the 1980s (International Health, Racquet, and Sportsclub Association, 1995). The 1980s also brought fitness centers, aerobics studios, fitness specialists, workout tapes, and the popularization and institutionalization of chic fitness clothing as everyday wear (Rader, 1997).

Jogging and long-distance running, as part of the new attention to fitness, made great strides in development and popularity during the 1970s and 1980s. For instance, in 1970 the first New York City Marathon attracted only 126 entrants. All were men (Cooper, 1997; Rader, 1999). By 1980 there were 16,005 men and women participants. By the mid-1980s the marathon had to limit participation to 20,000. The fitness craze and the popularity of running helped to fuel the growth of various running events, related products such as running magazines and books, and running apparel. The interest in running brought about the development of event management companies that specialized in the setup and management of running events. Other offshoot products included multievents such as triathlons, mega-distance races, biathlons, and iron man competitions.

The formal study of the sport industry expanded during the 1960s and 1970s, although it had its beginnings far earlier. In response to the growing interest in jobs and careers in the sport business industry, the Baseball Administration School at Florida Southern College in Lakeland, Florida, offered a program in baseball business administration in 1949 (Isaacs, 1964). A testament to the growing professionalization and formalization of education for jobs and careers in the sport industry, it just might have been the first sport management program at a college in the United States. Course titles in the program included The National Agreement (an analytical study of the governing association of the minor and major leagues); Player Contracts and Related Paperwork; Tickets and Tax Laws (a study of ticket pricing, taxes, and ticket sales and promotions); Legal Responsibility and Insurance; Finances, Accounting, and Payroll Systems; Park Maintenance (stadium facility management); Daily Game Operations; Concessions; and Promotion and Public Relations. These topics are similar to today's sport management curriculum standards (see chapter 2). It is unclear exactly when sport management education began or when the terms *sport(s) administration, sport management*, or *sport business* were first coined. Yet, before the creation in 1966 of the sports administration program at The Ohio University, a book by Stan Isaacs, a sport journalist in the 1950s and 1960s, titled *Careers and Opportunities in Sport* contained a chapter called "Careers in Sports Administration" (Isaacs, 1964).

Long before the creation of the baseball business administration program at Florida Southern College, A.G. Spalding was using sport management education to educate managers, organizers, and promoters of sport events as a means of promoting the Spalding line of sporting goods. In 1892 Spalding established Spalding's Athletic Library. Spalding describes the library as "the lead-

The popularity of long-distance running is evident in such events as the Chicago Marathon.

ing library series of its kind published in the world. In fact, it has no imitators, let alone equals. It occupies a field that it has created for itself" (p. ii). The library was extensive, with 123 titles covering numerous sport activities of the time. Although the books were designed to explain how to play particular sports, many included sport management material (Sullivan, 1907). For example, Spalding's *An Athletic Primer* includes chapters on how to perform track and field events, but also chapters on how to organize a track club, how to manage a track meet, and how to design facilities. In addition, one chapter describes how to pay particular attention to the spectators and keep them entertained and informed. In today's sport management education classrooms we call this a function of sport marketing.

From these humble beginnings, sport management education has become a growth industry, as evidenced in this book. There are scholarly associations and approximately 16 academic journals. The primary organization for the United States and Canada is the North American Society for Sport Management. There are over 200 undergraduate programs, over 80 master's programs, and 7 doctoral programs. Education provides a viable career for those interested in teaching and preparing those students whose jobs and careers will be in the sport business industry. Sport management education has helped to legitimize and professionalize careers in the sport business industry.

During the 1960s and 1970s, many new jobs were created for the support service businesses surrounding the sport industry, such as sport agents, sport marketing, professional club management, and sporting goods manufacturers. For example, in 1960 Mark McCormack started the International Management Group (IMG), a business that advises, manages, and represents athletes whose fame and popularity could bring hundreds, thousands, and eventually millions of dollars in sponsorship and endorsement deals (see chapter 16). When athletes hire agents to manage their business affairs and create potential earnings, the amount of dollars negotiated and the types of deals struck increase dramatically. For example, early records from Hillerich & Bradsby, makers of the Louisville Slugger bat, show that the company negotiated directly with athletes such as Pete Browning and Babe Ruth to put their names on bats. The deals were informal, often just verbal agreements, and athletes were minimally compensated (as mentioned earlier, Ruth received $100

and a set of golf clubs). Today, the negotiations take place between the athlete's agent and a company representative, and deals can be worth millions of dollars.

1980s: The Participation Revolution

In 1979 a young sport entrepreneur named Paul Fireman bought the North American distribution rights to Reebok. Within five years Fireman would own Reebok, changing the company during the 1980s so that it would become the number one seller of athletic shoes in the United States. Back in 1979 Reebok held a market share of slightly over 3% in the branded athletic footwear segment of the U.S. market. Fireman's first move was to import Reebok's high-quality, high-price running shoes to compete with Nike and Adidas. This strategy proved unfruitful as Nike and Adidas continued to outscore Reebok in the men's running shoe market. Reebok never achieved much above a 3% share of the market. In 1981 Fireman changed his strategy. He concluded that Reebok could not compete effectively in the men's shoe market against Nike and Adidas. Indeed, he decided that the company didn't need to. What Reebok needed, thought Fireman, was to tap into the burgeoning women's market for athletic footwear. In 1982 Reebok introduced the first athletic shoe specially designed for women. The Reebok Freestyle was an aerobic fitness shoe that catered to the growing women's interest in aerobic exercise (Quelch & Hiller, 1994; Rohm, 1999).

The Freestyle ushered in a period of phenomenal growth for Reebok. During the next five years the firm's sales grew from $3.5 million in 1982 to $1.4 billion in 1987. During this same period net income jumped from $200,000 to $165 million. Reebok became number one in sales by 1985, a position it held until overtaken by Nike in 1991. By 1987 Reebok held a 32.2% share of the branded athletic footwear market, a jump of nearly 30% in just five years. Between 1983 and 1987 Reebok ranked first among major U.S. companies in sales growth and earnings growth. Revenues reached $1.8 billion in 1989, and by 1992 the Freestyle had become the number one selling shoe in the industry (Quelch & Hiller, 1994; Rohm, 1999).

Reebok's success derived from its strategy of targeting women sport participants at a time when participation rates for women were growing dramatically. Between 1968 and 1980 high school girls' sport participation increased by more than 500%. Women collegians increased participation by nearly as much (Cahn, 1994; Guttman, 1991; Hult, 1989). According to a Wilson Sporting Goods study done at the end of the decade, eight out of ten girls were participating in sport (Figler & Whitaker, 1991). The feminist movement of the late 1960s and 1970s prompted the tremendous growth in the women's market for sport and sport products (Cahn, 1994). The fitness boom of the 1970s and 1980s discussed earlier also influenced women's interest. Women were very much a part of what Randy Roberts and James Olsen labeled the "sport and self movement" in the United States, which dominated the 1980s (Roberts & Olsen, 1989).

Increased participation by women was also a matter of public policy (Figler & Whitaker, 1991; Guttman, 1991; Hult, 1989). Title IX of the Education Amendments Act of 1972 and the follow-up Civil Rights Restoration Act of 1988 mandated increased opportunities for women athletes. Public institutions receiving federal funding had to increase opportunities for women to participate in sport. Increased participation translated into increased sales. Sporting goods manufacturers, distributors, and retailers, following the Reebok example, strove to do their bit for public policy by selling sport shoes, sport equipment, and sport apparel and prompting participation opportunities for women athletes.

Women were not the only ones to benefit from the participation revolution. Youth sports became more highly organized during the 1970s and 1980s. Little League Baseball grew exponentially, branching off into summer recreation leagues that established local rules and age limits for both boys and girls. Pop Warner Football became the participation model for the fall season, leading to flag football and other forms of age-group football. Age-group soccer soon followed and expanded to year-round participation via indoor facilities. Youth basketball became popular, as did youth swimming. Age-group tennis started during the decade as well. Organized youth sports dominated family leisure activities during the 1980s. In 1987 sport sociologists estimated that over 30 million children under age 16 were competing in organized sports. Participants needed apparel, equipment, and shoes. Youth sport leagues needed facilities, drafts, umpires, scoreboards, league coordinators, league structures, play-offs, and championships. In need of financing and sponsorships, youth sports became linked to local businesses. Youth sport

leagues became spectator sports as parents and relatives gathered to watch. Spectators also required facilities and concessions and equipment of their own. Sport industry entrepreneurs strove to meet all of these various needs and to make a profit (Roberts & Olsen, 1989).

In addition, an increasing number of adult Americans were participating in all kinds of recreational sports. In 1972 an article was published in the *New York Times* titled "Americans Spent More Money and More Time Just Playing." The article shed light on the numbers of people participating in sports and recreational activities in the United States. In addition, the article stated, "the leisure-time market now accounts for a total expenditure of $100 billion" ("Americans Spent More," 1972, p. 14). Recent studies of the sport industry have concluded that the largest segment of the industry is participation sports with expenditures on sporting goods being the second largest (of course, you can't play sports without equipment!). The Sporting Goods Manufacturers Association, for example, reported in 1999 that Americans spent $17.35 billion on sport equipment, $17.0 billion on recreational transport, $19.55 billion on sport apparel, and $8.73 billion on athletic footwear (Pitts & Stotlar, 2002).

The civil rights movements of the 1960s and 1970s resulted in the creation of sport organizations and events for nearly every minority group of people in the United States during the 1970s, 1980s, and 1990s. Sport organizations and events were created for groups such as African Americans, women, people with disabilities, lesbian and gay people, Hispanic Americans, American Indians, and people of different religions. Perhaps the largest group affected by civil rights was women. In 1972 Title IX of the Education Amendments Act was enacted (Rader, 1999). This amendment made illegal any act of sexual discrimination by schools and colleges that receive federal funding. Title IX and social change became the forces that addressed the inequity between men's and women's sports in school and university athletic programs and opened the doors for the growth and expansion of women's sport in the 1970s and through the 1980s and 1990s.

In 1978 the first women's professional basketball league was created. Called the Women's Professional Basketball League (WBL), it made history with its first game on December 9, 1978, in Milwaukee, Wisconsin, between the Milwaukee Does and the Chicago Hustle. The league lasted three years, folded, started again and went another three years, folded, and then repeated this again a few more times. It wasn't until the 1990s when two leagues were started, the ABL and the WNBA, that women's professional basketball would be popular enough for top echelons to proclaim that women's professional basketball now had enough commercial value along with major corporate support to finally become a mainstay in the industry.

Sporting goods companies were quick enough and sometimes lucky enough to capitalize on all of these trends. Shoe and apparel companies, in particular, benefited greatly. All one needed to go to a fitness center and work out, or to go jogging, was a T-shirt and shorts and a good pair of shoes. An example of this is found in the company today known in almost every corner of the world, Nike.

Started by a runner and originally named Blue Ribbon Sports in 1962, the Nike Company was begun at the right moment in history to capitalize on the early running and fitness movement (Strasser & Becklund, 1993). Philip Knight, Nike's founder, made some accidental and some brilliant decisions for the Blue Ribbon Sports Company during its early years in the 1960s and 1970s. Knight's original plan was to make a track and field shoe that would take over the U.S. market from the number one market share shoe made by Adidas in Germany and imported to the United States. Through several style changes, trials, failures, and materials innovations, the company slowly made manufacturing and marketing moves that would propel it to the top by the beginning of the 1980s. Among Nike's accomplishments were such shoe innovations as leather uppers, rubber soles, the waffle tread (actually inspired by a track coach's personal breakfast waffle iron), top athlete endorsements, use of the Olympics for promotion, and a dipped backstab (a cutout in the back upper to allow room for the Achilles tendon).

The Nike logo, called a Swoosh and now recognized all over the world, cost Nike a mere $35—the fee that Carolyn Davidson, a local art student at Portland State, charged for some logo sketches for Knight (Strasser & Becklund, 1993). During the 1970s Nike's revenues doubled and nearly tripled almost every year—$14 million in 1976, $71 million in 1978, $270 million in 1980, and more than $900 million in 1983 (Strasser & Becklund, 1993). The name Nike came from an idea that Jeff Johnson, Knight's first employee and also a middle-distance runner, had in the middle of the night (Strasser & Becklund, 1993). Blue Ribbon Sports had to come up with a name overnight for the first shoe manufactured for the company as their own first brand (earlier, Blue Ribbon Sports was distributing shoes from other companies) so that the shoe boxes could be printed. Johnson thought "Nike," the name of the winged goddess of victory from Greek mythology, was a perfect name for a running shoe. Additionally, with a stretch of the imagination, the Swoosh sort of looked like a wing. On June 18, 1971, the first Swoosh branded shoe went on sale (Strasser & Becklund, 1993).

From running shoes, Nike branched into soccer, tennis, football, and basketball shoes. Soon Nike added apparel and logo merchandise. Along the way, athlete endorsements, sponsorships, and naming deals made the name Nike a household word. Later, Nike negotiated the most lucrative endorsement deals with top name athletes Michael Jordan and Tiger Woods, which launched Nike to the top. In the final analysis, the strategies of the company, fueled by the fitness movement of the 1970s and 1980s, changed the sport business industry forever.

1990s: MJ as Brand and the Experience Economy

It began with the shoes. In 1984 when Nike first approached Michael Jordan, MJ played basketball in Converse and wore Adidas off the court (Wetzel & Yaeger, 2000). Nike pitchman Sonny Vacarro convinced Nike officials, including Phil Knight, that a Jordan signature shoe, the Air Jordan, would help the company regain its number one status in the industry. David Falk, Jordan's agent, agreed about the shoe's potential but demanded that Nike spend at least $1 million promoting the shoe and Michael Jordan. As Nike advertised and promoted its product, it would also be promoting Michael Jordan. By 1987 Nike was spending in excess of $5 million a year promoting Michael Jordan products (Wetzel & Yaeger, 2000).

Nike's investment paid off handsomely not only for the shoe company but also for Jordan. Jordan's athletic skills helped the process. Jordan's 63 points against the Celtics in a 1986 play-off game helped. Jordan emerged from the game as the new prototype superstar. Jordan's superiority, dash, and style were highlighted by the reigning superstar Larry Bird, who proclaimed, "That was God dressed as Michael Jordan" (Halberstam, 2000). The Spike Lee commercials ("It's Gotta Be the Shoes") begun in 1987 also helped. The commercials featured

71

Spike Lee as a nerdy basketball junkie who confronts Jordan on the basketball court and continually wonders aloud why Jordan wins. Lee concludes it's the shoes. Jordan, as himself, counters, "It's not the shoes" (Halberstam, 2000; Kellner, 2001). The humor is obvious. Jordan emerged from the commercial series as a talented, charming, beautiful, witty, and authentic superperson with a great smile and a mischievous wink (Halberstam, 2000). The commercials did more than sell shoes. They promoted Michael Jordan. Success fed success. Jordan's on-court exploits made him a more famous basketball player. Nike commercials made him a more famous person. By 1993 Nike had regained the number one position in athletic shoe sales (not just because of Air Jordan shoes), and MJ had become a brand name (Denzin, 2001).

By the mid-1990s Jordan had become an icon. Michael Jordan, or MJ, became associated with other brands: Air Jordan shoes, MJ Coca Cola, Jordan Quarter Pounders, MJ Quaker Oats and Wheaties, Jordan Ball Park Franks, the Jordan Fragrance (Bijan), the Jordan Brand Apparel, MJ Rayovac Batteries, and MJ/Hanes Underwear (Denzin, 2001). The MJ image of a gentle, kind, friendly, intelligent, dependable, wholesome, authentic family man with style and charm sold products globally (Denzin, 2001; Halberstam, 2000). Michael Jordan was the most recognizable person in the world according to Halberstam, who remarked, "You hear time and time again about people being in Borneo or somewhere and coming across a kid in a tattered Michael Jordan T-shirt" (Halberstam, 2000). Michael Jordan was transformed from superstar basketball player into super brand salesperson in the corporate world. Jordan as brand sold a vast array of rather mundane products (Halberstam, 2000). According to *Fortune* magazine, MJ helped to generate an estimated $10 billion in revenues for basketball, the media, and MJ's corporate partners (Halberstam, 2000).

Jordan made watching basketball or eating Wheaties an experience. Experiences are events that engage individuals in personal ways. Such engagement is the objective, the *raison d'être*, of what Pine and Gilmore (1999) dubbed the 21st-century experience economy. By offering consumers experiences instead of just products, marketers discovered that consumers responded by buying more and becoming brand loyal (Pine & Gilmore, 1999). When David Stern became commissioner of the NBA in 1984, he methodically set about improving the experience value of NBA basketball. Buoyed by great basketball and great stars, Stern added concertlike opening ceremonies to games. He speeded up game play, introduced flashier uniforms, improved halftime entertainment, and promoted giveaways for fans. He improved television coverage with more cameras, better angles, instant replay, zoom lenses, better announcers, and human interest segments. By adding showbiz and glamour to NBA basketball, Stern increased its appeal. He made it more entertaining by making it more experiential (Pine & Gilmore, 1999; Wolf, 1999).

The new experience economy had other effects on the sport industry. The 1980s and 1990s were an era of growing wealth and expansion in the United States. The sport business industry expanded horizontally with the introduction of many new types of businesses hawking goods, services, people, places, and ideas (Pitts & Stotlar, 2002). New companies focused on promotional merchandise and services, sponsorship management, event management, sport facility architecture and construction, sport marketing research, sport tourism, and athlete marketing and legal management.

The past two decades have also witnessed a boom in sport sponsorship. As corporations began to realize the potential of using sport for advertising, more sponsorship companies sprang up everywhere and numerous sport marketing and management service companies opened their doors for business to capitalize on this booming industry. By 1999 sport sponsorship expenditures reached $13.2 billion. Sales of licensed sport products reached $235 million. In the trading card industry, one company, Topps, paid out $229 million for licensing agreements (Pitts & Stotlar, 2002). The Super Bowl, for instance, is now a well-known launchpad for new corporate ad campaigns. And each year, college football bowl games have new titles, named for the companies willing to pay the highest bid for sponsorship and naming rights.

Women's sports grew exponentially, becoming more popular than ever at every level and every age. The new notion of the female athlete changed before our very eyes. The 1960s and 1970s had provided an all-out assault on sexism and the old traditional notions and limitations of genderized and sexualized roles. Now, with legislation and the women's rights movement making progress, women in sport charged ahead. However, the rights of women in sport would be met head-on by society's stronghold on old tradition. Not until the 1990s would women in sport in the United States become more comfortable with their muscularity and approach equality in pay to men. Along the way, it took Title IX, several lawsuits, and a series of events to reach this point. The 1973 Billie Jean King defeat of Bobby Riggs in tennis, dubbed the Battle of the Sexes, helped (Rader, 1999).

In 1992 women were only 34% of the U.S. Winter Olympics team but won 82% of the medals. The media reported this as a defeat of the men (Rader, 1999). In the past few Olympics, women's sports have been highly popular. The U.S. women's basketball team, softball team, and soccer team drew large crowds as they won the gold at the Olympics in the 1990s. In addition, the U.S. women's soccer team, having taken the grand prize of soccer at the Women's World Cup in 1998, became one of the most highly recognized and supported teams in the 1990s. The final match between China and the United States drew an incredible 90,000-plus crowd at the stadium and an estimated TV viewing audience of 40 million (Pitts & Stotlar 2002)). Many of the players' faces and names became household names.

Sports and recreational activities for the masses also boomed during the 1990s, further supporting the notion that sport feeds into the experiential economy. New, more experiential sports such as snowboarding, ice climbing, and sky dancing were invented. These new sports, and the new generation they represent, were dubbed "extreme sports" and "adventure sports." Aware of the trends toward experience, ESPN introduced the X-Games, a multisport event created especially for Generation X-ers and for TV.

Sport facilities in the 1990s conformed to the idea of adding value to the individual's experience. They became incredible complexes. From the smallest local parks and recreational softball complexes to the megasized multiple-use facilities, sport facilities in the 1980s and 1990s were engineering feats and works of architectural art. The largest ones included hotels, shopping centers, restaurants, garage parking, and children's playgrounds. Attempting to accommodate every need or desire of the loyal fan, the modern sport facility became a one-stop shop.

Globalization takes on a new meaning in the world of sport. On one hand, unique sports exist in nearly every region, with local people creating their own competitions and their own indigenous playing styles. On the other hand, some sports are introduced to people in other countries, become popular, and soon are mainstays of the culture. For instance, before 1980 practically no one played soccer in the United States. By the mid-1980s, the United States had a men's and women's national team and hosted the men's World Cup. In the 1990s the United States hosted the women's World Cup—one of the most attended and watched women's sport events in the United States.

In addition, easy movement across borders enhances the opportunities for athletes of different nations to participate in a plethora of sport events, both professionally and in amateur settings. The professional golf leagues are a good example of this. American golfers can travel to and compete in a number of golf tournaments in several countries. Likewise, golfers from around the world compete in U.S. tournaments. Another example is found in women's soccer. The women's World Cup and women's soccer in the Olympics are very popular events for soccer fans. Teams from around the world compete in these tournaments. Television and other media have made many of the players worldwide superstars. To capitalize on this global popularity, the first women's professional soccer association, the WUSA, brought players from around the world to join American stars in the inaugural season in 2001.

SUMMARY

This chapter provided sketches of some of the significant developments that took place between the 1870s and today and provided the foundation for the development of the sport business industry in the United States. The events, innovations, and entrepreneurs presented here are only a few, and we invite you to read about the many other events, innovations, and entrepreneurs who have been a part of the history of sport management and the sport business industry. History offers us many lessons that we can use today.

REVIEW QUESTIONS

1. What are some of the many ways that the history of sport business can be helpful to a sport business executive today?

2. Discuss the commercialization of sport throughout history and how it has influenced the sport business industry today.

3. Describe some events that significantly influenced and changed the sport business industry.

4. How have advances in manufacturing processes influenced the growth and development of the sport business industry?

5. How have advances in technologies influenced the growth and development of the sport business industry?

6. Describe the factors that have affected the growth and development of girls' and women's sports. Describe the factors that have influenced the growth and development of women's professional sports.

7. How has the mass media affected the sport business industry?

8. How have endorsement and sponsorship marketing affected the sport business industry?

REFERENCES

Aaker, D.A. (1991). *Managing brand equity*. New York: The Free Press.

Adelman, M.L. (1986). *A sporting time: New York City and the rise of modern athletics, 1820-70*. Urbana: University of Illinois Press.

Americans spent more money and more time just playing. (1972, December 31). *New York Times*, p. 14S.

Athletics as usual—only more so. (1917). *Sporting Goods Dealer, 37*, 26-31.

Athletic goods men draft code of fair trade practices. (1930). *Sporting Goods Dealer, 63*, 58-62.

Barnouw, E. (1966). *A tower in Babel*. New York: Oxford University Press.

Berlage, G.I. (1994). *Women in baseball: The forgotten history*. Westport, CT: Praeger.

Berlage, G.I. (2001). Baseball. In *The international encyclopedia of women and sports* (Vol. 1, pp. 95-101). San Francisco: Macmillan Reference.

Bernstein, M.F. (2001). *Football: The Ivy League origins of an American obsession*. Philadelphia: University of Pennsylvania Press.

Betts, J.R. (1974). *America's sporting heritage 1850-1950*. Reading, MA: Addison-Wesley.

Bradsby, F.W. (1922). The situation. *Sporting Goods Dealer, 47*, 48.

Bradsby, F.W. (1932). What about the future of our industry? *Sporting Goods Dealer, 66*, 84.

Bradsby, F.W. (March 1935). How you can use the Athletic Institute. *Sporting Goods Dealer, 72*, 44.

Brown, C.O. (1937, March). How the Athletic Institute operates. *Sporting Goods Dealer, 76*, 45.

Brown, L. (1992). *Girls of summer*. Toronto: HarperCollins.

Burk, R.F. (1994). *Never just a game: Players, owners, and American baseball to 1920*. Chapel Hill: University of North Carolina Press.

Burk, R.F. (2001). *Much more than a game: Players, owners, & American baseball since 1921*. Chapel Hill: The University of North Carolina Press.

By the numbers. (2002). *Street & Smith's SportBusiness Journal, 4*(37), 72.

Cahn, S.K. (1994). *Coming on strong: Gender and sexuality in twentieth-century women's sports*. New York: Free Press.

Calhoun, J.E. (1924). Dawn of the merchandizing era. *Sporting Goods Dealer, 52*, 60-62.

Candaele, K., & Wilson, K. (Producers), and Wallace, M. (Director). (1986). *A league of their own: A documentary* [Motion picture]. United States: Columbia Tristar Home Video.

Castle, J.A. (1926, January). Distribution of sporting goods reaches $90,000,000 a year. *Sporting Goods Dealer, 54*, 96-100.

Chaillaux, H. (1937, March). The American Legion's junior baseball program. *Sporting Goods Dealer, 76*, 48.

Cooper, P.L. (1997). The visible hand on the footrace: Fred Lebow and the marketing of the marathon. In S.W. Pope (Ed.), *The new American sport history: Recent approaches and perspectives* (pp. 386-401). Chicago: University of Illinois Press.

Davis, C.H. (1937). Let us cure this disease of lethargy. *Sporting Goods Dealer, 75*, 42-92.

Demand for all kinds of athletic equipment increased tremendously. (1917). *Sporting Goods Dealer, 36*, 26.

Denzin, N.K. (2001). Representing Michael. In D.L. Andrews (Ed.), *Michael Jordan Inc.* (pp. 3-13). New York: State University of New York Press.

Diogenes, Jr. (1924, December). What is wrong with the sporting goods industry and why? *Sporting Goods Dealer, 50,* 36-42.

Driving dull care away. (1917). *Sporting Goods Dealer, 37,* 66, 67.

Dumont, R. (1931). If we can get kid baseball kicking. *Sporting Goods Dealer, 65,* 77, 78-106.

Dumont, R. (1937, March). National semi-pro baseball congress. *Sporting Goods Dealer, 76,* 47.

Early days of athletic goods association recalled. (1935). *Sporting Goods Dealer, 72,* 131, 132.

Felker, C.T. (1930). Will baseball be killed by its friends? *Sporting Goods Dealer, 65,* 123.

Felker, C.T. (1936). Promotion the key to progress in 1936. *Sporting Goods Dealer, 74,* 106.

Fielding, L.W., & Miller, L.K. (2002). Historical eras in sport marketing. In B.G. Pitts & D.K Stotlar, *Fundamentals of sport marketing* (2nd ed.) (pp. 37-60). Morgantown, WV: Fitness Information Technology.

Fielding, L.W., & Miller, L.K. (1998a). The ABC trust: A chapter in the history of capitalism in the sporting goods industry. *Sport History Review, 29*(1), 44-58.

Fielding, L.W., & Miller, L.K. (1998b). The foreign invasion of the American sporting goods market. *Sport Marketing Quarterly, 7,* 19-32.

Fielding, L.W., Pitts, B.G., & Miller, L.K. (1990). Modern marketing in the sporting goods industry: The era of institutional development 1890-1910. *Completed Research in Health, Physical Education, Recreation and Dance.* Reston, VA: AAHPERD.

Fielding, L.W., Pitts, B.G., & Miller, L.K. (1991). The influence of the bicycle craze on the sporting goods industry 1893-1898; 1900-1910. *North American Society for Sport History Proceedings.*

Figler, S.K., & Whitaker, G. (1991). *Sport and play in American life.* Dubuque, IA: Brown.

Gilmore, J.A. (1931). What our association is striving to accomplish. *Sporting Goods Dealer, 64,* 129-131.

Gladden J. & Funk, D. (2002). Developing an understanding of brand associations in team sport: Emperical evidence from consumers of professional sport. *Journal of Sport Management, 64,* 54-81.

Gladden. J. & Wong, G.M. (1999). The creation and maintenance of brand equity—the case of the University of Massachusetts basketball. In M.A. McDonald, & G.R. Milne (Eds.), *Cases in sport marketing* (pp. 281-304). Boston: Jones & Bartlett.

Gorn, E.J., & Goldstein, W. (1993). *A brief history of American sports.* New York: Hill & Wang.

Got 'em guessing. (1922). *Sporting Goods Dealer, 47,* 134, 135.

A gratifying record. (1938). *Sporting Goods Dealer, 78,* 43.

Growth of sporting goods industry phenomenal. (1923). *Sporting Goods Dealer, 48,* 176-178.

Guttman, A. (1991). *Women's sports: A history.* New York: Columbia University Press.

Guttman, A. (1997). Mediated spectatorship. In S.W. Pope (Ed.), *The new American sport history: Recent approaches and perspectives* (pp. 366-385). Chicago: University of Illinois Press.

Halberstam, D. (1994). *October 1964.* New York: Villard Books.

Halberstam, D. (2000). *Playing for keeps: Michael Jordan and the world he made.* New York: Broadway Books.

Hardy, S.A. (1990). Adopted by all the leading clubs: Sporting goods and the shaping of leisure. In D.K. Wiggens (Ed.), *Sport in America: From wicked amusement to national obsession* (pp. 133-150). Champaign, IL: Human Kinetics.

Help Institute helps you. (1935). *Sporting Goods Dealer, 72,* 88.

Here's a campaign to boost baseball. (1935). *Sporting Goods Dealer, 72,* 88, 89, 178.

Hillerich & Bradsby. (1912-1917). *Baseball bats Order Book.* No. 2. The *Order Book* can be found in the Ekstrom Library Archives, University of Louisville, Louisville, KY.

Hillerich & Bradsby. (1920, 19 July). Minutes of the board of directors meeting.

Hillerich & Bradsby. (1939, 17 July). Minutes of the board of directors meeting.

Hult, J. (1989). Women's struggle for governance in U.S. amateur athletics. *International Review for the Sociology of Sport, 4,* 249-263.

International Health, Racquet, and Sportsclub Association (1995). *Industry data survey.* Boston: IHRSA.

Isaacs, S. (1964). *Careers and opportunities in sports.* New York: Dutton.

Johnson, R.S. (1999, April 12). Speed sells. *Fortune, 139,* 56-60, 62, 64, 66, 68, 70.

Johnson, S.E. (1994). *When women played hardball.* Seattle: Seal Press.

Kellner, D. (2001). The sports spectacle, Michael Jordan, and Nike: Unholy alliance? In D.L. Andrews (Ed.), *Michael Jordan, Inc.* (pp. 37-63). Albany, NY: State University of New York Press.

Large factories uphold dealer distribution policy. (1932). *Sporting Goods Dealer, 67,* 38, 39, 110.

Leacock, R.J. (1918, February). Leacock discusses trade conditions. *Sporting Goods Dealer, 27,* 41-45.

Levinson, D. (1921). David Levinson predicts drop in price of athletic goods. *Sporting Goods Dealer, 44,* 75, 76.

Lewis, G. (1973). World War I and the emergence of sport for the masses. *The Maryland Historian, 4,* 109-122.

Littlewood, T.B. (1990). *Arch: A promoter, not a poet: The story of Arch Ward*. Ames: Iowa State University Press.

A look into the future with R.J. Leacock. (1917). *Sporting Goods Dealer, 37,* 26-31.

Lucas, J.A., & Smith, R.A. (1978). *Saga of American sport*. Philadelphia: Lea & Febiger.

The markets. (1919). *Sporting Goods Dealer, 41,* 68.

Marshall, P. (Producer/Director). (1992). *A league of their own* [Motion picture]. United States: Columbia Pictures.

McMillan, V. (1935). Over sold and under promoted. *Sporting Goods Dealer, 72,* 100, 174.

Meek, A. (1997). An estimate of the size and supporting economic activity of the sports industry in the United States. *Sport Marketing Quarterly, 6*(4), 15-22.

Meek, J.T. (1928). De-bunking the sporting goods field. *Sporting Goods Dealer, 59,* 127, 128.

Miller, L.K., & Fielding, L.W. (1995). Resale price maintenance: A historical view of its impact on the sporting goods industry. *Journal of Legal Aspects of Sport, 5,* 1-27.

Moss, R.J. (2001). *Golf and the American country club*. Urbana: University of Illinois Press.

Necessity of athletics. (1917). *Sporting Goods Dealer, 37,* 70-72.

Noll, R.G. (1974). The U.S. team sports industry: An introduction. In R.G. Noll (Ed.), *Government and the sports business*. Washington, DC: Brookings Institution.

Once upon a time: Turning back the pages of Spalding's first ledger. (1947). *Sporting Goods Dealer, 96,* 128-130.

Oriard, M. (2001). *King football: Sport & spectacles in the golden age of radio & newsreels, movies & magazines, the weekly & the daily press*. Chapel Hill: The University of North Carolina Press.

Pine, J.B. II, & Gilmore, J.H. (1999). *The experience economy*. Boston: Harvard Business School Press.

Pitts, B.G., Fielding, L.W., & Miller, L.K.(1994). Industry segmentation theory and the sport industry: Developing a sport industry segmentation model. *Sport Marketing Quarterly, 3,* 115-124.

Pitts, B.G., & Stotlar, D.K. (2002). *Fundamentals of sport marketing* (2nd ed.). Morgantown, WV: Fitness Information Technology.

Porter, M.E. (1985). *Competitive advantage: Creating and sustaining superior performance*. New York: The Free Press.

Powers, R. (1984). *Supertube: The rise of television sports*. New York: Coward-McCann.

Quelch, J.A. & Hiller, T.B. (1994). Reebok International, Ltd. In J.A. Quelch & P.W. Farris (Eds.), *Cases in advertising and promotion management*. Boston: Irwin.

Quirk, J., & Fort, R.D. (1992). *Pay dirt: The business of professional team sports*. Princeton: Princeton University Press.

Rader, B.G. (1984). *In its own image: How television has transformed sports*. New York: The Free Press.

Rader, B.G. (1997). The quest for self-sufficiency and the new strenuosity. In S.W. Pope (Ed.), *The new American sport history: Recent approaches and perspectives* (pp. 402-416). Chicago: University of Illinois Press.

Rader, B.G. (1999). *American sports: From the age of folk games to the age of televised sports* (4th ed.). Upper Saddle River, NJ: Prentice Hall.

Retail sporting goods dealers' association. (1907). *Sporting Goods Dealer, 17,* 14.

Riess, S.A. (1989). *City games: The evolution of American urban society and the rise of sports*. Urbana: University of Illinois Press.

Robb, W. (1918, September). Robb sees bright prospects for athletics. *Sporting Goods Dealer, 37,* 31, 32.

Roberts, R., & Olsen, J. (1989). *Winning is the only thing: Sports in America since 1945*. Baltimore: Johns Hopkins University Press.

Robinson, P.R. (1909, January). Trade prospects for 1909. *Sporting Goods Dealer, 20,* 31, 32.

Rohm, A. (1999). Reebok (A). In M.A. McDonald & G.R. Milne (Eds.) (pp. 63-102), *Cases in sport marketing*. Boston: Jones & Bartlett.

Schuyler, C.J. (1929). A challenge to the sports goods industry. *Sporting Goods Dealer, 60,* 73-75.

Scudder, M. (1935). Speeding the growth of sports. *Sporting Goods Dealer, 72,* 94.

Seymour, H. (1960). *Baseball: The early years*. New York: Oxford University Press.

Smith, R.A. (1988). *Sports & freedom: The rise of college athletics*. New York: Oxford University Press.

Somers, D.A. (1972). *The rise of sport in New Orleans 1850-1900*. Baton Rouge: LSU Press.

Sperber, M. (1993). *Shake down the thunder: The creation of Notre Dame football*. New York: Henry Holt.

Spink, J.G.T. (1928). To sell more sporting goods, we must create more customers. *Sporting Goods Dealer, 57,* 73-75.

Spink, J.G.T. (1930). Just between us. *Sporting Goods Dealer, 63,* 39-40.

Spink, J.G.T. (1932). Just between us. *Sporting Goods Dealer, 66,* 38, 39, 116.

Strasser, J.B., and Becklund, L. (1993). *SWOOSH: The unauthorized story of Nike and the men who played there*. San Diego, CA: Harcourt Brace Jovanovich.

Sullivan, J.E. (Ed.). (1907). *Spalding's athletic library: An athletic primer*. New York: American Sports Publishing Company.

Taylor, A. (1927). Alex Taylor diagnoses some trade ills. *Sporting Goods Dealer, 58,* 144.

Tweedie, D.H. (1935). A fair share of America's recreation dollar for sporting goods. *Sporting Goods Dealer, 72,* 176.

Two centuries of sports business [poster insert]. (2000, April 17-23). *Street and Smith's SportsBusiness Journal.*

U.S. Bureau of the Census. (1939). *Biennial Census of Manufacturers.* Washington, DC: U.S. Government Printing Office.

U.S. Bureau of the Census. (1947). *Biennial Census of Manufacturers.* Washington, DC: U.S. Government Printing Office.

Value of sporting goods during peace and war. (1918). *Sporting Goods Dealer, 38,* 27-32.

Veeck, B. (1965). *The hustler's handbook.* New York: B.P. Putnam's Sons.

The voice of the trade. (1927). *Sporting Goods Dealer, 56,* 87, 163.

Voigt, D.Q. (1983). *American baseball: From postwar expansion to the electronic age.* University Park: The Pennsylvania State University Press.

Waddell, R.E. (1925). Industry needs reorganizing. *Sporting Goods Dealer, 52,* 222-223.

Wakefield, W.E. (1997). *Playing to win: Sports and the American military, 1898-1945.* Albany: State University of New York Press.

The war and its effect on sporting goods sales. (1917). *Sporting Goods Dealer, 35,* 28-31.

Watterson, J.S. (2000). *College football: History, spectacle, controversy.* Baltimore: The Johns Hopkins University Press.

Wetzel, D., & Yaeger, D. (2000). *Sole influence.* New York: Warner Books.

Winchester accomplishments. (1921). *Sporting Goods Dealer, 43,* 103-104.

Winchester makes 5000 items. (1925). *Sporting Goods Dealer, 53,* 169.

Wolf, M.J. (1999). *Entertainment economy.* New York: Random House.

Zimbalist, A. (1992). *Baseball and billions.* New York: Basic Books.

Chapter 4

Thinking Critically About Sport Management

Stuart M. Keeley and Janet B. Parks
Bowling Green State University

In a thought-provoking address to the North American Society for Sport Management (NASSM), Bob Boucher (1998) stated that "a true measure of whether [sport management] graduates are truly prepared is *not* the courses listed on their transcripts but whether they have been educated to *think* intelligently and *make decisions* about issues they will face in the dynamic world of managing a sport enterprise" (p. 81). Similarly, Janet Harris (1993) urged sport management educators to give greater emphasis to students' development of critical/reflective competencies. She surmised that such an emphasis would prepare professionals who would be liberated to "free themselves from traditional ways of identifying and solving problems, [and] to look at problems from new perspectives" (p. 322). In the same vein, Allan Edwards (1999) suggested that **critical reflection** should receive more attention than it currently receives in sport management so that we can find "new, less oppressive, and more just ways of creating and managing sport" (p. 79). The clear implication of all these suggestions is that, as the managers of the future, you will need exceptional *thinking* skills in order to make the decisions necessary to deal effectively and responsibly with the myriad challenges you will encounter.

critical reflection—Making judgments about whether professional activity is equitable, just, and respectful of persons (Edwards, 1999, p. 69).

We agree that sport managers of the 21st century will be called on to solve problems that we can't even conceptualize today. In order to develop the ability to make good decisions—decisions that are consistent with values and perspectives on which you have seriously reflected—you first need the ability to integrate critical thinking skills with the legal and ethical principles you will

learn in chapter 5. Such a need becomes obvious when you consider the types of issues that are facing future sport managers. Following are a few examples of contemporary issues:

- Should intercollegiate athletes receive salaries?
- Should intercollegiate athletes be tested for drugs?
- Should the Confederate flag be flown at athletic contests?
- Should male and female coaches be paid equal salaries if they coach the same sport?

79

- Should professional golfers with disabilities be permitted to ride in golf carts?
- Should boys' and men's sport programs be adversely affected in order for athletics programs to comply with Title IX?

You can probably think of many more such questions. How do you make good decisions about these and other issues? Good decisions are *not* based on expediency, the easy way out, or what will cause the least turmoil or make the most money. You are most likely to make good decisions if you make it a point to work toward a principled justification for your beliefs. Becoming a critical thinker is an important step toward providing such a justification.

The aim of this chapter is to provide you with helpful tools for thinking critically about issues relevant to sport management so that you can develop confidence in your ability to make decisions concerning such issues. First we will help you discriminate between critical thinking and other forms of thinking and to become aware of the essential components of critical thinking. In doing so, we will stress critical thinking dispositions and questions. We will define a set of critical thinking questions and then apply them to an essay concerning a controversial topic so that you can see critical thinking in action. Our hope is that when you have completed the chapter, you will be better prepared to solve problems and make decisions in sport management.

Becoming a Critical Thinker

As a professional, you will find yourself in many situations that require you to make decisions that affect a large number of people. Many times, these decisions must be made quickly. In all likelihood, you will base your decision on your own personal values while also considering the values of others. Two important components of critical thinking, therefore, are *conscious reflection* on personal values and *recognition of conflicting values*. The scenario described below clearly demonstrates the role of values in decision making—and the importance of knowing your values *prior* to a crisis that requires you to make an important decision.

Recognizing value conflicts and making judgments about your own preferred values are just two of the important ingredients for becoming a successful critical thinker. For example, in the basketball scenario, the values of competition, the integrity of the game, and convenience are in conflict with the values of compassion and respect for the individual. Considering your own preference with regard to this value conflict helps you make a more reflective decision on the issue. What is the best way to become better decision makers? An essential step is to develop *critical thinking skills*.

What *Is* Critical Thinking?

You probably have encountered the term *critical thinking* many times in your daily life and in the classroom. You may also have noticed that when the term is used, its meaning is often unclear. One reason for the confusion is that the term *critical thinking* means different things to different people. Thus, it is very important that you understand the meaning of critical thinking as we are using it in this chapter. Our definition is an adaptation of definitions that are widely used among scholars who systematically study critical thinking, and it should

When Tragedy Strikes

A high school basketball player collapsed during a tournament game. Rescue personnel administered mouth-to-mouth resuscitation and closed-chest heart massage for 90 minutes but to no avail. The young man was taken from the game on a gurney and subsequently was pronounced dead. The decision makers had two choices—to continue the game or to postpone the game.

If the decision had been your responsibility, what would you have done?

If you had been the coach of the injured player's team, what would you have recommended? What would you have thought if you had been the player's parent, a parent of a player on the opposing team, a student, or anyone else associated with the event?

On what values would you have based your recommendation or decision?

What additional information do you need in order to answer the question?

What value conflicts are you experiencing as you reflect on the decision you would make?

be very helpful to you in distinguishing between *critical* thinking and other kinds of thinking.

First, to better understand what we *do* mean by critical thinking, you need to understand what we do *not* mean. For example, critical thinking is not any of the following:

- *Just thinking*—It is "thinking," but it is a special form of thinking. For example, developing a good understanding of something is an important dimension of (just) thinking, but it is quite distinct from *critical* thinking.

- *Negative thinking*—To many people, critical thinking does not sound nice. It sounds negative. But critical thinkers are not naysayers! Critical thinkers are seeking something very positive—as solid a basis for their beliefs as they can find in a world full of uncertainty. Criticisms are simply a part of their search for better arguments. In this respect, critical thinking, if practiced appropriately, is positive, caring, and productive.

- *Creative thinking*—Certain aspects of critical thinking do require our best creative efforts. That is one of its appealing components. But critical thinking stresses making evaluative judgments rather than the imaginative leaps associated with brainstorming or generating novel ideas or strategies.

We have provided examples of what we do *not* mean; so what *do* we mean by critical thinking? A common feature of all critical thinking activity is systematic evaluation of arguments (reasons and their companion conclusions) according to explicit standards of rationality—careful thinking that helps us move forward in a continual, ongoing search to improve our opinions, decisions, or judgments. Critical thinking, as we use the term, refers to the following:

- The *awareness* of a set of interrelated critical questions
- The *ability* to ask and answer critical questions at appropriate times
- The *desire* to use those questions and to accept their results as a guide to behavior

Thus, the following equation captures the essence of critical thinking:

Critical thinking = Questioning skills + Desire to question and to accept the results of the questioning

Critical thinking can be practiced in a number of ways, some of which are much more desirable than others. For example, individuals might apply critical thinking with selfish motives, using their skills to support their own selfish interests. These individuals are not seeking solutions; rather, they are seeking to "destroy" the arguments of those who disagree with them. Such motivation interferes with the pursuit of furthering our understanding of an issue.

On the other hand, ideal critical thinkers possess a particular set of dispositions, or tendencies. While many dispositions facilitate the critical thinking process (see, for example, Facione, Facione, and Sanchez, 1995), we believe the set of three dispositions summarized by Ennis (2000) is an especially useful set for the critical thinker to pursue. For a more complete list of dispositions, see Ennis (1995). According to Ennis, ideal critical thinkers

- *Care* that their beliefs are true and that their decisions are justified; that is, they care to "get it right" to the extent possible.
- *Care* to present a position honestly and clearly, theirs as well as others'.
- *Care* about the dignity and worth of every person.

Note that caring is a central aspect of the critical thinking process. The ideal critical thinker is one who cares enough about what others have to say to make a very active attempt to discover and to listen to others' reasons and to be sensitive to others' feelings and levels of understanding. An important component of this caring is being truly and seriously open to points of view different from one's own, recognizing that one's own beliefs may not be sufficiently justified. Clearly, achieving this openness is more easily said than done.

Moving From the "Sponge" Approach to the "Panning for Gold" Approach

One approach to thinking about issues related to sport management is to think in a way similar to how a sponge reacts to water: by absorption. The problem with the *sponge approach* is that it is passive; it fails to provide you with a method for actively choosing which information and opinions to believe and which to reject, or which values to incorporate as your own personal values. If you were to rely solely on the sponge approach, you would remain dependent on the last expert that you encountered or the last argument that you read, or on the person who seemed to speak loudest. The sponge approach is also ineffective because experts often disagree for many reasons (e.g., differing values, training, and cultural backgrounds).

We think you would prefer a different model of learning than the sponge approach because you would rather choose for yourself what to believe and what to reject. To make your own choices, you should read and listen with a special attitude—a questioning attitude, assisted by a strong sense of curiosity. Such an attitude requires you to interact actively with information and arguments. We call this interactive style the *panning for gold approach*. Such an approach assumes that by actively "sifting" through all of the information you are bombarded with, you can choose what to believe with a sense of self-confidence; you can provide good justification for your beliefs. Such beliefs are the gold nuggets you are seeking.

To distinguish the gold from the gravel as you sift through information requires that you ask frequent questions and reflect on the answers—the essence of critical thinking. Using critical thinking as the method for panning for gold is a challenging task, but the reward is great. If you incorporate the interactive critical thinking process that we are emphasizing in this chapter, you can feel the same sense of pride in your reading and listening that you may normally get from successful participation in physical activities. You will no longer have to be dependent on experts. In fact, you will be able to challenge the opinions of experts, including your instructors, by asking critical questions about those opinions. You will, therefore, be able to construct your own knowledge and make your own decisions. You will have the satisfaction of knowing why you should either ignore or accept a particular bit of advice. As you learn to evaluate information and opinions systematically, you will feel like an active member of the growing field of sport management and not just a passive observer.

What Are the Critical Thinking Questions?

There is no single "correct" set of critical thinking questions. We will present eight selected critical thinking questions with a brief description of their meanings and suggestions for how to put them into practice. If you nurture the habit of asking these questions, you will be very successful in your "panning for gold" quest, and you will be better equipped to come up with your own questions as situations demand. Consequently, you will be in an excellent position to decide what to accept and what to reject. (Our discussion of each question is necessarily somewhat brief. For a more

in-depth discussion of the eight questions, see Browne & Keeley, 2001.)

The first set of questions will help you determine the *reasoning* of the argument. Some aspects of the reasoning will be stated (explicit), and some will be hidden (implicit). Before you can critically evaluate reasoning, you need to have as clear a picture of the reasoning as possible. Some communicators make their reasoning very clear; others present it in a very confusing manner.

Critical Thinking Question 1: What Are the Issues and the Conclusion?

Usually, writers and speakers are reacting to some issue, and they're trying to persuade you of their point of view on it. You start the critical thinking process by identifying the *issue* and the *conclusion*. Issues and conclusions will be either **descriptive** or **prescriptive**. Prescriptive conclusions will tend to be more greatly influenced by value preferences than will descriptive conclusions. For example, the claim that there should be more African American athletics directors (prescriptive) will be heavily influenced by values. Conversely, the claim that only 2.4% of all NCAA Division I athletics directors are African American (descriptive) will be much more dependent on empirical evidence, such as surveys of university athletics departments (Lapchick & Matthews, 2001). Look for the issue and conclusion at the beginnings and endings of essays, articles, or chapter sections. Titles and headings (especially in newspapers and magazines) are also excellent clues. Also, to help locate the conclusion, look for words that signal its presence, such as the following: *thus, therefore, consequently, hence,* and *but.*

descriptive—Concerns about the way the world is, was, or will be.

prescriptive—Concerns about the way the world should or ought to be.

Critical Thinking Question 2: What Are the Reasons?

Reasons are ideas that writers and speakers use to justify their conclusions. Reasons answer the *why* question: Why do you believe what you believe? Most reasoning is in the form "*This* (conclusion) because of *that* (reasons)." To discover reasons, you need to ask this: If the writers were sitting across from me, what reasons would they give to support their conclusion? When you have the combination of a reason or a set of reasons and a conclusion, then you have an argument. Thus,

Reasons + Conclusion = Argument

You should decide the merits of the conclusion on the basis of the quality of the reasons. Conclusions not supported by reasons are mere opinions, and thus they should usually be ignored—especially if they are controversial. Anyone who is trying to persuade you should have to answer the question, What are your reasons?

Critical Thinking Question 3: What Words or Phrases Are Ambiguous?

We can't determine whether we agree or disagree with someone's reasoning if key terms in the reasoning could have more than one meaning and those different meanings would influence how we would react. Such terms or phrases are *importantly ambiguous*. Critical thinkers attempt to clarify the meaning of key terms and phrases (those that are in the reasoning structure) that are ambiguous before making judgments about the quality of the reasoning. When faced with reasoning that is importantly ambiguous, ask for clarification if it is possible to do so. If you can't ask, then you will want to make a conscious effort to recognize how the changes in meaning will influence your reaction to the reasoning. For example, in evaluating a coach's success, if you define success solely as winning percentage, you may reach a different conclusion than if you define success as motivating athletes to achieve their full potential.

Critical Thinking Question 4: What Are the Value Conflicts and Assumptions?

Assumptions are ideas that individuals take for granted when they engage in reasoning. Assumptions are usually implicit in the reasoning, rather than explicit, so you have to "fill in the blanks." A full reasoning structure, with the blanks filled in, usually looks like the following diagram (adapted from M.N. Browne and S.M. Keeley, 2001, *Asking the right questions: A guide to critical thinking*, 6th ed. [Upper Saddle River, NJ: Prentice Hall]. By permission of M.N. Browne and S.M. Keeley.). Reasons support the conclusion only if the assumptions are reliable.

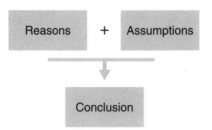

There are two kinds of assumptions—value assumptions and descriptive assumptions. As we use the term, **values** are abstract ideas about what individuals or groups care about. For example, honesty, compassion, competition, and justice are all values for most of us. In many cases, however, such as the basketball game in which the player collapsed, values are in conflict, such that embracing one value means rejecting another value. Such conflicts are pervasive in prescriptive issues, and within such issues individuals assume certain value preferences—*they take for granted that some values are more important than others*. The following reasoning example illustrates the influence of value conflicts and value assumptions:

Conclusion: Sport teams should cease using American Indian symbols and traditions, such as Indian ritual dances.

Reason: These practices are inaccurate, disrespectful, and offensive to American Indians and to others who are sensitive to such stereotyping.

This reason might be true, but in order for it to support the conclusion, a value assumption must be made: The value of *human dignity* is more important than the value of the *right to freedom of expression*; otherwise the writer would be less concerned about disrespect of Indians and more concerned about the rights of teams to promote whatever symbolic image they wished. Thus, within this controversy, the values of human dignity and freedom of expression are in conflict; and the writer has assumed that human dignity is the preferred value. Other writers might place higher value on the right to freedom of expression. When you encounter prescriptive conclusions, remember to search for the underlying value assumptions.

values—The unstated ideas that people see as worthwhile (Browne & Keeley, 2001, p. 62).

Critical Thinking Question 5: What Are the Descriptive Assumptions?

Descriptive assumptions are beliefs about how the world is, was, or will be, which, much like value assumptions, usually fill the gaps between reasons and conclusions and are usually unstated. We discover these important missing links—the glue that holds the reasoning together—by asking the question, What does the writer have to take for granted in order for the reason to support the conclusion or for us to believe that the reason is accurate? The following scenario illustrates the discovery of a descriptive assumption (Women's Sports Foundation, 2002):

Conclusion: Female athletes prefer to be coached by men rather than women.

Reason: Teams with male coaches have won more championships than teams with female coaches because female coaches aren't as intense and demanding as male coaches.

What descriptive beliefs need to be taken for granted in order for us to agree with the reasoning? A good way to discover such hidden beliefs is to ask, How could we disagree with the reasoning? In so asking, we discovered several beliefs taken for granted:

• *Assumption 1*: Teams coached by females have had the same recruiting resources as teams coached by males. It is possible, for example, that the schools willing to invest the most in the recruiting process have also tended to be schools hiring male coaches, and that is the cause of the difference in championships won.

• *Assumption 2*: It is acceptable to attribute standard characteristics to all members of a given group. If we accept that assumption, we also have to accept other stereotypes, such as "all football players are stupid," "all African Americans have rhythm," and "White men can't jump" (Women's Sports Foundation, 2002).

• *Assumption 3*: Men "know" the game of basketball better than women do. In fact, there is nothing inherent in basketball or in the nature of men or women that would allow us to conclude that one gender would know the game better than the other gender would.

Locating assumptions is well worth the hard thinking effort. Although usually hidden, assumptions are crucial to holding reasoning together. If the assumptions are faulty, as they are in the example, then you should reject the reasoning.

LEARNING ACTIVITY

Form a book club among sport management majors and read a book about issues in sport. Examples are presented in the "For More Information" section on pages 2-3, and you will find more titles in your library. Keep a journal and discuss your journal entries during club meetings. Encourage the club members to use critical thinking skills in the discussions. Pay special attention to finding assumptions.

Critical Thinking Question 6: Does the Reasoning Contain Fallacies?

Fallacies are mistakes in reasoning that usually don't seem to be mistakes. Often, they represent reasoning that requires erroneous or false assumptions. The following brief claim illustrates a fallacy: Either we raise *public* moneys to finance a sport stadium, or we will have to move the team to another city. This reasoning assumes there are only two choices. If, for example, it's possible to raise *private* moneys to build the stadium, then the assumption is false and there is a fallacy in the reasoning. There are several types of fallacies, and we recommend that you familiarize yourselves with them through some of the Web sites and books listed in the "For More Information" section on pages 2-3.

Critical Thinking Question 7: How Good Is the Evidence?

• Relaxation and imagery training enhance gymnastics performance in Olympic athletes.
• The graduation rate of nonathletes is higher than the graduation rate of athletes.
• The mandates of Title IX have forced several colleges to drop some men's sports.
• Participation in sport builds good character.
• If we accommodate athletes who are differently abled, then sports as we know them will be destroyed.

Should we believe these claims? Are they accurate? Are they facts or merely unsupported opinions? To evaluate such claims, we must ask the question, How good is the evidence?

All reasoning includes claims, or assertions, about the way the world is, was, or is going to be; these are descriptive beliefs. As critical thinkers we must decide which claims to believe. Because it is very difficult to establish the *absolute* truth or falsity of most descriptive beliefs, we find it most useful to view beliefs along a continuum of dependability. The greater the quality and quantity of evidence supporting a belief, the more we can depend on it and the more we can legitimately call the claim a "fact." Thus, for us, facts are beliefs that are supported with abundant evidence. The major difference between claims that are *opinions* and those that are *facts* is the present state of the relevant evidence.

Before we can judge the persuasiveness of a communication, we need to know which descriptive claims we can count on. How do we decide? We ask questions such as the following: Where's the evidence? How good is the evidence? What's your proof? How do you know that?

How good evidence is depends on what *kind* of evidence it is. Evidence comes in lots of forms, including the following:

Intuition

Appeals to authorities

Testimonials

Personal experience

Case studies and examples

Scientific research studies

Analogies

Each kind of evidence can be good evidence— when used appropriately. Learning to evaluate evidence well is a lifelong learning task. The more that you read and study across the various disciplines, the more familiar you will become with which kinds of evidence are most suitable for which kinds of descriptive claims. We can best help you at this point by briefly mentioning the most common kinds of evidence used in the field of sport management and alerting you to the strengths and weaknesses of such evidence. Even if you are not an expert on evidence, you can usefully ask the question, How good is the evidence? Let's examine the various kinds of evidence and some central questions that you can ask about each kind.

Appeals to Authority as Evidence

In today's world, the most common way to support a belief is to appeal to statements of an "expert," or of an authority. Purported experts appear everywhere—on TV, in magazines, on the Internet, and in your textbooks. Appeals to the statements of credible authorities are often valuable evidence. "Authorities," however, vary in degrees of exper-

tise, and they often disagree. Thus, we need to be highly critical when appealing to authority. Questions we need to ask when evidence is an appeal to authority include the following:

- How much expertise or training does the authority have on the relevant subject?
- Has the authority been in a position to have especially good access to pertinent information?
- Does the authority provide any specific information or reasons to support the claim?
- Is there good reason to believe that the authority is relatively free of distorting biases or influences?
- Has the authority developed a reputation for making dependable claims?

Personal Testimonials as Evidence

The editors of this book, of course, would be pleased to hear personal testimonials (see figure 4.1) from our readers. But praise from a single reader provides scant evidence for the quality of the book. After all, how typical is the reader? Does she have special expertise in reading such books? Does she have something to gain by her statement? As critical readers, we should be very wary of such evidence. Communicators often try to persuade us by quoting particular persons as saying that a given idea or product is good or bad, citing their personal experiences with the product. Such personal testimonials are always highly suspect as evidence because they are *highly selective, likely to be very biased, and void of any special expertise on the product or idea.*

Case Studies as Evidence

Case studies possess many of the same problems as personal testimonials. We define case studies as the report of detailed observations of a single individual or event made by another individual. They may be formal and systematic, such as the cases completed by Sigmund Freud, or they may

Dear Publisher:

This book on sport management has changed my life. I now truly understand the opportunities open to me in this field. I strongly recommend this book to anyone who plans a career in sport management.

Jane Feelgood, student

Figure 4.1 Personal testimonial.

be quite informal. Journalists, for example, often begin persuasive essays with vivid, rather informal, descriptions of individuals to whom they wish to refer. Often, such cases are presented to generate emotional reactions.

Single case studies usually can best be viewed as *striking examples*, or as *possibilities*, and not as proof or good evidence. Like personal testimonials, they are highly selective and subject to major biasing influences. They are difficult to generalize from. Be suspicious of case studies as evidence. Look for further evidence for the claim.

Scientific Studies as Evidence

"Research studies show . . ."

"Investigators have found . . ."

"A new study in the *New England Journal of Medicine* has shown . . ."

One kind of evidence that often carries special weight as support for beliefs or ideas is scientific research, which we define as a systematic collection of observations made by individuals who have followed some form of scientific methodology. In the field of sport management, such research studies are most likely to rely on surveys, in-depth interviews, or experiments.

Although the scientific method attempts to minimize many of the built-in biases in our observations of the world and in our intuitions, even the best of such studies have important limitations. Beliefs that appear to be scientific facts one day frequently turn out to be tomorrow's myths. Like appeals to any authority, we can't tell about the value of such findings until we ask lots of important critical thinking questions, such as the following:

- How reputable is the source of the report?

- Are any special strengths of the research mentioned?

- Is there any evidence that other researchers have found the same results? (Do not be overly influenced by a single study. Findings often vary from time to time and from researcher to researcher. In general, we should be most influenced by research findings that have been repeated by many researchers over a period of time.)

- How selective has the writer or speaker been in choosing studies to support a belief? Have relevant studies with contradictory results been omitted?

- Is there any reason for someone to have distorted the research or research interpretations? For example, are certain findings likely to personally benefit the researcher or the person citing the research?

- How far can we generalize, given the kinds of people or events studied? (Research results can be applied only to people and situations similar to those studied in the research.)

- Are there any biases or distortions in the way the surveys, questionnaires, ratings, or other measurements were used? Did interviewers ask leading questions? Did research participants know what kinds of answers were expected? Were survey questions ambiguous?

Analogies as Evidence

Our last kind of evidence is quite different from the others. Look closely at the form of the following brief argument, paying special attention to the reason supporting the conclusion.

"It's a mistake to hire a former star as a coach of an NBA basketball team. Look at what has happened the last several times teams hired great players to coach. They knew the game, but they just didn't know how to manage the players."

The evidence presented is a *comparison between two things* (hiring a star in the past and hiring a star today) to prove something about one of the things (the possible success of hiring a star now). When we compare something with which we are less familiar with something with which we are more familiar to support a conclusion, then we argue from **analogy**.

analogy—A form of logical inference in which we reason that if two things are alike in some ways, they are alike in other ways.

Analogies can stimulate insights, but they can also deceive us. For example, the previous analogy makes us consider potential problems with hiring a star athlete as a coach. But there are also possible important *differences*, which we need to consider. It is possible that recent stars are different from former stars in how they have tried to learn coaching methods for example. If so, this analogy may be faulty.

Because analogical reasoning is so common and has the potential to be both persuasive and faulty, you need to recognize such reasoning and know how to evaluate it systematically. To do so, try to focus on two factors: (1) the number of ways the two things being compared are similar and different and (2) the *relevance* of the similarities and the differences. Strong analogies will be ones in which the two things compared possess *relevant similarities* and lack *relevant differences*.

Try evaluating the following reasoning, in which an analogy provides the evidence:

"This baseball team needs a manager who will use very strict discipline. Baseball players are like children in a family. They need a strong parent who will set clear limits. Otherwise, they will keep testing the limits and disrupting the team."

Critical Thinking Question 8: What Significant Information Is Omitted?

What is *not* said by a writer or speaker is often as important as what *is* said. The information we receive is highly selective and incomplete. Communicators with limited space who are trying to persuade you are likely to select and use information that supports or confirms their view. Thus, you need to ask an important additional question before judging the quality of reasoning: What significant information is omitted or missing?

LEARNING ACTIVITY _____

Using an Internet search engine, locate two essays by credible authorities that provide arguments for different conclusions to an issue in sport or sport management (see issues on p. 79 for examples). Identify differences in value preferences, the selection of reasons, and the selection of evidence.

How do we discover something that is missing? You can ask many different questions to identify relevant omitted information, including many of the critical thinking questions described earlier. The following list, adapted from Browne & Keeley (2001), highlights some important kinds of omitted information:

- Arguments, research studies, examples, testimonials, or analogies that support conclusions that *differ* from the author
- Plausible definitions of key terms that differ from the author's definition
- Other value perspectives from which one might approach this issue
- Origins and details of "facts" and research findings referred to in the reasoning
- Omitted effects, both positive and negative, and both short and long term, of what is

advocated and what is opposed, including possible unintended consequences
- Context of quotes and testimonials that would provide a clearer sense of their meaning
- Possible benefits that authors might gain by convincing others of their position

By explicitly looking for missing information, you can decide whether you have enough information to judge the author's reasoning. If too much has been left out, which is often the case, you should be very cautious about accepting the conclusion. If you wish to make an informed judgment about the reasoning, then you will want to seek out more information.

LEARNING ACTIVITY _____

Go to your library and check out a copy of *Controversies of the Sports World* (1999) by Douglas T. Putnam. Find a chapter that covers a topic of interest to you, and, using the core critical thinking questions in this chapter, answer one of the issue-related questions at the end of the chapter.

Asking the Core Critical Questions

Let's go through the critical thinking steps with an example of a situation in which a sport manager needs to make a decision. Assume that you were recently named to the position of athletics director at a public high school with a long tradition of offering prayers over the microphone at athletic contests. Recently, however, some students and parents have challenged the prayers, and you aren't sure what to do. To add to the confusion, you receive a letter from a student's parents who are irate that you are even considering eliminating the prayers. What will you decide to do? Will you continue the tradition, eliminate it, or alter it? How will you make your decision? Perhaps reading the letter in figure 4.2 and the accompanying discussion will help you decide.

What Are the Issues and Conclusion? (Question 1)

The letter in figure 4.2 asks the question, Should prayer be permitted at public school contests? This is a prescriptive issue because it asks what *should* be done rather than what *is, was, or will be*

Dear Athletics Director:

Public prayer at public school athletic contests should be permitted because the First Amendment gives American citizens the right to freedom of speech and freedom of religion. Any restriction on a citizen's personal view or voice is a violation of these fundamental American rights. This country was founded on the principle of freedom of religion, and the young people of our country need to have opportunities to publicly proclaim their faith through prayer. As President Clinton stated, "I have never believed the Constitution required our schools to be religion-free zones, or that our children must check their faith at the schoolhouse door" ("Public Schools and Religion," 2000). Students have the same rights and liberties as all American citizens. In fact, we are sending students the wrong message when we allow open discussions about sex in our public schools but forbid discussions about God (MacLeod, 2000).

Research has revealed that most Americans believe in God and most support public prayer. For example, a 1999 *Newsweek* poll found that 94% of Americans believe in God while only 4% are atheists (MacLeod, 2000). Another 1999 poll found that 83% of Americans favored allowing students to say prayers at graduation ceremonies *(The Closet Atheist,* n.d.). A survey conducted in 2000 revealed that 74% of the respondents believed that "school prayer teaches children that 'faith in religion and God' is important" (Walsh, 2001).

Religion is also good for our health. Research financed by the Centers for Disease Control and Prevention found that people who attended church frequently had, on average, a life expectancy of eight more years than infrequent attendees (as cited in Myers, 2000). Moreover, religious people are 53% less apt to die of coronary disease, 53% less apt to commit suicide, and 74% less apt to die of cirrhosis (as cited in Myers).

Athletics plays a huge part in the lifestyles of many Americans. With athletics comes traditions, which often include prayer. The government does not have the right to forbid its youth from praying, particularly when it is such an integral part of the athletics tradition.

It is the right of American citizens to decide what they want to say when addressing any group publicly. Congressional sessions and other public meetings are opened with prayer, so why shouldn't athletic contests be started with prayer? People who want to pray have the right to believe in and say what they choose, even at public school events. If the government chooses to take any action against public prayer, some schools will continue practicing public prayer at all athletic events anyway. In Abernathy, Texas, the high school's head football coach, Dewayne Sexton, says that their locker-room tradition of prayer will not end: "We enjoy it and feel good about it; that's what we do" (Alford, 2000, p. 19). President George W. Bush agreed as he stated, "I support the constitutionally guaranteed right of all students to express their faith freely and participate in voluntary student-led prayer" (Mauro, 2000, p. 4). The fact is that people attend athletic contests voluntarily; so if they don't want to hear prayer, let them come late.

Angrily,
Chris and Pat Martin

Figure 4.2 This letter describes a prescriptive issue.

the state of the world. The major clue to the issue is the conclusion, which is stated in the first sentence: "Public prayer at public school athletic contests should be permitted."

What Are the Reasons? (Question 2)

Always try to restate each reason in your own words; when you can do that, you go beyond *reproduction* of a communicator's words to *understanding.* An important goal of critical thinking is in-depth understanding of reasoning.

The writers of this letter present several reasons, which we have listed here:

• *Reason 1: Restriction of personal voices violates the First Amendment, which guarantees freedom of speech and religion, and young people need to have opportunities to proclaim their faith publicly through prayer.* The supporting reasons are as follows:

1. President Clinton has argued that the Constitution doesn't require our schools to be religion-free zones.

2. Students have the same rights and liberties as all American citizens, and we send them a wrong message when we permit open discussions about sex but not about God.

- *Reason 2: Research shows that most Americans believe in God, and most support public prayer.* The supporting reasons are as follows:

    1. A 1999 *Newsweek* poll found that 94% of Americans believe in God.

    2. Another poll found that 83% of Americans favored student prayer at graduation ceremonies.

    3. A survey conducted in 2000 showed that 74% of respondents believed that "school prayer teaches children that 'faith in religion and God is important.'"

- *Reason 3: Religion is good for our health.* The supporting reason is that research by the Centers for Disease Control and Prevention found that regular church attendees lived eight more years than infrequent attendees, were less apt to die of coronary disease, and were less apt to commit suicide or to die of cirrhosis.

- *Reason 4: Prayer at athletic events is a long-standing tradition, and the practice of these traditions should be up to American citizens, not the government.*

- *Reason 5: Congressional sessions and other public meetings are opened with prayer; so why shouldn't athletic contests open with prayer?*

- *Reason 6: Even if the government acts against public prayer, some schools will continue to practice it anyway.* The supporting reason is that a Texas coach says that his locker-room tradition of prayer will not end.

- *Reason 7: President George W. Bush supports voluntary student-led prayer.*

- *Reason 8: People voluntarily choose to attend athletic contests; if they don't want to hear prayer, let them come late.*

These parents have presented numerous reasons to support their conclusion. We now need to *evaluate this reasoning* by asking further critical thinking questions.

Which Words or Phrases Are Ambiguous? (Question 3)

The place to look for important ambiguity is in the reasoning structure, which we have just completed; thus, our focus is on the reasons and the conclusion. Do you need more information about the meanings of certain terms or phrases before you decide whether to agree with the beliefs the parents state in the reasoning structure? For example,

in the conclusion, the phrase "public prayer at public school athletic contests" is importantly ambiguous. Although the meaning may at first seem obvious, our reaction to the conclusion and its supporting arguments may be affected by the choice of one of the following definitions of public prayer:

1. A school administrator asks those present at the contest to stand and join her in a prayer, which she reads over a microphone.

2. A student representative asks those present to join him in a moment of silent prayer.

If the parents were to mean the first definition, then we may be less willing to agree with them because the first definition seems to create a more coercive environment for those individuals who do not wish to join in. Notice that the term *public prayer* also is a key term of reason 2, and we should be reluctant to agree or disagree with this reason until we have a better sense of just what kind of public prayer most Americans support.

Another importantly ambiguous phrase is *freedom of religion*, which appears in reason 1. Just what does the First Amendment mean by guaranteeing freedom of religion? The extent to which that reason supports the conclusion will depend greatly on how broadly we interpret freedom of religion and how much we actually know about the U.S Constitution.

What Are the Value Conflicts and Assumptions? (Question 4)

What do these parents *care* about that leads them to take this position on the issue and to choose the reasons they use to support their conclusion? A central value assumption that links reasons 1 and 2, as well as reason 6, to the conclusion is a preference for the value of the *right of religious expression* over the value of *separation of religion and civil or government authority*. All of these reasons emphasize religious rights and activities while ignoring concern about the rights of students and other spectators to be free from the imposition of religious practices.

A value assumption that links reason 4 to the conclusion is a preference for *tradition* over *government intervention*. Also, for the results of public opinion polls in reason 2 to be supportive of the conclusion, we must assume that *majority rule* is an important value.

What Are the Descriptive Assumptions? (Question 5)

To get a more complete picture of the parents' reasoning, we need to know more than their value preferences. We also need to know what beliefs about the state of the world they take for granted. In order for reason 1 to support the conclusion, the parents must assume that schools cannot provide outlets for people to express their religious beliefs and to pray that would maintain a separation of church and state. This assumption is questionable because there are many ways for students to practice religious beliefs other than at school-sponsored events such as athletic contests.

Also, in order for reason 6 to support the parents' conclusion, the assumption must be made that because some people will ignore government acts, then such acts are wrong. For example, individuals frequently ignore government-regulated speed limits. Does that mean the speed limit laws should be abandoned?

Does the Reasoning Contain Fallacies? (Question 6)

Reasoning fallacies in this essay include several fallacies of irrelevance, including an appeal to common opinion, using the wrong reasons, and an appeal to questionable authority. Using the reason, for example, that a survey shows that most Americans favor student prayer at graduation ceremonies to support the belief that most Americans support public prayer urges us to accept a position simply on the grounds that a large number of people accept it. Broad public acceptance does not make a claim worthy of our acceptance. In addition, the first and third supporting reasons for reason 2 are irrelevant; they focus on belief in God and what school prayer teaches, not on support for public prayer, which is central to the reason. Also, reason 3 commits the fallacy of using the wrong reason; the issue is not about religion per se but about public prayer.

How Good Is the Evidence? (Question 7)

First, we need to ask the question, What kinds of evidence did the parents use? They used appeals to authority (e.g., President Clinton and President Bush), several research studies (see reasons 2 and 3), an analogy (see reason 5), and a personal testimonial (see supporting reason for reason 6). The credibility of these authorities for making

these particular judgments is questionable. For example, there is no reason to believe that either president has carefully studied the legal arguments on this issue, and there is good reason to believe that political considerations may be biasing their judgments. Not only are the surveys of questionable relevance, but because no information is given about sample size, breadth, and randomness, or about the wording and context of the survey questions, it is impossible to judge the generalizability of the results to large populations of Americans or to judge whether the questions were validly measuring the concepts referred to. For example, polls conducted with highly religious individuals would be expected to provide very different results from those conducted with groups of more secularly oriented persons. Also, the single testimonial from the Texas coach has very limited value because we have no idea how representative his view is of coaches in general. There is good reason to believe that coaches in Texas may have different attitudes toward public prayer than coaches in California or Vermont.

In summary, the evidence provided in this essay is very weak.

What Significant Information Is Omitted? (Question 8)

These parents have left out much information that could help us judge the persuasiveness of their reasoning. Information that we would like to see includes the following:

- A clearer definition of public prayer and freedom of religion

- Recognition and rebuttal of common counterarguments, such as the argument that school sponsorship of a religious message sends a message to some that they are "outsiders" and to others that they are "insiders" of the community

- President Clinton's actual reasons for his claim that the Constitution doesn't require our schools to be religion-free zones

- Further details about the most relevant surveys—especially information about the people surveyed, how the survey was presented to them, and the wording of the survey items

Can you think of other relevant research that was omitted?

It should be clear that the question of whether to include prayer in an athletic event cannot be answered with a "sound bite"—a simple yes or no. Regardless of your personal position on this issue, we hope the foregoing scenario provided a useful example of how to think about it. You can be certain that issues such as this are in your profes-sional future. If you begin now to reflect on your values and the values of others, develop critical thinking dispositions, and learn to ask and answer critical questions, you will be in a position to resolve them with greater confidence.

LEARNING ACTIVITY

Go to www.WomensSportsFoundation.org and click on "Issues and Answers." Choose any of the issues listed and read the accompanying articles. Critically analyze the ideas presented in the articles using the critical thinking skills presented in this chapter.

SUMMARY

Several scholars have suggested that sport man-agers of the future will be better prepared for their careers if they acquire critical thinking skills. Criti-cal thinking is different from *just* thinking, *negative* thinking, or *creative* thinking. It involves the aware-ness of a set of interrelated questions, the ability to ask and answer critical questions at appropriate times, and the desire to use those questions and to accept their results as a guide to behavior. Acquiring and developing critical thinking skills obliges you to engage in reflection, to demonstrate certain dispo-sitions, and to ask core critical questions. *Reflec-tion* implies evaluating your own values and the values of others. The critical thinking *dispositions* are caring that you "get it right," caring to present a position honestly and clearly, and caring about the dignity and worth of every person. The core critical *questions* involve identification of (1) the issues and the conclusion, (2) the reasons or justifications for the conclusions, (3) ambiguities, (4) value conflicts and value assumptions, (5) descriptive assumptions, (6) fallacies in the rea-soning, (7) the quality of the evidence, and (8) information that was omitted. Critical thinking skills can be used to solve problems in sport management and in personal decision making.

REVIEW QUESTIONS

1. Define "critical thinking" and explain the benefits of applying critical thinking skills to important issues in sport manage-ment.

2. What is the difference between learning *what* to think and learning *how* to think? Give examples of both types of activities as they can be applied to specific issues in sport management.

3. Identify an issue in sport on which experts have different opinions. What are the differ-ent opinions? Do you accept one opinion over another? Why or why not?

4. List the dispositions that critical thinkers should possess and indicate if you possess each of them. Explain your answers.

5. What are the core critical thinking ques-tions, and how would you use them in re-solving issues in sport management?

6. Choose one or more of the issues listed on page 79. What questions would you ask in reflecting on this/these issue(s)?

7. Reflect on the academic major of sport man-agement. Discuss how your values and per-spectives determine your personal beliefs about the choice of a major.

REFERENCES

Alford, D. (2000, August 7). Pregame prayer barred. *Christianity Today, 44*(9), 19-20.

Browne, M.N., & Keeley, S.M. (2001). *Asking the right questions: A guide to critical thinking* (6th ed.). Upper Saddle River, NJ: Prentice Hall.

Boucher, R.L. (1998). Toward achieving a focal point for sport management: A binocular perspective. *Journal of Sport Management, 12,* 76-85.

The closet atheist. (n.d.). Retrieved January 23, 2002, from www.geocities.com/closetatheist/stats.htm.

Edwards, A. (1999). Reflective practice in sport management. *Sport Management Review, 2,* 67-81.

Ennis, R.H. (1995). *Critical thinking.* Upper Saddle River, NJ: Prentice Hall.

Ennis, R.H. (2000). Super-streamlined conception of critical thinking. Retrieved January 23, 2002, from www.criticalthinking.net/SSConcCTApr3.html.

Facione, P.A., Facione, N.C., Sanchez, C. (1995). The disposition toward critical thinking. *The Journal of General Education, 44*(1), 1-25.

Harris, J. (1993). Using kinesiology: A comparison of applied veins in the subdisciplines. *Quest, 45,* 389-412.

Lapchick, R., & Matthews, K.J. (2001). 2001 Racial and gender report card, Center for the Study of Sport in Society, Northeastern University. Retrieved January 10, 2002, from www.sportinsociety.org/rgrc2001.html.

MacLeod, (2000, September). School prayer and religious liberty: A Constitutional perspective. *CWA Library.* Retrieved January 23, 2002, from www.cwfa.org/library/freedom/2000-09_pp_school-prayer.shtml.

Mauro, T. (2000). Supreme Court rules against prayer at Texas public school football games. *The Legal Intelligencer.* Retrieved January 29, 2002, from http://web.lexis-nexis.com/universe/document?_m=f1e1af65455bb1ac0153d8fb699c13ab&_docnum=7&wchp=dGLSzVlSlzV&_md5=712aeb778f80140a13f80a896dbce014.

Myers, D.G. (2000). On assessing prayer, faith, and health [Electronic version]. *Reformed Review, 53*(2), 119-126.

Public schools and religion. (2000, January 15-22). *America, 182*(2), 3.

Walsh, M. (2001, January 17). Public sees role for religion in schools. *Education Week on the Web, 20*(18). Retrieved January 23, 2002, from www.edweek.org/ew/ewstory.cfm?slug=18religion.h20.

Women's Sports Foundation. (2002). Do female athletes prefer male coaches? The Foundation's position. Retrieved January 10, 2002, from www.womenssportsfoundation.org/cgibin/iowa/issues/coach/article.html?record=3.

PART II

Social and Behavioral Foundations of Sport Management

A critical step in the process of becoming a responsible and effective manager of sport enterprises is the recognition of the significance of sport as a major social institution. The three chapters in this section, therefore, are designed to provide the foundation for an understanding of the legal, ethical, social, and psychological aspects of sport. An appreciation of the ramifications of these aspects of sport will increase the likelihood that you will make wise managerial decisions within the context of the broad social environment in which sporting activities occur.

In chapter 5 Lori Miller and Joy DeSensi introduce basic concepts related to ethical and legal aspects of sport management and explain why *legal* activities aren't always, by definition, *ethical*. After describing selected ethical and legal principles, the authors identify circumstances in which these principles may be in conflict. Exercises in this chapter give you opportunities to use the critical thinking skills you learned in chapter 4 and apply them to real-life situations that are likely to arise in sport.

Chapter 6 focuses on the role of sport sociology in the management of sporting activities. After defining sport sociology, Mary Jo Kane explains the nature and significance of sport in society. She describes selected theoretical explanations for the importance of sport in society and points out ways in which the study of sport sociology contributes to our understanding. Kane discusses ways in which sport reflects both good and bad aspects of society, how it can be used as a vehicle for social transformation, and how you can apply your knowledge of sport sociology in the management of sport.

Christine Green addresses the psyche of the sport consumer in chapter 7. She examines people's perceptions and attitudes toward sport and explains what motivates individual sport consumers. After discussing how consumer behaviors are influenced by groups of people, she suggests strategies for building and strengthening customer relations. The underlying theme of this chapter is that an understanding of how individuals make decisions about their consumption of the sport product will be valuable to sport managers as they compete with a multitude of other leisure-time diversions for the time and money of consumers.

FOR MORE INFORMATION

Ethics in Sport Management

- www.ausport.gov.au/info/ethics.htm
- www.sportsethicsinstitute.org/
- www.fedpubs.com/subject/social/sport_ethics.htm
- www.findlaw.com
- www.washlaw.com
- www.law.cornell.edu
- www.marquette.edu/law/sports/links.html
- www.ithaca.edu/sslaspa/links.htm

Professional and Scholarly Associations

- American Alliance for Health, Physical Education, Recreation and Dance (AAHPERD): www.aahperd.org

- American Sociological Association (ASA): www.asanet.org
- National Association for Girls and Women in Sport (NAGWS): www.aahperd.org/nagws/template.cfm
- North American Society for the Sociology of Sport (NASSS): http://playlab.uconn.edu/nasss.html
- Society for the Study of Legal Aspects of Sport and Physical Activity (SSLASPA): www.ithaca.edu/sslaspa/index.htm

- Tucker Center for Research on Girls & Women in Sport: www.tuckercenter.org
- Women's Sports Foundation (WSF): www.womenssportsfoundation.org

Scholarly Journals

- *International Review for the Sociology of Sport*
- *Journal of the Legal Aspects of Sport*
- *Journal of Sport & Social Issues*
- *Sociology of Sport Journal*

Chapter 5

Legal and Ethical Considerations in Sport Management

Lori Miller, Wichita State University
Joy T. DeSensi, The University of Tennessee

As you learned in chapter 4, sport managers are responsible for making numerous decisions on a daily basis. These decisions will be of various levels of importance and difficulty. All of them, however, will require you to engage in a process of decision making. Usually, your decisions will affect numerous **constituencies**, such as participants in your programs, your coworkers, your supervisors, the media, and parents of participants. All of these groups are entitled to hold you accountable for your decisions. Chapter 4 also exposed you to the benefits that critical thinking skills can produce when constituencies challenge the decisions that have been made and demand justification for chosen strategies. Now that you have acquired a fundamental understanding of the importance of critical thinking and have learned to ask the core critical questions, you can move on to a deeper understanding of two more disciplines you must consider when you make decisions: *ethics* and the *law*.

constituencies—Those individuals influenced by a particular decision.

The purpose of this chapter is to introduce you to situations that require sport managers to examine how legal and ethical principles can influence decisions. After explaining some selected ethical theories, we will briefly introduce select legal issues, discuss related ethical and philosophical considerations, and present questions for you to ponder.

Ethics

The terms *ethics* and *morality* are often used interchangeably, thus creating confusion. Strictly speak-

LEARNING OBJECTIVES

After studying this chapter, you will be able to do the following:

1. Identify legal issues affecting sport management operations.
2. Differentiate between the ethical theories of teleology and deontology.
3. Explain the rudimentary legal concepts associated with tort, federal civil rights legislation, constitutional issues, and contracts.
4. Identify ethical issues affecting sport management operations.
5. Identify situations in which legal and ethical issues may produce conflicting outcomes.
6. Engage in critical thinking and problem solving regarding sport management decisions containing both legal and ethical considerations.

ing, ethics is considered on the level of theory or principles, whereas morals are observed on the level of practice (Billington, 1988). In ethics, one appeals to rules or maxims as a way to justify certain moral decisions. Morals, on the other hand, are usually described as a special set of values that frame absolute limitations on behavior. "Do not steal," for example, would be a basic moral rule. As a sport manager, your morals matter to your families and friends. Your morals, however, might differ from the ethical principles you apply in refraining from "padding" the budget (DeSensi & Rosenberg, 1996). Beauchamp (1991) described morality as a "social institution with a code of learnable rules" (p. 6). The social nature of morality, its application of certain rules, and its expansive concerns separate it from ethics, which is embedded in theoretical concerns.

Ethics and Behavior

In making decisions, questions arise regarding how one *should* think and act. As shown in figure 5.1, decisions can reflect a variety of ethical and legal principles. The following ethical maxims offered by Laczniak (1983, p. 7; 1985, p. 10) are helpful guides for making decisions. We have added specific examples of each maxim to help you understand how a sport manager might put them into action.

- *The golden rule:* Act in the way you would expect others to act toward you (e.g., providing superior customer service to the fans attending a sporting event staged by your organization).

- *The utilitarian principle:* Act in a way that results in the greatest good for the greatest number of people (e.g., increasing resources as necessary and appropriate to pay for enhanced security at an athletic competition between two teams that are staunch rivals).

- *Kant's categorical imperative:* Act in such a way that the action taken under the circumstances could be a universal law or rule of behavior (e.g., enabling a person to cancel a contract within three days of signing).

- *The professional ethic:* Take only actions that would be viewed as proper by a disinterested panel of professional colleagues (e.g., requiring athletic trainers in your organization to be accredited by the National Athletic Trainers' Association).

- *The television test:* Always ask, Would I feel comfortable explaining to a national television audience why I took this action? (e.g., commenting on a recent allegation that a colleague had been arrested on criminal drug violations).

These maxims represent simple and quick considerations a sport manager may use when engaging in critical thinking practices and making decisions. In practice, sport managers should make decisions based on strong theoretical and philosophical convictions. We recommend an entire course in ethics related to sport management to develop this background. For now, the following summary of two ethical theories should be helpful.

Figure 5.1 Are these the principles that you believe a good sport manager should live by? Keep reading.

Reprinted from Wade Austin 1995.

Teleology and Deontology

The term *teleology* is derived from the Greek word meaning "end" and refers to evaluating the morality of actions or inaction on the basis of results or consequences. It is referred to as a results-oriented approach. For example, donating money for charity produces a greater degree of societal benefit than does giving the money as a bonus to one wealthy executive. **Utilitarianism**, which follows the work of Jeremy Bentham (as cited in White, 1988) and John Stuart Mill (1969), is a frequently used teleological theory. With this approach, the good of the group is considered above the good of the individual; therefore, decisions are made by selecting the action or inaction producing the greatest social benefit. The results-oriented approach is best explained by White's (1988) "no harm, no foul" example: If slight contact occurs in a basketball game and there is little or no harm, the greatest good is achieved by allowing play to continue.

utilitarianism—Action that tends to benefit society at the expense of individual interest(s).

The term *deontology* represents the concept of an individual duty owed to a person, organization, or society. **Kant's categorical imperative** serves as a prime example here. According to Kant (1959), we should act in such a way that our behavior under the circumstances could be a universal law or rule of behavior. As noted by Tuleja (1985), there are three ways to evaluate behavior within the framework of the categorical imperative:

1. The clearly moral action would be universalizable. That is, it would make sense, consistently, for everybody in a similar situation to take the same action.

2. The moral action would demonstrate respect for individual human beings. It would treat others not as means but as ends in themselves.

3. The moral action would be acceptable to all rational beings. If the action were made the basis of a universal law, receivers as well as initiators of the action would agree that it was appropriate (pp. 22-23).

Kant's categorical imperative—A rule, policy, value, behavior, or belief assumed to be "correct" or "right" by the majority of people.

Figure 5.2 shows a four-step process you could follow when trying to ascertain whether a particular decision is ethical. First, gather as many facts related directly and indirectly to the particular situation. Second, consider whether the action (1) has utility, (2) respects the rights of those involved, and (3) results in justice. If your response

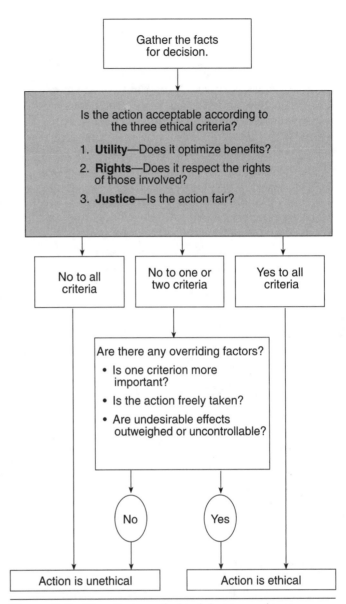

Figure 5.2 Flow diagram of ethical decision making.

Adapted from *Organizational Dynamics*, Autumn 1983, 73, M. Velasquez, G.F. Cavanagh, and D.J. Moberg. Copyright 1983, with permission from Elsevier Science.

to any of the previous questions is negative (i.e., the action does not have utility, does not respect the rights of others, or is unjust), the action is unethical. If the answer to all of the previous questions is yes, then you can conclude the action is ethical.

For example, if a baseball bat manufacturer decided to use inferior wood because the cost of materials was rising and the company was in financial jeopardy, this action must withstand critical evaluation. Facts that must be obtained include the costs to the manufacturer and consumer, the quality of the wood, the degree of financial difficulty being experienced by the company, and whether the product contains an increased risk of injury due to splitting wood, consumer injury, and so on. Analyze the acceptability of the above decision in terms of utility, respect for the rights of the concerned parties, and fairness. You must consider issues such as what and whose benefits are optimized. Is the action justified by the manufacturer selling an inferior product at a higher cost and ultimately making more money? Do both the manufacturer and consumer benefit from this action, or is one or both disadvantaged and placed in physical or economic jeopardy? Are the rights of those involved respected, or is there a potential risk of injury to the consumer? Is it fair for the manufacturer to know that the potential for injury exists, yet do nothing about it? In this example, there may be no overriding factors that would deem the decision ethical; therefore, if the answers to these questions are negative, the action would be unethical.

The Law

Each person probably has a different interpretation of the law. As defined by Black (1990), the law represents a "body of rules of action or conduct prescribed by controlling authority and having binding legal force" (p. 884). The law is an accumulation of rules and regulations that govern our behavior. Failure to abide by the defined rules of law results in either civil or criminal penalty. Yet the law is not arbitrarily defined by a remote set of judges, juries, and congressional representatives. Rather, the law is a reflection of society. A fundamental premise of the law includes the concepts of precedent. The doctrine of precedent (i.e., *stare decisis*) states that prior judicial decisions control subsequent decisions containing similar facts and questions of law (Teply, 1999). However, legal outcomes can differ over time based on differing fact scenarios, jurisdictional differences, or changed societal needs demanding an altered outcome (Shapo, Walter, & Fajans, 1999). Legislatures introduce statutes reflecting, in part, the desires of those they represent. For example, societal influences have spawned statutes governing drunk driving, ticket scalping, gambling, drug testing, and discrimination. The courts, in turn, decide disputes to determine if statutes were properly and legally interpreted and applied in accordance with our constitutional guarantees (Shapo, Walter, & Fajans, 1999).

In many ways, the law does serve to determine what is right and wrong, good and bad. As a result, many people believe that what is legal is, in fact, ethical. Unfortunately, decision making that combines *both* legal and ethical outcomes may be quite difficult to achieve. Henderson (1982) elaborated on this complexity by categorizing, and differentiating among, four separate legal and ethical outcome combinations. Henderson's model is presented in figure 5.3. Quadrant I reflects decisions that are both legal and ethical. Quadrant II reflects decisions that are ethical but illegal. Quadrant III reflects decisions that are unethical yet legal. Quadrant IV reflects decisions that are both unethical and illegal.

LEARNING ACTIVITY

1. Can you think of sport-related situations that represent each of the quadrants in figure 5.3?

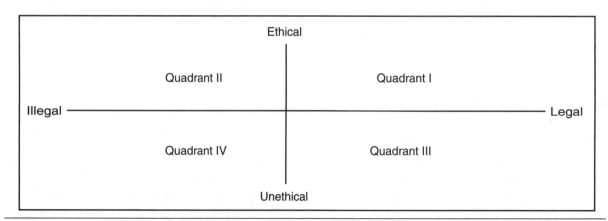

Figure 5.3 Legal and ethical considerations in decision making.

Where would you place the following: the use of restrictive covenants in employment contracts, drug testing, tobacco advertising, ticket scalping, discrimination against protected and unprotected classes of people, and professional sport team and league decisions regarding relocation?

2. What has shaped your thoughts over the years to lead you to believe that a given situation is legal or ethical?

The remainder of this chapter examines sport management situations that represent each of the quadrants in figure 5.3 as well as related legal and ethical doctrines. As you address the learning activities presented throughout the chapter, think about which quadrant each situation reflects and be able to defend your position.

Tort Law

Tort law, in particular the area of negligence, is based in deontological principles. Tort law represents a wrong done by one party to another and focuses on whether a particular individual(s) failed to perform appropriately based on an individual relationship with the injured plaintiff. The purpose of tort law is to remedy a wrong. Remedy for the wrong is provided by means of compensatory and/or punitive damages. Compensatory damages reflect monetary damages for medical bills, lost days of work, payment for hired hands, and pain and suffering. Punitive damages impose additional monetary costs to the defendant. Punitive damages serve to punish the defendant for his or her wrongdoing and make an example of the defendant's conduct so that others do not engage in similar acts. Punitive damages exceed monetary recourse beyond the costs of the actual injury.

In comparison to teleological theory, which promotes the greatest good for the greatest number of people, tort law focuses on what is good for the single injured plaintiff. While the plaintiff may recover for the incurred wrong, it is often the greater society who pays the costs associated with exorbitant damages as a company's increased expenses from litigation (e.g., enhanced insurance costs, attorney fees) are passed on to the consumer. Hence, it can be argued that tort law awards damages to a single injured plaintiff while imposing additional costs on consumers who never had, and never will have, any relationship to the plaintiff.

LEARNING ACTIVITY

Consider the following questions:

- Is tort law fair?
- Is it a form of justice that is in the best interests of society?
- What are the benefits associated with tort law?

A person may have a cause of action in tort as a result of the negligent or intentionally negligent acts of another. Unintentional torts (i.e., negligence), intentional torts (e.g., defamation, invasion of privacy, assault, battery, false imprisonment), and strict liability encompass the area of tort law.

Negligence

Negligence represents the failure to act as another reasonable, prudent professional would have acted in a like or similar circumstance. To prove negligence, a plaintiff must prove the following elements: duty, breach of duty, proximate cause, and injury. The duty is based on either a relationship with the plaintiff (e.g., coach/student-athlete, teacher/student, general manager of a sport team/spectator), voluntary assumption of a duty, or a duty imposed by a statute. Breach of duty represents an act that was not performed as another reasonable, prudent individual would have performed in the same or similar situation (i.e., failing to do something or failing to do something properly). Proximate cause relates to the actual linkage between the defendant's duty, breach of duty, and actual injury. For example, while the defendant may be negligent, the actual injury may have resulted from some other intervening act (e.g., lightning, unforeseeable acts of a third party). Defenses for negligence can include, but are not limited to, assumption of risk, comparative negligence, failure to meet one of the four elements of negligence, failure to meet procedural guidelines (e.g., statute of limitations), governmental immunity, volunteer immunity statutes, and recreational use immunity statutes.

LEARNING ACTIVITY

Do the following cases represent genuine cause of actions based in negligence? Why or why not? In your responses, consider whether the injuries were foreseeable. What ethical issues are involved?

1. A cheerleader is performing a pyramid during a time-out at a men's collegiate basketball

game. The woman on the top of the pyramid crashes to the hardwood floor as the pyramid collapses. She incurs significant injuries including a broken back and head injuries. There have been three other similar injuries in the past two years. The plaintiff alleges that the faculty sponsor is liable as well as the university. Specific allegations include negligent supervision and training. Does this cheerleader have a legitimate cause of action based in negligence? Should she have a cause of action? What defenses might apply to the school and the faculty sponsor?

2. A professional baseball team routinely employs the "Dizzy Bat Race" promotion during its home games. This promotion involves two people drawn from the spectators during the fifth inning who place their heads on bats, spin around five to six times, and then attempt to run the bases. The first one to run all the way around the bases wins the race and receives a free pizza from the local pizza restaurant. The ball team's management provides helmets, kneepads, and elbow pads for the fans to adorn as they participate in this promotion. During one of the promotions, a spectator becomes seriously disoriented and crashes to the ground headfirst. As a result of the fall, the spectator chips a tooth, breaks his nose, and requires stitches for a cut above his right eye. Does this spectator have a legitimate cause of action based in negligence against the team and its managers? Should he have a cause of action? What defenses might apply to the ball team or individual promotion coordinators?

3. A group of golfers is enjoying a Sunday afternoon game of golf when one member of the foursome is struck in the head with a flying golf ball. Who are the named defendants in this case? The golf course? The golf course managers? The person who fired the errant shot? Does it make any difference if the ball was hit by a nine-year-old who lives near the course and was not on the course as an invited, paying customer? Should the ethics for noncontact sports such as golf and badminton have different standards than contact sports such as football and wrestling? Why or why not?

Intentional Torts

Invasion of privacy, intentional infliction of emotional distress, and defamation are a few of the many intentional torts providing a plaintiff with a legitimate cause of action. There are four types of invasion of privacy including invasion of privacy based on intrusion, disclosure, false light intrusion, and commercial misappropriation. Invasion of privacy based on intrusion and disclosure require the plaintiff to prove similar elements. The plaintiff must prove that he or she has a genuine expectation of privacy that society recognizes as a legitimate privacy claim. False light intrusion can occur when, for example, the defendant reports surrounding facts or circumstances that taint or cloud the perception of the plaintiff. A claim of commercial misappropriation can evolve when a person attempts to make money from another's name or likeness. Intentional infliction of emotional distress requires the plaintiff to prove that the defendant's injurious conduct was made with either intent or a disregard for the consequences. In addition, the conduct must be held to be outrageous and the cause of severe emotional suffering. Defamation represents a "negative" false statement negligently made by an individual resulting in damage. The tort of defamation strives to protect an individual's right to his or her own reputation, pride, and integrity.

Similar to negligence, intentional torts strive to provide a remedy for the individual who has been wronged. Again, the deontological principles of ethics dominate. Two facets of the deontological theories include (1) duty and (2) individual rights. Tort law, in general, is decided according to these two principles. As explained by Morgan and Rotunda (2000), the deontological concept of duty reflects an understanding that "behavior is right or wrong, without regard to particular effects produced by the behavior in a given situation" (p. 21). The deontological concept of individual rights asserts that "individuals have certain human rights that lawyers should help preserve and protect . . . without regard to what the effect would be on the general happiness or well being of the rest of society produced by asserting the rights" (Morgan & Rotunda, 2000, p. 21). In other words, sport managers need to know what are professionally acceptable behaviors and how to serve individual sport fans, spectators, consumers, and clients. Failure to exercise judgment and make decisions based on these grounds reflects bad management and poor ethics and may result in legal liability.

LEARNING ACTIVITY

1. As you eagerly enter the Olympic venue to watch the races you have long awaited, a

security officer stops to search you and your belongings and take your fingerprints to run through FBI and police databases revealing prior criminal behaviors. Are you bothered by this intrusion? Is it ethical based on deontological or teleological principles? In what ways have individual and societal expectations of privacy changed over the past decade?

2. You are the university's sports information director. Although you like your current job, you have applied for a great job opportunity with a different university's athletics program. Days before your interview, chaos and confusion break out at your current school with rumor of a widespread scandal involving financial dishonesty, misrepresentation, and fraud. Faculty, student-athletes, boosters, and administrators are all allegedly involved. The local broadcast television station opens the nightly news show with the words, "Your local athletics department is in trouble and individual integrities are suspect." The next day the local newspaper alleges your knowing involvement as a disseminator of the university sport news and event happenings. You worry about how this debacle will influence your job prospects. A friend mentions suing for defamation. Is this advice worth taking? What ethical principles are involved?

Federal Civil Rights Legislation

The federal Constitution empowers Congress to enact legislation in a variety of subject areas (e.g., copyrights, patents, commerce). Congressionally enacted legislation reflects societal interests regarding future conduct about a variety of issues including, for example, discrimination and business practices (e.g., ticket scalping). Statutory language may appear general in nature because of its emphasis on governing future conduct (i.e., situations demanding statutory application that have not yet arisen). In turn, judges guide the application and interpretation of the statute with no legislative history through their written judicial opinions concerning the particular statutory-related dispute. The Americans with Disabilities Act and Title IX, both discussed briefly in the following sections, reflect federal legislation affecting sport management operations.

Americans with Disabilities Act

The Americans with Disabilities Act (ADA) prohibits discrimination against individuals with disabilities. Under the ADA, a person is defined as

having a disability if he or she has (1) a physical or mental impairment that substantially limits one or more major life activities, (2) a record of a disability, or (3) a perception of possessing a disability. Title I of the ADA prohibits discrimination in employment. Employers cannot discriminate against a person with a disability who meets essential job qualifications with or without a reasonable accommodation. Title III prohibits discrimination in places of public accommodation. In other words, all individuals must be granted access to places where the public congregates for purposes of recreation or leisure (e.g., bowling centers, health and fitness centers, skating rinks, sport arenas, and stadia). Participation can be denied in two situations: if accommodating the disabled individual poses a direct threat to other constituencies and if the accommodation creates an undue hardship by fundamentally changing the nature of the product offering (e.g., aerobic dance class), represents an excessive financial burden, or disrupts the environment itself.

The Casey Martin case, like most civil rights–related cases, focuses on what is "right" versus what might be in the best interests of society. Deontological ethical advocates would argue that the best interests of the individual should be pursued because this is the most humane and just behavior. After all, does it really matter whether Casey Martin uses a cart or not? The teleological ethicists, on the other hand, would ask questions such as, What impact will this have on the future of sport competitions? Will this decision prompt litigation, inviting ADA law suits against millions of sport event promoters who are unable and unwilling to change the rules of the game to accommodate every individual and his or her respective need?

Title IX

Title IX precludes discrimination based on sex in any education program receiving federal financial assistance.

A three-prong analysis is commonly used by the courts to ascertain if a Title IX violation has occurred. The first prong looks at the school's distribution of financial aid. The second prong evaluates "other" benefits, opportunities, and treatments within men's and women's sports programs. Areas evaluated include (1) provision of equipment and supplies; (2) scheduling of games and practice times; (3) travel and per diem allowances; (4) opportunity to receive coaching and academic tutoring; (5) provision of locker rooms

LEARNING ACTIVITY

1. Consider the well-known case, *PGA Tour, Inc. v. Martin* (2001) involving Casey Martin and the PGA Tour. Casey Martin has a congenital, degenerative circulatory disorder that makes walking extremely painful and laborious. Martin requested permission to use a cart during PGA Tour events. PGA denied his request, and Martin sued alleging PGA's violation for failure to comply with the ADA. The court considered key issues including whether a PGA tournament represented a place of public accommodation (i.e., the players themselves vs. the spectator availability) and whether riding in a cart would fundamentally alter the nature of the game itself. What are your thoughts? Was the PGA violating ADA provisions? What is in the best interests of society? The PGA? Casey Martin?

The Casey Martin-PGA case raises many questions about ADA compliance.

© Michael Zito/Sports Chrome USA

2. What type of disabilities should the government be regulating? Obesity? Stress?
3. Does the ADA legislation represent an intrusion into the realm of private business and free enterprise? Is the legislation necessary for ethical purposes or merely an expensive encroachment by government?

and dining facilities; (6) publicity and recruitment procedures; and (7) other support services provided (e.g., clerical or administrative). The third prong examines whether the interests and abilities of the underrepresented group have been accommodated. Specific attention under this prong is given to the proportionality of male and female students in the general student population versus the number of male and female students participating in athletics department programs, an institution's history and continuing practice of program expansion responsive to the interests and abilities of the underrepresented sex, and whether the institution has demonstrated that the athletic interests and abilities of its students have been effectively accommodated.

LEARNING ACTIVITY

Assume you are a senior high school female athlete aspiring to play varsity sport at a university 250 miles away. As a varsity soccer player averaging seven points a game throughout your high school career, your scholarship opportunities are plentiful in the fall of your senior year. Unfortunately, the university 250 miles down the road does not have a women's soccer program. Your grandfather, father, brother, and sister all attended this university, and you are enthusiastic about following this family tradition and becoming another loyal fan and alumna. In the spring you joyously celebrate the news that your school of choice has added women's soccer as one of its NCAA varsity sports. Along with the school's announcement of the new women's competitive opportunity, the school also announces its plans to eliminate the men's varsity wrestling team and the men's swim team. You are perplexed at this situation and wonder if the school's move to eliminate the men's teams is really necessary for compliance with Title IX. What are your thoughts? Is this ethical? Legal?

As you might have noticed by now, there are always counterpoints in both ethics and the law. The law is antagonistic by its very nature. Without controversy and a difference in perception, there would be no need for litigation. This wide variance of viewpoints is also prevalent in discussions regarding both ethics and morals. As we have seen earlier, views supporting deontological ethical theory often contradict views supporting teleological ethical theory. As summarized from a deontological perspective, Lumpkin, Stoll, and Beller (1999) stated, "inequality can never be legitimately defended or justified on the basis of scarcity of goods or an entitlement for those who earn more revenues" (p. 180). Some believe that women's sports programs do not deserve equity because of limited resources (i.e., there simply is not enough money to support program equipment needs, coaching salaries, facility demands), limited societal acceptance (i.e., society is not really interested in women's sports), prescribed gender roles (i.e., women should focus on being mothers and homemakers), and, of course, the summative statement "this is just the way it has always been done."

LEARNING ACTIVITY

Consider the issue of Title IX from both the plaintiff's and defendant's perspective. Why have women been discriminated against in the realm of athletics? Does Title IX reflect a subordination of women that requires legal intervention? Can, and should, sports administrators be expected to do the "right" thing? Is there a professional code of ethics that should exist for students desiring to be prospective sports administrators? Is there any merit to the term *reverse discrimination*?

Federal Constitution

As succinctly stated by Jesse Wilde (2001), the federal Constitution "governs American governments, not Americans" (p. 415). Although there may be similar regulatory outcomes within state constitutions or federal and state legislative acts, purely private organizations and those with whom they interact (e.g., employees, fans, clients) are not regulated or protected by the provisions within our federal Constitution. The intent of the Constitution was to protect the people from government's unwarranted intrusion, discrimination, arbitrary and capricious treatment, and infringement of liberty and property rights without due process. Sport organizations governed by the Constitution include state university athletics departments; federal, state, and municipally owned park and recreation departments; and possibly professional teams playing on state-owned property or property supported by taxpayers. The Constitution was not intended to govern the operations of the privately owned and operated sport organizations such as sporting good stores, health and fitness clubs, and private golf courses.

The passage of the Fourteenth Amendment in 1868 provided citizens with the same protections against unwarranted actions by state government. The provisions regulating the acts of the federal government as embodied within the first 10 amendments were "passed down" to the operations of state governments and also proscribed state-related unwarranted behaviors and intrusions on the people.

In chapter 4 you applied your critical thinking skills to the issue of school prayer at football games. In thinking about your decision, you considered moral and ethical aspects of the issue. That chapter did not, however, provide you with the legal context for your decision. Now you can complete the exercise by learning about the law and how its requirements interact with the moral and ethical aspects.

LEARNING ACTIVITY

1. Some individuals say that the most powerful influence associated with the president of the

The First Amendment and the Establishment Clause

The First Amendment to the federal Constitution passed in 1791 provides that "Congress shall make no law respecting an establishment of religion, or prohibiting the free exercise thereof." This portion of the First Amendment is often referred to as the Establishment Clause. The First Amendment, as applied to state public schools via the Fourteenth Amendment, has been interpreted as requiring a clear demarcation between any religious activity or practice and the public schools. In other words, a religious activity or practice is not to become entangled within an educational institution receiving state moneys or being governed by state employees. The government is not to promote or inhibit any religious practice(s).

Common law decisions have held that due to a student's impressionable mind, what might begin as a tolerance for religious expression can later become coerced indoctrination. Further, courts have considered the nature of events at which prayer is present (e.g., graduation ceremonies, high school football games). In holding against the constitutionality of the prayer, courts have concluded that attendance is not *totally* voluntary. In other words, attendance at graduation, while not compulsory, is such an ingrained part of the overall education experience that attendance becomes indirectly mandatory. The courts have held that a student's inability to attend a school-sponsored event comfortably due to religious beliefs provides a diminished educational experience in comparison to those attending freely and without opposition to religious activities.

Again, one can argue successfully from the perspective of either deontological or teleological ethics. Depending on the adopted ethical position, the outcome of your decision may vary. The deontological view, which is narrower and focused on individual duty and rights, would result in the school abandoning its rich history of prayer before the homecoming football game. In comparison, the more broad, society-interested perspective of teleology would conclude that society benefits as a blended population comes together not necessarily to support a specific religion but to recognize diversity, reflection, opportunity, and fair play. As mentioned earlier, the current legal position taken by the Supreme Court concludes that a prayer would violate Establishment Clause guarantees. However, as we have discussed, there is always a counterargument that may, over time, become the dominant controlling opinion of the Court.

United States is the ability to appoint justices to the Supreme Court. How does the president's appointment of members to the Supreme Court influence our society?

2. Why is an otherwise harmless activity such as prayer illegal in comparison to more obvious harms such as murder or misrepresentation?

3. Is it the responsibility of the public school to incorporate prayer as a means of producing a more ethical adult citizen?

Contracts

A contract represents an agreement between two or more parties to do, or not to do, a particular act. When a contracting party fails to abide by the terms of the agreement, the nonbreaching party has a legal cause of action. Contract law preserves and encourages the right of parties to make and enter into their own agreements as long as the contracts are legal, in accordance with public policy, entered into by those with capacity (i.e., of an appropriate age and without significant mental disability), and avoid the use of unequal bargaining power or economic duress. Common law and statutes require that a contract be fair but not necessarily equal. In other words, one party may clearly benefit by the terms of the contract itself. Recourse for breach of contract actions can include court-imposed injunctions, restoring the parties (or a party) to a contract to his or her precontract condition, reforming the contract so it better represents the intention of the parties or fairness, or total abandonment of the contract itself (i.e., rescission).

LEARNING ACTIVITY

You have decided to do something about that New Year's resolution to improve your physical and mental condition by engaging in a weekly exercise program. You decide to join the local health club. As part of the membership process, the health club asks you to sign a waiver that relieves the health club and its employees for their own acts of ordinary negligence. In essence, this waiver removes your right to sue if you should be injured by a wrong committed by the health club. If you choose not to sign the waiver, the health club can choose not to accept your membership. You remember that the purpose of tort law is to remedy a wrong. How can contract law supplant the tort law doctrine of remedying a wrong? Are public policy issues involved? Is the contract coercive in nature? Ethical?

Waivers are used quite frequently in sport management. For example, waivers are signed by health club members, spectators chosen to participate in a game's promotion, individuals renting sport equipment from the local sporting goods store, and people going on a white water rafting trip. In comparison to many of the previous illustrations, a strong teleological ethical theory emerges: Waivers jeopardize the legal rights of a few so that society may benefit. In sport and physical activity, the realm of possible injuries is exhausting, ranging from mild muscle strains to sprains, heat exhaustion, heat stroke, broken bones, and even death. If individuals were allowed to sue for the minor injuries inherent in sport and physical activity, the expense associated with owning and managing a sport or recreational organization would be exorbitant. Insurance costs, litigation-related fees (e.g., discovery, attorney fees, expert witness testimony), and damaged public relations could result in the cessation of the sport and recreational industry. Judicial and legislative approval of the signed waiver, while it denies an injured plaintiff recovery, benefits society through the continued solvency and sustained profitability of the sport organization.

LEARNING ACTIVITY

1. What do you think about the use of waivers denying a person the opportunity to recover for another's act of ordinary negligence?

2. What type of terminology and provisions would you want in your employment contract? What would differ if you were the employer instead of the employee?

SUMMARY

The daily decisions of sport managers profoundly influence employee and customer recruitment and retention as well as organizational solvency. Effective and efficient sport management requires managers who are cognizant of how their actions influence others. Considerations given to the "golden rule," the utilitarian principle, Kant's categorical imperative, the professional ethic, and the "television test" all can assist a decision maker striving to engage in prudent decision making. Further, the law (e.g., constitutions, statutes, common law) represents an extensive governance structure. Failure to comply with the law can bring both individual and organizational liability. Liability risk is heightened when professionals fail to act as another reasonable or like professional would act in a like or similar circumstance (i.e., acts of negligence). Further, office conduct and related policy including the maintenance of personnel files, communications with the media, and glancing through personal items of employees can subject an organization to invasion of privacy or defamation-related litigation. Contract development and use also contains legal, as well as ethical and moral, implications. Employers and employees both have a full and comprehensive understanding of contractual elements. Human resource legislation, while important for ethical and moral reasons, also imposes a financial burden on organizations in terms of needed compliance efforts (e.g., access for people with disabilities, opportunities for both men and women). Effective decision makers are able to consider both ethical and legal considerations when confronted with sport management dilemmas.

REVIEW QUESTIONS

1. Identify a sport management situation integrating one or more of the five ethical maxims (e.g., the golden rule, the utilitarian principle, Kant's categorical imperative, the professional ethic, and the television test).

2. Differentiate between teleology and deontology.

3. Why does society need laws governing behavior?

4. Identify the four elements of negligence that must be successfully proved by the plaintiff.

5. Elaborate on the concept of invasion of privacy, intentional infliction of emotional distress, and defamation.

6. Elaborate on how the Americans with Disabilities Act influences the sport industry.

7. Elaborate on Title IX and the influence it has had on the sport industry.

8. How has the Establishment Clause (i.e., the separation of church and state) influenced prayer before competitive events or practices?

9. Identify the benefits of contracts as applied to the following parties: (a) the sport organization, (b) the individual, and (c) society at large.

REFERENCES

Americans with Disabilities Act of 1990, 42 U.S.C.A. § 12101 et seq. (West, 1993)

Beauchamp, T.L. (1991). *Philosophical ethics: An introduction to moral philosophy* (2nd ed.). New York: McGraw-Hill.

Billington, R. (1988). *Living philosophy: An introduction to moral thought.* London: Routledge.

Black, M.A. (1990). *Black's Law Dictionary* (6th ed). St. Paul, MN: West.

DeSensi, J.T., & Rosenberg, D. (1996). *Ethics in sport management.* Morgantown, WV: Fitness Information Technology.

Henderson, V.E. (1982). The ethical side of enterprise. *Sloan Management Review, 23*(3), 37-47.

Kant, I. (1959). *Foundations of the metaphysics of morals* (L.W. Beck, Ed. and Trans.). Indianapolis, IN: Bobbs-Merrill (Original work published 1785).

Laczniak, G.R. (1985). Frameworks for analyzing marketing ethics. In G.R. Laczniak & P.E. Murphy (Eds.), *Marketing ethics: Guidelines for managers* (pp. 9-26). Lexington, MA: D.C. Heath. (Reprinted from *Journal of Macromarketing*, Spring 1983, pp. 7-18.)

Lumpkin, A., Stoll, S.K., & Beller, J.M. (1999). *Sport ethics: Applications for fair play* (2nd ed.). Boston: WCB McGraw-Hill.

Mill, J.S. (1969). *Utilitarianism.* In E.M. Albert, T.C. Denise, & S.P. Peterfreund (Eds.), *Great traditions in ethics: An introduction* (2nd ed.) (pp. 227-252). New York: D. Van Nostrand (Original work published 1861).

Morgan, T.D., & Rotunda, R.D. (2000). *Professional responsibility.* New York: Foundation Press.

PGA Tour, Inc. v. Martin, 532 U.S. 661 (2001).

Shapo, H.S., Walter, M.R., & Fajens, E. (1999). *Writing and analysis in the law* (4th ed.). New York: Foundation Press.

Teply, L.L. (1999). *Legal research and citation.* St. Paul, MN: West Group.

Title IX of the Education Amendments of 1972, 86 Stat. 235 (codified at 20 U.S.C. § 1681-1688 (1990).

Tuleja, T. (1985). *Beyond the bottom line: How business leaders are turning principles into profits.* New York: Facts on File.

White, T.I. (1988). *Right and wrong: A brief guide to understanding ethics.* Englewood Cliffs, NJ: Prentice Hall.

Wilde, T.J. (2001). State action. In D.J. Cotton, J.T. Wolohan, & T.J. Wilde (Eds.), *Law for recreation and sport managers* (pp. 415-426). Dubuque, IA: Kendall Hunt.

Chapter 6

Sociological Aspects of Sport and Physical Activity

Mary Jo Kane, University of Minnesota

An important step in becoming a successful sport manager is gaining an in-depth awareness of sport as an important cultural activity that permeates our society and influences both institutions and individuals in a multiplicity of ways. In order to understand the complex dynamics of how and why people participate in sport and physical activity, you must have knowledge about not only individual behavior (e.g., psychological aspects such as motivation) but also the social context in which that behavior occurs. Over the past three and a half decades, the scientific study of the social context of sport has been at the center of an academic discipline called *sport sociology*.

The purpose of this chapter is to provide a definition of sport sociology, delineate the nature and significance of sport, outline the role of social theory in that regard, and highlight several areas of scholarly inquiry within sport sociology, especially those areas most relevant to sport management as an academic field of study and a professional enterprise. The chapter ends with a discussion about the interplay between sport sociology and sport management.

Defining Sport

According to Eldon Snyder (1990), activities such as basketball, football, tennis, and golf are sports. However, Snyder also pointed out that a wide range of other kinds of physical activities are also considered sport. (See chapter 1 for a detailed discussion of "sport" versus "sports.") Such activities could include walking, fishing, and hiking. What is clear from these examples is that there exists a **continuum** of physical activity ranging from informal, playlike activity in a leisure setting, to the highly competitive, pressure-filled world of professional sport. Figure 6.1 depicts this continuum and in-

cludes some of the characteristics typically associated with such activity. Notice that as we move along the continuum, what distinguishes sport from other, more informal kinds of physical activity is the element of competition and the added dimensions of physical prowess and ability.

continuum—Continuous whole or series; an element or thing whose parts cannot be separated or separately discerned.

Defining Sport Sociology

Given that sport is such a significant part of contemporary U.S. society, it is not surprising that scholars would be interested in studying its scope and impact (Coakley, 2001). Beginning in the mid-1960s, researchers from academic fields such as sociology and kinesiology tried to do more than define sport and various aspects of physical activity—they also began to develop a scientific body of knowledge related to the nature and significance

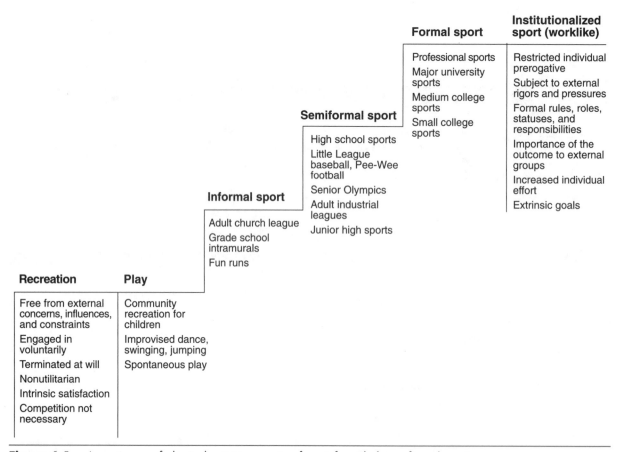

Figure 6.1 A continuum of physical activities ranging from informal play to formal sport.

Reprinted, by permission, from E. Snyder, 1990, *Sport and fitness management*, edited by J.B. Parks and Zanger (Champaign, IL: Human Kinetics).

of sport. This effort led to the emergence of a new academic discipline called sport sociology. According to Jay Coakley, sport sociology can be defined as the "subdiscipline of sociology that studies sports as parts of social and cultural life" (p. 4). Sport sociologists use sociological theories and concepts to examine social institutions and organizations (e.g., the International Olympic Committee), microsystems (e.g., women's professional basketball teams), or subcultures (e.g., gamblers) and to address such questions as, How do sports influence some of the most cherished American values such as loyalty, respect for authority, and honesty? As part of their analysis, sport sociologists do not typically focus on the behavior of specific individuals but examine instead the social patterns, structures, and organizations of groups actively engaged in sport and physical activity (McPherson, Curtis, & Loy, 1989).

An underlying assumption of sport sociology is that sport is a highly significant institution of the same magnitude as the economy, the family, the educational system, and the political structure. A fundamental goal of sport sociology is to describe the complex dynamics surrounding patterns of participation (e.g., the number of girls versus the number of boys involved in youth sports) and social concerns (e.g., an overemphasis on winning) that make up this important and all-pervasive institution (Nixon & Frey, 1996). It is important to keep in mind, however, that sport sociologists do far more than *describe* sport involvement by, for example, gathering data on how many people participate on an annual basis. Sport sociologists are ultimately concerned with understanding the social context in which this participation occurs, as well as the *meaning* of sport as a highly influential social, political, and economic institution (Siedentop, 1990).

The Role of Theory in Understanding Sport

When most people hear the word *theory*, they think of something that is boring, abstract, and in no way related to their everyday lives. But if we are to adequately understand the social context in which sport participation occurs, as well as the meaning underlying that participation, we must use one of the best analytical tools available to social scientists—theory. This is because theories help us "synthesize information about the social world and develop general explanations for how and why social life is organized in particular ways" (Coakley, 1998, p. 30). In short, theories allow us to make associations among facts and phenomena and organize them into meaningful patterns or explanations that help us make sense of our world.

The principal aim of scientific inquiry is to describe, explain, and predict human behavior. Theory is especially useful for these latter two aims. Most of us could describe how many professional golfers are White versus people of color. But how would we explain, let alone predict, this pattern of participation? By using social theory, we can **hypothesize** (and **empirically** test) that such patterns are a function of race (and racism), as well as social class.

hypothesize—To form a hypothesis, meaning to tentatively provide a logical foundation for further investigation; to assume or suppose.

empirical—Knowledge based on experimental method and observation versus theory or supposition.

Let us take the case of women's sports as a real-world example of how theory can help us not only understand the role and meaning of sport, but also create a more balanced and just society. We can easily establish that, historically, women's participation in sport was nowhere near men's participation. This was particularly true for certain team-oriented, combat sports such as football and wrestling. One theoretical perspective that allows us to explain such behavior has to do with *gender roles*. More specifically, the traditional relationship between sport and gender can be summed up in the following theory:

$$Sport = Male$$
$$Male \neq Female$$
$$\therefore Sport \neq Female$$

This theory allows us to explain why so few women (compared to men) played sports and to predict that when they did participate, especially in sports such as football, they would be stigmatized as "not real women." These kinds of theoretical observations led to a classical theory of sport

and gender developed in the 1960s by physical educator Eleanor Metheny. She argued that sports were considered sex-"appropriate" or "inappropriate" for females based on the physical and structural requirements of the activity in question. The more the sport allowed a female to conform to traditional expectations of femininity, the more appropriate or acceptable the sport was considered. Sports that required graceful, fluid body movements, along with minimal body contact with one's opponents, would be considered appropriate feminine behavior within a sport context (Metheny, 1965). Under this theoretical model, sports such as golf and figure skating would be considered "ladylike" activities, while sports such as rugby and football would be considered too "manly" for females.

Although Metheny's theory was quite useful in explaining the connections between sport and gender for many decades, a great deal has changed since the 1960s. Over the past four decades there has been a revolution in women's sports marked by an unprecedented increase in participation rates across a wide variety of sports and physical activities. The beauty of social theory is that, like society, it too is dynamic and ever changing. As a result, rather than categorizing and dividing sport along gender lines, we can now theorize it as a continuum of physical activity ranging from individual, aesthetic sports on one end to power-based team sports on the other. Conceptualizing sports in this fashion would help us explain why high-contact, physically aggressive team sports such as soccer and basketball—and sport icons such as Mia Hamm and Lisa Leslie—have become so socially accepted and widely popular.

LEARNING ACTIVITY

1. Can you think of any other areas of sport in which we might apply social theory?

2. How might you explain, meaning theorize, why males are much more likely than females to use steroids?

3. Why do you think Tiger Woods is one of the few people of color ever to succeed in professional golf?

As you can see, the questions—and the need for meaningful explanations—are endless. And remember, when you are trying to answer such questions, you are often using theory to provide those meaningful explanations. Maybe theories aren't so boring and irrelevant after all.

Rob Tringali, Jr./Sports Chrome USA

The aggressive play of Mia Hamm (left) is popular among fans of high-contact sports such as soccer.

Social Significance of Sport

Did you ever wonder why it is "News, Weather, and Sports"? Why not "News, Weather, and Technology"? Or education? Or even literature? Perhaps it is because sport is such a pervasive institution that influences almost every aspect of our daily lives. One measure of this influence is the vast resources invested in sport-related activities. As we all know, the sport and fitness industry has an enormous economic impact on U.S. society. With respect to discretionary spending alone, billions of dollars are spent annually on the sale of licensed sport products such as football jerseys and baseball caps. Television broadcasting giants ABC, CBS, ESPN, and Fox Sports "committed the staggering total of $18 billion over the next eight years" for the rights to broadcast National Football League games (Sandomir, 1998, paragraph 4). In the 2002 Super Bowl staged in New Orleans, Fox Sports generated

close to $200 million in advertising sales during its Super Bowl Sunday programming (Brockinton, 2002). And at the 2002 Winter Olympics in Salt Lake City, Utah, total expenses were approximately $70.4 million, with $32.8 million spent for all the Olympic sports and $37.6 million spent on the ceremonies alone (Associated Press, 2002).

We can also see the ways in which sport plays a central role in our society by how the attention athletes receive shines a spotlight on many of our nation's social ills. Indeed, sport has become so important to our national psyche that it is often sport figures who come to symbolize broader social concerns such as gang and date rape (football players at the University of Colorado and Darrell Russell of the Oakland Raiders), escalating acts of violence and aggression (the "hockey dad" Thomas Junta), and spousal abuse (Kirby Puckett and Jason Kidd) that may even end in murder (Ray Carruth and O.J. Simpson).

As these examples indicate, sport holds a place of great prominence in our society and has both positive and negative consequences. For instance, the positive outcomes of sport are reflected in its role as a unifier of people. Nowhere was this more evident than in the aftermath of September 11. All across the country, in sport stadia big and small, Americans came together and reaffirmed their strength and fortitude as we united as one nation. But sport has its dark side as well. The negative aspects of sport can be seen through—and even perpetuate—many of the ills that exist in the broader society such as sexism, racism, homophobia, and violence. An important point to keep in mind, however, is that in spite of all the negatives, sport has an incredible power to serve as a vehicle for social change. Not surprisingly, all of these aspects of sport have been areas of inquiry for sport sociologists.

Benefits of Sport

As we have discussed, sport can help to shape and maintain many social values held in high regard. Such values include hard work and fair play, self-discipline, sacrifice and reliance, and a commitment to one's self and to others. In short, sport can make contributions to the development and stability of individuals as well as to society as a whole.

Sport as a Socializing Agent

The socialization process refers to the various ways in which a society's dominant values, attitudes, and beliefs are passed down from generation to generation. A major component of the socialization process is **role learning**, meaning that young children learn to think and behave in accordance with the multiplicity of social roles available to them (Greendorfer, 2001). Because many of us are socialized into play, sport, and physical activity at an early age, they become an important incubator for mastering such roles as responsible neighbor, productive student and co-worker, loyal friend, and companion. A variety of research studies have provided empirical evidence that supports the significance of the socialization process in general and role learning in particular. These studies investigated the effects of play, games, and sport and discovered that involvement in such activities enabled children to learn about relationships both inside and outside a sport context (Coakley, 1993; McPherson et al., 1989). Indeed, Coakley (1998) argued that the socialization aspects of sport can be so far reaching that they affect even those individuals who do not actively participate. For example, spectators learn about the values and attitudes this society has toward a whole host of issues

ranging from respect for authority to teamwork to notions of citizenship. With this in mind, it's easy to understand how involvement in sport— whether as participants or as spectators—can influence a wide variety of individuals to think and behave in ways that enable them to contribute to the larger social agenda.

role learning—A social process by which children learn various roles and the characteristics associated with them such as neighbor, friend, student, sibling, daughter.

Sport as a Unifier of People

Sport can bring people together by giving them a sense of personal identity, as well as feelings of group membership and social identification (Coakley, 2001). Sport accomplishes this in numerous ways, from the individual level (an athlete who feels good about herself because she helped her team win) to the regional level (the rivalry between—and rabid fan support for—the Minnesota Vikings and the Green Bay Packers) to the national level (the entire nation rooting for Olympic athletes Marion Jones, Greg Louganis, and

Patriotic fans show that sport can serve as a unifier of people.

111

Jackie Joyner-Kersee). It seems apparent that few (if any) institutions have the ability to bring people together the way sport can. This is primarily because the popularity of sports cuts across race, social class, gender, and age barriers.

Because of its enormous visibility and appeal, sport also creates linkages among people that may transcend tension and conflict. In an era of increasing violence and hostility among Americans, it is essential that we not forget, or fail to use, sport as a vehicle by which we can bring individuals together as "team members" of a family, a neighborhood, a city, and a nation. As mentioned, nowhere was sport's ability to reach across great divides—and unite us in a common bond—more evident than in the aftermath of the tragedy of September 11. Even though some commentators argued that this unprecedented moment in U.S. history brought into sharp focus "what really mattered," it was nevertheless the case that sport events such as the World Series rallied the nation and gave us a sense of stability and familiarity in the "new normal" way of life post September 11. As **collective ritual**, sport played (and continues to play) an important role, both symbolically and tangibly, in our process of mourning and healing while reflecting the very best of America's values and character.

collective ritual—Groups of people engaging in a set (often traditional) form of rites and practices such as a religious ceremony or athletic event (e.g., the Super Bowl).

Dark Side of Sport

We have just discussed the various ways in which sport can produce highly beneficial outcomes not just for individuals but for society as a whole. This is not meant to suggest, however, that sport participation results only in good things. As is becoming increasingly and painfully apparent, sport involvement can have a darker side as well.

When individuals are denied the opportunity to experience feelings of competence and self-worth by achieving success in sports, the consequences can be very damaging. The abuses of youth sport programs, in which standards of excellence are often impossible to achieve given the physical, social, and psychological maturation levels of young children, are well documented (Williams, 2001). We also know that the pressure-cooker world of big-time athletics can distort and undermine fundamental values such as honesty and

integrity because of its "winning at all costs" mentality.

Recently, scholars and educators have alerted us to one of the most pressing (and dangerous) issues in all of sport—the prevalence of eating disorders. An alarming number of (mostly female) athletes and their coaches have bought into the dangerous—and potentially fatal—idea that in the world of competitive sport there is no such thing as being "too thin" (Anderson, 2001). This belief is fostered by the false assumption that reducing body fat and body weight will significantly improve an athlete's performance. How big is the problem? According to the National Association of Anorexia Nervosa and Associated Disorders, seven million women and one million men suffer from anorexia, bulimia, or some other form of binge eating disorder. According to sport psychologist Mark Andersen (2001), "prevalence rates for eating disorders among athletes are quite variable depending on the sport and who is doing the study" (p. 408). For example, one study discovered that only 8% of elite female athletes could be considered diagnosable with respect to an eating disorder, whereas another study found that close to 40% of intercollegiate female athletes had a disordered eating pattern (Andersen, 2001).

LEARNING ACTIVITY

Interview coaches, parents, and athletes about whether they have ever noticed that some female athletes may be struggling with eating disorders. If you were a coach or a fellow athlete, how would you deal with the situation?

In addition to the concerns just outlined, four areas of sport that reflect and contribute to some of the most troubling aspects of 21st-century America—sexism, racism, homophobia/heterosexism, and violence—will now be addressed as we highlight research findings from sport sociology.

Sexism in Sport

In the wake of the modern feminist movement begun in the early 1970s, a number of women's roles expanded into areas traditionally occupied by men; the world of sport was no exception. In 1972, **Title IX** of the Education Amendments Act was passed. This landmark federal legislation was designed to prohibit sex discrimination in educational settings (Brake, 2001; Masteralexis, 1995). Since its passage and implementation, enormous changes in the world of women's sports have taken place. There have been substantial gains in the number of sports offered, access to athletic scholarships and facilities, and overall athletic budgets. In terms of participation rates, close to three million females are now involved in interscholastic sports nationwide compared to only 300,000 before Title IX. And at the intercollegiate level, 40% of all participants are female compared to only 15% who participated in the early 1970s (Post, 2002).

Title IX—Federal legislation amended to the 1964 Civil Rights Act: "No person in the United States shall, on the basis of sex, be excluded from participation in, be denied the benefits of, or be subjected to discrimination under any education program or activity receiving Federal financial assistance."

It is clear that in the wake of the implementation of Title IX, millions of girls and women participate in a wide variety of sport and physical fitness activities. Change is also reflected in the ever-increasing acceptance of young girls' involvement in sport: According to a national survey sponsored by the Sporting Goods Manufacturers Association (SGMA), girls aged 6 to 17 are extremely active in organized sports. Noting that approximately 11.5 million girls are members of an organized team, Gregg Hartley, vice president of SGMA, observed that: "The flood of girls into team sports is one of the major sports trend [nationwide] in the past decade" (Sporting Goods Manufacturers Association, 2001, paragraph 10). Women are also making great strides at the professional level. In the last few years we have seen the rise of new professional sport leagues such as the Women's National Basketball Association (WNBA) and the Women's United Soccer Association (WUSA). Another marker of change? Twenty years ago the annual prize money in women's tennis was $250,000; today that number is $50 million (Lewis & Sommerfeld, 2001).

Although women have made enormous progress in sport, it would be a mistake to assume that they have attained equality. For example, in 1999, 27 years after the passage of Title IX, women received approximately 40% of athletic scholarships at the intercollegiate level even though they represented 53% of all undergraduates nationwide (Suggs, 1999). Athletic budgets, salaries for coaches and athletic administrators, and access to facilities were nowhere near an equitable ratio: At the college level alone, women received only 32% of recruiting bud-

gets and 36% of operating budgets. In addition, coaches of women's teams received just 28% of the total salary expenditures on coaches (Suggs, 1999). Finally, sportswomen lagged far behind their male counterparts in leadership roles in women's athletics (Acosta & Carpenter, 2002; Kane, 2001) and in mass media coverage of women's sporting events (Dalton, 1999; Duncan & Messner, 2000).

In spite of these drawbacks, most people would argue that Title IX has been a tremendous success. But Title IX also has its critics. Opponents of the law point out that they support women's athletics and acknowledge that Title IX has played an important role in the tremendous growth of women's sports. But they also argue that as institutions attempted to comply with Title IX, many men's sports such as baseball and wrestling were dropped in order to achieve statistical balance. Though it is certainly the case that some men's nonrevenue sports have been eliminated in the wake of Title IX, a recent nationwide study commissioned by the Women's Sports Foundation indicated that since 1972 women gained a net increase of 1,658 sport programs, while men's sports had a net increase of 74. Only in Division I was there a net decrease in men's sports (Women's Sports Foundation, 2001).

It is true that some men's sports have been dropped as a way to comply with Title IX. But those decisions are not mandated by the statute; they were made at the local level by athletic administrators. When these administrators are faced with a decision to right a wrong and enforce Title IX, they are not required to drop a men's sport in order to do so. They could pursue alternative cost-cutting strategies such as prohibiting men's football and basketball teams from staying in hotels the night before every home game, a routine nationwide practice in big-time athletics programs. The revenue saved from this (and many other) unnecessary expenditures could save a men's nonrevenue team. Instead, athletics directors pit women's sports against men's, distract us from taking a closer look at the financial decisions made in men's major sports, and create unwarranted hostility toward Title IX.

Leadership Roles

In terms of leadership positions in women's sports, females have lost far more than they have gained in the wake of Title IX. Before 1972 over 90% of all head coaches in women's athletics were female; today that figure stands at just 44%, a statistic that represents an all-time low (Acosta & Carpenter, 2002). And even though the overall number of head coaching jobs in women's sports has increased by approximately 1,000 since the mid-1980s, Acosta & Carpenter (2002) found that, between 2000 and 2002, there were 361 new head coaching jobs for women's teams; men were hired for 90% of them.

The picture for women in administrative positions is even bleaker: Whereas before Title IX women occupied the vast majority (over 90%) of all athletics director positions in women's athletics, more recent data show that figure to be approximately 18% (Acosta & Carpenter, 2002). It is worth noting that 18.8% of all intercollegiate programs for women in this country do not employ a single woman in any administrative position (Acosta & Carpenter, 2002). We should also remember that these figures are confined to women's athletics: It has been 30 years since the passage of Title IX, yet in men's intercollegiate athletics, women continue to occupy less than 2% of all head coaching positions (Gogol, 2002). These results make it undeniably clear that with respect to leadership opportunities, men have fared far better under Title IX than have women. It is even more troubling to see that women have not only been denied admission into leadership roles in men's sports but have actually lost ground in their own domain.

Some have suggested that this employment trend occurred because men are better qualified than women, but this belief is not supported by empirical evidence. Research studies have indicated that women are often as or more qualified than their male counterparts. In a nationwide investigation, Acosta and Carpenter (1988) asked those most responsible for recruiting and hiring college head coaches—athletics directors—to list the reasons for the dramatic decline in the number of women coaches since the passage of Title IX. Their findings indicated that male athletics directors perceived the four most important reasons to be (1) lack of qualified female coaches, (2) failure of women to apply for job openings, (3) lack of qualified female administrators, and (4) time constraints due to family obligations. Researchers empirically tested two such beliefs—that women are less qualified and are more restricted than men because of family obligations (Hasbrook, Hart, Mathes, & True, 1990). Interestingly, these researchers discovered that female coaches were *more* qualified in terms of coaching experience with female teams, professional training, and professional experience. They further discovered that male coaches were *more* restricted due to family

responsibilities. These findings suggest that harmful stereotypes can disadvantage females who want to become coaches because "the beliefs expressed by male athletics directors appear to be based more on a gender-stereotypic bias about female competence than on any objective data" (Stangl & Kane, 1991, p. 49).

LEARNING ACTIVITY

Do a survey of the colleges and universities in your state or region to determine how many women versus men occupy head coaching positions. Does it matter if the sport is revenue producing (e.g., basketball) versus nonrevenue producing (e.g., track and field)?

Why does it matter that there are fewer and fewer women in leadership positions? Because, as many scholars and educators have pointed out, coaches can (and do) serve as important mentors and role models. If young women athletes never see other women serving in leadership positions, they may think that they don't belong, and so they don't apply. The importance of having women in head coaching positions is supported by recent research. In a study examining male and female college athletes, researchers discovered that females who were coached by women were more likely to be interested in entering the coaching profession than were females who were coached by men (Everhart & Chelladurai, 1998).

Media Coverage of Female Athletes

Many female athletes have become household names as a result of sport media coverage over the past three decades. Billie Jean King, Martina Navratilova, Mia Hamm, Venus and Serena Williams, Jennifer Capriati, and Karrie Webb immediately come to mind. In spite of such progress, numerous research studies continue to demonstrate that sportswomen and men are treated very differently by the media in two important ways. First, sportswomen are given significantly less coverage across all of mainstream media, and second, when female athletes are given coverage, they are stereotyped in ways that emphasize their femininity and physical attractiveness rather than their accomplishments as highly skilled and dedicated athletes.

With respect to the *amount of coverage*, even though participation rates for a variety of women across an array of activities have increased tremendously, sportswomen continue to be grossly underrepresented in overall media coverage (Kane

& Greendorfer, 1994). This is true whether we examine time periods in relationship to Title IX, the age of the athlete, her race, or the type of sport in which she is involved (Kane, 1996). Would you be surprised to learn that women represent approximately 40% of all participants nationwide yet still receive only 6 to 8% of total sport coverage? A study conducted by the Amateur Athletic Foundation of Los Angeles in the mid-1990s illustrates this point: Examining sport coverage on three local network affiliates (ABC, CBS, and NBC) in Los Angeles, researchers discovered that sportswomen received only 5% of the overall coverage (Duncan, Messner, & Jensen, 1994). In a follow-up study released by this same organization, researchers found that little had changed in the ensuing years: In early-evening and late-night TV news shows, women's sports received only 8.7% of overall sport coverage. Interestingly, this result was better than what the authors discovered about ESPN's nationally recognized *SportsCenter*—coverage of women's sports there was a dismal 2.2% (Duncan & Messner, 2000).

Women's lack of representation is not confined to network broadcasting. Two recent studies of print journalism reveal similar results. In a study that looked at three different kinds of newspaper coverage—*The New York Times, The Tennessean,* and *USA Today*—investigators found that coverage of male athletes outnumbered females by seven to one, and that for every picture of a female athlete there were five pictures of male athletes (Shields, Gilbert, & Finklestein, 1997). Three years later, an examination of two of those newspapers revealed that very little had changed even though women's participation rates were continuing to skyrocket: In *USA Today* men's sports received close to five times as much coverage as women's sports, and in *The New York Times* men received a "staggering 10 times as much space as women" (Eastman & Billings, 2000, p. 202).

The second pattern that has been discovered by sport media scholars involves *type of coverage.* Again and again, male athletes are portrayed in ways that emphasize their athletic strength and competence, while female athletes are represented with images that highlight their femininity and physical attractiveness (Daddario, 1994; Davis, 1997; Kane & Lenskyj, 1998; Kane & Parks, 1992). For example, female athletes are significantly more likely than male athletes to be portrayed off the court, out of uniform, and in highly passive and sexualized poses. In one of the most powerful forms of media representations—photographic images—female athletes are routinely portrayed

as ladies first and athletes second if at all. In a groundbreaking study that examined sport photographs of female athletes participating in the 1984 and 1988 Olympic Games, Margaret Duncan (1990) discovered that popular illustrated magazines with large circulations throughout North America—*Time, Newsweek, Life, Sports Illustrated,* and *Macleans*—produced photographs that emphasized the sexual appeal of highly elite sportswomen. More specifically, Duncan found that Olympic female athletes were portrayed in ways that emphasized their physical (i.e., sexual) appearance and were photographed in poses that displayed them as sexual objects for male pleasure and desire. For example, a cover photograph on *Newsweek* pictured Olympic sprinter Florence Griffith Joyner bent over and posing for the camera in a way that invited the viewer to focus primarily on her body parts, especially her uncovered thigh. We can think of numerous examples in which female athletes are portrayed in such a manner: Jenny Thompson, Brandi Chastain, and of course Anna Kournikova, who has generated the greatest amount of corporate sponsorship ever given to any female athlete even though she has never won a professional singles tennis championship.

LEARNING ACTIVITY

Write a class paper on the amount and type of coverage given to female athletes on your local television stations. Does the coverage support or contradict research findings at the national level?

The amount and type of media coverage that sportswomen receive is not a trivial matter. By creating the impression that females are largely (if not mostly) absent from the sporting scene and by treating the female athletes we do see and read about in ways that denigrate them and their athletic endeavors, the media marginalize women's sport involvement. This in turn denies them the status, power, and prestige that are routinely given to male athletes. Why are athletic females treated in this manner? A number of scholars have suggested that it is because of the long-standing and deep-seated connection between women's sports and the fear of a so-called lesbian presence. In short, it involves the "image problem" surrounding women's athletics. Sport scholar Pat Griffin (1992) argued that the pressures on sportswomen to conform to traditional notions of femininity has to do with a widespread concern that they are, or appear to be, heterosexual: "The underlying fear is not that a female athlete or coach will appear too plain or out of style; the real fear is that she will look like a dyke or, even worse, is one" (p. 254). To counteract such fears, female athletes have gone to great lengths to assure themselves and others that sport can (and should) be highly consistent with traditional notions of femininity and heterosexuality. As a result, female athletes routinely engage in practices that counteract the notion that the sport experience masculinizes young girls and women. Such practices include wearing makeup, even on the court, and having long hair.

According to Griffin (1992), sportswomen are also routinely encouraged, and in many cases required, to "engage in the protective camouflage of feminine drag" (p. 254). By "feminine drag," Griffin means that athletic females are often pressured to behave in ways that reinforce the notion that they are pretty, feminine, and heterosexual. For example, female athletes may be required by coaches and administrators to embrace a "feminine image" by wearing skirts or dresses when traveling to out-of-town games and by wearing makeup and jewelry (Krane, 1997; Theberge, 2000). Given such an environment, it is not surprising that we see so many images of female athletes that emphasize their femininity and sexuality rather than their accomplishments as highly skilled sportswomen.

Homophobia/Heterosexism in Sport

Sport sociologists are just beginning to address two of the most oppressive aspects of sport—homophobia and heterosexism. According to Griffin and Genasci (1990), homophobia "is the irrational fear or intolerance of homosexuality, gay men or lesbians, or even behavior that is perceived to be outside the boundaries of traditional gender role expectations" (p. 211). They defined heterosexism as the "societal assumption that heterosexuality is the only acceptable, sanctioned, and normal sexual orientation" (p. 211).

Homophobia and heterosexism are rampant in both women's and men's athletics. In terms of men's sports, Brian Pronger (1990) pointed out that being a male athlete and being gay is seen as a contradiction in terms. This is because traditional definitions of masculinity are synonymous with being a male athlete, and, as most of us were taught to believe, being an athlete and being a man means being physically tough and courageous. It is therefore not surprising that gay men are seen as the antithesis of "manliness" because homophobic assumptions stereotype them as soft, passive, and nonathletic.

Although homophobia is present in both women's and men's athletics, fears or concerns about homosexuals have long been associated with women's sports. Such fears range from historical assertions that women's participation will harm their reproductive capacity (and make them unable to fulfill what are presumed to be "appropriate" heterosexual roles such as wife and mother) to modern-day claims that athletic involvement will turn women into men (Cahn, 1994). One example of this latter (though false) assertion is the commonly held belief that female athletes, particularly those who engage in more "masculine" sports, are (or will become) lesbians.

Sport sociologists are becoming increasingly aware of how much homophobic stereotypes prevent female athletes from gaining recognition, status, and respect. This is because being pejoratively labeled a lesbian is to be stigmatized as abnormal or deviant and to be threatened with the loss of employment, career, and family (Blinde, Taub, & Han, 1994; Griffin, 1998, 2001; Krane, 1996, 1997). It is important to point out that this labeling process affects *all* female athletes, homosexual and heterosexual alike (Iannotta & Kane, 2002). Helen Lenskyj (1992) conducted one of the earliest studies that specifically addressed homophobia in women's sports. She found that sport and physical education climates were so hostile not only to lesbians, but to women in general that the majority of lesbians, whether they were players, coaches, administrators, or faculty, kept their sexual orientation invisible.

A number of scholars have confirmed Lenskyj's initial findings. More recent research has demonstrated how homophobic beliefs and practices touch the lives of female coaches and athletes on a routine, day-to-day basis. As mentioned, athletes may be pressured by coaches to project a so-called feminine image by wearing skirts or dresses when traveling and by wearing makeup (Krane, 1997; Theberge, 2000). Coaches often insist that athletes conform to such standards through pejorative language meant to stigmatize lesbians (e.g., "don't look butch" or "don't look or act like men") (Griffin, 1998; Krane, 1997). Players suspected of being lesbian may be dismissed from their position on the team—and lose their scholarship—or could be passed over in the selection of elite teams (Griffin, 1998; Theberge, 2000). In an attempt to avoid such damaging outcomes, athletes may police the sexual practices of teammates, reporting suspicion of "lesbian activity" to a coach or an administrator. Finally, gossiping about the sexual orientation of teammates or women on other teams or commenting negatively about women who appear butch or masculine are two ways that female athletes try to avoid a "lesbian label" (Griffin, 1998; Iannotta & Kane, 2002; Krane, 1997).

Female coaches are also at risk. Behaviors related to their personal lives are often monitored by administrators, colleagues, and even their own athletes. For example, coaches have reported being watched and followed home by colleagues to observe their living arrangements (Wellman & Blinde, 1997). They have also reported dating and engaging in sexual relationships with men to reduce suspicion about their sexual orientation (Griffin, 1998). Private phone calls are often made by search committee members to determine a female applicant's sexual orientation (Nelson, 1991; Wellman & Blinde, 1997). Finally, "negative recruiting," a practice that involves a coach suggesting to a potential athlete or her parents that another coach or team has a "lesbian" reputation, is used to dissuade recruits from playing for a rival coach (Galst, 1998; Iannotta & Kane, in press).

Given such an oppressive environment and the strong (and understandable) desire of many lesbians to keep their private lives private, it is not surprising that issues surrounding homophobia and heterosexism rarely surface in the world of sports, at least on a public scale. But recently, two well-publicized incidents brought homosexuality out of the closet. The first incident involved women's professional golf. In May 1995 former CBS Sport's golf analyst Ben Wright was quoted as making derogatory remarks about the so-called negative influence of lesbians on the women's professional golf tour. Stating that "lesbians in the sport hurt women's golf" and that "when it [the presence of lesbians] gets to the corporate level, that's not going to fly," Wright also demeaned female athletes in general by suggesting that they are "handicapped by having boobs" that get in the way of their backswing (Gerdes, 1996, p. 1). Wright initially denied having made such remarks but was fired in January 1996 after it was widely reported that others had overheard him making such comments. It should be taken as a sign of social progress that such oppressive and stereotypic attitudes about lesbians in particular and women in general were taken seriously. It is also important to keep in mind that what hurts women's sports is not the presence of lesbians; it's the presence of homophobia.

Another instance that revealed the stereotypes (and the dangers) surrounding gay athletes occurred in 2001 when Brendan Lemon, the gay editor of *Out Magazine*, revealed to his readers that he had been having a relationship with a major league baseball player. Though his revelation did not result in a firestorm of slurs and derogatory remarks about homosexuals (a sign of progress?), it did generate numerous jokes on television. On a more positive note, it also started a public—and in many ways sympathetic—discussion about what would happen to a gay man if he did come out of the closet, especially if he were still playing. Given that no professional male athlete has ever revealed being gay during his career, one has to wonder if it will take the courage and tenacity of a Jackie Robinson to break the "gay barrier" in men's athletics. As Billy Bean, former professional baseball player and gay man, remarked: ". . . a lot of people really, they go to the lowest common denominator and think that just because a person is a homosexual, he is all about sex, and not that he is a human being. . ." (ESPN.comPage2, 2001, paragraph 68).

Racism in Sport

Since Jackie Robinson broke the color barrier in Major League Baseball in the 1940s, minorities have made important progress in all levels of sport. Despite this, racism remains deeply entrenched throughout the sport world. For example, a number of research studies have discovered a phenomenon called "**stacking**," whereby minority groups are steered into or away from certain player positions that are directly linked to status, power, and prestige (Johnson & Johnson, 1995). A recent examination of stacking in Major League Baseball revealed that Latino players dominated middle infield positions, African Americans were overrepresented in outfield positions, and white players were predominantly in "the most central position of catcher, as well as the other infield positions" (Margolis & Piliavin, 1999, p. 16).

stacking—A disproportionate allocation of athletes to central (e.g., quarterback) and noncentral (e.g., offensive tackle) positions as a function of their race or ethnicity.

Another example of stacking is found in the National Football League: Even though 68% of all NFL players are African Americans, in 2001 only a handful of starting quarterbacks (e.g., Daunte Culpepper, Donovan McNabb, and Kordell Stewart) were Black. Minorities are also underrepresented at all levels of sport leadership positions. Tony Dungy (Indianapolis Colts) and Herman Edwards (New York Jets) are the only Black head coaches among the 32 teams in the NFL. Lapchick and Benedict (1993) reported that in the early 1990s, there were no Black general managers in either the NFL or MLB; heading into the 1996 season, the NFL had only two general managers of color, while MLB had one. The National Basketball Association has shown the greatest progress: In 1996 six out of 29 general managers were African American. Lapchick and Benedict also found that as of the early 1990s the highest management positions in professional sports—chair of the board and president/CEO—were overwhelmingly dominated by White males. More recent figures reveal a moderate increase in leadership positions in professional sports: Currently, there are 20 head coaches or managers of color across the NBA, NFL, and MLB. As Lapchick and Matthews (2001) pointed out: "This is nearly 45 percent higher than the previous best among the big three sports in past [studies]" (p. 11). The authors also noted that in spite of such progress, minority representation in leadership positions remains low and that White males continue to dominate the upper echelons of ownership and management.

Minority representation is even lower when we examine intercollegiate athletics. At the Division I level, only 2.4% of all athletics directors are African American men. In terms of head coaching positions in major sports such as men's football and basketball, African Americans occupy just 2.1% and 21.6%, respectively, of these leadership roles (Lapchick & Matthews, 2001). And even though there are some well-publicized instances of Black men being hired in prestigious head coaching positions—the recent hiring of Tyrone Willingham at Notre Dame being one example—the overall employment record remains abysmal.

The lack of minorities in important leadership positions is often based on racial myths and stereotypes. Some of you may remember the insensitive remarks made by Al Campanis in the late 1980s when he appeared on ABC TV's *Nightline* program hosted by Ted Koppel. Campanis appeared on the program to pay tribute to Jackie Robinson. He was asked to do so because he had been part of the Los Angeles Dodgers baseball organization since the early 1940s and had helped to develop the Dodgers' reputation for recruiting and playing minorities. But Campanis sparked a national controversy when he explained that MLB did not (in 1987) have any African American gen-

eral managers or managers because African Americans "may not have some of the necessities" for these particular occupations (Nixon & Frey, 1996, p. 240). Though Campanis apologized for his remarks the next day, calling the incident "the saddest of my career" (Associated Press as cited in Nixon & Frey, 1996, p. 240), he was nevertheless forced to resign shortly thereafter.

Stereotypes regarding racial minorities in sport are not confined to beliefs about leadership abilities. As Derrick Jackson (1989) pointed out, there is a popularly held belief that African American athletes owe their success to their "natural" abilities, suggesting that they have some genetic advantage over Whites when it comes to achievement in sports. In contrast, White athletes are said to achieve excellence because of their discipline, intelligence, and hard work. Sport scholar Jay Coakley argued that such beliefs are based on racist assumptions. Drawing a parallel with the dominance of Canadians in hockey, Coakley comments:

There have been no claims that white Canadians owe their success in hockey to naturally strong ankle joints, instinctive eye-hand-foot coordination, or an innate tendency not to sweat, so they can retain body heat in cold weather... However, when athletes with black skin excel or fail at a certain sport, regardless of where they come from in the world, many people look for genetic explanations consistent with dominant racial ideology (Coakley, 2001, p. 249).

Racial minorities are also stereotyped in media coverage. In the previously mentioned 1994 study by the Amateur Athletic Foundation of Los Angeles, Margaret Duncan and her colleagues found what they called a "hierarchy of naming" pattern whereby those members of a less powerful group (minorities and women) were frequently referred to by their first names only, while those in more powerful groups (White men) were referred to either by their last or their full names. In 90% of the cases in which male athletes were referred to on a first name only basis, the athlete in question was a person of color. Some examples from professional sports will bring this point closer to home. All of us know who "Michael," "Magic," and "Shaq" are, but we do not think of Kurt Warner, Larry Bird, and Wally Szczerbiak as "Kurt," "Larry," and "Wally." Although certainly not intentional, this type of coverage can reflect and perpetuate a lack of respect toward minority athletes.

LEARNING ACTIVITY

Keep a journal when watching televised sports and identify the number of times announcers refer to athletes of color by their first names only. Compare this coverage with that given to White athletes.

One of the more recent examples of the racial stereotypes that abound in the world of sports indicates that racism reaches far beyond beliefs about African Americans and touches almost all racial and ethnic groups. In 1999 then Atlanta Braves relief pitcher John Rocker shared his beliefs about—not to mention his disgust with—a variety of minority groups during an interview with *Sports Illustrated*. Rocker attacked African Americans, Asians, Vietnamese, Latina/os, and homosexuals with comments such as:

> [Riding on a New York subway is] like you're riding through Beirut next to some kid with purple hair next to some queer with AIDS right next to some dude who just got out of jail for the fourth time right next to some 20-year-old mom with four kids. It's depressing. (Pearlman, 1999, paragraph 6)

Although Rocker did receive ovations in some ball parks (Henning 2000, paragraph 2), in general his remarks were widely denouced, both inside and outside the sport world. He soon became too much of a liability for the Braves and was traded to another team, though some critics (and cynics) suggested it was more for his declining performance than for his outrageous remarks.

Violence in Sport

A number of sport sociologists have argued that violence is institutionalized in men's athletics (Curry, 1991; Melnick, 1992; Messner, 1992). For example, Mike Messner and Don Sabo (1994) pointed out that in recent years the image of male-athlete-as-hero has changed into one of an out-of-control, irresponsible, greedy individual who is often physically and sexually abusive toward women. Examples of this latter image are rampant throughout sports. Football players and recruits at the Universities of Colorado and Georgia have recently been accused of gang rape. And in spite of its storied history and clean-cut image, Nebraska's football team also has a history of sexual abuse toward women (Ray, 1996).

In addition to team members engaging in such sordid practices, stories of violence and sexual assault by individual athletes could fill a police blotter on an almost weekly basis. In the late 1990s NBA player Latrell Sprewell attacked his coach,

P.J. Carlesimo, and threaten (Sprewell) wasn't traded to a 2001). Star linebacker Ray Le (though later acquitted of) Although O.J. Simpson was murdering Nicole Brown, a did find that he willfully and w death of Ronald Goldman and also committed battery with malice and oppression against Nicole Brown; Simpson was ordered to pay the Goldmans $8.5 million in damages (Online News Hour, 1997). Simpson was also convicted of spousal battery in the late 1980s (Nelson, 1994). Professional golfer John Daly pleaded guilty to a misdemeanor harassment charge after he was arrested for "allegedly hurling his wife against a wall, pulling her hair and trashing the house" (Nelson, 1994, p. 133). Rae Carruth is serving time in prison for charges related to the murder of his girlfriend, Kirby Puckett and Jason Kidd have been accused of beating their wives, and we are all familiar with the rape conviction and ongoing rape allegations surrounding Mike Tyson.

LEARNING ACTIVITY

Identify three current examples from professional sport in which athletes have gotten into trouble with law enforcement. As a sport manager, what specific strategies would you use to try and reverse this all-too-troubling trend?

Why is this happening? A number of scholars suggest that for many males a central part of the sport experience is the glorification of violence—a glorification that encourages men to equate their physicalness with behavior that demeans, intimidates, and sexualizes others (Kane & Disch, 1993; Melnick, 1992; Messner & Sabo, 1994). In one of the few empirical studies that has examined the incidence and rate of sexual assault perpetrated by male athletes, Crosset, Benedict, and McDonald (1995) discovered that male intercollegiate athletes, and in particular those who participate in football and basketball, were implicated in a disproportionately high number of sexual assault allegations. Their study strongly suggests that men's sports, especially team sports that emphasize the physical domination and subjugation of others, have become a place where males learn far too often that violence is an "acceptable" way to relate to and control others, particularly when those others are women and homosexual men. As we begin to learn more about the athletic experience

119

males, it is important to ask ourselves whether the current model of men's sports fosters attitudes and practices of physical and sexual assault that endanger us all.

Sport as a Vehicle for Social Transformation

Even though the issues outlined in the previous section represent some of the most problematic aspects of sport, it is equally true that sport can help us overcome injustice, prejudice, and oppression. Structured and reinforced with appropriate social values, the sport experience can instill individuals with a strong desire and commitment to make significant contributions to their society. Indeed, numerous scholars have pointed out that sport, because of its enormous visibility and popularity, frequently serves as a catalyst for protesting society's ills and bringing about significant social change. Perhaps the most celebrated example of sport as a vehicle for change occurred in 1947 when Jackie Robinson broke the color barrier in Major League Baseball and paved the way for countless athletes of color to participate across all levels of sport. We can only imagine what sport—and all of society—would be like were it not for the contributions of Muhammad Ali, Arthur Ashe, Marion Jones, Magic Johnson, Walter Payton, Serena and Venus Williams, and Michael Jordan to name a few.

Another area (and era) in which sport became a catalyst for change involved the turbulent 1960s. This period was marked by social unrest, assassinations of political and social leaders such as John and Robert Kennedy and Martin Luther King Jr., and demonstrations in the streets over U.S. involvement in Vietnam. Against this backdrop, the 1968 Summer Olympic Games took place in Mexico City. During the Games, two Black athletes—Tommie Smith and John Carlos—who had won the gold and bronze medals in the 200-meter dash, used the awards ceremony to protest racial injustice. During the national anthem, Smith and Carlos lowered their heads and raised their black-gloved, closed fists in a gesture that was widely seen (and criticized) as a "Black power salute." Though they were stripped of their medals and vilified back in the United States, their protest brought to light many of the injustices faced by African Americans and (in some quarters) revealed the hypocrisy of America as the land of the free. As author John Gettings (2002) pointed out, their protest repre-

sents not only one of the most memorable moments in Olympic history but a milestone in the civil rights movement.

LEARNING ACTIVITY

Identify and discuss two recent examples in which sport has served as a catalyst for important social or political change.

In the early 1990s sport—and a celebrated sports figure—again transformed our culture. Near the peak of his career, Magic Johnson stunned not only the NBA but all of America with the revelation of his HIV positive status. Before his shocking announcement, many Americans were aware that thousands of people had died from AIDS and that millions more were infected with the deadly disease. We were even aware that such celebrities as Hollywood icon Rock Hudson and Freddy Mercury, lead singer for the rock band *Queen,* had died of complications due to AIDS. But in the early 1990s AIDS education, treatment, and research had not been an issue that had overtaken our public consciousness. Magic Johnson's medical condition and his subsequent retirement from professional basketball demonstrate the power and widespread appeal of sports. In the wake of his press conference, the AIDS epidemic became *the* national story. As a result, Magic Johnson helped us see AIDS as an American tragedy and enabled us to move beyond the stereotypic and inaccurate perception that AIDS was confined to gay men and that contracting AIDS was synonymous with a death sentence.

One final example of sport as a vehicle for change is women's increasing and widespread participation in sport and physical activity. Before the early 1970s and the passage of Title IX, many segments of society—including many kinds of sporting activities—were considered off-limits to the majority of females. But women and sympathetic men began to push for greater opportunities and a more level playing field for those females who wanted to participate. Such participation has made a difference in the lives of countless girls and women, their families, and their communities. Sport sociologist Mary Duquin (1989) argued that sport can serve as an ideal setting for experiencing feelings of self-worth and empowerment. Through the physical, social, and intellectual challenges found in sport, women, like men, learn about their physical potentials; test their ambitions, goals, and dreams; and realize their ability to create their destiny not only in sport but in society as a whole.

Implications for Sport Managers

Sport sociology has a number of implications for sport managers. We have already discussed how individuals can gain feelings of competence and empowerment through the sport experience. We have also examined broader social issues such as the way mainstream media portray women athletes and how race (and racism) are perpetuated throughout the sports world. At the same time, however, we have seen how organized sport can unify cities and nations and transcend bigotry and oppression. What all of these scenarios have in common is *people*. And knowing about people is critical to one's success as a sport manager. For example, Snyder (1990) pointed out that the management of sport and physical activity ultimately depends on people becoming involved, whether as spectators or active participants. A sport manager's ability to get people involved in—and stay committed to—such activity requires a basic understanding of the social context of sport and the meaning attached to that context.

A few examples that relate directly to the positive and negative aspects of sport illustrate this point. Not long ago in the city of Minneapolis, sport managers were concerned with the lack of sport participation by adolescent African American females. They soon discovered that low par-ticipation rates were not due to a lack of interest but to major barriers such as gender-role stereotyping and safety concerns that affected girls far more than boys (Steiner, 1991). Managers discovered that, unlike their brothers, adolescent girls were expected to take care of younger siblings when the parent, who was often a single mother, was at work. This particular barrier was solved by providing day care at the local parks and recreation facilities. Another barrier sport managers discovered was that adolescent girls often lacked transportation to and from the facility; this was particularly problematic for attendance at evening programs. This problem was solved when sport managers got volunteers to provide transportation. By developing a creative and aggressive outreach program, participation rates skyrocketed.

Another example of the interplay between sport sociology and sport management relates to the notion of sport as a unifier. Over the past few years there has been a resurgence of interest in minor league baseball. In many ways this resurgence can be linked to the larger social context and meaning of sport. The players' strike that occurred in Major League Baseball in the mid-1990s—and another possible strike that threatened the game a decade later—has left many fans disgusted with and angry over what they see as the greed, arrogance, and insensitivity of both players and owners. As a result, fans have turned away in record numbers. In this vacuum, many minor league and semiprofessional teams united cities around the country by attracting fans eager to return to a time when sport was thought to be played for the love of the game.

Case Study

A final example of how sport sociology has direct implications for sport management involves a recent situation at the University of Minnesota in which sport managers relied on research findings to guide their decision making. Anthony Brown is the assistant director of the Department of Recreational Sports; his boss, James Turman, is the director. They recently submitted a long-range proposal for recreational sport facilities to the U of M's planning office. To inform their decisions regarding number of participants, design issues, and other pertinent factors related to on-campus sport facilities, they examined longitudinal survey data from the National Sporting Goods Association. Findings from this survey provide nationwide participation rates related to age, gender, geographic location, and popularity of activity. Brown and Turman concluded that exercise for fitness and physical appearance will remain very popular among college students. They also used these research data to conclude that in team sports, interest in basketball will remain strong, soccer will continue to grow, and participation in extreme sports and outdoor pursuits such as snowboarding and skateboarding will be on the rise. Brown's and Turman's use of research findings had a direct impact on their facility and program master plan—more soccer fields, facilities for roller hockey and in-line skating, a skateboard park, and inclusion of a climbing wall as well as another basketball gymnasium in the rec center addition.

SUMMARY

Sport sociology involves the scientific study of the social context of sport. Though sport sociologists study the various ways in which people participate in sport, they are primarily interested in the meaning of sport and its influence on our social, political, and economic institutions. Sport management is directly linked in theory and practice to sport sociology because both areas are influenced by the cultural and societal aspects of sport and physical activity.

Sport has great prominence in our society, shaping and perpetuating many important social values. The social benefits of sport include teaching children valued social roles and unifying diverse groups of people as they root for a particular team. Sport can also engender feelings of self-worth and a sense of empowerment. But there are negative aspects of sport as well, such as sexism, racism, homophobia, and violence both in and out of sport settings. Finally, sport may serve as a vehicle for social transformation. Sport figures can enhance awareness of and sensitivity to social problems such as AIDS, alcoholism, and drug abuse.

Understanding and appreciating the field of sport sociology will provide an important foundation for understanding the field of sport management. In order to be effective, sport managers must be aware of the social aspects of sport. Considering that sport managers work with individuals in social settings, it is imperative that they understand both the individual and the social environment because individuals and the environment are continuously interacting and affecting each other. The sport manager can play an integral role in developing positive sport environments. By doing so, individuals will more fully and effectively participate in all aspects of sport and physical activity as athletes, fans, clients, or consumers. As we have seen throughout this chapter, sport is a much-loved institution. The challenge (and the excitement) for sport managers is to harness that love in ways that emphasize not only sound management skills but also a sense of social responsibility that enriches us all.

REVIEW QUESTIONS

1. What is the definition of sport sociology, and how (and why) is it related to examining the social context of sport?

2. Why are social theories so important for understanding the meaning of sport in our daily lives? Give one specific example to support your position.

3. How and why do sports come to symbolize broader social concerns throughout our society? List three social causes or concerns in which this has happened.

4. What do we mean when we say that sport is a socializing agent? How does participation in sport allow us to learn important societal roles?

5. Why do eating disorders tend to affect female athletes at significantly greater rates than male athletes?

6. What is Title IX, and how has it influenced participation patterns for girls and women on a nationwide basis? Why is it considered such a landmark moment in the history of women's sports?

7. What are some of the major criticisms of Title IX? What do the proponents of Title IX say to counteract these criticisms?

8. Why has there been such a dramatic decline in the number of women in key leadership positions in sports over the past three decades? As a sport manager, identify three specific strategies you would use to reverse this trend.

9. Identify the various ways in which female athletes are given different kinds of media coverage than that given to male athletes. State the reasons you think this may be the case.

10. List two recent examples of racism in professional sports. Do you think stereotyping happens more often to African Americans or Hispanics, or is it just a different type of stereotyping?

11. Outline specific ways in which homophobia prevents sportswomen from gaining respect and status in the sport world. Explain how homophobia can negatively affect *all* women

in sports, not just those individuals who are gay.

12. Why are male athletes much more prone to violent behavior on and off the court than are female athletes? How does this tie into societal expectations about maleness and masculinity?

13. Identify the ways in which sport can serve as an important catalyst for social change.

Give two current examples to support your case.

14. Discuss how and why sport sociology has a number of significant implications for sport managers. How would you use both social theory and research findings from sport sociology to become a more effective sport manager?

REFERENCES

Acosta, R.V., & Carpenter, L.J. (1988). *Perceived causes of the declining representation of women leaders in intercollegiate sports: 1988 update.* Unpublished manuscript, Brooklyn College, Brooklyn, NY.

Acosta, R.V., & Carpenter, L.J. (2002). *Women in intercollegiate sport: A longitudinal study—twenty-five year update 1977-2002.* Retrieved September 13, 2002, from http://www.aapherd.org/nagws/template.cfm?template=acostacarpenter.html.

Andersen, M.B. (2001). When to refer athletes for counseling or psychotherapy. In J.M. Williams (Ed.), *Applied sport psychology: Personal growth to peak performance* (4th ed.) (pp. 401-415). Mountain View, CA: Mayfield.

Anderson, K. (2001, May-June). Starving to win. *Sports Illustrated for Women,* 88-95.

Associated Press. (2002, January 11). The Associated Press: Olympic budget. Retrieved July 15, 2002, from http://2002.ksl.com/news-3716i.php?p=1.

Blinde, E.M., Taub, D.E., & Han, L. (1994). Sport as a site for women's group and societal empowerment: Perspectives from the college athlete. *Sociology of Sport Journal, 11,* 51-59.

Brake, D. (2001). The struggle for sex equality in sport and the theory behind Title IX. *University of Michigan Journal of Law Reform, 34*(1, 2), 13-149.

Brockinton, L. (2002). Fox eyeing $200M Super Bowl ad take. *Street & Smith's SportsBusiness Journal.* Retrieved January 27, 2002, from www.sportsbusinessjournal.com/stories/1999-08-23/headline1.html.

Cahn, S.K. (1994). *Coming on strong: Gender and sexuality in 20th century women's sports.* New York: The Free Press.

Coakley, J.J. (1993). Social dimensions of intensive training and participation in youth sports. In B.R. Cahill & A.J. Pearl (Eds.), *Intensive participation in children's sport* (pp. 77-94). Champaign, IL: Human Kinetics.

Coakley, J.J. (1998). *Sport in society: Issues & controversies* (6th ed.). Boston: WCB McGraw-Hill.

Coakley, J.J. (2001). *Sport in society: Issues & controversies* (7th ed.). Boston: WCB McGraw-Hill.

Crosset, T., Benedict, J., & McDonald, M. (1995). Male student-athletes reported for sexual assault: Survey of campus police departments and judicial affairs. *Journal of Sport & Social Issues, 19,* 126-140.

Curry, T. (1991). Fraternal bonding in the locker room: A profeminist analysis of talk about competition and women. *Sociology of Sport Journal, 8,* 119-135.

Daddario, G. (1994). Chilly scenes of the 1992 winter games: The mass media and the marginalization of female athletes. *Sociology of Sport Journal, 11,* 275-288.

Dalton, L. (1999, May/June). Girl power: Women's sports score more fans, media coverage. *Gannetteer,* pp. 12-13.

Davis, L. (1997). *The swimsuit issue and sport: Hegemonic masculinity in* Sports Illustrated. Albany, NY: SUNY Press.

Duncan, M.C. (1990). Sport photographs and sexual difference: Images of women and men in the 1984 and 1988 Olympic Games. *Sociology of Sport Journal, 7,* 22-43.

Duncan, M.C., & Messner, M.A. (2000, September). *Gender in televised sports: 1989, 1993 and 1999.* Los Angeles: The Amateur Athletic Foundation of Los Angeles.

Duncan, M.C., Messner, M.A., & Jensen, K. (1994). *Gender stereotyping in televised sports: A follow-up to the 1989 study.* Los Angeles: The Amateur Athletic Foundation of Los Angeles.

Duquin, M.E. (1989). The importance of sport in building women's potential. In D.S. Eitzen (Ed.), *Sport in contemporary society* (3rd ed.). (pp. 357-362). New York: St. Martin's Press.

Eastman, S.T., & Billings, A.C. (2000). Sportscasting and sports reporting: The power of gender bias. *Journal of Sport & Social Issues, 24,* 192-213.

ESPN.comPage 2. (2001, June 3). *Outside the lines: The gay dilemma.* Retrieved November 14, 2001, from http://sports.espn.go.com/page2/tvlistings/show62transcript.html.

Everhart, C.B., & Chelladurai, P. (1998). Gender differences in preferences for coaching as an occupation:

123

The role of self-efficacy, valence, and perceived barriers. *Research Quarterly for Exercise in Sport, 69*, 188-200.

Galst, L. (1998, October 26). The sports closet. *Ms., 9*(2), 74-78.

Gerdes, R.S. (1996, January 17-23). CBS golf analyst booted. *Focus Point,* pp. 1, 3.

Gettings, J. (2002). Olympics: Civil disobedience. *Infoplease.com.* Retrieved February 4, 2002, from www.infoplease.com/spot/mm-mexicocity.html.

Gogol, S. (2002). *Hard fought victories: Women coaches making a difference.* Terra Haute, IN: Wish.

Greendorfer, S. (2001). Gender role stereotypes and early childhood socialization. In G.L. Cohen (Ed.), *Women in sport: Issues and controversies* (2nd ed.). (pp. 3-23). Reston, VA: National Association for Girls and Women in Sport.

Griffin, P. (1992). Changing the game: Homophobia, sexism and lesbians in sport. *Quest, 44*, 251-265.

Griffin, P. (1998). *Strong women, deep closets.* Champaign, IL: Human Kinetics.

Griffin, P. (2001). Homophobia in women's sports: The fear that divides us. In G.L. Cohen (Ed.), *Women in sport: Issues and controversies* (2nd ed.). (pp. 279-290). Reston, VA: National Association for Girls and Women in Sport.

Griffin, P., & Genasci, J. (1990). Addressing homophobia in physical education: Responsibilities for teachers and researchers. In M.A. Messner & D.F. Sabo (Eds.), *Sport, men and the gender order* (pp. 211-221). Champaign, IL: Human Kinetics.

Hasbrook, C.A., Hart, B.A., Mathes, S.A., & True, S. (1990). Sex bias and the validity of believed differences between male and female interscholastic athletic coaches. *Research Quarterly for Exercise and Sport, 63*, 259-267.

Henning, L. (2000). Braves silence Tigers in Rocker's return. *The Detroit News* [Online], March 15. Available:www.detnews.com/2000/tigers/0003/15/G01-16634.htm.

Iannotta, J., & Kane, M.J. (2002). Sexual stories as resistance narratives in women's sports: Reconceptualizing identity performance. *Sociology of Sport Journal, 19,* 347-369.

Jackson, D. (1989, January 22). Calling the plays in black and white. *The Boston Globe,* pp. A30, A33.

Johnson, B.D., & Johnson, N.R. (1995). Stacking and "stoppers": A test of the outcome control hypothesis. *Sociology of Sport Journal, 12*, 105-112.

Kane, M.J. (1996). Media coverage of the post Title IX female athlete: A feminist analysis of sport, gender and power. *Duke Journal of Gender Law & Policy, 3*(1), 95-127.

Kane, M.J. (2001). Leadership, sport, and gender. In S.J.M. Freeman, S.C. Bourque, & C.M. Shelton (Eds.), *Women on power: Leadership redefined* (pp. 114-146). Boston: Northeastern University Press.

Kane, M.J., & Disch, L.J. (1993). Sexual violence and the reproduction of male power in the locker room: The "Lisa Olson incident." *Sociology of Sport Journal, 10,* 331-352.

Kane, M.J., & Greendorfer, S. (1994). The media's role in accommodating and resisting stereotyped images of women in sport. In P. Creedon (Ed.), *Women, media and sport: Challenging gender values* (pp. 28-44). Thousand Oaks, CA: Sage.

Kane, M.J., & Lenskyj, H.J. (1998). Media treatment of female athletes: Issues of gender and sexualities. In L. Wenner (Ed.), *MediaSport: Cultural sensibilities and sport in the media age* (pp. 186-201). London: Routledge.

Kane, M.J., & Parks, J.B. (1992). The social construction of gender difference and hierarchy in sport journalism—Few new twists on very old themes. *Women in Sport and Physical Activity Journal, 1,* 49-83.

Krane, V. (1996). Lesbians in sport: Toward acknowledgment, understanding, and theory. *Journal of Sport & Exercise Psychology, 18,* 237-246.

Krane, V. (1997). Homonegativism experienced by lesbian collegiate athletes. *Women in Sport and Physical Activity Journal, 6,* 141-163.

Lapchick, R., & Benedict, J. (1993, Summer). 1993 racial report cards. *Center for the Study of Sport in Society Digest, 1,* 4-9. Boston: Northeastern University.

Lapchick, R.E., & Matthews, K.J. (2001). *Racial and gender report card.* Boston: Northeastern University, Center for the Study of Sport in Society.

Lenskyj, H. (1992). Unsafe at home base: Women's experiences of sexual harassment in university sport and physical education. *Women in Sport and Physical Activity Journal, 1,* 19-33.

Lewis, N., & Sommerfeld, M. (2001, September 6). Flexing their muscles for charity. *Chronicle of Philanthropy.* Retrieved October 13, 2001, from http://philanthropy.com/free/articles/v13/i22/22000101.htm.

Margolis, B., & Piliavin, J.A. (1999). "Stacking" in Major League Baseball: A multivariate analysis. *Sociology of Sport Journal, 16,* 16-34.

Masteralexis, L.P. (1995). Sexual harassment and athletics: Legal and policy implications for athletic departments. *Journal of Sport & Social Issues, 19,* 141, 153.

McPherson, B.D., Curtis, J.E., & Loy, J.W. (1989). *The social significance of sport.* Champaign, IL: Human Kinetics.

Melnick, M. (1992, May-June). Male athletes and sexual assault. *Journal of Physical Education, Recreation and Dance, 63*(5), 32-35.

Messner, M.A. (1992). *Power at play: Sports and the problem of masculinity.* Boston: Beacon Press.

Messner, M.A., & Sabo, D.F. (1994). *Sex, violence and power in sports.* Freedom, CA: The Crossing Press.

Metheny, E. (1965). *Connotations of movement in sport and dance.* Dubuque, IA: Brown.

Nelson, M.B. (1991). *Are we winning yet? How women are changing sports and sports are changing women.* New York: Random House.

Nelson, M.B. (1994). *The stronger women get the more men love football: Sexism and the American culture of sports.* New York: Harcourt Brace.

Nixon, H.L., & Frey, J.H. (1996). *A sociology of sport.* Belmont, CA: Wadsworth.

Online News Hour. (1997, February 5). Verdict of O.J. Simpson civil trial. Retrieved July 16, 2002, from www.pbs.org/newshour/bb/law/february97/simp_2-5.html.

Pearlman, J. (1999, December 23). At full blast [Electronic version]. *Sports Illustrated Online.* Retrieved March 15, 2000, from http://sportsillustrated.cnn.com/features/cover/news/1999/12/22/rocker/.

Post, J. (2002, April 18). Share your Title IX story with us. Retrieved July 15, 2002, from www.womenssportsfoundation.org/cgi-bin/iowa/issues/inv/article.html?record=887.

Pronger, B. (1990). Gay jocks: A phenomenology of gay men in athletics. In M.A. Messner & D.F. Sabo (Eds.), *Sport, men and the gender order* (pp. 141-152). Champaign, IL: Human Kinetics.

Ray, B. (1996, January 26). Unforgiven: Passage of time can't hide NU's problems. *Daily Nebraskan Online.* Retrieved July 17, 2002, from www.unl.edu/DailyNeb.arch/zzzzz/1-96/1-26-96/opinion/ray.html.

Sandomir, R. (1998, January 17). Anatomy of a TV deal: Getting CBS back in the game. *New York Times on the Web.* Retrieved January 27, 2002, from http://users.primushost.com/~bcompain/COMM497F/cbs_sports.htm.

Shields, S., Gilbert, E., & Finklestein, I. (1997, January). Media coverage of girls and women in sport: Integrating research into the undergraduate curriculum. Paper presented at the National Association of Physical Education and Higher Education Conference, Savannah, GA.

Siedentop, D. (1990). *Introduction to physical education, fitness and sport.* Mountain View, CA: Mayfield.

Snyder, E. (1990). Sociology of sport. In J.B. Parks & R.K. Zanger (Eds.), *Sport and fitness management* (pp. 213-222). Champaign, IL: Human Kinetics.

Sporting Goods Manufacturers Association. (2001, May 1). *New survey: 54% of US youngsters play organized sports.* Retrieved December 20, 2001, from www.sgma.com/press/2001/press988721108-30622.html.

Stangl, J.M., & Kane, M.J. (1991). Structural variables that offer explanatory power for the underrepresentation of women coaches since Title IX: The case of homologous reproduction. *Sociology of Sport Journal, 8*, 47-60.

Steiner, A. (1991, April 9). Park plan targets girls' self image. *The Minnesota Women's Press, 1*, 6-7.

Suggs, W. (1999, May 21). More women participate in intercollegiate athletics [Electronic version]. *Chronicle of Higher Education.* Retrieved February 2, 2002, from http://chronicle.com/free/v45/i37/37a00101.htm.

Theberge, N. (2000). *Higher goals: Women's ice hockey and the politics of gender.* Albany, NY: State University of New York Press.

Walton, T. (2001). The Sprewell/Carlesimo episode: Unacceptable violence or unacceptable victim? *Sociology of Sport Journal, 18*, 345-357.

Wellman, S., & Blinde, E.M. (1997). Homophobia in women's intercollegiate basketball: Views of women coaches regarding coaching careers and recruitment of athletes. *Women in Sport and Physical Activity Journal, 6*, 63-82.

Williams, J.M. (2001). (Ed.). *Applied sport psychology: Personal growth to peak performance* (4th ed.). Mountain View, CA: Mayfield.

Women's Sports Foundation. (2001, April 2). The Women's Sports Foundation gender equity report card. Retrieved September 3, 2002, from www.womenssportsfoundation.org/cgi-bin/iowa/issues/inv/article.html?record=190.

Chapter 7

Psychology of Sport Consumer Behavior

B. Christine Green, University of Texas at Austin

Imagine that you have developed a new sport. Who will play your sport? Who might watch it? The success of your new sport depends on your ability to attract customers. You need to know everything you can about your customers. You need to know what they want, what they need, what they think, and what's important to them. Most important, you want to know *why* they make the choices that they do. The study of consumer behavior enables you to do just that.

Consumer behavior can be defined as "the behavior that consumers display in searching for, purchasing, using, evaluating, and disposing of products and services that they expect will satisfy their needs" (Schiffman & Kanuk, 1991, p. 5). Consumer behavior helps you to understand the personal and group factors that influence consumer decisions and how purchase decisions are made. A good understanding of current and potential consumers enables an organization to develop products and services to better meet the needs of customers and to develop marketing strategies to attract and retain customers.

The purpose of this chapter is to provide an overview of consumer behavior in sport. You will learn about individual factors influencing sport consumption in the first section. This section describes the motives for active (i.e., sport participation) and passive (i.e., sport spectation) sport consumption, and examines consumers' perceptions and attitudes toward sport. The second section examines group influences on the sport consumer. In this section you will examine the impact of reference groups, socialization processes, and sport subcultures on consumer decision making. Ways to build and strengthen relationships between customers and sport organizations are discussed in the third section. The final section introduces you to the decision process and examines the influence of situational influences on purchase decisions.

LEARNING OBJECTIVES

After studying this chapter, you will be able to do the following:

1. Identify key motives for sport participation and spectation, and differentiate between the two.
2. Define consumer perception.
3. Describe the components of consumers' attitudes toward sport.
4. Differentiate between consumer involvement and identification.
5. Analyze the value of consumer loyalty.
6. Explain the ways in which groups can influence the consumption behaviors of individuals.
7. Discuss the process of consumer decision making in sport.
8. Identify the situational factors that can influence the decision-making process.

Understanding the Individual as a Sport Consumer

Think for a minute about buying a gift for each of your best friends. Would you buy each one the same gift? Probably not. How, then, do you decide on the gift best suited to each of your friends? Most likely, you will consider what you know about each friend. What does she like? What might he need? How does she feel about certain types of products? Does he have a favorite brand? The more you know about your friend, the easier it is to choose the perfect gift. The same is true for sport businesses. In order to sell more tickets, to sell more tennis rackets, or to entice more players and teams to join a league, sport organizations need to know about their customers. The more a sport organization knows about its customers, the better it is able to design products and services to meet the needs of those customers, to design marketing messages that attract new customers and keep existing customers coming back, and to target messages to individuals most receptive to those messages.

Even though no two individuals are exactly the same, people often have some characteristics in common. It is standard practice in marketing to try to group or segment people on the basis of common characteristics. In marketing terms, groups sharing a number of common characteristics are called **market segments**. Marketers then choose to focus their efforts on one or more of the identified market segments. The selected market segments are referred to as **target markets**. Products and services are designed to meet the needs of the target market. For example, many sporting goods manufacturers differentiate male consumers from female consumers. As a result, golf clubs come in men's and women's models. This makes sense from the standpoint of size and strength. On average, men are taller and stronger than women; women's clubs are shorter and lighter than those designed for men. Thus, women's clubs are designed to meet the physical needs of women golfers. Some golf bags are also designed and marketed as distinctly for men or distinctly for women. On the surface, there seems to be no need to distinguish men's bags from women's bags. Certainly there is no physical need. Rather, the distinguishing characteristics of the two models are style and color. The bags are designed to appeal to the different style needs, preferences, perceptions, and attitudes of male and female golfers.

market segment—A portion of the population that is distinctive in terms of its needs, characteristics, or behavior.

target market—A market segment or segments identified as the focus of an organization's marketing efforts; a segment chosen to allow an organization to attain its marketing goals most effectively and efficiently.

Gender is just one of a multitude of characteristics that marketers use to define a target market. Age, ethnicity, education, and income levels are demographic characteristics that can also be used to define a particular target market. Although **demographic segmentation** can be useful, it tends to rely on stereotypical images of particular groups. Segmenting based on demographic characteristics alone would be like trying to plan a party for a group of female African American college students that you've never met. What kind of food would they like? What drinks would you provide? What kind of music would they enjoy? What would they like to do at the party? Because you don't know them, all you would have to rely on would be stereotypes, which are often inaccurate and sometimes offensive. Now consider planning the same party for the same women, only they are your friends and you know them personally. So, in addition to knowing that they are similar in age and educational background, you also know what they like and don't like. Because you know how your friends think and feel, you know what to give them at your party. When considering demographic segmentation, keep this dynamic in mind.

demographic segmentation—Dividing the market into groups based on demographic variables such as age, sex, family size, income, occupation, education, religion, and ethnicity.

Marketers also seek to understand the way customers (and potential customers) think and feel. This allows them to further define their potential market segments. Grouping people on the basis of their psychological differences is called **psychographic segmentation**. Common psychographic measures include consumer needs and motives, perceptions, learning experiences, attitudes, interests, and opinions. By getting inside the head of the consumer, marketers are better able to meet the needs of their target market. Suppose, for example, that you have been asked to market a summer sport camp to high school girls. What kinds of sports would you offer at the camp? Would you provide elite coaching or recreational instruction? These are questions about the design of your products and services. As a sport marketer, you would want to design your products and services to meet the needs of your chosen target market. It would help to divide the market of high school girls into smaller, more homogeneous groups based on the girls' motives to participate in sport. So, you might divide this group into three subgroups: (1) athletes who want to enhance their sport skills, (2) players who want to be with their friends or meet new friends, and (3) individuals trying to lose weight and increase their overall fitness. Notice that these three groups are seeking different benefits from their camp experience.

psychographic segmentation—Dividing a market into different groups based on social class, lifestyle, or personality characteristics.

For the first market segment, you might offer elite coaching in a single sport. You might also provide sessions on strategies and tactics, physical training, and how to get a college scholarship. However, if you designed your camp in this manner, do you think it would be attractive to the other two groups? Probably not. A camp designed for the second group would need to provide plenty of opportunities to socialize. It could offer instruction in a number of sports and might leave plenty of time for informal activities. Elements of a camp targeting the third group might include a focus on cardiovascular exercise, diet, and nutrition. The key, from a marketing standpoint, is choosing a market segment that fits the products and services that you have to offer or adapting your product to the needs of your target market.

Alternatively, understanding your target market can help you attract customers to an existing product by using messages that appeal to the needs of the target market. Consider once again the sport camp for high school girls. It is possible to design a camp (i.e., product) that could meet the needs of all three groups. Let's say that the camp will offer two sessions of volleyball instruction per day, will include diet and nutrition counseling, and will provide a different social event each evening. Although you now have only one product to sell, you can appeal to each of the three psychographic segments based on their motives for participating in sport. You might emphasize the quality of the coaches in your communications with group 1, the social schedule in advertising targeted at group 2, and the nutrition counseling in a brochure designed to attract girls in group 3. The key aspect of marketing your camp, whether you choose to appeal to one market segment or to all three, is to understand the needs of the customer and to design your products, services, and marketing communications in a way that appeals to the needs of the chosen target market or markets.

Sport consumers are often usefully segmented on the basis of their motives, perceptions, and attitudes. These are built from experiences, which may depend on people's interests and opinions. The following sections describe each of these psychological constructs and explore the ways that each can be used to better understand the sport consumer.

Consumer Needs and Motivation

The fulfillment of needs is the essence of a marketing orientation (Shank, 2002). Everybody has needs. We are born with innate physiological needs—the need for food, water, air, clothing, and shelter. The fulfillment of these needs is required for life. We also have acquired needs such as the need for esteem, affection, or power. These needs are not necessary for life and tend to vary from culture to culture and from person to person. These needs are better described as wants and desires. Motivation can be defined as "the driving force within individuals that impels them to action" (Schiffman & Kanuk, 1991, p. 69). The driving force exists in response to an unfulfilled need. The key to the success of a sport organization is to identify and satisfy customers' unfulfilled needs better or faster than the competition. Consequently, successful marketers define their target markets by the needs they are trying to satisfy. While individual needs and motives will vary, researchers have identified some common motives for sport participation.

Participant Motivation

Over 100 motives for participating in sport have been identified by researchers (Green, 1996). Fortunately, the reasons people give to explain their participation can be usefully grouped into three key motives: (1) achievement motivation, (2) social motivation, and (3) mastery motivation (Roberts, 1992). The need to compete, to win, and to be the best are examples of achievement motivations. These needs nearly always require an element of social comparison. To attract participants motivated by achievement goals, sport marketers could emphasize the competitive elements of their programs. A competitive league structure and playoff opportunities would be important to players motivated by achievement. These players may also value **extrinsic rewards** such as MVP awards, all-star games, and trophies. Standard programs do a good job of catering to achievement-motivated participants. However, many programs stop there, reaching only a narrow market segment—participants with a need for achievement. Sport marketers can attract participants from a much larger pool of potential players by catering to other motivations.

extrinsic rewards—Rewards given to an individual by someone else.

Marketing efforts directed toward participants seeking social opportunities through their sport participation highlight the social interactions among participants. Advertisers of both sport and nonsport products often use images of athletes enjoying themselves during and after competitions. Many clubs offer coeducational sport in an attempt to provide more extensive social interactions between men and women. Runners clubs clearly cater to social motivations. Consider the following excerpt from the Austin Runners Club Web site (n.d.):

> *Are you tired of running alone? Want to meet new people? Well, Austin Runners Club has the answer for you. ARC offers club runs four days a week. These group runs are for everyone of all abilities. The runs are usually about four-six miles long and run at various paces. After each run there is a gathering at a restaurant or pub for food and good conversation.*

Unlike most sports, running does not require others to train with, and you can compete without being a part of a team. But that doesn't mean that people don't run for social reasons or that runners don't value social interactions. Clearly, that is not the case. The Austin Runners Club excerpt highlights two very important elements of club membership for socially motivated runners: (1) you can run with a group and thus don't have to run alone, and (2) the socializing continues after the run and thus is not limited to the training session itself.

The third key motivational category for participation in sport is mastery motivation. Skill development, learning, and personal challenge appeal to mastery-oriented participants. Programs offering instruction, coaching, or mentoring can often appeal to these participants. Like achievement seekers, mastery-motivated participants may seek competition. But for these participants, competition is for **intrinsic reward** and is less about winning and more about challenging oneself. Training and instruction take place regularly in elite

sport settings and in most sport programs designed for children and teens. But what about programs designed for adults? While instruction is not the only way to appeal to mastery-motivated participants, it is certainly an underused element of adult sport programs. Mastery is intrinsic to timed sports such as swimming and track, and to individually scored sports such as golf and bowling, but can be built into a variety of sport settings through goal setting. Adventure sports such as rock climbing and mountain biking routinely use mastery appeals in their advertising. The advertisement for OuterQuest (n.d.) illustrates the way marketers can incorporate mastery appeals into their advertising (see figure 7.1).

instrinsic rewards—Rewards received by an individual from the experience itself.

We have identified three fundamental motives for sport participation: achievement, social, and mastery motives. We have also discussed ways in which sport marketers can appeal to each of the three types of motives. Now think of the things that motivate you to participate in your favorite sport. Chances are that you are motivated by more than one thing. It is important to note that people have multiple motives for participating in sport. Rarely do people take up running just to socialize with others. Nor is it likely that you would join a volleyball team just to best your competition. In marketing your sport to current and potential participants, you would do well to provide elements to appeal to each of the motives and to communicate in ways that highlight benefits appealing to each motivational segment. Consider the example in "A Swim Club in Crisis" on the following page.

Spectator Motivation

Interestingly, the reasons people give for watching sport are quite different from their reasons for

If you are looking for high adventure and great exercise, then you should try mountain biking. Regardless of whether you are completely new to the sport or an experienced biker seeking new skills and terrain, we have a mountain biking course that is perfect for you! Beautiful rolling hills and mountain paths surround the Washington area, and mountain biking is the perfect way to explore and enjoy these natural resources. Use your own bike or borrow one from our quality fleet of front suspension Specialized™ bikes; either way, a great ride and quality instructors await you at OuterQuest.

Figure 7.1 Mastery appeal by OuterQuest.

Reprinted, by permission, from Camp OuterQuest. Available: http://www.teamouterquest.com.

A Swim Club in Crisis

A small suburban swim club was in trouble. Although the club enjoyed moderate success in the local summer swim league, there was substantial turnover of membership from summer to summer. Each year almost half the families from the previous season did not return. The club conducted a survey at the end of one of its seasons and discovered that there was a great deal of variation in why families joined the club. Some wanted their children to win ribbons, medals, and trophies (achievement motivation); some found that the club was a good way to get to know other people in the community (social motivation); and some wanted their children to improve their swimming skills (mastery motivation). The club had always assumed that its primary task was to help children become winning competitive swimmers. The club focused on achievement by helping its swimmers to find a specialty event and to train to win in that event. All members were required to compete at weekend swimming meets. Although there was a team picnic at the end of the season, the club did little else to foster social interaction among its members.

After the survey, the club changed its policies. Coaches implemented special coaching to help swimmers who wanted to develop swimming skills beyond their primary competitive events (mastery motivation). Members who did not want to compete were not required to enter weekend swimming meets. The club also introduced more social events for members, including pizza parties and midseason picnics (social motivation). Within two years, the club had grown from 62 families to over 300 families, and members typically stayed with the club for several years. By developing its programs to appeal to multiple motivations, the club increased its membership, improved its financial position, and also became league champion.

Scenario: Recruiting Speedskaters

You have just been hired as the development officer for a regional speedskating organization. Your objective is to increase participation in speedskating. Your organization does not have a large marketing budget, but it does have strong links to U.S. Speedskating, the national governing body for the sport. As a result of this relationship, your organization depends on the marketing efforts of U.S. Speedskating. The excerpt from their Web site shown in figure 7.2 illustrates their current marketing campaign. To leverage the national marketing campaign to recruit new skaters in your region, you have a three-part task:

1. Analyze the benefits of speedskating that are being used in the national marketing campaign.

   To do this, begin by categorizing the reasons listed in the advertisement on the basis of potential motives to participate. The three main categories of participant motivation are clearly represented in the advertisement. For example, achievement motives are highlighted by items such as, "Because you can win an Olympic medal! Because you dream about representing your country in competition! Because you might earn a scholarship for college!" Similarly, social motives appear in the ad. Examples include "Because your friends skate! Because you can meet new friends! Because you like a supportive, social, team environment!" Lastly, mastery appeals are also embedded in this ad. Consider the following: "Because you'll learn to skate even faster than you already can! Because you want to be a better inline skater!"

2. Design one or more speedskating programs and services that meet the needs represented by the motives from task 1.

   You could design a single program that tries to deliver all of the benefits described. Alternatively, you might design three programs. The first could be highly competitive and emphasize achievement. This might include opportunities to compete against skaters within the region and outside the region. It might also include a representative team that would compete nationally. A second program could be designed to appeal to social motives. This program would be the most team oriented and inclusive of all interested skaters. It could also include social (nonskating) events with other people in the program. Socially motivated skaters might also

(continued)

(continued)

enjoy traveling to events in which they could meet new people. Yet another program might focus on providing mastery-oriented benefits. This program could emphasize improvement and might include individualized instruction, support services such as nutrition and weight training, and assistance with goal setting and goal planning.

3. Develop brochures and an advertisement that will attract participants to your newly designed programs.

The marketing materials for each program would provide information about the program that would highlight the main benefits of that program. So the achievement program would highlight the representative and competitive opportunities for skaters. It might include images of club skaters receiving medals or an action shot of a skater crossing the finish line first. The social program, on the other hand, would use images of team members enjoying themselves, while the brochure for the mastery program might include testimonials from skaters who have made dramatic improvements in their times. In any case, the images and text for the brochures and any supporting advertisements should be designed to highlight the particular benefits that potential skaters seek through participation.

Why Should I Try It?

Because you already love to skate! Because it's fun! Because it's fast! Because you are always moving! Because it's like flying without leaving the ground! Because you'll learn to skate even faster than you already can! Because all you have to do is skate! Because your friends skate! Because you can make new friends! Because you can travel, see new places and new people! Because you can win an Olympic medal! Because you need a sport to do in the winter! Because you want to cool off in the summer! Because you want to be a better inline skater! Because you want an individual sport that you can customize to your needs and goals! Because you want a fast, fun, social recreational activity! Because you want a sport you can do for life! Because you want to beat your Dad or Mom in a race! Because you want a lot of variety and options—short track, long track, pack, time trials, marathon, sprints, indoor, outdoor, intense, recreational, . . . Because you like a supportive, social, team environment! Because it will keep you out of trouble! Because you dream about representing your country in competition! Because you like the speed! Because you like the wind in your face! Because you like to glide fast and far! Because you want a sport that is internationally widespread! Because you want to cross-train for other sports! Because you want to bring the Olympic Spirit to your hometown! Because you want to join the 2002 Winter Olympic Hometeam! Because you want a sport that builds character and self-esteem! Because you want a sport that helps you spend time together as a family! Because you might earn a scholarship for college! Because it will help you get into great shape! Because if you don't, you'll never know if it was your talent, your passion! Because it's fun! Because you already love to skate! Just try it! Won't you join us? Go to the start . . . click on the graphic to return to the home page and contact us. Ready?

This site developed and maintained by U.S. Speedskating in partnership with members of the ASU to promote the growth of the sport and the benefits it brings its participants in the United States.

Figure 7.2 Speedskating advertisement.

Reprinted, by permission, from the U.S. Speedskating. Available: http:www.usspeedskating.org.

participating in sport. Like participation motives, spectator motives vary considerably. Eight core motives have been found to capture the many reasons given for attending sport events (Wann, Melnick, Russell, & Pease, 2001):

1. Diversion from everyday life
2. Entertainment value
3. Self-esteem enhancement
4. Eustress
5. Economic gain
6. Aesthetic value
7. Need for affiliation
8. Family ties

Each motive is discussed in the following sections.

Diversion

For many, watching sport is a way to escape from everyday life. It is a **diversion** from the stress or boredom of one's own life. Like other forms of entertainment, such as movies and theater, sport spectating allows people to let their cares slide away as they lose themselves in the drama and spectacle of the contest. To appeal to consumers' desires to escape from everyday life, sport marketers should emphasize what anthropologists call liminality or liminal space (Turner, 1986). Liminality can be defined as social space outside normal rules that is characterized by a heightened sense of community. In other words, liminal space is a place where normal rules don't apply; it is a place where social boundaries disappear. As social boundaries break down, there is an increased sense of connection and bonding with other participants. Sport settings often provide liminal experiences. Where else can you go where it is acceptable (and even encouraged) to scream and yell, clap and stamp your feet, and hug complete strangers? Similarly, sport spectators have a ready-made community—other fans of the team. In essence, fans form a community of support for the team and also for one another. For fans attracted to sport as an escape from their daily lives, sport marketers can build appeals around images that emphasize the unique behaviors and social relationships found at sport events. Other entertainment options (e.g., movies and concerts) can provide an escape from everyday life, but few can match the liminality common at most sport events.

diversion—A distraction from a course or activity.

Officially Sanctioned Events: Super Bowl XXXVI Weekend

- Coca Cola and America Online present the NFL Experience
- Celebration in the Oaks
- Toys for Tots Golf Skills Competition
- Global Junior Championship VI
- 5th Annual NFL Alumni Super Bowl of Golf Showcase
- "Kickoff to Rebuild 2002"—A Rebuilding Together Community Event
- Total Renaissance Woman Brunch and Tea
- Super Bayou Give Back of the Stars Weekend: Teen Rally and Rap Session
- Mascitec Experience—An Interactive Career Exploration Program for Students
- Game Day New Orleans Gridiron Celebrity Hoops
- 2002 Super Bowl Breakfast
- 4th Annual NFL Alumni Sporting Clays Team Challenge
- Gridiron Glamour
- Shades of Pink: A Reflective Salute to Breast Cancer Research
- NFL Alumni Player of the Year Awards Dinner
- Taste of the NFL
- Super Bayou Give Back of the Stars Weekend: The Celebrity Sorriere on the Bayou
- Super Bowl XXXVI Gospel Celebration
- Super Bowl XXXVI
- The Players Gala New Orleans 2002

Figure 7.3 Ancillary entertainment at the Super Bowl.

Entertainment

Not surprisingly, many fans are motivated to attend a sport event for its entertainment value. Closely related to the escape motive just discussed, the entertainment motive is driven by a desire for drama and excitement. Sport marketers can take advantage of the uncertainty built into sport contests to highlight the drama to fans. Further, sport marketers can hype critical player matchups and rivalries to add intensity to the drama. Increasingly, sport events offer entertainment well beyond the sport contest itself. For example, figure 7.3 lists the 20 officially sanctioned events offered on Super Bowl XXXVI weekend in New Orleans (Greater New Orleans Sports Foundation, n.d.).

Self-Esteem

Most of us have felt the glow and satisfaction of a favorite team's victory. Basking In Reflected Glory (BIRGing), as first labeled by Cialdini and colleagues

(1976), is a key driver of attendance for fans seeking to enhance their self-esteem. Fans seek to enhance their self-esteem by associating themselves with a successful team or player. In effect, the success of the team rubs off onto the fan. Similarly, fans may attempt to maintain their self-esteem by disassociating themselves with the team after a loss or poor performance. This has been described as Cutting Off Reflected Failure, or CORFing (Snyder, Lassegard, & Ford, 1986). Sport marketers can attract new fans that jump on the bandwagon when a team is winning but must be careful to develop a relationship with these new fans that use the team to enhance their own self-esteem. Remember, as a marketer you have no control over the competitive performance of your team or its athletes, so it is dangerous to base your marketing efforts solely on appeals to self-esteem enhancement. However, you might initially appeal to this market segment through opportunities to BIRG and then develop complementary strategies to retain these fans in times when the team is less successful.

Eustress

Eustress is a form of positive stress or arousal. Fans motivated by **eustress** seek excitement and stimulation. Marketers should appeal to all five senses in efforts to reach fans motivated by eustress. Music, chants, and sound effects can provide auditory stimuli; scoreboards, lighting, movement, and color can provide visual stimuli. Even the smell of hotdogs or automobile exhaust can be stimulating to fans. In many cases, arousal is linked to the suspense associated with prior experience. For example, arousal levels increase when fans are anticipating the first pitch of a baseball game or when the gun goes off at a track meet. As a sport marketer, you can capitalize on existing moments and create new moments of anticipation. For example, clowns often perform prior to the bull-riding competition in rodeo. Initially intended to distract the audience, rodeo fans know that the clown act signals that it is time for the bulls to take center stage. As a result, the tension begins to build as the audience's arousal levels increase.

eustress—Positive levels of arousal provided to sport spectators.

Economic Gain

Economic gain is a powerful motive for a small but growing group of people. While betting on sports is not a new phenomenon, it has become more commonplace since the advent of Internet gambling. Sport gambling has risen alarmingly on college campuses, in part due to the availability of Internet access (Jenkins, 2000). Although ethically you may not want to design your marketing appeals to encourage gambling, it is of interest to explore this motivation. A fan with a bet on a game has a vested financial interest in the game's outcome. Further, this fan is interested not just in who won but also in the margin by which the game was won. Interestingly, these fans could remain interested and involved in a lopsided game when most fans have long left for the parking lot. For many sport gamblers, it is the point spread that matters. Sport marketers may want to consider ways to encourage this same level of interest in the game without encouraging gambling. In fact, **fantasy** and **rotisserie leagues** are one way to do this. Rotisserie baseball teams draft players from across the league. As a result, these fans follow players (and teams) from across the league. Their fantasy team's performance is based on the performance of players on many major league teams. Thus, they have a stake in the outcome of nearly every game played.

fantasy/rotisserie leagues—Virtual leagues governed by a set of rules by which sport fans can draft players from professional teams onto their own imaginary teams and play weekly games against their friends in a league that rewards the team with the best record. Wins are determined by the aggregate statistics of the individual players on each team. For more information, see www.fantasyindex.com/How2Play.html.

Aesthetic Value

Many fans are motivated by the innate beauty of athletic performance. The aesthetic motive is most clearly associated with sports such as ice dancing and rhythmic gymnastics; however, fans of all sports report being fascinated by the aesthetic elements of the sport. Soccer fans, for example, repeatedly mention the pure beauty of well-executed skills. Although it may be less difficult to market stylistic sports by appealing to fans' appreciation for the aesthetics of the sport, marketers can make good use of aesthetic appeals across a variety of sport contexts. Remember, beauty is in the eye of the beholder. Some will see beauty in a linebacker flattening a receiver across the middle, some in the aerial antics of a skateboarder, and still others in the perfect tee shot. To appeal to aesthetic motives, sport marketers should reconsider the elements of skill and beauty in the sport and then highlight those elements using visual imagery, commentary, or music.

Affiliation

People like to be a part of something, to feel that they belong. Attendance at a sport event can provide this feeling. Think about attending a WNBA game between the Washington Mystics and the Indiana Fever. You might feel a sense of belonging with several groups. You may feel that you belong to a group of basketball fans or to a group of Mystics fans. While these are perhaps the most obvious groups, there could be others. Many WNBA fans consider attendance as a way of being a part of the women's movement (McDonald, 2000). Others may be motivated to attend because their friends attend; that is, attendance is a way to be part of a social group. As a sport marketer, you can help fans to feel a part of something when they attend your events.

Family Ties

Similar to the affiliation motive, some people attend sport events in order to spend time with their families. Sports have the ability to appeal to everyone in the family in some way. Marketers can take advantage of this by appealing to the need for family togetherness. As family schedules become increasingly hectic, sport events provide a ready source of wholesome, exciting family fun. Minor league baseball and women's basketball have been very successful in fulfilling the need for family ties (Rogers, 2000).

LEARNING ACTIVITY

Attend a sport event. Ask the people seated around you why they chose to attend the event. Compare their reasons with the motives discussed in the text.

Participant and Spectator Markets

Many people believe that the best place to find fans for a sport team is among players of that sport. While there is some overlap between fans and participants of any particular sport, it varies from sport to sport and is much less common than one might think (Burnett, Menon, & Smart, 1993; Milne, Sutton, & McDonald, 1996). For example, 18.1 million Americans played soccer in 2000 (Soccer Industry Council of America, 2000), yet average attendance at men's Major League

Soccer matches was less than 14,000 in the same year (Major League Soccer, 2002). Given the number of soccer players in the United States, you might expect higher attendance figures for professional soccer matches. Yet, if you compare the key motives for participation with those for spectation, it is clear that playing sport and watching sport are driven by different needs. Consequently, you wouldn't expect active sport consumers (i.e., players) to also be passive consumers of sport (i.e., spectators), nor would you expect spectators to be active participants of the sport.

However, needs and motives do not fully explain consumers' sport choices. The degree to which a sport is seen to meet a particular need or motive depends on each consumer's perceptions and experiences. Consumers must recognize the opportunity to watch or to participate in a sport as a means to fulfill a need or motive. That depends on past experiences and the ways those experiences are perceived. The following section considers the role of consumer perceptions.

Consumer Perceptions

Each of us perceives the world in our own way. Many Americans perceive the sport of curling as an unusual and uninteresting winter sport. The 1.5 million curlers throughout the world would hardly agree with this perception. Similarly, you might consider football to be an exciting, physically challenging game, while your friend thinks of it as brutish and violent. Whose perception is correct? Although perceptions often do not correspond to reality, individuals tend to act and react on the basis of perceptions rather than on the basis of objective reality. In fact, marketers spend billions of dollars trying to alter people's perceptions of their products and services. So where do our perceptions come from, and how can sport marketers shape customers' perceptions of their products?

Perception can be defined as a process by which a person selects, organizes, and interprets stimuli in order to create a meaningful picture of the world. A stimulus can be any input to any of the senses. Stimuli can be physical inputs from the surrounding environment such as sights, sounds, smells, tastes, sensations, or they can be cognitive inputs such as expectations, motives, and learning as a result of previous experience. Let's examine each of the three facets of perception—selection, organization, and interpretation (Kardes, 1999).

Selection

Consider the following scenario. A group of friends attended a college basketball game together. Afterwards, they were discussing the game at the local pizza shop. Dan, a former high school basketball player, was regaling Steve with a play-by-play account of what he called "the most beautiful fast break I've ever seen." No one else in the group even recalled seeing the play under discussion, including Steve. Steve is a high school volleyball coach. He had been very impressed with the strategy used by the visiting team. David, a musician with little interest in team sports, talked incessantly about the entertainment at the game—the halftime show, the pep band, the cheerleaders, and the crowd chants. It was almost as if the three friends had attended entirely different events. Each had focused his attention on different elements of the game: Dan on the physical play, Steve on the coaching strategies, and David on the nonsport entertainment. This is an example of selective attention: choosing (often subconsciously) to pay attention to elements that are relevant to one's needs, attitudes, and experiences. In other words, people tend to be aware of stimuli that meet their needs and interests and filter out stimuli that are less personally relevant.

Organization

People rarely attend to each stimulus individually. Rather, stimuli are grouped together and perceived as a unified whole. Sport teams have taken advantage of the grouping effect by associating their team with particular images. For example, many team mascots are chosen to imply desired characteristics to the team. As a result, American football teams tend to choose mascots such as Bears, Vikings, and Cowboys in the hope that fans will then associate their team with strength, aggression, and toughness. Similarly, advertisements for a variety of products and services use sport imagery to associate their products with desired characteristics. For example, soft drink ads often show people enjoying a soft drink while watching or playing a sport in order to associate the drink with fun, energy, excitement, or camaraderie.

Interpretation

People are selective about the stimuli they perceive and then organize the stimuli into patterns and groupings. Ultimately, however, perceptions depend on each individual's interpretation of the stimuli. The interpretation, and consequently the perception, is uniquely individual. Consider the sport of underwater hockey, a hockey game played on the bottom of a swimming pool by teams wearing masks, snorkels, and fins. If you were shown a photograph of people playing underwater hockey and then asked your impression of the sport, your perception would be influenced by your prior experiences. Your prior experiences help to form particular expectations

Mascots such as Muddy of the Toledo Mud Hens baseball team provide nonsport entertainment during athletics events.

Courtesy of the Toledo Mud Hens Baseball Team

Figure 7.4 Model of attitude formation.

that may provide alternatives that you would use to interpret the stimuli presented. The broader your experiences, the more interpretations and alternatives you have to draw on. Although you may not have been familiar with underwater hockey, you might draw on your knowledge, experience, and attitudes toward ice hockey. Someone else might draw on his or her experience and attitudes toward water sports more generally.

People tend to generalize their experiences and attitudes from one product to another or even from one category to another. When these generalizations are positive, it is commonly called a "halo effect" (Mara, 2000). Licensing is a prime example of sport marketers taking advantage of halo effects to sell products. Team logos appear on everything from clothing to golf balls to baby bottles. At least one university offers dog collars, slippers, and sink strainers with their team's logo.

Consumer Attitudes

As the previous section indicates, experiences and existing attitudes greatly influence our perceptions of various sports, teams, athletes, and other sport products and services. Marketing efforts are often directed at shaping people's perceptions of a particular product, service, or brand. Essentially, this is a task of forming (in the case of a new product or service) or changing (in the case of an existing product or service) customers' attitudes about the product or service. But what exactly is an attitude, and how do we form our attitudes? In its simplest form, an attitude can be an expression of your inner feelings that reflects whether you like or dislike something. Your attitudes are based on your previous experiences (behavioral component), feelings (affective component), and beliefs (cognitive component) about an object (Shank, 2002). These three components work together to formulate an attitude (see figure 7.4).

Attitudes Get a Workout

Consider the case of Maria. Maria doesn't like health clubs. Let's examine the three components to see how Maria's attitude toward health clubs may have been formed.

First, we'll examine the cognitive component of attitude—Maria's knowledge of and beliefs about health clubs. Maria believes that health clubs are expensive. She also believes that health clubs are for fit people. These beliefs may or may not correspond to your own beliefs about health clubs and may or may not be true. In fact, much of Maria's knowledge of health clubs comes from two sources: infomercials for home exercise equipment, which highlight the cost savings of home equipment, and magazine ads for a national health club chain that features ultrafit-looking young professionals working out in a state-of-the-art health club. Now add to these beliefs Maria's feelings about health clubs—the affective component. These feelings are often based on an emotional reaction to one's knowledge, experience, and beliefs. Maria is afraid of health clubs. Her feelings of intimidation stem from her belief that health clubs are only for fit people and from her previous experience with a personal trainer. Her experience is part of the behavioral component and is based on her actions. Last year Maria wanted to get in shape. She contacted a personal trainer whom a friend had recommended. In two months of training, Maria pulled several muscles, sprained an ankle, and felt tired and run down from the flu. Maria's experience with the personal trainer was not a pleasant one. It is easy to see how this experience, combined with her feelings and beliefs, created a very negative attitude toward health clubs.

(continued)

(continued)

You might think that it would be nearly impossible to recruit Maria to join a health club. Selling Maria a membership would require a change in Maria's attitude toward health clubs. The three components of attitude offer the sport marketer three points of leverage to change an attitude. Each would require a different approach:

- Maria's belief that health clubs are expensive could be changed through accurate price information, discount promotions, or alternative pricing strategies such as monthly payments rather than annual fees. One might also use testimonials and photos of ordinary-looking, less-than-fit members in brochures and advertisements.
- Emotional appeals emphasizing fun, safety, or comfort might help to overcome Maria's fear of health clubs.
- A free trial membership could go a long way toward negating Maria's prior experience with the personal trainer.

Although these are just a few of the many possible tactics available, each could make a difference. Together, they may work to change Maria's attitude.

LEARNING ACTIVITY

Choose two sports, one that you have a positive attitude toward and one that you have a negative attitude toward. For each sport, develop a list for each component of your attitude. Compare the lists for each sport.

Group Influences on the Sport Consumer

This section examines the external factors influencing sport buying behavior. Each of us is influenced by the people closest to us, by the groups with which we choose to associate, and by the broader society in which we live. Take a moment and think about choosing to play on an intramural team at your university. The types of sports offered are typically those sports valued by your national culture. Consequently, American university students might choose to play basketball, while British students may choose to play cricket and Malaysian students may choose to play badminton. Further, the choice to play or not to play intramural sport can be greatly influenced by your membership in a group. Physical education majors would be expected to value sport participation highly, but music majors might not. If you choose to participate, your choice of sport may then be influenced by your close friends.

Clearly, each of us will be influenced by different people and will value the opinions of different groups. Thus, each of us has our own reference groups. Reference groups serve as a benchmark for evaluating our participation and purchase decisions. These are the people and groups who influence our perceptions, attitudes, and behaviors by providing us with a valued point of comparison. Reference groups can be either direct or indirect. Direct reference groups are those groups requiring face-to-face interaction; indirect reference groups do not require direct contact. Each is discussed in the following sections.

Direct Reference Groups

Family and friends exert a great deal of influence on the attitudes, values, and perceptions that we develop. Think about your own sport participation. Who first encouraged you to play sport? Children are commonly introduced to a sport by their parents or teachers (Brustad, 1996). Later, one's peers play a more powerful role in participation choices (Horn & Weiss, 1991). Similarly, you probably shared your first moments as a fan of your favorite team with friends or family members. Furthermore, your choices are usually reinforced by your friends and family. For example, if you are a tennis fan, you may watch the U.S. Open with your family, you may attend a local tournament with friends, or your brother may give you a tennis shirt for your birthday. Each of these actions subtly reinforces your attitudes and behaviors regarding tennis.

Although friends and family can be a powerful influence on one's sport choices and purchases, they are not alone in their influence. Nearly everyone is part of a larger group of some kind. Some of these groups offer formal membership (e.g., sport teams, special interest clubs, service groups), but most do not (e.g., high school sophomores, business majors, residents of a particular neighborhood). The point is that the group shares something in common and the group's values serve as a point of evaluation for one's own attitudes and behaviors.

Social class can sometimes place invisible boundaries on our choices by delineating what is appropriate and inappropriate behavior. Social class often serves as a referent when choosing to participate (or not participate) in a particular sport (Raudsepp & Viira, 2000). We tend to associate certain sports with participants of a particular social class. Golf, sailing, and polo, for example, are often associated with upper-class participants, while bowling and pugilistic sports such as boxing are more likely to appeal to working-class participants.

Social class tends to serve as a global referent; that is, it affects one's choices and behaviors across a variety of settings. But not all reference groups have global influence. Consider the following example. Judy is an executive at XYZ Corporation. During the week, she interacts with other high-level executives, wears a suit to work, and makes thoughtfully informed decisions about the direction of her company. Her primary reference group is other executives. During work hours, Judy's behavior is constrained by what is seen as appropriate behavior by others like her. But this reference group is not the only influence on Judy's behavior. Judy is also an athlete. On the weekend, she is a football player. Her reference group in this situation is other football players. In her team setting, Judy's behavior is no longer influenced by the unwritten rules of appropriate executive behavior. In fact, Judy the executive would not make a very good linebacker. While the football subculture may value the thoughtfully informed decisions of an executive, it is more likely to value big hits, aggression, and trash talk—behaviors that would be entirely inappropriate in Judy's work setting. In this example, Judy physically interacted with others in both the executive subculture and the subculture of women's football. However, a subculture does not require direct interaction to serve as a reference group.

Indirect Reference Groups

Indirect reference groups can be highly influential. They may consist of individuals such as athletes, coaches, actors, or politicians; alternatively they may be groups or subcultures. In either case, the individual or group's influence is not the result of direct face-to-face contact. Instead, these are often **aspirational reference groups**—groups in which a person is not currently a member but aspires to be a member. Gatorade's "Be Like Mike" advertising campaign featuring Michael Jordan is perhaps the most unabashed use of an aspirational reference group to sell a product, but there are numerous, albeit subtler, examples of advertisements that use athletes as aspirational referents.

aspirational reference group—A group to which an individual wishes to belong.

Subcultures can operate in much the same way as aspirational reference groups. Let's assume for the moment that you want to be a surfer. Even before you learn to surf, chances are that you will be influenced by what you know about surfers and the surfing subculture. You may buy *Surfing* magazine, watch surfing events, and talk to people who surf. Your knowledge of the surfing subculture, however superficial, may influence the style and brand of clothing you choose to wear, the music you listen to, or even the way you style your hair. Marketers are more than willing to sell you products that help you to look and feel as though you belong to the group.

As a marketer, you can take advantage of the ability of reference groups to change consumers' perceptions, attitudes, and purchase behaviors. But for the reference group to wield its influence, it must be able to (1) make the person aware of your product, (2) provide a chance for the person to compare himself or herself with the group, (3) influence the person to adopt attitudes and behaviors consistent with the group, and (4) support the person's decision to use the same product or service as the group (Schiffman & Kanuk, 1991).

Your choice of reference groups is affected by your perceptions and past experiences. Your choice of reference groups can affect your preferences for particular sports and the sport choices that you make. In other words, the reference groups you choose are based, in part, on what you have learned, and the reference group may also have an effect on what you learn subsequently. This is an effect of consumer socialization.

Consumer Socialization

We have seen that family, friends, teachers, and other reference groups can affect your decisions about participating in sport and about watching sport. Yet, the effect of people who are significant in your life reaches even further. Through them you learn not merely *what* you prefer, but also *how* to consume what you prefer. Let's assume that you want to watch a baseball game. You have several choices. You could watch a game played by a local Little League team. You could watch a minor league game. You could watch a major league game. If you choose a major league game, you could attend the game or watch it on television. If you attend the game, you could sit in the bleachers, behind home plate, or behind a dugout. The choices you make will be influenced, in part, by what you have learned about the ways to watch baseball. If when you were first learning to enjoy watching baseball, your family or friends typically preferred to watch on television, you will be more likely to choose to watch on television. On the other hand, if going to the ball game was something that your family or friends treated as a valuable choice, then you are likely to consider going to the game to be preferable to watching it on television.

As we grow and mature, we learn how to consume the sport that we prefer. Both direct and indirect reference groups influence the ways in which we consume sport. Think of your own expectations of appropriate behaviors at a baseball game. Your early experiences attending with friends or family may have been the beginning of lifelong rituals. For example, Tom has season tickets to watch the Baltimore Orioles. When he was young, his father took him to watch the Washington Senators. Three things were always part of the baseball experience for Tom. One, he always took his baseball glove to the game; two, his father always bought him peanuts and a hotdog at the ballpark; and three, they always hollered at the umpire. Tom has continued these rituals as an adult. Unintentionally, he has also taught his own children that baseball games require one to bring a glove, eat peanuts and hotdogs, and yell at the officials. This is an example of socialization through modeling. Just as Tom did as a child, Tom's children watched their father's behavior at baseball games and began to copy his behavior. Prompting and reinforcement can further assist in the socialization process. For example, Tom might prompt his daughter to bring her glove or ask if she would like some peanuts. Similarly, he might reinforce her jibes at the umpire by laughing or praising her comments.

Each of these processes—modeling, prompting, and reinforcing—also occur via indirect reference groups. Spectators seen on television broadcasts and in movies often influence our attitudes and consumption behaviors. Advertisements can prompt behaviors or reinforce our perceptions of appropriate ways to enjoy the game. Over time, we

are socialized into a way of consuming sport that is shaped by our reference groups, both direct and indirect. Sport marketers are also interested in ways to socialize customers into particular consumption patterns. One of the most effective ways to influence the attitudes and behaviors of customers is to build and nurture relationships with them.

LEARNING ACTIVITY

Interview two family members and two friends to determine what role the family and other reference groups had on their choice to become a fan of a particular team.

Building a Relationship With the Consumer

In the previous sections we identified key internal factors and external influences on sport consumers. In practice, it is difficult to isolate distinct influences of either internal or external forces. Rarely are sport consumption decisions influenced solely by any one force. Rather, one's internal attitudes, perceptions, and experiences are formed and interpreted by one's relationship to a reference group or membership in a particular subculture. Two processes, involvement and identification, highlight the ways in which internal and external forces combine to influence our sport decisions.

Consumer Involvement and Identification

Consumer involvement has been characterized as a combination of one's interest in a sport product (e.g., team, athlete, sport), and the degree to which one considers the product an important part of one's life (Park & Mittal, 1985). Many sport participants become highly involved with their sport. Correspondingly, they think about, talk about, and read about their sport frequently. They tend to feel more deeply about their sport than do less involved participants. Involvement is valued by sport marketers because high levels of involvement are associated with increased purchasing and consumer loyalty (Kerstetter & Kovich, 1997).

As a marketer, you can facilitate participants' involvement. Imagine for a moment that you are the owner of a local ice rink whose main clientele consists of current and former ice hockey players.

How can you deepen their involvement with ice hockey? First, you may want to find ways to stimulate their interest in the sport. Think back to the earlier discussion of participant motivation. You know that your clients may be participating for a variety of reasons. Consequently, they may be interested in different aspects of the sport. Some participants may like the camaraderie of the team atmosphere, some may be interested in the skating skills, some may like the strategic elements, and still others may like the physicality of the sport. As a sport marketer, you can build excitement and interest around multiple elements of the sport, thereby broadening participants' interest in the sport as a whole. Further, you could provide products and services such as lessons, magazines, videos, equipment, and other expertise. In this way, you offer your customers materials to engage their thinking about the game and provide fodder for hockey-related conversations. Lastly, you should consider providing space for those conversations to take place. Waiting areas, eating areas, and locker rooms are informal spaces where participants can socialize and share the ice hockey subculture. Involvement does not occur in a vacuum; it is through interactions with others that players learn to value the sport.

The more one becomes involved with a sport, a team, or some other sport product, the more it becomes a part of one's identity. Consequently, involvement and identification are closely related. The process of identification occurs as your role (as a participant or as a fan) becomes central to your personal sense of self—that is, your identity (Shamir, 1992). Hence, the statements "I am a Red Sox fan" and "I am a scuba diver" are expressions of identification with a team and with a sport, respectively. These roles may be a part of your self-identity (the way you see yourself) or a part of your social identity (the way others see you) (Sirgy, 1986). In either case, identification is a form of attachment, and, like any attachment, its object varies.

The most common object of identification is the team, particularly when the team is also representative of a community. College teams often inspire high levels of identification, particularly among students and alumni. But identification can occur at any level of sport. Entire communities exhibit deep emotional attachments to high school football teams in Texas and communities in other

Highly identified fans.

parts of the country. Further, athletes and coaches can also be objects of identification. Advertisers often take advantage of consumers' attachments to individual athletes and coaches by using them in their ads. For example, the "Got Milk?" ad campaign featured pictures of famous athletes sporting milk moustaches. The National Dairy Council counted on consumers identifying with athletes such as Marion Jones, Tony Meola, and others (see www.whymilk.com/celebrities/index.htm). The logic goes like this: If they like milk and you identify with them, then you should be drinking milk too.

Highly identified consumers attend more games, are less sensitive to price, and invest more time and effort in being a fan (Sutton, McDonald, Milne, & Cimperman, 1997). They tend to purchase and display licensed products. Also important, they tend to be more tolerant of performance slumps and losing seasons. As performance is beyond the control of sport marketers, the desirability of highly identified fans is obvious. These are not fair-weather fans; these fans are loyal.

Consumer Loyalty

There are few industries other than sport in which customer loyalty carries such a high level of emotional and psychological investment. You have only to think about the public outrage when Art Modell moved his NFL franchise from Cleveland to Baltimore to get a feel for the loyalty of Cleveland Browns fans. Many people become fans as children and follow a particular team all of their lives. This is the essence of brand loyalty—constant preference for one brand over its competitors (Baldinger & Rubinson, 1996). The traditions and rituals of sports and sport teams provide consumers with psychological (and often emotional) hooks to maintain loyalties. For many, team loyalty provides a sense of community and belonging that is difficult to find in our modern society (Stone, 1981). For sport marketers, loyalty is a way to shortcut the decision process, to reduce the alternatives available to consumers, and to stimulate continued team-related spending. Let's now examine the decision-making process for a typical purchase.

Consumer Decision Making in Sport

You make hundreds of decisions each day. You decide when to get out of bed in the morning, what to wear, how to comb your hair, and whether to eat breakfast. Your sport-related decisions are equally varied. You decide whether to participate in sport, which sports you will try, whether you will watch sport, which sport, which team, who you will cheer for, whether you will purchase season tickets, and if you will wear your team jersey. The list of decisions seems endless. Some decisions are easily made; others require much thought. In any case, the decision-making process has a fairly common progression. It begins with the recognition of a need or problem that spurs one to gather information about potential solutions. Alternatives are then evaluated, with the "best" alternative leading to purchase. The purchase experience is then followed by a period of postpurchase evaluation that will influence future purchase decisions (see figure 7.5). Notice that decision making does not happen in a void. Rather, it is influenced by each of the internal and external factors already discussed. It is further influenced by the situation in which the decision occurs. In this section we will first examine the situational factors influencing the decision-making process, then explore the decision process itself, and finish with a discussion of postpurchase evaluation.

Situational Factors

A situation is a set of factors outside of the individual consumer and removed from the product or advertisement of the product that the consumer is purchasing. Marketers need to know how purchase situations influence consumers in order to develop marketing strategies that enhance the purchase of their products. The five categories of **situational influence** are (1) physical surroundings, (2) social surroundings, (3) task requirements, (4) temporal perspective, and (5) antecedent states (Kardes, 1999). The physical surroundings include the geographic location, décor, sound, smells, lighting, weather, and crowding. It is easy to see, for example, how the weather would influence your decision to play tennis. Social surroundings deal primarily with the presence of other people who could have an impact on your decision. For example, if you want to go to a movie, but the group that you are with prefers to go bowling, it is likely that you will comply with the group and find yourself at the bowling alley.

situational influence—The influence arising from factors that are particular to a specific time and place and are independent of individual customers' characteristics.

Task requirements speak to the context of the purchase (that is, the intent or requirement of the

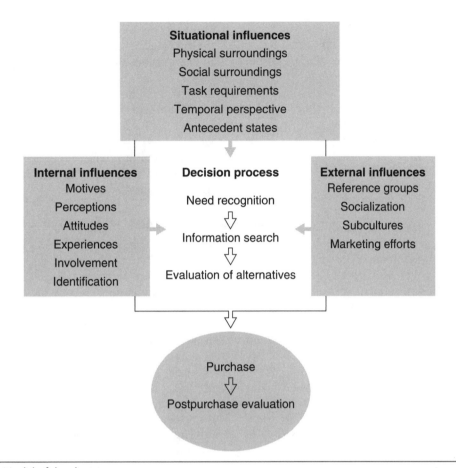

Figure 7.5 Model of the decision process.

purchase). Consider the purchase of a pair of running shoes. If you are purchasing them for yourself, you may be more concerned with performance functions than with price. However, what if you are purchasing them as a gift? You may be more concerned with price and attractiveness than with actual performance.

The fourth category is temporal perspective. Time pressures, the time of day, and the season of the year are all examples of potential temporal influences. Most sports are associated with particular times of the year. These associations become entrenched in the minds of consumers. Marketing a sport outside of its traditional season can be difficult, as we saw with the failure of the USFL, an alternative professional football league with league play beginning in the spring.

Lastly, antecedent states can affect the decision process. These encompass momentary moods, such as anxiousness, excitement, or even hunger; and momentary conditions, such as cash on hand, fatigue, or illness. If you have ever attended a sport event and wondered, on your return home, why on earth you purchased a gigantic foam finger, you

have probably experienced the influence of excitement on the purchase decision process. Let's look more closely at this process.

Decision Process

Each of us arrives at a decision in a slightly different way. We begin with motives, perceptions, attitudes, and experiences that are uniquely our own. We are influenced by reference groups and subcultures that are important to us, and we have been socialized in different ways. As a result, we interpret and react to marketing efforts in varied ways. Despite these differences, the steps in the decision process are remarkably consistent from consumer to consumer.

Need recognition is the first step in the decision process. This is likely to occur when you are faced with a problem or realize a difference between an actual state and a desired state. This can be as straightforward as the need to replace a worn-out softball glove or as complex as a desire to change one's lifestyle in order to fit in time for exercise. In the first case, the need is obvious: The equipment no longer works, so it must be replaced.

In the second case, the need is less straightforward. What aspects of one's lifestyle need to be changed in order to begin exercising? For example, do you need to wake earlier to make time to exercise? Maybe you need to give up another activity or spend less time at work. In this case, the need emerges from the gap between the current lifestyle and the desired lifestyle.

need recognition—Perception of a difference between a desired state and the actual situation; the first stage of the decision-making process.

Once the need has been identified, the consumer seeks information that helps to resolve the problem or fulfill the need. Prior experience or brand loyalty may provide the consumer with enough information to determine alternatives. For example, Casey's satisfaction with his old glove might be all the information necessary to decide to purchase the latest model of the same glove. If he is loyal to a particular brand, he may limit his search by collecting information only about products produced by that company. He may ask the opinion of respected members of his reference group or be influenced by the acceptability of a brand or style within his softball subculture. He may search out information on the Internet, in magazines, or via the local sport store. In any case, he will collect enough information to determine his purchase options. Potential purchases fall into one of several decision sets. Casey's list of potential products is called the "awareness set." This represents all of the alternatives of which Casey is aware. Not all of these products will be considered. The group of gloves that will be evaluated in the next step is called the "evoked set." The gloves that are not being considered, due to an unpleasant experience or negative information, are called the "inept set." Lastly, the "inert" set consists of the products for which Casey has a neutral evaluation.

When evaluating items in the evoked set, consumers tend to use two types of information: (1) a list of the potential products from the evoked set and (2) the features and characteristics that will be used to evaluate those products (Schiffman & Kanuk, 1991). This has important implications for sport marketers. First, it is imperative that consumers are made aware of your product or service. You may manufacture the best glove on the market, but it will never make consumers' evoked sets unless they are aware that it exists. Second, you need to understand which features are important to your target market. It is useless to provide the highest quality of leather for your softball

gloves if consumers evaluate them on the basis of their fit and price.

Consumers make their purchase decision based on an evaluation of products within the evoked set. It is important to note that the evoked set is influenced by both internal and external forces. These forces also influence the relative value attached to product attributes. As you can see, the final purchase decision is based on your personal evaluation of particular products and their attributes.

Postpurchase Evaluation

You might think that the process ends with the purchase, but there is yet another step in the process—the postpurchase evaluation (Shank, 2002). As consumers use a product, they evaluate it with respect to their expectations. Let's return to the example of Casey and the softball glove. Casey will have developed expectations about the performance of his new glove. He might expect that it will look good, break in easily, and fit his hand well. After using the glove for several practice sessions, he will evaluate the glove's actual performance. If the glove performs as or better than expected, Casey will be satisfied with his purchase. But if the glove does not fit well or is difficult to break in well, then he may be dissatisfied with his purchase. From a marketing standpoint, Casey's satisfaction is important for two reasons. One, his satisfaction will affect his future purchases of the product, and two, it will affect word-of-mouth communication about the product and the brand.

An important part of the postpurchase evaluation is consumers' attempts to reassure themselves that they made the right decision. In other words, they question their own judgment. This is called **cognitive dissonance**. Consumers attempt to reduce postpurchase cognitive dissonance in several ways. They may rationalize their decision as being a wise choice (e.g., this is definitely the best softball glove because it fits so well). They may seek out marketing materials that confirm their decision while avoiding advertisements for competing products. They may try to persuade others to make the same purchase, or they may seek out others who are satisfied with their purchase of the same product. Each of these strategies reinforces their satisfaction with the purchase. Consequently, it is important to offer services and information after the sale in order to reduce consumers' cognitive dissonance. Similarly, it is easier and more cost effective to sell to existing customers than it is to recruit new customers. Consequently, reducing consumers' cognitive dissonance in the postpurchase period is an effective strategy to increase repeat purchases.

cognitive dissonance—Feelings of anxiety or doubt that can occur after an important decision has been made.

LEARNING ACTIVITY

Consider participating in a new sport. Follow your decision-making process from beginning to end. What information did you collect? From whom? How did you evaluate your alternatives?

SUMMARY

The study of consumer behavior in sport helps you understand your customers. A better understanding of your customers helps you develop products and services that meet their needs and to design marketing strategies to attract new customers and retain existing customers. This chapter explored the individual and group factors that influence sport consumption. Individual factors examined were motives, perceptions, and attitudes. The influence of reference groups, socialization processes, and subcultures were identified as the primary group factors that affect decisions to purchase sport products and services.

However, it is rare that sport consumption decisions are influenced by only one force. Typically, group and individual influences work simultaneously to exert influence over a purchase decision. Two processes, involvement and identification, combine internal and external influences, often resulting in increasing levels of customer loyalty. Customer loyalty results in repeat purchases at a minimal cost to the sport marketer. This occurs because loyalty shortcuts the decision process by reducing the time and energy needed to collect the necessary information to make a good decision.

The last section of the chapter identified five situational factors that can have an impact on the decision process: physical surroundings, social surroundings, task requirements, temporal perspective, and antecedent states. These factors, in combination with the individual and group factors already discussed, exert influence at each stage of the decision process. The recognition of a need or problem is the first step in the process. Once a need is identified, the consumer seeks information about potential products and services that can fulfill that need or solve the problem. The consumer then develops a set of possible purchase options and evaluates each prior to making the purchase.

However, the process does not end with the purchase. Customers can evaluate their purchase in two ways. They often evaluate their purchase in reference to prepurchase expectations. If performance meets or exceeds their expectations, then customers are satisfied. Interestingly, customers tend to reassure themselves that they made the right purchase. This is an attempt to reduce cognitive dissonance. Sport marketers can help customers to feel good about their purchase by providing information after the purchase that highlights the benefits and attributes of the product or highlights the use of the product by valued members of customers' reference groups.

As a sport marketer, it is your job to entice customers to purchase your products, attend your games, compete in your events, and use your services. The consumer decision process identifies the steps in the process. As a marketer, you can use your knowledge of the situational, group, and individual factors that can influence each step in the decision process to design products, services, and marketing campaigns to meet the needs of your customers.

REVIEW QUESTIONS

1. List and explain the key motives for sport participation. Give an example of each.

2. List and explain the key motives for sport spectation. Give an example of each.

3. You and a friend attend a basketball game at your university. Why might you and your friend have different perceptions of the game?

4. List the three components of an attitude.

5. As a sport marketer, how would you try to change a negative attitude toward your product?

6. What is the difference between consumer involvement and fan identification?

7. Why are loyal fans important to a sport organization?

8. Identify potential group influences on an individual's decision to attend a sport event.

Give an example of the way each would exert influence on the decision.

9. Describe the decision process of parents choosing a youth sport program for their child.

10. What would you do to reduce postpurchase cognitive dissonance?

REFERENCES

Austin Runners Club home page. (n.d.). Retrieved January 5, 2002, from www.austinrunners.org/home.shtml.

Baldinger, A.L., & Rubinson, J. (1996). Brand loyalty: The link between attitude and behavior. *Journal of Advertising Research, 36*(6), 22-34.

Brustad, R.J. (1996). Parental and peer influence on children's psychological development through sport. In F.L. Smoll & R.E. Smith (Eds.), *Children and youth in sport: A biopsychosocial perspective* (pp. 112-124). Madison, WI: Brown & Benchmark.

Burnett, J., Menon, A., & Smart, D.T. (1993). Sports marketing: A new ball game with new rules. *Journal of Advertising Research, 33*(5), 21-33.

Cialdini, R.B., Borden, R.J., Thorne, A., Walker, M.R., Freeman, S., & Sloan, L.R. (1976). Basking in reflected glory: Three (football) field studies. *Journal of Personality and Social Psychology, 34*, 366-375.

Greater New Orleans Sports Foundation. (n.d.). Sports calendar. Retrieved February 3, 2002, from www.superbowlxxxvi.org/sbhost/calendar.htm.

Green, B.C. (1996). A social learning approach to youth sport motivation: Initial scale development and validation (Doctoral dissertation, University of Maryland, 1996). *Dissertation Abstracts International, 60*.

Horn, T.S., & Weiss, M.R. (1991). A developmental analysis of children's self-ability judgements in the physical domain. *Pediatric Exercise Science, 3*, 310-326.

Jenkins, C. (2000, March 13). Caught in gambling's web: Colleges fear students easy targets for Internet sports betting sites. *USA Today*, p. 1C.

Kardes, F.R. (1999). *Consumer behavior and managerial decision making*. Reading, MA: Addison-Wesley.

Kerstetter, D.L., & Kovich, G.M. (1997). An involvement profile of Division I women's basketball spectators. *Journal of Sport Management, 11*, 234-249.

Major League Soccer. (2002). MLS statistics archive. Retrieved January 7, 2002, from www.mlsnet.com/archive/stats.html.

Mara, J. (2000). The halo effect. *Brandweek, 41*(20), 86-88.

McDonald, M.G. (2000). The marketing of the Women's National Basketball Association and the making of postfeminism. *International Review for the Sociology of Sport, 35*, 35-47.

Milne, G.R., Sutton, W.A., & McDonald, M.A. (1996). Niche analysis: A strategic measurement tool for managers. *Sport Marketing Quarterly, 5*(3), 17-22.

OuterQuest. (n.d.). Home page. Retrieved January 7, 2002, from www.teamouterquest.com/.

Park, C.W., & Mittal, B. (1985). A theory of involvement in consumer behavior: Problems and issues. *Research in Consumer Behavior, 1*, 201-231.

Raudsepp, L., & Viira, R. (2000). Sociocultural correlates of physical activity in adolescents. *Pediatric Exercise Science, 12*, 51-60.

Roberts, G.C. (Ed.). (1992). *Motivation in sport and exercise*. Champaign, IL: Human Kinetics.

Rogers, M.H. (2000, August). Playing with family values: The attractions of minor league baseball. *Stadia, 4*, 34-38.

Schiffman, L.G., & Kanuk, L.L. (1991). *Consumer behavior* (4th ed.). Englewood Cliffs, NJ: Prentice Hall.

Shamir, B. (1992). Some correlates of leisure identity salience: Three exploratory studies. *Journal of Leisure Research, 24*, 301-323.

Shank, M.D. (2002). *Sports marketing: A strategic perspective*. Upper Saddle River, NJ: Pearson Education.

Sirgy, M.J. (1986). *Self-congruity: Toward a theory of personality and cybernetics*. New York: Praeger.

Snyder, C.R., Lassegard, M., & Ford, C.E. (1986). Distancing after group success and failure: Basking in reflected glory and cutting off reflected failure. *Journal of Personality and Social Psychology, 51*, 382-388.

Soccer Industry Council of America (2000). National soccer participation survey. North Palm Beach, FL: Author.

Stone, G. (1981). Sport as a community representation. In G.R.F. Lüschen & G.H. Sage (Eds.), *Handbook of social science of sport* (pp. 214-245). Champaign, IL: Stipes.

Sutton, W.A., McDonald, M.A., Milne, G.R., & Cimperman, J. (1997). Creating and fostering fan identification in professional sports. *Sport Marketing Quarterly, 6*, 15-22.

Turner, V. (1986). *The anthropology of performance*. New York: PAJ Publications.

Wann, D.L., Melnick, M.J., Russell, G.W., & Pease, D.G. (2001). *Sport fans: The psychology and social impact of spectators*. New York: Routledge.

PART III

Organizational and Managerial Foundations of Sport Management

Aspiring sport managers must be familiar with theories of organizational behavior, management, and leadership and be able to apply these theories in practical settings. The two chapters in this section, therefore, address the behavior of sport organizations and the attributes of managers and leaders in the sport industry. The underlying theme of this section is that managers have a responsibility to themselves, their employees, and their constituents to appreciate and apply theoretical concepts that will improve the effectiveness and efficiency of the workplace as well as the quality of the sport product or experience.

In chapter 8 Jerome Quarterman describes the characteristics of organizations, defines organizational behavior, and provides an overview of the interdisciplinary nature of organizational behavior. He then presents examples of what research has taught us about organizational behavior and explains how sport managers can use theories of organizational behavior to increase the satisfaction and productivity of their employees. He concludes with an explanation of three levels of analysis that have been employed in studies of organizational behavior: individual behaviors, small group behaviors, and processes and structures within the organization.

Chapter 9 examines the concepts of management and leadership in sport organizations. First, Jerome Quarterman and Ming Li define management and leadership. They point out similarities between the two functions as well as differentiating between the expectations of managers and those of leaders. Quarterman and Li discuss several theories associated with management and leadership, describe competencies needed by managers and by leaders, and explain the various roles played by each. Finally, the authors present a classification system for different types of managers. The information in this chapter will be useful to you regardless of the setting in which you eventually pursue a career.

FOR MORE INFORMATION

Professional and Scholarly Associations

- North American Society for Sport Management (NASSM)
- Sport Management Council/National Association for Sport and Physical Education (NASPE)/American Alliance for Health, Physical Education, Recreation and Dance (AAHPERD)

Professional and Scholarly Publications

- *Athletic Business*
- *European Sport Management Quarterly*
- *International Journal of Sport Management*
- *Journal of Sport Management*
- *Sport Marketing Quarterly*
- *Street & Smith's SportsBusiness Journal*

Electronic Databases

- Business Source Premier
- Lexis-Nexis Academic
- SBRnet Sports Business Research Network
- SPORT Discus

Chapter 8

Sport Organization Managers and Organizational Behavior

Jerome Quarterman, Florida State University

The workplace of the sport industry has become increasingly complex due to the dramatic increase in the size of sport organization staffs and the diversity among staff personnel.

Sport organization staffs are composed of a variety of part-time employees, volunteers, student interns, full-time professionals, and full-time nonprofessionals (Lamke, 1991). The diverse makeup of staffs has required managers to have strong skills in dealing with human behaviors in the workplace (organizational behaviors).

Understanding how people behave in organizations is essential to your career success as a future employee in the sport industry. As a subordinate, superior, staff member, manager, owner, or even CEO, you will no doubt encounter personnel problems and issues in the workplace. While no foolproof methods exist for making you highly effective when difficult situations arise, the study of organizational behavior offers useful principles (Bobbitt & Behling, 1981; Nadler & Tushman, 1980; Wofford, 1982). These principles can help you understand why individuals and groups behave as they do in certain situations. Your increased understanding will in turn help you improve or maintain good relations with others in the workplace, which will increase your personal satisfaction and productivity.

This chapter will introduce some of the basic principles of organizational behavior and explain the ideas and concepts in the context of managing others in the workplace of the sport industry. The chapter opens with the development of a definition of the term *organization* and discusses the common features of organizations in general and

sport organizations in particular. This is followed by a comprehensive overview of organizational behavior, including its role as a field of study and its interdisciplinary nature. Next we explore the nature of organizational behavior in the context of the sport industry.

The chapter ends by addressing some of the questions students often ask about the relevancy of studying organizational behavior, including its relevancy to the sport industry.

Defining Organization

A prerequisite for understanding organizational behavior is a solid understanding of the term organization. When we hear the term, we may think of businesses such as the Nike Corporation, Reebok International, the YM/YWCA, the National Football League (NFL), or the National Collegiate Athletic Association (NCAA). As you can see, the term encompasses a wide variety of organizations (see figure 8.1). Our concern here is what these myriad groups have in common.

LEARNING ACTIVITY

Describe each of the businesses in figure 8.1 as an organization. What characteristics do these organizations have in common?

The term *organization* has been defined by a variety of organizational science theorists for nearly two-thirds of a century. Barnard (1938) defined the term as "a system of consciously coordinated activities or forces of two or more persons" (p. 73). Since this initial definition, several writers have followed with other interpretations of the term. Table 8.1 lists these scholars, the dates of their work, and the key parts of their definitions. While the definitions differ, they do share the following five features:

1. A collection of individuals and groups
2. Goal orientation
3. Deliberate structure
4. Deliberate coordination
5. Identifiable boundary

Building on the aforementioned definitions and common features, I propose a working definition of **sport organization**.

sport organization—A deliberately structured and coordinated system of individuals and groups with special skills and talents in the sport industry working together to achieve a common set of goals.

This definition implies that organizations in the sport industry are composed of people working together in formal groups (such as departments, task forces, ad hoc committees, standing committees, work shifts, and teams) to accomplish the goals and objectives of the organization in the most effective and efficient manner. The following sections will discuss the features of this definition in more detail by using the organizational chart of a fictitious professional baseball team as an example (see figure 8.2).

- **Sport organizations are deliberately structured.** Sport organizations need a logical and systematic arrangement of people and resources. The baseball team's organizational chart shows two major sections: a business section and a baseball section. On the business side, the division is made up of a vice president (general manager) and three departments: public relations, corporate sales, and marketing. These divisions and departments, or those in any organization, were not hastily formulated but carefully determined and coordinated in order to construct an effective and efficient organization.

- **Sport organizations are deliberately coordinated.** This feature implies that the work among the individuals and groups in sport organizations must be coordinated in a patterned relationship. For example, the work in the professional baseball program was not assigned randomly but as needed to achieve the predetermined goals and objectives. Without coordination, the baseball program would not be able to achieve its goals.

- **Sport organizations exist as a system of individuals and groups.** Organizations in the sport industry do not operate without the human element. Individuals and groups of people with special skills are the lifeblood of these organizations. Human resources are needed to activate the nonhuman resources (e.g., scoreboards, computers, etc.) in a baseball program. While the infield, the signage, the lights, and the seats are tangible, none of these resources can be activated without the human element. If we took away the interactions among the individuals and groups of the baseball program, the program would have no life. The system of humans gives life to the baseball program as an organization.

- **Sport organizations are made up of people with special skills.** This feature implies that individuals and groups are selected because they bring special skills, knowledge, and competencies to an organization. Each member of an organization is selected with a skill or competency that will assist the organization in achieving its goals such as the ones mentioned in the next feature.

- **Sport organizations are goal (task) oriented.** This feature implies that sport organizations exist for a reason. Goals refer to a future state toward which an individual, group, or organization itself strives. Goals are held by individual players (such as striving to maintain a .300 batting average for

Figure 8.1 Sport organizations come in many sizes, shapes, and forms.

Table 8.1   Definitions of Organization

Author(s)	Definition
Nahavandi & Malekzadeh, 1998	"two or more people who cooperate and coordinate their activities in a systematic manner to reach their goals." (p. 3)
Narayanan & Nath, 1993	"an arena where human beings come together to perform complex tasks so as to fulfill common goal(s)" (p. 4)
Reitz, 1987	"a social unit that has been deliberately designed to achieve some special goals" (p. 87)
Schermerhorn, Hunt, & Osborn, 1994	"a collection of people working together in a division of labor to achieve a common purpose" (p. 12)
Vasu, Stewart, & Garson, 1990	"human beings working individually and in groups toward the goal in a system that has identifiable boundaries" (p. 3)
Newstrom & Davis, 1997	"the study and application of knowledge about how people—as individual and as group—act within organizations" (p. 5)

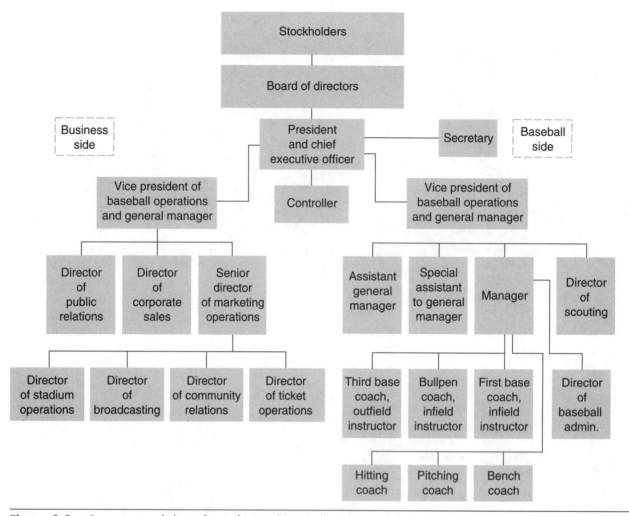

Figure 8.2 Organizational chart of a professional baseball team.

the season), staff members (such as striving to enjoy a satisfying work experience), or the organization itself. Typical annual organization goals for a professional baseball organization may include

- winning the World Series,
- increasing corporate sales by 30%,
- selling all stadium seats for all home games, or
- providing high levels of job satisfaction for all employees (i.e., players, administrators, and professional and nonprofessional staff members).

Now that we have a conceptual definition of the term *organization* in general and *sport organization* in particular, the task is to define and analyze the concept of organizational behavior. Organizations do not run themselves, people do; therefore, the concern is about human behavior in organizations. The concept is commonly expressed as organizational behavior. As with the term *organization,* there appears to be no general consensus on the definition of *organizational behavior.* The term seemingly has as many definitions as authors. A content review of definitions of organizational behavior is provided in a number of textbooks and perspectives of organizational behavior. All such definitions are arbitrary in nature and scope (Cummings, 1978). An all-encompassing operational conceptual definition has been offered for the purpose of this chapter.

organizational behavior—A field of study that systematically investigates the impact of individual behavior, small group behavior, inter-organizational structures, and inter-organizational processes on an organization (in our case within an organization of the sport industry).

Parts of this definition will be highlighted throughout the remaining sections of this chapter.

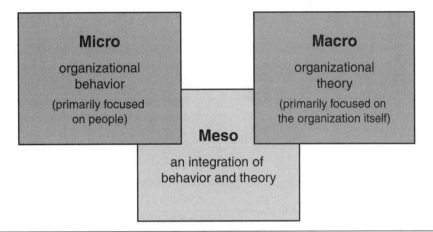

Figure 8.3 The micro/macro distinction.

Adapted from the work of Daft, 2001; House, Rousseau & Thomas-Hunt, 1995.

As you continue to study this chapter, you should gain a deeper understanding of the concept of organizational behavior in the context of the behaviors, attitudes, and performances of people in organizations of the sport industry. In the next part of our discussion a distinction has been made between the concepts of organizational theory and organizational behavior.

Organizational Behavior Versus Organizational Theory

Organizational behavior and organizational theory are the two most common perspectives from which organizational life can be studied (Daft, 2001; Narayanan & Nath, 1993; Steers & Black, 1994; Vecchio, 1991; Wagner & Hollenbeck 1992). As a field of study, organizational behavior is focused on the behaviors, attitudes, and performances of people within an organization (Vasu, Stewart, & Garson, 1990). Organizational theory as field of study is focused on the whole organization or one of its major subsystems (Vasu, Stewart, & Garson, 1990; Steers & Black, 1994).

The study of organizational theory constitutes a macro view of organizations, whereas the study of organizational behavior constitutes a micro view (Daft, 2001; Nahavandi & Malekzadeh, 1998; Steers & Black, 1994). To further explain, "organizational theorists are concerned with the total organization ability to achieve the goals effectively; thus, they must not only consider how it is structured but also how it is situated in a broader sociopolitical and economic context" (Slack, 1997, p. 8). Usually the focus is outside the boundaries of an organization (e.g., competition between two or more organizations or guidelines imposed on

an organization from a governing agency), and the primary focus for managers is macro in nature.

Unlike organizational theory, the study of organizational behavior is primarily focused on the behaviors of individuals, small groups, and interpersonal processes within the boundaries of an organization. When decisions and actions of managers are primarily influenced by intergroup politics, learning style, personality, the learning style of an individual, or interpersonal conflict, the primary focus of managers is micro in nature.

The micro and macro perspectives do overlap in some instances. When one of the two perspectives extends over the other, the topics are discussed in an integrative manner and are referred to as the meso perspective (Daft, 2001; House, Rousseau, & Thomas-Hunt, 1995). For example, the topic of communication is a micro concern when the focus is on a supervisor and the subordinates within an organization. However, the topic is of macro concern when the focus is on a supervisor and the print or broadcast media from outside of the organization (see figure 8.3). In this chapter, the primary focus is organizational behavior that places the people component in the forefront of analysis and the organization itself as a contextual or background component. After clarifying the meaning of organizational behavior and distinguishing it from organizational theory, it should be easier to sketch what it is as a field of study and as an academic subject.

Organizational Behavior As a Field of Study

Organizational behavior emerged during the 1960s as a body of knowledge dedicated to better understanding and managing people in the workplace (Bobbit & Behling, 1981; Bobbitt, Breinhold, Doktor, & McNaul, 1978; Wofford, 1982). As a field of study the primary objective of organizational behavior is to develop and implement a scientific body of knowledge about human beings and their performances (Szilagyi & Wallace, 1980). As Wofford (1982) noted: "Organizational behavior is a systematic attempt to understand the behavior of people in organizations, the effects of the organization on behavior, and the effects of behavior on the organization and its effectiveness" (p. 5). As a mature field, organizational behavior offers a new and emerging field like sport management an opportunity to borrow its definitions, concepts, and theories. This is important because a large portion of research in sport management has rested on organizational theory (e.g., structural and procedural components, guidelines, rules, regulations, procedures, policies, programs, job descriptions, etc.). As noted by several contemporary writers in sport management articles (Koehler, 1988; Olafson, 1990; Parkhouse, Ulrich, and Soucie, 1982; Parks, 1992; Paton, 1987), missing from the body of knowledge in the sport management studies is the concerted effort to understand management and leadership from a manager's perspectives. Because of this concern, there is need to closely study the behaviors of managers as they interact with individuals, small groups, and participate in interpersonal processes in organizations of the sport industry.

Unique Features of Organizational Behavior Studies

A careful examination of the writings of behavioral and social science scholars has revealed the unique features of organizational behavior as a field of study. For our purposes, two of these features will be discussed: (1) the interdisciplinary nature of organizational behavior (Hunsaker & Cook 1986) and (2) the units or dimensions for analyzing human behavior in organizations (Cummings, 1978; Bobbitt, Breinhold, Doktor, & McNaul, 1978; Szilagyi & Wallace, 1980).

The Interdisciplinary Nature of Organizational Behavior

Organizational behavior is interdisciplinary in that it draws from the knowledge base of the behavioral and social sciences (Hunsaker & Cook, 1986; Szilagyi & Wallace, 1980).

The **behavioral sciences** are composed of four dominant disciplines: psychology, social psychology, sociology, and cultural anthropology, (Daft & Steers, 1986; Luthans, 1991; Robbins, 1996; Szilagyi & Wallace, 1980; Vecchio, 1991). Table 8.2 offers definitions and summaries of specific studies on topics from the behavioral sciences. Of the four disciplines, psychology has had the greatest impact on the study of organizational behavior (Szilagyi & Wallace, 1980).

behavioral sciences — A group of disciplines (psychology, sociology, social psychology, and cultural anthropology) that guide the nature and scope of human behavior.

In addition to the behavioral sciences, the **social sciences** are also important in making the study of organizational behavior more manageable. The social sciences are composed of three dominant disciplines: political science, history, and economics (Hunsaker & Cook, 1986; Robbins, 1996). Table 8.3 gives definitions and examples of some of the primary topics addressed in the social sciences. In sport management, we can apply what has been learned from research in each of the disciplines in the behavioral and social sciences. By using this approach the knowledge base for sport management studies can be strengthened.

social sciences — A group of disciplines (political science, history, and economics) that guide the nature and scope of group behavior.

Studying Organizational Behavior via Units of Analysis

Behavioral and social scientists have suggested strategies for classifying organizational behavior into categories called **units of analysis** (Babbie, 2001; Cummings, 1978; Lofland & Lofland, 1995; Luthans, 1991; Robbins, 1996; Rosenberg, 1968; Szilagyi & Wallace, 1980). The unit analysis behavior construct is typically divided into three levels: the individual level, the group level, and interpersonal processes within an organization. (Cummings, 1978; Nahavandi & Malekzadeh, 1998; Szilgyi & Wallace, 1980). Figure 8.4 presents a conceptual integrative framework of the organizational behavior construct in context of the aforementioned units for analyzing human behavior. Examining organizational life according to such units can make teaching and research more manageable in the field of sport management.

Table 8.2　The Behavioral Sciences From an Organizational Behavior Perspective

Behavioral science	Definition	Example of research topic
Psychology	A behavioral science that focuses primarily on the impact of individual behavior	Personality formation Social perception Coping with stress Job involvement Organizational commitment Organizational citizenship behavior Learning styles Job satisfaction Leadership effectiveness Management competencies
Sociology	A behavioral science that focuses primarily on the impact of relationships within and between small groups	Group dynamics Work teams Organizational culture Organizational power Intergroup conflict Group development Group decision making
Social psychology	A behavioral science that focuses primarily on the impact of individual behavior within groups	Intergroup conflict Stereotyping prejudice Group cohesiveness Group conformity Sport spectating
Cultural anthropology	A behavioral science that focuses primarily on the impact of behavior of people from different cultures, subcultures, and social classes	Organizational culture Cultural diversity Workplace diversity Organizational communication Organizational environment

Table 8.3　The Social Sciences From an Organizational Behavior Perspective

Social science	Definition	Example of research topic
Political science	The study of how governmental and public policy influence the behaviors of individuals and groups within an organization	Allocation of power Group conflict Conflict resolution Office politics Coalitions Negotiation/bargaining Labor relations Antitrust laws Networking
History	The study of how past and current events of an organization influence the behaviors of individuals and groups within an organization	Present events Past events
Economics	The study of how scarcity and choices of goods and services produced by an organization influence the behaviors of individuals and groups within an organization	Labor relations Compensation programs Game attendance Financial impact Scarcity of land Scarcity of labor Scarcity of capital

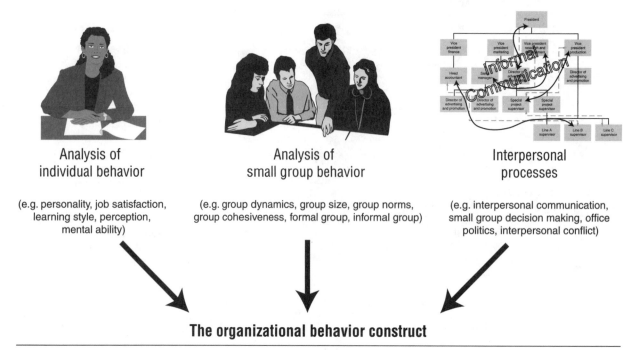

Analysis of individual behavior	Analysis of small group behavior	Interpersonal processes
(e.g. personality, job satisfaction, learning style, perception, mental ability)	(e.g. group dynamics, group size, group norms, group cohesiveness, formal group, informal group)	(e.g. interpersonal communication, small group decision making, office politics, interpersonal conflict)

The organizational behavior construct

Figure 8.4 An integrative framework of organizational behavior constructed via units of analysis.

Adapted from the works of Hunsaker & Cook, 1986; Szilagyi & Wallace, 1980.

units of analysis—A dimension that classifies the organizational behavior concept as to whether its primary focus is the behavior of individuals, small groups, or the interpersonal process within an organization.

This framework is conceptual in nature and scope and does not contain scientific evidence to predict specific behaviors. However it does portray the general nature of organizational behavior in a coherent and orderly manner. As presented in the framework, the **individual level of analysis** is focused on the behaviors of groups of individuals as individuals (Babbie, 2001). This level of analysis implies that each person is different in terms of such factors as attitudes, values, personality, perceptions, work commitment, and so on. This means that as future managers of organizations in the sport industry, you will be confronted with the challenges of achieving the organization goals through the efforts of a diverse group of individuals. Having this type of knowledge about others as well as yourself, would seemingly shape your behavior into being a more effective and efficient manager.

individual level of analysis—Primarily focused on how individuals behave as they work in pursuit of organizational goals.

Unlike the individual analysis, the **group level of analysis** is focused on the behaviors of small groups. Very seldom do people work solely as individuals in organizations. For our purpose, we are primarily concerned about small groups in the work place. Social psychologists (Michener & DeLamater, 1999) have defined the term *small group* as any group in size where its members can interact face-to-face with one another. There is no designated number of members which make a small group as long as the group size allows for interactions among all of its members. Thus a group may be considered small with 50-100 members provided each member was positioned so that he/she could interact directly with any one or all of the other members. Organizations take on a variety of elements in reference to the groups for which they are composed. Two such elements are formal groups and informal groups. (Dunham & Pierce, 1989). Formal groups are those created by owners and managers within an organization to achieve its goals. For example, ad hoc committees, standing committees, task forces, and project teams are formal groups. Informal groups are groups that emerge spontaneously in response to common interests or shared values of individuals within an organization (Dunham & Pierce, 1989). Figure 8.5 presents the formal groups as structured by managers into four major divisions: *finance, marketing, research and development,* and *production.* However, as illustrated

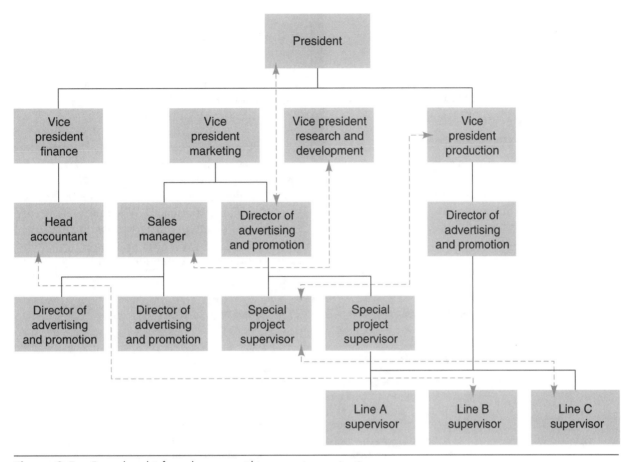

Figure 8.5   Formal and informal groups within a sport organization

by the dashed lines there exists an informal group within the organization. The group is made up of employees who have lunch together each day and discuss sports and politics. Both the formal and informal groups are important to an organization.

group level of analysis—Primarily focused on how small groups within an organization behave as they work in pursuit of organizational goals.

The third unit for analyzing behavior is the **interpersonal processes.** This level is focused on interpersonal processes and group dynamics within an organization. These are on-going activities that give life to an organization (small group leadership, interpersonal communications, small group decision making, individual decision making, personal power, office politics, and interpersonal conflict, etc.) (Ivancevich & Matteson, 1989; Steers & Black, 1994). The aforementioned classification of organizational life is a guide to help analyze human behavior in the context of sport organizations, while adhering to guidelines of the

organizational behavior construct. The focus of study is primarily on the selected organization and not the behavioral or social science disciplines. The organizational behavior construct is not perfect; however, it replaces guesses, hunches, and common sense with a well-researched body of knowledge and guidelines for managing human behavior in the work place (Johns, 1996; Kreitner & Kinicki, 1995; George & Jones, 1995). This approach has been given prominence throughout the remaining sections of the chapter. As you study the selected research investigations taken from the sport management literature, you should gain a better understanding of the organizational behavior constructs (e.g., behavior, social sciences, and units of analysis) in reference to managing others in organizations of the sport industry.

interpersonal processes—Focused on interpersonal processes and group dynamics within an organization.

None of the levels is more important than the others; rather each has its place in helping us understand behavior in the workplace. All employees—managers and non-managers alike—can benefit from a working knowledge of these units of analysis.

Organizational Behavior Research in Context of Sport Management Studies

Table 8.4 displays scientific investigations conducted in the field of sport management where the focus was primarily related to individual and group behavior analysis. Each of the selected studies was categorized as a topic within the organiza-

tional behavior construct and as a topic within one of the topics studied by psychologists. The first study examined relationships between second-tier intercollegiate athletics directors and their subordinates among transformational leadership, organizational commitment, and organizational citizenship (Kent & Chelladurai, 2001).

The next study by Koehler (1988) focused on job satisfaction. She examined the level of 19 measures of job satisfaction among corporate fitness managers. The third study addressed occupational stress among athletics directors of NCAA member institutes (Copeland & Kirsch 1995). The aforementioned scheme is an example of how sport management research may be presented in a more systematic, logical, and coherent manner under the guidelines

Table 8.4 Behavioral Science Research in Sport Management (Psychology)

Behavioral science	Summary
Organizational commitment	"This study tested the propositions that (a) perceived leader-member exchange quality (LMX) between second level managers (e.g., associate, assistant athletics directors) and their subordinates would be associated with perceived transformational leadership behaviors (TL) of the athletic director, and (b) subordinates' organizational commitment (OC) and organizational citizenship behavior (OCB) would be correlated with both perceived TL and LMX . . . . Correlational and regression analyses showed that the three dimensions of TL were significantly correlated with LMX. Additionally, the dimensions of TL and LMX were differentially related to OC and OCB." (Kent & Chelladurai, 2001, p. 135)
Job satisfaction	"Drawing from the content of organizational behavior for use in the study presented here, items of measure for job satisfaction include ability utilization, achievement, activity, advancement, authority, company polices/practices, compensation, co-workers, creativity, independence, moral values, recognition, responsibility, security, social service, social status, supervision-human relations, supervision-technical, variety, and working conditions. The corporate fitness managers participating in this study reported their level of general job satisfaction to be an average of 78.67 out of a possible 100 points. The factors shown to be significantly more satisfying than all other factors at the .05 level were social service and moral values. Additionally, although not significantly different from each other, both factors of advancement and compensation were revealed to be significantly more dissatisfying at the .05 level than all other factors." (Koehler, 1988, p. 100)
Coping with stress	"Increasing demands among contemporary administrators of intercollegiate athletics may potentially create role overload and lead to occupational stress (OS). The purpose of this study was to identify perceived stress levels of intrinsic administrative tasks among NCAA Division I ($n = 37$), II ($n = 27$), and III ($n = 44$) head athletic directors (ADs), and to determine if these perceptions varied by divisional status. . . . [there were] no significant differences ($p > .05$) in general perception of job stress across divisions; ADs across divisions reported perceived evidence of, and quick recovery from, OS *almost always* using a mean cutoff of 3.5. Significant differences ($p \leq .05$) for task-related stress were revealed between Divisions I and II in policy decision making and fund raising. Budget demands and firing rated highest as almost always (3.5 cutoff) stressful across divisions." (Copeland & Kirsch, 1995, p. 70)

Behavioral science	Summary
Interpersonal power	"This study examines the differences among 308 municipal and county park and recreation supervisors and their perceptions of their immediate bosses' power as well as their satisfaction with their bosses' supervision. The six sources of power investigated are expert, reward, referent, legitimate, coercive, and upward influence. The modifying variables considered are sex, length of experience in the profession, and length of time served under an immediate superior. The findings suggest that experienced supervisors are satisfied with bosses who had expert, referent and upward influence. Dissatisfied supervisors and ineffective superiors tend to result from a supervisory relationship built upon a coercive base of power." (Beeler, 1985, p. 54)

of the organizational behavior construct by a unit or dimension of analysis. The studies in Table 8.4 were focused on the behaviors of groups of individuals as individuals and were analyzed from a micro perspective within the scope of psychology.

Middlemist and Hitt (1981) developed a theoretical model in support of the units of analysis (figure 8.6). According to these authors, interactions among individuals, groups, and the organizational factors are the primary mechanisms for increasing an organization's health in terms of

- **employee satisfaction,**
- **employee productivity,** and
- **organizational effectiveness.**

A fourth element, **organizational efficiency**, has been added to the model.

employee satisfaction—Feelings that individuals and group have about their jobs and the conditions of the workplace.

employee productivity—The output of goods and services resulting from individuals and groups within an organization.

organizational effectiveness—The degree to which the goals of the organization are accomplished.

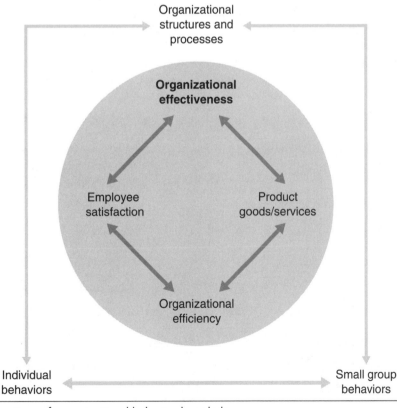

Figure 8.6 Assumptions of organizational behavior knowledge.

Adapted, by permission, from R.D. Middlemist and M.A. Hitt, 1981, *Organizational behavior: Applied concepts* (Chicago: Science Research Associates, Inc.), 7.

organizational efficiency—The degree to which the goals of an organization are accomplished without wasting resources.

Questions Often Asked About the Study of Organizational Behavior

Three questions that often surface about the study of organizational behavior by students are: Why study organizational behavior when it is seemingly common sense? Why study organizational behavior in the context of the sport industry? and How is organizational behavior helpful to managers? While such questions are very simple ones, there is no general consensus among behavioral and social sciences as to how each should be answered. Therefore, the responses that follow are not conclusive in nature.

• **Why study organizational behavior when it is seemingly common sense?** The most common rationale for studying organizational behavior is that it offers a set of guidelines based on empirical evidence (Greenberg & Baron, 1997; Vecchio, 1986-87). Decisions based on such evidence are generally better than those based on gut feelings or intuition. Gut feelings, hunches, and intuition are helpful only under a narrow set of circumstances. For example, when we ask five persons the best way to handle a specific behavior problem, we will perhaps get five different answers. While organizational behavior principles are not perfect, they result in positive consequences in the workplace more often than do gut feelings and intuition.

• **How is organizational behavior helpful to managers?** Organizational behavior provides managers with a way of systematically thinking about the complex nature of human behavior in the workplace. Lorsch (1987) listed three primary ways in which organizational behavior is helpful to mangers: (1) it provides managers a way to systematically view the different ways employees behave in the workplace; (2) it provides managers with a set of well-defined concepts and constructs that help them analyze work experiences; and (3) it offers managers tools and techniques for dealing with workplace problems. Knowledge of organizational behavior enables sport organization managers to better handle a full range of human behaviors in the workplace.

From an understanding of organizational behavior, managers may develop a better mind-set for taking actions and making decisions with tangible or overt organizational elements as well as intangible or covert elements (Wofford, 1982). Overt activities are those that are observable and apparent in the workplace. They are usually production-related issues conveyed in the organizational structure and system, such as long- and short-range plans, mission statements, goals, rules, regulations, policies, procedures, controlling resources, profits, and so on. Covert activities are

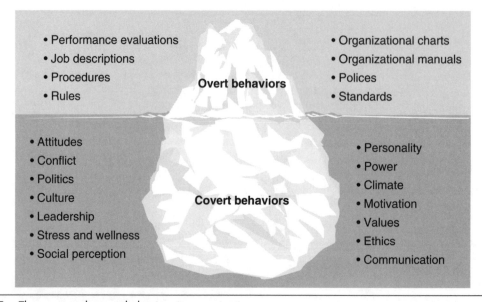

Figure 8.7   The overt and covert behaviors in organizations.

Adapted from R.J. Selfridge and S.L. Sokolik, 1975, "A comprehensive view of organizational development," *MSU Business Topics* 23(1):46-51.

not as easily observable or as apparent as overt activities. They are usually people-related issues. The iceberg analogy in figure 8.7 can help us better understand the dynamics of overt and covert activities. Managers can use the iceberg analogy to analyze the causes and effects of both overt and covert activities. Realizing that some workplace dynamics are more easily observable than others can be a first step in effective management.

- **Why study organizational behavior in the context of the sport industry?** The most common

response is that students may find it easier to understand organizational behavior principles and concepts when specific examples are used from sport management. For example, in this chapter the concepts of organizational behavior were partially explained via topics in the sport management literature (see table 8.4). Also, organizations in the sport industry are very diverse in nature as explained in chapter 1. Students may find it easier to understand organizational behavior when it is being discussed in the context of the segment of the sport industry in which they are interested.

SUMMARY

This chapter introduced a number of important concepts about the study and application of organizational behavior in the context of the sport industry. *Organization* was defined as a collection of people brought together in deliberately structured and coordinated ways to achieve a common set of goals. Five common features of organizations were discussed in the context of the sport industry:

1. a collection of individuals and groups,
2. goal orientation,
3. deliberate structure,
4. deliberate coordination, and
5. an identifiable boundary.

There is no general consensus among behavioral and social scientists regarding the definition of organizational behavior.

Organizational behavior in the sport industry was defined as a field that systematically investigates the impact of individual behavior, small group behavior, and the organization itself in the sport industry. The primary objectives of organizational behavior knowledge are to increase employee satisfaction, employee productivity, organizational

effectiveness, and organizational efficiency. Organizational behavior is interdisciplinary in nature because it draws from both the behavioral sciences (psychology, sociology, social psychology, and cultural anthropology) and the social sciences (economics, political science, and history).

From these sciences three levels of analysis for human behavior were derived:

- the individual level,
- the group level, and
- interpersonal processes.

Each of the levels exists as a distinct entity; however, each complements the others. Management theorists maintain that all three levels of analysis are important and that managers can use each level as a tool to strategically analyze the behaviors of employees in the workplace. Organizational behavior provides managers ways to systematically deal with the complex nature of human behavior in the workplace.

Applying the tools of organizational behavior in the workplace can have positive consequences for managers, their staffs, and their organizations.

LEARNING ACTIVITY

Select an article that was guided by psychology, sociology, social psychology, or cultural anthropology (table 8.2) from a journal in sport management research.

- List the reference of the article (APA style or choice of instructor)
- Describe the topic
- Describe the purpose of the study
- Describe the major findings of the study

Explain how this study can be categorized in the context of each of the following

- The organizational behavior construct
- The micro perspective
- The level (unit) of analysis

The article should come from one of the following journals:

- *Journal of Sport Management*

- *Sport Marketing Quarterly*
- *Journal of Park and Recreation Administration*
- *European Sport Management Quarterly*
- *Cyber Journal of Sport Marketing*
- *International Journal of Sports Marketing and Sponsorship*

- *International Journal of Sport Management*
- *Journal of Sports Economics*
- *Journal of Sport Tourism*
- *International Sports Journal*
- *Sport Management Review*
- *Korean Journal of Sport Management*

REVIEW QUESTIONS

1. Why is it important to define the term *organization* in the context of the field of sport management?
2. Explain how the field of organizational behavior contributes to the study of sport management.
3. Define the term *organizational behavior* in the context of the sport industry.
4. What is meant by unit of analysis?
5. What levels of analysis are usually studied in organizational behavior?
6. Compare and contrast the micro, meso, and macro perspectives of organizational behavior.
7. Which of the behavioral sciences are typically studied in organizational behavior?
8. How does a course in organizational behavior benefit you as a student in the field of sport management?

REFERENCES

Babbie, E. (2001). *The practice of social research* (9th ed.). Belmont, CA : Wadsworth.

Barnard, C.I. (1938). *The functions of the executive.* Cambridge, MA: Harvard University Press.

Beeler, C.S. (1985). Differences among recreation and park supervisors and their perceptions of power. *Journal of Park and Recreation Administration, 3*(4), 54-63.

Bobbitt, H.R., & Behling, O.C. (1981). Organizational behavior: A review of the literature. *Journal of Higher Education, 52*(1), 29-44.

Bobbitt, H.R. Jr., Breinhold, R., Doktor, R., & McNaul, J. (1978). *Organizational behavior: Understanding and prediction* (2nd ed.). Englewood Cliffs, NJ: Prentice Hall.

Copeland, B.W., & Kirsch, S. (1995). Perceived occupational stress among NCAA Division I, II, and III athletic directors. *Journal of Sport Management, 9,* 70-77.

Cummings, L.C. (1978). Towards organizational behavior. *Academy of Management Review, 3,* 90-98.

Daft, R.L. (2001). *Organization theory and design* (7th ed.). Cincinnati, OH: South-Western College Publishing.

Daft, R. L., & Steers, R. M. (1986). *Organizations: A micro/macro approach.* Glenview, IL: Scott Foresman.

Dunham, R.B., & Pierce, J.L. (1989). *Management.* Glenview, IL: Scott Foresman.

George, J.M., & Jones, G.R. (1995). *Understanding and managing organizational behavior* (3rd ed.). Reading, MA: Addison-Wesley.

Greenberg, J., & Baron, R.A. (1997). *Behavior in organizations: Understanding and managing the human side of*

work (6th ed.). Upper Saddle River, NJ: Prentice Hall.

House, R., Rousseau, D.M., & Thomas-Hunt, M. (1995). The meso paradigm: A framework for the integration of micro and macro organizational behavior. *Research in Organizational Behavior 17*(1), 71-114.

Hunsaker, D.L., & Cook, C.W. (1986). *Managing organizational behavior.* Reading, MA: Addison-Wesley.

Ivancevich, J.M., & Matteson, M.T. (1989). *Organizational behavior and management* (2nd ed.). Homewood, IL: Irwin.

Johns, G. (1996). *Organizational behavior: Understanding and managing life at work* (4th ed.). New York: Harper Collins.

Kent, A., & Chelladurai, P. (2001). Perceived transformational leadership, organizational commitment, and citizenship behavior: A case study in intercollegiate athletics. *Journal of Sport Management, 15,* 135-159.

Koehler, L.S. (1988). Job satisfaction and corporate fitness managers: An organizational behavior approach to sport management. *Journal of Sport Management, 2,* 100-105.

Kreitner, R., & Kinicki, A. (1995). *Organizational behavior* (3rd ed.). Chicago: Irwin.

Lamke, G.G. (1991). Human resource management in recreational sports. *NIRSA Journal, 16*(1), 42-45.

Lofland, J., & Lofland, L.H. (1995). *Analyzing social settings: A guide to qualitative and observation analysis* (3rd ed.). Belmont, CA: Wadsworth.

Lorsch, J.W. (1987). *Handbook of organizational behavior.* Englewood Cliffs, NJ: Prentice Hall.

Luthans, F. (1991). *Organizational behavior* (6th ed.). New York: McGraw-Hill.

Middlemist, R.D., & Hitt, M.A. (1981). *Organizational behavior: Applied concepts.* Chicago: Science Research Associates.

Michener & Delameter, J.D. (1999). *Social psychology* (4th ed.). Fort Worth: Harcourt Brace.

Nadler, D.A., & Tushman, M.L. (1980). A model for diagnosing organizational behavior. *Organizational Dynamics Journal, 2,* 35-41.

Nahavandi, A., & Malekzadeh, A.R. (1998). *Organizational behavior: The person organization fit.* Upper Saddle River, NJ: Prentice Hall.

Narayanan, V.K., & Nath, R. (1993). *Organization theory: A strategic approach.* Homewood, IL: Irwin.

Newstrom, J.W., & Davis, K. (1997). *Organizational behavior: Human behavior at work.* (10th ed.). Boston: McGraw-Hill.

Olafson, G.A. (1990). Research design in sport management: What's missing, what's needed? *Journal of Sport Management, 4,* 103-120.

Parkhouse, B., Ulrich, D., & Soucie, D. (1982). Research in sport management: A vital rung of this new corporate ladder. *Quest, 34,* 176-186.

Parks, J.B. (1992). Scholarship: The other "bottom line" in sport management. *Journal of Sport Management, 6,* 220-229.

Paton, G. (1987). Sport management research: What progress has been made? *Journal of Sport Management, 1,* 25-31.

Reitz, H.J. (1987). *Behavior in organizations* (3rd ed.). Homewood, IL: Irwin.

Robbins, S.P. (1996). *Organizational behavior: Concepts, controversies, applications* (7th ed.). Englewood Cliffs, NJ: Prentice Hall.

Rosenberg, M. (1968). *The logic of survey analysis.* New York: Basic Books.

Schermerhorn, J.R., Hunt, J.G., & Osborn, R.N. (1994). *Managing organizational behavior* (5th ed.). New York: Wiley.

Slack, T. (1997). *Understanding sport organizations: The application of organization theory.* Champaign, IL: Human Kinetics.

Steers, R.M., & Black, J.S. (1994). *Organizational behavior* (5th ed.). New York: Harper Collins.

Szilagyi, A.D., & Wallace, M.J. (1980). *Organizational behavior and performance.* (2nd ed.). Santa Monica, CA. Goodyear.

Vasu, M.L., Stewart, D.W., & Garson, G.D. (1990). *Organizational behavior and public management* (2nd ed.). New York: Marcel Decker.

Vecchio, R.P. (1991). *Organizational behavior* (2nd ed.). Chicago: Dryden Press.

Vecchio, R.P. (1986-87). Some popular (but misguided) criticism of the organizational behavioral sciences. *Organizational Behavior & Teaching Review, 10*(1), 28-34.

Wagner, J.A. III, & Hollenbeck, J.R. (1992). *Management of organizational behavior.* Englewood Cliffs, NJ: Prentice Hall.

Wofford, J.C. (1982). *Organizational behavior: Foundations for organizational effectiveness.* Boston: Kent Publishing.

Chapter 9

Managing and Leading Sport Organizations

Jerome Quarterman, Florida State University
Ming Li, The Ohio University

This chapter examines two important concepts in management theory in the context of sport organizations: management and leadership. After defining management and leadership, we will then analyze the nature and scope of each. We will also differentiate between management and leadership by comparing them. The theoretical approaches that have been proposed by management theorists for the study of leadership will be surveyed, as well as the competencies needed by managers. The chapter ends with the description of a system used to classify managers and the characteristics of successful leaders.

Differences Between Management and Leadership

In chapter 8 you became familiar with the concepts of organizations and organizational behaviors. How managers use skills in management and leadership is very much essential to the success or failure of organizations in the sport industry. During the latter 1990s, the sport industry was estimated as a $213 billion industry and ranked sixth among all industries in the United States (Broughton, Lee, & Nethery, 1999). Clearly such a large and competitive industry is in need of sound and balanced leadership and management approaches. The question is, How does one define and distinguish between management and leadership? The literature offers many definitions of both management and leadership (Hemphill & Coons, 1957; Katz & Kahn, 1978; Robbins, 1996; Schermerhorn, Hunt, and Osborn, 1994). Kotter (1990) maintained that the processes of management and leadership are two "distinctive and

complementary systems of action . . . both are necessary for success in an increasingly complex and volatile business environment" (p.103).

Researchers usually define the concepts of **management** and **leadership** based on their own perspectives. Hersey and Blanchard (1988) provided one of the most comprehensive definitions of management as "the process of working with and through individuals and groups to accomplish organizational goals" (p. 3). They defined leadership as "the process of influencing the activities of an individual or a group in effort toward goal achievement in a given situation"(p. 83). The hypothetical organizational chart for the business side of a professional baseball team in figure 9.1 illustrates these definitions.

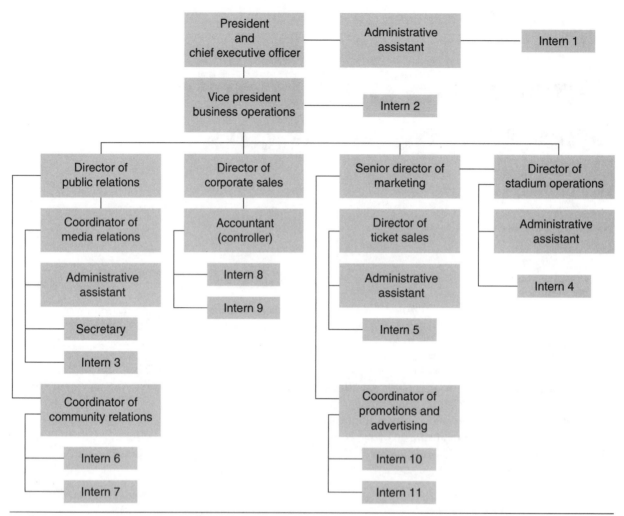

Figure 9.1 Partial organization chart—business side of a hypothetical professional baseball team.

management—The process of working with and through individuals and groups to accomplish organizational goals.

leadership—The process of influencing individual and group behavior for some desired results.

While managers are often leaders, not all leaders are necessarily managers. As you can see, the term *leader* is broader than the term *manager* since all employees will act as leaders at some time. Anytime a person attempts to influence the behaviors of others, regardless of the reason, that person is considered a leader. For example, an intern may have special skills using the Excel program on the computer to draw charts and graphs. When the intern assists the controller or the director, she is considered a leader for the given time. When others rely on a person, that

person is a leader, even if he is not in a management position.

Organizations in the sport industry are very dynamic and require managers with special skills and talents in both management and leadership. The topics of management and leadership will be discussed as separate entities in the next two sections of this chapter. The section that follows will then integrate the two concepts in a discussion of managerial leaders in sport organizations.

Management as a Process in Sport Organizations

Over the years, in management textbooks, management journals, and speeches, management scholars have addressed the practice of management as a process. The **process approach** implies that managers use a set of ongoing interactive activities, commonly known as the underlying processes of management, for accomplishing the goals and objectives of their respective organizations, departments, or work units. Such processes were first introduced more than six decades ago as POSDCORB (Gulick & Urwick, 1937).

POSDCORB is the acronym that describes the underlying processes of

- planning,
- organizing,
- staffing,
- directing,
- coordinating,
- reporting, and
- budgeting.

process approach—Using a set of ongoing interactive activities, commonly known as the underlying processes of management, for accomplishing the goals and objectives of an organization, department, or work unit.

Subsequent scholars whittled Gulick and Urwick's original seven processes down to four: *planning, organizing, directing,* and *controlling,* with some scholars adding a fifth: *staffing* (Drucker, 1967, 1974; Hersey & Blanchard, 1988; Koontz & O'Donnell, 1976; Mahoney, Jerdee, & Carroll, 1965; McFarland, 1974). In this chapter we will address these five processes of management in our discussion of sport organizations. Figure 9.2 offers a developmental model of the management process approach based on the works of the previously mentioned theorists.

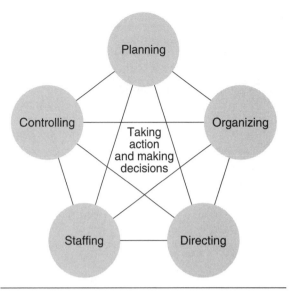

Figure 9.2 The management process approach.

Contemporary sport management theorists use the process approach to describe the management of sport organizations (Leith, 1983; Mullin, 1980). Although the models differ from one scholar to another, most generally agree about the nature of the management process. Typically, the process starts with planning and ends with controlling or evaluating. Managers engage in the activities in different sequences, however, with some performing several activities simultaneously as they carry out the responsibilities of their jobs. The element that is universal in all of the processes, however and whenever they are performed, is decision making. Table 9.1 offers definitions of each of the underlying processes, followed by examples of how a general manager of a private sport club might practice them.

Table 9.1 Management Process of a General Manager in a Private Sport Club

Underlying process	Definition	Example
Planning	Developing and implementing goals, objectives, strategies, procedures, policies, and rules to produce goods and services in the most effective and efficient manner.	The general manager of a private sport club predicts the increase in enrollment at the start of the new year and arranges for the facility to be open 18 hours per day instead of 15 hours.
Organizing	Arranging resources (i.e., human, financial, equipment, supplies, time, space, informational) for producing goods and services in the most effective and efficient manner.	After conducting an assessment, the general manager establishes a work unit for teaching golf at the club. A full-time coordinator is appointed who will coordinate three teaching pros and a new golf course with an adequate budget.

(continued)

Table 9.1 *(continued)*

Underlying process	Definition	Example
Staffing	Recruiting, selecting, orienting, training, developing, and replacing the employees needed to produce goods and services in the most effective and efficient manner.	The general manager advertises the positions: three teaching pros, one maintenance person, and one administrative assistant. The general manager then holds interviews, checks references, makes job offers, and selects the staff needed for the golf program.
Directing	Influencing members (subordinates, peers, and supervisors) as individuals and groups to produce goods and services in the most effective and efficient manner.	The general manager encourages the golf teaching pro to prepare weekend course packages for local executives who have expressed an interest in learning golf skills.
Controlling	Evaluating whether the employees are on task and making progress toward achieving the goals and adhering to the guidelines and standards for producing goods and services in the most effective and efficient manner.	After three months the general manager monitors the progress of the new golf program with the coordinator and discusses possible ways to make the program more attractive to lure new members.

Theoretical Approaches to the Study of Leadership

Management and leadership theorists have developed several theories to explain how leadership is carried out in organizations. Knowledge and approaches for understanding leadership theory have progressed through several distinct phases over the years. Four of the most common theoretical approaches to leadership will be discussed in this section: the trait approach, the behavioral approach, the situational (contingency) approach, and the new leadership theories of the 1990s (transactional and transformational) (Bass, 1985; Burns, 1978; Yukl, 1989).

Trait Approach to Leadership

The trait approach is based on a set of universal characteristics associated with effective leaders. The traits of a leader may be classified in the areas of personality, abilities, and physical attributes (Wofford, 1982). Personality is associated with social and personal traits. This approach attempts to develop a logical link between the personality traits of leaders and effective leadership. The basic assumption of the theory is that good leaders may share some common personality traits. If those personality traits could be identified, they may be used as criteria in leader identification. For example, David Stern, Paul Tagliabue, and Bud Selig may have some personality traits in common. The diagnosis of those commonalities may provide people in professional sport with ideas about whom to hire as the commissioner of a professional sport league. General knowledge, fairness, and intelligence are among the traits most frequently mentioned. The people who challenge this approach argue that the possession of those personality traits does not always guarantee that a person will become a good leader. Being intelligent, for example, does not guarantee that a per-

Coach Tyrone Willingham is a self-confident charismatic leader who can convince his coaching staff and players to successfully achieve the goals of the Notre Dame football program.

© AP Photo/Joe Raymond

son will be a good leader. In short, the studies of leaders' personality attributes represent the early work on leadership.

Behavioral Approach to Leadership

The creators of the behavioral approach to leadership believe that people need more than certain personality traits to be effective leaders. According to this approach, effective leaders demonstrate one of two major styles or dimensions: consideration and initiating structure (Kerr & Schriesheim, 1974). **Consideration** describes the extent to which leaders have relationships with subordinates. Such relationships are established on the basis of mutual trust, respect, and consideration of subordinates' ideas and feelings. Considerate leaders care about their employees and strongly promote camaraderie in the workplace.

consideration—The extent to which leaders have relationships with subordinates that are based on mutual trust, respect, and consideration of subordinates' ideas and feelings.

Initiating structure describes the extent to which leaders are likely to establish goals and structure their subordinates toward the attainment of those goals. Managers who mainly pay attention to nonpeople factors such as organizational structure and policies and are concerned about how to get the job done demonstrate the style of initiating structure.

initiating structure—The extent to which leaders establish goals and structure their subordinates toward the attainment of those goals.

The results of studies comparing the leadership styles of consideration and initiating structure were not conclusive in terms of which was more effective. However, researchers did agree that effective leadership styles are situational and that different work situations and subordinates demand different leadership styles.

Situational (Contingency) Approach to Leadership

Unlike the trait and behavioral approaches, the common theme of this approach is that there is no single best style of leadership for every situation. Effective managers are those who can change their leadership styles to meet the needs of their followers and the given situation.

There are several models of the situational approach to leadership: Fiedler's Contingency Model (Fiedler, 1967), the Path-Goal Model (Evans, 1970; House, 1971), and the Situational Model (Hersey, Blanchard, & Johnson, 2001).

• *Fiedler's Contingency Model*: Fiedler developed the first situational theory of leadership in 1967. He postulated that the performance of a group depends on the interaction between leadership style and situational variables. Leadership style is determined by a measurement instrument called the Least Preferred Coworker (LPC). This is a projective technique in which a manager leader is asked to think about the individual with whom the leader can work the least well. It is the individual who the manager leader has had the most difficulty in getting a task completed. It is not about an individual that the leader likes better. It is about identifying the leader as being primarily task-oriented (e.g., being highly concerned about getting tasks done through his or her subordinates) or the leader as being relationship-oriented (e.g., being highly concerned about developing a good working relationship with the subordinates). High scores on the instrument are associated with a relationship leadership style and low scores with a task leadership style (Ayman, Chemers, & Fiedler, 1997).

• *Path-Goal Model*. Like Fiedler's model, this model attempts to determine the most appropriate leadership style for different situations. Developed by House (1971), it focuses on how a leader influences followers' perceptions about work goals, self-development goals, and path-goal accomplishment (House, 1971; House & Mitchell, 1974, 1997). The theory has two general propositions. First, the degree of subordinates' acceptance of a certain leadership style depends on whether they believe such behavior is an immediate source of satisfaction or instrumental to future satisfaction. Second, the leader's behavior is motivational and affects the satisfaction and efforts of subordinates (House & Mitchell, 1997). Two **contingency variables** moderate the relationship between leadership behavior and subordinate satisfaction: the personal characteristics of the subordinates and "the environmental pressure and demands with which subordinates must comply in order to accomplish the work goals and to satisfy their needs" (House & Mitchell, 1997, p. 262).

contingency variables (Path-Goal Model of Leadership)—The variables that moderate the relationship between leadership behavior and subordinate satisfaction.

• *Situational Leadership® Model.* The third model in the situational approach to leadership is the Situational Leadership model developed by Hersey, Blanchard, & Johnson (2001). Unlike Fiedler's and House's models, this model is comprised of four patterns of communication that managers may choose to use in talking to their followers: telling, selling, participating, and delegating (see figure 9.3). In order to decide which leadership style is most appropriate, managers must be able to assess the readiness of the follower(s) and the ability and willingness of the follower(s) to perform a task. Once managers have identified the readiness level of the person or group they are attempting to influence, they can then choose the most appropriate leadership style. Telling and selling are both primarily leader-oriented and one-directional communications. Participating and delegating are primarily follower-oriented and two-directional communications (Hersey, Blanchard, & Johnson, 2001). From this model a manager's primary style can be determined. The primary style is defined as the behavior pattern managers use most often when attempting to influence the behavior of others.

Transactional and Transformational Approaches to Leadership

Unlike the trait, behavioral, and situational approaches, the transactional and transformational approaches have more to do with a leader's impact on the organization than with leadership effectiveness with individuals and groups within the organization. The transactional and transformational approaches focus primarily on relationships that managers develop with members in their respective organization (see table 9.2).

Transactional leadership refers to three types of exchanges that occur between leaders and followers: contingent rewarding, management by exception (active), and management by exception (passive) (Bass, 1985; Doherty, 1997). Leaders reward or discipline followers in exchange for the followers performing a mutually agreed-upon task.

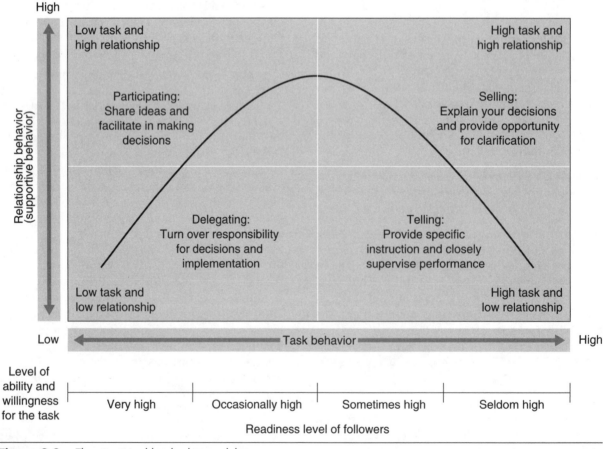

Figure 9.3 The situational leadership model.

Table 9.2 Transformational and Transactional Leadership

Transformational leadership

Factor	Primary role of managerial leader
Charisma (idealized influence)	Shares a vision and a sense of vision with followers.
Inspirational motivation	Increases the optimism and enthusiasm of followers.
Intellectual stimulation	Encourages followers to consider new ways to look at old methods and problems.
Individualized consideration	Gives personal attention to followers and makes each feel important.

Transactional leadership

Factor	Primary role of managerial leader
Contingent reward	Gives followers a clear understanding of what is expected of them, then arranges to exchange the rewards. Occurs when the leader and the staff member(s) "agree on what the [staff] needs to do to be rewarded or to avoid punishment" (Bass, 1995); the managerial leader is constantly in contact with the staff members.
Management by exception	Monitors followers' performances and takes corrective action when mistakes or failures are observed. The managerial leader has no basic contact with the staff. Staff only hear from the managerial leader when something goes wrong.
Laissez-faire leadership	Little or no leadership or contact is made with the staff members.

Adapted from the works of Bass, 1985.

Transformational leaders raise the consciousness of their followers about the importance of outcomes and how to reach those outcomes by going beyond their own self-interests. Transformational leaders are charismatic or exhilarating, influential, inspirational, intellectually stimulating, and individually considerate. While most managers engage in both transactional and transformational leadership behaviors, they do so in different amounts (Bass, 1985).

During the 1990s several studies were conducted on various topics of management and leadership by writers in sport management. Tables 9.3 and 9.4 present seven examples of such studies. Reported in table 9.3 are studies in managerial competencies (Danylchuk & Chelladurai, 1999); and leadership effectiveness and transformational leadership (Wallace & Weese, 1995; Weese, 1995, 1996). Table 9.4 presents four studies including topics in leader behavior (Branch, 1990); managerial leadership (Soucie, 1994); and transformational/transactional leadership behavior (Doherty, 1997; Doherty & Danylchuk, 1996).

Managerial Leadership

Contemporary management theorists suggest that both management and leadership are essential to the professional preparation of those who aspire to practice as supervisors and managers in sport organizations. **Managerial leadership** combines management and leadership into a coherent, integrated concept. Bennis and Nanus (1985) asserted that "managers are people who do things right and leaders are people who do the right thing" (p. 21). Kotter (1990) argued that "management is about coping with complexity and leadership is about coping with change" (p. 103). He maintained that both management and leadership are needed for a successful business. Good management skills are needed to maintain "a degree of consistency and order," and good leadership skills are needed to "produce movement" in a business (p. 103). The approach seems most logical since the aforementioned theorists professed that managers must be skilled in both management and leadership (see figure 9.4).

managerial leadership—The combination of management and leadership into a coherent, integrated concept.

Recently, sport management theorists have begun to integrate leadership and managerial behaviors into a single concept. Soucie (1994) suggested that effective leadership and management should be an integrated approach called

Table 9.3 Examples of Managerial/Leadership Research in Sport and Recreational Management Studies

Example of topic in contemporary sport management	Research
Managerial competencies	"This study described and analyzed the managerial work in Canadian intercollegiate athletics. The directors of 37 Canadian intercollegiate athletic departments responded to a questionnaire eliciting perceived importance of, time devoted to, and percentage responsibility for 19 managerial activities carried out by athletic departments. These managerial activities were largely patterned after Mintzberg's (1975) description of managerial work and were verified by a group of experts. Results showed that financial management, leadership, policy making, disturbance handling, revenue generation, and athlete affairs were perceived to be the most important and most time consuming activities. Information seeking, maintenance activities, and league responsibilities were rated the least important. The athletic directors reported that they were largely responsible for the more important tasks with average percent responsibility of 55%. The average responsibility assigned to assistant directors was 29.5%, and this limited responsibility was significantly but inversely related to the importance of the tasks." (Danylchuk & Chelladurai, 1999, p. 148)
Leadership effectiveness	"This study was undertaken to investigate the links between transformational leadership, organizational culture, and employee job satisfaction within the 69 Canadian YMCA organizations. The results . . . allowed the researchers to conclude that significant differences in organizational culture existed between the YMCA organizations led by high transformational leaders and YMCA organizations led by low transformational leaders. In addition, the YMCA organizations led by high transformational leaders administered organizations that carried out the culture-building activities of managing change, achieving goals, coordinated teamwork, and customer orientation to a greater degree than YMCA organizations led by low transformational leaders. No significant differences in employee job satisfaction levels existed between the YMCA organizations led by high transformational leaders and those led by low transformational leaders." (Wallace & Weese, 1995, p. 182)
Transformational leadership	"The purpose of this preliminary investigation was to explore the relationships that exist between transformational leadership (measured by the Leadership Behavior Questionnaire), organizational culture (measured by the Culture Strength Assessment), and organizational effectiveness (measured by the Target Population Satisfaction Index) in the campus recreation programs of both the Big Ten and Mid-American Conferences ($N = 19$). The directors of these programs were given considerable levels of job autonomy to lead their respective programs as well as the opportunity to alter and/or imbed a desired culture during their administration. Significant differences were uncovered in both conferences for executive transformational leadership and organizational effectiveness. However, no significant relationship was uncovered between transformational leadership and organizational effectiveness. A significant relationship was discovered between organizational culture strength and organizational effectiveness." (Weese, 1996, p. 197)

Table 9.4 Examples of Managerial/Leadership Research in Sport and Recreational Management Studies

Example of topic in contemporary sport management	Research
Leader behavior— consideration and structure	"The purpose of this study was to examine athletic director and selected assistant perceptions of leader behavior to determine whether their perceptions contributed significantly to the prediction of intercollegiate organizational effectiveness. Findings indicate that effective athletic organizations have leaders who are more predisposed to

Example of topic in contemporary sport management	Research
	goal and task accomplishment than to developing good interpersonal relationships with their subordinates. Contemporary leadership theory and management philosophy suggests that organizations that can accomplish both are most effective. Athletic directors may want to adjust their leadership behaviors to meet the managerial demands of today's intercollegiate athletic program." (Branch, 1990, p. 161)
Managerial leadership	"The purpose of this article is to (a) express a perspective regarding leadership, (b) draw lessons from the leadership literature, (c) gain insights from research about leadership effectiveness, and (d) infer from this literature prescriptions for practicing sport administrators. The article reviews the research literature that pertains to (a) leadership influence and power, (b) leadership traits and skills, (c) leadership behaviors, (d) situational leadership, and (e) charismatic and transformational leadership." (Soucie, 1994, p. 1)
Transformational/ transactional leadership behavior	"This study examined the effect of various leader characteristics on the transforma-transformational/transactional leader behavior (Bass, 1985) and impact of inter-university athletic administrators (*n* = 32), as rated by their coaches (*n* = 114). . . . Differences in transformational/transactional leader behavior were observed for the leader characteristics of gender and age, where female and younger athletic administrators were found to exhibit transformational leader behavior more often, and transactional leader behavior less often, than their male and older counterparts, respectively. Gender and age also were associated with the coaches' perception of leader effectiveness and their frequency of extra effort." (Doherty, 1997, p. 275)
Transformational/ transactional leadership behavior	"This study examined the leader behavior of inter-university athletic administrators according to Bass's (1985) transformational/transactional leadership model. . . . Coaches' satisfaction with leadership, perceived leader effectiveness, and extra effort were positively and strongly associated with transformational leadership and contingent reward behavior, whereas negative relationships were observed for management-by-exception (passive) and nonleadership behaviors. Leader behavior was not associated with the coaches' commitment to the athletic department." (Doherty & Danylchuk, 1996, p. 292)

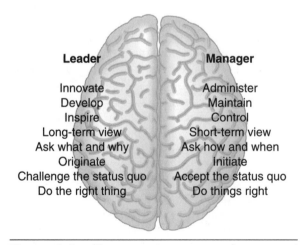

Figure 9.4 The integrative concept of managerial leadership.

"managerial leadership" (p. 3). He maintained that management and leadership may be qualitatively different but that each complements the other,

creating more effective and efficient managers in sport organizations. Quarterman (1998) also proposed a conceptual approach to the leader–manager dichotomy. His exploratory efforts raised concerns for the study of the concept of managerial leaders (managerial leadership) from an integrative perspective. Figure 9.4 illustrates the combination of the two separate entities into one entity of managerial leader. While it is desirable to view the concepts of leading and managing as distinct processes, leaders and managers do not constitute two different types of people (Kotter, 1990). It appears that the most successful managers in sport organizations are those who are able to combine relatively high degrees of managerial and leadership skills based on the situation. Organizations in the sport industry need individuals with special skills and talents who can dynamically assume the roles of both manager and leader.

Leaders of sport organizations use several managerial skills and assume a variety of managerial roles. Empirical studies have provided methods to identify and describe the skills that managers use (Katz, 1974) and the roles they assume (Mintzberg, 1973, 1990) as they carry out the processes of management.

Managerial Leadership Skills

The term *skill* reflects the idea that one's ability to perform managerial tasks is not innate. It can be learned and developed through experience and formal training. Katz (1974) identified the skills needed by managers of all types of organizations as conceptual, interpersonal (human), and technical.

Conceptual skills are required for managerial leaders to see the sport organization as a whole and to see the relationships among the parts that make up the whole organization. For example, the commissioner of the National Basketball Association (NBA) uses conceptual skills to compare the total market share of goods and services produced by the NBA with the market share produced by each individual professional team that comprises the NBA.

conceptual skills—The ability to see the organization as a whole and the relationship among the parts that make up the whole organization.

Managerial leaders use **interpersonal skills** to interact with others and to coordinate individual and group efforts in achieving an organization's goal. Specifically, this implies that the manager must be able to work with both internal and external constituents. For example, the director of campus recreation at a university who is confronted by minority students dissatisfied about how the facility is governed will need to use interpersonal skills to deal constructively with such criticism.

interpersonal skills—The ability to interact with others and to coordinate individual and group efforts in achieving an organization's goal.

Technical skills include the specialized knowledge, tools, techniques, and resources used in achieving an organization's goals. Managerial leaders must be able to perform certain technical skills as well as show their subordinates how to perform the skills. For example, the marketing director for a national athletics footwear firm would have to be efficient in preparing the annual report or annual budget for the marketing division of the firm. She must also be able to teach others who work in the division how to prepare such reports.

technical skills—The specified knowledge, tools, techniques, resources used in achieving an organization's goal.

All managerial leaders use conceptual, interpersonal, and technical skills, but they use them in varying degrees. For example, top managers often devote a major portion of time to long-range planning; therefore, they will typically spend more time using conceptual skills than will middle and supervisory managers. Paul Tagliabue, commissioner of the NFL, is a good example of a top-level manager who is recognized for using conceptual skills. "I don't want to be involved in things that are repetitive and things that are day-to-day," Tagliabue says. "If it involves a new concept, then I want to know the concept is being implemented the way I conceived it, not the way someone else dreamed of it. I don't want to micromanage" (Weisman, 1993, p. 2c). On the other hand, supervisory sport managers spend most of their time directing (motivating, leading, and communicating) nonmanagerial staff; therefore, these supervisors use more technical skills than do top-level or middle-level managers. Interpersonal skills are important to managers at *all* levels of sport organizations because it is the responsibility of the managers to design ways for others to do the work. They work with and through others to attain the goals of the organization.

In this example, supervisory (first-level) managers are identified as using more technical skills in sport activity performance and in producing the services of the club (e.g., showing the workers new teaching techniques, setting up equipment). However, the owners (executive directors or general managers) will use fewer technical skills and will spend far more time using conceptual skills (e.g., developing and implementing long-range goals and monitoring the resources used by the club) and interpersonal skills. When considering middle-level management, theoretically the need for interpersonal skills is magnified more than technical and conceptual skills. Technical skills are needed, however, substantially less than by first-line managers and more than by top-level managers. Theoretically, middle managers also need some conceptual skills, however, more than by the first-line managers and less than by top-level managers.

Figure 9.5 shows the distribution of skills used by managers. Notice that technical specialists must be well trained in technical and interpersonal skills to perform their jobs and produce the services offered by the sport club. This does not mean, however, that technical specialists can't or shouldn't use conceptual skills; in fact, the best ones will.

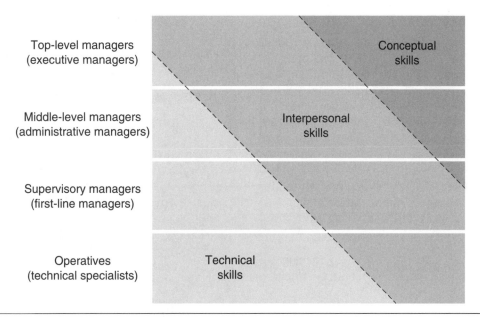

Figure 9.5 Typical distribution of skills used by managers. Administrative directors (middle-level managers) spend significant amounts of time using technical, interpersonal, and conceptual skills. Note that all three managerial levels use interpersonal skills equally. Unlike managers, nonmanagers (also known as operatives or technical specialists) spend large amounts of time utilizing technical skills. These are the individuals who are responsible for producing the goods and services in organizations of the sport industry.

Managerial Roles

In addition to using a range of skills, managerial leaders must assume a variety of roles as they carry out the traditional processes of management (Mintzberg, 1973, 1990). Mintzberg defined a *role* as a set of expected behaviors associated with a managerial position. Based on Mintzberg's theory, the typical manager portrays 10 roles, which are classified into three categories: interpersonal, informational, and decisional.

Interpersonal Roles

Mintzberg (1990) identified three specific **interpersonal roles**: figurehead, leader, and liaison. When managerial leaders engage in these roles, they are primarily involved in interpersonal relationships with others. As **figureheads**, managers perform a variety of symbolic and ceremonial duties. Examples of the figurehead role are showing up at a subordinate's wedding, welcoming visitors to an organization, representing the organization at a public function, and cutting the ribbon for a new facility. One illustration of a top executive acting as a figurehead is a government official throwing out the first ball to open the men's professional baseball season.

interpersonal roles—Roles involving interpersonal relationships with others.

figureheads—Managers acting in symbolic and ceremonial ways.

The *leader* role relates to managerial leaders' relationships with their subordinates. As leaders, managers recruit, select, train, motivate, evaluate, and direct the subordinates' energies and efforts toward accomplishing the organization's goals. Leaders are also responsible for coordinating the work of subordinates. Examples of the leader role are conducting a workshop on computer programming for the support staff and rewarding staff for outstanding job performance. The director of ticket sales exhibits the role of leader when providing flexible working hours for the telemarketing staff.

The **liaison** role refers to a managerial leader's ability to develop and cultivate relationships with individuals and groups outside the work unit or organization. For instance, coordinators of concessions usually maintain contact with vendors to determine when there will be special sales on certain supplies. Directors of campus recreation often meet with peer directors to discern how they will vote on an important issue before the official voting sessions. These managerial leaders are acting in the liaison role.

liaison—Managers in the role of developing and cultivating relationships with individuals and groups outside the work unit or organization.

Informational Roles

When managerial leaders exchange and process information, they engage in the informational role. These roles include monitor, disseminator, and spokesperson. As **monitors**, managerial leaders scan the environment for information that can affect the organization. They collect information from a variety of sources, including subordinates, peers, superiors, contacts, news media, electronic mail, the Internet, gossip, and hearsay. A supervisor who has coffee lounge conversation with other supervisors about the organization's plans to downsize the support staff is engaging in the monitor role.

monitors—Managers in the role of scanning the environment for information that can affect the organization.

As managerial leaders collect information, they become the nerve centers of their work areas. When they transmit the information to others, they are disseminators and spokespersons. As **disseminators**, managers selectively pass on information to others in the organization or work unit. A supervisor who attends an athletic conference meeting and then informs the subordinates of the rule changes that have been enacted is engaging in the role of disseminator.

disseminators—Managers in the role of passing information on to others in the organization or work unit.

As **spokespersons**, managerial leaders transmit information to persons or groups outside their respective organizations or work units. For example, the director of public relations of the professional baseball organization outlined in figure 9.1 who speaks to the local Rotary Club luncheon might tell the members about the upcoming season and special events. In this type of situation, the director is assuming the role of spokesperson for the baseball organization.

spokespersons—Managers in the role of transmitting information to persons or groups outside the manager's respective organization or work unit.

Decisional Roles

Decisional roles may be exhibited in four specific categories: entrepreneur, disturbance handler, resource allocator, and negotiator. As **entrepreneurs**, managerial leaders search for ways to effect change and improve an organization. A manager who provides the latest computer technology for the ticket office is acting in an entrepreneurial role. The director of operations of a professional football team who finds and uses information worldwide is also fulfilling an entrepreneurial role.

entrepreneurs—Managers in the role of searching for ways to effect change and improve an organization.

As **disturbance handlers**, managerial leaders respond to unexpected situations that might disrupt the organization's normal operation. Usually, managers must react to such disruptions immediately. For example, if all the support staff of a sport marketing agency became ill with influenza and could not report to work during the week of a major tennis tournament sponsored by that agency, the normal operation of the tournament would be affected. The event manager at the agency would need to hire temporary help and recruit volunteers to handle the disturbance effectively.

disturbance handlers—Managers in the role of responding to unexpected situations that might disrupt the organization's normal operation.

As **resource allocators**, managerial leaders determine how best to allocate resources such as people, money, equipment, supplies, time, and information to each employee, group, or work unit, or to the entire organization. For example, the coordinator of marketing and promotions of a state sport festival must provide the support staff and assistants with adequate office supplies to develop literature for informing the public about upcoming events.

resource allocators—Managers in the role of determining how best to allocate resources to each employee, group, or work unit, or to the entire organization.

As **negotiators**, managerial leaders confer with persons inside or outside the work unit or organization to obtain concessions or to agree on pivotal issues. Bargaining and reaching an agreement with subordinates, a regulatory agency, an interest group, or a vendor are examples of the negotiating roles. A purchasing manager for the Women's National Basketball League who negotiates with a vendor for lower prices and faster delivery times on equipment and supplies illustrates the negotiator role.

negotiators—Managers in the role of conferring with persons inside or outside the work unit or organization to obtain concessions or to agree on pivotal issues.

© Frances M. Roberts

As an executive for major league baseball, Bud Selig must negotiate with a variety of external and internal constituents.

All managerial leaders, from top executives to first-line supervisors, perform decisional roles. However, the degree to which managers perform each role will vary according to the managerial level. For example, Pavett and Lau (1983) found that the disseminator, figurehead, negotiator, and spokesperson roles are closely associated with top-level managers. On the other hand, the leadership, resource allocator, and disturbance handler roles are more closely associated with first-line supervisory managers (Kerr, Hill, & Broedling, 1986). Table 9.5 illustrates the role delineation revealed in a study of athletic conference commissioners (Quarterman, 1994).

Major Dimensions for Classifying Managerial Leaders

While all managers have formal authority for directing the work activities of others, different managers possess different degrees of authority. In the hierarchy of an organization, managers are usually classified as (1) top-level managers, (2) middle-level managers, or (3) supervisory-level managers (Glueck, 1980).

Table 9.5 Adaptation of Mintzberg's Managerial Roles for Intercollegiate Athletic Conference Commissioners

Role	Description of role	Examples
Interpersonal figurehead	Performing ceremonial duties on behalf of the conference	Welcoming dignitaries, greeting visitors, participating in groundbreaking ceremonies
Leader	Influencing subordinates to get the work done at the conference office	Conducting performance evaluations, acting as a role model in the workplace, praising an employee for doing a good job
Liaison	Maintaining a network of outside contacts to gather information for the conference	Attending meetings with peers, listening to the "grapevine," participating in conference-wide meetings
Informational monitor	Perpetually scanning the environment for information that may prove useful to the conference	Lobbying for information at an NCAA meeting, staying in contact with other commissioners by telephone, reviewing the athletic literature
Disseminator	Transmitting information received by individuals and/or groups outside the conference	Sending information to the coaches and athletic directors, having a review session on NCAA rules with the athletic directors.
Spokesperson	Transmitting information to individuals and/or groups outside the conference	Speaking at community and professional meetings, briefing the state legislature about athletics

(continued)

Table 9.5 *(continued)*

Role	Description of role	Examples
Decisional entrepreneur	Searching for new ideas and implementing changes for the betterment of the conference	Initiating a new marketing concept for increasing revenue, bringing new technology to the conference
Disturbance handler	Making decisions to deal with unexpected changes that may affect the conference	Resolving a conflict among member institutions, dealing with changes in game schedules
Resource allocator	Making decisions concerning resource use—people, time, money, space, or the conference	Making a decision about a tournament site, adding or deleting a sport program
Negotiator	Bargaining with individuals, groups, or organizations on behalf of the conference	Negotiating a television contract, negotiating with vendors

Reprinted, by permission, from J. Quarterman, 1994, "Managerial role profiles of intercollegiate athletic conference commissioners," *Journal of Sport Management* 8(2):131-132.

• *Top-level managerial leaders*—This is the smallest group of managers. **Top-level managerial leaders** are also known as executive or senior-level managers, and they have the most power and authority. They are usually responsible for the total organization or a major part of it.

top-level managerial leaders—The executive or senior-level managers of an organization who have the most power and authority.

• *Middle-level managerial leaders*—**Middle-level managerial leaders** (also known as administrative-level managers) are usually selected by top-level managers. Therefore, they are responsible *to* top-level managers and responsible *for* supervisory-level managers and sometimes for technical specialists. To their subordinates, the middle-level managers are the source of information and solutions to problems because they know the technical side of the products and services. Consequently, a middle-level manager is often considered half generalist and half specialist (Petit, 1975). The managerial leaders at the middle level are, in general, responsible for (1) managing a department or unit that performs an organizational function (Petit, 1975) and (2) ensuring that the assigned tasks are done efficiently. Middle-level managers are unique because they must be both leaders and followers. They are connected to supervisors and to subordinates, both of whom are also managers.

middle-level managerial leaders—Managers who are selected by and responsible to top-level managers. They are responsible for supervisory managers and sometimes for technical specialists.

They also are commonly referred to as administrative-level managers.

• *Supervisory-level managerial leaders*—Theoretically, **supervisory-level managerial leaders** (also known as first-line managers or supervisors) report to middle-level managers and are responsible for nonmanagerial employees. Although such coordinators make up the largest number of managers, they have the least amount of authority. They are primarily responsible for a single area in a work unit, division, or department in the sport organization.

supervisory-level managerial leaders—Managers who report to middle-level managers and are responsible for nonmanagerial employees.

In addition to the title of coordinator, supervisory-level managers may have any one of the following titles:

• Supervisor
• Department supervisor
• Department head
• Assistant director
• Chair
• Assistant manager
• Unit supervisor

Regardless of the title used for supervisory managerial leaders, they are primarily responsible for supervising other employees (including lower-level managers as well as nonmanagers). It is their job to communicate with, inspire, and influence the other members in the organization to get the job done in the most effective and efficient way. This makes their positions unique because they are the main source of contact between the nonmanagerial technical specialists and management. Examples of the titles of managers at different levels in three selected sport organizations are shown in table 9.6.

LEARNING ACTIVITY

Review an issue of *Athletic Business, Fitness Management,* or the *NCAA News.* Find an example of a job listing for each of the following: (1) a first-line super-visory manager, (2) a middle-level manager, and (3) a top executive in a setting associated with sport organization management.

Characteristics of Successful Managerial Leaders

In a 1988 issue of *Fortune* magazine, management consultants, business school professors, and CEOs of America's largest companies identified seven key skills needed to be an effective and efficient leader (Labich, 1988). The generalized concepts of these skills are relevant for managerial leaders in sport organizations (see table 9.7).

Table 9.6 Titles for Managerial Leaders at Different Levels in Three Typical Sport Organizations

Levels of management	Professional baseball organization	Investor-owned health and fitness club	NCAA Division I-A intercollegiate athletics program
Top-level managers	President Chief executive officer Vice presidents • Business operations • Baseball operations	Owner(s) General managers Regional directors • Corporate wellness • Health promotion	Board of trustees University president Athletics director (AD) Head football coach Senior associate AD
Middle-level managers	Director of public relations Director of corporate sales Director of marketing operations Team manager Director of scouting	Site managers • Corporate wellness • Health promotion	Head coaches—major sports Associate ADs • Director of fund-raising • Director of development
Supervisory-level managers	Director of stadium operations Director of broadcasting Director of community relations Director of baseball administration	Coordinators (supervisors) • Aerobics • Fitness • Golf • Pro shop • Weight training	Assistant AD Sports information director Coordinator of athletic training Marketing director Academic coordinator

Table 9.7 Characteristics of Successful Leaders

They trust their subordinates.	A good leader will make use of employees' energy and talent. The key to a productive relationship is mutual trust.
They develop a vision.	Employees want to follow a visionary leader. They want to know where they are going and why.
They keep their cool.	Leaders demonstrate their mettle in crisis and under fire. They inspire others to remain calm and to act intelligently.
They are experts.	Employees are much more likely to follow a leader who radiates confidence, is intuitive, and continues to master the profession.

(continued)

Table 9.7 *(continued)*

They invite dissent.	A leader is willing to accept a variety of opinions and integrate them.
They simplify.	Leaders focus on what is important and reach elegant, simple answers to complex problems by keeping the details to themselves.
They encourage risk.	Leaders encourage employees to take chances and readily accept error.

Source: Labich, 1988.

Scenario: Learning How to Be an Effective Managerial Leader

Several years ago two students graduating from the sport management program at American Sport Marketing Institute were hired by Marketing International, a sport marketing firm, as project assistants. Two years later they were both promoted to project managers. As opposed to being paid for performing their specialty in designing promotional materials, they were now being paid for being managers supervising two different projects. At the end of the first six months, one of them, Antonio Demopolis, was experiencing considerable success and enjoying his new managerial job. Dolores Hayashi, the other manager, was not so successful. She was experiencing problems in meeting schedules and deadlines. There was unrest among several project representatives under her. She was also becoming discouraged and frustrated. Her immediate superior was concerned about her situation.

Antonio had adapted well to his new role. He realized that, in a way, he was embarking on a new and different career within the firm and had adjusted accordingly. More specifically, whether it was because of his personal insight or because he received help from his superior, he perceived his role and function to be different from what it used to be. Among the many things he did after being appointed manager was to delineate what objectives needed to be accomplished; the availability of the people in his unit to work toward those objectives; and the skills, strengths, and weaknesses of those individuals. He reviewed the work flow in his unit and formulated priorities and schedules. Through various meetings, he attempted to communicate these priorities and schedules to his subordinates, and he instilled his personal philosophy, which valued teamwork highly. He shared and discussed problems with his project assistants frequently. In addition, he was actively involved with helping individuals in his unit to set proper goals and realistically evaluate their performance.

In contrast, Dolores became overwhelmed by her new role. When she realized that she was no longer expected to complete the actual work for the project as she was used to, she became confused. She believed that to get each project done, she as a manager needed to make sure every aspect of the project was completed properly. As a result, she checked every assignment completed by her subordinates. When she found an error, she made the correction herself. She became convinced that checking was the only way to ensure that no mistakes were committed. Dolores's obsession with detail led her to spending more time to make sure things were done right. Because she became so involved in checking, she neglected her other responsibilities. She did not file workload recording reports and employee evaluations on time. In addition, her staff assumed less responsibility for their work. They became passive, and two-thirds of her staff changed jobs and left the firm within a year.

1. What processes of management did Antonio demonstrate?

2. What management skills did Dolores lack? What were her strengths?

3. If you were the top manager, how would you help Dolores improve her performance? How could you capitalize on her ability to check details?

SUMMARY

Management and leadership are two distinct yet complementary systems of action. Management refers to the process of working with and through individuals and groups to accomplish organizational goals, and leadership is defined as a process of influencing individual and group behavior for some desired results. Contemporary management theorists have cited five underlying processes that guide the concept of management as planning, organizing, directing, staffing, and controlling. Four of the most common theoretical approaches to leadership are trait, behavioral, situational, and transactional/transformational.

Managerial leadership is a term that integrates management and leadership into a coherent concept. The manager–leader dichotomy serves as a way of thinking for managers of sport organizations.

Conceptual, interpersonal, and technical skills are three types of managerial skills needed by managerial leaders. Conceptual skills are the ability to see the organization as a whole and the relationship among the parts that make up the whole organization. The ability to interact with others and to coordinate individual and group efforts in achieving an organization's goal is referred to as interpersonal skills. Technical skills are concerned with the specified knowledge, tools, techniques, and resources used in achieving an organization's goal.

Managerial leaders in sport organizations commonly assume three basic roles: interpersonal, informational, and decisional. When managerial leaders perform the interpersonal role, they are primarily involved in interpersonal relationships with others. When they exchange and process information, they engage in the informational role. When executing the decisional role, managerial leaders search for ways to effect change and improve an organization, respond to unexpected situations that might disrupt the organization's normal operation, or determine how best to allocate resources.

Managerial leaders in sport organizations are classified as top-level managerial leaders, middle-level managerial leaders, and supervisory-level managerial leaders. The executive or senior-level managers of an organization who have the most power and authority are called the top-level managerial leaders. The middle-level managerial leaders are those individuals selected by and responsible to top-level managers. They are responsible for supervisory managers and for technical specialists. They also are commonly referred to as administrative-level managers. Supervisory-level managerial leaders are the managers who report to middle-level managers and are responsible for nonmanagerial employees.

REVIEW QUESTIONS

1. Explain the differences between the terms *management* and *leadership.*

2. Explain the differences between leaders and managers in organizations of the sport industry.

3. Briefly review each of the approaches to the study of leadership.

4. Explain the managerial skills used at each level of management in a sport organization.

5. Explain the managerial roles sport managers assume as they carry out the traditional processes of management.

6. Explain the major dimensions for classifying managerial leaders.

7. What skills are needed for a leader to become effective and efficient?

REFERENCES

Ayman, R., Chemers, M.M., & Fielder, F. (1997). The contingency model of leadership effectiveness: Its levels of analysis. In R.P. Vecchio (Ed.), *Leadership: Understanding the dynamics of power and influence in organization* (pp. 351-380). Notre Dame, IN: University of Notre Dame Press.

Bass, B.M. (1985). *Leadership and performance beyond expectation.* New York: Free Press.

Bennis, W., & Nanus, B. (1985). *Leaders: The strategies for taking charge.* New York: Harper & Row.

Branch, D. (1990). Athletic director leader behavior as a predictor of intercollegiate athletic organizational effectiveness. *Journal of Sport Management, 4,* 161-173.

Broughton, D., Lee, J., & Nethery, R. (1999). The answer: $213 billion. *Street & Smith's SportsBusiness Journal, 2*(32), 23, 26.

Burns, J.M. (1978). *Leadership.* New York: Harper & Row.

Danylchuk, K.E., & Chelladurai, P. (1999). The nature of managerial work in Canadian intercollegiate athletics. *Journal of Sport Management, 13*(2), 148-166.

Doherty, A.J. (1997). The effect of leader characteristics on the perceived transformational/transactional leadership and impact of interuniversity athletic administrators. *Journal of Sport management, 11*(3), 275-285.

Doherty, A.J., & Danylchuk, K.E. (1996). Transformational and transactional leadership in interuniversity athletics management. *Journal of Sport management, 10*(3), 292-309.

Drucker, P.F. (1967). *The effective executive.* New York: Harper & Row.

Drucker, P.F. (1974). *Management: Tasks, responsibilities, practices.* New York: Harper & Row.

Evans, M.G. (1970). The effects of supervisory behavior on the Path-Goal relationship. *Organizational Behavior and Human Performance,* 277-298.

Fiedler, F.E. (1967). *A theory of leadership effectiveness.* New York: McGraw-Hill.

Glueck, W.F. (1980). *Management* (2nd ed.). Hinsdale, IL: The Dryden Press.

Gulick, L., & Urwick, L. (1937). *Papers on the science of administration.* New York: Institute of Public Administration.

Hemphill, J.K., & Coons, A.E. (1957). Development of the leader behavior description questionnaire. In R.M. Stogdill & A.E. Coons (Eds.), *Leader Behavior: Its description and measurement.* Bureau of Business Research. Columbus, OH: The Ohio State University.

Hersey, P., & Blanchard, K.H. (1988). *Management of organizational behavior: Utilizing human resource* (5th ed.). Englewood Cliffs, NJ: Prentice Hall.

Hersey, P., Blanchard, K.H., & Johnson, D.E. (1996). *Management of organizational behavior: Utilizing human resources* (7th ed.). Upper Saddle River, NJ: Prentice Hall.

Hersey, P. Blanchard, K.H., & Johnson, D.E. (2001). *Management of organizational behavior: Leading human resources* (8th ed.). Upper Saddle River, NJ: Prentice Hall.

House, R. J. (1971). A path-goal theory of leader effectiveness. *Administrative Science Quarterly, 16,* 321-328.

House, R.J., & Mitchell, T.R. (1974). Path-goal theory of leadership. *Journal of Contemporary Business, 3,* 81-97.

House, R.J., & Mitchell, T.R. (1997). Path-Goal Theory of Leadership. In R.P. Vecchio (Ed.), *Leadership: Under-* standing the dynamics of power and influence in organizations (pp. 259-273). Notre Dame, IN: University of Notre Dame Press.

Katz, R.L. (1974). Skills of an effective administrator. *Harvard Business Review, 52*(5), 90-101.

Katz, D., & Kahn, R. (1978). *The social psychology of organizations* (2nd ed.). New York: Wiley.

Kerr, S., Hill, K.D., & Broedling, L. (1986). The first line supervisor: Phasing out or here to stay? *Academy of Management Review, 11,* 103-114.

Kerr, S., & Schriesheim, C. (1974). Consideration, initiating structure, and organizational criteria—An update of Korman's 1966 review. *Personnel Psychology, 27,* 555-568.

Koontz, H., & O'Donnell, C.J. (1976). *Management: A systems and contingency analysis of managerial functions* (6th ed.). New York: McGraw-Hill.

Kotter, J.P. (1990). What leaders really do. *Harvard Business Review, 68*(3), 103-111.

Labich, K. (1988, October 24). The seven keys to business leadership. *Fortune, 118*(10), 58-62, 64, 66.

Leith, L.M. (1983). The underlying process of athletic administration. *The Physical Educator, 40,* 211-217.

Mahoney, T.A., Jerdee, T.H., & Carroll, S.G. (1965). The job(s) of management. *Industrial Relations 4*(2), 97-110.

McFarland, D.E. (1974). *Management: Principles and practices* (4th ed.). New York: Macmillan.

Mintzberg, H. (1973). *The nature of managerial work.* New York: Harper & Row.

Mintzberg, H. (1975). The manager's job: Folklore and fact. *Harvard Business Review, 53*(1), 49-61.

Mintzberg, H. (1990). The manager's job: Folklore and fact, *Harvard Business Review, 68*(2), 163-176. (Reprinted from *Harvard Business Review, 53*(1), pp. 49-61, 1975.)

Mullin, B.J. (1980). Sport management: The nature and utility of the concept. *Arena Review, 4*(3), 1-11.

Pavett, C.M., & Lau, A.W. (1983). Managerial work: The influence of hierarchical level and functional speciality. *Academy of Management Journal, 26,* 170-177.

Petit, T.A. (1975). *Fundamentals of management coordination: Supervisors, middle managers, and executives.* New York: Wiley.

Quarterman, J. (1994). Managerial role profiles of intercollegiate athletic conference commissioners. *Journal of Sport Management, 8,* 129-139.

Quarterman, J. (1998). An assessment of the perception of management and leadership skills by intercollegiate athletics conference compressions. *Journal of Sport management, 12*(2), 146-164.

Robbins, S.F. (1996). *Organizational behavior* (7th ed.). Englewood Cliffs, NJ: Prentice Hall, p. 413.

Schermerhorn, J.R., Jr., Hunt, J.G., & Osborn, R.N. (1994). *Managing organizational behavior* (5th ed.). New York: Wiley.

Soucie, D. (1994). Effective managerial leadership in sport organizations. *Journal of Sport Management, 8,* 1-13.

Wallace, M., & Weese, W.J. (1995). Leadership, organizational culture, and job satisfaction in Canadian YMCA organizations. *Journal of Sport Management, 9,* 182-193.

Weese, W.J. (1995). Leadership and organizational culture: An investigation of Big Ten and Mid-American Conference Campus recreation administrations. *Journal of Sport Management, 9*(2), 119-134.

Weese, W.J. (1996). Do leadership and organizational culture really matter? *Journal of Sport Management, 10,* 197-206.

Weisman, L. (1993, November 29). Tagliabue likes to see big picture. *USA Today*, pp. 1C-2C.

Wofford, J.C. (1982). *Organizational behavior: Foundations for organizational effectiveness.* Boston: Kent Publishing Company.

Yukl, G. (1989). Managerial leadership: A review of theory and research. *Journal of Management, 15*(2), 251-289.

PART IV

Selected Functional Areas of Sport Management

The sport industry offers a wide variety of career opportunities to aspiring sport managers. Each of these opportunities requires an understanding of all of the concepts discussed thus far in this book. Each segment of the industry also requires additional, specific skills and abilities. The purpose of the chapters in this section is to introduce you to nine segments of the sport industry in which possibilities exist for you. These nine segments are representative of settings in which you could find careers in sport, but they are not, by a long shot, a complete inventory of sport-related job possibilities. If you take advantage of the additional resources included in the reference lists in each chapter and the "For More Information" section on pages 186-188 you will discover many more opportunities available to you in the world of sport.

In chapter 10 Wayne Blann and Ketra Armstrong explain the importance of the relationship between a sport marketing plan and the organization's mission and core values. The authors then discuss the elements of a SWOT analysis and explain how it can be used to assess present and future market climates. Blann and Armstrong present information on the various dimensions of sport products and events, define product positioning and market niches, and explain the communication of product images. They also cover marketing segmentation, pricing and promotion strategies, distribution channels, and the packaging and selling of sport products. The theme of socially responsible sport marketing runs throughout the chapter.

Clay Stoldt, Catherine Pratt, and Jason Jackson address publicity and public relations in chapter 11. After identifying a number of sport-related career opportunities in the communication industry, they provide an insightful discussion of important ethical issues associated with the field. The authors then identify the skills and knowledge required to pursue such careers, delineating the responsibilities of professionals involved in sport media relations, community relations, and other types of public relations positions in sport organizations. The authors conclude with essential information on how advances in communication technology are affecting the practice of public relations in sport.

In chapter 12 Tim DeSchriver and Dan Mahony introduce basic principles of microeconomics and macroeconomics. They relate economic theory to the sport industry and explain the concept of economic impact analysis as it is used in sporting events and facilities. DeSchriver and Mahony further explain the business structure of sport organizations and introduce the basic tools of financial management. They present several professional opportunities associated with economics and financial management.

Rob Ammon and David Stotlar address sport facility and event management in chapter 13. After delineating the steps required for effective facility management, they differentiate between public and private facilities and point out similarities and differences between *event* management and *facility* management. Real-life scenarios illustrate the importance of proper planning for sporting events. Ammon and Stotlar conclude with a discussion of risk management concerns for managers of sport facilities and events.

Intercollegiate athletics is the topic of chapter 14. First, Robertha Abney and Ellen Staurowsky define intercollegiate athletics and present a brief overview of its history in the United States. Then, the authors discuss governing bodies associated with intercollegiate athletics, identify several administrative positions and related responsibilities within intercollegiate athletics departments, and discuss current challenges in college sport. Finally, they present a number of professional associations, organizations, and publications related to intercollegiate athletics.

In chapter 15 Jay Gladden and Bill Sutton define, explain, and discuss the development of professional sport. The authors then address the unique characteristics of professional sport, such as its governance structure and the relationship between labor and management. The significance of television for pro sport is also presented, as is a discussion of the major revenue sources for a professional sport team. Gladden and Sutton then describe several types of employment opportunities available in pro sport.

Mark McDonald and Bill Sutton present information about the role, scope, and impact of sport management and marketing agencies in chapter 16. The authors differentiate between types of agencies and explain the evolution of each. They further define the functions of these agencies and discuss career opportunities associated with them.

Chapter 17 addresses one of the newer career fields, sport tourism. Heather Gibson describes tourism and the tourism industry and then explains the intersection of tourism and sport. The author provides a thorough explanation of the different types of sport tourism: active sport tourism (e.g., traveling to participate in physical activities), event sport tourism (e.g., traveling to watch sporting events), and nostalgia sport tourism (e.g., traveling to sport museums or halls of fame). Gibson concludes with a discussion of the sociocultural, economic, and environmental impacts of sport tourism.

In chapter 18 Ted Fay explains the development of the international sport industry with respect to sport federations, leagues, corporations, and events. He discusses the power structure and processes of the international sport industry, including linkages within the industry. Fay addresses the import–export exchange process regarding sport products, services, and personnel throughout the world and identifies resources as well as the knowledge and skills necessary to compete for a job in the international sport marketplace.

An appreciation of the wide diversity of opportunities available in the sport industry will enable you to plan your professional life more realistically. Rather than concentrating only on the chapters that address the careers in which you are *currently* interested, we hope you will study the material in *each* of the nine career chapters and reflect on the possibilities each area might hold for you. Who knows? As you learn more about the possibilities that exist, you might develop new interests and revise your career goals!

FOR MORE INFORMATION

Marketing: Professional and Scholarly Associations

- Academy of Marketing Sciences
- American Marketing Association
- American Sports Data, Inc.
- Direct Marketing Association
- International Sports Marketing Association
- Licensing Industry Merchandisers Association (LIMA)
- Society of Consumer Affairs Professionals

Public Relations Professional Organizations

- College Sports Information Directors of America (CoSIDA)—www.cosida.fansonly.com
- Female Athletic Media Relations Executives (FAME)—www.personal.psu.edu/staff/m/j/mjh11/FAME/index2MJ.html
- Football Writers Association of America—www.footballwriters.com
- International Association of Business Communicators—www.iabc.com
- National Association of Collegiate Directors of Athletics (NACDA)
- National College Baseball Writers Association—www.sportswriters.net/ncbwa/
- Public Relations Society of America—www.prsa.org
- United States Basketball Writers Association—www.usbwa.org

Facility Management Professional Associations

- International Association of Assembly Managers
- National Recreation & Park Association
- National Swimming Pool Foundation
- U.S. Golf Association
- YMCA of the USA

Facility Management Internet Sites

- International Association of Assembly Managers: www.iaam.org/

- International Facility Management Association: www.ifma.org
- Job opportunities: www.JobsinSports.com
- Rock concerts and crowd safety: www.crowdsafe.com/reports.html
- TeamWork Online www.teamworkonline.com/
- Stadium and venue news: www.stadianet.com/go.php

Tourism Associations

- Audubon International's Cooperative Sanctuary System, Golf Program: www.audubonintl.org/programs/acss/golf.htm
- British Tourism Authority Sport Tourism Initiative: www.visitbritain.com/sport
- Canadian Sports Tourism Initiative: www.canadatourism.com/en/ctc/ctx/partnerships/NicheProducts/sports_initiative.cfm
- Canadian Tourism Commission: www.canadatourism.com
- Committed to Green Foundation for environmental management of sports: www.committedtogreen.com/
- Tourism Sport International Council: http://sptourism.net/
- Travel Industry Association of America: www.TIA.org
- U.S. Olympic Committee: www.usoc.org
- World Tourism Organization: www.world-tourism.org
- World Travel and Tourism Council: www.wttc.org

Special Issues of Journals on Sport Tourism

- *Journal of Vacation Marketing*, 1998, vol. 4, (1)
- *Tourism Recreation Research*, 1997, vol. 22, (1)
- *Visions in Leisure and Business*, 1999, vol. 18, (spring)
- *Current Issues in Tourism,* 2002, vol. 5, (1)
- *Journal of Sport Management*—2003
- *Journal of Sports Tourism*

Sport Tourism Companies or Attractions

- World Golf Village: www.wgv.com
- LPGA Hall of Fame: www.worldgolf.com/wglibrary/history/lpgahoff.html
- National Baseball Hall of Fame: www.baseballhalloffame.org
- Disney's Wide World of Sports: www.dwws.disney.go.com
- Basketball Hall of Fame: www.hoophall.com/
- Women's Basketball Hall of Fame: www.wbhof.com/main.html
- Olympic Museum, Geneva, Switzerland: www.olympic.org/uk/passion/museum/index_uk.asp
- Pinehurst Resort, North Carolina: www.pinehurst.com/
- American Skiing Company: www.peaks.com/
- Intrawest Ski Company: www.intrawest.com/
- Norwegian Cruise Lines: www.ncl.com

Conferences and Special Events

- National Association of Sports Commissions: www.sportscommissions.org
- National Girls and Women in Sports Day—www.sportsforwomen.com
- North American Society for Sport Management Conference—www.nassm.org
- Women's Sports Foundation Summit—www.sportsforwomen.com
- Women's Sports Marketing Conference—www.sportsforwomen.com
- National Association of Collegiate Marketing Administrators Conference—www.ncaa.com

Professional and Scholarly Publications

- *Advertising Age*
- *Amusement Business*
- *Athletic Business*—www.athleticbusiness.com
- *Athletics Administration*
- *Club Industry*
- *CoSIDA Digest*—www.cosida.fansonly.com/genrel/info.html
- *Facility Manager*

- *Fitness Management*
- *Journal of Communication Management*—www.henrystewart.com/journals/hspindex.htm
- *Journal of Marketing*
- *Journal of Public Relations Research*—www.erlbaum.com/Journals/journals/JPRR/jprr.htm
- *Journal of Sport Management*—www.unb.ca/web/sportmanagement/jsm.htm
- *Marketing Communications*
- *National Aquatics Journal*
- *NCAA News*—www.ncaa.org
- *PR Week*—www.prweekus.com/us/index.htm
- *Prep to Win*—www.preptowin.com
- *Psychology and Marketing*
- *Public Relations Strategist*—www.prsa.org/prpubs.html
- *Special Events Report*
- *Sport Marketing Quarterly*—www.fitinfotech.com/smq/smqpage.html
- *Sports Illustrated*—www.cnnsi.com
- *Sports Market Place*—www.sportmarketplace.com
- *Stadia*
- *Street & Smith's SportsBusiness Journal*
- *Team Marketing Report*
- *Team Marketing Report Newsletter*
- *The Chronicle of Higher Education*—www.chronicle.com
- *The Sponsors Report*
- *The Sporting News*—www.sportingnews.com
- *The Sports Business Daily*
- *The Women's Sports Experience*—www.lifetimetv.com/wosport

Sport Finance Books

- Fried, G., Shapiro, S., & DeSchriver, T. (2003). *Sport finance.* Champaign, IL: Human Kinetics.
- Helyar, J. (1994). *Lords of the realm.* New York: Ballantine Books.
- Livingstone, J.L., & Grossman, T. (Eds.). (2002). *The Portable MBA in finance and accounting* (3rd ed.). New York: Wiley.
- Noll, R.G., & Zimbalist, A. (Eds.) (1997). *Sports, jobs, and taxes: The economic impact of sports teams and stadiums.* Washington, DC: Brookings Institution Press.
- Quirk, J., & Fort, R.D. (1997). *Pay dirt: The business of professional team sports.* Princeton, NJ: Princeton University Press.
- Quirk, J., & Fort, R.D. (1999). *Hard ball: The abuse of power in pro team sports.* Princeton, NJ: Princeton University Press.
- Staudohar, P.D. (1996). *Playing for dollars: Labor relations and the sports business* (3rd ed.). Ithaca, NY: ILR Press.

Professional Teams

- National Basketball Association, www.nba.com
- Women's National Basketball Association, www.wnba.com
- National Hockey League www.nhl.com
- Major League Baseball, www.mlb.com
- National Association of Professional Baseball Leagues, www.minorleaguebaseball.com
- American Hockey League, www.theahl.com
- East Coast Hockey League, www.echl.com
- Women's United Soccer Association, www.wusa.com
- National Football League, www.nfl.com
- Arena Football League, www.arenafootball.com

Chapter 10 _____

Sport Marketing

F. Wayne Blann, Ithaca College
Ketra L. Armstrong, The Ohio State University

Marketing is one of the most complex and yet most important functions influencing the overall success of sport organizations. Through their marketing efforts, sport organizations must package, promote, and deliver products to their consumers in a profitable manner. You probably have heard the term *sport marketing* in many contexts, and you might be wondering exactly what it means. That's a good question because sport marketing is composed of several elements, and the term *sport marketing* frequently is used incorrectly. People tend to define marketing in terms of their experiences, instead of recognizing one of the most important roles of marketing—carrying out the mission of an organization.

Some corporate executives might describe sport marketing as selling goods and services to generate a profit. But sport marketing is *more* than selling. People working in advertising and public relations might consider sport marketing as obtaining Super Bowl tickets for clients or entertaining a corporate sponsor at the U.S. Open Golf Tournament. But sport marketing is *more* than advertising and public relations. Individuals providing services for professional athletes might view sport marketing as arranging for athletes to attend the grand opening of a shopping mall or arranging to have corporate executives play tennis with Andre Agassi or Steffi Graf. But sport marketing is *more* than community relations.

Pitts and Stotlar (2002) defined sport marketing as "the process of designing and implementing activities for the production, pricing, promotion and distribution of a sport product or sport business product to satisfy the needs or desires of consumers and to achieve the company's objectives" (p. 79). Marketing is a complex function, and sport marketing is even more complex because sport has certain characteristics that make the product unique. A brief examination of some unique sport qualities proposed by Mullin, Hardy, and

LEARNING OBJECTIVES

After studying this chapter, you will be able to do the following:

1. Recognize how a marketing plan is linked to an organization's mission statement and core values.
2. Assess the present and future market climate for a sport or event by conducting a SWOT (strengths, weakness, opportunities, and threats) analysis.
3. Analyze the dimensions of a sport product, such as the game itself or an event.
4. Define product positioning and market niche.
5. Communicate images and messages of a sport product in ethical and socially responsible ways.
6. Define market segmentation and identify viable target audiences.
7. Discuss how sports are distributed to consumers.
8. Define packaging and selling a sport product.
9. Explain what is meant by the "promise" of a marketing plan.
10. Identify two sport marketing needs in the 21st century.

Sutton (2000) will show how sport as a product differs from other goods and services and therefore why it must be marketed uniquely.

1. Aspects of the sport experience are intangible. For example, you cannot touch the actual competition that takes place between two football teams. (You can, however, touch products associated with the experience such as equipment, the stadium, hats, T-shirts, videos, etc.) In addition,

Brooks (1994) pointed out that the sport product has an intangible dimension that is internally generated and represented by the psychic side of sport—participants' emotions and experiences. Examples include

- the high individuals experience when running their personal best time,
- the thrill individuals feel when winning a contest,
- the satisfaction individuals derive when overcoming challenges posed by competitors or the environment, and
- the pride individuals or teams feel when they compete to the best of their ability.

2. Sport is subjective and heterogeneous because the impressions, experiences, and interpretations about a sporting event may vary from person to person. If two individuals attend the same field hockey game, one may view the game as low scoring and unexciting. Yet, the other person may appreciate the strategy involved in the game and consider it interesting. It is difficult for a sport marketer to predict what impressions, experiences, and interpretations consumers will have about sporting events.

3. Sports are inconsistent and unpredictable because of injuries to players, the emotional state of players, the momentum of teams, and the weather. These factors contribute to the uncertain outcome of sports. Sport marketers have little control over these factors, yet the unpredictability has great appeal to spectators.

4. Sport is perishable because the sport event as it is being played is what spectators want to see. Few people are interested in seeing yesterday's soccer match or field hockey game. Consequently, marketers must focus on advance ticket sales. If the team's performance is poor or not up to expectations, gate receipts will suffer. Based on the perishability of sport competitions, sport marketers often offer tangible items (such as T-shirts, souvenirs, merchandise, etc.) that serve as lasting reminders of the overall sport experience.

5. As alluded to in the discussion of the intangible aspects of sports, sport involves emotions. Some spectators become emotionally attached to their teams and are referred to as fanatics or fans. Other consumers might purchase licensed products with team logos and uniform replicas as a way of identifying with their teams. Consumers often do not display such heightened emotions or psy-

chological attachment to other goods or products (such as vacuum cleaners). Like sport itself, sport consumers are unique as a result of their emotional connection to sport.

Given these unique characteristics, what factors should we consider in making decisions about packaging, promoting, and delivering sport products? Who will be attracted to the products, and how will the packaging, promoting, and delivering of the products influence the consumers' experiences and perceptions? What changes will be needed in the packaging, promoting, and delivering of sport products in the future? We will address these questions in this chapter. You will learn about the necessity of developing marketing activities that are responsive to the needs of society; the elements of the marketing mix; how to select consumers for sport; how companies develop socially responsible sport marketing plans; and the integrated process involved in packaging, positioning, promoting, and delivering sport to consumers. In addition, you will learn to appreciate the dilemmas faced by sport managers in implementing sport marketing plans. Finally, we will discuss future challenges and trends in sport marketing.

As you will learn, marketing sport is a challenging but exciting undertaking. Nevertheless, sport marketing decisions should be based on sound and rational information. The sport industry was last estimated at $213 billion (Broughton, Lee, & Nethery, 1999), making it the sixth largest industry in the United States. A number of resources are currently available that offer valuable information and insight regarding sport, marketing, and the marketing of sport. See the "For More Information" section on page 186.

Ethics and Social Responsibility

Every sport organization has a purpose for existing. This purpose is defined in its mission statement, which represents the core values of the organization. Sport does not exist in isolation; rather, it is influenced by societal issues and trends. Therefore, the mission statement of a sport organization must also consider the values and beliefs that are most prevalent in the environments in which it operates.

Since marketing is critical in encouraging consumers to purchase an organization's products or engage in an organization's activities and events, sport marketers should also acknowledge societal norms and concerns and should not engage in any exploitive or unethical practices (Laczniak, Burton, & Murphy, 1999). Sport marketing practices should therefore be derived from and consistent with the mission statement and core values of the organization to ensure that the overall packaging, promotion, and delivery of sport will be done in a socially responsible manner. Marketing in an honest and ethical manner that creates a distinctive and socially responsible image is the best way to position a sport product in the market. Being ethically and socially responsible will also increase the likelihood of the organization achieving marketing success and customer satisfaction.

Developing a Sport Marketing Plan

Marketing plans serve as road maps or game plans for an organization's marketing activities. Having a well-developed marketing plan is key to the marketing success of sport organizations. The four primary elements of a marketing plan—product, price, place, and promotion—comprise the **marketing mix**. These elements are well established in the marketing industry and are universally known as the four Ps.

- *Product*—A tangible good (object), a service, or an intangible quality that satisfies consumers' wants or needs.

- *Price*—The value of the product and the costs the consumer must accept to obtain the product. Consumers determine the value of a product by balancing the expected benefits of buying the product against the expected costs of the product. When the benefits derived from a product exceed the costs attached to the product, then consumers believe the product has value.

- *Place*—The distribution channels that allow consumers to access or obtain the product.

- *Promotion*—The integrated communication and public relations activities that communicate, inform, persuade, and motivate consumers to purchase the product.

marketing plans—Comprehensive frameworks for identifying and achieving an organization's marketing goals and objectives.

marketing mix—The elements of product, price, place, and promotion, which are manipulated by

sport marketers in striving to achieve marketing goals and objectives.

To maximize their success, marketers develop strategic plans to manipulate the four Ps in a variety of ways depending on the mission of the organization and the fluctuations of the market (Pitts & Stotlar, 2002). This manipulation is critical to carrying out a marketing plan successfully. However, to devise a comprehensive plan for achieving marketing goals and objectives, factors beyond the four Ps must be considered. In this chapter we present a 10-step process for developing a sport marketing plan called the 10 Ps—purpose, product, projecting the market, position, players, package, price, promotion, place, and promise. This process, shown in figure 10.1, illustrates that, while the four Ps are central to the marketing plan, they

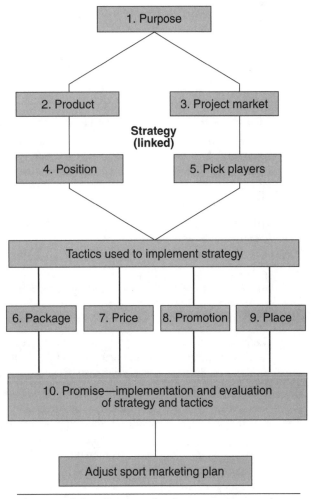

Figure 10.1 Steps in developing a sport marketing plan.

Adapted, by permission, from B.G. Pitts and D.K. Stotlar, 2002. *Fundamentals of sportmarketing* (2nd ed.). Morgantown, WV: Fitness Information Technology, Inc. 87.

must be integrated with other elements to achieve optimal sport marketing success.

Step 1: Identify the Purpose of the Sport Marketing Plan

Step 1 involves clarifying the purpose of the sport marketing plan and linking the plan to the organization's mission and core values. Before packaging, promoting, and delivering can occur, sport marketers must establish a context to provide an orientation and direction for what they are trying to accomplish and how they expect to do so. Establishing a context requires sport managers to examine the organization's core values as described in its mission statement. If the organization does not have a mission statement, then a mission statement that identifies core values must be written. It is important that all individuals in the organization be involved in the process of writing a mission statement so that everyone will be committed to carrying out the mission and acting in

accordance with the core values. Covey (1989) says, "an organizational mission statement is important because it creates in people's hearts and minds a frame of reference, a set of criteria or guidelines by which they will govern themselves. . . . They have bought into the changeless core of what the organization is about" (p. 143).

A sport marketing plan derived from and consistent with the organization's mission statement and core values is necessary to ensure that the packaging, promotion, and delivery of sport will be conducted in socially responsible ways. The National Basketball Association's (NBA) mission, presented in figure 10.2, provides a good example of a mission statement with core values.

The mission of the Cincinnati, Ohio, River Front Classic (RFC), which is a football event featuring two historically Black colleges/universities (HBCU) is to become a successful, nationally renowned corporate and community partner for the benefit of students through the presentation of events that promote education. This event uses

---

The NBA's mission is to be the most respected and successful sports league organization in the world.

We aim to achieve our mission, and thereby continue to enhance the economic value of our teams, by
working to make basketball the most popular global sport and to maintain the NBA's position as the best in basketball; creating and maximizing business opportunities and relationships arising from basketball; and capitalizing on our key assets and strengths—our people, skills, experience, reputation, and innovative and entrepreneurial spirit—to expand beyond basketball into related activities worldwide.

We have a commitment to excellence
We do every task as well as it can be done, reflecting quality and attention to detail at every stage—from inception, to planning, to execution.

We strive at all times to live by and act in accordance with the following core values:

Innovation We encourage entrepreneurship and innovative thinking. We create opportunities and do not merely react to those that come our way. We aim always to be on the cutting edge and ahead of all competition.

Integrity We conduct ourselves in accordance with the highest standards of honesty, truthfulness, ethics, and fair dealing.

Respect We value our individuality and diversity. We are civil and respectful to each other, to our fans, customers, and business associates. We take pride in our success, but we are not arrogant.

Social responsibility We recognize and embrace our responsibility—as a corporate citizen in the world, in the United States, and in local communities to support causes that help people to achieve an improved quality of life.

Teamwork We work hard together in a true cooperative spirit and without regard for departmental lines or individual goals. Our priority is always to provide the best possible service to all our constituencies.

Workplace environment We believe in equal opportunity, the importance of job satisfaction, and that each employee has an important role in achieving our mission. We empower each employee to make job-related decisions commensurate with the employee's experience and level of responsibility. We promote and reward our employees solely on the basis of merit, and we evaluate not only achievement but also whether the employee's conduct reflects conformity with our mission and values.

Figure 10.2 Mission statement of the National Basketball Association.

Reprinted, by permission, from the National Basketball Association.

HBCU football as the centerpiece for integrating sport, entertainment, business, and education. A substantial percentage of the proceeds of the event are donated to the respective universities that participate in the event. The RFC marketing plan, which includes student development initiatives, educational programs, corporate opportunities for Black businesses, and uplifting activities for the Black community, is in direct alignment with its mission statement and is an illustration of ethical and socially responsible sport marketing.

In addition to having the mission statement to guide the marketing planning process, marketers must also have clearly defined goals and objectives that will determine the overall success of the marketing plan. Goals refer to the general summary statements of expected outcomes, and objectives refer to the specific activities that will enable the marketer to obtain the expected outcomes. When the goals and objectives are achieved and are in alignment with the organization's mission, the marketing plan is deemed a success.

Step 2: Analyzing the Sport Product

In step 2, the marketer analyzes the sport product and determines whether the product is a tangible good, a game or event, or a service. The sport product is three dimensional (Pitts, Fielding, & Miller, 1994). It is composed of tangible goods, support services, and the game or event itself (see figure 10.3). Goods include tangible items such as clothing (e.g., shoes, aerobic apparel) and equipment (e.g., automobiles and car parts, tack used in horse racing, mountain bikes). Support services include activities or programs that are ancillary to sport but necessary for its operation (e.g., game officials, athletic trainers, sport psychologists). The game or event itself is composed of two dimensions: the core product and product extensions (Mullin, Hardy, & Sutton, 2000).

The core product of the event is the actual competition (e.g., the players and coaches on the competing teams, the sport activity itself, and the facility in which the competition takes place). Brooks (1994) proposed the following tangible elements in the core sport product:

- The type of sport—football, basketball, gymnastics
- The participants—athletes (beginner, elite, professional), coaches (volunteer, part-time salaried, full-time professionals), and the

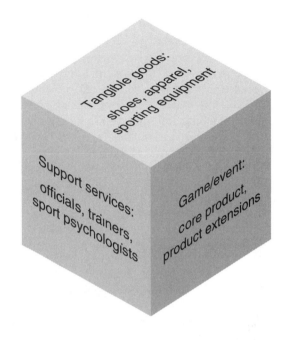

Figure 10.3 Three dimensions of the sport product.

environment (challenging golf courses, difficult mountains)
- The team—Notre Dame, Michigan, Dallas Cowboys

The product extensions are the supplemental ancillary items, such as the mascot, music, halftime entertainment, concessions, bands, cheerleaders, and so on, that are associated with the overall sport experience. Because of the flair and excitement of product extensions that are created around the core product, sport events are often viewed as a form of entertainment (e.g., NBA All-Star Game, Super Bowl, World Series, NCAA Final Four Basketball Championships, etc.).

As mentioned in the introduction of this chapter, the unique characteristics of sport as a product as well as the unique emotions experienced by sport consumers make marketing sport a challenging yet exciting endeavor. You must fully understand and appreciate the elements of the core product of sport as well as the core product extensions before you can develop an appropriate and effective marketing plan.

Step 3: Projecting the Market Climate

As mentioned previously, sport does not exist in isolation; it is profoundly influenced by market conditions. Therefore, step 3 is analyzing the past and current market climate to project and forecast the future market climate to see how it may affect sport marketing practices. Assessing the sport climate requires examining internal and external factors as they affect marketing efforts. For example, **internal factors** affecting the climate of Major League Baseball include players, owners, team management, and staff personnel. The media, corporate sponsors, advertisers, spectators, and the federal government represent examples of **external factors** that affect the climate of Major League Baseball.

internal factors—Factors inside a sport organization that affect the sport marketing climate (i.e., players, owners, team management, and staff personnel).

external factors—Factors outside of a sport organization that affect the sport marketing climate (e.g., media, corporate sponsors, advertisers, spectators, federal regulations, regulations of sport governing bodies).

Major League Strike

In 1994 Major League Baseball (MLB) was having one of its best years ever. Several players were striving to break long-standing records, and teams that had not contended for a league championship in many years were leading their leagues in the standings. Newly aligned divisions had created another tier of play-offs and wild card possibilities. This created great interest among spectators, which resulted in increased attendance and heightened press coverage. The game was reinvigorated and seemed to be making strides to reclaim its place as America's national pastime. Then the dispute between players and owners regarding possible implementation of a salary cap resulted in the longest players' strike in the history of U.S. professional sport.

The strike ended the 1994 season on August 11; there were no league championships and no World Series. Even the beginning of the 1995 season was delayed because the dispute between players and owners remained unresolved. MLB withdrew its participation in the newly formed Baseball Network and thus limited its television market. Finally, the courts forced the league to begin operations in May 1995 because the players and owners still had not settled their differences. In the fall of 1996 the owners and the players' association signed a new collective bargaining agreement. Although the terms of the agreement did not resolve the problems, it did provide stability for the league through the year 2000.

From a marketing perspective, MLB was faced with a disaster following the 1994 players' strike. The spectators viewed the players and owners as selfish and greedy and believed they did not care about the fans or the game. The situation had serious negative financial consequences for everyone directly or indirectly involved with the industry. Team management and staff personnel; the media; corporate sponsors and advertisers; food, beverage, and lodging businesses; and other support services in the communities all lost in the process. MLB needed a new marketing strategy to promote and sell the game.

LEARNING ACTIVITY

Using the MLB case study, analyze baseball's past market climate to project the future market climate. You might ask, What impact has the media had on baseball in the past? What impact will the media have on baseball in the future? What actions have been taken by the federal government in the past regarding the baseball industry, and what actions might the federal government take in the future? What kinds of relationships have advertisers and sponsors had with baseball owners in the past, and what benefits did each party derive? How might the relationships of advertisers and corporate sponsors with baseball owners change in the future?

Assessing the past market climate enables managers to identify factors associated with successful or failed marketing efforts. On the other hand, forecasting the future market climate requires reexamining the organization's mission. Assessing the (internal) strengths and weaknesses of an organization or event and the (external) opportunities and threats faced by an organization or event is called a **SWOT analysis** (Rowe, Mason, & Dickel, 1986). A SWOT analysis usually results in developing a new mission statement, which, in turn, will affect the marketing plan.

SWOT analysis—A management technique available to sport marketers to help them assess the strengths, weaknesses, opportunities, and threats of their organization.

For example, an assessment of the market climate of MLB between 1990 and 1995 might reveal the following information: escalating player salaries, confrontations between players and owners, federal court actions to settle disputes between players and owners, declining TV viewership, declining ticket sales, and the public's growing disenchantment with the game. A SWOT analysis of the future market climate of MLB might forecast the following:

- *Strengths*—History, tradition (America's national pastime), established spectator markets
- *Weaknesses*—Game too slow and too long, lack of TV viewership resulting in loss of advertisers and corporate sponsors
- *Opportunities*—Improve marketing of star players, interleague competition to stimulate team rivalries and spectator interest, new stadia
- *Threats*—Popularity of professional basketball and football; lack of interest in baseball among youth, women, and minority ethnic groups; erosion or loss of antitrust exemption

Given this past, present, and future market analysis, MLB may need to reexamine its mission statement and core values and determine a new mission.

Step 4: Positioning the Sport Product

Step 4 involves positioning the sport product. According to Shank (2002) positioning is defined as fixing your sport entity in the minds of consumers in the target market. The objective of positioning is to differentiate the sport product from competing products by creating a distinctive image of the product. Distinctive images are created in

SWOT Analysis of Women's Professional Basketball

An examination of the SWOT for two professional women's sport leagues such as the Women's National Basketball Association (WNBA) and the now defunct American Basketball League (ABL) provides another illustration of the manner in which internal and external factors may influence marketing success. The major strength of the WNBA was that it was a product of the NBA; however, a weakness of the ABL was its ownership by a small group of private investors. Consequently, the WNBA had the financial backing (from the NBA) to absorb the deficits (a strength), whereas the ABL had a limited budget and did not have the financial resources to absorb the financial losses incurred (a weakness). WNBA teams were located in large cities that were considered major U.S. markets (an opportunity); ABL teams were located primarily in midsize, medium-market cities (a threat). The WNBA games were held in NBA arenas (a strength), whereas the ABL games were held in collegiate and other smaller venues within their respective cities (somewhat of a weakness). Another major strength of the WNBA was its national media distribution (NBC, ESPN, and Lifetime); a major weakness of the ABL was its regional media distribution (Regional Sports Channels, Prime Network, and Black Entertainment Television). The ABL did not allow its players to participate in other basketball leagues (a weakness that limited players' appeal and exposure), whereas the WNBA allowed its players to participate in other professional women's basketball leagues (a strength that maximized the players' appeal and exposure). The WNBA season of competition was held during the summer months and did not compete with other girls'/women's basketball leagues (an opportunity), whereas the ABL season of competition was held during the "traditional" winter months, competing with girls' high school basketball and women's college basketball games (a threat).

The key to marketing success is for an organization's strengths and opportunities to outweigh its weaknesses and threats. Applying the SWOT analysis to the WNBA and ABL illustrates why the WNBA is still in existence and the ABL suspended operations midway through its third season. As did the marketers of the WNBA, sport marketers should therefore examine the present market conditions and seek to maximize their products' or events' strengths and opportunities and minimize their weaknesses and threats.

consumers' minds based on (1) the type of consumers that purchase the product, (2) the design of the product as well as the benefits offered by the product, (3) the price of the product, and (4) where the product/event takes place (i.e., the arena or facility). Products are often positioned by means of verbal and nonverbal communications to consumers. Sport images can be communicated through logos, symbols, and messages through TV and radio advertisements, public service announcements, jingles, press releases, news articles, and feature articles. For example, in 1995 Reebok developed a new TV advertisement about girls' participation in sport (see figure 10.4). This advertisement communicated a distinctive image to capture the attention of girls and women sport participants, spectators, and volunteers.

A sport product perceived by consumers as being unique is well positioned to compete successfully in selected markets, provided the images are positive. For example, posters and other printed materials used to promote the 1994 Gay Games showed camaraderie and support among the participants, which helped communicate an image of unity. This positioned the 1994 Gay Games for success with consumers in particular markets. The unique image also conveyed messages that were positive and socially responsible. Likewise, the Paralympics does an excellent job in communicating positive images of elite world-class athletes who are physically challenged by showing that these individuals can compete in athletic events just like athletes who are not physically challenged. The New Orleans, Louisiana, Bayou Classic (the largest and most popular Black college sport event in America) has been positioned as a sociocultural and festive entertainment event that contains market features that are particularly salient to the Black community. Many Black consumers who are not football fans attend the Bayou Classic in record-breaking numbers because of the image they have of the event as one that is exciting and culturally relevant (Armstrong, 1998, 2002).

As mentioned previously, the type of consumers that are attracted to an event may also contribute to the event's positioning. For example, ESPN's X-Games, NBC's Gravity Games, and so forth are sport events that attract Generation X-ers (individuals born between 1965 and 1976). Based on the needs and interests of the consumers of these events, the events contain daring and high-energy activities that contribute to their overall image. The effective positioning of sport events contributes enormously to their marketing success.

In their landmark work on public relations theory, Grunig and White (1992) suggested that effective communication practices consisted of several elements: (1) open and honest communications with the public, (2) images and messages that are socially responsible, (3) cooperation with the public and response to their interests, and (4) good faith relationships with the public. (See "Renaming the Washington Bullets" on p. 197.)

Along the same lines, in order to respect the sacred values and customs of many American Indians, a number of colleges and universities have replaced nicknames of their mascots and eradicated promotional gimmicks that reflected aspects of American Indian traditions and practices. Viewing marketing as a means of honest verbal and nonverbal communication that creates a distinctive and socially responsible image of a sport product is the best way to position a sport product in the market.

Positioning the sport product also involves establishing a specific niche for the product in the market. There are six distinct markets for sport. Primary markets are composed of (1) participants, (2) spectators, and (3) volunteers; and secondary markets are composed of (4) sponsors, (5) advertisers, and (6) athletes' endorsement of products and licensed products (Brooks, 1994). Examples of niches in primary markets include the following:

- Participants—Athletes, coaches, and game officials
- Spectators—Stadium attendees, television viewers, radio listeners, and newspaper or magazine readers

Video: Scenes from high school, many focusing on girls' sports: team practice, competition, traveling on the bus, hanging out at school, ultimately capturing moments of closeness among the players.

Audio: (girl) If you don't play . . . you can hang out . . . you can watch . . . you can brush your hair a lot . . . but you can never say, "I was a player." And you can never say, "I was on the team." And worst of all, you can never do all this incredible, exciting . . . hilarious stuff . . . with these girls who are like sisters. So all I'm trying to say is . . . my question is . . . wanna play?

Video: Just Another chance to Play on Planet Reebok.*

Figure 10.4 Images that encourage girls' participation in sport.

*Reprinted, by permission, from Reebok International Ltd.

Renaming the Washington Bullets

A story about the Washington Bullets demonstrates how Grunig and White's (1992) four steps might be applied. During the 1995-1996 season, Abe Pollin, owner of the Washington Bullets, decided the team nickname conveyed a negative image because bullets had nothing to do with basketball but everything to do with people being injured or killed by shooting incidents in Washington, D.C. and the surrounding communities. Pollin used open and honest communications with the public about the need to change the team's nickname (step 1). He involved the public in a promotional contest to determine a new team nickname, one that would convey a positive and socially responsible image of the team (step 2). The contest was an example of an organization working cooperatively with the public and responding to the public's interest (step 3). A corporate sponsor contributed prizes for some contestants, thus generating interest and publicity and establishing a good faith relationship with the public (step 4). Moreover, an antiviolence campaign was launched in conjunction with the team nickname contest. This campaign communicated the message that the Washington Bullets organization was a good corporate citizen wanting to help the community solve an important social problem. The promotional nickname contest resulted in the team being renamed the Washington Wizards.

- Volunteers—Social hosts at sports events, statisticians, team managers

Secondary markets include the following:

- Advertisers—Use sports to target and communicate their products to large groups of spectators (e.g., stadium banners and signs, TV and radio advertisements)
- Corporate sponsors—Use sports to target and communicate positive and distinctive images about their products to large groups of spectators (e.g., Cadillac as sponsor of golf tournaments, Volvo as sponsor of tennis tournaments)
- Athletes' endorsement of products and licensed products—Use sports personalities and celebrities or distinctive symbols, logos, or trademarks to have consumers perceive products as popular or prestigious

Step 5: Picking the Players: Analyzing and Targeting Consumers

In step 5, the marketer analyzes the market and targets consumers, a process that we can envision as "picking the players" that will allow the marketing plan to be a success. This involves grouping consumers according to common characteristics. As mentioned previously in the discussion of the unique aspects of sport, sport consumers are heterogeneous and have different wants, needs, interests, and behaviors regarding sport. To appeal to the uniqueness of sport consumers, marketers must have information about them. According to Francese (1993), market research is conducted to obtain information about sport consumers in four areas: demographics, psychographics, media preferences, and purchasing behavior (see figure 10.5).

Information collected through market research enables marketers to segment consumers into clusters according to selected characteristics. This process is called market segmentation and is used to identify target audiences. Demographic segmentation refers to clustering sport consumers based on their age, gender, income, race/ethnicity, education, and place of residence. Psychographic segmentation refers to appealing to consumers' attitudes, interests, and lifestyles (see chapter 7). Market segmentation based on media preference would cluster consumers based on their sport media preferences (such as television, radio, Internet, and magazines/publications). Purchasing behavior as a means of market segmentation refers to grouping customers according to the frequency of usage behavior (such as how often or how frequently they attend an event or purchase a product).

Market segmentation allows the sport marketer to identify smaller clusters of sport consumers who may exhibit similar wants, needs, and interests regarding sport. This process involves target marketing, which is zeroing in on specific consumers who are most likely to find the product appealing rather than attempting to sell products to all consumers. Target marketing involves identifying specific consumer groups that will most likely buy the product and therefore help sport organizations meet the goals and objectives of the marketing plan. For example, a sport equipment manufacturer might identify the primary target

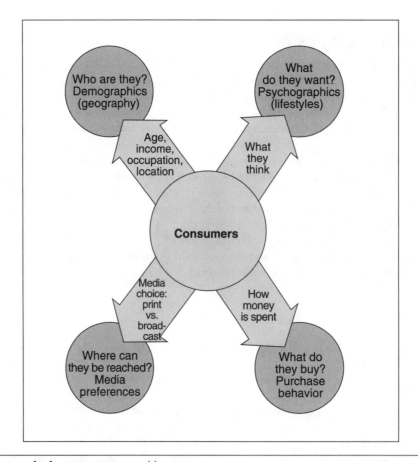

Figure 10.5 Types of information generated by consumers.

Reprinted, by permission, from Francese, P. (1990). How to manage consumer information. In D. Crispell (Ed.), *The insider's guide to demographic know-how* (pp. 9-14), Ithaca, NY: American Demographics Press.

audience as males 12 to 16 years of age who are interested in in-line skating and who watch MTV.

Due to the growth of ethnic minority populations and the increased ethnic diversity of sport consumers, sport marketers have begun to increase their awareness of the need to devise marketing strategies to reach Black, Hispanic, and Asian consumers (Armstrong, 1998; Hofacre & Burman, 1992; McCarthy & Stillman, 1998). Moreover, research has indicated that ethnic minorities do have affinities for certain sports (Bernstein, 1999), and their spending power as consumers is increasing. According to the Selig Center for Economic Growth, a research organization at the University of Georgia, the total Black annual buying power in 1999 was $533 billion (up 72.9% since 1990), Hispanic buying power was $383 billion (up 84.4% for the same time period), and Asian buying power was $229 billion (up 102%). These characteristics have made ethnic minority populations economically attractive and potentially profitable consumer segments for sport marketers.

In addition to awakening to the ethnic minority markets, sport marketers have also realized the importance of devising marketing strategies to appeal to female consumers. Until recently, women were not viewed as a viable target market for men's sports. However, with women's increased purchase of men's sport teams' merchandise, women's increased spectatorship of men's sports (such as the NBA, NFL, MLB, and NHL), the growth of women's sports, and the financial gains women have made as consumers along with their general influence over family purchases and consumption decisions, they have also become an important target market for sports (Barbano, 1998; Sutton and Wattlington, 1994). Moreover, the Title IX generation (women and girls born after 1972) is young, female, and relatively affluent. These are three of the most highly desirable attributes sought by marketers.

Another group of consumers that has attracted the attention of sport marketers are the Generation X consumers (individuals born between 1965 and 1976). These consumers have exhibited behaviors that differ from other markets and illustrate how demographics (age) and psychographics (attitudes and interests) may interact to influence sport consumer behavior (Turco, 1996). As al-

Courtesy of Celso Rodriguez, *El Tiempo*, Toledo, Ohio

In response to the increased diversity of sport consumers, sport marketers are devising marketing strategies to reach Black, Hispanic, and Asian consumers.

luded to previously, sport events such as the X-Games and the Gravity Games illustrate that Generation X-ers are a target market to be reckoned with. In addition, consumer characteristics such as race/ethnicity, age, and gender may be integrated or combined to create specific target markets.

Once target audiences are identified, a marketer can develop a strategy to reach them. The strategy involves customizing the elements in the marketing mix to appeal to the wants, needs and interests of the target markets. A key to success in product positioning (discussed in step 4) is communicating an image for the product that will appeal to the target audience. For example, the 1994 Gay Games and Paralympics advertisements communicated honest and positive images that encouraged participants, spectators, and sponsors from specific target markets to get involved in these events. Regarding Black college sports events such as the River Front Classic and Bayou Classic previously discussed, advertisements and core product extensions were effective because they were specifically designed to appeal to the target market (i.e., the Black community). In the case of the X-Games and Gravity Games, they were also customized to appeal to Generation X-ers.

Picking the players is a critical aspect of the marketing plan. Without consumers, sport organizations would not be successful in reaching their marketing goals and objectives. Therefore, it is important that sport marketers target the right groups of consumers. Criteria for selecting the "right" (i.e., viable) target markets include factors such as the size of the target group, the amount of resources available to the target group, and whether the target group is accessible to the organization. The determination of whether a target market is acceptable varies among sport organizations largely based on the organization's marketing goals and objectives. For example, a target market of 100 students for a football event that attracts over 100,000 consumers may not be considered an acceptable size to warrant specific marketing attention. However, a target market of a hundred students for a fitness club with a membership of approximately 200 is an acceptable size and may make a big impact on the fitness club's overall success. With the changing demographic representations, psychographic profiles, media preferences, and purchase behaviors of sport consumers, picking the right players is often a challenging undertaking for sport marketers. Nevertheless, it is necessary for marketing success.

Once marketers have identified the target consumers for their product, they must engage in a number of strategies that will help draw targeted consumers to the sport organization. Steps 6 through 10 of the 10 Ps process will describe strategies that help marketers successfully attract their target audiences.

Step 6: Packaging the Sport Product

Packaging the sport product includes presenting the product in the best possible manner to encourage selected target audiences to purchase it. Because consumers differ, it is necessary to present the product in different ways. Packaging tangible or industrial sport products involves explaining the benefits of the products, such as the strength and longevity of metal bats, the comfort and safety of helmets, and the expanded sweet spot of oversize tennis rackets. However, packaging the core product of sport (the game or event itself) involves communicating about the expectations of the product and providing information before the point of purchase. For example, sport marketers might package the game or event as family entertainment and offer family ticket plans. Or marketers might package sport as a good place to make business contacts and offer business ticket plans. A sport organization might want to be seen as caring about the community and thus offer group discount ticket plans for social service and charitable organizations.

Another aspect of product packaging is the manner in which product extensions (discussed in step 2) are included in the overall sport experience. For instance, music, halftime promotions, and entertainment contribute to the overall packaging of a sport event such as a basketball game. There may be consumers who are not specifically attracted to the core product (the basketball game); instead they may be attracted to the way the core product is packaged (i.e., with music, fun, excitement, and entertainment).

In addition, it is important to note that another aspect of the sport product is the associated licensed merchandise. Many sport teams and events offer goods such as hats, T-shirts, jackets, and other apparel as well as nonapparel items such as watches, novelty items, memorabilia, and decorative items that are perceived as extensions and representations of the teams. Sport consumers' affinity to teams' licensed products is noteworthy. Based on research by the National Sporting Goods Manufacturers Association, Shank (2002) reported that total U.S. retail sales for licensed products for the four major professional sport leagues (i.e., the NBA, NFL, MLB, and NHL) and colleges and universities more than doubled in less than a 10-year time span (increasing from $5.35 billion in 1990 to $10.95 billion in 1999). Therefore, sport marketers should be mindful of the various tangible and intangible extensions of their sport products or events.

Packaging the sport product to secure financial support from corporations is an especially important aspect of the marketing plan called sponsorship. Sponsorship involves an agreement between a sport organization or event and a corporation wherein the corporation pays a fee to the organization or event to acquire the rights to affiliate with the organization or event. Sponsorships can help corporations increase sales, change attitudes, heighten awareness, and build and maintain positive relationships with consumers. A sport marketer must conduct research to learn what benefits corporations are seeking through sponsorship. This information is necessary before beginning negotiations with corporate sponsors. In negotiations, marketers must be flexible about modifying packages to meet the interests and needs of the corporate sponsor. However, flexibility does not mean that the sport product should be misrepresented or that claims of benefits should be exaggerated. The exchange between the sport organization and the corporate sponsor must be honest and fair in order to maintain and strengthen a trusting relationship (McCarville & Copeland, 1994).

Sponsorships of women's sport products provide unique opportunities for corporations to communicate to women that they honestly care about women's issues. By sponsoring women's sports, corporations can demonstrate that they are not simply promoting their products but that they are taking a special interest in women and they want to generate goodwill among women. For instance, State Farm Insurance Company sponsors women's professional skating, tennis, golf, college basketball, and college volleyball with a magazine ad that says, "We will insure that girls will always get to play." According to David E. Jacobson, senior editor of *International Events Group Sponsorship Report*, the message is most important in women's sponsorship (Shank, 2002).

The way a product is packaged either directly or indirectly influences or is influenced by every other aspect of the 10 Ps process outlined in this chapter (such as who will be attracted to the product or event, its relevance to the current market climate, what its price should be, how it should be promoted, and how it will be delivered). Therefore, it is important for sport marketers to understand how all the different elements that contribute to product packaging influence the success of the marketing plan.

Step 7: Pricing the Sport Product

Step 7 is determining the value of the product by assigning it a price. Price is the element that is most visible and flexible because of discounts, rebates, and coupons. According to Pitts and Stotlar (2002), marketers should consider four factors when developing a pricing strategy:

1. Consumer—Analyze all aspects of the consumer, including demographics, psychographics, purchasing behaviors, and media preferences.

2. Competitor—Analyze the consumer's perception of the product value compared with all competing products, and analyze the competitors' prices.

3. Company—Analyze the costs involved in producing the product (materials, equipment, salaries, rent) and set a minimum price to cover the costs.

4. Climate—Analyze external factors, such as laws pertaining to pricing, government regulations, the economic situation, and the political situation.

Normally, money is exchanged for products. In sport marketing, however, trading is a common practice. According to Gray (1996), sport organizations or events frequently trade tickets, stadium signage, and scoreboard advertisement for goods and services. For example, marketers of a tennis tournament might make trades with corporate sponsors to include tickets for tennis balls, stadium signage for food and beverages for a hospitality tent, and scoreboard advertisement for the use of vehicles to transport players and officials.

The value of a product is determined by factors other than price. Each consumer has attitudes, preferences, beliefs, and a certain amount of expendable money. Besides price, these factors influence how individuals determine the value of a product. Because the value of a product is unique to each consumer, it is important to develop a pricing strategy that will appeal to as many different consumers as possible. For example, sport franchises set different prices for corporate season ticket holders, charitable organizations, group ticket purchasers, mini-season ticket purchasers, family ticket purchasers, and single ticket purchasers.

Consumers tend to equate price with value. Therefore, a new sport franchise should price tickets comparable to competing products (other sporting events, movies, theater, other entertainment) rather than set a lower price. Consumers might equate a lower price with an inferior product.

Corporate sponsorships in sport.

© S. Varone/Photo Network

Lead time is important to sport pricing. There are more day-of-the-game or walk-up sales at a Major League Baseball game than at an NBA basketball game because there are many more games and seats available at lower prices in baseball than in basketball (Mullin, Hardy, & Sutton, 2000).

Sport pricing is complex and critical to the success of the marketing plan. However, price is one aspect of the marketing plan that may be readily changed (i.e., slightly increased or slightly decreased). For example, it is not unusual for sport organizations to alter their prices to attract different consumers (e.g., students may pay a different price for event tickets than the general public pays). Sport organizations may also change prices according to the market environment (i.e., lowering prices during a recession or economic downturn) or the team's performance (i.e., as a team's performance dramatically improves, so may the price of game tickets increase). In the final analysis, sport marketers must determine how consumers perceive the value of the product compared with all other competing products and determine an appropriate price.

Step 8: Promoting the Sport Product

Step 8 involves communicating the product's image to the selected target audiences. Promoting sport products involves implementing a mix of activities that will best (1) communicate the desired image of the product to the target audiences, (2) educate and inform the target audiences about the product and its benefits, and (3) persuade the target audiences to purchase the product. Elements that compose a promotion strategy (i.e., the promotional mix) include advertising, publicity, activities and inducements, public relations (including community relations and media relations), personal selling, and sponsorship.

• *Advertising*—One-way paid messages about the sport product (newspapers, magazines, TV, radio, direct mail, scoreboards, in-arena signage, pocket schedules, game programs, posters, outdoor advertising, the Internet).

• *Publicity*—Nonpaid communication about a sport product in which the sponsor is usually not identified and the message reaches the public because it is newsworthy (news releases, TV and radio public service announcements).

• *Activities and inducements*—Promotions to encourage consumers to purchase the sport product (giveaways, coupons, free samples, cash refunds, contests, raffles).

• *Public relations*—Overall plan for communicating a positive image about a product to the public, including implementing community and media relations activities and programs. For example, through their "Be Fit" campaign, the WNBA seeks to communicate the importance of being physically active. Moreover, the WNBA players, coaches, and administrators are involved in a number of public relations activities that promote awareness of breast cancer and the need for women to take an active role in early detection. Both of these examples contribute to the WNBA's positioning as a socially responsible sport organization that seeks to address some of the issues that directly or indirectly affect their consumers, both male and female.

• *Community relations*—Activities and programs to meet the interests and needs of the public and, by so doing, establish good faith relationships with the public (youth sport clinics, athlete autograph signing opportunities, collecting food items at sport arenas to help people in the community). For example, the National Hockey League established the Diversity Task Force in 1994 to introduce economically disadvantaged children of diverse ethnic backgrounds to the game of hockey. The Diversity Task Force implemented several grassroots community relations programs to reach specific target audiences: The Annual Willie O'Ree All-Star Game, named after the first Black player in the NHL, celebrates the successes of the individual inner city programs, as their top players, ages 10 to 12 years old, compete in an East-West game; the Diversity Task Force Campership program provides economically disadvantaged youth with the opportunity to attend summer hockey camps throughout North America and receive on-ice hockey instruction; and the Coolest Kids Ice Hockey Tournament features regional boys and girls selected from teams that participated in the summer hockey camps program organized by the Diversity Task Force. With the growing need for sport organizations to be socially responsible, community relations activities that garner favorable relationships with the public are essential for marketing success.

• *Media relations*—Maintaining networks and positive relations with individuals in the media to obtain positive media exposure for a sport product (schedule informal and formal information sessions with media representatives). Because of the pervasive influence the media has on marketing success, sport marketers must make concerted efforts to create a positive relationship between their sport event and the media. This may be accomplished by providing the media with press releases, having news conferences, having media day events (in which the media are invited to interact with the players, coaches, and administrators), providing media guides for the respective sport events, and so on. Each of these activities promotes active involvement from the media, which will subsequently contribute to relationship building with the community.

• *Personal selling*—Direct face-to-face communication with individuals, groups, or organizations to sell tickets, luxury suites or boxes, or sponsorships. Personal selling is one of the most important activities in the promotional mix because it is the revenue-producing element. Sport marketers consider personal selling to be unique and highly effective because it involves face-to-face interaction with the target audiences rather than mass communication to thousands of consumers. A personal interaction with consumers allows salespeople to adapt messages based on feedback, communicate more information to the target audience, guarantee that the target audience will pay attention to the message being delivered, and develop a long-term relationship with the target audience. Successful salespeople realize they must adapt their sales pitch according to the selling situation. For instance, selling women's sports is different from selling men's sports. Research shows that the majority of people who watch women's sports are either young career professionals with daughters or older, retired persons with high levels of disposable income. These spectators value the following aspects of sport: quality sport, exemplary graduation rates, high standards of ethical conduct, and articulate young athletes who make contributions to their communities (Lopiano, 2002). In making their sales presentations, salespeople should emphasize these values. For instance, the sales pitch might emphasize hardworking players giving 100% effort, dedicated players who are serious students, talented young athletes who are well spoken, caring athletes who give back to their communities, and an honest sports program. Personal selling complements the other promotional activities by educating consumers about what they are experiencing and pointing out the benefits they are deriving.

• *Sponsorship*—A form of promotion that involves the partnership between sport organizations or events and corporate entities. Sponsorship agreements allow sport organizations and corporations to meet their marketing objectives. Sponsorship has exceeded traditional forms of promotions (Shank, 2002) and has become quite lucrative. For example, an estimated 67% (which is approximately $5.9 billion of the $8.7 billion spent on all sponsorships) is spent on the sponsoring of sport events (Shank, 2002). Corporations make expensive investments in sport for a number of reasons, such as (1) to establish or improve their image (via association with high-visibility events), (2) to promote their products, thereby increasing sales, (3) to display goodwill, and (4) to obtain access and exposure to the events' target markets. For example, sport events such as the Super Bowl, the Olympics, and the NCAA football and basketball championships are especially attractive to corporate sponsors. Sport events also benefit from the sponsorship arrangement because the corporations often provide sport events with products, services, and financial resources. Obtaining sport sponsorships is important for the overall marketing success of sports because sponsorships often provide sport marketers with the resources necessary to package (as discussed in step 6), promote, and deliver their events.

Promotions are perhaps the most visible aspect of the marketing plan and are related to every aspect of the 10 Ps process. For example, promotions communicate something about the consumers, the product, packaging and position, the price, and the channels in which the product will be distributed. The successful use of the various promotional elements presented in this chapter therefore requires an understanding of the following:

• The factors that influence the thoughts, perceptions, and actions of the target audience
• Clear promotional objectives (regarding sales, promoting awareness, etc.)
• The appropriate promotional mix tool (radio, television, newspapers, etc.) to use given the uniqueness of the sport product or event
• Other aspects of the marketing plan coordinated with the promotional mix elements to create an integrated strategy that will achieve the marketing goals and objectives

Step 9: Placing the Sport Product

Step 9 is analyzing the place of the sport product. **Place** refers to the location of the sport product (stadium, arena), the point of origin for distributing the product (ticket sales at the stadium, sales by a toll-free telephone number), the geographic location of the target markets (global, national, regional, state, communities, cities), and other channels that are important to consider regarding

Nike Sponsorship of The Ohio State University

The essence of sport sponsorship may be illustrated in the case of The Ohio State University (OSU) and Nike. Largely due to (1) the popularity of OSU among sport consumers throughout the United States, (2) the high national visibility of OSU athletics, and (3) the tradition of excellence and success experienced by OSU athletes, Nike entered into a sponsorship with OSU valued at $11.4 million (in which Nike contributed $8.4 million worth of equipment for OSU's athletic teams and $3 million in cash to the OSU account). These product and financial contributions made an enormous contribution to OSU's athletic teams and events. Nike received the promotional license or right to have its logo placed on the uniforms of OSU athletic teams and also received the right to sell Nike products and apparel throughout OSU's campus. Any exposure for OSU athletics also meant exposure for Nike. Thus, the sponsorship between OSU and Nike created a win–win relationship, in which both entities received promotional benefits. Sport marketers seeking sponsorships from corporations must be sure that their sport events will

1. enable the corporations to obtain a competitive advantage and meet their marketing goals and objectives,
2. be a good fit with the image and philosophy of the corporation, and
3. provide a link to the consumers the corporation is seeking to attract.

Therefore, sport marketers are usually required to develop sponsorship proposals outlining what the sport event offers sponsors, what the sport event expects to receive from sponsors, and how the win–win situations will be implemented and evaluated.

---

how target audiences may access the product (such as time, day, season, or month in which a product is offered, as well as the media distribution outlets consumers may use). Factors related to the physical location of the sport can have a favorable or unfavorable impact on the marketing plan. To ensure a favorable impact, the sport facility must be easily accessible (highway systems, parking, walkways, ramps); have an attractive physical appearance (well maintained and painted); have a pleasant, convenient, and functional environment (quick and easy access to concessions, clean bathrooms, smoke-free and odor-free environment); and have safe and pleasant surroundings (adequate public safety and security personnel, attractive neighborhood).

place—The comprehensive manner in which sport is distributed to consumers.

Sport is unique in the way it is distributed to consumers. The production and consumption of the product occur simultaneously for spectators attending sport events in stadia or arenas. The sport product is also distributed to consumers, nationally and globally, through the electronic media of television (regular cable and pay-per-view), radio, and Internet broadcasts.

Ticket distribution is another critical aspect of sport distribution. The objective of a ticket distri-

bution system is to make consumer purchases accessible, easy, quick, and convenient. Some approaches used by sport organizations include using outside companies such as Ticket Master; ticket outlets at local banks, shopping malls, and grocery stores; mobile van units that transport ticket personnel and operations to various locations throughout the community; on-site stadium and arena ticket sales with expanded hours of operation, toll-free telephone numbers, and will-call pickup arrangements.

Place is a critical aspect of the marketing plan. A sport product may be packaged with exciting extensions, communicated effectively to the target audiences, and offered at a reasonable price, but if the consumers cannot access the event (e.g., due to time or location barriers), the marketing of the event will not be a success. Therefore, the overall objective of placing (and thus distributing) the sport product is to facilitate consumers' ability to take part in the sport experience (or purchase the sport product) in a timely and convenient manner, thereby promoting marketing success.

Step 10: Promise of the Sport Marketing Plan

Step 10 is evaluating the extent to which the marketing plan met its promise to help achieve the organization's mission. This evaluation requires obtaining feedback (from inside and outside the organization) about the marketing plan. The feedback must then be analyzed and evaluated. The evaluation should focus on determining the extent to which the plan helped the organization achieve its mission by acting in accordance with the core values of the organization. For example, Reebok might establish a mission "to diversify its products to appeal to girls and women" based on a core value of "establishing positive relationships with all segments of the community." Obtaining feedback from girls and women about the Reebok TV advertisement would be a good way to evaluate this element of the marketing plan. The evaluation might conclude that the TV advertisement achieved the mission and did so in a manner that was consistent with the core values. To evaluate the effectiveness of the marketing plans for some of the Black college sport events that specifically seek to empower the Black community sociologically and economically, marketers may evaluate the number of students who attended the event, examine the financial contributions the events made to the respective HBCU universities, and examine the economic contributions of the event to the local economies.

In some cases, a marketing plan might not have a clear purpose linked with the organization's mission and core values. In these cases, an evaluation of the marketing plan might show that it is not helping the organization achieve its mission or, even worse, that it is reflecting poorly on the organization. For example, the Washington Redskins might establish a mission to "be the most respected and successful football team in the NFL" based on a core value of "being civil and respectful to each other, to fans, and business associates." Obtaining feedback from fans, business associates, and others might indicate that the team nickname Redskins is offensive to some people. An evaluation of the team nickname, as an element of the marketing plan, might conclude that the nickname is not helping the organization achieve its mission and, even worse, is communicating a negative image of the organization. In this case, the management of the franchise might consider selecting a new team nickname that will communicate a positive image and be viewed as socially responsible. The mission and core values of the organization should be considered in selecting a new team nickname.

As these examples indicate, linking the purpose of the marketing plan to the organization's mission and core values helps ensure that the plan will be socially responsible. Sport marketers who develop marketing plans linked to the organization's mission and core values are being proactive. According to Covey (1989), "reactive people are driven by feelings, by circumstances, by conditions, and by their environment. Proactive people are driven by values—carefully thought about, selected, and internalized values" (p. 72). Sport marketers who are proactive will achieve the promise of the marketing plan because their actions will be socially responsible and will help fulfill the mission of the organization.

Challenges and Directions in Sport Marketing

In many segments of the sport industry, sport marketers are pressured to increase their product sales in order to generate increased revenues for their organizations. This pressure poses a challenge. Because sport marketers are involved in persuading consumers to buy, they run the risk of exaggerating or misrepresenting their products in an effort to sell them. Today, and in the future, sport marketers should recognize this risk and monitor their marketing strategies to ensure that they communicate honest images and messages about their products that are consistent with the core values of their organizations.

Also, even though sport is quite popular, sport marketers must not market sport based on the "Field of Dreams" supposition: "If you build it, they will come!" This means that the overall excitement and popularity of sport will not replace the need for strategic marketing decisions. Moreover, as competition (with movies, arts, entertainment, etc.) for consumers increases, and as sport organizations are required to be more profitable, sport marketers will need to increase their understanding of basic marketing principles as applied to the sport industry.

Sport, like other businesses, operates in a global market and must respond to the rapidly changing racial and ethnic demographics in the societies in which it operates. One factor that sport marketers must be aware of is the influence of race and ethnic identity on sport consumption. A person's race or ethnicity generally exerts a profound influence on that person's thoughts, attitudes, and behaviors, including those that pertain to sport consumption. Racial and ethnic influences may be internal (factors within individuals that may influence sport consumption behaviors) or external (factors that are prevalent in a sport setting or environment that may influence sport consumption behaviors) (Armstrong, 2001, 2002). In addition to the diversity of sport consumers based on race and ethnicity, sport consumers' wants and needs may also differ based on a variety of other factors such as gender (e.g., the unique tastes of females compared to males) and age (e.g., the interests of senior consumers compared to those of the younger Generation X-ers).

The changing demographic and psychographic characteristics of sport consumers will increase the overall diversity to which sport marketers must respond as they seek to develop successful marketing plans. The trend of increased diversity in the national and global market will pose a special challenge and yet a unique opportunity for sport managers and marketers in the 21st century (Armstrong, 2001; DeSensi, 1994). The increased diversity in the environments in which sport oper-

ates will require not only that sport marketers be equipped with marketing fundamentals, but also that they have the skills to adapt them to multicultural sport consumers. This requires developing appropriate and acceptable intercultural communications, packaging features, positioning strategies, and distribution channels to reach culturally diverse consumers in domestic and international environments (Armstrong, 2001; McCarthy & Stillman, 1998; Sutton & Wattlington, 1994; Turco, 1996).

Sport marketers of the future will need to examine ways of attracting a diverse base of sport consumers and create multicultural sport spectating and participating experiences. To help achieve this objective, directors of college and university sport management programs must recruit, financially support, and graduate students from demographically and psychographically diverse backgrounds to ensure a pool of culturally diverse, qualified applicants from which leaders in the sport industry can hire sport marketers.

SUMMARY

This chapter outlined a 10-step process you can use in developing a sport marketing plan (see figure 10.1). The core of this process includes the primary elements in marketing, traditionally known as the four Ps and called the marketing mix (product, price, place, and promotion), but also includes additional factors such as organizational, environmental, and consumer-related considerations (purpose, projecting the market, positioning, picking the players, packaging, and promise). A sport marketing plan will most likely succeed when marketing is viewed as a comprehensive process of packaging, promoting, and delivering sport to consumers in a manner that satisfies

consumers' wants and needs and simultaneously meets the sport organization's marketing goals and objectives. Tactical marketing mix strategies (product, price, promotions, place) should therefore communicate a distinct, positive, and honest image of a product and the consumers to whom it is targeted. Such strategies will enable the sport organization to establish a favorable position among its niche of targeted consumers in the market and will subsequently fulfill the promise of socially responsible marketing that is linked to and consistent with the mission and core values of the organization.

REVIEW QUESTIONS

1. Explain how a context for a sport organization is established and why establishing a context is important in developing a sport marketing plan. (Refer to purpose, mission statement, and core values in the explanation.)

2. Explain how a SWOT analysis is used in analyzing a sport organization and its market in an effort to forecast the future market climate.

3. Explain the three dimensions of a sport product and the ways in which a sport product is unique.

4. Explain how positioning a sport product utilizes other promotion activities to help fix an image of a sport product in the minds of consumers.

5. Explain why a sport product/event should be promoted in ethical and socially responsible ways. Give examples of ethical and socially responsible promotion activities of a selected sport product.

6. Explain what methods are used to segment the market to identify viable target audiences for a sport product.

7. Describe strategies that can be used to most effectively distribute a sport product to consumers.

8. Explain the role of packaging in selling a sport product to specific target audiences. Give examples of packaging a sport product for a particular target audience.

9. Explain the two sources used to obtain feedback about a sport marketing plan and describe some individuals or groups from each source that can help evaluate a sport marketing plan.

10. Describe two sport marketing needs in the 21st century.

Job Opportunities

Assistant Director, Special Events and Promotions

Responsible for writing press releases, developing mailing lists, making telephone calls, and assisting with the implementation of special events promotions. Candidates must have strong writing, oral, and computer skills and knowledge of the sport industry.

Assistant Sport Marketing Director

Assist ticket coordinator in all aspects of ticket sales and promotions; assist event director with planning and execution of on-site advertising and operations; assist volunteer coordinator in organization and administration of event volunteer workers. Candidates must have communication, organizational, and sales skills.

Assistant Public Relations Director

A professional sport league office is seeking a self-motivated individual with at least three years' experience working in a public relations office with a professional sport team. A bachelor's degree in sport management/communications is required. The candidate must also demonstrate excellent writing and computer skills. Job responsibilities include writing press releases; preparing and distributing daily sport circulation reports; compiling, organizing, and printing statistics for media guide publications for special events such as the All-Star Game Series and League Championship Series; and preparing written materials for press conferences.

Coordinator of New Business Development

A new professional women's ice hockey league, is seeking an individual with at least five years' management experience with a professional sport team or league office. A bachelor's degree in sport management, management, or marketing is required. Demonstrated skills in strategic management planning, marketing, and community relations are desirable. Job responsibilities include working with the vice president of marketing and special events in developing strategic plans for expanding markets and spectator audiences, strengthening and expanding community grassroots involvement in the sport, and attracting new corporate sponsors.

Tournament Operations Manager

A sport management firm responsible for marketing a professional women's tennis tournament is seeking an individual with one to three years' experience in professional sport tournament operations. A bachelor's degree in sport management is preferred. Job responsibilities include assisting the tournament director with food and beverage operations, managing facilities, and coordinating and servicing on-site booth operations for corporate sponsors. Excellent planning, organizational, interpersonal, and communication skills are required.

Director of Marketing

A major university is seeking an individual with three to five years' experience in marketing or sport marketing. A bachelor's degree in marketing or sport management is preferred. Previous work experience in an NCAA Division I athletics department or with a professional sport team is desirable. Job responsibilities include ticket sales and promotions, promoting individual sport teams, securing

(continued

(continued)

corporate sponsorships, selling stadium advertising space and program advertisements, and developing and implementing other marketing and promotions strategies.

Director of Community Relations

A new expansion team in a minor ice hockey league is seeking a creative and highly motivated individual to develop and implement a community relations program. A bachelor's degree in sport management is preferred. Job responsibilities include arranging speaking engagements for coaches and players, organizing youth ice hockey clinics, organizing appearances of coaches and players with charitable organizations, and developing other strategies for involving coaches and players in community activities and events. The individual must have excellent planning and organizational skills with the ability to handle details.

Director of Marketing and Promotions

A new professional sports team is looking for an individual to direct marketing and promotions. This position includes raising awareness and interest in a sport never played professionally in this area. Applicants must have at least five years of experience with sport promotion/marketing; preference will be for candidates with previous professional sport promotion/marketing experience. The marketing and promotions director will report directly to the team owner and work closely with the general manager and other team personnel.

REFERENCES

Armstrong, K.L. (1998). Ten strategies to employ when marketing sport to Black consumers. *Sport Marketing Quarterly, 7*(3), 11-18.

Armstrong, K.L. (2001). Creating multicultural sport spectating experiences: Marketing the sociology of sport consumption. *International Journal of Sport Management, 2,* 183-204.

Armstrong, K.L. (2002). An examination of the social psychology of Blacks' consumption of sport. *Journal of Sport Management, 16,* 267-288.

Barbano, S. (1998, February/March). Women's sports market perspective: Women as spectators of men's sports. *Women's Sport Market Report, 3*(1), 1, 8.

Bernstein, A. (1999). Study: Hispanic tastes are varied, strong. *Sports Business Journal, 2*(28), p.7.

Brooks, C.M. (1994). *Sports marketing: Competitive business strategies for sports.* Englewood Cliffs, NJ: Prentice Hall.

Broughton, D., Lee, J., & Nethery, R. (1999). The answer: $213 billion. *Street & Smith's SportsBusiness Journal, 2*(32), 23, 26.

Covey, S.R. (1989). *The seven habits of highly effective people.* New York: Simon and Schuster.

DeSensi, J.T. (1994). Multiculturalism as an issue in sport management. *Journal of Sport Management, 8,* 63-74.

Francese, P. (1990). How to manage consumer information. In D. Crispell (Ed.), *The insider's guide to demographic know-how* (pp. 9-14), Ithaca, NY: American Demographics Press.

Gray, D.P. (1996). Sport marketing: A strategic approach. In B.L. Parkhouse (Ed.), *The management of sport: Its foundation and application* (pp. 249-289), St. Louis, MO: Mosby.

Grunig, J.E., & White, R. (1992). Communication, public relations and effective organizations. In J.E. Grunig (Ed). *Excellence in public relations and communications management.* Hillsdale, NJ: Erlbaum.

Hofacre, S., & Burman, T.K. (1992). Demographic changes in the U.S. into the twenty-first century: Their impact on sport marketing. *Sport Marketing Quarterly, 1*(1), 31-36.

Laczniak, G., Burton, R., & Murphy, P. (1999). Sports marketing ethics in today's marketplace. *Sport Marketing Quarterly, 8*(4), 43-53.

Lopiano, D. (2000). Marketing Trends in Women's Sports and Fitness. Women's Sports Foundation. www.lifetimetv.com/search/frameset/shtm.

McCarthy, L.M., & Stillman, W.P. (1998). Marketing sport to Hispanic consumers. *Sport Marketing Quarterly, 7*(4), 19-24.

McCarville, R.E., & Copeland, R.P. (1994). Understanding sport sponsorship through exchange theory. *Journal of Sport Management, 8,* 102-114.

Mullin, B.J., Hardy, S., & Sutton, W.A. (1993). *Sport marketing.* Champaign, IL: Human Kinetics Publishers.

Pitts, B.G., Fielding, L.W., & Miller, L.K. (1994). Industry segmentation theory and the sport industry: Developing a sport industry segmentation model. *Sport Marketing Quarterly, 3*(1), 15-24.

Pitts, B.G., & Stotlar, D.K. (2002). *Fundamentals of sport marketing* (2nd ed.). Morgantown, WV: Fitness Information Technology.

Rowe, A.J., Mason, R.O., & Dickel, K.E. (1986). *Strategic management: A methodological approach*. New York: Addison-Wesley.

Shank, M.D. (2002). *Sports marketing: A strategic perspective* (2nd ed.). Upper Saddle River, NJ: Prentice Hall.

Sutton, W.A., & Watlington, R. (1994). Communicating with women in the 1990s: The role of sport marketing. *Sport Marketing Quarterly, 3*(2), 9-14.

Turco, D.M. (1996). The X Factor: Marketing sports to Generation X. *Sport Marketing Quarterly, 1*(1), 21-24.

Chapter 11

Public Relations in the Sport Industry

Clay Stoldt, Wichita State University
Catherine Pratt, Bowling Green State University
Jason Jackson, EyeJax Foundation

Most of us who fantasized about a career in sport eventually realized that professional participation as an athlete was beyond our talents. This reality, however, did not necessarily diminish our interest in and enjoyment of sports, nor does it have to eliminate a career primarily focused on sport. Many of you might find a career in sport **public relations** both enjoyable and rewarding. Organized sport organizations, from small colleges to professional franchises, from YMCAs to the Olympics, need individuals who can help foster strong relationships between the organization and its most important **publics** (Cutlip, Center, & Broom, 1994). While in some ways public relations can be considered part of the job of every employee, a substantial number of sports administrators are employed specifically as public relations professionals. Their titles vary, but they usually include words such as *media relations*, *community relations, information, publicity*, or *communication*.

public relations—An organizational function that fosters the development of positive relationships between the organization and its most important publics.

publics—Groups of people who are affected in varied ways by an organization.

In this chapter you will learn about three primary aspects of sport public relations. First, you will learn about communication in general—the basic skills, the general framework, and the application of those concepts to public relations practice. Second, you will learn about the most common sport public relations jobs. These jobs are in media relations, community relations, and several other areas (Jackowski, 2000; Mullin, Hardy, &

Sutton, 2000). The media relations section of the chapter will include a brief overview of the relatively unique relationship between sport and the mass media. The third area discussed in this chapter focuses on community relations in sport, and the fourth section considers other public relations positions in the industry. The fifth section examines the impact of communication technology on sport, specifically the practice of sport public relations. Finally, since understanding and appreciating socially responsible behavior is a bottom-line requirement for a successful career in sport public relations, each of the sections will highlight some relevant ethical issues involved in the practice.

Communication Basics

Sport public relations positions include collegiate sports information director, community relations director for a professional sports team, or corporate communication manager for a fitness and recreation facility or sporting goods manufacturer. Regardless of the setting, all the occupational choices in this chapter share a common denominator: the ability to communicate effectively. Creating a message that accurately and effectively communicates your ideas to the audience you want to reach is the foundation for success in sport public relations.

The most basic skills you need to develop are your writing and speaking abilities. Writing effectively means that you must be able to track down and organize information and record it in a way that interests and informs readers. This means that sentences must be grammatically correct, wording must be succinct, and ideas must flow from one point to another. Speaking effectively also entails organizing information. Strong speakers are able to boil large amounts of information down into key points that they repetitively emphasize, and they are able to build on those points with additional information and humorous or insightful stories (Gregory, 2002). They also connect with their audiences by using appropriate gestures and body language. Because of the variety of audiences that public relations practitioners routinely must reach, failure to develop effective communication techniques is usually a prelude to unproductive or even counterproductive efforts.

LEARNING ACTIVITY

Who is the best public speaker you have ever heard? Was this person a sport figure? Chances are, the speaker you're thinking of used effective communication techniques. Based on your experience with that speaker, and perhaps others, make a list of the qualities that characterize effective public speakers.

Not all communication is successful communication. Remember the popular game "Gossip" or "Telephone" that involved whispering a sentence to the person in the next seat, who then whispered it to the next person, continuing until the message had been passed along by everyone playing the game? The outcome was usually a final message that differed radically from the original whispered communication. Although this distortion or miscommunication might be amusing in a game, the results are not so funny when we fail to communicate our message in situations in which accurate communication is important.

So how do you become an effective communicator? There's the old joke: How do you get to Carnegie Hall? Practice, practice, practice! Even when you interview for an entry-level job in the sport public relations field, you will be expected to have already developed strong communication skills and gained some related experience. You may get some of this experience through experiential learning activities in your classes, but that probably will not be enough to distinguish you competitively. You will likely need to volunteer with a sport organization (e.g., in media relations or community relations) or with a mass media outlet (e.g., a campus newspaper or radio station) to get the repetition necessary to hone your skills adequately. Significant volunteer experience will likely position you to gain a high-quality internship where you can continue to build the skills necessary for a successful career in the field.

Certainly, experience is a critically important ingredient. But just communicating without understanding the essentials of the process and what has been learned about effective communication means that you waste a lot of time reinventing the wheel! You can avoid mistakes and eliminate wasted effort if you understand the established principles of effective communication and public relations.

General Communication Models

Communication scholars have suggested that theoretical ideas are easier to understand if they are presented as a diagram or model. Hundreds of communication models, from basic to sophisticated, have been developed to help explain how we communicate, how we ought to communicate, obstacles to communication, and communication effects. The most well-known and useful models share an approach that treats **communication** as a process. Most feature identifiable components arranged to explain the process. The most commonly accepted components are

- the source,
- the message,
- the channel through which the message is delivered, and
- the receiver.

When combined with the concepts of encoding, decoding, feedback, and noise, these components offer a useful description of the communication process with a practical advantage: The better we understand the process, the more likely we are to communicate well.

communication—A process by which messages of meaning are shared by senders and receivers. Communication takes place at multiple levels—interpersonally, in groups, and via the mass media.

The model in figure 11.1 is based on the work of communication scholars such as Harold Lasswell, Wilbur Schramm, Claude Shannon, and Warren Weaver (Severin & Tankard, 1997). In this model, the communication source could be a person addressing the crowd at a community gathering, the individual(s) or organization that produces a brochure, the author of a written news release, or the speaker at a news conference. The message in each of these cases is the denotation and connotation of the spoken or written words and pictures that the sender produces. While channels can be described literally (e.g., broadcast or cable channels), communication scholars usually use the term to describe the delivery system or the way in

which the message gets from the sender to the receiver (i.e., spoken word, gestures, over-the-air broadcast television, film, etc). Thus, the channel through which a message is delivered could be face-to-face spoken words (with accompanying voice, expression, and gesture cues) or the printed words (with accompanying graphics and layout). The receiver of the communication could be one or several individuals listening to a speaker, the readers of a magazine, or visitors to a Web site.

The *encoding* and *decoding* components of the communication process refer to the inescapable fact that every sender and receiver of communication assigns meaning to the communicated message. This meaning may or may not be readily apparent. Think about the times you've heard or seen something that didn't communicate the intended message. Key words may not have been familiar or the speaker's language may have been communicating one message while her facial expressions communicated another. Think, too, about instances in which you thought you knew the meaning of some communication, but later you discovered your interpretation was incorrect. (Just think back to a recent test or assignment in which your poor grade was a direct result of not understanding what the instructor expected.)

Noise accounts for elements that interfere with the reception of the message. It can be literal; fans yelling at a sporting event may drown out the field announcer relaying an important message. Noise can also be figurative; a poorly printed brochure would certainly hinder communication effectiveness and thus be a form of noise. Another example

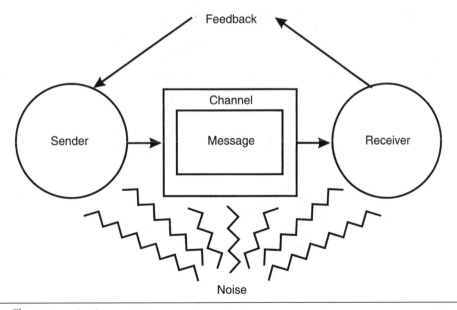

Figure 11.1 The communication process.

of figurative noise would be personal problems that might distract you from focusing on the problem at hand, impairing your ability to speak or write well. The goal in communicating is to minimize controllable noise and cut through uncontrollable noise so there are as few impediments as possible in the communication process.

Feedback refers to communication that the receiver sends back to the sender through deliberate or inadvertent responses. Feedback helps the communicator understand whether the correct message was received. It provides information for future communication. Phone calls concerning a change in the services offered by a recreation facility, fans erupting in cheers at a spirit rally, or the defeat of a municipal ballot initiative to help fund your team's new sports arena are all examples of feedback.

It is also important to remember that even the best-intentioned and best-fashioned communication may be ignored, misinterpreted, or forgotten. The terminology for these communication pitfalls is selective attention, selective perception, and selective retention. *Selective attention* refers to the tendency we all have to seek communication that relates to topics in which we already have an interest. *Selective perception* refers to interpreting information in a way that reinforces what we already believe. *Selective retention* describes our inclination to remember those things we find comfortable and useful, forgetting the things we dislike or that make us uncomfortable. Each concept feeds on the basic human need to avoid conflict or cognitive dissonance—the emotional or intellectual discomfort we feel when messages conflict with our strongly held beliefs. Effective communication requires an understanding of human nature and of people's need to protect themselves through strategies such as selective attention, perception, and retention.

To simplify our communication model, we can also look to Schramm (1954), who argued that for communication to exist, the sender and the receiver must share something: a common language, vocabulary, or interest in or understanding of the subject being communicated. The more the sender and receiver share, the easier it is for them to communicate effectively. Schramm's point is a useful one to consider when you communicate. Ask yourself how much you and the receiver of your communication share. If you can increase the level of shared interest, you will increase the likelihood that your communication efforts will be successful.

Models of Public Relations Practice

While the model in figure 11.1 and Schramm's model present general communication concepts, they also have a direct relationship with many of the key ideas underlying public relations work. For example, some of the country's most prominent public relations scholars have argued that public relations practitioners work under four basic models of communicating (Grunig & Grunig, 1992): two **one-way models** and two **two-way models**. These are summarized in table 11.1. The assumptions made about the communication process and the organization's purpose in communicating usually drive the decision as to which model to employ.

one-way model of public relations—A communication model focusing exclusively on the flow of information from the sport organization to its publics.

two-way model of public relations—A communication model focusing on communication give-and-take between a sport organization and its key publics.

Table 11.1 Four Models of Public Relations and Communication

Model	Purpose	Nature of communication
Press agentry publicity	Propaganda	One-way; complete truth is not always essential
Public information	Dissemination	One-way; truthful disclosure of information
Asymmetrical	Scientific persuasion	Two-way; imbalanced effects
Symmetrical	Mutual understanding	Two-way; negotiated effects

Source: Grunig, J.E., & Grunig, L.A. (1992). Models of public relations and communication. In J.E. Grunig (Ed.), *Excellence in communications and public relations management* (pp. 285-325). Hillsdale, NJ: Erlbaum.

The first model is a one-way publicity/press agentry model. Organizations using this model do not seek input from their key publics, but they are extremely concerned about "getting their message out there." Sometimes they are even willing to push the envelope regarding what may be appropriate or ethical in order to get attention. If you've ever watched a news conference promoting an upcoming boxing match turn into a melee, you have seen this model in action at its worst. The boxers, and sometimes the promoters, are willing to risk their credibility, not to mention the well-being of anyone caught in the middle of the fracas, in exchange for the "buzz" the prematch fight will generate among the public. There are many ethical applications of this model as well. It is interesting to note that Grunig suggests that the entertainment industry (one could argue that sport falls into that category much of the time) usually adheres to the limited one-way model in which feedback is limited to things such as ticket sales.

The second one-way model is the public information model. Organizations using this model are not as outrageous in seeking public attention. Instead, they offer effective service to members of the mass media and the general public by providing information in a credible manner. For example, they may assist members of the mass media in setting up interviews, or they may provide a variety of other services to members of the media covering a sport event. Many professional organizations and college athletics programs have sports information offices to perform these functions. They hope that by offering such services, they will be more likely to receive greater amounts of favorable publicity.

Two-way communication models are based on the assumption that the most effective forms of communication require input from target publics. In other words, communication requires give and take. For example, if the owner of a sport team wants the community to vote in favor of a tax increase to help fund a new stadium, that owner would be smart to gather some information regarding public sentiment toward the team and public projects in general before attempting to craft public relations messages. In such an example, the owner is using the first two-way model, the asymmetrical approach. Its goal is to scientifically use information about a public to more effectively communicate and get that public to behave as desired. In the case of our example, the desired outcome would be the community voting yes for the tax increase to fund the new stadium.

The second two-way model is the symmetrical approach. It too employs planned information-gathering techniques to communicate more effectively, but it recognizes that the outcome of the communication process will likely mean that both the organization and the public must change their positions or behavior. In other words, the second model is about negotiating mutually acceptable solutions.

Media Relations in Sport

The mass media devotes considerable attention to sport. Because of that, most sport managers find that working with members of the mass media is an important part of their job. In many cases, sport organizations hire individuals specifically to manage media relations because the work necessary to provide good service to the media requires the complete attention of one or more staff members. Regardless of your level of interest in media relations, you need a good understanding of the relationship between sport and the mass media if you want to be an effective sport manager.

Sport and the Mass Media

The relationship between sport and the **mass media** has been described as "symbiotic" (Leonard, 1998), meaning that the two entities are frequently interdependent. Each party uses the other for its own gain.

mass media—Organizations of professional communicators who deliver messages to large audiences simultaneously or quickly over large geographic areas. The mass media possesses delivery systems capable of transcending the time and space limitations inherent in interpersonal and group communication settings.

Sport organizations use the mass media to gain public exposure for their events, facilities, and product offerings. The game preview you hear about on the local television news tonight may help sway you to attend that game rather than go to a movie as you had originally planned. The newspaper story about the latest in exercise equipment being installed at a nearby fitness center might entice you to tour the facility and maybe even buy a membership.

Publicity in the mass media can be an asset or a liability for sport organizations. Positive publicity is the best of all worlds for sport managers. It is less costly than other methods of promotion because the airtime or airspace is free. It also tends to be more credible than other methods of promotion because consumers know the message is not paid for by the sport organization. On the other hand, negative publicity is difficult to manage for the same reason. Since sport managers do not control the content of the media's message, they cannot mandate that the media *not* print or broadcast embarrassing stories. Accordingly, many sport organizations have developed crisis communication plans. These plans help sport managers plan ahead for tragic or embarrassing situations such as an accident involving team members or an incident in which a member of a team is arrested. Crisis communication plans help sport organizations be **proactive** (i.e., following previously defined strategies) rather than **reactive** (i.e., scrambling to "spin" the situation in a desperate attempt to look good) in their media relations efforts (Stoldt, Miller, Ayres, & Comfort, 2000).

proactive—Advance planning that allows individuals or organizations to prepare for contingencies they will likely face in the future. From a public relations perspective, this means developing strategies to prevent or manage future problems the organization deems probable or important.

reactive—Dealing with problems only after they have developed. From a public relations perspective, this means failing to anticipate and plan for difficult issues that the organization will likely face.

Just as it is in the sport organization's best interest to cultivate positive coverage in the mass media, it is often in the mass media's best interest to provide considerable sport coverage. Given intense public interest, sport helps sell newspapers and magazines, draw audiences to radio and television newscasts, and generate traffic for Web sites. Therefore, media organizations frequently devote considerable resources to sport journalism.

Sport journalists are a diverse lot. Some work as reporters, covering news and writing articles for a newspaper or magazine. These journalists are members of the **print media**. Others work for a radio, television, or cable outlet, covering and packaging reports on sport-related topics. These individuals help make up the **electronic media**. More and more, both print and electronic sport journalists are having some of their work appear on the Internet. The World Wide Web is just one aspect of the new technologies changing the field of sport journalism and public relations. Although the most prominent area of coverage has traditionally been professional and top-division collegiate sport, individuals working for the media outlets in sport journalism cover a variety of topics, including nearly every recreational sport activity.

print media—Organizations that mass-produce printed publications for distribution into homes, offices, and businesses. Members of the print media include newspapers of various types (e.g., daily, weekly) and general and specialized magazines.

electronic media—Organizations that transmit radio or television signals through the air or via cable into homes, offices, and businesses. Members of the electronic media include commercial and noncommercial (i.e., public) broadcasting stations and cable networks or stations.

Much of the sport content within the mass media comes in the form of news or feature coverage. However, the broadcast media also devotes significant resources to live coverage of sport events as entertainment programming. These events frequently draw large audiences who possess characteristics that are highly desirable to advertisers (e.g., income, education level). The size of these audiences is commonly measured using ratings and shares. Ratings represent the percentage of the population overall (e.g., all households with televisions) that watches a particular program. Shares represent the percentage of the "tuned in" population (e.g., all households using television at a given time) that watches a particular program. Super Bowl and Olympics broadcasts account for many of the highest-rated television programs ever. Given the ability of sport programming to draw large audiences, many broadcast entities are willing to pay large amounts of money in the form of rights fees to have the exclusive privilege to carry the events. For example, the National Football League's 1998 television deals with Fox, CBS, ABC, and ESPN call for the league to receive $17.6 billion in rights fees over an eight-year period (Perman, 1998).

What Media Relations Specialists Do

Sport **media relations** professionals who work for a team, facility, or organization are responsible for creating, coordinating, and organizing information about that entity and disseminating it to the public indirectly through the mass media or

The Print Media

Newspapers reach a substantial portion of the U.S. population on a daily basis. Recent readership figures indicate that more than a hundred million adults, or better than 50% of the adult population, read at least a portion of a newspaper each day (Newspaper Association of America, 2000a). Over the span of a typical workweek, 65% of the adult population will read a newspaper, and 60% of all adults read at least a portion of a Sunday newspaper. Sport coverage draws a significant number of those readers. In fact, research indicates that the sport section ranks number two in readership (43% of adults) behind general news (70% of adults) (Newspaper Association of America, 2000b). Sport magazines are also prevalent in the marketplace. These magazines range in scope from more general interest periodicals such as *Sports Illustrated* and *The Sporting News* to more specialized publications such as *Golf Digest*.

The Electronic Media

There is no shortage of radio and television stations in the United States and no shortage of audience members willing to listen and watch. Research indicates that 99% of American homes have radios and 98% have television sets (*Broadcasting and Cable Yearbook*, 2001). In fact, 75% of U.S. homes have more than one TV set, and 86% have a videocassette recorder. Cable television is common as well, with 68% of homes being connected. Serving these households are 12,717 radio stations (4,685 commercial AM stations, 5,892 commercial FMs, and 2,140 noncommercial FMs) and 1,663 television stations (567 commercial VHF stations, 721 commercial UHFs, 125 noncommercial VHFs, and 250 noncommercial UHFs). There are also 11,800 cable systems operating in the United States. Most offer 60 or more channels. These organizations would not be in business without a large market for programming. The average U.S. household watches seven hours and 29 minutes of television each day.

While some television and radio stations are noncommercial or educational, most are commercial. Television stations are either affiliated with a network (e.g., ABC, CBS, NBC, Fox, UPN, WB) or operate as independent stations with limited or no network affiliation. Most major network affiliates have local news and thus sport programming. Television networks have additional sport personnel to cover events on a regular or special basis (e.g., the NFL, Wimbledon). Obviously, ESPN and its sister channels require a large number of sport reporters and anchors to handle their all-sport format. Some programs that air on ESPN, however, are sold to the network as a package complete with announcers and commentators under contract to the company producing the programs, not the network airing them. Radio stations are less likely to have full-time sport broadcasters on staff, but in large markets, the top stations may have someone who handles sport reporting. Sport talk radio stations tap into a radio network's all-sport programming or have local broadcasters they employ on a full- or part-time basis.

through direct channels (e.g., organizational Web site). Some organizations have staffs large enough to include separate information and promotion functions, but many organizations employ a single individual who handles information, promotion, media relations, customer or fan relations, and miscellaneous marketing and other public relations duties. Success as a media relations professional requires a genuine interest in the field, strong interpersonal and written communication skills, and the perseverance to unearth and secure internship and entry-level job opportunities in a highly competitive field.

media relations—An organizational activity resulting in the creation, coordination, and organization of information and the dissemination of it to the public through the mass media.

Those who have studied sport media relations (Chamberlin, 1990; Nichols, Moynahan, Hall, & Taylor, 2002; Stoldt, 2000) indicate that the duties of sports information directors at colleges or universities include the following:

- Writing news releases
- Updating hometown newspapers
- Writing feature stories
- Filing game reports
- Writing, editing, and laying out brochures
- Preparing game programs

A sports information director for a college athletics program can be your first position in sport media relations.

- Overseeing promotional activities
- Compiling records and statistics
- Organizing a photo file system
- Planning and conducting press conferences
- Answering requests from publications and organizations
- Managing a press box staff and managing the press box on game day
- Developing and updating crisis communication plans
- Maintaining the athletics program's Web site
- Any other duties assigned by the athletics director or other supervisor

Chapter 14 has more detailed information on the duties and career paths of collegiate sports information jobs. Media relations specialists in professional sport perform many of these same functions, although for major league teams, staff responsibilities might be spread among more individuals. Sports communicators who work with sport recreation facilities also perform some of these functions, but the focus is on the community opportunities available at the facility and the events or activities scheduled.

LEARNING ACTIVITY

You may be surprised to find how much of the information sport broadcasters share with their audiences comes from materials provided to them by the participating sport organizations. Pick a major pro or college sport event that will soon be televised. Visit the Web site of one of the teams participating in the game. Download the game notes (often available in Adobe Acrobat Reader). When you later watch the game on television, notice how many of the same facts and figures are shared with the audience!

Careers in Media Relations

There are thousands of colleges and universities and hundreds of major and minor league professional sports teams in North America, not to mention one or more sport, fitness, health, or recreation facility in most North American cities. Each enterprise needs to get information to the public, and many of them employ at least one communication specialist to handle the job. This means there are many opportunities for you to be employed as a media relations professional. You must remember, though, that the field is so popular and so

In Profile

Name: John Humenik

Title: Assistant athletics director—sports information, University of Florida

Education:

- Bachelor's degree in business administration (management) with a minor in communications, Clarion University, 1974
- Master's degree in business administration, Clarion University, 1975

Professional Background:

- Sports information director, Clarion University, 1975
- Assistant sports information director, Princeton University, 1976-77
- Sports information director, Princeton University, 1977-1980
- Director of sports information, University of Michigan, 1980-82
- Sports information director, University of Florida, 1982-88
- Assistant athletics director, University of Florida, 1988-present

Job Responsibilities:

- Coordinates the information operations of the Florida athletics program
- Coordinates news coverage, media operations, media services, publications, publicity, and general public relations for a 20-sport program
- Manages a staff of 10 full-time sports information employees

Career Highlights:

- In 1998, was the first person ever to receive the Enberg Award, named for acclaimed sportscaster Dick Enberg and given to a person who provided exceptional leadership in promoting the values of education and athletics. Subsequent winners have been former North Carolina basketball coach Dean Smith, NBA legend Bill Russell, and NFL Hall of Famer Alan Page.
- Information director from 1996 for Florida's national championship football team.
- On-site communications coordinator for Florida men's basketball teams that advanced to the 1994 and 2000 Final Fours.
- Director for information campaign that resulted in quarterback Danny Wuerffel winning the 1996 Heisman Trophy, the nation's highest individual college football honor

Advice to students: "I've always felt that to be successful in this profession you must always look at what we do as a profession and not a job. There is a big difference between the two. What we do is a special responsibility and privilege that demands a high level of dedication and commitment, and those we work for and with have a right to expect that from us."

competitive that your career success depends on recognizing and sometimes *creating* opportunities to get your foot in the door. Prospective employers will be looking for a solid educational preparation that includes strong communication skills. Typical majors are sport management, journalism, public relations, and communications. Beyond your basic education, however, you should capitalize on the opportunity to secure volunteer or internship experiences so that when you graduate you will have more on your résumé than just the name of your degree.

A good internship can do more than simply give you experience; it can also give you a network of practitioners to contact for job opportunities, not to mention essentials such as letters of reference. While some top-level professional teams offer internship opportunities, because the competition to be involved in the "glamorous" world of professional sport is so intense, these internships are hard to come by. Your best bet would be to try minor league teams or teams in sports other than football, basketball, baseball, and hockey. Don't forget to look for internship opportunities with community recreational facilities such as the YMCA and YWCA and Jewish Community Centers. Tight budgets and limited staff resources can make these organizations appreciate dedicated volunteer and internship help.

Your first full-time job will probably be as an assistant sports information director or an assistant promotions director at a college, a team, a governing body, or a facility. You could also start at the director's level with a smaller organization, but you would probably also be a one-person staff. If you do your job well and keep your ear tuned for advancement opportunities, you should have the opportunity to advance to a higher-level position or move to a larger organization. The first job you get should provide you with a broader network of contacts that will be valuable as you prepare to move into positions with larger organizations or into a manager or director job. You may also need to evaluate your willingness to relocate. Your pool of opportunities will expand if you are willing to move to organizations in a range of regions.

The competitive nature of sport media relations jobs cannot be overstated. Although the number of available positions has increased as colleges, facilities, and teams recognize the connection between publicity and profit, the number of individuals competing for the jobs has also increased. Salaries are not always commensurate with similar communication positions in the corporate world because of the many people who seem willing to work in sport almost for free. In addition, sport media relations professionals are frequently called on to work long hours. "First one to arrive, last one to leave" is a common reality in the profession. Work schedules totaling 60 to even 80 hours a week are not uncommon during a particular season, and for those working at the collegiate level, sport seasons usually run about 10 months.

Ethical Issues in Media Relations

Media relations professionals frequently deal with a variety of ethics-related issues. Perhaps the most sensitive issues center on privacy. Media relations professionals have access to a great deal of information—much of it personal. If you work in the field, you need to be sensitive to this and release only information that will not compromise people's right to privacy. For example, it is unethical (not to mention illegal) for a college media relations professional to publicly release student-athlete grade point averages. The exception to this might be the

authorized release of information in the event a student-athlete earns academic all-star recognition. The College Sports Information Directors of America (CoSIDA) is a professional organization with a prescribed code of ethics (see http://cosida.fansonly.com/genrel/info.html) designed to guide members as they wrestle with privacy-related and other ethical issues.

Another ethics-related issue relevant to media relations has to do with the one-way and two-way models discussed earlier. Many sport managers think the job is limited to publicity: getting coverage of their team or event or practicing "damage control" when something negative happens or is suspected. But a more complete or sophisticated approach to media relations would classify generating publicity as only one aspect of the work. Sport organizations that rely predominantly on a one-way flow of information may violate the boundaries of ethical relationships with their key constituents. In other words, it is tough for two parties to have a healthy relationship if only one does all the talking!

Community Relations in Sport

Community relations activities tend to center on charitable initiatives, and they often complement media relations work (Lesly, 1998). One community relations professional notes that while media relations publicizes what happens on the field of competition, community relations promotes what happens off the field (S. Tate, personal communication, February 13, 2002).

community relations—An organizational activity designed to build relationships with residents and civic-minded organizations in the geographic area in which the sport organization is located.

Sport organizations engage in community relations activities for many reasons. First, community relations has traditionally been viewed as a long-term investment in the sport organization's image (Mullin, Hardy, & Sutton, 2000). Sport organizations seen participating in charitable outreach programs and other worthy undertakings are likely to be perceived in a positive manner by various constituents. Second, many sport organizations are finding that effectively planned community relations efforts can result in new revenue in the short term. For example, if a player or coach from your organization makes an appearance at an

© Frances M. Roberts

Public appearances made by professional athletes such as Al Leiter of the New York Mets are an important part of community relations in sport.

educational assembly for schoolchildren, you can provide the kids with complimentary tickets for an upcoming game. However, the tickets may stipulate that each child must be accompanied by an adult who purchases his or her own ticket to the game. Finally, community relations is the socially responsible thing for sport organizations to do. Even if your sport organization did not receive long-term image enhancement or short-term revenue gains from your community relations efforts, such activity would be prudent since it is in your organization's best interest to function in a thriving, vibrant community.

LEARNING ACTIVITY

Visit the Web site of the sport organization of your choice and see if it contains information on community relations initiatives. Many sport organizations, particularly high-level professional franchises, do offer such information online. Upon reviewing the site, prepare a brief presentation for your class. Questions you'll want to answer during the presentation include the following:

- What community relations activities has the organization implemented?
- Who has been involved in those activities?
- Do the community relations activities listed seem to be a good fit for the sport organization?
- If you were to suggest one other community relations initiative for the organization, what would it be? Why?

What Community Relations Professionals Do

Sport community relations professionals who work for a team, facility, or organization are responsible for creating, organizing, and executing charitable initiatives and other programs designed to involve the organization in community enhancement. Some organizations have staffs large enough to include community relations specialists who work in their assigned areas on a full-time basis. Many others employ a single individual or a small staff with other public relations or marketing responsibilities in addition to community relations. Like other

221

sectors of the public relations field, success as a community relations professional requires strong communication and interpersonal skills as well as the determination to seek out opportunities to gain experience and make important contacts in the field.

A common form of sport community relations activity is the donation of money to various charities. Some sport organizations, particularly those at the major professional level, execute a variety of fund-raising events throughout the year and then donate the proceeds of those fund-raisers to charitable organizations. For example, the NHL's Dallas Stars donated more than $300,000 to various charities in their metropolitan area in 2000 (Dallas Stars, 2000). The Stars funded those donations through fund-raising events such as a "Casino Night" where donors can join with players and coaches for an evening of games, prizes, food, and beverages. Another example is New Balance, a shoe and apparel company that makes donations to various charities and executes a product donation program for people in need who are located near their main facilities (New Balance, 2001). Charities benefiting children and young people are commonly favored by sport organizations. Sometimes the sport organization's contributions are as simple as autographed merchandise that can then be auctioned off by the charity in its own fund-raising activities.

A second form of community relations activities commonly employed by sport organizations is initiatives to better the community via direct contact. For example, some organizations cultivate youth sport participation by constructing sport venues (e.g., ball fields in the inner city) and sponsoring clinics. Others may engage in partnerships with charitable organizations to advocate important messages (e.g., "stay in school") or generate an important service (e.g., building a home with Habitat for Humanity). These initiatives take place at multiple levels from the professional sport league to the member franchise to the individual player or coach. In addition, some sport organizations are looking to take their community relations efforts to a new level of effectiveness by creating strategic partnerships with corporate sponsors to more effectively serve their communities. The Washington franchise of the National Football League has developed one such "leadership council" in which the team and its corporate partners pool resources to maximize the benefit of their community relations programs for all parties involved (Schoenfeld, 2000).

A third form of common community relations activity does not directly benefit charitable organizations but does enable the sport organization to build relationships with various constituents through direct contact. Many community relations professionals coordinate speaking appearances by other members of their organizations. Still others organize promotional events such as the annual winter caravans many Major League Baseball teams stage to rally support during the off-season. Some organizations, particularly those at the minor league level, find that the most popular personality at such appearances is usually the team mascot.

Careers in Community Relations

Community relations activity is common in a wide range of sport organizations from professional entertainment organizations to colleges and universities to for-profit fitness centers to sporting goods manufacturers. The larger the organization and the greater its resources, the more likely that organization will be to have one or more employees assigned specifically to community relations. For example, MLB's Kansas City Royals has four employees working full-time in community relations. One of their minor league affiliates, the Wichita Wranglers, has no one working full-time in community relations. Those responsibilities fall under the job description of the director of marketing.

On balance, there are fewer full-time positions in community relations than in media relations in sport. One primary reason is that hundreds of colleges and universities hire at least one full-time employee in sports information. Many community relations responsibilities are delegated to the student life skills division of the athletics department. Still, community relations is a viable career option within sport. In fact, some believe that the community relations function will grow considerably in the coming years (Jackowski, 2000). If so, sport organizations will likely be looking to increase the number of community relations specialists they employ and increase the resources they are willing to devote to the function.

Competition is fierce for sport community relations positions, so if you're hoping to work in the field, you must distinguish yourself competitively by finely honing your communication skills and by securing significant volunteer and internship experience before applying for an entry-level job. Employers are looking for applicants with proven track records in successfully executing commu-

In Profile

Name: Shani Tate

Title: Director of community relations, Kansas City Royals

Education:

- Bachelor's degree in business administration, University of Missouri—Columbia, 1996
- Master's degree in public administration with an emphasis in economic development, University of Missouri—Kansas City, 1998

Professional Background:

- Intern with Sprint/United Telephone, 1991-93
- Intern in baseball operations and then special markets, Kansas City Royals, 1997-98
- Manager of community relations and special markets, 1998-2000

Job Responsibilities:

- Works with players, coaches, and front office personnel to further enhance the image of the organization as a responsible corporate and community citizen
- Responsible for planning, budgeting, publicity, implementation, and postevaluation of in-stadium promotions and community events
- Assumes leadership role in planning, managing, and evaluating Royals' business practices that promote diversity
- Serves as executive director of Royals Charities, the official foundation of the ball club
- Manages a staff of three other full-time employees

Career Highlights:

- Selected to participate in the Major League Baseball executive development program. Only two individuals per franchise are annually chosen to take part in the prestigious program.
- Seeing Royals Charities grow from a financial base of $6,000 to $400,000 during her tenure. Royals Charities issued $255,000 in grants to worthy organizations during 2001.
- The everyday reward of making a difference in people's lives by virtue of the charitable ventures of the Royals' organization

Advice to students: "Set measurable goals and work to obtain valuable public relations experience by maximizing educational opportunities, working on internships—paid or unpaid—and volunteering with nonprofit organizations. Find something you're passionate about, and make it your job. This makes it much easier to go to work every day."

---

nity relations initiatives. The good news is that with a little creativity and a good dose of initiative you can gain this experience while you are still in school. Keep in mind that many sport organizations do not have the resources to hire full-time employees in community relations. Rather than pinning your hopes on a major league organization or industry leader in fitness or equipment, consider volunteering for a local minor league organization, a nonmajor college or university, or a lo-

cally owned fitness business. They would likely welcome your help in carrying out some of the initiatives they have already planned or creative ideas of yours.

Thoroughness is the key, however. Most community relations efforts are hard work. Your credibility depends on your ability to see the project(s) through to completion. You should also carefully document the results of your efforts. While it may be true that many community relations activities are worthy endeavors, key decision makers are more likely to value them (and your efforts) if you can document results such as the attendance at a special event; the publicity the initiative generated; or letters, phone calls, and e-mails of appreciation from the constituents served.

If and when you are fortunate enough to secure a job in community relations, you will likely start in one of two places. You will be either a public relations/marketing generalist with a smaller organization or a lower-level member of a small community relations staff with a larger organization. As you gain experience, expand your network of contacts, and document your effectiveness in community relations endeavors, you will likely have the chance to advance to higher-level positions or larger organizations. There is some sentiment in the field that, if you want to work with a major professional franchise, the best way to start is by gaining volunteer, internship, or entry-level experience with a major professional franchise.

Community relations professionals in sport will likely be paid less than their counterparts in other industries. This is largely because of the demand for jobs in the field. There may also be the perception that community relations in sport is somehow easier than it is in other professions because of the great interest the mass media has in many sport organizations. While there is some truth to that at the high-profile professional and college levels, community relations professionals in sport also face some challenges unique to the industry. One is that because of their public visibility, many sport organizations receive far more requests for help from worthy organizations than they can possibly fulfill. Saying no to deserving organizations is a difficult but necessary part of the job. In addition, some community relations professionals find it challenging to match community relations initiatives with the interests of key individuals within the organization such as high-profile coaches and athletes. However, when the work is completed effectively, the benefits are significant for all parties involved.

Ethical Issues in Community Relations

Community relations professionals are frequently confronted with a couple of ethical issues. One is keeping their priorities straight. Sport organizations are in a relatively unique position to capitalize on the publicity that often accompanies their community service initiatives. For example, sport figures making visits to patients in a children's hospital may make for good press and moving visual images. Seeking publicity for such ventures clearly enhances the sport organization's reputation within the community. However, when publicity rather than service becomes the sole force behind a community relations initiative, an ethical boundary has been crossed. As stated by Peak (1998), "the benefits of a community relations program should be in the program, not the publicity" (p. 130).

A second ethical issue confronted by community relations professionals is giving credit where credit is due (Peak, 1998). While sport organizations may want to publicize the good deeds done by their member managers, coaches, and athletes, they should be careful to distinguish individual community relations initiatives from organizational programs. In addition, sport organizations that team with other businesses in the community on charitable initiatives must be careful to share the spotlight. This may be difficult since the sport organization is frequently the more prominent player in the mix. Nonetheless, a less self-serving approach to publicity is often the best if generating goodwill within the community at large and with corporate partners in particular is the sport organization's priority.

Other Public Relations Positions

Many sport organizations employ public relations professionals in positions that are not limited to media relations or community relations. Job titles and scopes of responsibility vary from one organization to another. However, some of the more common "other" public relations positions may be described as follows:

• Corporate communications: As noted by Deeter (1993), corporate communications work frequently intersects with multiple public relations areas. These may include marketing communication such as media placement in support of a promotional effort, employee communications, community relations, and customer relations. Corporate communications positions tend to be more common in sport organizations with relatively large public relations staffs.

• Creative specialists: These public relations practitioners possess specialized skills in design, layout, graphic arts, and other technical skills. Within college athletics departments they frequently work with the sports information office, collaborating with their colleagues to produce media guides, game programs, posters, and other printed materials.

• Employee/volunteer relations: Internal constituents are easily overlooked, but they are critical to the sport organization's success. Some public relations professionals specialize in employee or volunteer relations. Their jobs are to build strong internal relationships by creating forums for communication and staging special events (e.g., volunteer appreciation day). Volunteer relations positions are more prevalent in settings such as a state amateur sport festival in which a large volunteer workforce is critical to the event's execution.

• Web site manager: These sport communicators specialize in managing their organizations' Web sites. They may update online information, respond to inquiries from visitors to the Web site, facilitate discussion forums, and serve as liaisons with other staff members whose functions include Web site interests (e.g., sports information, marketing, ticket sales).

Depending on the setting, other public relations jobs in the industry may also focus on investor relations, government relations, or relations with governing bodies within the industry.

Communication Technology and Its Impact on Sport

When the electronic media, particularly television, gained widespread use in the last century, it changed sport in a profound way. Instead of having to wait to read about a sport event in the morning newspaper, we could watch it live or catch highlights on cable programs such as ESPN's *SportsCenter*. The influx of television dollars into professional competitive sports and such amateur sport events as the Olympics has affected everything from salaries to rules. Television was the impetus behind night baseball and obviously plays a central role in making the Super Bowl a super event! Some people even think our national sport shifted from baseball to football because the pace and segmented action in football made for better television.

Similarly, the new communication technologies emerging today are changing and will continue to change the way we relate to sport. We now no longer have to wait for *SportsCenter* to go on the air to catch up on the day's events. We can simply punch up our favorite sport news Web site on the Internet and get updates on games just completed and even those in progress. And if we're watching a live broadcast of a game on television, we can expand our game experience by going online for "enhanced" coverage where we can track game statistics and respond to various poll questions regarding the contest.

Emerging Technologies

The technological advances of recent years make this an exciting and challenging time for sport public relations professionals. We now possess the capacity for instantaneous communication and access to a pool of information that perhaps should more accurately be renamed an ocean.

The **Internet** is a global computer network offering access to information housed on a multitude of smaller networks linked by a common set of computer protocols or standards (Holtz, 1999). Even those of us who are not computer gurus may frequently rely on the Internet for communication. **E-mail** allows us to transmit messages to designated individuals over the Internet. Senders and receivers of e-mail must have specific designations or e-mail addresses in order to properly

---

Growth of the Internet

The growth of the Internet has been the single most important development in sport communications in recent years. As of 2000 more than 300 million people worldwide were using the Internet (World Almanac, 2002). In addition, it has been estimated that 39% of the U.S. population goes online to access sports information ("*SportsBusiness Journal*/ESPN Sports Poll," 2001). Not surprisingly, sport Web sites such as espn.com, sportsline.com, and nfl.com frequently draw heavy traffic.

While most speculate that the Internet will continue to grow through the early 2000s, some believe that growth will be largely dictated by the rate at which broadband technologies are adopted (Liberman, 2001). If that technology, which allows for high-quality receipt of Internet video, becomes widespread, the medium's growth could continue at a rapid pace. In fact, one technology group now estimates that 80% of U.S. homes will have broadband Internet access by 2010 ("Communications Today," 2001).

direct their communication. However, it is relatively simple and inexpensive (some organizations offer free e-mail service) to gain such an address. Many of us who now use e-mail can scarcely remember how we functioned without it.

Internet—A global network providing access to computers around the world with an ever-expanding menu of services. "Surfing the Internet" has entered our culture's jargon to describe the use of Internet services and capabilities.

e-mail—A form of communication available electronically via the Internet. E-mail allows online computer users to transmit messages to individuals with specific designations (i.e., e-mail addresses).

Another dimension of the Internet is the **World Wide Web,** a collection of Web sites that we can access through a browser such as Internet Explorer or Netscape Navigator. Surfing the Web is now a "user-friendly" experience. All we have to do is point and click. That is to say, we can access all sorts of information by simply clicking on the appropriate link appearing on our computer screen that connects us to the Web site we want to visit. The World Wide Web allows us to select content from a vast array of sources (some of them credible and ethical, some of them not). It also allows for a two-way flow of information as we can send messages by participating in an online discussion, responding to surveys, or sending messages to

online content providers via e-mail. Sport-related Web sites such as espn.com (ESPN's Web site) and nfl.com (the National Football League's Web site) frequently provide information and interactive forums (e.g., discussions, online games) and sell products (e.g., tickets, merchandise).

World Wide Web—A collection of Web sites accessible to online computer users via an Internet browser.

If you are interested in pursuing a career in sport public relations, you need to become familiar with this technology. Marshall McLuhan, whose 1966 *Understanding Media: The Extensions of Man* was embraced, ignored, and recently revived by communication scholars and media enthusiasts, said, "The medium is the message." He was right. The technological advancements of recent years have changed our world. Technology isn't an option in sport communication; it is the absolute—or virtual—reality.

LEARNING ACTIVITY

Investigate the computer technologies available at your school, in particular any instructional sessions available free to students either through direct instruction or computer-assisted instruction. Become familiar with some of the most basic computer applications that would be of value to sport public relations professionals and keep track of any innovations that

---

Case Discussion

Congratulations! You have just landed your first full-time paid position in sport public relations. Specifically, you have just been named the director of public relations for a minor league professional basketball franchise. As such, you are responsible for coordinating all aspects of the organization's public relations efforts. These include media relations, community relations, and other public relations activities.

One of your first priorities is to significantly upgrade the team's Web site. So far, the Web site has been pretty basic, including general information such as the team's schedule and results. You now have the opportunity to work in conjunction with a technical specialist to expand the site. Your part of the equation is content—what to include and how to organize it. As you consider the possibilities, think about the following questions:

- How could the work you'll be doing in media relations significantly expand the content you make available to visitors of your Web site?

- What aspects of your community relations program would you want to highlight on the Web site?

- How could you expand the site's function to make it a tool for a two-way flow of information?

You are likely to find some great ideas by visiting the Web sites of similar organizations and seeing how they are using those sites as public relations tools.

received publicity during this school term. What are the implications of the innovation for sport public relations professionals?

Implications for Sport Public Relations Professionals

The emergence of these new technologies has already had a major impact on the way many sport public relations professionals practice their profession, and it seems certain that more changes are on the way. In fact, some communication experts believe the communication technologies that have recently emerged hold the potential to revolutionize the field.

One advantage that many sport organizations have already realized through the Internet is the ability to disseminate messages to a mass audience quickly and inexpensively without having to go through the mass media. Only a few years ago, sport media relations professionals were completely reliant on the mass media to convey messages that originated with the sport organization through news releases. If the media did not use the releases, the information simply was not available to the public. Now, sport public relations practitioners can post that information on organizational Web sites where interested parties can access it at their convenience. Or they can e-mail the information to a distribution list of interested parties who have previously provided their addresses to the organization. This offers a level of message control previously unattainable in the field.

Additionally, the Internet provides a forum for a two-way flow of communication with the public. Many sport organizations are only now beginning to take advantage of this opportunity. However, some sport managers are doing some simple but innovative things. For example, Mark Cuban, the controversial owner of the NBA's Dallas Mavericks, allows fans to e-mail him directly, and he even takes time to reply! Cuban made his fortune in new technology, and now he is using technology to engage in direct communication with his publics. In fact, the Internet may be one of the most effective tools available to public relations professionals trying to manage relationships with multiple constituents (Holtz, 1999).

Of course, new technology frequently has a way of making things more complicated, and sport public relations professionals are also finding this to be true. Media relations specialists in particular are dealing with a couple of troublesome issues. First, they are finding that more and more print journalists are able to post information online about games in progress. This has raised concerns among broadcast media outlets that have paid rights fees for what they believed to be the exclusive right to carry live game information. The broadcast partners are calling on sport organizations to deny journalists the rights to post play-by-play updates as they happen (Schoenfeld, 1999). Media relations professionals are now developing policies that seek to find a balance between the interests of Web site journalists and broadcast partners. Another issue they are facing is the growing amount of noncredible information (e.g., false rumors about a sport organization) and nonauthorized credible information appearing on the Web. One college football team even discovered video of its practices on the Internet the week before a game against a conference rival (Matuszewski, 2000)! These issues, and others, will call on sport public relations professionals to adjust their strategies as new technologies continue to develop.

SUMMARY

Public relations in sport presents an exciting and viable career option for prospective sport managers. At its best, the public relations function allows sport organizations to build healthy relationships with their key constituents. Jobs in the field include positions in media relations, community relations, and other related areas. Regardless of the specific job, however, strong written and oral communication skills are a necessity. Since competition for sport public relations jobs is fierce, it is also crucial that you gain substantial volunteer and internship experience while you are still in college.

Given the relatively unique relationship between the mass media and sport, a high number of media relations positions are available in the field. Sport media relations professionals disseminate information to the public through the mass media or through organizational Web sites. They also manage additional media requests, service the media during games or events, and manage records and statistics.

Sport community relations professionals generate goodwill for their organizations. They coordinate organizational participation in charitable endeavors, fund-raisers that benefit various nonprofits, and public appearances by managers and players. They also coordinate special promotional events. By carefully executing these activities, they enhance their communities and their organizations' reputations within their communities.

Advancements in technology are changing the way sport public relations professionals operate. Relatively recent developments such as the Internet afford opportunities to reach constituents directly, instantaneously, and interactively. Web technology is also calling on sport public relations professionals to meet new challenges as the amount of sports information available to consumers escalates rapidly.

REVIEW QUESTIONS

1. How would you define *public relations*? Why is public relations so important to sport organizations?

2. What skills and experiences are most important to prospective public relations professionals? If you were to begin planning now for a career in sport public relations, what sort of experiences should you seek out?

3. Describe the work of sport media relations professionals. What sorts of tasks are a part of their job descriptions? What are the advantages and disadvantages of their jobs?

4. Describe the work of sport community relations professionals. What sorts of tasks are a part of their job descriptions? What are the advantages and disadvantages of their jobs?

5. What are some of the other public relations positions sometimes available in sport organizations?

6. What emerging technologies are having an impact on sport public relations professionals? What do you see as the greatest opportunities and threats these technologies bring to the profession?

7. What are some of the common ethical issues facing sport public relations professionals? How can professional codes of ethics help sport public relations practitioners?

Job Opportunities

Assistant Sports Information Director

Midsize university with Division I athletics program for a wide variety of men's and women's sports is looking for an addition to its sports information staff. The successful candidate will have a bachelor's or master's degree in journalism or a sport-related field with at least two years of sports information experience with a college, facility, or professional sport team. Superior oral and written communication skills a must! Primary responsibilities include writing and editing press guides and programs. The position requires extensive evening and weekend work. Salary is commensurate with experience.

Promotions Director

Health facility in urban area seeks a self-motivated individual with three to five years of experience working promotion or public relations with some experience in a sport- or fitness-related field. A bachelor's degree in journalism, communication, or sport management strongly preferred. Strong writing and speaking skills, good organization, and a high level of creativity and flexibility a must. Job responsibilities include special events planning, media relations, membership promotion, and marketing. The individual will work closely with the facility director and the facility's 20-member community board.

Community Relations Assistant

Major-level professional sport franchise seeks qualified applicant to assist in all aspects of the team's community relations program. These include, but are not limited to, off-season promotional tours, fan festivals, charitable fund-raisers, special appearances, ticket donations, and research projects as needed. Qualifications include two years of related experience. Excellent communication skills required. Must be proficient in word processing and database management software. Must be a self-starter, well organized, and willing to work flexible hours that frequently include evenings and weekends.

Director of Public Relations

Sport-related entertainment company in major market seeks qualified applicant to generate public exposure that will result in increased revenue. The successful applicant will work to promote ticket sales for more than 25 varied sport events each year. Specific responsibilities include media relations, Web site management, and promotional event planning and execution. The ideal candidate possesses five years or more of experience in sport promotion. Excellent communication, interpersonal, and organizational skills required.

Corporate Communications Assistant

Sporting goods manufacturer seeks team-oriented communicator to assist in various public relations initiatives. Specific responsibilities include producing employee newsletter, creating other promotional materials, and assisting in the execution of a product donations program. Bachelor's degree in a related field required. Solid oral and written communication skills a necessity. Must be able to meet deadlines and handle multiple project assignments simultaneously.

Director of Communications

Professional sport league office seeks qualified candidate to manage all aspects of the league's public relations and to serve as a resource for member clubs as necessary. Responsibilities include producing league publications (e.g., official league magazine), writing support materials for league video productions, and managing the league's Web site. Must possess strong communication skills and be adept with job-related computer programs. Candidates with diverse public relations experience in minor league sports may be particularly well suited to this position.

REFERENCES

Broadcasting and cable yearbook. (2001). New Providence, NJ: R.R. Bowker.

Chamberlin, A. (1990). Sports information. In J.B. Parks & B.R.K. Zanger (Eds.), *Sport & fitness management: Career strategies and professional content* (pp. 63-72). Champaign, IL: Human Kinetics.

Communications Today. (2001, December 20). *World Wide Web turns 10*, 7 (237). Retrieved November 15, 2002, from www.telecomweb.con/

Cutlip, S.M., Center, A.H., & Broom, G.M. (1994). *Effective public relations* (7th ed.). Englewood Cliffs, NJ: Prentice Hall.

Dallas Stars. (2000). *Community report.* Arlington, TX: Author.

Deeter, W.R. (1993). Great communicators: The growing importance of corporate communications. In B.J. Morgan (Ed.), *Public relations career directory* (5th ed.) (pp. 53-58). Detroit: Gale Research.

Gregory, H. (2002). *Public speaking for college and career* (6th ed.). New York: McGraw-Hill.

Grunig, J.E., & Grunig, L.A. (1992). Models of public relations and communication. In J.E. Grunig (Ed.), *Excellence in public relations and communication management* (pp. 285-325). Hillsdale, NJ: Erlbaum.

Holtz, S. (1999). *Public relations on the net.* New York: American Management Association Publications.

Leonard, W.M. II. (1998). *A sociological perspective of sport* (5th ed.). Needham Heights, MA: Allyn and Bacon.

Lesly, P. (1998). The nature and role of public relations. In P. Lesly (Ed.), *Lesly's handbook of public relations and communications* (5th ed.) (pp. 3-18). Lincolnwood, IL: NTC Contemporary.

Liberman, N. (2001, June 25-July 1). Once-hot Web hits a cool spell. *Street & Smith's SportsBusiness Journal, 4,* 44.

Jackowski, M. (2000, October 2-8). Repair, rebuild relationships with your community. *Street & Smith's SportsBusiness Journal, 3,* 40-41.

Matuszewski, E. (2000). Tangled Web. *College Sports Information Directors of America Digest, 50*(2), 7.

McLuhan, M. (1966). *Understanding media: The extensions of man.* New York: McGraw-Hill.

Mullin, B.J., Hardy, S., & Sutton, W.A. (2000). *Sport marketing* (2nd ed.). Champaign, IL: Human Kinetics.

New Balance. (2001). *Community involvement: Giving guidelines.* Boston: Author. Retrieved February 12, 2002, from www.newbalance.com/aboutus/cmnty/guidelines.html.

Newspaper Association of America. (2000a). *Highlights.* Vienna, VA: Author. Retrieved February 1, 2002, from www.naa.org/marketscope/audiencesheets/highlights.html.

Newspaper Association of America. (2000b). *Section readership by gender.* Vienna, VA: Author. Retrieved February 1, 2002, from www.naa.org/marketscope/readership2000/1t_Gender/genderT1.html.

Nichols, W., Moynahan, P., Hall, A., & Taylor, J. (2002). *Media relations in sport.* Morgantown, WV: Fitness Information Technology.

Peak, B. (1998). Community relations. In P. Lesly (Ed.), *Lesly's handbook of public relations and communications* (5th ed.) (pp. 113-136). Lincolnwood, IL: NTC Contemporary.

Perman, S. (1998, January 26). Thrown for a loss by the NFL. *Time, 151,* 52-53.

Schoenfeld, B. (1999, September 27-October 3). Vikings take issue with journalism's new speed. *Street & Smith's SportsBusiness Journal, 2,* 21.

Schoenfeld, B. (2000, November 20-26). Snyder, Skins take charity to a new level. *Street & Smith's SportsBusiness Journal, 3,* 24.

Schramm, W. (1954). How communication works. In W. Schramm (Ed.), *The process and effects of mass communication* (pp. 3-26). Urbana: University of Illinois Press.

Severin, W.J., & Tankard, J.W., Jr. (1997). *Communication theories: Origins, methods and uses in the mass media* (4th ed.). White Plains, NY: Longman.

SportsBusiness Journal/ESPN Sports Poll. (2000, June 11-17). *Street & Smith's SportsBusiness Journal, 4,* 13.

Stoldt, G.C. (2000). Current and ideal organizational roles of NCAA Division I-A sports information professionals. *The Cyber-Journal of Sport Marketing, 4*(1). Retrieved May 24, 2000, from www.cjsm.com/vol4.stoldt41.htm.

Stoldt, G.C., Miller, L.K., Ayres, T.A., & Comfort, P.G. (2000). Crisis management planning: A necessity for sport managers. *International Journal of Sport Management, 1,* 253-266.

World Almanac. (2002). *Internet basics.* Mahweh, NJ: Primedia Reference. Retrieved January 17, 2002, from OCLC FirstSearch database at http://newfirstsearch.oclc.org.

Chapter 12

Finance, Economics, and Budgeting in the Sport Industry

Timothy D. DeSchriver, University of Massachusetts, Amherst
Daniel F. Mahony, University of Louisville

Sport is one of the most diverse industries in the business world. It is composed of subindustries such as professional sports, collegiate athletics, facility management, health and fitness, and sporting goods. This diversity makes it somewhat difficult to measure the overall economic size of the industry. For example, should the sale of a pair of hiking boots be considered sport spending? Should the $50 million that Coca-Cola spends to be an official Olympic Games sponsor be considered sport spending?

The lack of an exact definition of the sport industry has led to a variety of measures of the size of the sport industry. As noted in chapter 1, Meek (1997) estimated that the cumulative spending on sport-related goods and services in the United States was $152 billion in 1995. Based on this estimate, sport was the 11th largest industry in the United States, larger than both the insurance and legal services industries (Meek, 1997). More recently, *Street & Smith's SportsBusiness Journal* estimated that the size of the sport industry was approximately $212.53 billion in 1997, with an annual growth rate of 9.9% (Broughton, Lee, & Nethery, 1999). While the U.S. Department of Commerce does not estimate the overall size of the sport industry, it does provide some financial information on the size of specific sectors within the sport industry (see table 12.1). For example, in 1997 approximately $1.34 billion was spent at skiing facilities such as Steamboat Springs Resort in Colorado and Camelback Mountain in Pennsylvania. The skiing industry also employed over 58,000 full-time workers.

While the actual dollar amount that can be attributed to the sport industry may be debatable, all of the estimates make it very clear that sport contributes a great deal to the U.S. economy. Sport

LEARNING OBJECTIVES

After studying this chapter, you will be able to do the following:

1. Explain the basic principles of microeconomics and macroeconomics.
2. Relate the theories of economics to the sport industry.
3. Discuss the concept of economic impact analysis and its relationship to sport events and facilities.
4. Describe the business structures of sport organizations.
5. Identify the basic tools of financial management.
6. Recognize the basic elements of financial statements for sport organizations.
7. Identify the various professional and career opportunities in the sport industry that are related to economics and financial management.

and recreation produce billions of dollars in sales and employ hundreds of thousands of workers. In addition, the sport industry has experienced significant growth in recent years, which has increased its importance within the U.S. economy (Mahony & Howard, 2001).

All of this growth and expansion leads us to this chapter's discussion of the economic and financial issues related to the sport industry. Now that we have briefly discussed the size and scope of the industry, we will spend the rest of the chapter presenting basic principles of economics and financial management, addressing their relationship

231

Table 12.1 Economic Activity of Selected Sport Industry Sectors

Sport industry subsector	Sales level	Number of full-time employees
Skiing facilities	$1.34 billion	58,513
Golf courses and country clubs	$8.63 billion	160,118
Fitness and recreational sport facilities	$7.94 billion	256,397
Professional sport teams and clubs	$7.81 billion	33,330
Racetracks (horse and dog)	$4.14 billion	44,880
Agents and managers for artists, athletes, and public figures	$2.41 billion	13,239

Source: 1997 Economic Census. (2001). U.S. Department of Commerce.

to the sport industry, and discussing career opportunities related to the financial management of the sport industry.

Current Financial Situation in the U.S. Professional Sport Industry

One segment of the sport industry that has seen tremendous growth over the past decade is professional sports. For example, Major League Baseball (MLB) in 2001 had operating revenues in excess of $3.5 billion (CBS News, 2001). Throughout the last decade, major professional men's sport leagues have seen their revenues increase over 10% annually. Despite this growth in revenue, there are economic problems. In particular, MLB has seen a widening gap between the high- and low-revenue teams. In 2001 the New York Yankees generated over $240 million, making them the highest revenue team in MLB, while the Montreal Expos ranked last in revenue with only $34 million. This is an economic concern because all teams, regardless of revenue, compete for the same players. The current revenue disparity makes it very difficult for teams who have older stadia or are located in small markets, such as the Expos, to acquire the best players and be competitive on the field. In the long run, this disparity may lead to a decrease in overall fan interest in Major League Baseball.

To try to avoid this problem, most professional men's leagues attempt to equalize the differences in team revenues through revenue sharing. For example, all of the traditional four major men's leagues (National Basketball Association, National Hockey League, Major League Baseball, and National Football League) share revenue from national television rights fees and merchandise sales.

Therefore, even though a team such as the New York Giants may be more popular than the Cincinnati Bengals, they both receive the same amount of money from the NFL's $2 billion annual television deals, the league's largest single source of revenues. Revenue sharing equalizes team revenues and allows teams in smaller markets to compete financially with the big market teams. This is very important for professional sports leagues. Unlike other industries, professional teams within a single league both compete and cooperate. While their teams attempt to beat each other on the field, team managers must cooperate in order to ensure financial success for all teams. If teams start to struggle financially, this would have a negative impact on the success of the league.

As you may have already noticed, professional men's sport leagues are heavily reliant on the media. For example, teams in the NFL generate more money from their national and local media deals than they do from gate receipts. Table 12.2 shows the amount of money that some professional leagues and college events generate from media rights. An interesting facet of these media deals is the financial connection between media companies such as AOL/Time Warner, News Corporation, and Disney and professional sport. For example, News Corporation owns the Fox Sports Network and its regional affiliates along with the FX cable station. In addition, it also owns the Los Angeles Dodgers. Therefore, when the Dodgers negotiate their local television rights deals, they are actually signing a deal with a fellow corporate subsidiary. Currently, teams such as the Chicago Cubs, Atlanta Braves, New York Rangers, and Texas Rangers are all owned by individuals or corporations that are involved in the media industry.

Despite the fact that most major professional men's sport leagues have seen media and other revenues grow substantially over the past decade,

Table 12.2 Sport Television Rights Deals

Property	Network(s)	Annual average	Length
NFL	CBS, Fox, ABC, ESPN	$2.2 billion	1998-2006
NBA	NBC, TNT, TBS	$660 million	1999-2002
MLB	Fox, FSN, ESPN	$652 million	2001-2006
NHL	ABC, ESPN	$120 million	1999-2004
NASCAR	NBC, TBS, Fox, FSN	$400 million	2001-2008
NCAA Men's Basketball Tournament	CBS	$545 million	2003-2013
Bowl Championship Series	ABC	$100 million	2002-2006

Sources: Major sports TV rights deals. (2001). [Online]. Available: www.sportsvueinc.com/facts/TV.htm; & Stewart, L. (2000, 27 October). October belongs to Fox. *Los Angeles Times*, p. ID.

this has not guaranteed overall profitability. Here, it must be stated that a business's profits are determined by both revenues and costs. The following equation can be used to calculate the profit level for a sport organization:

Profit = Total revenues – Total costs

Thus, while MLB has seen tremendous growth in revenues over the past decade, owners still claim to be losing money . They base this claim on cost increases in areas such as team payroll, travel expenses, and coaching and staff salaries. In December of 2001 Commissioner Bud Selig released financial information for the league showing that the 30 teams combined lost $232 million in the 2001 season (CBS News, 2001). While the accuracy of this number has been widely questioned, it is certainly true that some teams are not profitable because revenue growth has not kept up with large increases in team operating costs. Specifically, team owners have been unable to control their spending on players. The average player salary in Major League Baseball was over $2.1 million for the 2001 season. The most noteworthy salary is probably that of Alex Rodriguez, the shortstop for the Texas Rangers. Texas's owner, Tom Hicks, signed Rodriguez to a 10-year, $252 million contract beginning with the 2001 season. At $25 million per year, Rodriguez's salary is almost as much as the total payrolls of teams such as the Montreal Expos and the Minnesota Twins.

Like MLB owners, the National Hockey League owners have also had difficulty controlling player salaries. This has led to substantial losses for teams that have not been able to increase their revenues. However, in the NFL and NBA, owners have been able to negotiate agreements with players through the collective bargaining process, thus helping to control salaries. For these leagues, the amount of money that owners spend on players' salaries is based on the level of revenues they produce. Therefore, player salaries will increase only if the teams are generating additional revenue. This makes it much more difficult for NBA and NFL owners to become as financially stressed as some owners in the NHL and MLB, and it is why team profitability is more consistent in the former two leagues.

Current Financial Situation in U.S. College Athletics

Rising costs are also an important issue in collegiate athletics. Most collegiate athletics programs, even at the Division I level, do not produce enough revenue to cover their costs. A 1999 study of the finances in collegiate athletics (Fulks, 2000) found that only 71% of Division I-A athletics departments had revenues that exceeded costs, and in many cases this profit occurred only because the university provided institutional resources to the athletics department. It should be noted that the athletics departments at many universities rely on financial support from the overall university budget in order to cover all of their costs. In addition, the percentage of schools at which costs exceed revenues increases at the Division I-AA, II, and III levels.

Unfortunately, many other athletics departments face a similar situation. This is becoming increasingly true as costs increase in areas such as team travel, equipment, coaches' salaries, and grants-in-aid. Some colleges and universities have also seen their costs increase as they increase opportunities for women. In response to the financial pressure from increasing costs in all areas of collegiate athletic spending, some athletics departments have taken measures such as the elimination of sport teams and the reduction of scholarships. For example, in the spring of 2002 the University of Massachusetts, Amherst, was forced to eliminate seven varsity sports due to a $2 million budget deficit.

The rising costs have also put additional emphasis on the need to increase revenues. Athletics administrators have turned to private donations, corporate sponsorship, television, and merchandising for additional revenue. At the Division I level, athletics administrators have used television rights fees and ticket sales to help their financial situation. Within the past decade schools such as Penn State, Florida State, Virginia, and Texas A&M have all expanded their football stadia to increase ticket sales revenue and to meet spectator demand. A university such as Penn State can generate over $2 million in ticket revenue from one home football game at 106,537-seat Beaver Stadium ("Beaver Stadium," 2001). However, not all institutions are able to find additional revenue sources so easily. Many athletics departments are increasingly relying on student fees and other forms of institutional support to avoid large budget deficits. While this is true even at the Division I-A level, it becomes increasing common at lower Division levels in the NCAA and at NAIA schools where other revenue sources are more limited.

The largest single source of revenue in collegiate athletics is the annual Men's Basketball Championship. Beginning in 2003, CBS will pay the NCAA over $500 million per year for the right to televise three weeks of men's basketball in March (CBS, 1999). The $500 million will be about 90% of the overall revenues generated by the NCAA. Division I universities are quite pleased with this new deal because over 75% of this money is distributed from the NCAA to them. This will be a large increase over the $100 plus million per year received in the current contract (NCAA, 2001). This additional revenue will definitely help big-time college athletics departments pay for their growing expenses.

LEARNING ACTIVITY

List as many costs and revenue sources as you can think of associated with operating the following sport organizations:

- Professional sport franchise
- Collegiate intramural program

Economics of Sport

Many people are somewhat intimidated by the word *economics*. For some, it brings back memories of studying how intangible items such as widgets and utils are produced and sold. However, this stereotype is far from the whole story. Economics is one of the few academic disciplines that can be applied to almost any human action. Within the field of sport management, economics can help us understand issues such as the price paid by consumers for a pair of shorts in a sporting goods store, the escalating salaries of Major League Baseball players, and the decision made by a high school athlete to forgo college and play professionally.

Definition of Economics

The **economics of sport** may be defined as the study of how people within the sport industry deal with scarcity. This statement leads to the obvious question: What is scarcity? **Scarcity** is present in today's world because there are not enough resources to meet the wants and needs of society. For example, a health club may want 200 different machines available to its members. Unfortunately, due to the scarce amount of resources available to the club management, it may have the ability to provide only 50 machines. Economics helps determine how the health club management will decide to distribute its scarce resources not only on machines but also on staff salaries, rent, utilities, and office supplies.

economics of sport—The study of how people within the sport industry deal with scarcity.

scarcity—The basic economic problem facing all societies. A product is considered scarce if people want more of the product than is freely available for consumption.

Scarcity is an important issue in sport management because it is encountered by all managers. Managers have a maximum quantity of resources available for their use. Even the ultra-rich New York Yankees have a maximum amount of resources that they are willing to devote to players' salaries. It should be noted that the most successful managers are the ones who make the best use of these limited resources. While the fact that the Yankees have the most resources gives them an advantage in winning the World Series, it does not guarantee a championship, as was demonstrated in the 2001 World Series when they lost to the Arizona Diamondbacks. Their management must make wise decisions on how to allocate these resources most efficiently in order to be successful.

The limited resources available to managers are used to produce **goods** and **services** that are then sold to consumers. Goods and services are exchanged through the **economic interaction** of individuals and organizations. For example, the purchase of a new mountain bike at a store is an example of economic interaction. One product of value, a mountain bike, is exchanged for another product of value, cash. It is important to mention that not all economic interactions involve cash. For example, a business may provide free equipment, such as basketballs, to a three-on-three basketball tournament organizer in exchange for advertising space on the event T-shirt.

goods—Tangible products such as a pair of soccer cleats, a tennis racket, or a mountain bike.

services—Intangible products such as marketing advice, business consulting, and financial planning.

economic interaction—The exchange of one product of value for another product of value.

Transactions such as those just described occur in **markets**. A market may be an actual physical location such as a sporting goods store or a bicycle shop. It may also be an intangible idea such as a computerized stock exchange or the market for players in the WNBA. For teams such as the New York Liberty and the Miami Sol, there is a market where players are bought and sold, but the market is not an actual physical location. These markets are the core of economic activity. Without markets, goods and services could not be exchanged.

markets—Arrangements by which economic exchanges among people or businesses occur.

Economics has been traditionally separated into two areas of study: macroeconomics and microeconomics. The following sections will discuss these two areas and relate them to the sport industry.

Macroeconomics and the Sport Industry

Macroeconomics can be thought of as the "big picture" of economics. Topics such as economic growth and recession, the unemployment rate, and interest rates all come under the study of macroeconomics. While an individual sport business may be more focused on issues such as profits, employee costs, and the price of its product, it should also be concerned with the macroeconomic environment in which it operates. For example, companies such as Spalding, Rawlings, and New Balance that produce sport products may see their labor costs increase when unemployment is low. In another instance, country clubs may experience an increase in membership applications due to a strong economy. Both of these scenarios show how macroeconomic conditions may affect individual sport organizations.

macroeconomics—The study of the problems and workings of the economy as a whole (Taylor, 2001).

The year 2000 marked the ninth consecutive year of positive economic growth in the United States. It was the longest economic expansion in U.S. history. As stated earlier, the sport industry was similar to most other industries in that it saw unprecedented financial growth during those nine years (Mahony & Howard, 2001). Indeed, many young sport managers had never experienced an economic recession. As the year 2000 turned into 2001, it became obvious that the U.S. economy was entering a downturn. Some sport managers struggled as they faced a difficult business environment. Companies such as MVPsports.com and Quokka Sports went out of business due in part to the downturn in the economy.

Real Gross Domestic Product (GDP)

The most important aspect of macroeconomics is the measurement of the value of goods and services produced by a country, as explained by the **real gross domestic product (GDP)**. For the year 2000, the real GDP of the United States was approximately $9.3 trillion (Taylor, 2001). As mentioned earlier, there have been several estimates of the sport and recreation industry's real GDP. From these studies, let's assume that the sport industry's real GDP is about $200 billion. From this assumption, the sport and recreation industry composes approximately 2% of the overall real GDP for the United States. To put this in perspective, $2 out of every $100 of production is on sport- and recreation-related goods and services.

real gross domestic product (GDP)—The value of all the goods and services newly produced in a country during some period of time, adjusted for inflation.

It must also be recognized that the real GDP fluctuates over time. Over the course of several years, these fluctuations are known as **business cycles**. Overall, an economy is usually in either a state of economic **expansion** or **recession**. Most economists state that real GDP must decline for a minimum of six months for the economy to be in a state of recession. At some point, an economy will switch from expansion to recession. The point at which real GDP hits its highest point before it starts to decline is known as a **peak**. On the other end, the point at which real GDP hits its lowest point and then begins to increase is the **trough**. Figure 12.1 provides a graphic representation of the business cycle.

business cycles—The highs and lows in the level of economic activity over several years.

expansion—A period in which there is positive economic growth.

recession—A decline in economic activity, or real GDP, that lasts for a minimum of six months.

peak—A point at which economic activity has reached a temporary maximum level.

trough—A point at which economic activity has "bottomed out" at its lowest level.

Successful sport managers must have the ability to determine how economic expansions and recessions will affect their individual businesses. Many retail businesses such as sporting goods stores see declines in sales during periods of recession and vice versa during expansions. Ironically, many economists believe that some sport events experience increased ticket sales during recessions. Sport events, especially minor league sports, are fairly inexpensive. Therefore, during a recession, consumers who may have less spending money than usual may attend low-cost sport events such as minor league baseball and hockey games.

Interest Rates

Interest rates are another important aspect of macroeconomics. The **interest rate** is the amount that financial institutions, such as banks, charge when they lend money. It is presented as a percentage of the amount of money loaned (Baumol & Blinder, 1986). For example, a business may borrow $1,000 from a bank for a year at an interest rate of 5%. At the end of the year, the business will owe the bank $1,050:

$$\$1,000 + (1,000 \times .05) = \$1,050$$

interest rate—The amount a financial institution charges when it lends money. It is stated as a percentage of the amount borrowed.

The interest rate is important because many sport organizations must borrow money in order to operate. For example, two people wanting to open a new sport marketing agency may need to borrow money to start their business. They do not, most likely, have enough money to pay for

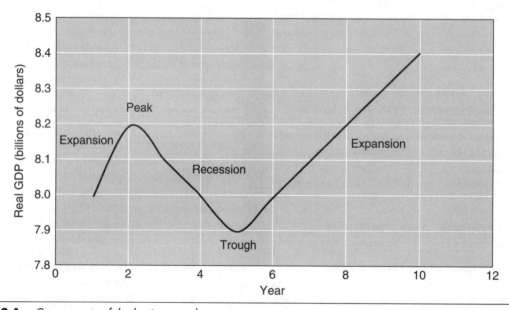

Figure 12.1 Components of the business cycle.

start-up costs on items such as computers, rent, utilities, and office supplies. Therefore, they will borrow money from a financial institution. The owners believe the agency will generate sufficient revenues to pay for all their operating costs and also the annual payment to the bank for the money that was borrowed plus the interest.

Recently the professional sport industry has seen a boom in new-facility construction. Cities such as San Francisco, Detroit, Los Angeles, and Boston have all built new stadia or arenas in the past five years. In every case, the team's ownership has been forced to borrow some money to pay for their share of the construction expenses. For the New England Patriots' new Gillette Stadium, team ownership borrowed $312 million to pay for their share of the $350 million total construction cost (Kaplan, 2000). When dealing with such large sums of money, a change in the interest rate of only 1% means a difference of millions of dollars. Clearly, when borrowing funds, the general goal of the sport manager should be to obtain the lowest possible interest rate.

Inflation Rate

Another aspect of macroeconomics that sport managers should be concerned with is the inflation rate. The **inflation rate** is the percentage increase in the overall price level of goods and services over a given period of time, usually one year (Taylor, 2001). For example, if the current inflation rate is 4%, we would expect that a product that costs $100 today will cost approximately $104 in one year. Inflation is closely tied to the real GDP. Historically, we have seen inflation increase just prior to periods of economic recession, and it has decreased during and after recessions. Since inflation measures the general trend of prices, it has a great effect on sport organizations. A collegiate athletic program may see its costs for items such as equipment, uniforms, and gasoline rise due to inflation. In order to remain profitable, the program may raise ticket prices or attempt to attract new corporate sponsorship dollars. Both of these actions would be attempts to increase revenues. If the program does not increase its revenues, it will become less profitable as costs rise due to inflation.

inflation rate—The percentage increase in the overall price level of goods and services over a given period of time, usually one year.

As you can see, macroeconomics plays an important role in the field of sport management. The field of macroeconomics is quite complex, however, and this section has provided only some of the basic concepts. An introductory course in macroeconomics will offer much more in-depth information.

LEARNING ACTIVITY

How do you believe an economic recession would affect the following aspects of the sport industry?

- Corporate sponsorship of sport events
- Luxury sailing vessels
- Minor league professional hockey games

Microeconomics and the Sport Industry

Microeconomics is the study of the behavior of individual businesses and households (Keat & Young, 2000). It uses economic theories to explain specific industries such as sport and recreation, automobile manufacturing, and health care. Microeconomics studies variables such as price, revenues, costs, and profits for individual industries and organizations. For example, microeconomics helps to explain why you may walk into two sporting goods stores and see different prices for the same model of running shoe.

microeconomics—The study of the behavior of individual businesses and households.

Supply–Demand Model

Microeconomists often use models to explain the behavior of producers and consumers. These models are simplified descriptions of how markets operate. There are two fundamental aspects of a market: demand and supply. The supply–demand model is the most widely used and most powerful model in economics. As you will see, an accurate supply–demand model can provide information on the amount of a product or service that consumers are willing to buy at different prices, the amount suppliers are willing to produce at different prices, and the final price that consumers will pay.

We will begin by discussing demand. **Demand** is the relationship between the price of a product and the amount of the product that consumers are willing to buy. The amount that consumers are willing to buy at various prices will be referred to as the **quantity demanded**. In general, consumers will demand less of a product as its price increases, and they will demand more

237

Table 12.3 Demand Schedule for Athletic Shoes	
Price	**Quantity demanded**
$140	2
$120	4
$100	6
$ 80	8
$ 60	10
$ 40	12
$ 20	14

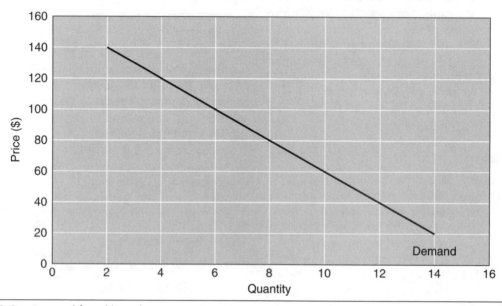

Figure 12.2   Demand for athletic shoes.

of a product as its price falls. This is known as the **law of demand.** Demand can be shown through either a tabular or graphic representation. Let's use the example of a hypothetical market for athletic shoes. Table 12.3 shows the quantity of athletic shoes demanded by consumers at different price levels. The same relationship is graphically illustrated in figure 12.2. As you can see, the demand curve is downward sloping. This will always be true due to the law of demand.

demand—The relationship between the price of a product and the amount of the product that consumers are willing to buy.

quantity demanded—The amount of a product that consumers are willing to buy at various price levels.

law of demand—Consumers will demand less of a product as its price increases and more of a product as its price falls.

The other side of the supply–demand model is supply. **Supply** is the relationship between the price of a product and the amount of the product that suppliers are willing to produce and sell. The amount that suppliers are willing to produce and sell at various prices is known as the **quantity supplied.** Overall, suppliers will increase production as the price of the product increases and decrease production as the price falls. This is referred to as the **law of supply.** Similar to demand, we can represent supply in both tabular and graphic forms. Let's continue with the athletic shoe example. Table 12.4 shows the quantity of athletic shoes supplied by businesses in the mar-

Table 12.4 Supply Schedule for Athletic Shoes

Price	Quantity supplied
$140	14
$120	12
$100	10
$ 80	8
$ 60	6
$ 40	4
$ 20	2

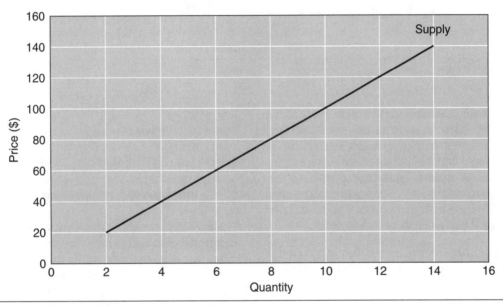

Figure 12.3 Supply of athletic shoes.

ket at various prices, and figure 12.3 presents the information in graphic form. It is important to note that the supply curve will generally have this upward-sloping shape. Again, this is because suppliers will increase production as the price they can charge for their product increases.

supply—The relationship between the price of a product and the amount of the product that suppliers are willing to produce and sell.

quantity supplied—The amount that suppliers are willing to produce and sell at various price levels.

law of supply—Suppliers will increase production as the price of the product increases and decrease production as the price falls.

The last phase of the supply–demand model is to determine **market equilibrium**. By analyzing

tables 12.3 and 12.4, you can determine that at a price of $80 consumers are willing to buy eight pairs of athletic shoes and suppliers are willing to produce and sell eight pairs of shoes. Thus, this would be the market equilibrium. Graphically, market equilibrium is represented by the intersection of the supply and demand curves. Figure 12.4 shows that at the intersection of the supply and demand curves the equilibrium price and quantity are $80 and eight pairs of shoes, respectively.

market equilibrium—The price at which the quantity demanded equals the quantity supplied.

You may wonder what would happen if the price of athletic shoes were $100. Notice that at a price of $100, consumers are willing to buy 6 pairs of shoes and suppliers are willing to sell 10 pairs of shoes. Under these circumstances, the market is

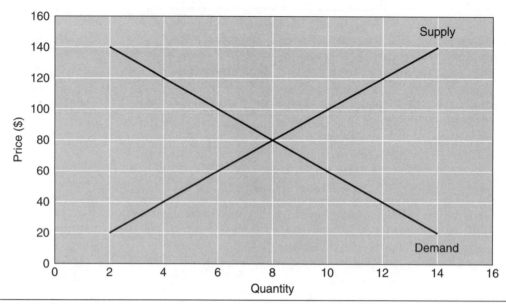

Figure 12.4 Athletic shoe market.

not in equilibrium. We would refer to this situation as a **market surplus** because producers are willing to sell more shoes than consumers are willing to buy. Conversely, it is also possible to have a market shortage. A **market shortage** occurs when consumers are willing to buy more athletic shoes than suppliers are willing to produce and sell. This would occur if the price were at $60.

market surplus—A price at which the quantity supplied of a product is greater than the quantity demanded.

market shortage—A price at which the quantity demanded of a product is greater than the quantity supplied.

As you can see, the supply–demand model is a very powerful tool in microeconomics. It helps us determine the quantity demanded and supplied of a product at various prices and the equilibrium price and quantity. Additionally, it can also show whether the market is in a state of surplus or shortage.

Market Structures

The structure of markets is another important aspect of microeconomics. As we said earlier, all products are sold in markets. There are many different types of markets within the sport industry. For example, the market for the purchasing of stadium naming rights is much different from the market for athletic footwear. Economists attempt to group markets based on characteristics such as the number of sellers, the ability of sellers to differentiate their products from those of the competition, and the ability of producers to enter and exit the market. In general, individual markets can be separated into four categories: perfect competition, monopolistic competition, oligopoly, and monopoly .

Perfectly competitive and **monopolistically competitive markets** have the greatest number of organizations involved in the market. In addition, companies that produce and sell their product in a perfectly or monopolistically competitive market have little or no control over the price they may charge. If one producer attempts to sell its product at a price that is higher than that of its competition, consumers will simply buy from the competition. Therefore, in the long run, it is very difficult for companies in highly competitive markets to make relatively large profits. In most major cities the fitness industry is a good example of a highly competitive market. Consumers have their choice of dozens of fitness centers. If one center attempts to increase its prices dramatically, consumers will simply shift to the competition.

perfectly competitive market—A market that has a large number of suppliers and consumers; all suppliers produce an identical product, information is shared by all parties, and the market is easily entered and exited by suppliers.

monopolistically competitive market—A market that has a large number of suppliers and consumers; information is shared by all parties, the market is easily entered and exited by suppliers, and the product may be differentiated across suppliers.

Oligopolistic markets are characterized by a small number of suppliers. A good example of an oligopoly is the sport drink industry, 90% of which is controlled by Gatorade, Powerade, and Allsport (Keat & Young, 2000). Given the low number of producers, these three companies have greater control over the prices they charge to consumers. Thus, it is somewhat easier for them to make a profit compared to a company in a perfectly competitive market.

oligopolistic market—A market that has a small number of suppliers and a large number of consumers.

The final type of market is a **monopoly**. A monopoly is a market in which only one company sells the product. For example, the NCAA has the market over the televising of collegiate basketball championships. It is the only organization that sells that product. Therefore, the television networks must compete against each other in order to purchase this unique product. Because of the popularity of its product, the NCAA Men's Basketball Tournament, and the monopoly power that it has, the NCAA makes over $500 million per year from CBS for the exclusive television rights.

monopoly—A market that has only one supplier of the product.

LEARNING ACTIVITY

Develop examples of at least two markets within the sport industry that you would consider to be highly competitive. Also, provide two examples of sport-related markets that are oligopolies and two examples of markets that are monopolies.

Economic Impact of Sport Events and Facilities

With the growth of the sport industry, major sport events seem to take place on a weekly basis. While these events bring enjoyment to a community, they can also bring a substantial amount of economic activity. Community leaders believe that events such as the Olympics, the Super Bowl, and the NCAA Final Four will stimulate their local economies due to increased spending by out-of-town visitors. This spending will, in turn, increase local tax revenues and produce jobs (Howard &

Crompton, 1995). While major events such as those mentioned may produce millions of dollars for a local economy, smaller events such as road races, soccer tournaments, and festivals may also increase economic activity.

Sport economic impact studies are estimates of the change in the net economic activity in a community that occurs due to the spending attributed to a specific sport event or facility (Turco & Kelsey, 1992). These studies are very helpful in measuring the increase in revenues, tax dollars, and jobs due to a sport event or facility. For example, Rishe (2001) estimated that the 2001 NCAA Division I Women's Basketball Final Four had an economic impact of approximately $16 million on the St. Louis, Missouri, metropolitan area. In addition, the event generated about $6 million in labor income and $1 million in tax revenue. As you can see, while it may not attract the level of interest that the Super Bowl may attract, the NCAA Women's Final Four still has a significant economic impact on a community.

sport economic impact studies—studies of how expenditures on sport teams, events, or facilities economically affect a specific geographic region.

Economic impact studies are conducted by collecting information on the spending patterns of visitors to a sport event or facility. A researcher may distribute surveys to event spectators to determine how much they spent on things such as hotels, rental cars, food, game tickets, and merchandise. These data are then used to determine the overall new economic activity. Most often, computer software packages such as RIMS II and IMPLAN are used by researchers to calculate the final economic impact.

Economic impact analysis is often used by civic leaders when deciding to construct new sport facilities. Most new facilities are funded in part by public money from sources such as taxes and lottery revenues. For example, $169 million of public funds were used in Pittsburgh to build PNC Park, the home of the Pittsburgh Pirates. Also, about 75% of the $498 million it cost to build Safeco Field in Seattle came from public funding. Team owners, business community members, and civic leaders defend the use of public funds by stating that the new facilities will generate economic activity, tax revenues, and jobs. Thus, economic impact studies are an invaluable tool in the fight to obtain public funding.

There is some disagreement on the ability of sport events and facilities to generate economic activity. A study completed by the Maryland Department of Fiscal Services concluded that PSINet Stadium in Baltimore, Maryland, generates only about $33 million per year in economic benefits for the State of Maryland. In addition, the stadium only produced an additional 534 full-time jobs for the state. In comparison to other projects in the state, the new job creation is quite small. For example, Maryland's Sunny Day Fund for economic development cost taxpayers $32.5 million and produced 5,200 full-time jobs (Zimmerman, 1997). However, it must be noted that, while the Sunny Day Fund cannot produce a Super Bowl winning team like the 2001 Baltimore Ravens, proponents of the public financing of sport facilities also argue that the facilities and teams generate intrinsic benefits for a community that cannot be measured in dollars and cents.

Because economic impact studies are far from an exact science, the results are always in question. An economic impact analysis can be misrepresented in several different ways. As stated earlier, economic impact should include spending only from out-of-town visitors, not the spending of local residents who attend the games. For some events, economic impact results can be grossly overestimated if the spending of locals is also included. The spending by locals should not be included because even if the event did not occur or the facility did not exist, locals would most likely spend their money elsewhere in the community such as at a restaurant or movie theater.

As you can see, economic impact analysis is a very important topic in the economics of sport. Economic impact studies have received a significant amount of media attention as civic leaders and team owners have used them to justify the use of public funding for new sport facilities. It must be remembered that an economic impact study is only as good as the methods used to generate its results. Educated readers should always ask two questions when seeing the results of an economic impact study: (1) *Who* conducted the research? and (2) *How* was the research conducted? Unfortunately, economic impact studies may be manipulated to generate a wide variety of results. For example, a proponent of a new facility may greatly overestimate the economic impact, while a critic of the same facility may underestimate the economic impact. Ironically, the two sides may be using the same statistical information; they are simply analyzing it in very different ways.

LEARNING ACTIVITY

Conduct an Internet search to find the results of at least one economic impact study that was conducted for a sport event or facility.

Overview of Financial Management

Financial management is the "application of skills in the manipulation, use, and control of funds" (Mock, Shultz, Shultz, & Shuckett, 1968). In other words, financial management is how an organization deals with money-related matters. Generally, the functions of financial management are broken down into two broad areas—determining what to do with current financial resources (i.e., money) and determining how to procure additional financial resources (Mock et al., 1968). For example, in a given year the Chicago Bears earn a profit of $10 million. The question for the financial manager is, What should the Bears do with that money? The Bears could use the money to sign a high-priced free agent, to renovate their practice facility, or to increase the salaries of current employees. They could also invest the money or distribute the money among the current owners.

Even after the organization decides how to use the money, the financial manager must decide the method for distributing the money. For example, the Bears may decide to spend the money on a free agent. However, they still must structure the player's contract. The financial manager would try to determine the differences in cost between giving the player a large signing bonus up front and structuring the deal in such a way that the player will not receive most of the contract until a few years into the future. Choosing what to spend the money on and how to spend the money has some significant long- and short-term implications for the team. For example, in 1996 the Dallas Cowboys won the Super Bowl but put themselves in a difficult position by signing players to contracts that required large payments toward the ends of the contracts. This left them with little room under the salary cap to sign new players in later years.

While the example of the Bears allows for an interesting discussion, few sport organizations have the "problem" of deciding how to spend excess money. Because many sport organizations are struggling financially (Mahony & Howard, 2001), two of the key roles of the financial manager in sport is determining how much money will be needed to meet long-term obligations and how to procure those funds. While most involved with sports immediately think of selling tickets or merchandise as ways to increase available funds, a number of other means are available. For example, good investments can result in significant amounts of interest for the organization. Also, some sport teams have begun to sell stock in the team to raise funds; many leagues have collected large fees from expansion teams. Both of these actions generate revenue for all teams in the league.

Structure of Sport Businesses

In order to make financial decisions, the organization must understand its structure and current nature. This section will discuss how sport organizations are structured. We will also introduce the basic financial statements that people inside and outside the organization use to determine the current financial strengths and weaknesses of the sport organization.

Profit Versus Nonprofit Organizations

One of the key distinguishing characteristics of organizations is whether they are for-profit or nonprofit organizations. There are a number of examples of each within the sport industry. Profit-oriented organizations include sporting goods companies (e.g., Nike, Wilson, Callaway Golf), professional sport teams (e.g., Los Angeles Dodgers, New York Liberty, Dallas Mavericks), and some sport participation facilities (e.g., miniature golf courses, bowling alleys, health clubs). Traditionally, the primary goal in a profit-oriented company, as the name would suggest, is to produce a profit. While the owners may have other purposes (e.g., helping clients improve their health, winning championships), the pursuit of profit is generally the primary goal of the owners, and it is what drives many financial decisions.

In contrast, the pursuit of profit as the primary goal is a violation of the laws governing nonprofit organizations. Some nonprofit organizations in sport include most sport teams below the professional level (e.g., college, high school, youth), some membership clubs (e.g., YMCAs, private golf courses), and municipal sport organizations (e.g., municipal golf courses, community pools). The primary purpose of these organizations is generally to encourage sport participation among those who would not be served adequately by for-profit organizations. For example, a community pool can provide swimming opportunities for children whose families cannot afford to build a pool or buy a membership in a club with a pool. While nonprofit organizations cannot pursue profitability as a primary goal, they can be profitable. Some people believe that nonprofit organizations must end up with no profit at the end of the year, but this is not true. However, laws do govern what they can do with this profit. For example, a nonprofit ski slope cannot give a bonus to an executive based on profitability, but it can reinvest the money in new ski lifts in order to better serve its nonprofit purpose.

Sole Proprietorships, Partnerships, and Corporations

While nonprofit organizations do not have owners, a distinguishing feature among profit-oriented companies is the partnership structure. Among profit-oriented companies in sport, many organizations (e.g., Nike, Churchill Downs, Boston Celtics, Callaway Golf) are corporations. Corporations have multiple owners who own stock (i.e., an ownership share) in the company. In some cases, the stock is publicly traded, so anyone can buy an ownership interest in the company. However, some corporations have only a limited number of stockholders, and the stock is not publicly available.

The main advantage of the corporate structure is that the owners' liability is limited to the amount they invested. If you have $1 million invested in Nike, you cannot lose more than $1 million even if Nike is sued. This may not sound like a big advantage, but if your net worth as an individual is $100 million, this limited liability becomes very important. However, there are disadvantages as well. It is costly to incorporate a business, and corporations are essentially double taxed by the government. When a corporation makes a profit, its profits are taxed as are the individual owners when they receive their share of the earnings (i.e., dividends).

One alternative structure is a partnership. Partnerships are organizations in which two or more people provide the resources needed for the organization to operate. Examples of partnerships include many locally owned sporting goods stores, sport agent firms, sport travel companies, and some professional sport teams. Some people prefer partnerships to corporations because they are less expensive and easier to form and the owners are taxed only once. However, owners in partnerships do not have limited liability. For example, if you invest $1 million in a partnership and the partnership is sued, your potential liability is not limited to $1 million. In other words, you can lose everything, even if the mistake leading to the lawsuit was made by your partner. If you are worth $100 million, this is obviously a significant risk. There are some alternative structures (e.g., subchapter S corporations, limited liability partnerships) that are designed to avoid the major disadvantages of both partnerships and corporations, but organizations wishing to use these structures must meet specific regulations. A discussion of these regulations is beyond the scope of this chapter.

The final general structure is a sole proprietorship. Examples of sole proprietorships in sport would again include many locally owned sporting goods stores and sport agent firms. There are also a growing number of small Web-based companies that have only one owner. Sole proprietorships are similar to partnerships with a few differences. First, there is only one owner in the sole proprietorship instead of multiple owners. Second, the sole proprietorship is even easier to set up than the partnership. Third, while the sole proprietor still has unlimited liability, he or she is no longer liable for the actions of a co-owner. However, few people have the resources to be a sole proprietor, so this structure is not available to everyone.

Single-Entity Structure

As is discussed throughout this book, the sport industry is unusual or unique in some areas. One example is the use of the **single-entity structure** in professional sports. While professional sport teams are all members of a particular league and often share certain revenue sources and expenses, each team is generally operated as a separate entity. However, some new sport leagues (e.g., MLS, WNBA, WUSA) have gone with a single-entity structure. The advantage of using the single-entity structure in these fledgling leagues is that it allows the leagues to work together more efficiently and make decisions that focus more on what is good for the league than on what is good for an individual team. In addition, it allows the league to set limits for player salaries in a way that would be illegal if they were not using the single-entity structure. The long-term success of this structure is still unknown, but it is expected to be increasingly popular with new leagues.

single-entity structure—The configuration of a professional sport league in which all of the teams work together as a single unit.

Financial Statements

While the structure of the business will have some impact on how the business reports financial information, almost all sport organizations develop certain financial statements for their organizations on a regular basis. While it is beyond the scope of this chapter to discuss every detail included in financial statements and all of the ways the information in these statements can be examined in order to better understand the organization's current financial situation, we will provide a brief overview of the major financial statements and the useful information provided in these statements.

Balance Sheet

In figure 12.5 you will find the balance sheet for Couch Sporting Goods (CSG). In this example, Gary Couch is the sole proprietor of a sporting goods store. The balance sheet reflects the financial condition of the organization as of a particular date. Although the balance sheet is generally reported at the end of a given financial period (e.g., the end of the year), a financial manager can generate a balance sheet any time such information is needed. The balance sheet includes three categories—assets, liabilities, and owner's equity. Assets are the financial resources of the company and include both current assets and long-term assets. Current assets are generally items that are cash or expected to be converted into cash within the next year to meet current obligations. Long-term assets are items that are not expected to be turned into cash during the next year. Some examples include CSG's land, building, and equipment. All of these items are recorded at the price paid for them, and some are reduced as their value declines (i.e., accumulated depreciation). Long-term assets also include CSG's long-term investments, which may include investments such as government bonds that will not be converted to cash for a number of years.

Liabilities are obligations to pay money to others for goods or services. In other words, liabilities are what are owed to others. Current liabilities are those that are due to be paid in the next year (i.e., current obligations), while long-term liabilities are those that are due sometime after the current year. Owner's equity is Gary Couch's share of the business's resources. It includes both the money Gary has personally put into the company (i.e., paid-in capital) and Gary's earnings from the sporting goods store that he decided to leave in the company (i.e., retained earnings). As you can see in figure 12.5, total assets are equal to liabilities plus owner's equity. This is always true. Logically,

Couch Sporting Goods
Balance Sheet
December 31, 2002

Assets:
Current assets:

Cash	$265,000
Accounts receivable	150,000
Inventory	300,000
Prepaid expenses	50,000
Total current assets	765,000

Long-term assets:

Land	200,000
Building	70,000
Equipment	75,000
Less: Accumulated depreciation	40,000
Long-term investments	50,000
Total long-term assets	435,000

Total assets	$1,200,000

Liabilities:
Current liabilities:

Accounts payable	$250,000
Notes payable	150,000
Accruals payable	100,000
Total current liabilities	500,000

Long-term liabilities:

Notes payable	200,000
Bonds payable	200,000
Total long-term liabilities	400,000

Total liabilities	900,000

Owner's equity:

Paid-in capital	200,000
Retained earnings	100,000
Total owner's equity	300,000

Total liabilities and owner's equity	$1,200,000

Figure 12.5 Balance sheet for Couch Sporting Goods.

all of the resources (i.e., assets) either belong to the owner (i.e., owner's equity) or are owed to another entity (i.e., liabilities).

Income Statement

In figure 12.6 you will see the income statement for Couch Sporting Goods. The income statement provides the financial results of the organization's operations over a specific period of time. As with the balance sheet, the income statement is often reported at the end of the year but can be generated at any point and for any period of time. For many people, the income statement is the most important financial statement because it gives the user the organization's "bottom line" (i.e., the net profit or net loss). While completely understanding

Couch Sporting Goods
Income Statement
For the Period Ending December 31, 2002

Net sales	$1,200,000
Cost of sales	600,000
Gross profit	600,000
Operating expenses:	
Salaries	150,000
Rent	10,000
Utilities	5,000
Insurance	50,000
Advertising	10,000
Payroll taxes	20,000
Depreciation	5,000
Total operating expenses	250,000
Net operating income	350,000
Other income (expenses):	
Land sale	50,000
Interest income	2,000
Interest expense	(7,000)
Total other income (expenses)	45,000
Net taxable income	395,000
Income tax expense	100,000
Net income	$295,000

Figure 12.6   Income statement for Couch Sporting Goods.

the organization's financial situation requires a thorough examination of all of the financial statements, the bottom line gives the user a quick assessment of the organization and its success in achieving the primary goal of profit-oriented companies—profitability.

The income statement includes two categories—revenues and expenses. Revenue is the inflow of value to the business. It is important to note that revenue is the inflow of value and not the inflow of cash. Therefore, revenue is recorded when the good or service is delivered, not when the cash is received for that transaction. For example, when the New York Rangers sell a ticket to a December 4 hockey game in July, they do not recognize the revenue from that sale until the game is played on December 4. Likewise, if

customers are given tickets for the December 4 game with the promise that they will pay for them in January, the revenue is still recognized on December 4, not when the cash is received in January.

At the top of the income statement for Couch Sporting Goods (CSG) are net sales. This represents the amount of merchandise that CSG sold in 2002. Note that some other revenue items (e.g., land sale, interest income) are recorded toward the bottom of the income statement. These items are separated from the net sales because most financial analysts are more concerned with revenue from the company's main business, which is generally more useful for predicting future revenue. This will become clearer to you when you take a class in sport finance.

The expenses are generally separated into four categories: direct expenses (or cost of sales), operating expenses, other expenses, and income tax expense. Again, the income statement is much more useful to analysts if the expenses are recorded in this way. Direct expenses, or cost of sales, are expenses that can be directly matched to the main source(s) of revenue. For example, cost of sales is the total cost to CSG of all of the items sold in 2002. Operating expenses are other normal business expenses, such as salaries, rent, and utilities, that cannot be directly matched to specific revenue items. Other expenses are expenses that occur outside of the normal business operations for a given company. Items such as interest expense and unusual losses are often recorded here. For example, if CSG lost $10,000 in

a lawsuit, it would report that loss as an other expense. Finally, income tax expense is the amount the company pays to the Internal Revenue Service (IRS) related to the profits for the year. After subtracting all of the expenses from all of the revenue, the income statement provides the net income (loss) at the bottom of the statement; this is the "bottom line."

Statement of Cash Flow

The final financial statement we are going to discuss is the statement of cash flow, shown in figure 12.7. The purpose of the statement of cash flow is to show the inflow and outflow of cash during a given period of time. As previously discussed, the income statement does not record revenue and expenses when the cash is received or disbursed.

Couch Sporting Goods
Statement of Cash Flow
For the Period Ending December 31, 2002

			Operating activities
Net income			**$295,000**
Other additions (increases in cash)			
Depreciation	5,000		
Increases in accounts payable	50,000		
Increases in accruals payable	20,000		
Subtractions (decreases in cash)			
Increase in accounts receivable	(25,000)		
Increase in inventory	(75,000)		
Net cash flow from operations		270,000	
Long-Term Investing Activities			
Acquisition of fixed assets		(20,000)	
Financing activities			
Increase in notes payable	20,000		
Increase in bonds payable	30,000		
Removal of cash by owner	(150,000)		
Net cash flow from financing		(100,000)	
Net increase in cash		$150,000	
Cash at the beginning of the year		115,000	
Cash at the end of the year		$265,000	

Figure 12.7 Statement of cash flow for Couch Sporting Goods.

Scenario: Columbus University

Karen Petho, a longtime assistant athletics director, has finally received the opportunity to be an athletics director. Although she was very excited on the day of her appointment (January 1, 2003), she quickly found that her job at Columbus University was not going to be easy. Columbus University is a public institution in Seattle, Washington. The school has about 25,000 students and is ranked by *Barron's Guide to Colleges* as very competitive. The athletics department is a member of the NCAA (Division I-A). The CU Bears are also a member of the Big West Conference. The school is best known for its men's basketball team, which won the national championship many years ago and still remains a consistently strong performer. Currently, the Bears have 20 athletics teams (men's football, men's and women's basketball, men's and women's track, men's baseball, women's softball, men's and women's fencing, men's and women's golf, men's and women's tennis, men's wrestling, men's and women's volleyball, men's and women's gymnastics, and men's and women's lacrosse). With the exception of the men's basketball program, most of the other sport teams are average based on national standards in Division I-A.

The Columbus University athletics department, unlike many Division I programs, has generally produced enough revenue to cover its expenses without help from university funds or student fees. However, the program is beginning to have some major problems with its budget. The university now provides approximately $3 million in support, and about $1 million is funneled from student fees to the athletics department. Even with this money, the budget for revenues is projected to be about $26 million per year for the next four years, with the costs exceeding $31 million each year. Given this scenario, what options are available to help the athletics department balance its budget for the next four years? Discuss some revenue areas that may be increased and some expenses that may be reduced in order to balance the budget.

Additionally, the income statement focuses on items of value that are not cash in nature, such as depreciation. However, it is important for financial managers to specifically monitor the inflow and outflow of cash. Too much money in the form of cash may mean the organization should direct more of its money to interest-earning investments or expand its business operations. Too little in cash may mean the company needs to borrow money or limit some its expenditures. The statement of cash flow allows financial managers to monitor cash-related activity and make these types of decisions. Figure 12.7 shows that Couch Sporting Goods was able to increase its cash-on-hand significantly in 2002. Because of the small size of this company, CSG may want to shift some of that cash to long-term investments that would earn more interest for the company or look to expand the business.

LEARNING ACTIVITY

Identify three different types of business structures in the sport industry. Find financial statements for these businesses and look for similarities and differences. You can find the financial statements for many businesses at http://finance.yahoo.com or on companies' Web sites.

Sources of Revenues and Expenses for Sport Organizations

A variety of revenues and expenses are typical in the sport industry. However, these "typical" revenues and expenses will vary depending on the type of sport organization. In this section we will discuss briefly some of the business types in the sport industry and then examine some sources of revenues and expenses in these businesses.

Types of Sport Organizations

As previously discussed, there are many different types of sport organizations with many different goals. Some of the organizations are geared toward encouraging sport participation. These include youth sport organizations, community recreation, and high school sports. Other organizations seek to make a profit by providing participation opportunities for individuals that are not offered, or not offered as well, by nonprofit organizations. These include sport facilities that rent their facilities to participants (e.g., bowling alleys, health clubs), organizations that seek to train individuals (e.g., personal trainers, others that provide lessons in a particular sport), and organizations that provide the equipment necessary to participate in a certain sport (i.e., sporting goods companies).

In addition, many companies focus more on the sport spectator. These include both professional sports (e.g., WNBA, NASCAR, PGA) and "big-time" college sports. While these organizations make a large portion of money from sport spectators, other companies benefit from sport spectating as well. These include independent sport facilities that host sport events, the sport media that bring sport events and information related to sport events to the consumer (e.g., television, radio, magazines, the Internet), and companies that sell products licensed by these professional and college sport organizations.

The obvious diversity of the sport industry leads to a variety of revenue and expense sources. Some of these are fairly common across these companies. For example, many sport organizations are involved in some way with product sales on the revenue side and salaries, building costs, and supplies on the expense side. The next two sections will focus on types and aspects of revenues and expenses that are unique in the sport industry.

Sources of Revenues

Some of the revenue sources that are unique in sport are a number of items related to game attendance (e.g., concessions, personal seat licenses, luxury suite rentals, booster club donations), media rights, sponsorships, and licensing. While events outside of sport typically see the ticket price as the major source of revenue related to event attendance, this is not always true. The total price of attendance is often much greater than the cost of the ticket. Consider the following:

1. Most sport organizations charge fans an additional fee for parking during the event.

2. Fans typically spend money on concessions at the stadium. Purchasing hotdogs, beer, soda, and so on is considered by many fans to be an important part of the game experience.

3. Some professional and college sport teams are now charging fans for personal seat licenses. The personal seat license is a charge to the fan for the right to buy a particular seat. For example, a fan may buy a personal seat license for 10 years for $5,000. The fan must then pay for season tickets each year for the next 10 years. If the season ticket price is $500 per year, the fan will actually end up paying $10,000 (5,000 + [500 × 10]) over 10 years

for the privilege of watching games from that particular seat.

4. A fan who wants a nicer setting for watching games may decide to rent a luxury suite. Similar to the personal seat license, the fan must still purchase tickets for the game after paying the cost of renting the luxury suite.

5. College sport fans must often donate money to the athletics department in order to buy the best seats and in some cases to buy any seat. Therefore, the college sport fan may donate $1,000 each year in order to buy two $200 season tickets. In this case, the fan is actually paying $1,400 ($1,000 + $200 + $200) for the season tickets, or $700 per seat.

Because of the increasing cost of attending games (Howard, 1999), many sport spectators watch or listen to most games at home. Because of the large audience for sports outside of those attending games, many professional sport teams make a large percentage of their revenue from media contracts. For example, the National Football League (NFL) recently signed an eight-year contract worth $17.6 billion for the television rights to their games (Mahony & Howard, 2001). In addition, big-time college sports receive large amounts of money for their broadcasting rights. The NCAA's contract for the men's basketball tournament is at the top of the list with an 11-year contract worth $6.2 billion, a 252% increase from the current contract (Hiestand, 1999). Because the tournament is only 10 days long, this means the NCAA will receive an average of over $50 million per day for the broadcast rights. In many cases the television stations may make little or no money directly from the broadcast of sport events. However, they believe broadcasting games will be beneficial because they can use the broadcasts to promote other programming and they benefit from a positive association with sports.

Another group looking to take advantage of the positive association with sport events, leagues, teams, and players is corporate sponsors. Sponsors are paying approximately $8 billion a year to sponsor sport events, leagues, and teams (Howard, 2000) because they believe that if they are associated with these sport organizations, people will have a more positive image of their company and will be more likely to buy their products or services. The largest sums of money, such as the $300 million paid by Reliant Energy to the Houston Texans, have generally been paid for naming rights of stadiums ("Stadiums and arenas," 2002).

Likewise, corporations pay large amounts of money to athlete endorsers to help promote their products and services. For example, Nike became the dominant force in the athletic footwear industry at the same time the career of its top endorser, Michael Jordan, was taking off.

A final group looking to take advantage of the positive feelings sport spectators have about teams and players is the sellers of licensed products. Once a rather small industry, sport licensed product sales became big business during the 1980s (Howard & Crompton, 1995). While most people immediately think of player jerseys and team hats, the licensed products industry includes a variety of products, including video games, blankets, framed pictures, and sport equipment. While most of the money from these sales goes to the producers of these products, sport organizations do receive a percentage of these sales.

Sources of Expenses

Two sources of expenses that are most critical for most sport organizations are the cost of sport facilities and the cost of salaries. Sport facilities can be very expensive. While most sport organizations try to get local communities to help pay for stadia, many are finding they have to pay at least part of the cost. This results in long-term debt payments, which can affect the financial stability of the organization for many years. Sport facilities are also costly to maintain. This is particularly a problem in large open-air facilities that may not be used for much of the year but must be maintained year-round. Sport facilities also tend to become "obsolete" fairly quickly. If an organization has to make debt payments for 30 years, it may end up making payments on a facility that it is no longer using. In some cases, large sport facilities have been torn down before reaching their 30th birthday. All of these factors combined mean any organization making the decision to build a new facility must fully and carefully explore all of the options available. For example, some sport organizations have been able to offset some of the cost of a new facility by collecting personal seat license and luxury suite rental fees prior to the beginning of construction.

The increase in salaries in both professional and college sports during the last 30 years has been dramatic (Howard & Crompton, 1995). Players' and coaches' salaries often make up more than 50% of the expenses in professional sports, and college coaches are often by far the highest-paid employees on campus. As previously discussed, Alex Rodriguez recently signed a contract with the Texas Rangers that will pay him approximately $25 million per year, while Rick Pitino became one of the highest-paid college basketball coaches in the United States when he signed a deal with the University of Louisville worth about $2 million per year. While many suggest that the salaries are "worth it" because of the revenue that players and coaches bring in for an organization, some have questioned this assumption. Zimbalist (1999) found that even the best college coaches are worth less than $200,000 extra per year, and it is hard to explain how one player is capable of generating an additional $25 million per year in revenue. Therefore, while profits are important to these organizations, it is vital to understand that some of these salaries are not related to the bottom line. Some organizations may pay more than they can afford because the owner or university official cares more about winning than about profits. The strong desire in sports to win has probably led many sport organizations to make foolish financial decisions.

LEARNING ACTIVITY

Pick three sport organizations. Use sources such as Web sites to identify as many sources of expenses and revenues as possible for each. Compare and contrast the revenues and expenses for these three sport organizations.

Careers in Financial Management for Sport Organizations

There is an increasing variety of jobs related to financial management in sport. In the past, financial management jobs in sport were generally not very complicated. Many organizations had business managers who were basically bookkeepers. They recorded all receipts and distributions of money and made sure the organizations' financial records were in order. While these jobs still exist, many jobs today involve far more sophisticated financial management skills. For example, the Cleveland Indians' decision to issue public stock required sophisticated financial skills that the typical bookkeeper would not possess. Likewise, players' contract negotiations require that both the team and player hire someone with a strong understanding of financial management. As the sport industry becomes more sophisticated at all levels, the need for individuals with more sophisticated financial skills will become increasingly greater.

A number of jobs are available for individuals who are interested and have ability in the area of financial management. Some of the jobs that require financial management skills include ticket or box office manager, staff accountant, and athletics business manager. Because more sophisticated financial management skills are needed for some activities, many professional teams and other larger for-profit sport organizations will have individuals in positions of assistant general manager or vice president for financial operations with such skills. This is particularly true if the general manager or president does not possess the strong financial management skills necessary to make some of the more complicated financial decisions. For particularly complicated financial decisions, some sport organizations hire outside consulting firms to help with those decisions. A number of companies provide such advice, and some, including many of the major accounting firms, have individuals who specialize in sport consulting.

As a student of sport management, you must understand that the skills needed for many of these jobs, particularly those requiring highly sophisticated financial skills, will require you to take classes beyond the typical undergraduate sport management degree. One class in sport finance will not be enough to prepare you to handle a public stock offering.

LEARNING ACTIVITY

Talk to two people in sport organizations involved with financial management. Determine their educational background, experience, and current job responsibilities.

SUMMARY

This chapter focused on the financial and economic aspects of sport organizations. The sport industry is one of the largest industries in the world. While estimates may vary, the sport industry is believed to generate over $150 billion in sales in the United States alone. In order to understand information such as this, sport managers must familiarize themselves with both macroeconomic and microeconomic concepts. A successful sport manager needs to understand economic concepts such as supply and demand when determining the amount of a product to supply and the price at which the product should be sold. Additionally, we have shown that a market is an economic system in which products are bought and sold. Sport managers must recognize which of the four general markets (perfect competition, monopolistic competition, oligopoly, and monopoly) they are operating in. Another important economic concept that has been discussed is economic impact studies. These studies are critical in determining the amount of economic activity that is generated from a sport team, event, or facility. Economic impact studies are widely used by team owners, politicians, and activist groups when making decisions on the construction of a new sport facility or the acquisition of a sport franchise.

We have seen in this chapter that sport organizations are structured in a variety of ways, including as corporations, partnerships, and sole proprietorships. The sport industry even uses some unique formats, such as the single-entity structure in some professional sport leagues. Owners must examine the advantages and disadvantages of each potential structure before deciding which is best for their organization. Regardless of which structure is chosen, each organization will need to develop basic financial statements, such as a balance sheet, income statement, and statement of cash flow. Owners and others will use these statements to evaluate the company's financial position and financial success. In particular, many observers are interested in the company's revenues and expenses and their impact on the company's profitability. As discussed, many of the revenue and expense items in sport have grown at a rapid pace, which has made financial management in sport very challenging.

REVIEW QUESTIONS

1. Describe the difference between macroeconomics and microeconomics.

2. What is an interest rate? Why is it important to sport organizations that are in the process of getting started?

3. What are the four types of market structures? Provide sport examples of each.

4. Explain the meaning of economic impact.

5. Construct supply and demand curves from table 12.5 showing the supply and demand for tennis rackets.

Table 12.5 Supply and Demand for Tennis Rackets

Price	Quantity demanded	Quantity supplied
$250	3	18
$225	6	16
$200	9	14
$175	12	10
$150	15	8
$125	18	5

6. From table 12.5, determine the market equilibrium price and quantity for tennis rackets. What would happen if the price level were $150?

7. What are the different types of structures of businesses in the sport industry? Give examples of each.

8. What is the main purpose of each of the financial statements?

9. What type of useful information can be found in each financial statement?

10. What are the major sources of revenues and expenses in the sport industry? How are they different from or similar to those of nonsport organizations?

11. What types of positions are available in financial management in the sport industry? How are they similar and different?

Job Opportunities

Associate Director, Athletics/Finance

Bachelor's degree in accounting, business administration, finance, or related field required, with five to eight years of experience in managing a complex accounting operation. Advanced degree preferred. Previous significant experience in budgeting and expense analysis required, as are strong interpersonal, supervisory, written, and oral communication skills, as well as computer skills, including Excel, database management, and word processing. Certified Public Accountant highly preferred.

Athletics Ticket Manager

Duties: Administer all aspects of the athletics ticket office; manage and supervise ticket office staff; design ticket applications; coordinate sales and distribution; assign seats; maintain a system of internal controls to ensure that accounting and auditing procedures are followed; maintain computer ticketing system; compile game reports; and maintain cash flow. Qualifications: Experience in ticket office procedures, knowledge of basic accounting principles, demonstrated management skills, and excellent interpersonal skills. Bachelor's degree preferred with experience in a college sport arena. Willingness to work extended days, weekends, and holidays.

Accounting Manager

Local entertainment group seeks an individual who will be responsible for all accounting, budgeting, and reporting for the parent company. The ideal candidate will be a solution-finding, hands-on financial manager with solid accounting, diplomatic, interpersonal, and leadership skills. Past work experience in accounting and financial management of an organization or business is desired. A bachelor's degree in accounting, finance, or business is a minimum requirement.

Accountant

This position is responsible for maintaining some accounting and all accounts receivable requirements for an NBA team. Essential duties and responsibilities include: Assist in the preparation of monthly preliminary internal financial records. Assist in the preparation and monthly monitoring of annual budget, including variance analysis, monthly forecasting for revenue accounts, and some expense accounts. Support accounts payable with coding accruals, journal entries, and assessment of sales and use tax. Prepare game audit reconciliations. Prepare ticket tests for home games. Assist with monitoring cash flow. Assist senior accountant with various ad hoc projects. Timely invoicing of sponsorship deals, broadcast contracts, executive suite contracts, and other miscellaneous accounts. Record deposits. Make collection calls. Prepare cash reconciliations for ticket system. Prepare monthly ticket accounts/ receivable report. The successful candidate will have two years or more of accounting and accounts receivable experience; excellent attention to detail and organization skills; extensive computer knowledge, including Excel; and ability to work in a high-pressure environment with strict deadlines. We are looking for a team player with a customer service focus.

REFERENCES

Baumol, W.J., & Blinder, A.S. (1986). *Economics: Principles and policy, macroeconomics* (3rd ed.). New York: Harcourt Brace Jovanovich.

Beaver Stadium Information Page. (2001). [Online]. Available: www.gopsusports.com.

Broughton, D., Lee, J., & Nethery, R. (1999, December 20-26). The answer: $213 billion. *Street & Smith's SportsBusiness Journal,* 23-26.

CBS News (2001, December 6), *Baseball's profits and losses.* Retrieved November 20, 2002, from http://www.cbsnews.com/stories/2001/12/06/sports/main320297.shtml

Fulks, D.L. (2000). *Revenues and expenses of Divisions I and II intercollegiate athletic programs: Financial trends and relationships-1999.* Indianapolis, IN: The National Collegiate Athletic Association.

Hiestand, M. (1999, November 19). CBS locks in college hoops for $545M. *USA Today,* p. C1.

Howard, D.R. (1999). The changing fanscape of big-league sports: Implications for sport managers. *Journal of Sport Management, 13,* 78-91.

Howard, D.R. (2000, January 20). *Stadium financing in the new millennium.* Paper presented at the International Sports Summit, New York.

Howard, D.R., & Crompton, J.L. (1995). *Financing sport.* Morgantown, WV: Fitness Information Technology.

Kaplan, D. (2000, December 18-24). Pats' tab for stadium is highest ever. *Street & Smith's SportsBusiness Journal, 3,* 1, 48.

Keat, P.G., & Young, P.K. (2000). *Managerial economics: Economic tools for today's decision makers* (3rd ed.). Upper Saddle River, NJ: Prentice Hall.

Mahony, D.F., & Howard, D.R. (2001). Sport business in the next decade: A general overview of expected trends. *Journal of Sport Management, 15,* 275-296.

Meek, A. (1997). An estimate of the size and supported economic activity of the sports industry in the United States. *Sport Marketing Quarterly, 6*(4), 15-21.

Mock, E.J., Schultz, R.E., Shultz, R.G., & Shuckett, D.H. (1968). *Basic financial management: Text, problems, and cases.* Scranton, PA: International Text Company.

NCAA. (2001). 2001 NCAA Annual Report. Retrieved November 14, 2002 from http://www.ncaa.org/library/membership/membership-report/2001/30-38.pdf.

Rishe, P. (2001). Economic impact report: 2001 NCAA Division I Women's Basketball Final Four. Retrieved November 14, 2002, from www.sportsimpacts.com.

Stadiums and arenas under construction. (2002, March 4-10). *Street & Smith's SportsBusiness Journal, 4*(46), 24-25.

Stewart, L. (2000, September 27). October belongs to Fox. The Los Angeles Times, p. 1D.

Taylor, J.B. (2001). *Economics.* Boston: Houghton Mifflin.

Turco, D.M., & Kelsey, C.W. (1992). *Conducting economic impact studies of recreational and parks special events.* Arlington, VA: National Recreation & Park Association.

University of Massachusetts Athletic Department Annual Report. (2001). Amherst, MA: University of Massachusetts.

Zimbalist, A. (1999). *Unpaid professionals: Commercialism and conflict in big-time college sports.* Princeton, NJ: Princeton University Press.

Zimmerman, D. (1997). Subsidizing stadiums: Who benefits, who pays? In R.G. Noll & A. Zimbalist (Eds.), *Sports, Jobs and Taxes.* Washington, DC: Brookings Institution Press.

Chapter 13

Sport Facility and Event Management

Robin Ammon, Jr., Slippery Rock University
David K. Stotlar, University of Northern Colorado

The differences between sport and entertainment events have diminished to the point where these productions have more in common with each other than they have variations. Not only are these events similar, but the skills and competencies required to *manage* them are also similar.

Students from a variety of majors, including sport management, are finding opportunities to schedule events, work with facility operations, oversee facility finances, equip facilities with TV and video connections, provide maintenance and custodial services, conduct facility marketing and promotions, engage in event merchandising, and provide risk management services. While a plethora of sport facility and event management positions are available in the real world, an interested student must have the desire and determination to learn the necessary skills to be an effective manager.

What types of skills and knowledge should a facility or event manager possess? This chapter will answer this question while providing examples pertaining to facility management, event management, and risk management. Each area is unique, but they are also interwoven to the point that it is sometimes difficult to identify which skill is being performed at any time. In fact, most of the time at least two and perhaps three of them are occurring simultaneously. Due to the symbiotic relationship among facility, event, and risk management, many of the skills and competencies will be similar. The facilities themselves, however, come in a variety of shapes and sizes.

Types of Facilities

The many types of sport facilities can be categorized in many ways (see table 13.1). Some facilities

are single purpose in that they are designed for only one sport. Minute Maid Park (Houston Astros) and Heinz Field (Pittsburgh Steelers) are examples of single-purpose facilities. Aquatic areas and water parks are also designed as single-purpose facilities, as are softball complexes, golf courses, bowling alleys, motor sport tracks, and skating rinks. While some facilities are not single purpose, they are specialized. For example, ice arenas can be used for figure skating competitions, ice hockey, curling, and instructional and recreational skating, but certainly not for soccer matches.

Some facilities are multipurpose; in addition to hosting professional and intercollegiate sport competitions, these large spaces are used for a variety of events, such as concerts, ice skating competitions,

Table 13.1 Types of Sport Facilities

Type of facility	Example
Single purpose	Softball complex, bowling alley
Single purpose, specialized	Ice arena
Multipurpose	Large stadium (e.g., Bank One Ballpark), high school field house
Nontraditional	Skateboard park, convertible indoor/outdoor facility

motocross races, home and garden shows, and recreational vehicle shows. Originally, these types of events were held in outdoor facilities; however, in recent years, many covered stadia and large arenas have been built. You might be familiar with some of these, such as Bank One Ballpark in Phoenix, Invesco Field at Mile High Stadium in Denver, Staples Center in Los Angeles, and Phillips Arena in Atlanta. Movable stands and convertible floors enable these massive facilities to accommodate a variety of events, from small gatherings to large concerts, ice extravaganzas, conventions, athletic events, and festivals. Covered or not, most of these multipurpose facilities have large video screens and video monitors that provide close-ups, instant replays, and special features to entertain the spectators.

Not all facilities have roofs and walls, however. Golf courses, ski areas, and amusement parks are also classified as sport/entertainment facilities. In addition, not all facilities contain large seating areas for spectators. A fitness center might provide activity spaces for gymnastics, swimming, tennis, racquetball, and jogging and a cardiovascular area, as well as fitness machines and free weights. Finally, in some situations, the facility's purpose is broad and incorporates many sports or activities. For example, a multipurpose high school gymnasium might be designed for interscholastic sport practices and competition, physical education classes, school plays, and graduation ceremonies.

Nontraditional facilities have also grown in popularity. The increasing appeal of adventure activities has produced indoor rock climbing centers, and the once criticized activity of skateboarding now has its own parks complete with half-pipes and various jumps. Snowboarding, once banned at most ski areas, is now reaching mainstream popularity with many ski areas promoting special events only for boarders. Amusement parks and water sport parks are becoming extremely popular throughout the world. In fact, the largest-grossing Disney Park in 2001 was in Tokyo, Japan. Some

stadia in Europe, such as Chelsea Stadium in England, include hotel rooms similar to those contained in the SkyDome in Toronto, Ontario. One team in England's Premier Soccer League, West Ham United, has gone as far as to convert its luxury suites into hotel rooms that can be rented to the general public. Some international stadia have become involved in the scheduling of nontraditional events. The new 60,000-seat indoor stadium near Essen, Germany, has a retractable roof and a sliding field. The field will be used when Germany hosts the 2006 Men's Soccer World Cup. With the field removed, an artificial lake can be set up for indoor windsurfing with the interior blowers creating various wind conditions (Cameron, 2001).

Regardless of the size or type of the facility or the kinds of events it hosts, one factor remains consistent: In order to maintain a safe and enjoyable environment, managing the facility and event properly is of paramount importance.

Facility Management

Facility managers need various administrative skills in order to operate facilities efficiently and effectively. The coordination of these "standard operating procedures" (SOPs) is critical with today's multipurpose facilities. The terrorist attacks that occurred on September 11, 2001, forever changed the way facilities are managed. Customer service and safety, while considered important before the attacks, are now utmost priorities for facility managers. These two issues must be of paramount concern when planning, administering, coordinating, and evaluating the day-to-day operations of a facility.

Facility Personnel

The *facility director* or *facility manager* is directly responsible for most sport and entertainment facilities. This individual is mainly responsible for the creation of the facility's SOPs and ensuring that these procedures are administered correctly. At one time, when municipalities that owned the facilities appointed many of these directors, these directors "owed" their jobs to a politician and may not have been experienced in facility management. Today, however, large private management corporations manage many of the large facilities across the country. Thus, directors are now considered experts in the field of facility management and can be thought of as chief executive officers (CEOs).

The *operations manager* reports directly to the facility director and is responsible for all personnel, procedures, and activities related to the facility. This person has a variety of responsibilities such as defining the roles, responsibilities, and authority of facility staff; recruiting personnel to coordinate the various areas of the facility; coordinating personnel, policies and procedures, and activities within the facility; evaluating facility operations; and making recommendations to the facility director.

The *event coordinator* is usually directly responsible for managing the individual events, which vary greatly from concerts to ice shows, political rallies, and athletic events. While the type of event varies a great deal, the event coordinator's responsibilities usually include the following:

- Transporting, assembling, erecting, and storing equipment as directed
- Establishing a control system for venue and equipment logistics (e.g., inventory management, storage, transportation of equipment)
- Recruiting, training, and supervising specific personnel
- Assisting in maintaining venues and equipment throughout the event
- Facilitating ticketing and ticket distribution at venue sites and evaluating venue and equipment operations

While the event coordinator manages the event for the facility, the facility director is ultimately responsible for the successful outcome of the event.

Privatization

An unprecedented boom in the number of new sport/entertainment facilities in the United States has occurred over the past 10 to 15 years. The trend began with professional team facilities and has now spread to universities and the minor leagues. A number of new sport/entertainment facilities have also been erected overseas. Individuals who are not in the facility management business often own these new facilities, or they are publicly managed. As a result, the operational efficiency of these facilities is often less than optimum, causing a drain on financial resources. Variables such as political red tape, inefficient management, and even patronage (hiring individuals in repayment for political favors) have caused these financial concerns. In the majority of these cases, gross operating expenses exceed gross revenues, causing many of these facilities to operate at a break-even point or even a deficit. As you can imagine, this situation has led to services and events being reduced or eliminated. The bottom line is that many public assembly facilities have displayed an operating loss year after year. Until recently, many city officials accepted these losses as the normal course of doing business (Farmer, Mulrooney, & Ammon, 1996).

In the past 10 years this trend has changed as many facilities have turned to private companies to handle their management tasks. **Privatization** is the term used to describe this move from public to private management. Private owners or municipalities still own the facilities, but they **outsource** the *management* of their facilities to professionals who specialize in facility management.

privatization—Moving the management of facilities from the public sector to private companies or organizations.

outsource—The subcontracting of services to an independent contractor.

The future of privatization contains many possibilities, but currently the main reason a facility would use a private management group is for the creation of new revenue sources. In addition, private management companies usually are able to improve tenant relations by enhancing the physical property and hiring more efficient and accountable employees. Private management companies have negotiating savvy they can bring to bear on tenants, promoters, and concessionaires. They are able to negotiate lucrative deals based on multiyear contracts that encompass several arenas. The clout of private management frequently leads to more bookings at a lower price than a single facility can achieve. Thus, the priority for a private management company is to make the facility profitable.

The four major private facility management companies in the United States currently are as follows:

1. Spectacor Management Group (SMG), a joint venture company owned by Hyatt Hotels and ARAMARK Corporation
2. Clear Channel Entertainment (which used to be known as SFX)
3. Global Spectrum
4. ARAMARK/Ogden

Once a municipal facility has decided to use a private management company, the facility manager negotiates the contract, which normally runs from three to five years. The contract usually will specify a base management fee plus incentives. An average annual management fee would probably be in the neighborhood of $100,000. This base fee normally covers the site supervision by private management company personnel and any support necessary from the corporate offices.

LEARNING ACTIVITY

You are the event manager of an 18,000-seat municipally owned arena in a midsize city in the central United States. The facility has not shown a profit in the past three years, and you have been asked to make a presentation to the city council describing the advantages and disadvantages of hiring a private company to manage the facility. At this meeting the council expects you to make a recommendation as to which option they should choose. What will you say?

Event Management

Every event is a *product*, an *outcome*, and an *occurrence*. An event will occur in a specific year and month, on a specific date, and at a specific place. All preparation must be completed before the event begins. The total effort is much like the preparation of an actor who is waiting in the wings for the cue to go on stage. The pressure for perfection in event management is quite high. Many students feel that obtaining a 90% (A) grade for academic work constitutes excellent performance. However, if you are managing an event for 70,000 people and your satisfaction level is 90%, you will have 7,000 dissatisfied patrons. Events come in many shapes and sizes, from a small corporate 5K run to the New York Marathon, from an 18-hole community fund-raising tournament to the Mas-

ters, from a Little League baseball game to the World Series. Event management includes the planning, coordinating, staging, and evaluating of an event. Most events have similar components regardless of their scope. Successful event management requires attention to each of the following areas:

- Recruitment and training of personnel
- Planning emergency medical services
- Risk management
- Facility rental and venue logistics
- Alcohol management and training
- Box office management and ticketing
- Food service management and catering
- Building maintenance
- Marketing, advertising, and public relations
- Hospitality and VIP protocol
- Securing proper permits and licenses
- Contract negotiations with promoters
- Merchandise, concession, and novelty sales
- Crowd management
- Parking and traffic control
- Evaluating the final result

Whether the event is a small golf tournament or the NFL Super Bowl, many components are crucial to the success of the event depending on the nature of the event, the time, the place, and the clientele. Donna in the scenario on p. 259, for example, would have no need for a box office or ticket management because there would be no seated audience. On the other hand, a ticket to the Super Bowl is a prized possession. Think of the preparation of the stadium maintenance crew for an NFL play-off game! Even Donna had to deal with parking logistics for the tournament. Marketing and merchandising are strategic assignments for both Donna and the NFL. Good recruitment policies for both volunteer and paid personnel are also an important element in event management. Finally, training event personnel will make or break the success of the production. A good training program will pay for itself many times over by providing quality performance for a quality event.

Event Personnel Assignments

Establishing an organizational structure for events should be one of the first steps in event management (Steadman, Neirotti, & Goldblatt, 2001). This will ensure that there is no confusion regarding

Scenario: Depressed Donna

Donna Clark was the activities coordinator for the Department of Parks and Recreation in a midsize town in western Pennsylvania. She had decided to conduct an 18-hole golf tournament called The Spring Swing as a fund-raiser for the Parks and Recreation Department. The tournament was to be held at the local public course. During the two weeks before the tournament, Donna conducted preliminary planning meetings with her Parks and Recreation staff and local volunteers. She also touched base with the golf course administrators, making sure they remembered about the tournament. She was confident that most logistics were in place and that the golf tournament fund-raiser would be a success.

On Friday, the day before the tournament, the grounds keeper responsible for the public course notified Donna that an underground cistern used to irrigate the course had flooded, making the number 10 tee box unplayable. The grounds keeper informed Donna that the situation occurred almost every spring. After several discussions, Donna decided to construct a temporary tee box next to the course parking lot. The head grounds keeper assured Donna there would be no problem with constructing the tee box before the start of the next day's tournament.

Friday at 4:00 P.M., after solving the flooding problem, the only remaining pretournament agenda items were the delivery of the various trophies and the catering setup for the tournament lunch. Eighteen teams had prepaid a $160 entry fee, which included a buffet lunch and six categories of trophy awards. Tammy Wannabe, Donna's assistant, convinced her to go home while Tammy awaited the tardy trophies.

Around 7:30 P.M., after a relaxing dinner, Donna received several disturbing phone calls. Patty Poser called to explain that the trophy manufacturer had production problems and the plates on the tournament trophies read "Sing Spring" not "Spring Swing." She apologized profusely but said little could be done at this late date. No sooner had Donna hung up the phone than Mike Munchy, the caterer, called. He explained to Donna that because the tee box had been switched to the parking lot, there was not enough room to set up the tent for the buffet lunch. Unfortunately, when the company that was contracted to set up the tent discovered there wasn't enough room, they had gone home. Mike explained that he had called the subcontractors to get them to return to the course, but the company was closed and would not open until the next morning at 10:00 A.M. The tournament was scheduled to begin at 8:00 A.M.

Donna had not anticipated these problems, and she was stunned and confused. In addition to everything else, the grounds keeper called again and said that the water leak on number 10 was more severe than expected and the first 210 yards of the 380-yard par 4 was unplayable. Donna was paralyzed with indecision. What should she do?

---

tasks and responsibilities for the event. Because of the varied nature of events, no two events will have identical organizational structures. However, many elements are common across the industry of event management. Figure 13.1 shows a typical event structure for a moderately large (2,000 to 3,000 participants) sporting event.

Event Personnel Job Descriptions

An event management structure contains a variety of positions. For the sake of brevity, however, we will discuss only two of the levels of authority illustrated in figure 13.1.

Event Coordinator

The event coordinator is responsible for the overall administration of the event. Some of the re-

sponsibilities include developing operational and strategic plans, preparing the financial statements and budgets for approval, and anticipating problems and implementing solutions. The coordinator is responsible for hiring and recruiting division managers and coordinators and defining their roles, responsibilities, and authority. The coordinator also needs to provide administrative support for division managers and coordinators in the overall planning for each area. The coordinator also must prepare an event manual with guiding principles, policies and procedures, roles and responsibilities, and so on. This manual should clearly define the roles, responsibilities, and authority of each division manager as well as facilitate communication among the divisions. The coordinator assumes responsibility for organizational structure

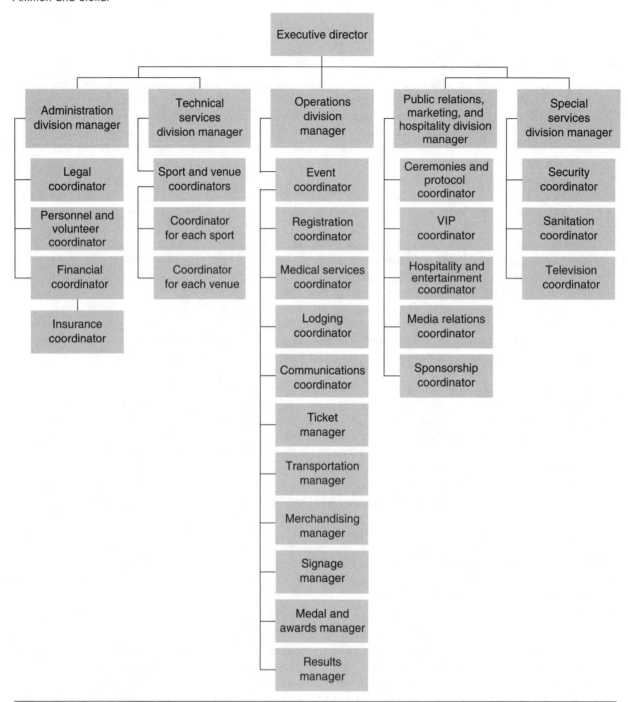

Figure 13.1 Event management structure.

duties not specifically assigned to division managers or coordinators. The coordinator approves all overall plans, strategies, and budgets while at the same time monitoring the financial and human resources (e.g., budget, revenues and expenditures, and staff and volunteers). The coordinator is ultimately accountable for all aspects of the event.

Administration Division Manager

The administration division manager is responsible for clerical activities associated with the general administration of the event office and other administrative duties as defined by the event coordinator. This person's responsibilities include maintaining contacts, as directed, with administration division coordinators. Administration division coordinators include legal, financial, insurance, and personnel and volunteer coordinators. This manager coordinates personnel, policies and procedures, and activities within the administration division and provides the necessary support to coordinators and committees within the divi-

Sport Facility and Event Management

sion. The administration division manager communicates with other division managers while facilitating communication among all administration coordinators and among other division personnel as directed. The person in this position also supervises clerical personnel, evaluates the administration division, and makes recommendations to the event coordinator, to whom he or she reports directly.

Technical Services Division Manager

The technical services division manager is responsible for designing the basic framework or structure within which the event can be effectively managed. These activities include, but are not limited to, venue operations and sport logistics and event specifications. This person defines the tasks and responsibilities for sport and venue administrative and technical needs as well as the various operational, logistical, and sanctioning needs of all sports. These tasks are accomplished through the development of a formal, workable structure and planning process that clearly illustrates the order of responsibility and authority. The technical services division manager also assigns tasks and responsibilities in conjunction with the operational, logistical, and sanctioning needs of all sports. The technical services division manager reports directly to the event coordinator.

Operations Division Manager

The operations division manager is responsible for all personnel, procedures, and activities contained in the operations division. These include items such as registration, lodging, medical services, communications, merchandising and concessions, transportation, signage, medals and awards, and results. The operations division manager is also responsible for clearly defining the roles, responsibilities, and authority of each coordinator and manager while recruiting personnel to coordinate each operations area. The person in this position helps coordinators and managers complete their assigned tasks and assists them in the overall planning for each area. He or she coordinates personnel, policies and procedures, and activities within the operations division and facilitates communications among all operations coordinators and managers and among other division personnel, as needed. The operations division manager communicates with other division managers while supervising personnel and approving policies. Finally, he or she evaluates the operations division and makes recommendations

to the event coordinator, to whom he or she reports directly.

Public Relations, Marketing, and Hospitality Division Manager

The public relations, marketing, and hospitality division manager works at the direction of the event coordinator in all matters pertaining to public relations, marketing, and hospitality. This person is responsible for personnel, procedures, and activities contained in this division, including, but not limited to, ceremonies and protocol, sponsorship, VIP services, media and public relations, and hospitality entertainment. He or she recruits personnel to coordinate each activity and helps staff complete assigned tasks and responsibilities. While coordinating personnel, policies, procedures, and activities within the division, this manager also assists other divisions with public relations, marketing, and hospitality needs. The public relations, marketing, hospitality division manager develops, implements, and manages the overall event marketing plan and facilitates communications among other divisions' personnel as needed. He or she evaluates the public relations, marketing, and hospitality division and makes recommendations to the executive director. This person reports directly to the event coordinator.

Special Services Division Manager

The special services division manager is responsible for all personnel, procedures, and activities contained in the special services division. These include security, sanitation, and television. This manager is responsible for developing and implementing plans for each special services area. He or she recruits personnel to coordinate each special services area while clearly defining the roles, responsibilities, and authority of each coordinator and committee. The special services division manager coordinates personnel, policies and procedures, and activities within the special services division while assisting the coordinators in the overall planning for each area. This manager supports the coordinators and committees within his or her division, while also facilitating communication among special services coordinators and other divisions as needed. He or she supervises personnel, approves policies, and evaluates the special services division, making recommendations to the event coordinator, to whom he or she reports directly.

An effective organizational structure facilitates effective event planning. All events—from Donna's golf tournament to the World Cup—need effective event management plans. A management plan should include six basic steps: scheduling, negotiating, coordinating, staging, settling with the promoter, and evaluating. The event coordinator will ultimately be responsible for developing this plan.

Scheduling the Event

Scheduling an event entails a reservation process in which events are planned according to the philosophy of the facility. Since most facilities maintain a profit-oriented philosophy, an event coordinator will try to schedule the largest number of events without overburdening the facility or employees. Securing and contracting one specific event or attraction is known as **booking** an event.

scheduling—A reservation process for a facility's events.

booking—Securing and contracting one specific sport or entertainment event.

Scheduling conflicts always occur with facilities that produce a variety of events. The facility's reputation is built on how its managers handle such conflicts. One public relations conflict may have to do with the type of event. An act such as Marilyn Manson or Insane Clown Posse, for example, may be considered too controversial for some areas of the country. However, these types of events may produce a large profit margin due to increased ticket sales and the accompanying concession and merchandise expenditures. Thus, the facility management's booking decisions can be almost a balancing act.

Facility managers often have to ask themselves, Does the facility *want* or *need* to book this event? In this context *want* relates to making money, and *need* relates to community satisfaction. In making such decisions, managers must remember that the facility has a reputation to uphold in the community; they must *not* let personal opinion get in the way of booking a show. The event travels on to the next tour date, while the manager must remain to face any criticism or controversy, which may affect future ticket sales.

Negotiating the Event

Once an event is formally scheduled, preliminary negotiations occur between the event coordinator and the promoter or representative of the event. These negotiations determine the terms of the event contract for items such as the rental price of the facility. Most facilities use a "**boilerplate**" document, which addresses the specific terms between the promoter and the facility or event manager. This type of document uses standard language and a fill-in-the-blanks format similar to most apartment leases to divide up the expenses and profits from the event. Normally a prearranged percentage known as a "**split**" is used to divide up revenue from the sale of tickets, merchandise, and sometimes concessions. These financial negotiations are a critical factor in establishing the cost of an event. If the dollar amount is too high, additional negotiations ensue to determine which costs to eliminate and which splits to modify.

boilerplate—Generic document that uses standard language and a fill-in-the-blank format.

split—A prearranged percentage used to divide various sources of revenue.

Coordinating the Event

After the preliminary negotiations with the promoter are completed and the **cost analysis** is calculated, the event coordinator sits down and studies all aspects of the event. The event coordinator is responsible for meeting sport- or entertainment-specific venue and equipment needs as requested by the appropriate managers or promoter. The person in this role will need to transport, assemble, erect, and store equipment while establishing procedures and guidelines for the rental, purchase, storage, and transportation of venue equipment. Securing a warehouse area for equipment storage and distribution as well as establishing a control system for venue and equipment logistics (e.g., inventory management, storage, and transportation of equipment) is of crucial importance. Once these items are completed, the event coordinator begins recruiting, training, and supervising the personnel who will assist in maintaining the venues and equipment throughout the event.

cost analysis—An estimation of the revenue and expenses of an event.

During this time the event coordinator designs a plan or **work order** for all employees to follow. This instrument is the game plan for the event. It documents all the requirements discussed with the promoter or other company representative. Anything not documented will be the responsibility of the event coordinator. The work order also defines the time it will take to do each assigned task. As this plan develops, problems pertaining to the original contract may occur, causing the contract to be revised. Orientation meetings will be scheduled with various staff to address the specific concerns of the work order such as type of seating, search policy, and alcohol policy. In addition risk management concerns need to be discussed. In a recent study, for example, 98% of facility managers identified slips and falls as the most common injury while 95% of the facility managers mentioned that these cases were normally settled out of court (Ammon & Fried, 1998).

work order—A document that illustrates all requirements of the event.

In the scenario on page 259, Donna failed to plan properly. One secret to successful planning is the ability to plot the event's time restrictions. Coordinators should start with the date of the event and calculate the time needed for each step, from last-minute tasks just before the event back to the initial meeting for the event. Additional time for emergencies should be added into the work order schedule.

Various preliminary planning meetings should take place with all staff members and other individuals whose cooperation is critical to the success of the event. In "Depressed Donna's" case, people such as personnel from the athletics department, campus police, and local volunteers should have been consulted, informed, and involved at each step along the way. During this process, any necessary permits should be obtained, a factor Depressed Donna neglected to consider. In addition, the organizers must continually anticipate potential problems, thus avoiding surprises such as the ones Donna had to face.

Staging the Event

After much planning and anticipating, the day of the event arrives. In small events such as golf tournaments, the event coordinator makes certain that items such as longest-drive and closest-to-the-pin markers are in place and that each group has received its electric carts or caddies. Finally, refreshments, award tables, and portable toilets should be properly located. For large events such as concerts and ice shows, an entire day is usually allowed for load-in and setup once the truck(s) carrying the equipment for the event arrive.

At the designated hour on the day of the event, the doors or gates are opened, the crowd flows inside, and the event begins. At this point, the event coordinator discovers if he or she was effective in planning and coordinating the many facets of staging the event, including parking, seating, alcohol policies, and crowd control.

Parking

As with every plan, the various groups involved must be allowed to provide input into the work order. With regard to parking and traffic, campus, city, county, and state law enforcement agencies should have input. Some parking spaces may be lost due to weather (mud or large puddles of water) or because of special promotions such as fireworks, and traffic flow problems may exist due to limited access. Providing bus and emergency access lanes will diminish the total number of vehicles that can park at the event. Intersections with higher than normal accident rates must be identified, and extra officers should assist out-of-town fans through these problem areas. Posting adequate signs on major thoroughfares to direct arriving spectators also decreases potential problems. Altering the duration of signal lights during ingress and egress assists vehicular traffic through most congested areas. In addition, notifying local residents and businesses of event-day traffic plans helps community relations. Finally, establishing emergency routes for police, fire, and medical personnel may quickly and safely avert dangerous situations.

Seating

Many facilities in the United States use reserved seats during various events. With a reserved ticket a spectator is assured of a specific seat, in a specific row, in a specific section at the event. With the use of trained ushers and an effective crowd control plan, most events encounter minimal problems with this type of seating. Other types of seating are not as easy to manage. General admission (GA) seating is a first come, first served process that sometimes causes fans to line up outside for hours before the facility opens, in the hope of gaining that prestigious front row seat. Festival seating is a type of GA seating, but it is actually a misnomer because no actual seats exist. Festival seating allows spectators to crowd together standing shoulder to shoulder in open floor space. Unfortunately, this type of seating has proven tragic in several instances. In 1991 three teenagers died in Salt Lake City at an AC/DC concert due to a crowd surge. Ironically, legislation that prohibited festival seating in Salt Lake had been passed but was not enforced. More recently, in June 2000 during a

Pearl Jam set at the Roskilde Festival near Copenhagen, nine concertgoers near the front of the stage were crushed after the crowd surged (Baugus, 2002). While festival seating allows promoters to sell more tickets than reserved or general admission seating, it is the most deadly and injurious of seating arrangements and continues to be a controversial topic in event management.

Alcohol Policies

Prior to September 11, 2001, some experts believed alcohol to be the biggest concern for facility and event managers (Tierney, 2001). A potential liability exists if intoxicated patrons create dangerous situations for themselves and others. Some people argue that revenue generated from beer sales is worth the risks. Some universities with small facilities would find it difficult to generate a profit without beer sales (Ammon, 1995). Others have determined that alcohol is not worth the liabilities even given the increased revenue. During the 2001 NFL season, games in Cleveland and New Orleans were briefly halted after fans protested game officials' calls by littering the fields with plastic beer bottles. These plastic bottles had become a lucrative trend the year before. Miller Brewing Company found that the use of plastic bottles helped to reduce spillage from cups, kept the beer from going flat, and obviously increased brand awareness (Hiestand & Woods, 2001).

Some government officials have become concerned enough to legislate "dram shop laws." These statutes provide plaintiffs who have been injured by an intoxicated individual with a cause of action to sue the defendant plus the owners of the bar or restaurant where the defendant became drunk.

The ability to foresee alcohol risks that could prove harmful to patrons is a reasonable way to reduce liability. Employing specific crowd control techniques may limit the abuse of alcohol at facilities and events. Erecting signs prohibiting alcohol from being brought into the stadium and training crowd management staff at facility entrances to confiscate any alcohol beverages brought into the facility may prohibit intoxicated individuals from entering the facility.

Facility and event managers can help curtail alcohol incidents by requiring servers and crowd control staff to be trained in Training for Intervention Procedures by Servers of Alcohol (TIPS), developed by the founding director of the National Institute on Alcoholism and Alcohol Abuse, or Techniques for Effective Alcohol Management (TEAM), a program of the National Highway Transportation Safety Administration. Concessionaires should check IDs thoroughly and wristband those who are of legal age, while at the same time enforcing a two-beer limit to any fan at one time and reducing the size of servings to 12 ounces. Facility and event managers should eliminate beer sales at a specific point during the event and create a designated driver program for fans who drink too much.

The presence of alcohol at sporting events is controversial, but Miller and Anheuser-Busch are two of the five largest spending sport advertisers on television. Moreover, drinking beer at sport events has been occurring for over a hundred years. It has become a part of the culture of sport spectatorship, and many spectators consider it a right. As Carmen Policy, the president of the Cleveland Browns, stated after the beer bottle throwing incident during the 2001 NFC season at Cleveland Browns Stadium, "I think beer is a part of sports, just like it is part of family picnics" (Hiestand & Woods, 2001, p. 3A). Therefore, until something much more serious than plastic bottles on a couple of NFL fields occurs, alcohol will continue to be a part of sport.

Crowd Management

A facility or event manager does not need to have large numbers of spectators to mandate a crowd management plan. Whether employed at a small high school basketball game, a local YMCA, or the NCAA Division I soccer championships, every facility or event manager should have a crowd management plan.

First of all, facility and event managers must try to provide as safe and enjoyable an environment as possible. This is accomplished by implementing various risk management components. The crowd control plan must be an integral element of a larger risk management plan.

Trained and competent staff to carry out the plan is the first component of an effective crowd control plan. Some facilities conduct the crowd control duties themselves. This is known as **in-house** security or crowd control. Other facilities contract out or outsource crowd control services to independent contractors.

in-house—Services provided by the facility staff.

An emergency plan for all spectators is the second component of an effective crowd control plan. To ensure accessibility for all citizens, Congress passed the **Americans with Disabilities Act (ADA)** in 1992. The ADA has had a major impact on sport, entertainment, and arts facility design. Not

Planning for traffic and crowd control is an important facet of the event coordinator's job.

only must an emergency plan be designed and implemented, but also the courts will ask for documentation of when the plan was practiced. Sport and entertainment event managers must be familiar with requirements of the ADA as they pertain to facility features such as signage, restrooms, telephones, parking, and shower stalls. Furthermore, event managers must also develop plans for the evacuation of spectators with disabilities or special needs. The plan must have an *anticipatory* and a *reactionary* component. The anticipatory component pertains to inspections and preventive maintenance, while the reactionary component pertains to the procedures implemented after an emergency occurs. Emergencies take many forms such as medical problems (life-threatening and minor injuries), impending weather (lightning, tornadoes), natural disasters (earthquakes, floods), fire, bomb threats, power loss, and in today's society, terrorist activities.

Americans with Disabilities Act (ADA)—Legislation that provides civil rights for citizens with disabilities by prohibiting discrimination in places of public accommodation (White, 1999).

The third component of an effective crowd control plan should address the procedures necessary to eject disruptive, unruly, or intoxicated patrons. The ejection duties should remain the responsibility of *trained* crowd control staff and, in some jurisdictions, police officers, sheriff's department personnel, or state troopers. These individuals must understand the concepts of the "reasonable person theory" (see chapter 5) and "excessive force," and understand that they may be sued for negligence if they eject patrons incorrectly. Ushers should not undertake these duties if they are not trained in proper crowd control procedures. Removing disruptive or intoxicated fans will provide a safer environment for the remaining spectators and help to protect the facility or event manager from potential litigation (Ammon & Unruh, 2001).

A competent communication network is the fourth component in an effective crowd control plan. Communication is critical in providing spectator safety, enjoyment, and security. The use of a centralized area for representatives from each group involved in the management of an event (law enforcement, maintenance, medical, and security) will facilitate communication and improve decision making.

The creation and use of proper signage is the fifth and final component of crowd control. Informational and directional signs build a support network between fans and facility management staff. Spectators appreciate being treated fairly and if previously informed will normally abide by facility directives pertaining to no smoking sections, alcohol policies, and prohibited items. Directional signs have a number of important uses. As spectators approach the facility, road signs can indicate the correct exits and provide relevant parking information. Other signs serve to indicate the correct gate or portal, as well as directing ticket-buying patrons to the box office. Signage will also help facility patrons locate concession stands, first-aid rooms, telephones, and restrooms. Informational signs regarding prohibited items assist patrons in making decisions before entry (Ammon & Unruh, 2001).

Settling With the Promoter

While the event is in progress, the promoter and the event coordinator sit down together for the **settlement**. This process involves reconciling the revenues versus the expenses and dividing any resulting profit between the promoter and the facility representative according to the split as determined during the preliminary negotiation phase (Farmer et al., 1996).

settlement—Reconciling the expenses and revenues of an event and dividing the profits according to a contracted arrangement.

Evaluating the Event

After the event is over and the crowd has filed out, the equipment used in the event is gathered up and put away or stored in trucks, and the cleanup of the facility commences. Usually another entire day is permitted for the load-out. Interestingly, this element was overlooked in the management of the 1994 U.S. Olympic Festival in St. Louis. Some of the venues were booked only until the day of the last event. This necessitated the frantic dismantling and loading of sport equipment from the venues into trucks because the venues were scheduled for other events on the following day. The trucks were subsequently unloaded and the equipment was inventoried and returned to suppliers and sponsors as needed. This could have been avoided had the managers permitted time for equipment load-out.

Immediately after the event, the event coordinator meets with the management team to evaluate the entire process. **Documentation** of the entire process is critical, not only for protection against subsequent litigation but also for reference in planning future events. In the following scenario we will see how a prepared event manager would conduct a golf tournament.

documentation—Completing detailed records describing the event.

LEARNING ACTIVITY

The Volvo International Tennis Championships are scheduled for your facility. Prepare an event management plan. Begin by listing all the activities that need to take place before the event. Include such items as reserving the facility, advertising, hotel accommodations, ticket printing and sales, and personnel scheduling. Next, place all the activities in the sequence in which they must occur. Now, calculate the time needed to accomplish each task. Finally, place the items on a project calendar that shows each activity in sequence, the time required to complete it, and the overall chain of events.

Risk Management

The impact of the terrorist attacks on September 11, 2001, has been felt throughout the world, but we should not let it change our way of life. In order to make facilities and events as safe as possible, facility and event managers must be proficient in many areas. In order to successfully stage an event, no area is more important than understanding and implementing an effective risk management plan.

The events of September 11, 2001, will forever affect the sport industry. It is estimated that professional sport teams will spend an additional $30 million in security costs in 2002, which breaks down to approximately $235,000 per team among the four major sports (Williams, 2001).

The 2002 Winter Olympics in Salt Lake City, Utah, was one of the greatest challenges in sport venue security since September 11. Due to the terrorist activities at the 1972 Munich Games and the pipe bomb at the 1996 Atlanta Games, as well as the events of September 11, security for the Olympics was unusually high. "The federal government is coordinating the operation, which will use the Secret Service, the FBI, the Utah National Guard, and state and local police to protect 2,400

Scenario: Dynamic Donna

Donna Clark was the activities coordinator for the Department of Parks and Recreation in a midsize town in western Pennsylvania. She was conducting an 18-hole golf tournament called The Spring Swing as a fund-raiser for the Parks and Recreation Department. The tournament was to be held at the local public course. A year ago, when the project had been assigned, Donna had planned the event in detail using a work order that included times, schedules, deadlines, and committees. In-depth formal planning meetings had also been held with the course grounds keeper during which a variety of "what if" scenarios had been discussed and alternative plans implemented. A temporary tee box 170 yards from the green had been constructed two weeks before the tournament, turning the hole into a par 3, just in case the annual spring flooding occurred. The trophies were outsourced by contract with delivery guaranteed two weeks before the tournament. The marketing plan was successfully implemented (see chapter 10), and news releases and interviews were well received by both the print and broadcast media (see chapter 11). All project personnel were well prepared and on task. Every committee coordinator performed well. After the golf tournament, Donna's team of volunteers and the course administrators evaluated the event. All comments, complaints, and suggestions for improvement were included in Donna's event folder for implementation next year. The golf tournament was a success with a great turnout and good weather! By the way, Donna has been working on more than this event. The annual Fourth of July 5K road race is coming up, and she is ahead of schedule with her event planning.

athletes and hundreds of thousands of visitors" (Woodward, 2002, p. 19). The number of security personnel was in excess of 10,000, and the resultant cost approached $400 million, but the 2002 Olympics were tragedy free.

What Is It?

Risk management has been defined as the control of financial and personal injury loss from sudden, unforeseen, unusual accidents and intentional torts (see chapter 5) (Ammon, 1993). The loss or "risk" can be physical or financial in nature. Physical risks may vary in severity from insect bites or sprained ankles on the less severe side to death or paraplegia on the most severe side. Financial risks also are prevalent and will vary from the less severe types of minor vandalism to the most severe risks of fire or theft. Obviously, one goal of a risk manager should be to reduce the monetary losses and physical risks while managing a sport facility. This goal is not only a difficult one but one that must be monitored constantly.

LEARNING ACTIVITY

Think about why there are more lawsuits in sport and recreation today than 10 to 15 years ago. How could risk management help eliminate some litigation cases?

Identification of Risks

A well-trained staff educated about proper risk management procedures can help a facility or event manager identify potential risks. They may be aware of risk locations, and they are in constant communication with fans or clients who also witness many of the various risks prevalent in a sport facility.

Technological Advances in Risk Management

Risk management techniques are continuously changing and improving. Different types of technology assist the facility manager in reducing facility risks. One example is the use of bar codes on tickets. This allows facility and event management officials to track the sale and use of a ticket. Where was it originally purchased and by whom? "Smart cards," already in use in some hockey, basketball, and baseball facilities, gather fan preferences through the use of surveys in exchange for discounts on concession items and merchandise. While some individuals in our society may see the use of a national "smart card" as an infringement on their personal right to privacy, the technology already exists to attach a digital photo, fingerprint, or even a DNA profile to these identification cards (Scanning the Masses, 2002).

SUMMARY

The World Cup, the Olympics, concerts, and high school track meets all have two common denominators: They take place in some type of facility, and they are events. All facilities and events need individuals to manage them.

The management of many sport and entertainment facilities is being outsourced to four main private management companies. These private management companies have been successful in raising the profit margin of many sport and public assembly facilities across the United States.

Event management includes several important tasks for an event to be successful. An event coordinator needs to know and understand how these tasks relate to the successful completion of every event. Scheduling and booking an event begins the overall process, and a cost analysis is a critical element in this initial operation. After the event coordinator has decided that the event will be held, the necessary contracts need to be signed, and the event manager must create and communicate a work order to the others on the event management team. Items such as seating, crowd management, alcohol policies, settlement, and event evaluation must be carried out for an effective event.

In light of recent terrorist activities, risk management has become a tremendously important responsibility for all personnel working with facilities and events. The duty to provide a safe and enjoyable environment creates the need for sport management individuals who can anticipate potential areas of loss and injury and can take action to decrease them. Interested sport management students with knowledge of law and facilities can obtain a position in the facility or event risk management field.

The number of facilities has grown exponentially in recent years, and each of these facilities schedules sport and entertainment events with global implications. However, the terrorist attacks on September 11, 2001, have changed the facility and event management industry dramatically. On top of that, the economic surge of the late 1990s has ceased, requiring some areas of sport to undergo questionable downsizing as our society entered a period of recession. Because of these various events, the future of facility and event management is not as clear as once imagined. As revenues have slowed, profit margins have been affected. The influence this domino effect has on facility and event management needs to be continually monitored.

REVIEW QUESTIONS

1. Name a single-purpose facility. Name a multipurpose facility. List the types of personnel who would be involved in facility management at either type of facility.

2. Currently, four companies privately manage more than 300 facilities nationally and internationally. List these four companies. Why would a facility choose to contract with one of these companies?

3. What is a work order similar to? What is the purpose of a work order? Who compiles the work order?

4. Why does the management team need to meet and evaluate the overall production once the event has been completed? Why should all the proper documentation be completed at this meeting?

5. Why is employing trained individuals to reduce facility risks a less expensive alternative than reacting to potential disasters or litigation without such individuals? How can a large amount of this litigation be avoided?

6. Even though sport and entertainment productions continue to be extremely popular and continue to result in extensive media coverage, what two recent occurrences may affect future travel and spending at these events?

Job Opportunities

Food and Beverage Manager

Looking for a general manager to oversee all aspects of our small arena concession business. Major responsibilities include event day operations, developing and implementing operation and inventory controls, training programs for concessions employees, and special projects. The candidate must have excellent organizational and interpersonal skills.

Event Coordinator

Established mid-Atlantic municipal arena seeking applications for hands-on event coordinator with additional responsibility of employee training. Include résumé and salary history.

Director of Arena Operations

Full-time position available for a director of operations responsible for day-to-day operation of the arena, including ticketing, guest relations, security, and first aid. Duties will also include ensuring guest satisfaction through employee hiring and training, design of safety and risk management programs, and the day-to-day supervision of six managers and staff.

Promotion Manager

Currently seeking an enthusiastic, creative, and results-oriented promotion manager who is eager to promote live sporting events. Will be responsible for researching assigned markets; ticket pricing and sales; setup; media planning, buying, and negotiating; local sponsorship sales; and event publicity planning and coordinating. Candidate must have a degree in marketing or sport management. Travel required.

Operations Manager of Water Park

This position reports to the corporate offices in New Jersey and is responsible for the day-to-day operations of the water park. Primary responsibilities include facility maintenance, aquatics, park services, guest services, and admissions. Secondary responsibilities require supervising group services and marketing.

Sport Facility Manager

Professionally based sport and entertainment group seeking individual to manage its stadium and ancillary facility development process. The ideal candidate should possess experience in facility development and start-up, along with related aspects such as concession negotiations and supervision of facility architectural firms. Facility operations experience a plus.

Branch Manager and Guest Services Managers of XYZ Event Management Company

Event staffing company is seeking dynamic individuals to fill immediate and future openings in major arenas and stadiums. Proven management skills and hands-on experience in the crowd and facility management industry preferred. Financial management and budgetary planning experience a plus. Communication and leadership skills are necessary to excel in this rewarding environment.

Public Facility Manager

Edwards Amphitheater is seeking a public facility professional to assume the position of facility manager. This position requires supervising marketing and box office personnel, negotiating with all outside promoters, and coordinating all self-promoted events. In addition, the facility manager will supervise and oversee all group sales and special events. Individuals should possess a background in facility management.

REFERENCES

Ammon, Jr., R. (1993). Risk and game management practices in selected municipal football facilities (Doctoral dissertation, University of Northern Colorado, 1993). *Dissertation Abstracts International, 54,* 3366A.

Ammon, Jr., R. (1995, April-June). Alcohol and event management: Two sides of the same coin. *Crowd Management, 1*(4), 16-19.

Ammon, Jr., R., & Fried, G. (1998). Assessing stadium crowd management practices and liability issues. *Journal of Convention & Exhibition Management, 1*(2-3), 119-150.

Ammon, Jr., R., & Unruh, N. (2001). Crowd management. In D.J. Cotton, J.T. Wolohan, & T.J. Wilde (Eds.), *Law for recreation and sport managers* (2nd ed.) (pp. 329-339). Dubuque, IA: Kendall/Hunt.

Baugus, R.V. (2002, January/February). Roskilde organizers learn from 2000 tragedy. *Facility Manager, 18*(1), 24, 26.

Cameron, S. (2001, December 17-23). Tales from Europe: Scottish dilemma, naked truth, and indoor windsurfing. *Street & Smith's SportsBusiness Journal, 4*(35), 19.

Farmer, P., Mulrooney, A., & Ammon, Jr., R. (1996). *Sport facility planning and management.* Morgantown, WV: Fitness Information Technology.

Hiestand, M., & Woods, S. (2001, December 19). Fan conduct rises on NFL agenda: Some see violence at recent games as precursor to soccer-style hooliganism. *USA Today,* 3A.

Scanning the masses: Taking a look at face recognition technology. (2002, January/February). *Facility Manager, 18*(1), 29-30.

Steadman, G., Neirotti, L.D., & Goldblatt, J.J. (2001). *The ultimate guide to sports marketing.* New York: McGraw-Hill.

Tierney, R. (2001, September 24). Zumwalt examines the new threat. *Amusement Business, 113*(38), 1, 4.

White, H. (1999). Planning and designing the facilities. In T. Sawyer (Ed.), *Facilities planning for physical activity and sport of sport: Its foundation and application* (9th ed.) (pp. 11-28). Dubuque, IA: Kendall/Hunt.

Williams, P. (2001, December 10-16). Clubs will continue to pay for security. *Street & Smith's SportsBusiness Journal, 4*(34), 26.

Woodward, S. (2002, February 4-10). Security effort is always Olympic event. *Street & Smith's SportsBusiness Journal, 4*(42), 19, 23.

Chapter 14

Intercollegiate Athletics

Robertha Abney, Slippery Rock University
Ellen J. Staurowsky, Ithaca College

From the intrigues of the Bowl Championship Series (BCS) to the Madness of March, college sport occupies as prominent a place in the American sports scene as any professional or Olympic-level sporting enterprise. The fate of favored and favorite teams is the subject of much attention. Internet chat rooms churn out speculation about who will be recruited by whom, what team will come out on top, and which shoe company has reached an agreement with which university for a multiyear, multimillion-dollar sponsorship deal. Through sport media coverage, which includes television, radio, and print, players and coaches become celebrities, while the games themselves serve to entertain millions of fans around the country.

There is much more to college sport than meets the eye. The financial stakes are high, as evidenced by the $6 billion agreement the National Collegiate Athletic Association (NCAA) reached with CBS in the spring of 2002 for the broadcast rights to the men's Division I basketball tournament and selected other championships. Of equal importance are the reputations of the schools that sponsor these programs. The purpose of this chapter is to provide an overview of the contemporary college athletics program in the 21st century and to create a snapshot of what goes on behind the scenes. After reading this chapter, you should have a better understanding of the organizations that govern and regulate college sport, how college athletics programs operate, and the kinds of careers you might wish to pursue in this segment of the sport industry.

LEARNING ACTIVITY

Visit the NCAA Web site at www.ncaa.org/finances. Locate the revenues and expenses data for the association. Using the charts provided, track how the revenue from the $6 billion is distributed to the NCAA membership.

LEARNING OBJECTIVES

After studying this chapter, you will be able to do the following:

1. Define intercollegiate athletics.
2. Demonstrate an understanding of the events surrounding the development of intercollegiate athletics.
3. Describe the purpose of organizations governing intercollegiate athletics.
4. Identify key athletic administrative personnel within intercollegiate athletics departments.
5. Identify the duties of the various administrators who manage intercollegiate athletics departments.
6. Discuss several current challenges within intercollegiate athletics.
7. Identify key associations, organizations, and publications related to intercollegiate athletics.

Governance of Intercollegiate Athletics

Most secondary and postsecondary educational institutions in North America provide varsity athletics programs for their students. In secondary schools these programs are called *interscholastic* athletics. Programs offered by four-year colleges, universities, and junior and community colleges are known as *intercollegiate* athletics. Initially, intercollegiate athletics was student controlled. They began with class games that eventually became intercollegiate contests. In fact, they were so low-key that, when the owner of a railroad proposed the idea of a regatta between the Yale and Harvard boat clubs in 1852, "The crew members thought of it as a 'jolly lark' which provided them with an eight-day, all-expense paid vacation on Lake Winnipesaukee" (Lucas & Smith, 1978, p. 197). This unpretentious event marked the beginning of intercollegiate athletics in the United States.

The nature of intercollegiate athletics quickly changed from social interactions to highly competitive events. By 1905 football competition had become so intense that some individuals urged that the sport be reformed or abolished. One way of implementing reform was to establish associations to govern intercollegiate athletics.

National Collegiate Athletic Association (NCAA)

Prompted by deaths and charges of brutality in college football, President Theodore Roosevelt hosted the White House Conference on Football in 1905. Roosevelt summoned coaches, faculty, and alumni representatives from Harvard, Yale, and Princeton to the conference. The purpose of the conference was to encourage the representatives to carry out both the letter and the spirit of the football rules. Roosevelt's decree led to the formation of the Intercollegiate Athletic Association of the United States (IAAUS), which was officially constituted on March 31, 1906, and became known as the National Collegiate Athletic Association (NCAA) in 1910 (NCAA, 2002).

The NCAA headquarters is located in Indianapolis, Indiana. With a membership of more than 1,200 colleges, universities, conferences, and sport organizations dedicated to the sound administration of intercollegiate sport, it is the largest and most influential governing body in the field. Each NCAA member institution is classified as Division I, II, or III (see figure 14.1). Division classification is based on several criteria, among them the size of the financial base, the number and types of sports offered, the focus of the program, and the existence of athletic grants-in-aid. Examples of Division I, II, and III athletics department organizational charts are shown in figures 14.2, 14.3, and 14.4, respectively.

Athletics programs at Division I schools are major financial enterprises that generate significant revenue. They must offer at least seven sports for men and seven for women (or six for men and eight for women), and they must have at least two team sports for each gender. Division I schools offer full grants-in-aid based on athletic ability, are highly competitive, and consider many athletic contests as entertainment for spectators. Depending on their resources, Division I programs may be financed through student fees, gate receipts, television revenues, **licensing revenues,** and private donations. Division I colleges and universities are further divided into Divisions I-A (117 active members), I-AA (123 active members), and I-AAA (85 active members), each with specific classification criteria (NCAA, 2002).

licensing revenues—royalties paid to athletics departments by second parties in return for the right to produce and sell merchandise bearing a logo or other mark associated with its sports program (Irwin, 2001)

Division II institutions must offer at least four sports for men and four for women and must have two team sports for each gender. The 270 active member institutions in Division II offer grants-in-aid based on athletic ability, but fewer per capita than do Division I schools. Division II schools are financed by their institutions in the same way as academic programs on campus and focus primarily on regional competition. In Division III, with 410 members, the focus is on participation rather than competition or entertainment. In these schools, which must offer at least five sports for women and five sports for men, including two team sports for each gender, athletic scholarships are not offered. Athletes are treated the same as other students with respect to admission policies, academic advisement, and scholarships. Participation opportunities for student-athletes are the primary concern of these programs, and they generally focus on regional and conference competition (NCAA, 2002).

Other National Governing Bodies

The National Junior College Athletic Association (NJCAA) was conceived in Fresno, California, and became a functioning organization in 1938. The NJCAA seeks to promote and supervise a national program of junior college sports and activities consistent with the educational objectives of junior colleges. Its membership comprises approximately 550 institutions. It is organized into 24 geographic regions and is headquartered in Colorado Springs, Colorado (Karlin, 1995; NJCAA, 2002).

Established in 1940, the National Association for Intercollegiate Athletics (NAIA), located in Olathe, Kansas, has approximately 360 member institutions (NAIA, 2002). It is open to four-year and upper-level two-year colleges and universities in the United States and Canada. With an emphasis on academic achievement, the NAIA is also dedi-

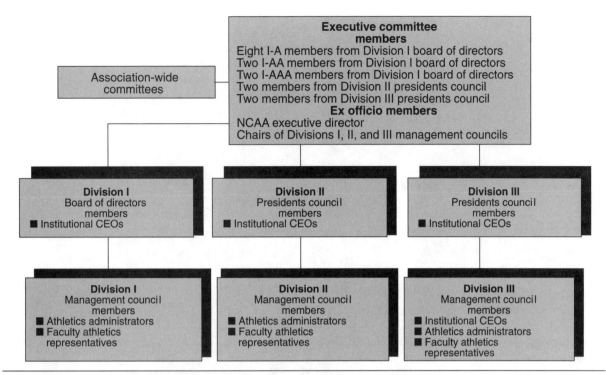

Figure 14.1   NCAA organizational chart/governance structure (1997).

Data from NCAA News, August 4, 1997, 34(20).

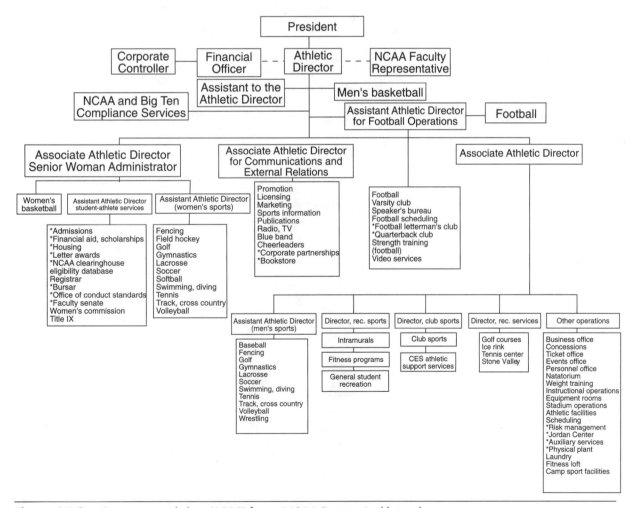

Figure 14.2   Organizational chart (1995) for an NCAA Division I athletics department.

Reprinted, by permission, from Penn State University.

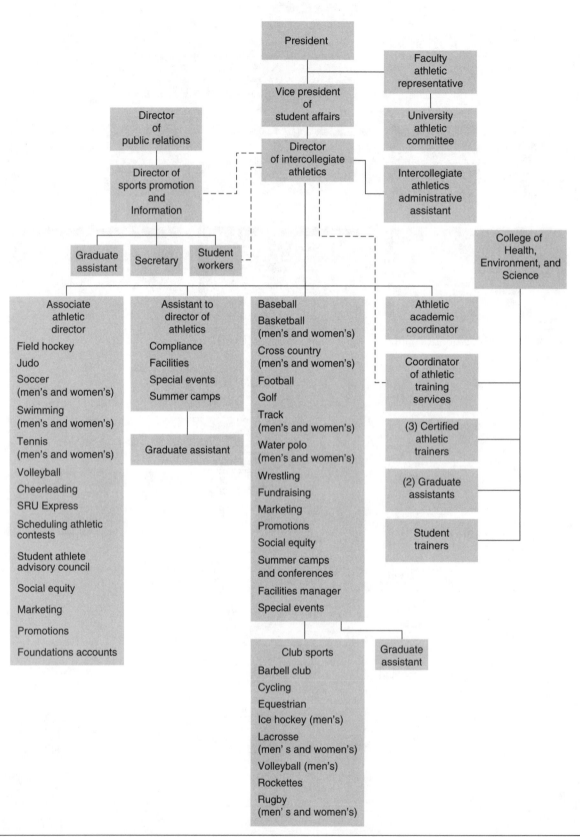

Figure 14.3 Organizational chart for an NCAA Division II athletics department.

Reprinted, by permission, from Slippery Rock University.

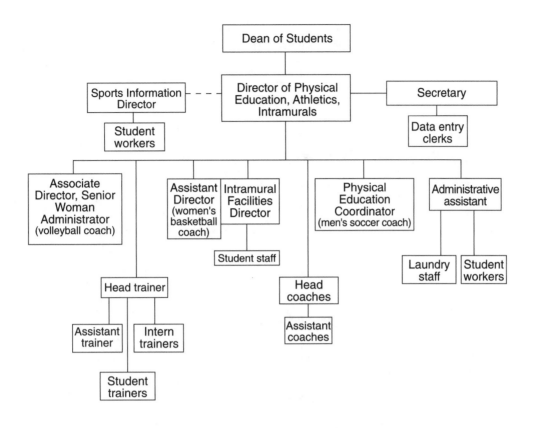

	Varsity programs (21)	
	Men (11)	Women (10)
Fall (7)	Cross country Football Soccer	Cross country Field hockey Soccer Volleyball
Winter (6)	Basketball Swimming, diving Indoor track	Basketball Swimming, diving Indoor track
Spring (8)	Lacrosse Tennis Outdoor track Baseball Golf	Lacrosse Tennis Outdoor track

Figure 14.4 Organizational chart for an NCAA Division III athletics department.

Reprinted, by permission, from Kenyon College.

cated to respect, integrity, responsibility, servant leadership, and fair play. The NAIA was the first national organization to offer postseason opportunities to black student-athletes (1948). It was also the first national organization that sponsored men's intercollegiate athletics to offer athletic championships for women's sports (1980). It has started a Champions of Character program to continue its emphasis on the development of integrity through athletics (NAIA, 2002). The organizational chart for the NAIA is depicted in figure 14.5.

Another organization governing intercollegiate athletics is the National Christian College Athletic Association (NCCAA). Incorporated in 1968 and located in Greenville, South Carolina, the NCCAA focuses on "the promotion and enhancement of intercollegiate athletic competition with a Christian perspective." The NCCAA has 112 member institutions in two divisions. Division I consists of 52 liberal arts institutions, and Division II consists of 60 Bible colleges (NCCAA, 2002).

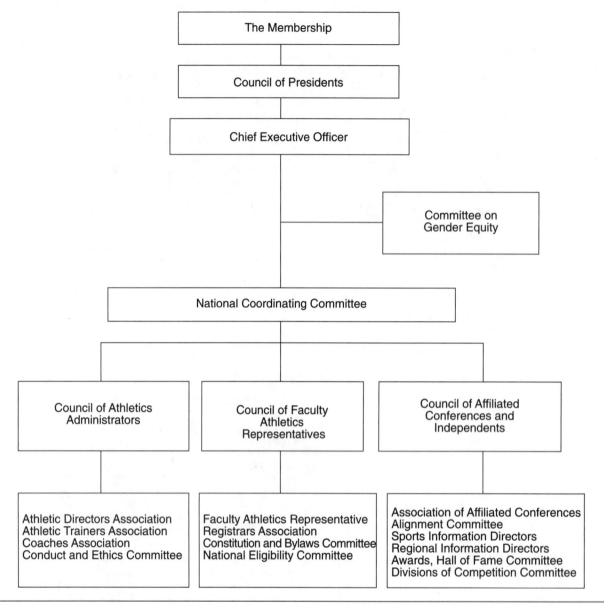

Figure 14.5 NAIA organizational chart (1993).

Reprinted, by permission, from NAIA.

A national governing body exclusively for women's intercollegiate sport emerged in 1971 when the Association for Intercollegiate Athletics for Women (AIAW) was established by women physical educators from colleges and universities across the country (Morrison, 1993). During its 10-year existence, the AIAW provided many opportunities for women athletes, coaches, and administrators. The organization also offered several national championships, many of which received television coverage. Eventually, however, the NCAA and the NAIA expanded their structures to include women's athletics, and in 1982 the AIAW was dismantled. Currently, both men's

and women's intercollegiate athletic programs exist under the auspices of the same governing bodies.

Conferences

A conference is a group of colleges or universities that governs the conduct of its member institutions' athletics programs. The first athletic conference, the Intercollegiate Conference of Faculty Representatives, was established in 1895; later it became known as the Western Conference or the Big Ten Conference. In addition to establishing rules of competition and conducting conference championships, conferences have functions related to the following areas:

- Communication within and beyond the membership
- Scheduling
- Officiating
- Crowd control and contest management
- Compliance and enforcement (rules and regulations)
- Eligibility of student-athletes
- Television contracts
- Informational services
- Merchandising (e.g., procuring commercial sponsorship of conference championships)
- Endorsement of an exclusive line of clothing or equipment
- Conducting surveys of its members
- Fostering collegiality among member institutions
- Record keeping (Kinder, 1993)

Examples of conferences are the Central Intercollegiate Athletics Association (CIAA), Mid-America Intercollegiate Athletics Association (MIAA), the Ivy League, the Atlantic Coast Conference (ACC), the Mid-Eastern Athletic Conference (MEAC), the Pennsylvania State Athletic Conference (PSAC), the Mid-American Conference (MAC), the Southeastern Conference (SEC), the Southwestern Athletic Conference (SWAC), the Eastern College Athletic Conference (ECAC), the New York State Women's Collegiate Athletic Association (NYSWCAA), the Atlantic Women's Colleges Conference (AWCC), and the Big Ten Conference. A typical conference organizational chart is presented in figure 14.6.

The ECAC is the nation's largest athletics conference. It was founded in 1938 as the Central Office for Eastern Intercollegiate Athletics. In 1983 the Eastern Association of Intercollegiate Athletics for Women (EAIAW) was merged into the ECAC structure. This merger greatly increased ECAC's membership base.

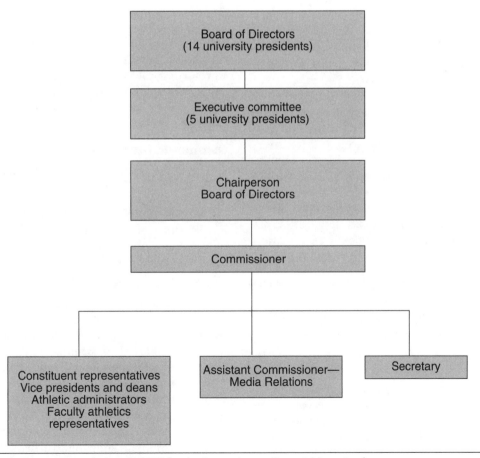

Figure 14.6 Organizational chart (1977) for the Pennsylvania State Athletic Conference.

Reprinted, by permission, from the Pennsylvania State Athletic Conference.

Membership within the CIAA, MEAC, and AWCC conferences is unique in comparison to the major conferences. The member institutions within the CIAA and MEAC are exclusively historically Black colleges and universities, and women's colleges are exclusively comprised within the AWCC. The AWCC is a fairly new conference. It was formed in 1995. It is committed to promoting the highest level of excellence for women in academics and athletics. The membership requirements are that the college be a women's college, accredited, four-year, liberal arts institution, and NCAA Division III member. There are eight institutions within the AWCC.

Institutional Governance

Since the founding of the NCAA in 1910, the question of who controls athletics on college campuses has been a point of contention. The history of college sport is replete with stories of repeated academic and financial scandals that have led to college sport being described periodically as out of control and in need of reform. Prior to 2001, the most significant college athletic reform movement in recent memory was initiated by the Knight Commission on Intercollegiate Athletics in the late 1980s. In response to one of the most scandal-ridden and publicly embarrassing moments in college sport history, a moment in which just over half of the Division I-A programs (57 of 106) had been censured, sanctioned, or put on probation for major violations of NCAA rules, the commission proposed a **"one-plus-three model" for intercollegiate athletics** (Knight Foundation Commission on Intercollegiate Athletics, 1991). This model emphasized the necessity for college presidents to control intercollegiate athletics and to direct their attention to three things: academic integrity, financial integrity, and independent certification of athletics programs.

institutional governance—The process by which athletics departments are held accountable to the rules and regulations governing the conduct of intercollegiate sports.

one-plus-three model for intercollegiate athletics—A model of intercollegiate athletic reform proposed by the Knight Commission that emphasized individual presidential control over three areas: academic integrity, financial integrity, and independent certification of athletics programs.

Ten years after the unveiling of the "one-plus-three" model, the Knight Commission met to as-

sess the progress made in implementing it. Whereas they acknowledged that some of the goals set out in the late 1980s had been achieved, they also found that problems in big-time college sport had not diminished and, in fact, had actually increased. A decade after their report was issued, there was no appreciable reduction in the number of Division I-A schools penalized for NCAA violations. As the commission noted, "more than half the institutions competing at the top levels continue to break the rules. Wrongdoing as a way of life seems to represent the status quo" (Knight Foundation Commission, 2001).

Among the most glaring of these problems that the commission cited were repeated academic improprieties (e.g., **academic fraud**, low graduation rates), a "financial arms race" (e.g., excessive spending and poor financial accountability), and escalating commercialization as evidence of "the widening chasm between higher education's ideals and big-time college sports" (Knight Foundation Commission, 2001). This time around, the commission proposed another "one-plus-three" model of athletic reform. The centerpiece of this model is no longer individual college presidents but a coalition of presidents representing the most powerful athletics conferences that the commission believes have the potential to achieve a reform agenda that includes academic reform, a de-escalation of the athletics arms race, and a de-emphasis of the commercialization of intercollegiate athletics.

academic fraud—Inappropriate conduct in academic areas such as tutors writing papers for athletes, athletes receiving copies of tests in advance, changing athletes' grades so they can remain eligible, and other practices that violate principles of academic honesty.

Other Athletic Reformers: Faculty, Scholars, Students, and Athletes

The Knight Commission is not alone in its concern about the effect of college sport on the integrity of higher education (Sack & Staurowsky, 1998; Sperber, 2000). The commission's model of reform, however, is only one among a number to be discussed in recent years. Well-respected college administrators James Shulman and William Bowen (2001), in their book *The Game of Life,* documented that the overemphasis on winning, money, and professionalization found in big-time programs has seeped into every aspect of the educational system within the United States, reaching all the way to the elementary school level. Shulman and Bowen reported that even among institutions traditionally known for maintaining a balance between academics and athletics, such as the Ivy League and private liberal arts colleges, progressively more resources have been allocated to intercollegiate athletics programs over the years to the detriment of the academic experience of students on those campuses. They concluded that presidents, trustees, alumni, faculty, and students should seriously reconsider the role athletics plays on college campuses and reallocate resources accordingly.

Even before the Knight Commission reconvened in the year 2000, the Drake Group, comprised of scholars from around the country who study college sport, met to develop a reform platform for intercollegiate athletics (Lords, 2000). In response to the reality that "college athletics has been transformed into a multi-billion dollar entertainment industry that has compromised the academic mission of the university," members of the Drake Group have strongly advocated for faculty to play a more forceful role in preserving academic integrity and safeguarding against the corrosive effect of big-time college sport on the daily practices of higher education. Among the Drake Group's proposed solutions are a recommendation that public policy makers consider requiring public disclosure of academic information about athletes, that institutions offer academic support and counseling services equally to all students rather than have special services located in athletics departments, and that consideration be given to replacing one-year renewable scholarships that place athletes in dependent relationships with coaches with need-based financial aid.

At Rutgers University a group of faculty, students, and alumni known as the Rutgers 1000 have organized to contest the continuing practice of the university in pursuing a big-time athletics program that drains money away from the academic programs at the institution. College athletes themselves have also felt the necessity of advocating on their own behalf. Under the leadership of former UCLA football player Ramogi Huma, the Collegiate Athletes Coalition was formed in January 2001. With both support and money from the United Steelworkers of America, the coalition has targeted full health care coverage, better life insurance plans, reductions in class-disrupting mandatory practices and workouts (including ones that are falsely labeled "voluntary"), increased in-season stipends, and

greater flexibility in the restrictions governing employment (Farmer, 2001).

LEARNING ACTIVITY

The fact that a variety of approaches are being suggested to resolve the problems that exist in intercollegiate athletics should not be viewed as a discouraging sign. Rather, solutions come through earnest exploration and debate coupled with a sincere willingness to fix the problem. As aspiring young professionals, you will be in a position to make a difference. How might you go about addressing an aspect of the problem? Locate an article about college athletic reform. Critique the article and offer your own views about what needs to be done.

Intercollegiate Athletics Administrators

As a student, you may want to find a definitive answer to the question of what athletics administrators do. To some degree, athletics administrators resemble typical managers in other business settings and industries. Athletics administrators must be able to execute the fundamental managerial functions of planning, organizing, staffing, directing, coordinating, reporting, and budgeting.

However, the definitive answer to the question of what athletics administrators do is elusive because of the unique nature of athletics departments and how they are structured within specific colleges and universities. For example, the athletics department at the University of Texas was referred to by *Fortune* magazine writers Johnson and Danehy (1999) as "Longhorn Inc." and athletics director DeLoss Dodds as the chief executive officer (CEO) responsible for overseeing a "business" that had an operating budget of $45.3 million. In contrast, an athletics director at a Division III institution or junior college, with responsibility for a budget of less than $1 million, faces different job demands and responsibilities. In many respects, this can be thought of as the distinction between major corporations and locally owned businesses. Both require managerial skills and savvy, but the demands on the leaders of the enterprises vary markedly.

In chapter 9 you learned about top-level, middle-level, and supervisory-level or first-line managers. As figures 14.2, 14.3, 14.4, and 14.7 show, you can find all three types of managers in most intercollegiate

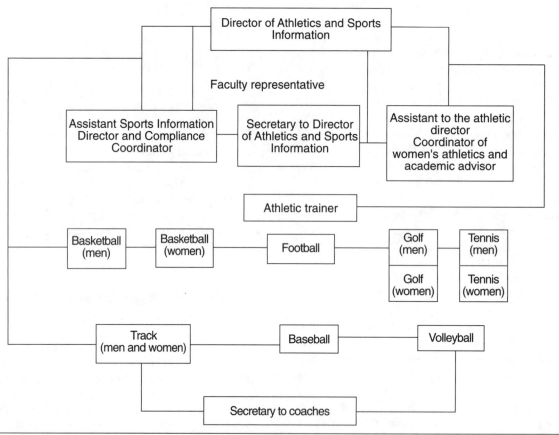

Figure 14.7 Mississippi Valley State University Athletic Department organizational chart.

Reprinted, by permission, from Mississippi Valley State University.

athletics departments. An important point to remember is that many administrators will have assistants. These assistant positions are the ones that novice athletics administrators often pursue and occupy at the beginnings of their careers.

As a general rule, the more prominent the athletics department is, the larger the annual operating budget will be, and the more complex the organizational structure is, the larger the full-time and part-time athletics department staff will be. Thus, administrators working in Division I-A colleges and universities will occupy positions with narrowly defined responsibilities. Alternatively, in athletics departments in Divisions II and III, as well as at the junior and community college levels, administrators may be responsible for a wider array of responsibilities. As a consequence, individuals employed in those settings might also have to perform duties other than those related to their athletics management role, such as teaching in sport-related areas, coaching, or working in student life.

The size of the school and athletics department are not the only factors that can affect the ap-

proach taken by athletics administrators to their jobs. Most of what we know about intercollegiate athletics management today pertains to traditionally White institutions. While management functions overlap significantly in every athletics department, we cannot assume that what we know about intercollegiate athletics management based on that information can be uniformly generalized and applied to historically Black colleges and universities (HBCUs), such as Tennessee State, Mississippi Valley State, Howard University, South Carolina State, Florida A&M, Tuskegee University, and Grambling University. *USA Today* sportswriter Bryan Burwell (1993), for example, noted that events such as the **Bayou Classic** and other **HBCU** men's football classics offer a "radical cultural departure" from the prevailing image of men's college football. In contrast to the vast majority of highly publicized men's college football games, audiences for these events are composed primarily of people of color. The events themselves are often staged as cultural festivals with step shows, beauty pageants, and music performances scheduled in conjunction with the games. Researcher

Ketra Armstrong's (1998, 2000) work on marketing sport to Black consumers also reinforces this point.

Bayou Classic—Considered to be the "grand-daddy" of historically Black men's college football rivalries, this game features Grambling versus Southern University. Other events between the two schools in track and field and women's basketball are labeled "classics" as well.

HBCU—This acronym refers to historically Black colleges and universities.

The notion that not all athletics programs fit the dominant model of college sport management is borne out not only in the HBCUs but also in women's college athletics programs. Typically located in small liberal arts institutions and falling under the rubric of Division III, the women's athletics program in schools such as Smith, Bryn Mawr, Mt. Holyoke, and Mills College adopt management models that are consistent with single-sex women's education institutions.

Due to the variability of the college sport marketplace, no two positions are identical nor are the job titles used to describe them. As you explore career opportunities in this sector, you will discover that while two individuals may hold the same job title, their actual jobs may differ considerably. When you begin to search for internships or positions in intercollegiate athletics, study each job description carefully to determine if the responsibilities of the position match your career interests and your areas of expertise. This investment of time and attention will yield a more satisfying result in the end and increase the likelihood that you will be successful in your search. The following sections offer overviews of positions that can be found in typical athletics departments along with outlines of job responsibilities for each of the positions discussed.

Athletics Director (AD)

In a book about strategic planning for college athletics programs (Yow, Migliore, Bowden, Stevens, & Loudon, 2000), ADs were described as "pilots [of a major airliner], responsible for taking off, landing, conferring with the navigator, and communicating with the air traffic controller" (p. 3). The metaphor is an apt one. An AD assumes oversight for the following: budget and finance, facilities, risk management, television contracts, compliance with laws and regulations of national and conference governing bodies, academic progress of college athletes, communication with the media, schedul-

ing, marketing games and other events, corporate sponsorships, ticket sales, community relations, alumni relations, campus relations, fund-raising, and personnel management, including the hiring and termination of coaches (Karlin, 1995).

Whereas historically the role of the AD was one of providing leadership and direction for the athletics program in the creation of playing opportunities for athletes, the ever-increasing demands of revenue generation have reshaped the emphasis ADs place on certain responsibilities. Several researchers in recent years have documented the growing importance of fund-raising within the overall scheme of what an AD is expected to do (Curtis, 2000; Staurowsky, 1996). Further, the transformation of college sport into mass-mediated spectacle with high visibility has, in turn, transformed the responsibilities of the AD and other administrators within an intercollegiate athletics department (Nichols, Moynahan, Hall, & Taylor, 2001).

Obviously, not all of these duties can be performed by the AD. Thus, it is not surprising that athletics directors who work in the "major" conferences (SEC, ACC, Conference USA, Big East, and Big 10) identify delegation as the key interpersonal skill needed to run a successful athletic team or organization. The vast majority of these ADs also believe that the abilities to influence and motivate individuals are essential leadership skills (Christian, 2000). These skills are reflective of the organizational structure in which middle-level and first-line administrators in charge of specific areas report to, and are supervised by, an AD. In most Division I institutions, the AD reports directly to the university president or through a vice president to the president. There is greater variation in reporting lines at the Division II and III levels, with ADs potentially reporting to administrators such as the vice president of student affairs, the dean of health and human services, or the chair of the department of physical education.

Associate or Assistant Athletics Director

Associate and assistant ADs are clearly middle managers. These titles generally represent either the level of administrative responsibility assigned to the individual in the role or the level of seniority and experience the individual has. In many respects, the associate or assistant AD supports the AD in achieving the overall mission of the department by working closely with the AD and overseeing specific areas, such as marketing, fund-raising, event management, facilities management, or

281

In Profile

Name: Gene Smith

Title: Director of Athletics, Arizona State University

If there were a prototype for the 21st-century athletics director, Gene Smith might well be it. Growing up in Cleveland, Ohio, Smith attended Chanel High School, where he distinguished himself in football, basketball, and track while receiving the football team's most valuable player award. Smith went on to pursue a bachelor's degree in business administration at the University of Notre Dame, where he also played defensive end for the Irish, achieving distinction once again as a member of the Associated Press 1973 national championship team.

It was at Notre Dame that Smith would go on to make a successful professional transition from player to coach. Notably, Smith was serving as an assistant coach in the program during the 1976-1977 season when the Irish were recognized as the undisputed national champions. Following his coaching experience, Smith chose to make a career move, becoming a marketing representative for IBM, a decision that would eventually lead to his hiring as the director of athletics at Eastern Michigan University and Iowa State.

In 2000 Smith was hired as Arizona State University's (ASU) 18th director of athletics. In that capacity, he is called upon to demonstrate command of an array of organizational management skills in the running of a Division I-A athletics department that is a member of the PAC-10 Conference. He has had to handle numerous personnel decisions, including the hiring of coaches in the sports of men's football, soccer, and wrestling; women's golf; and men's water polo. Smith provides the vision and leadership for an athletics program with 22 sports, 500+ athletes, a staff of close to 150 (many of whom are charged to execute marketing and information management functions), and a $30 million budget. Notably, during his time at ASU, Smith participated in the successful completion of a major athletics development project, a $30 million capital campaign. One of the major projects funded in part through that campaign was the construction of the $19 million Ed and Nadine Carson Student-Athlete Center, which opened in May 2002.

The authors thank Mark Brand, assistant director of athletics and sports information director at ASU for his assistance in the completion of this profile.

---

athletics communications. In large athletics departments, several individuals will be designated as associate or assistant ADs. Senior associates usually serve as the second in command within an athletics department and assume responsibility for the overall operation of the department in the absence of the AD. As mentioned previously, in order to determine what people in these positions do, you have to read their job descriptions or speak with them directly.

First-Line Managers

First-line managers are responsible for specific work groups in the athletics department. These managers typically report to an associate or assistant AD. It should be noted that many of these positions have emerged within the past two decades. These positions include academic coordinator, business and finance manager, compliance officer, development and public relations director, event and facility manager, marketing and promotions director, sports information director, ticket manager, and senior woman administrator. Brief descriptions of these jobs follow.

Academic Coordinator

According to the National Association of Academic Advisors for Athletes (N4A), fewer than 10 full-time academic advisors for athletes existed in 1975. As of 2002 the N4A had a membership of over 550 (NAAAA). This phenomenal growth has been due to the passage of NCAA bylaw 16.3.1, which requires all Division I programs to offer academic support and tutoring services to athletes, and the Academic Enhancement Fund Program, which allocates $50,000 per year to each Division I athletics program in support of these programs (www.ncaa.org/enhancement).

Athletics academic advisement services are designed to assist athletes in addressing the dual and sometimes conflicting demands of being both a student and an athlete. As is the case with all of the areas we have addressed, the structure of these offices and the range of services they provide can vary from one institution to another. In general, athletics academic offices provide assistance to athletes in the broad areas of admission, academic orientation, academic standards, registration, financial aid, housing, and student life. The academic coordinator monitors the academic activities of athletes and maintains records on their academic progress. In order to do their jobs effectively, academic coordinators work closely with coaches, faculty, the compliance officer, and other administrators.

One of the programs that the athletics academic support office may offer to athletes is the CHAMPS-Life Skills Program (Challenging Athletes' Minds for Personal Success). This program was created through the collaborative efforts of the NCAA Foundation and the Division I-A Athletic Directors' Association. The program is built around five "commitment statements" that address academic excellence, athletic excellence, personal development, career development, and service to the community (www.ncaa.org/edout/champs_lifeskills/program.html).

Individuals who have an interest in working as an athletics academic advisor need to understand the business of college sport and regulations that impact on athletes and be equally familiar with the processes of social adaptation and human development, academic performance assessment, and career guidance strategies. In large athletics programs, the athletics academic support services staff might include several academic counselors, mentors, and tutors, some of whom will be undergraduate and graduate students.

Business and Finance Manager

The business and finance manager for an intercollegiate athletics department recommends and implements policies, procedures, and methods of accounting that ensure strict compliance with sound business practices in accordance with the rules and regulations of the institution, conferences, and the national governing body. As the financial officer for the athletics department, the business manager assists the AD in preparing, administering, and monitoring the budget. This includes determining charges and arrangements associated with the rental of athletics facilities by both internal and external groups. Business managers oversee the processing of all reimbursements and payments while assuming responsibility for the creation, generation, and distribution of monthly financial statements for the review of the AD, middle-level managers, coaches, and staff members. Depending on the athletics department, the athletics business and finance office may also be responsible for handling the payment of wages to part-time and student personnel hired to assist with athletic and special events. Further, this office may be charged with the task of arranging housing, hotel, and meal accommodations for teams. Business and finance managers must have a solid background in the area of financial accounting.

Compliance Officer

Compliance with NCAA regulations is not the sole responsibility of the person designated in an athletics department to serve as the compliance officer or coordinator. Compliance is technically a shared responsibility among all parties who come in contact with the athletics program, including the AD, coaches, current athletes, prospective athletes, boosters, and alumni, as well as representatives from various campus offices (e.g., admission, financial aid, residence life, health services). The process of compliance in its contemporary form evolved in the 1990s in conjunction with the development of the NCAA program certification process.

Broadly stated, the role of compliance coordinators is to develop educational processes that help everyone directly or indirectly involved with the athletics program understand and comply with the rules of the institution, the national governing body, and the conference. The span of responsibilities compliance officers may be assigned include assessment of student initial eligibility, continuing eligibility, and transfer eligibility as well as adherence to regulations governing athlete recruitment. Because of the complexity of rules, compliance coordinators are often given the task of developing and implementing record keeping methods to demonstrate that compliance in various areas is monitored. Much of this record keeping is done via computer software programs. Compliance officers play a crucial role in the formulation of compliance reports that must be submitted to the NCAA on a regular basis.

Individuals who have an interest in working in the compliance area must be detail oriented and have an exhaustive understanding of NCAA and conference rules and regulations along with the management and communication skills necessary to effectively explain rules and regulations. Although a law degree is not a requirement for this type of position, the nature of the job lends itself to someone with this kind of interest and background.

Development and Public Relations Director

Depending on the institution, the process of raising money from friends of an athletics program is called athletics fund-raising, development, or advancement. Athletics fund-raising organizations may be called fan clubs, booster clubs, friends associations, alumni clubs, or athletic foundations. Athletics development officers are responsible for raising funds to support various aspects of the athletics department by identifying and implementing fund-raising projects and cultivating potential and current donors. In athletics fund-raising, several basic principles apply. You want to encourage people who donate to your program to continue to donate, and hopefully donate more over time, while searching out and contacting new donors to expand your financial base. The importance of development efforts to college athletics programs cannot be underestimated. For the fiscal year 1999, 17% of the revenue generated by Division I-A programs came from alumni contributions, which translates into millions of dollars in support (Fulks, 2000). This type of position requires a combination of marketing, management, and media relations skills.

One element that is extremely important in this area is vigilance with regard to the donors involved with your program. This is an area in which the potential for rules violations has proven to be high. It is not unusual for donors and friends of athletics programs to offer athletes under-the-table payments, improper gifts, and other benefits that violate NCAA rules. As a result, athletics development officers are required to show the steps they take to educate friends of the program about rules and regulations governing athletics programs so as to avoid problems in this area.

Event and Facility Manager

In recent years, there has been a marked expansion of athletics facilities on college campuses. Due to the limitations of space and resources, pressure has been placed on athletics departments to find ways for facilities to serve the multiple needs of campus constituencies and to generate income through the rental and use of multipurpose facilities for special events, such as concerts. The position description for an event and facility manager reflects this trend. Facility scheduling, maintenance, improvements, and contest management are the major duties assigned to event and facility managers (Farmer, Mulrooney, & Ammon, 1996; Solomon, 2001). Because so many people use athletics facilities, and for so many different activities, facility and event managers must be attentive to the reduction of risk and liability while finding ways of being user-friendly through creating as much availability and accessibility as possible. One of the major responsibilities of the event and facility manager is game management for home athletics events. This entails arranging for appropriate levels of security at games; hiring, training, and supervision of ushers; marking and lining of fields and courts; arrangements for ticket sellers and ticket takers; management of the time schedule of the game, including such things as the National Anthem, bands, and half-time shows; and attendance to the needs of game officials. A more detailed description of event and facility management is presented in chapter 13.

Marketing and Promotions Director

In the summer of 2001 the University of Oregon purchased a 10-story billboard in New York City's Times Square on which it displayed a picture of its Heisman Trophy nominee, quarterback Joey Harrington. The cost of that billboard was a tidy $250,000. Yes, as in a quarter of a million dollars. Although the amount of money invested in the Harrington campaign was unusual, the promotion itself was not. For the Heisman alone, schools routinely invest $15,000 to $20,000 to promote their nominees (Posnanski, 2001). Marketing and promoting the contemporary college athletics program happens at all levels and is motivated by the need to generate interest in the program through enhanced visibility, increased attendance, and expanding revenue streams (see chapter 12).

Marketing and promotions directors may be responsible for promoting ticket sales for individual games, nonrevenue sports, season packages, and championship events along with a complete line of apparel, fan support merchandise, and items for retail sale via direct mail and through the university's bookstore and concessions area. Marketing and promotions directors are also charged with identifying potential corporate sponsors, developing sponsorship proposals, and ensuring that proposals are implemented according to agreements reached with sponsors (Irwin, Sutton, & McCarthy, 2002). In an age in which product branding, merchandising, and licensing have become such integral parts of the marketing of intercollegiate athletics programs, marketing and promotions directors must have a comprehensive understanding of trademark licensing and be familiar with trademark principles, terms, and definitions used in trademark law (Pitts & Stotlar, 2002).

Sports Information Director

Media have played a significant role in the development and evolution of all forms of sport in the United States, including college sport. The popularity and revenue-generating potential of college football and men's basketball are not, as some seem to believe, accidental or happenstance. Rather, the intensity of the interest and financial investment in those sports is the result of a long-standing relationship between college sport and the media (Oriard, 2001). The emergence of the NCAA and the formalization of college football in 1910 coincided with an era in which newspapers were struggling to gain a foothold in U.S. popular culture. As John Marrs (1998) noted, "serious-minded newspaper editors of the 1920s found sports too popular to fight and sports coverage claimed 40% of all local news space" (p. 5).

The advent of televised sport in the mid-1950s dramatically changed the relationship between college athletics departments and journalists. Prior to the 1950s, sport publicists sought to gain coverage for their teams in newspapers and on radio. Television introduced the element of revenue-generating potential through access to national audiences and immediate, live game coverage. Emblematic of the changing times, the NCAA published its first public relations manual for intercollegiate athletics in 1954. Reflecting the background and training of the NCAA's first executive director, Walter Byers, who had been a journalist, the association went on to persuade colleges and universities that they needed to have a full-time sport publicist on staff while simultaneously pursuing television contracts to enhance the public profile of college sport (Byers, 1995; Marrs, 1998).

The introduction of 24-hour-a-day, every-day-of-the-week sport coverage, along with the Internet, emerging technologies, and the increase in women's sport, has substantially affected the way communications are managed and handled by intercollegiate athletics programs (Nichols,

Moynahan, Hall, & Taylor, 2001). Sports information directors, also referred to as athletics communications specialists, sport publicists, and college sport public relations directors, are responsible for both technical and management functions. As a public relations practitioner, a sports information director must be adept at developing an array of publication materials, including media guides, press releases, recruiting brochures, game programs, feature stories, and newsletters, along with the background work (e.g., research, interviews with coaches and players) to support those publications. In addition to executing the technical demands of the job, sports information directors are also responsible for managing budgets, organizing events, and supervising personnel. Successful sports information directors need to have excellent writing and research skills, a vast understanding of mass communication and media technologies, an awareness of (and an ability to) appeal to internal and external audiences, and a capacity to maintain a calm demeanor while working in high-stress/high-pressure situations. For more information about sports information directors, see chapter 11.

LEARNING ACTIVITY

Identify a story about a college athletics program, coach, or athlete from a media source. Based on the information in the story, track the source of the story. Did the story originate with a press release distributed by the sports information office? Was it a feature idea suggested by the sports information director to the writer of the story? Were the statistics in the story drawn from a media guide or game program?

Ticket Manager

The primary responsibilities of the ticket manager are coordinating all ticket operations, designing the ticketing plan, and accounting for all money expended and received for tickets. A major resource for the ticket manager is the International Ticketing Association (INTIX). Members of INTIX include a vast array of businesses and organizations in sport and entertainment fields around the world (e.g., amphitheaters, ballet and opera companies, festivals, sport teams, state fairs, theaters, and universities). Ticketing software and hardware development workers, ticket agents and printers, and Internet-based ticketing companies also belong to INTIX. INTIX sponsors an annual conference as well as an intensive certification program to help people in the industry stay current on trends and techniques to provide the best service possible to consumers. Additional information can be found at www.intix.org.

Senior Woman Administrator (SWA)

When you read through biographies of people working in intercollegiate athletics, you may come across the term *senior woman administrator*. The term itself is not a position title per se, but it does designate "the highest-ranking female administrator involved with the conduct of a member institution's intercollegiate athletics program" (Earle, 2001, p. 22). The purpose of the senior woman administrator concept is to ensure that women have a role in the decision-making process in college sport while also ensuring that women's interests at the campus, conference, and national levels are represented. Research about senior woman administrators reveals that 79% of Division I SWAs serve in some administrative role within their departments, occupying assistant, associate, or senior associate athletics director positions. However, in other divisions, fewer senior woman administrators have significant administrative responsibilities (Claussen & Lehr, 1999). Oftentimes this means that SWAs in the lower divisions are designated as such but have little decision-making power and serve only as figureheads.

Who is a Senior Woman Administrator?

The highest ranking female administrator involved with conducting a member institution's intercollegiate athletics program. She should be a full-time institutional employee who has demonstrated an interest in athletics.

What is the purpose of appointing a Senior Woman Administrator?

To involve female administrators in a meaningful way in the decision-making process in intercollegiate athletics. The position is intended to ensure representation of women's interests at the campus, conference, and national levels.

Who appoints the Senior Woman Administrator and to whom does she report?

Generally, the athletics director or the university president appoints the SWA, and the SWA usually reports to the athletics director.

Figure 14.8 NCAA senior woman administrator.

Reprinted, by permission, from NCAA brochure *Senior Woman Administrator*.

The concept of the senior woman administrator can sometimes be confusing. Although some SWAs are assigned sole responsibility for women's athletics programs and teams, the range of responsibilities assigned to SWAs can encompass all that goes on in a coeducational athletics department. According to Jane Meyer, the senior associate director of athletics at the University of Iowa, the scope of responsibilities for SWAs should contribute to the decision making regarding the following areas: business affairs/budget management, Equity in Athletics Disclosure Act (EADA) oversight, personnel decisions, gender equity/Title IX, athlete welfare, promotions/sponsorship/marketing/development, legislation process at the NCAA and conference levels, strategic planning, and formulation of a mission or philosophy for the department. In recent years steps have been taken to designate an SWA within athletics conferences as well. See figure 14.8 for more information.

LEARNING ACTIVITY

Based on what you've learned about the history of college sport and women's access to administrative positions, why is an SWA needed in intercollegiate athletics departments and conferences?

Equipment Manager

According to the Athletic Equipment Managers Association (AEMA), equipment managers purchase equipment; fit equipment such as football helmets; check, clean, and inspect uniforms and equipment to reduce wear and risk of injury while preserving the life of the equipment and garments as part of the budget management process; and establish a comprehensive accountability system that includes inventory (pre- and postseason), reconditioning, and storage. As is the case with all of the other positions mentioned in this chapter, there is a significant management component to an equipment manager's job (Olson, 1997). Effective communication with top-level, middle-level, and first-line administrators is absolutely essential. Equipment managers are expected to develop educational programs for the purposes of training professional and student staff (Momentum Media, 1999).

Since 1991, AEMA has promoted a certification program for equipment managers to ensure a high standard of performance and professional preparation. As of 1999, there were 481 certified athletic equipment managers in the United States (Momentum Media, 1999).

Athletic Training Staff

In most athletics programs, you will find a head athletic trainer and any number of assistant athletic trainers, depending on the size of the institution. Athletic trainers are responsible for ensuring the proper care, treatment, and prevention of injuries for all student-athletes at home and away athletic contests. It is the responsibility of the athletic training staff to assign personnel to all home and away events for which an athletic trainer is appropriate and to provide the necessary staff for all championship events. Decisions related to practice, competition, treatment, therapy, and rehabilitation are usually coordinated with the full participation of the student-athlete, the head coach, the athletic training staff, and other appropriate medical personnel.

Most full-time athletic trainers apply for certification from the National Athletic Trainers' Association (NATA), the primary professional organization for athletic trainers. Graduate and undergraduate athletic training students frequently work in the school's athletic training program as part of the NATA certification process. The NATA Board of Certification (NATABOC) has identified six performance domains (i.e., areas of responsibility) in which athletic trainers must be competent: prevention; recognition, evaluation, and assessment; immediate care; treatment, rehabilitation, and reconditioning; organization and administration; and professional development and responsibility (NATABOC, 1999). While most of these domains are directly associated with the prevention and care of injuries, the organization and administration domain requires athletic trainers to be competent in managerial tasks such as planning, writing policies and procedures, compliance with standards, management of finances and personnel, and maintenance of records. It is important, therefore, for prospective athletic trainers to take course work in business and management in order to acquire the skills necessary to function effectively in these roles. It would also be a good idea to take teaching methods courses because opportunities to teach athletic training courses in academic units such as sport management or physical education frequently arise.

The Commission on Accreditation of Allied Health Programs (CAAHEP) accredits athletic training curricula. Among other requirements, this organization mandates that programs offer formal instruction in the following areas: assessment of injury/illness, exercise physiology, first aid and emergency care, medical conditions and disabilities, health care administration, anatomy, human physiology, kinesiology/biomechanics, medical ethics and legal issues, nutrition, pathology of injury/illness, pharmacology, professional development and responsibilities, psychosocial intervention and referral, risk management and injury/illness prevention, strength training and reconditioning, statistics and research design, therapeutic exercise and rehabilitative techniques, therapeutic modalities, and weight management and body composition (CAAHEP, 1998-2002). CAAHEP also encourages the inclusion of course work in general education, multicultural diversity, liberal arts, and the humanities in the curriculum. Study in these areas not only will help students become better trainers but also will prepare students for later academic and career growth, such as course work in teacher education, graduate school, entrepreneurship, and research (CAAHPEP, 1998-2002).

Administrators in Governing Bodies

Administrative positions in conferences and national governing bodies parallel many in colleges and universities. The major difference between them is that administrators in conferences and governing bodies must consider the welfare of many institutions and the conference as a whole, rather than focusing on a single university. As explained in chapter 9, conference commissioners in all NCAA divisions perform their duties within three major role classifications: interpersonal, informational, and decisional (Quarterman, 1994). Examples of these functions are shown in table 9.5. You will notice they are similar to the roles of an AD, except that the AD is acting on behalf of the university and the commissioner is acting on behalf of the member institutions. The organizational charts in figures 14.1, 14.5, and 14.6 contain additional positions in the NCAA, the NAIA, and conference offices, respectively.

Careers in Intercollegiate Athletics Administration

For some people, money, praise, prestige, and short workweeks are motivational factors for pursuing a career in intercollegiate athletics. Actually, those are the least likely benefits for the vast majority of positions. Intercollegiate athletics

In Profile

Name: Carolyn Schlie Femovich

Occupation: Executive director, the Patriot League

What to do with 17 years of management experience at the NCAA Division I level? Become the executive director of a Division I conference, of course.

Carolyn Schlie Femovich started her career in intercollegiate athletics while a graduate teaching assistant at Indiana University. From there she was selected in 1975 to serve as an assistant professor and head coach of women's basketball and tennis at Gettysburg College. In 1978 she became the coordinator of women's athletics. After four years in that position, she was hired at the University of Pennsylvania (Penn) as an associate athletics director. In 1986 Femovich was appointed senior associate athletics director, a position she would hold until her selection as executive director of the Patriot League in 1999. As a senior associate at Penn, Femovich played a significant leadership role in the management of a highly successful Ivy League program. Among her responsibilities at Penn, Femovich participated in strategic planning and facilities development, human resource management, and event as well as budget planning.

Femovich's previous experience was most important in ensuring her success as executive director of the Patriot League. During her tenure with the Patriot League, she has worked to establish a strategic direction for the conference while increasing league visibility, marketability, and fiscal security. Indicative of the need for college sport managers to participate in the governance of intercollegiate athletics, Femovich currently serves as the Patriot League representative on the NCAA management council. Previously, she chaired the NCAA basketball marketing subcommittee and was a member of the NCAA Division I business/finance cabinet and the Division I women's basketball committee. A measure of her influence can be seen in the primary role she played in bringing the NCAA Women's Basketball Final Four to Philadelphia in the spring of 2000. Additionally, she is currently chair of the prestigious Honda Awards Program, a program that honors the top collegiate woman athlete of the year.

At the time of Femovich's hiring as executive director of the Patriot League, she was one of just two women to hold the position of commissioner of a Division I conference that met the needs of both male and female athletes.

The author would like to thank the media relations staff at the Patriot League for their assistance in the preparation of this profile.

administrative positions do not typically pay high salaries, you have to contend with "Monday morning quarterbacks" who are always willing to tell you how you could improve your performance, the hours are long, and the work is challenging. Rewards for your efforts might occasionally include the excitement of watching your teams in conference, regional, or national championship tournaments. More frequently, however, athletics administrators feel sufficiently rewarded to know that they are doing something they enjoy and, at the same time, touching the lives of young men and women and making a difference.

Career paths in intercollegiate athletics vary widely. There are no established paths that you can set out on to end up where you thought you were going. The following discussion of career paths of ADs and first-line administrators is designed to help you gain insight into this competitive career field.

Becoming an Athletics Director

The traditional path to the AD position has been from collegiate athlete to collegiate coach to AD. Currently, however, there are at least two alternatives to that path. In some cases, athletics departments are recruiting successful businesspeople to take the helms of their financially challenged departments. In other situations, individuals who aspire to be ADs are gaining formal education through sport management programs (Berg, 1990).

Although there is no one best path to the AD position, the appropriateness of the athlete-to-coach-to-AD path has been challenged, particularly for NCAA Division I institutions. Reflecting widely held sentiments, Cuneen (1992) stated that "managerial expertise and business acumen have become such essential characteristics for directors of major collegiate athletic programs that the long-standing career path of player to coach to athletic director is no longer sufficient" (p. 16).

She suggested that prospective ADs should pursue a doctoral curriculum to prepare them for job responsibilities such as business management, strategic planning, marketing, facility management, legal aspects of sport, finance, accounting, organizational theory, and personnel management.

Fitzgerald, Sagaria, and Nelson (1994) examined the career patterns of 200 athletic directors in NCAA Division I, II, and III institutions. They found that most respondents had been either college athletes or college coaches. Consistent similarities ended with that observation, however, as career paths differed unpredictably within divisions and between genders. ADs in HBCUs have followed a slightly different path (Quarterman, 1992). Like their counterparts in predominately White institutions, most administrators at HBCUs were intercollegiate players and coaches before becoming ADs. The difference is that most of them also have teaching experience and are faculty members or coaches while they are serving as ADs. According to Quarterman, the career experiences of ADs in HBCUs (athlete to coach or instructor to AD) are similar to those of ADs in NAIA and NCAA Division II and III institutions.

First-Line Administrators

First-line administrators, such as marketing directors, academic coordinators, and sports information directors, spend their entire careers within a work unit focused on one aspect of the program. For these administrators, career advancements are typically in the form of a vertical move from assistant director of a work unit to director of that unit. Occasionally, first-line administrators will relocate to similar positions at other universities (i.e., a horizontal or lateral move) to advance their careers. Other first-line administrators, particularly in NCAA Division I programs, might move into associate or assistant AD positions (Fitzgerald et al., 1994; Quarterman, 1992). As these administrators move vertically, whether to director of the work unit or to associate or assistant AD positions, they will be expected to perform additional managerial and administrative functions.

Job Satisfaction

Intercollegiate athletics administrators have reported a high degree of satisfaction with most aspects of their jobs (Parks, Russell, Wood, Roberton, & Shewokis, 1995). Middle-level and first-line administrators, however, tend not to be satisfied with their salaries and their promotion opportunities (Parks et al., 1995). Dissatisfaction with salaries is probably a reaction to salaries in intercollegiate athletics being lower than salaries for managerial positions in other industries. The appeal of sport is so strong, however, that many individuals are content to work long hours for low pay. Moreover, the benefits that come with university employment (e.g., vacation time, life and health insurance, travel opportunities, access to academic courses, retirement benefits, association with student-athletes) are excellent, frequently offsetting modest salaries.

The dissatisfaction of athletics administrators with opportunities for promotion is probably a reflection of the career paths in intercollegiate athletics. In this field, you typically start out as an assistant to a first-line administrator (e.g., assistant director of marketing) and eventually work your way up to the director of marketing position. Only in rare instances does this path lead to the top position (i.e., AD). Consequently, first-line administrators might not perceive many opportunities for promotion.

Academic Preparation for Athletics Administration

The typical AD has at least one degree beyond the baccalaureate. In 1994, 85% of the ADs in NCAA I, II, and III institutions held master's degrees, with 21.5% of them possessing doctorates (Fitzgerald et al., 1994). Quarterman (1992) found that more than 95% of the ADs in HBCUs held master's degrees, and 36% of them had doctorates. An advanced degree was also prevalent among NCAA Division I-A middle-level and first-line administrators. Parks and colleagues (1995) found that more than 60% of these administrators held either master's or doctoral degrees. It is clear that if you want to pursue a career in intercollegiate athletics, a master's degree will probably be necessary.

You can begin your career path in athletics administration by studying sport management at the undergraduate level; engaging in practica, service learning, or field experiences in athletic administration; or volunteering or completing an internship with an athletics department or a conference office. Your program should provide you with knowledge about sport in society and the role of athletics in institutions of higher education as well as an understanding of the business and technical aspects of the field. If you aspire to a position in an HBCU, NAIA, NCAA II, or NCAA III institution, it would be a good idea to develop a field of academic or coaching expertise too

289

because you will probably be a professor or a coach as well as an administrator (Quarterman, 1992).

Practica, field experiences, volunteer positions, and internships will give you practical experience, one of the most valuable assets you can acquire. While you are observing, learning, and performing career-related tasks for an athletics department or conference office, you are proving your competencies to professionals who are working in the positions for which you strive. In some cases, an internship serves as a stepping-stone to a job with either the internship organization or another organization. While the actual tasks performed may be menial, the observations that can be made and the interaction with professionals in the field can be invaluable for ongoing professional development. Volunteer for as many related events as possible to gain experience that can be reflected on your résumé. Potential employers want to see real accomplishments and the practical work experience obtained through practica, field experiences, volunteering, service learning, and internships. The internship is vital to your career development.

Next, you should select a graduate school that will complement the knowledge and experience you gained at the undergraduate level. If you have no experience in intercollegiate athletics, an important element of the master's degree might be an internship with the university athletics department or conference office. This experience will permit you to learn more about the day-to-day operations of athletics administration. If you perform well, you will also begin to develop a valuable network of professionals who can vouch for your ability when you are looking for a job. If you want to be an AD, particularly at a major institution, you should include doctoral study in your professional preparation plans.

Current Challenges

Numerous challenges await the next generation of intercollegiate athletics administrators. Major concerns include diversity, gender equity, racial equity, homophobia, financial stability, ramifications of the socioeconomic status (SES) of student-athletes, program cost containment, corporate sponsorship, institutional control of athletics, academic integrity, and financial compensation for athletes. This list is not exhaustive, nor does space allow us to present any of these challenges in its entire complexity. In fact, we will discuss only the first three here. If you wish to explore these topics in more depth, a good place to begin would be other chapters in this book that address the specific concerns in which you are interested.

Diversity

Current discussions of affirmative action and equal opportunity might lead a person to believe that a gender and racial balance has been achieved in intercollegiate athletics administration, particularly at the middle-level and first-line positions. On the contrary, recent studies of NCAA member institutions have shown a marked *lack* of diversity in athletics administrative personnel. For example, 92% of the 200 ADs in Fitzgerald and colleagues' 1994 study were White, and 71.5% of them were men. Parks, Russell, and Wood (1993) found a similar racial and gender imbalance among 402 NCAA Division I-A top-level, middle-level, and first-line administrators, where 92% of the respondents were White and 83% were male. The gender and racial imbalance found in these two studies presents a major challenge to the next generation of sport managers, who will be responsible for equalizing opportunities in intercollegiate athletics administration. In the more enlightened age of the 21st century, intercollegiate athletics administration should reflect greater participation, not only by women and minorities but also by people with differing abilities, a population that is currently underrepresented in athletics administration (Abney & Richey, 1992).

Gender Equity

Title IX of the Education Amendments Act of 1972 requires athletics administrators to ensure equity in scholarship support, number of women coaches, promotion of women's athletics, salaries, scheduling of women's games, inclusion of women administrators up to the highest levels, and budgets (Tillman, Voltmer, Esslinger, & McCue, 1996). The Equity in Athletics Disclosure Act of 1994, which went into effect in October 1996, requires institutions of higher education to make public all information *by gender* about participation rates of student-athletes and expenditures associated with coaching salaries, grants-in-aid, recruiting costs, and equipment (U.S. Department of Education, 2002). Although this legislation enhances efforts to enforce the provisions of Title IX, equity in athletics is as much a moral responsibility as it is a legal mandate. The next generation of athletics administrators will be challenged to expand opportunities for women while controlling the costs associated with providing a quality athletics experience (Howard & Crompton, 1995).

Racial Equity

With the increase in participation rates, the implementation of affirmative action policies, the passage of Title IX, and the Civil Rights Restoration Act of 1988, one would anticipate an increase in the opportunities for minorities in coaching and managerial positions in intercollegiate athletics. This is not the case. African American male and female coaches and administrators have not attained parity and remain underrepresented in college athletics (Brooks & Althouse, 1993).

Abney and Richey (1991) investigated barriers Black women administrators face in HBCUs and traditionally White institutions. In both settings, the women reported "inadequate salary," "lack of support groups," and "being a woman" as obstacles to their career development. The women who worked in HBCUs identified the additional barriers of "sexism" and "low expectations by administrators." The women who worked in the White institutions reported that "being Black" was an additional obstacle to their development as was the "lack of cultural and social outlets in the community."

In the 21st century, athletic be increasingly sensitive to t and race on an individual's Abney and Richey (1992) sur stated, "For minority wome of Title IX, there must be in that are knowledgeable, committed, and to the differences and the hiring of minority women. Until this occurs, opportunities will remain limited" (p. 58).

LEARNING ACTIVITY

Following the September 11, 2001, terrorist attacks in New York and Washington, athletics directors, managers, and sport administrators at all levels were faced with several challenges. One of those challenges was whether to cancel athletic contest(s) in the days and weeks following the attacks. Interview an athletics administrator and a coach at your institution. Ask that person to discuss the positive and negative factors related to canceling athletic contests following the terrorist attacks.

SUMMARY

Intercollegiate athletics began in the 1850s as class games and evolved into highly competitive programs. These programs are regulated by national governing bodies and conferences. The first line of control, however, lies with the institution. The Knight Foundation Commission on Intercollegiate Athletics (1991) issued a report calling for presidential control, academic integrity, financial integrity, and certification. Athletics administrative positions include athletics director, associate and assistant athletics director, academic coordinator, business and finance manager, compliance officer, development and public relations director, event and facility manager, marketing and promotions director, sport information director, and ticket manager. Additional personnel include the equipment manager and the athletic training staff. The SWA (senior woman administrator) is the NCAA designation given to the highest-ranking female athletic administrator.

Career paths in intercollegiate athletics vary widely. Most administrators have at least one academic degree beyond the baccalaureate. Individuals who want to become ADs in major institutions should consider earning a doctorate. Challenges with which intercollegiate athletics administrators must deal include diversity, gender and racial equity, homophobia, financial stability, ramifications of differences in socioeconomic status (SES) of student-athletes, cost containment, corporate sponsorship, institutional control, academic integrity, and financial compensation for athletes.

REVIEW QUESTIONS

1. How much is the CBS broadcast deal for the NCAA men's Division I basketball tournament and selected other championships worth?

2. When was the NCAA founded?

3. In the 1980s, what organization initiated a call for intercollegiate athletic reform?

4. Describe that organization's "one-plus-three" model for intercollegiate athletics.

5. What did Shulman and Bowen, authors of the book *The Game of Life*, conclude about the effect of big-time college sport programs on education?

6. What is the Drake Group?

7. Are intercollegiate athletics administrators just like other managers in business settings? Explain your answer.

8. Identify two factors that can affect how athletics administrators approach their jobs.

9. Identify three key skills that athletics directors who work in "major" conferences believe are necessary to run a successful program.

10. An academic coordinator may be asked to run something called the CHAMPS-Life Skills Program. What is this program?

11. What does a business and finance manager oversee in an athletics department?

12. What are athletics development officers required to do to demonstrate that they have educated donors about NCAA rules and regulations?

13. What is the Equity in Athletics Disclosure Act of 1994?

14. Discuss several challenges that intercollegiate athletics administrators must face during the 21st century.

15. What is the purpose of the senior woman administrator?

Job Opportunities

Assistant AD

Assistant Athletics Director for Media Relations. Duties include coordinating and supervising media relations for 17 intercollegiate sports including copywriting, designing, and editing media guides and game programs; coordinating interviews and press conferences; writing stories, game notes, and press releases; overseeing all media operations at athletic events; supervising media relations staff; overseeing department's Internet application. Qualifications: Bachelor's degree required and five years' experience in collegiate athletics administration.

Associate AD

Associate Athletics Director for an NCAA Division II program that sponsors cross-country running and skiing, rifle, basketball (men's and women's), and women's volleyball and Division I men's ice hockey. Responsibilities include: Assisting the athletics director with daily departmental operations; direction of coaching, facility, and sports medicine staff; education and enforcement of NCAA, conference, and university policies and regulations; sports programs and game scheduling; academic advising; liaison to booster clubs and Intercollegiate Athletic Committee; promote collaboration with community; advisor to student-athlete board. Bachelor's degree in administration or relevant experience required, master's preferred.

Academic Counselor

Academic Counselor—Division I Athletics: We invite candidates to apply for this full-time, fixed-term 12-month position. The counselor will monitor the academic progress of students on the men's and women's basketball teams, softball team, and baseball team. This will include supervision of study hall, tutorials, and other academic assistance. The counselor will be responsible for end-of-the-year and term-to-term outcome reports. The counselor will assist in the communication of eligibility issues between the Compliance Office and the students in compliance with university, conference, and the NCAA rules and regulations. The counselor will also assist the NCAA Life Skills staff and the university's Student Affairs staff with the coordination and creation of programming for all students. The position will be responsible for coordinating the Student-Athlete Orientation Program, assisting with orientation classes for student-athletes, monitoring the Learning Zone, and coordinating tutor requests and other academic requests. Master's in education, college personnel, higher education administration, counseling, or other related field required. Two years' experience working with a diverse college population in a counseling/advising capacity. Applicants with experience in a major university setting (NCAA Division-I) with experience working with student-athletes are preferred. Organizational skills and interpersonal/communication skills essential. Some evenings and weekends required.

Sports Information

Twelve-month renewable contract position available at an NCAA Division I-A institution. Responsibilities: design and create media guides, news releases, and other publications for athletics programs; assist in the updating of the Internet Web site; other duties as assigned by the director. Minimum qualifications: bachelor's degree by date of employment; at least two years of work in a sports information, athletics communications, or media relations type office; good organizational and management skills; working knowledge of the Internet. Preferred qualifications: bachelor's degree in journalism, telecommunications, or related field; three to five years of experience.

Public Relations

A California university is seeking an Assistant Director for Community and Youth Programs. Qualifications include strong organizational skills; excellent computer skills (including MS Word, MS Excel, MS Access, MS Publisher, and Web design); professional and friendly demeanor; strong interpersonal skills; and team orientation. General knowledge of NCAA rules and regulations preferred. The assistant director functions as the division's primary computer support entity, while also serving as a significant resource in the areas of marketing and promotions, as well as financial affairs. Operating under minimal to general supervision, the position assumes the lead role in all computer-related issues ranging from Web design, to database management, to desktop publishing, while also functioning as a vital liaison in the areas of public relations and community outreach. This is a 12-month, contract position with comprehensive health (medical, dental, optical) and retirement benefits.

Athletic Marketing

An NCAA Division I institution has an immediate opening for the position of Director of Athletic Marketing. This is a full-time 12-month position. Responsibilities include but are not limited to: developing and implementing comprehensive marketing plans to increase attendance at home events, soliciting and maintaining corporate sponsorships, managing and fulfilling sponsorship agreements, coordinating and managing game day event operations, developing and designing various athletic publications, creating and organizing advertising, managing community relations program, and serving as a liaison to university student organizations and community groups for the Athletics Department. Qualifications: Bachelor's degree required, master's degree preferred; a minimum of three years' experience in NCAA Intercollegiate Athletics is desired; strong oral and written communication skills; experience with computers with proficiency in desktop publishing preferred (Pagemaker, Illustrator, Photoshop); ability to work a flexible work schedule including some evenings and weekends; ability to organize multiple tasks, meet deadlines, and plan schedules. The successful candidate will be a person of integrity with high ethical standards and exhibit a strict adherence to NCAA, university, and departmental rules and regulations. Salary is commensurate with qualifications and experience.

Promotions

A midwestern university is seeking qualified applicants for a Director of Promotions position. Directs the daily promotional activities for 18 varsity sports with emphasis on football, men's/women's basketball, volleyball, and special events. Responsible for developing promotional plans for all revenue sports; developing effective ticket sales strategies; designing and copying all ticket brochures; disseminating ticket sales/advertising materials throughout the university and community; overseeing the copy, design, production, and placement of all print, television, radio, and billboard ticket advertising; planning and implementing special athletic events; and supervising of staff. A bachelor's degree, preferably in marketing, communications, management, or related field of study, is required. Three years' experience in promotions or event management is required. Athletic promotions experience is preferred. Word processing, desktop publishing, excellent oral and written communication and editing skills are required. Ability to effectively interact with and serve diverse customers, organize and prioritize multiple tasks to produce high-quality work with attention to detail, meet established deadlines, and take initiative to see projects through to completion is necessary. Interest in and knowledge of sports preferred.

(continued)

(continued)

Ticket Office

Athletics Ticket Manager—Manages operations and supports ticket office personnel, especially supervising all operations of the Paciolan System. Responsibilities include upholding, creating, and implementing policies and procedures that produce optimum customer service and efficient ticket operations; performing and managing financial activities of the office from processing orders to reconciling transactions with university records; overseeing the allocation of seating for all sports in conjunction with customer priority level; coordinating all ticket printing, packaging, and delivery for individual customers and game day sales. Must have great foresight with planning, financial and auditing knowledge, and excellent communication skills. Requires understanding customer needs; knowledge of ticketing operations and sport management policies and procedures; in-depth understanding of Paciolan system; fluency in Windows and Microsoft Office; general understanding of the role of the department within the university. Requires good interpersonal/leadership skills, data entry skills, telephone communication skills, and a general understanding of basic accounting procedures. Undergraduate degree or equivalent experience required; master's degree preferred. Five plus years of related experience required.

Compliance

A major college conference invites applications for the position of Assistant Director of Compliance and Championships. Responsibilities include: administering the NLI, secondary violations, interpretations, rules education, eligibility and squad lists, NCAA legislative issues; administrative management for select Conference championships, awards, merchandising and other duties as assigned. Qualifications: Candidates must have a bachelor's degree; minimum of two years' professional experience in collegiate athletics or related field; excellent interpersonal, writing, and computer skills. Salary commensurate with qualifications.

Development

The booster club of a Florida university is accepting applications for the position of Assistant Director of Development. Bachelor's degree required plus at least two years of successful development-related experience and knowledge of intercollegiate athletics required. Excellent leadership, communication, and organizational skills are necessary. Position requires some weekend work, after hours work, and travel.

Primarily responsible for assisting with the day-to-day operations of the booster club's annual fund, administering major donor recognition and benefits, and coordinating away game donor travel. Some identification, cultivation, and solicitation of donors is involved. Must work closely with a variety of university and athletics department staff. Must also assist with other duties in the athletics development office as assigned.

These position descriptions were fictionalized from positions found at www.ncaa.org/employment.html.

REFERENCES

Abney, R., & Richey, D.L. (1991). Barriers encountered by Black women in sport. *Journal of Physical Education, Recreation and Dance, 62*(6), 19-21.

Abney, R. & Richey, D.L. (1992). Opportunities for minorities. *Journal of Physical Education, Recreation and Dance, 63*(3), 56-59.

Armstrong, K.L. (1998). Ten strategies to employ when marketing sport to Black consumers. *Sport Marketing Quarterly, 7*, 11-18.

Armstrong, K.L. (2000). African-American students' response to race as a source cue in persuasive sport communications. *Journal of Sport Management, 14*(3), 208-226.

Berg, R. (1990). The roads less traveled. *Athletic Business, 14*(11), 44-47.

Brooks, D.D., & Althouse, R.C. (1993). Racial imbalance in coaching and managerial positions. In D.D. Brooks & R.C. Althouse (Eds.), *Racism in college athletics: The African-American athlete's experience* (pp. 101-142). Morgantown, WV: Fitness Information Technology.

Burwell, B. (1993, November 26). Bayou Classic gives tradition a new beat. *USA Today*, p. 5C.

Byers, W. (with Charles Hammer). (1995). *Unsportsmanlike conduct: Exploiting college athletes.* Ann Arbor, MI: University of Michigan Press.

Christian, H. (2000). *Leadership styles and characteristics of athletic directors.* Unpublished doctoral dissertation, University of Alabama. Dissertation Abstracts Online. Retrieved November 20, 2002 from http:www.lib.umi.com/dissertations/results?set_num=1.

Claussen, C.L., & Lehr, C. (1999). *RACI chart descriptions of the authority of senior woman administrators.* North American Society for Sport Management, Vancouver, British Columbia.

CAAHEP (1998-2002). *Standards and guidelines for an accredited educational program for the athletic trainer.* Retrieved November 15, 2002, from http://www.caahep.org/standards/at_01.htm.

Cuneen, J. (1992). Graduate-level professional preparation for athletic directors. *Journal of Sport Management, 6,* 15-26.

Curtis, M. (2000). *A model of donor behavior: A comparison between female and male donors to men's and women's athletics support organizations at Division I NCAA-affiliated institutions within the Big Ten.* Unpublished dissertation, The University of Iowa.

Earle, J. (2001). *2001-2002 NCAA Division I manual.* Indianapolis, IN: NCAA Publishing.

Farmer, P., Mulrooney, A., & Ammon, Jr. R., (1996). *Sport facility planning and management.* Morgantown, WV: Fitness Information Technology, Inc.

Farmer, S. (2001, January 18). Union may put label on colleges: Labor: United Steel Workers get behind effort by former UCLA linebacker to get better treatment for athletes. *Los Angeles Times,* p. 1D.

Fitzgerald, M.P., Sagaria, M.A.D., & Nelson, B. (1994). Career patterns of athletic directors: Challenging the conventional wisdom. *Journal of Sport Management, 8,* 14-26.

Fulks, D. (2000). *Revenues and expenses of division I and II intercollegiate athletics programs: Financial trends and relationships.* Indianapolis, IN: NCAA Publishing.

Howard, D.R., & Crompton, J.L. (1995). *Financing sport.* Morgantown, WV: Fitness Information Technology.

Irwin, D. (2001). Sport licensing. In B.L. Parkhouse (Ed.), *The management of sport* (3rd ed.) (pp. 353-364), New York: McGraw-Hill.

Irwin, R., Sutton, W., & McCarthy, L. (2002). *Sport promotion and sales management.* Champaign, IL: Human Kinetics.

Johnson, R.S., & Danehy, M. (1999, December 20). How one college program runs the business: Inside Longhorn, Inc. *Fortune,* p. 160.

Karlin, L. (1995). *The guide to careers in sports.* New York: E.M. Guild.

Kinder, T.M. (1993). *Organizational management administration for athletic programs* (3rd ed.). Dubuque, IA: Eddie Bowers.

Knight Foundation Commission on Intercollegiate Athletics. (1991, March). *Keeping faith with the student athlete: A new model for intercollegiate athletics.* Charlotte, NC: Author.

Knight Foundation Commission on Intercollegiate Athletics. (2001, June). *A call to action: Reconnecting college sports and higher education.* Retrieved November 25, 2002 from www.ncaa.org/databases/Knight_commission/2001_report/2001_knight_report.html.

Lords, E. (2000, April 7). Professors' group seeks to reform college sports. *The Chronicle of Higher Education, 46*(31), p. A58.

Lucas, J.A., & Smith, R.A. (1978). *Saga of American sport.* Philadelphia, PA: Lea & Febiger.

Marrs, J.M. (1998). *The phantoms of the arena: A history of collegiate athletic publicity, 1911-1961.* Unpublished doctoral dissertation, University of Washington.

Momentum Media (June/July 1999). *AEMA marks a quarter century.* Retrieved November 18, 2002, from http://www.momentummedia.com/articles/am/am1104/bbaema25.htm.

Morrison, L.L. (1993). The AIAW: Governance by women for women. In G. Cohen (Ed.), *Women in sport: Issues and controversies* (pp. 59-78). Newbury Park: Sage.

NAAAA (2002). *N4A history.* Available online at www.nfoura.org/about/about_history.php

NATABOC (1999). *Role delineation study: Athletic training profession* (4th ed.) Omaha, NE: Author.

Nichols, W., Moynahan, P., Hall, A., & Taylor, J. (2001). *Media relations in sport.* Morgantown, VA: Fitness Information Technology.

Olson, J. (1997). *Facility and equipment management for sport directors.* Champaign, IL: Human Kinetics.

Oriard, M. (2001). *King football: Sport and spectacle in the golden age of radio and newsreels, movies, and magazines, the weekly and daily press.* Chapel Hill, NC: University of North Carolina Press.

Parks, J.B., Russell, R.L., & Wood, P.H. (1993). Marital and other primary dyadic relationships of intercollegiate athletics administrators. *Journal of Sport Management, 7,* 151-158.

Parks, J.B., Russell, R.L., Wood, P.H., Roberton, M.A., & Shewokis, P. (1995). The paradox of the contented working woman in athletics administration. *Research Quarterly for Exercise and Sport, 66,* 73-79.

Pitts, B.G., & Stotlar, D.K. (2002). *Fundamentals of sport marketing* (2nd ed.). Morgantown, WV: Fitness Information Technology.

Posnanski, J. (2001, August 26). Hawking the Heisman: Hey kid, want college football's top prize? Your school had better make one heck of a sales pitch and hope it pays off. *The Kansas City Star,* p. L9.

Quarterman, J. (1992). Characteristics of athletic directors of historically Black colleges and universities. *Journal of Sport Management, 6,* 52-63.

Quarterman, J. (1994). Managerial role profiles of inter-collegiate athletic conference commissioners. *Journal of Sport Management, 8,* 129-139.

Sack, A.L., & Staurowsky, E.J. (1998). *College athletes for hire: The evolution & legacy of the NCAA amateur myth.* Westport, CT: Praeger Press.

Shulman, J.L., & Bowen, W.G. (2001). *The game of life: College sports and educational values.* Princeton, NJ: Princeton University Press.

Solomon, J. (2001). *An insider's guide to managing sporting events.* Champaign, IL: Human Kinetics.

Sperber, M. (2000). *Beer and circus: How big-time college sport is crippling undergraduate education.* New York: Henry Holt.

Staurowsky, E.J. (1996, October). Women and athletic funding raising: Exploring the relationship between gender and giving. *Journal of Sport Management, 10,* 401-416.

Tillman, K.G., Voltmer, E.F., Esslinger, A.A., & McCue, B.F. (1996). *The administration of physical education, sport, and leisure programs* (Rev. ed.). Boston: Allyn and Bacon.

U.S. Department of Education (2002). Equity in Education Disclosure Act. Retrieved November 15, 2002, from http://www.ed.gov/offices/OPE/PPI/eada.html.

Yow, D.A., Migliore, R.H., Bowden, W.W., Stevens, R.E., & Loudon, D.L. (2000). *Strategic planning for collegiate athletics.* Binghamton, NY: The Haworth Press.

Professional Sport

James M. Gladden, University of Massachusetts, Amherst
William A. Sutton, National Basketball Association

Professional sport is any sport activity or skill for which the athlete is compensated. Compensation can be in the form of a salary, bonuses, reimbursement for expenses, or any other forms of direct payment. The activity being performed can be a team sport such as basketball, a dual sport such as tennis, an individual sport such as figure skating or skateboarding, or a sport entertainment performance such as the Worldwide Wrestling Federation (WWF). Although these professional sports usually imply the presence of spectators, an audience is not a criterion by which professional sport is defined. For example, some sport organizations such as the Ladies Professional Golf Association (LPGA) and the Professional Golf Association (PGA) have a classification of membership called the **teaching professional**. Although these professionals might occasionally compete in tournaments for prize money, they typically earn their livings instructing others in the skills and strategies of the game. Their skills, therefore, might be directed to a small group of students or perhaps only one individual. Teaching pros also are involved in clinics, lessons, club management, and merchandising ventures, all of which can be lucrative revenue sources. Table 15.1 presents a representative list of North American professional sports.

teaching professional—A professional athlete who focuses primarily on teaching other athletes the intricacies of the sport. Most prevalent in golf, teaching professionals also compete in tournaments but typically do not compete on such high-profile tours as the PGA or LPGA Tour.

Professional sport events such as the Super Bowl, World Series, Masters, Indianapolis 500, Wimbledon, Kentucky Derby, and X Games now occupy the core of the world sport mentality. Although we have mentioned both team sports and sports featuring the individual thus far, this

---

LEARNING OBJECTIVES

After studying this chapter, you will be able to do the following:

1. Define, explain, and discuss the development of professional sport.
2. Describe the unique facets of professional sport, including its governance and the labor–management relationship professional team sports depend on.
3. Document the significance of the relationship between television and professional sport.
4. Describe the major revenue sources for a professional sport team.
5. Identify the types of employment opportunities available in professional sport.

---

chapter will concentrate on professional team sports because of their profound economic impact and the number of job opportunities they provide. Most jobs associated with professional individual sports are found in sport management and marketing agencies (see chapter 16). The purpose of this chapter is to provide information and insight about four primary aspects of professional team sport—its historical development, its unique aspects, its revenue sources, and the variety of career opportunities associated with pro sport.

Nature of Professional Sport

David Guterson (1994) described professional sport in this way:

Like money, it is something we love, a first waking thought and a chronic passion, as well as a vast sector of the economy, a wellspring for myth and

Table 15.1 Representative List of North American Professional Sports

Auto racing	Football	Skateboarding
Baseball	Golf	Skiing
Basketball	Hockey	Snowboarding
Billiards	Horse racing	Soccer
Bodybuilding	Ice skating	Surfing
Bowling	Motocross	Tennis
Boxing	Racquetball	Triathlons
Curling	Rodeo	Volleyball

totem, and a media phenomenon of the highest order. Our sports can fend off the brute facts of existence, temporarily arrest the sadness of life, briefly shroud the inevitability of death and provide the happy illusion of meaning through long enchanted afternoons. . . . Sport is a language we all speak. Sport is a mirror. Sport is life. Through sport we might know ourselves. (p. 38)

Guterson's description accurately portrays the powerful role professional sport occupies in many people's everyday lives. Professional sport exemplifies sport at its highest level of performance, and it generates the majority of coverage attributed to sport through the print and electronic media. As packaged events, professional team sports (e.g., men's and women's football, men's hockey, men's and women's soccer, men's baseball, women's softball, and men's and women's basketball) provide considerable entertainment and pleasure for spectators. As such, demands on the three principals that form the professional sport industry—labor, management, and governance—are complex, diverse, and ever changing. **Labor** continues to aggressively protect and procure additional resources for its membership, which are the professional athletes. **Management**, or the owners of professional teams, is trying to win back some leverage and control lost to labor over the past three decades. Finally, **governance**, made up of the professional sport leagues, attempts to regulate, but not completely control, both labor and management.

labor—A term that typically refers to the collective group of athletes in team sports that unionize in order to bargain collectively with the league owners (management).

management—When referring to the collective bargaining process, management refers to the collective group of ownership that is negotiating with the players, or labor.

governance—In professional team sport, this is the league structure that exists to oversee both the competitive and business elements of the sport. The National Football League, the National Basketball Association, and the Women's United Soccer Association are all forms of governance.

History of the Major American Professional Sports

Professional sport can be traced to ancient Greece where, beginning with the Olympic Games in 776 B.C., a class of professional sportsmen known as "athletai" existed. These athletai were well-paid men recruited from mercenary armies and trained exclusively for brutal competition (Freedman, 1987). In exchange for competing and winning, athletai often received remuneration in the form of prizes and money. Although the notion of amateurism might suggest that professional sport did not exist before the late 19th century, an element of professionalism has pervaded sport throughout its development.

Although baseball is often considered America's national pastime, it was not the first sport professionals played. Boxers, jockeys, and runners were paid for their prowess during the early and mid-19th century. Baseball, however, was the first *team* sport to employ professionals. In 1869, the Cincinnati Red Stockings became the first professional baseball team. Their appearance was closely followed in 1871 by the National Association of Professional Base Ball Players, the first professional sport league (Rader, 1983). In 1876 William Hulbert formed the National League, the precursor to Major League Baseball as we know it today. Middle-class entrepreneurs owned these early teams, and stadia were constructed as a matter of civic enterprise (White, 1996). This is a contrast to the corporate ownership and publicly financed stadia and arenas that exist today.

It was not until after the turn of the 20th century that another sport formed a recognized professional league. In 1917 the National Hockey League emerged after the National Hockey Association of Canada Limited suspended its operations (National Hockey League, 1996). This was closely followed in 1921 with the creation of the National Football League. The National Basketball League (NBL), founded in 1937, was the first professional basketball league. In 1949 the National Basketball Association resulted from a merger between the NBL and the Basketball Association of America (BAA) (Staudohar & Mangan, 1991).

Although professional team sport has been in existence for more than 100 years, it has not been until the past 55 years that professional sport opportunities existed for many minority segments of the American population. In fact, professional sport opportunities were segregated until 1947, when Jackie Robinson broke baseball's color line with the Brooklyn Dodgers. Before 1947 African American players played in separate, segregated professional leagues. The Negro Baseball League was founded in the late 1800s as an outlet for African American baseball players who were not allowed to play in the all-White major leagues. The league afforded players such as Satchel Paige, Josh Gibson, and even Jackie Robinson an opportunity to play. In addition, most owners, club managers, reporters, and umpires in the Negro leagues were also African American. The demise of the Negro leagues began with the integration of professional baseball in 1947; they ultimately ceased operations in the late 1950s.

Professional sport outlets for women have arisen only in the past 60 years. In the 1940s the first women's professional league, the All-American Girls' Baseball League (AAGBL), was formed. Created in 1943 in response to the decreased player quality in Major League Baseball during World War II and the vast popularity of women's amateur softball, the AAGBL played 11 exciting seasons before folding in 1954 due to poor management (Browne, 1992). Since 1954 there have been a number of other women's professional leagues, mainly in the sport of basketball. From 1979 to 1991 there were four attempts to capitalize on the growing participation and interest of women in basketball: the Women's Professional Basketball League (1979-1981), the Women's American Basketball Association (October-December 1984), the National Women's Basketball Association (October 1986-February 1987), and the Liberty Basketball Association (February-March 1991). Each league was unsuccessful due to financial difficulty ("A History," 1996).

The past 10 years has seen a resurgence of interest in women's professional sport. In 1996 two women's professional basketball leagues were formed: the American Basketball League (ABL) and the Women's National Basketball Association (WNBA). The ABL played two and a half seasons before folding halfway into the 1998-99 season due to financial difficulties, which were at least partially due to the competition from the NBA-sponsored WNBA, which still exists today. In June 1997 the Women's Professional Fastpitch (WPF) softball league began. Finally, during the summer of 2001 the Women's United Soccer Association (WUSA) began play.

LEARNING ACTIVITY

The American Basketball League (ABL) ceased operations midway through its third season. Using either library research or research available on the World Wide Web, identify at least three reasons that the ABL did not succeed.

As professional sport progressed throughout the 20th century, its success was largely tied to the media, which served both to promote and to finance professional sport. As early as the 1920s baseball games were broadcast on the radio. By the mid-1930s radio networks were paying $100,000 to carry the World Series (Rader, 1983). The popularity of professional sport (mainly baseball) on the radio reached its apex in the 1940s and 1950s. During the 1950s televised sporting events became commonplace.

In 1961 the Sports Broadcasting Act was passed by Congress, and the relationship between the media and professional sports changed dramatically. Until that time, antitrust law had prohibited leagues from negotiating network television contracts on behalf of their members. However, the leagues felt it was important to the financial viability of their member teams to negotiate a collective (on behalf of all league teams) agreement. This rationale suggested that, as opposed to negotiating contracts with individual teams, the major television networks (ABC, CBS, NBC) would pay significantly larger sums of money if leaguewide rights were offered. As a result, the NFL successfully led a lobbying effort to create an exemption in antitrust law. The Sports Broadcasting Act of 1961 gave sport leagues an exemption from antitrust law, granting them the right to collectively negotiate fees with the networks. This legislation paved the way for the leaguewide, highly lucrative television deals that pervade professional sports today (Gorman & Calhoun, 1994).

299

Unique Aspects of Professional Sport

Four aspects of professional sport distinguish it from other industries: interdependence, structure and governance, labor–management relations, and the role of the electronic media.

Interdependence

The central premise that differentiates professional team sport from any other business organization is the need of the teams to compete and cooperate simultaneously (Mullin, Hardy, & Sutton, 2000). In other words, the teams depend on one another to stage the games that constitute the product. In his classic work on the NFL, *The League*, David Harris (1986) describes this unique situation as **League Think**. According to former commissioner Pete Rozelle:

> *One of the key things that a sports league needs is unity of purpose. It needs harmony. . . . When you have unity and harmony and can move basically as one, you can have a successful sports league. The objective of "League Think" is to reverse the process by which the weak clubs get weaker and the strong clubs get stronger. Favorable results are a product of the degree to which each league can stabilize itself through its own competitive balance and league wide income potential. (pp. 13-14)*

League Think—Pioneered and most effectively implemented by the National Football League, this represents the notion that teams must recognize the importance of their competition and share revenues to ensure that their competitors remain strong.

When teams function together collectively, some teams sacrifice the potential for higher revenue in the interest of league stability. For example, the Dallas Cowboys and Oakland Raiders typically sell a disproportionate amount of NFL licensed merchandise. However, this money is pooled and shared equally with the other 30 NFL teams. Therefore, the presence of the Dallas Cowboys and Oakland Raiders in the collective bargaining agreement increases the revenue generated for all NFL member teams. Due to their existence in large television markets, the New York Giants and Chicago Bears function in much the same way during television negotiations. The key is that all members make sacrifices and concessions for the long-term benefits and growth of the league.

Although each major professional sport league differs in the extent to which it shares revenues, each league pools its revenues to some extent. For example, NFL teams all share equally in their national television packages (cable and network), whereas baseball teams share only their national contracts and keep all the revenue from their local agreements. These local agreements can vary significantly in the amount of revenue produced. **Large market teams** (teams that exist in large cities and negotiate large local television packages) such as the New York Yankees have local broadcast packages that are significantly larger than **small market teams** (teams that exist in smaller cities) such as the Kansas City Royals. Over the past 10 years the disparity in local media revenues has created significant discrepancies in the amount of money different Major League Baseball (MLB) teams are able to pay their players. This has resulted in a situation in which MLB's large market teams have a much better chance of reaching the play-offs and winning the World Series.

large market teams—Professional teams that exist in cities where the population is very large and the potential for lucrative local media contracts is very high.

small market teams—Professional teams that exist in midsize or smaller markets (for professional sport) whose potential for local media contracts is not that high.

LEARNING ACTIVITY

Using your library resources, find an article that discusses the local broadcasting agreements in Major Leage Baseball. In that article, which team makes the most money from local broadcasting agreements? Which team makes the least?

Structure and Governance

Each professional sport typically has its own structure and system of governance, typically referred to as "the league office," which usually involves the following components:

1. League commissioner
2. Board of governors or committee structure composed of the team owners
3. A central administrative unit that negotiates contracts and agreements on behalf of the league. The central administrative unit also assumes responsibility for scheduling, li-

censing, and other functions, such as coordinating publicity and advertising on behalf of the teams as a whole.

For example, at this writing, Major League Baseball is composed of 30 teams situated in two leagues (National and American—see table 15.2). Each league consists of three divisions (East, Central, and West). Each league has a president, who reports to a commissioner. The commissioner is responsible for representing the interests of all parties associated with professional baseball. These parties include owners, players, fans, television networks, corporate sponsors, host cities and venues, and the minor leagues. Contrast this organizational structure to mainstream business. There is no authority over the manufacturers of candy that represents the interests of both Hershey's and M & M Mars as they attempt to make money.

Baseball is unique in its extensive minor league system, which provides an elaborate development system that prepares players to participate in the major leagues. Each major league team has at least four affiliate teams in the minor leagues. As long as they meet certain standards in terms of the size of their facilities, owners of minor league teams enter into contractual relationships with major league clubs whereby the minor league team becomes an "affiliate" of the major league team. The major league team pays the player salaries, while the minor league affiliate is responsible for all franchise operations (including sales and facility management) and travel expenses for the players (Tannenbaum, 1994). Recently, some major league teams have purchased minor league teams, thus eliminating the independent owner that acts as an affiliate. Therefore, rather than let independent affiliates of the major league team make money, major league franchises become the owners of the minor league franchise and reap the financial benefits that result.

The cultivation of minor league systems is increasingly popular among the other major professional sport leagues as the following examples illustrate:

- The American Hockey League (AHL) is the premier development league for the National Hockey League (NHL).
- NFL Europe (formerly known as the World League of American Football) is a summer professional football league in Europe that serves as a training ground for future NFL players.
- In 2001 the NBA introduced the National Basketball Development League (NBDL), an NBA-owned minor league for professional basketball.

Over the past 10 years a variation on the typical league structure and governance has emerged—that of the **single-entity structure**. In the single-entity structure, the league is the owner of all of the teams in the league. Popularized by Major League Soccer upon its formation, this structure is also employed by the WUSA, NBDL, and to a certain extent, the WNBA. Under the single-entity structure, there are no team owners. Rather, individual investors pay for the right to "operate" teams. Along these lines, players are not hired by the teams but by the league. One of the unique

Table 15.2 Organization of Major League Baseball

National League East	National League Central	National League West	American League East	American League Central	American League West
Atlanta Braves	Chicago Cubs	Colorado Rockies	Baltimore Orioles	Chicago White Sox	Anaheim Angels
Florida Marlins	Cincinnati Reds	Los Angeles Dodgers	Boston Red Sox	Cleveland Indians	Oakland A's
Montreal Expos	Houston Astros	San Diego Padres	New York Yankees	Detroit Tigers	Seattle Mariners
New York Mets	Milwaukee Brewers	San Francisco Giants	Tampa Bay Devil Rays	Kansas City Royals	Texas Rangers
Philadelphia Phillies	Pittsburgh Pirates	Arizona Diamondbacks	Toronto Blue Jays	Minnesota Twins	
	St. Louis Cardinals				

features of this governance structure is that it allows the league to control costs since it is the employer of all of the athletes. While the legality of single-entity structures has been challenged under antitrust law (*Fraser et al. v. Major League Soccer*, 2000), thus far the courts have refused to deem the structure in violation of antitrust law.

single-entity structure—A new form of league governance in which teams are owned by the league and the players sign contracts with the league. Single-entity structures are in place in the WNBA, MLS, and WUSA, for example.

Labor–Management Relationship

Five unique circumstances and conditions are related to the labor–management relationship in North American professional sport. Some aspects are the opposite of common business practices and philosophies. However, such idiosyncrasies are considered essential by the participating parties to preserve the financial stability of the professional sport product. In the following sections we will examine each element and explain its uniqueness and significance to professional sport.

Baseball's Antitrust Exemption

Perhaps most unique among the conditions in professional sport is Major League Baseball's exemption from the rules and regulations of the Sherman Antitrust Act. The Sherman Antitrust Act was created to prohibit companies from dominating their respective markets in interstate commercial activity, thus creating a monopoly in which consumers have only one product choice, rather than having several products from which to choose. Normal businesses are prohibited by law from attempting to eliminate all competitors from the marketplace. For example, many recent corporate mergers in the telecommunications and airline industries have been scrutinized by the federal government to determine if they result in decreased competition.

However, as a result of the U.S. Supreme Court's ruling in the *Federal Base Ball Club of Baltimore, Inc. v. National League of Professional Base Ball Clubs* (1922), Major League Baseball was granted an exemption to antitrust law. In its decision, the court deemed that baseball was local in nature and did not involve the production of a tangible good and thus was not subject to interstate commerce law. In effect, this granted Major League Baseball the right to undertake strategies that would prevent the establishment of competitive

leagues. This exemption gives pro baseball team owners significant leverage over the cities in which they operate. Recently, this has led owners to threaten to leave their host cities if new stadia are not built. Although Major League Baseball's exemption from antitrust regulations has been challenged on several occasions, the courts have not overturned the decision.

LEARNING ACTIVITY

Justice Oliver Wendell Holmes is responsible for the opinion of the court that granted an antitrust exemption to baseball (*Federal Base Ball Club of Baltimore, Inc. v. National League of Professional Base Ball Clubs*, 259 U.S. 200, 1922). Find the case in your local law library or on the Web through LexisNexis, read the opinion, and construct an argument for repealing this exemption.

Collective Bargaining

Workers involved in interstate commerce, which includes all professional team sports (except Major League Baseball because of its antitrust exemption), are covered by the National Labor Relations Act (NLRA). The NLRA provides three basic rights that are the center of labor relations policy in the United States: (1) the right to self-organization, to form, join, or assist labor organizations; (2) the right to bargain collectively through agents of one's own choosing; and (3) the right to engage in concerted activities for employees' mutual aid or protection (Staudohar, 1989). In professional team sports, the NLRA provides players the right to join a union, to have a basic player contract (establishing a minimum salary, benefits, and working conditions) negotiated collectively by union representatives, and to strike or conduct other activities that help achieve objectives. The term *collective bargaining* is used because all active league players are in the bargaining unit and thus form a collective unit for negotiating and bargaining with their respective leagues. Teams join together as a league in bargaining with the players' union so that the negotiated contract in each sport applies to all teams uniformly.

Greenberg (1993) suggested that common elements of a collective bargaining agreement (the agreed-upon settlement by all parties) might include the following:

- Specification of contract length
- Compensation (minimum salary), which also includes pensions and other fringe benefits

- Rules for use of labor—in pro sports this would cover the number of games played in a week, starting times related to travel, and most important, free agency
- Individual job rights—seniority, time served, and possibly morals clauses related to conduct and drug testing
- Rights of union and management in the bargaining relationship—collecting union dues, providing for union security, and so on
- Methods for enforcing, interpreting, and administering the agreement—details grievance procedures, arbitration, no-strike clauses, and so on
- Rules for agent certification
- Option clauses
- Injury protection and safety issues
- Economic benefits such as severance pay, travel expenses, meal allowances, and so on
- Discipline—suspensions, fines, dismissal, and so on

Professional athletes employed by teams that exist within single-entity structures have taken advantage of their ability to bargain collectively to varying degrees. The WNBA players have the only players union among the single-entity leagues. As a union, the WNBA players have achieved a collective bargaining agreement with the league that stipulates such things as salaries and benefits. Beyond this though, the union has not taken any substantive legal action against the league. In contrast, rather than unionize, MLS players decided to file a lawsuit charging antitrust practices on behalf of management.

Free Agency

Free agency is the ability of players, after fulfilling an agreed-upon (through a collective bargaining agreement) number of years of service with a team, to sell their services to another team with limited or no compensation to the team losing the players. Thus the terms *free agent* and *free agency* have evolved to signify the relative freedom all professional team sport players have to move from one team to another.

However, professional team sport still imposes significant restrictions on its labor. For example, players do not immediately become free agents. Instead, free agency is a negotiated item in the collective bargaining agreement of all professional team sport leagues. The collective bargaining agreement recognizes the investment the team has

incurred in developing the player, while also recognizing the fair market value of the player in the open market. Thus, the collective bargaining agreement provides free agency after the player has played an agreed-upon (by both labor and management) number of years.

Therefore, rights are granted to the team that initially drafts a player for a specified time. Following that specified period, players are free to seek employment from the highest bidder. Free agents may also be classified according to talent and years of service to a particular team. Based on such classifications, the team signing a particular player may or may not be required to provide compensation to the team losing the player. Again, this is different from mainstream business practices. For example, mandating that a brand manager for Procter & Gamble work for three years before being allowed to take a job with Kraft is unheard of.

The implementation of free agency in the mid-1970s had a profound effect on the economics of professional sport. Given the freedom to negotiate with the highest bidder, salaries of professional athletes escalated astronomically. In 1976, when the players first earned the right to become free agents, the average salary in professional baseball was $46,000. In 2000 the average salary in Major League Baseball was nearly $2 million ("Putting the Past," 2001). Similar salaries exist in the other men's major professional sport leagues (NHL, NFL, NBA). At the time of writing, average salaries for women's professional sport teams were much lower. See figure 15.1 for a graph depicting the salary growth in each of the four major professional sport leagues from 1993 to 2000. The increased power of the players unions and increased salaries of players led to increased labor stoppages in the professional sport leagues. With player salaries continually increasing, owners of professional sport teams are facing revenue-generating challenges. Such concerns have led owners to take an increasingly tough stance during collective bargaining negotiations. As a result of management–labor salary disputes, work stoppages have become a frequent occurrence.

These problems have not yet surfaced within leagues with single-entity structures. Because the league owns the teams and controls player movement within the single-entity structure (and the courts have recently suggested that they are not engaging in antitrust practices), free agency does not exist. As a result, salaries are still quite modest in single-entity leagues (such as MLS, WUSA, and

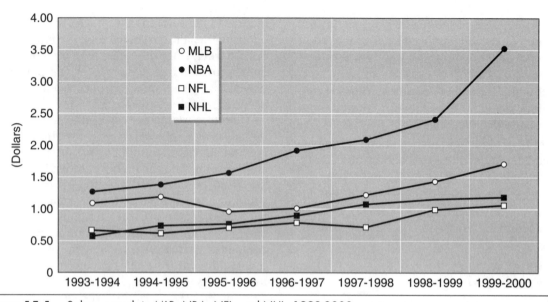

Figure 15.1 Salary growth in MLB, NBA, NFL, and NHL: 1993-2000.

Source: Based on data provided by *Street & Smith's SportsBusiness Journal,* January 31- February 6, 2000, p. 29.

the WNBA) as opposed to the leagues with individually owned teams. The ability of the single-entity leagues to keep salaries low may also be due to the fact that these new leagues are fighting for survival. Therefore, it is in the best interests of both the players and the league to keep salaries at a level that allows the league to keep costs manageable. For example, if the WNBA players were to fight for significantly higher salaries, this could impact the profitability of the league to the extent that it might cease to exist. This would eliminate the only major professional basketball league for women in the United States and force American women to seek professional opportunities overseas (as was the case before the introduction of the ABL and WNBA).

Salary Caps

With the onset of free agency in the 1970s, the professional sport industry allowed players to sign with the highest bidder. Therefore, the richest teams could afford the best players. Consequently, the spending on player salaries increased greatly, as already noted. In response, salary caps were created to protect owners from one another by setting a ceiling on player payrolls. According to Gary Roberts, editor of *The Sports Lawyer,* the owners in every sport claim that the inherent need for every team to be successful on the field, coupled with the reality that half the teams will always lose, will inevitably fuel an upward escalation of salaries that will make profits impossible for many league members, especially those in smaller

markets (Roberts, 1995). This is exactly what has happened in Major League Baseball. Between 1995 and 1999 teams whose payrolls were in the top 25% of all MLB payrolls won all 158 postseason games (Rofe, 2000a). One way that the leagues, owners, and players have worked together to keep costs down is through the implementation of salary caps.

Salary caps are agreements in which both labor and management share the revenues generated by the league. Pioneered by the NBA in 1983 and implemented for the 1985-1986 season, the salary cap guaranteed that the NBA players would receive 53% of all gross revenues. Since then, the NFL and Major League Soccer (MLS) have both adopted salary cap structures. These agreements are designed to provide greater **parity** between teams in large cities (markets), such as the New York Knicks and Los Angeles Lakers, and small market teams, such as the Portland Trailblazers and Milwaukee Bucks. A salary cap places a limit on the total compensation (salaries and bonuses) that a team can use for player salaries. All teams in the league must comply with the provisions of the salary cap. Salary caps are put into effect through the collective bargaining agreement and also include a minimum player salary.

parity—Also known as competitive balance, refers to the notion that every team has a legitimate chance to win the championship based on the resources available.

To illustrate the salary cap and how it works, we will examine the salary cap structure of the NBA.

In general terms, the salary cap is calculated, subject to certain adjustments, by multiplying projected "basketball-related income" (which generally includes all income received by teams as a result of basketball operations [e.g., ticket sales, sponsorship, television revenue, etc.]) by 48.04%, subtracting player benefits, then dividing the result by 29 (the number of teams in the league). The minimum team salary is then calculated by multiplying the salary cap by 75%.

The most notable exception to the salary cap is the qualifying veteran free agent exception, or as it is most commonly called, the Larry Bird Rule. The Bird Rule permits a team to re-sign its own free agent for any amount up to the maximum player salary if he played for the team for some or all of each of the prior three seasons. This rule was implemented to make it more financially attractive for free agents to remain with their current teams, providing a stable team for the hometown fan base. An unintended consequence of the Bird Rule was that teams began to exceed the salary cap with much more regularity and much higher numbers of dollars than previously anticipated. Thus, the NBA has created a **luxury tax** (implemented starting with the 2002-03 season) system that will tax teams in excess of the cap. The system permits teams to exceed the cap and sign free agents (their own and those of other teams) but places a higher cost on them through the tax. While Major League Baseball does not currently (at the time of writing) have a salary cap, it too has a luxury tax for those teams exceeding a set salary level.

luxury tax — A penalty levied on teams that exceed the salary cap. Teams must pay taxes to the league based on how much they exceed the salary cap. Luxury tax revenues are then split among small market teams or among the teams that do not exceed the salary cap.

LEARNING ACTIVITY

Disputes between labor and management in professional sport have sometimes resulted in work stoppages, either in the form of a strike (initiated by the players) or a lockout (initiated by the owners). In both cases, the players negotiate for better benefits, including a better pay scale, while the owners claim they are losing money because the players' salaries are too high. However, it would seem that both sides should ultimately work together if professional sport is going to succeed. Why then is there such a long history of problems between labor and management in nearly all of the professional sports? Prepare a 10-minute speech highlighting your response. Also, in this speech, identify who you think is right.

Player Draft

In accordance with the principles of League Think, the player draft is designed to be an equitable system for distributing new talent among all league members. The draft provides each professional sport league with a mechanism for the teams with poor records to have an advantage over teams with winning records in acquiring the most talented new players. Through the draft, teams voluntarily agree to restrict competition for new talent. As a result, the destination and salary of a new player are determined solely by the team that drafts the player. Phenomena such as the player draft do not exist in other areas of the labor market. Just imagine a scenario in which top law school graduates were restricted as to whom they could work for and where they could work by an annual draft held by law firms throughout the country!

Recent collective bargaining agreements in men's basketball and men's football have sought to limit the number of rounds of the draft. This limiting would result in fewer players being drafted and more players being free agents to sign with anyone offering them a contract. The players union would prefer that this would be the case for all players but recognizes the need for some type of equal and formal player distribution to maintain competitiveness among the members of the league.

While a player draft exists in leagues that have single-entity structures, it is a modified draft. For example, in Major League Soccer, the league allocates the best players (called "marquee players") among the teams as means of maintaining competitive balance. After the marquee players have been allocated, the teams then draft from the remaining pool of players available (*Fraser et al. v. Major League Soccer*, 2000).

Role of the Electronic Media

Whether it is network television, cable television, radio, or the Internet, the electronic media plays a critical role in driving the popularity of professional sport and generating additional revenue for professional sport teams. While radio was the first electronic medium to bring professional sport to the masses, television (both network and cable) has had a profound impact on the development of professional team sport over the past 50 years. As we move forward in the 21st century, new media sources such as satellite television and the Internet could be the next important horizons in broadening the reach of professional team sport and the enhancement of league revenue streams.

Importance of Television

No single factor has influenced the popularity of sport, the escalation in player salaries, free agency, and the growth and increase of corporate involvement in professional sport more than television. Television is also responsible for helping professional sport become more than just competition and athleticism—it has helped professional sport become entertainment.

Entering its 27th season in 1996, ABC's *Monday Night Football* was the pioneering effort to package pro sport as entertainment. This prime-time extravaganza sought to reach more than just traditional football fans by adding analysis, commentary, special guests, additional camera angles, video replays, graphics, and highlights to enhance the event and broaden its appeal to women and other nontraditional viewing groups (Roberts & Olson, 1995). Based on the success of *Monday Night Football*, the ultimate television sport spectacle, the Super Bowl, was created. Born from the rivalry and merger of the National Football League and the American Football League, the Super Bowl has become one of the most successful televised events of all time, viewed by millions around the world.

As a result of the success in packaging sport for entertainment, **hallmark events** such as the Super Bowl, along with baseball's World Series, All-Star Games, and the NBA Finals, are now shown during prime time (8-11 P.M.). Additionally, these events are also telecast in many other countries. For example, the 2000 WNBA All-Star Game was televised in 154 countries and described in 23 languages (Brockinton, 2000a). Such hallmark events also can provide an identity as well as a source of tourism revenue for a city or region. Hallmark events affect the perception of a town or region through media coverage of the event, most notably television coverage. Further, hallmark events contribute economically through expenditures relating to lodging, local transportation, and tourism, such as entertainment and shopping (see chapter 17).

hallmark events—Highly visible events that are attended by many people and watched by even more on television (and now followed on the Internet). Examples of hallmark events include the WNBA All-Star Game and the Super Bowl.

On the other side of the coin, professional sports (and in this case men's football) need television for two reasons. First, as already discussed, the leagues and member teams receive significant revenue outlays from network and cable television agreements. Second, television enhances the enjoyment associated with watching professional sport events. Consider the following factors in viewing a football game:

- Given the proximity to the action in a large stadium, the action in a football game can be difficult to follow.
- Only a certain number of fans can attend the game in person.
- Football with its numerous formations and free substitution can be confusing. In supporting football, television offers commentary and explanation, many replays, isolations, and other variations of camera angles, all of which allow the viewer to more effectively understand and follow the game.
- Television provides an expansive (and increasingly international) audience, regardless of the weather.

Emerging Sources of Media Coverage

Imagine that you grew up in Chicago and now live on the East Coast. Based on where you grew up, you are an ardent follower of the Chicago professional sports teams (Bulls, Bears, Cubs, White Sox, Blackhawks, and Fire). However, unless these teams make the play-offs, rarely are you able to follow your team through radio broadcasts or radio and cable television broadcasts. This is a dilemma faced by millions of North Americans today. Increasingly, there are solutions for the problems faced by the sport fan described in this scenario. Most notably, satellite television and the Internet have greatly increased the access of sport fans to a full menu of sport events.

Satellite technology and satellite television providers such as DirecTV and Echo Star have worked with the leagues to create packages whereby the average sport fan can access any game during the season by either paying an up-front fee for season-long access or subscribing (paying a one-time fee) on a game-by-game basis. For example, in 2002, for $149.99, owners of a satellite television system receive "NFL Sunday Ticket," which provides them with access to all NFL games on a given Sunday.

The Internet is also affording fans increased access to games of interest. Currently, fans can access radio broadcasts of their favorite games, typically through league-run Web sites. For example, in the scenario described earlier, the Bears

Table 15.3 Number of Visitors to MLB, NBA, NFL, and NHL Web Sites During Busiest Months

League	Busiest month	Number of visitors
MLB	October	501,000
NBA	May	2,744,000
NFL	October	6,685,000
NHL	April	993,000

Source: Based on data presented in *Street & Smith's SportsBusiness Journal,* March 19-25, 2001, p. 27.

fan living on the East Coast could listen to every Bears game by tuning in through NFL.com. Because the leagues are able to negotiate collectively on behalf of the teams and the Internet rights could become increasingly valuable, the leagues have recently moved to being exclusive providers of radio broadcasts, whereas teams used to provide such a service through their Web sites as well. This allows the leagues to increase the number of "hits" or visits to their Web site during the season. Table 15.3 depicts the number of visitors MLB, the NBA, NFL, and NHL received during their busiest months in 2000. In 2001 Major League Baseball became the first Web site to charge its listeners for the right to listen to broadcasts. For $9.99 each, 115,000 subscribers accessed the radio broadcast of Major League Baseball games from all over the country (Liberman, 2001). Such charges may become more frequent in the future, particularly as technology allows greater access to video broadcasts of games on the Internet.

LEARNING ACTIVITY

Using the World Wide Web, locate the schedules and determine whether you can listen to the next game of the following teams:

- Los Angeles Sparks (WNBA)
- Denver Nuggets (NBA)
- Kane County Cougars (Minor League Baseball)
- Houston Texans (NFL)
- Carolina Courage (WUSA)
- Hartford Wolfpack (Minor League Hockey)

Revenue Sources for Professional Sport Teams

While the revenue sources for sport organizations were discussed in chapter 12, there are some unique aspects to generating revenue in professional sport that require discussion. Pro sport has three primary constituencies: management, labor, and the fans. Each has a unique perspective regarding revenue sources. Management regularly claims that teams are not making money or have a hard time making money due to the exorbitant salaries paid to the players (refer back to figure 15.1). For example, Major League Baseball commissioner Bud Selig claimed that 25 out of the 30 teams lost money during 2001 (King, 2001). On the other hand, labor (the players) will suggest that, although salaries have increased, teams have remained profitable and franchise values have increased dramatically (Zimbalist, 1992). In addition, players will cite the fact that owners regularly underestimate their profits in the interest of keeping players' salaries low. From the fans' perspective, both sides are often seen as greedy. Fans frequently suggest that escalating players' salaries have led owners to increase the price of tickets, concessions, and parking. Regardless of the point of view, professional teams are under constant pressure to generate revenue. Beyond what was discussed in chapter 12, some unique aspects of revenue production exist in the areas of media contracts, gate receipts, licensing/merchandising revenues, and sponsorship.

Media Contracts

The details of the national media contracts for a variety of sport leagues are presented in table 15.4. However, there are two important distinctions that we must make with respect to media revenues in professional sport. First, the NBA, NHL, and MLB allow their member teams to negotiate **local television contracts**. In the case of MLB, this leads to great disparities in the incomes of its member teams (Howard & Crompton, 1995). The NFL, under the notion of League Think, does not allow local television deals, except for preseason games. Finally, the national television revenues for the NHL are not distributed equally—Canadian teams receive a smaller portion due to their lack of influence on U.S. television markets.

local television contracts—Agreements made between professional teams and local television

Table 15.4 Media Contracts of Various Professional Sport Leagues

League	Network	Amount	Number of years	Expires
NFL	Fox	$4.4 billion	8	2005
	ABC	$4.4 billion	8	2005
	CBS	$4 billion	8	2005
MLB	Fox	$2.5 billion	6	2006
	ESPN	$851 million	6	2005
NHL	ABC/ESPN	$600 million	5	2003–2004
NBA	NBC	$1.75 billion	4	2001
	TNT/TBS	$890 million	4	2001
MLS	ABC	Revenue sharing	6	2003

Source: Data garnered from *Street & Smith's SportBusiness Journal*, October 2-8, 2000, p. 59.

stations and regional sport networks. These agreements provide teams with additional media revenue beyond what they receive from the national television contract.

Second, toward the end of the 20th century and now at the beginning of the 21st century, media revenues began to plateau after a period of rapid escalation. This is at least partially due to the proliferation of sport programming now available. Given the growth and capabilities of both cable television and satellite television, there has been a dramatic increase in the amount of sport programming available to the average viewer. For example, 21,000 hours of sport programming was available from 13 national networks in 1994. By 2000 more than 87,000 hours of sport programming was available from 20 different national networks (Brockinton, 2000b). Given the increased choices available to the average sport fan, the number of viewers tuning in to the telecasts of professional sport events has recently declined, making it more difficult for the leagues to negotiate lucrative television contracts.

Gate Receipts

As late as 1950, gate receipts and concessions accounted for more than 92% of the typical pro team's revenue (Gorman & Calhoun, 1994). With the increasing importance of media revenues, however, pro teams have become less reliant on gate receipts, although gate receipts remain the major source of revenue for minor league professional sports. In addition, they are the most prevalent source of revenue for start-up professional leagues such as MLS and the WUSA (Horovitz, 1996). The majority of the gate receipts are retained by the home team. However, to varying degrees depending on the league, a portion of the gate receipts are given to the league (to cover league operating expenses), and a portion of the proceeds may be given to the opposing team.

In the future, teams can increase gate receipts by increasing attendance or increasing ticket prices. The ability to increase attendance varies dramatically by both team and league. For example, in the inaugural WUSA season (2001), the Carolina Courage filled 92.2% of their seats ("WUSA Attendance Final," 2001). In contrast, the Bay Area CyberRays filled only 29.6% of their seats. Based on these figures, it would stand to reason that the CyberRays have more potential for growth than the Courage. Table 15.5 provides a sampling of attendance information from a variety of professional sport leagues. As is evidenced by this table, there is more room for attendance growth in MLB, MLS, the WNBA, and the WUSA than there is in the NFL, NBA, and NHL. In addition, given the rapid escalation of ticket prices since the early 1980s, it may not be possible to increase the price of tickets. For the 2000-01 NBA season, the average price of an NBA ticket was $51.02 while the average price of an NFL ticket during the 2000 season was $48.97 (Frank, 2000). Considering the other costs associated with attending a professional sport event (parking, concessions, souvenirs, etc.—see chapter 12), it has become extremely expensive for a family to attend a major professional sport event.

Licensing and Merchandising Revenues

Licensing revenues are generated when leagues and teams grant merchandise and apparel manufacturers the right to use their names and logos. In return for that right, the leagues and teams receive

Table 15.5 Attendance Information From Selected Major Professional Sport Leagues for the Season Ending in 2001

League	Average attendance	Percent of capacity	Number of teams at 90% of capacity or greater
NFL	61,191	90.0%	17 out of 31
NHL	16,563	90.4%	18 out of 30
NBA	16,778	86.1%	13 out of 29
MLB	30,073	64.6%	5 out of 30
MLS	14,964	64.6%	1 out of 12
WNBA	9,074	46.9%	0 out of 16
WUSA	8,103	59.3%	1 out of 8

Source: Derived from various issues of *Street & Smith's SportsBusiness Journal* during the year 2001.

a royalty (i.e., a percentage of the selling price) for each item sold by the manufacturers. These agreements have been an increasingly lucrative source of revenue for pro teams. Between 1980 and 1996, sales of NFL merchandise increased 400% (Howard & Crompton, 1995). Licensing programs, administered by the league offices, distribute the revenue equally among the teams. Recently though, domestic licensing revenues have begun to plateau as the market for such merchandise has become saturated. For example, from 1995 to 1999, retail sales of NFL licensed merchandise increased only slightly, from $2.8 billion to $3.0 billion ("On the Racks," 2000). In response to this decline, pro sport leagues are looking to overseas markets for increased merchandise sales. Typically employed as one of the first strategies used in entering foreign markets, retail promotions and marketing pro sport apparel has successfully generated additional revenues.

Sponsorship

During the 2001 season, Major League Baseball (the league, not including team efforts) generated $125 million through **sponsorship** sales (Lefton, 2001). In 2000 the WNBA was seeking $3.5 million for a league sponsorship package (Bernstein, 2000). At the team level, the San Diego Padres generated $12.2 million from sponsorship sales for the 1999 season (Rofe, 2000b). One major benefit of a professional team sponsorship deal is visible corporate signage. The demand for signage locations visible to the television viewer has led sport marketers to continually seek new and innovative display techniques. **Rotating signage**, stationary signage around the playing area, and **virtual signage** during television broadcasts are devices

used to increase revenues. Additionally, one way that teams are helping to fund these facilities is by selling the **naming rights** to these facilities. For a large sum of money, the stadium will agree to include the name of the corporation in the name of the facility. For example, the WNBA's Washington Mystics play in the MCI Center. In order to obtain these naming rights, MCI agreed to pay $44 million over 20 years ("Naming Rights Deals," 2001). A sampling of naming rights deals throughout professional sport is presented in table 15.6.

sponsorship—The acquisition of rights to affiliate or directly associate with a product or event for the purpose of deriving benefits related to that affiliation or association (Mullin, Hardy, & Sutton, 2000, p. 254).

rotating signage—A form of sign that is placed on scoreboards and adjacent to playing surfaces that can rotate the advertisements shown.

virtual signage—Signage that is generated via digital technology and placed into a sport event telecast so that it appears as though the sign is part of the playing surface or adjacent to the playing surface.

naming rights—When a company pays for the right to have its name on a professional sport facility. For example, United Airlines paid for the right to have the stadium where the Chicago Bulls and Blackhawks play be called the United Center.

LEARNING ACTIVITY

Identify the minor league baseball or hockey franchise nearest to your surrounding area. Attend at

Table 15.6 Sampling of Recent Naming Rights Deals for Professional Sport Arenas

Building	Company	Teams	Amount paid	Years of contract
Reliant Stadium	Reliant Energy	Houston Texans (NFL)	$300 million	30
FedEx Field	Federal Express	Washington Redskins (NFL)	$205 million	27
Phillips Arena	Phillips Electronics	Atlanta Hawks (NBA) Atlanta Thrashers (NHL)	$185 million	20
American Airlines Arena	American Airlines	Miami Heat (NBA) Miami Sol (WNBA)	$42 million	20
Comerica Park	Comerica Bank	Detroit Tigers (MLB)	$66 million	30
Verizon Wireless Arena	Verizon Wireless Inc.	Manchester (NH) Monarches of the American Hockey League (AHL)	$11.4 million	15
Colisee Pepsi	PepsiCo	Quebec Citadelles (AHL)	$1 million	10
Fifth Third Field	Fifth Third Bank	Dayton Dragons of the Midwest League (A baseball)	$6.5 million	20
Louisville Slugger Field	Louisville Slugger	Louisville River Bats of the International League (AAA baseball)	$2 million	Indefinite

Source: Data generated from tables presented in *Street & Smith's SportsBusiness Journal*, August 13-19, 2001.

United Airlines paid for the right to have the home of the Chicago Bulls and Blackhawks be named the United Center.

© Bruce Leighty

least one of its games. Take notes on everything you witness, including stadium operations, ticket sales, concessions sales, stadium design, and the visibility of team personnel. Based on past experiences with major league sports (MLB, NFL, NBA, and NHL), how are the facets of minor league operations different from major league operations? How are they similar?

Career Opportunities in Professional Sport

Like any business, professional sport organizations constantly attempt to upgrade their efficiency through their personnel. In searching for new employees, management often looks to sport management and administration programs, searches other professional sport organizations, or considers individuals working in the corporate sector who may have skills essential to the sport industry.

The organizational hierarchies of professional sport are far from uniform. Employment oppor-

tunities vary greatly in terms of titles and responsibilities not only from sport to sport but also from team to team within the same sport. Additionally, a variety of jobs are available at the league level. For example, see "A Day in the Life of Shelby Reed" for a description of someone who works in the NBA office. Some professional sport organizations have a single owner (e.g., Art Modell owns the Baltimore Ravens), and others may have several owners (e.g., both Ted Leonsis and Michael Jordan have ownership stake in the Washington Wizards, Washington Mystics, and Washington Capitols). An example of the structure of an organization owning more than one team is presented in figure 15.2, which depicts the four businesses owned by RDV Sports, including the Orlando Magic of the NBA and the Orlando Miracle of the WNBA. Still others may be corporately owned (for example, Comcast owns the Philadelphia Flyers and Philadelphia 76ers).

Particularly with the rise of the WNBA, owners increasingly own multiple teams across different sport leagues. WNBA teams are controlled by the

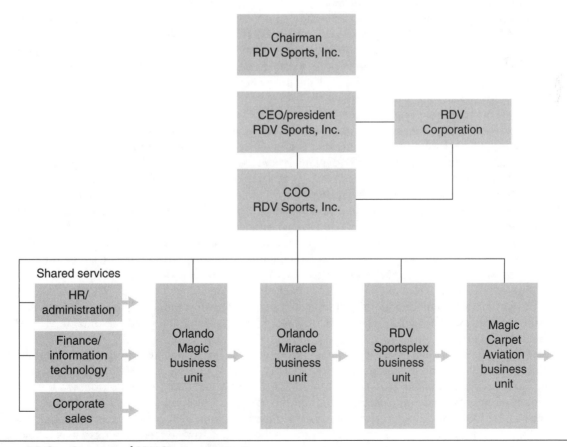

Figure 15.2 Overview of RDV Sports organization.

Reprinted, by permission from RDV Sports, 2002.

NBA team owner in that same market. In cases in which multiple teams are owned by one owner or owners, some of the same personnel might be used to fill positions in both organizations. This used to be the premise for the WNBA, which operates during the summer when the NBA arenas are more available. However, more recently, the WNBA has moved away from sharing staff with the NBA and has begun creating its own business staff. Figure 15.3 depicts the model of the WNBA team

A Day in the Life of Shelby Reed

I entered a sport management master's degree program in the fall of 2000 with the vague aspiration to work in sport marketing. It is safe to say that I had no exact idea of what I wanted to do. I didn't even know what I wanted to do first (maybe sport marketing, maybe corporate sponsorship, maybe team marketing), but I knew I wanted to learn everything about the business of sports. That's how I describe what my days have been like for the past year and a half—I am soaking it all up.

After some career counseling from my professors, I decided to take a job in the Associates Program at the NBA league office in New York. I was assigned to the marketing and team business operations department. I have had an exceptional experience! My responsibilities are challenging and exciting. They are project oriented, as opposed to ongoing, which fits my personality. This also makes each day at the NBA a very different learning experience.

The first project I was assigned to was compiling organizational charts from all NBA teams. This project was challenging because some teams are not as time conscious or as accommodating as others are. Many teams gave me the run-around, some just said no to my request, and others did not give me what I asked for. The org charts are used as a resource for the account managers (NBA staff that work with individual teams to improve their marketing activities and revenues), so when they prepare to visit a team, they know the structure of the organization.

The second project I worked on was a recap of the WNBA/'N SYNC promotion that took place July 20-24, 2001. I compiled all meeting agendas/notes and communications among Jive Records, the WNBA league office, and each WNBA team. It was important for us to document every detail of the development of this promotion in order to make improvements on any future league-wide or Jive Records partnered promotions. From all the promotion details, I wrote executive summaries for internal purposes and for Jive Records.

The best part of my experience at the NBA is the opportunity I have had to work with some of the best sport marketers in the industry, the account management team. The account management strategy is to constantly evaluate teams and the effectiveness of their staff and strategies/ideas. Because account managers are always traveling, I serve as a point-person for them. I prep the account managers for their visits with ticket sales numbers and market research analysis. I organize a weekly conference call and take notes, and I update a travel calendar every week.

I am also the point-person for our department's "Best Practices" program. This program combines the knowledge of the account managers and the experience of the teams to determine the best ideas for conducting and analyzing market research, managing databases, improving customer retention, increasing new sales, selling groups, developing individual game themes/promotions, and reducing the number of people who don't show up to games. My job is to gather ideas from account managers and gather additional information from the contact at the teams. Once all the details are available (and the team gives permission), we share the information with other teams. In the past few months, we have written a "Best Practice" checklist for the teams' self-assessment and an explanation of "Best Practice" strategies.

In the past six months I have had the opportunity to write several programs. Using the experience of the account managers, I created a model for building and using a fan database. This task was overwhelming at times, considering I knew nothing about databases, but the account managers were very helpful. Through this project, I learned what it takes to build an effective database and how to use it to market directly to fans. I also helped write models for building an in-house telemarketing program and enhancing a fan's experience from every point at which they interact with the team.

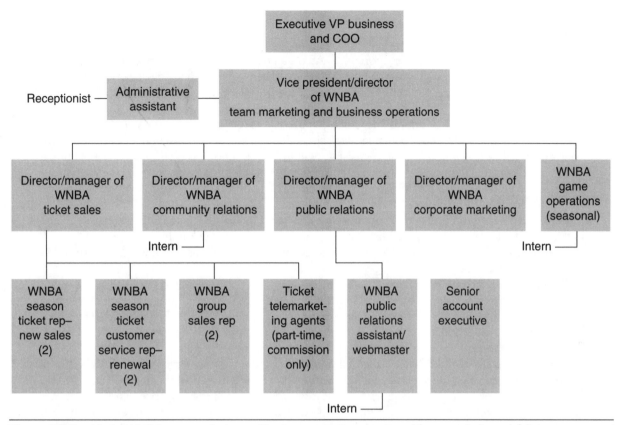

Figure 15.3 Model WNBA team marketing and business operations structure. (These are dedicated, full-time, year-round positions unless otherwise stated.)

Adapted, by permission, from the Women's National Basketball Association.

marketing and business operations departmental structure.

Common Categories of Work Responsibility

There are a variety of positions within any professional sport organization. The types and existence of positions vary from team to team and sport to sport. For example, Major League Baseball teams employ more people in player personnel than the National Basketball Association or the National Football League because of their extensive minor league systems. In addition, minor league organizations (Minor League Baseball, the International Hockey League, and the East Coast Hockey League) will typically employ fewer people than major league organizations (NFL, NBA, MLB, NHL). This section highlights a variety of positions that may be available within any professional sport organization. With respect to major professional sport teams, there is typically a group of executives that may include the following:

- Chief executive or operating officer (CEO or COO)—Responsible for the day-to-day functioning of the entire organization, both on the field (performance) and off the field (revenue generation)

- Chief financial officer (CFO)—Responsible for the organization's accounting and financial planning

- General counsel—Responsible for overseeing all legal matters associated with the team including, but not limited to, player contracts, liability issues, and marketing contracts

- General manager—Typically responsible for acquiring, developing, trading, and releasing talent, as well as creating a development system for young players

Beyond these executive positions, jobs with professional sport teams can typically be separated into two categories:

1. Player personnel
2. Business

313

Case Study

The phone rang in Tonya Mertz's apartment. As a senior in the Sport Management Program at Southeastern University, Tonya was hoping that this would be a return phone call about an internship. It was late April, and Tonya was hoping to start her career by interning with a professional basketball team for the summer.

"Hi, Tonya, this is Kristin Carter of the Chicago Power [a recent entry into the WNBA]. I'm calling to offer you an internship in our community relations department. As we discussed in the interview, your basic responsibilities will include assisting with all of our charitable efforts and events in the community. We want the people of Chicago to know that the Power cares about the community. Your background working in the community with your team at Southeastern is what convinced us that you were right for this internship. What do you think?"

"Kristin, I am flattered and excited about your offer," said Tonya. "But I would like a little bit of time to think about it. Would it be possible to think about this over the weekend?"

"No problem, Tonya. We would love to have you on our staff this summer. I will look forward to hearing your response on Monday," concluded Carter.

Tonya hung up the phone thinking that the opportunity was very interesting and well suited to her skills and experiences. As a four-year starter on the Southeastern basketball team, Tonya's career had just concluded. Knowing that she was not quite good enough for the WNBA, Tonya decided to parlay her passion for basketball into a career in professional basketball. This opportunity with the Power could provide the start she was looking for . . . until the phone rang again.

"Hello, Tonya. This is Paul Butterworth of the Little Rock Lasers [a new team in the NBA's National Basketball Development League]. I'm calling to offer you an internship position in marketing. As you know, we are a new organization. So, while this is an internship, we are poised to integrate you into the workings of our ticket sales, corporate sales, and promotions efforts. I think you will be hard pressed to find an organization that will give you more responsibility as an intern."

Tonya was stunned, but she collected herself enough to say, "Wow, Mr. Butterworth, that sounds great. I am thrilled by your offer. But would you mind terribly if I took the weekend to think about it?"

"No problem, Tonya. I will wait for your call on Monday." With that Butterworth hung up.

Tonya did not know what to do. She was stunned. Five minutes ago, she was all but headed for Chicago. Now another company was offering her an internship. What should she do?

Based on what you learned in this chapter and what you can garner from outside research, consider the following questions:

1. What does Tonya need to consider prior to making a decision?
2. What are the advantages and disadvantages of each opportunity?
3. What are the opportunities for growth with each opportunity?

Player Personnel Positions

A variety of jobs focus on player personnel or putting the best possible team on the field or court. A description of these jobs follows. However, before examining each of the individual jobs on this side of the professional sport organization, it is important to note the difficulty and competitiveness associated with these positions. Because many of the positions require an intricate knowledge of the sport, being a former athlete, and quite often a former professional athlete, in the particular sport may be a prerequisite for success. The player personnel department (called "basketball operations") for the Orlando Magic is depicted in figure 15.4.

• *Player personnel.* This department is involved in identifying, evaluating, and developing potential and current players. In baseball, this department would also be involved in observing players assigned to the minor leagues. Typical jobs in this area include being a scout, in which researching potential draft picks and upcoming opponents are central responsibilities. The pinnacle position within the player personnel side of the organization is typically the general manager position. The general manager is the final decision maker on drafting and trading decisions.

• *Medical, training, and team support.* These individuals assume responsibility for the physical (and sometimes mental) preparation and readi-

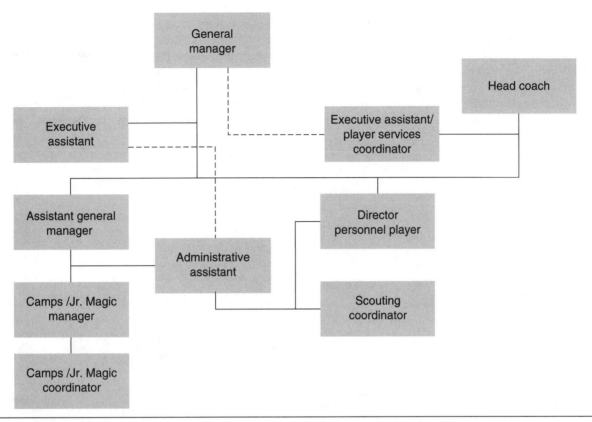

Figure 15.4 Organizational chart of the Orlando Magic basketball operations department.

Reprinted, by permission, from RDV Sports, 2002.

ness of the players. Responsibilities include medical care, treatment of injuries, rehabilitation, dental care, nutrition, strength training and conditioning, career counseling, and aftercare programs.

• *Coaching staff.* This group concentrates on all activities occurring between the lines. In other words, they are primarily concerned with coaching, managing, and training the players on their rosters.

• *Player education and relations.* People in these positions are typically responsible for educating players on a variety of issues including financial management, substance abuse, nutrition, image management, and additional higher education. Additional responsibilities may include working as a liaison between the team and players with respect to player appearances in the community.

• *Video support staff.* Responsibilities of the video support staff include producing and editing videos, purchasing and maintaining video hardware and software products, supervising and coordinating satellite feeds, and coordinating all broadcasting originating at the home facility. The video support staff also is responsible for filming games and maintaining the team's library of game films and player evaluation videos.

• *Equipment and clubhouse staff.* These personnel maintain, clean, order, repair, distribute, inventory, ship, and pack all uniforms and equipment. They also negotiate with manufacturers and sales personnel for equipment and uniforms. It is their responsibility to determine the suitability of the product and to make appropriate recommendations regarding purchasing. In addition, these personnel have security responsibility for the locker room both at home and on the road.

• *Stadium and facility staff.* This group is responsible for the maintenance, upkeep, and repair of the playing surface. They are also responsible for preparing the team's offices, locker rooms, training facilities, practice facilities, and playing fields. They must be familiar with artificial surfaces as well as natural grass playing surfaces. The stadium and facility staff ensures that the playing surface is safe and works in inclement conditions to make the field playable. In terms of playing surfaces and related areas, these individuals are the liaisons between the venue management team and the professional franchise.

Business Positions

In contrast to the player personnel side of the organization, the business side of the organization does not have any control over team performance issues. However, people in these positions play a very important role in the organization in that they are responsible for generating revenue, marketing, developing a fan base, and working with the many customers of the organization. An example of the Miami Heat's business operations is depicted in the organizational chart in figure 15.5.

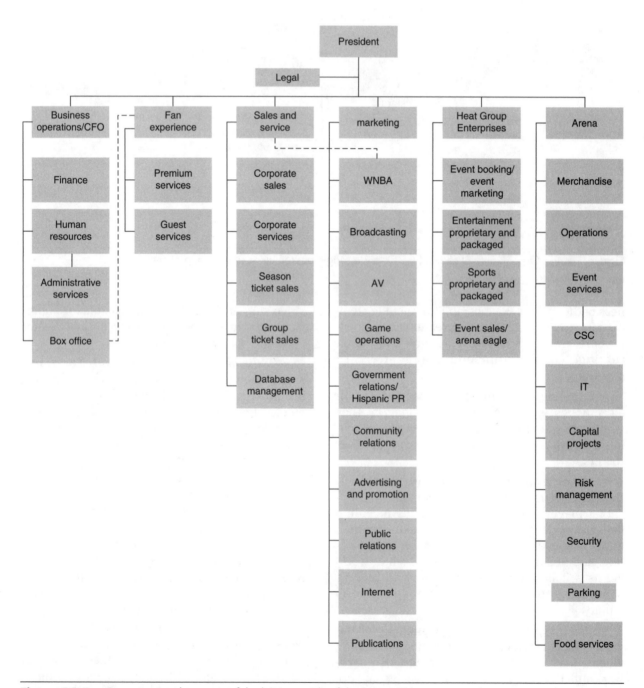

Figure 15.5   Organizational structure of the business side of the Miami Heat.

Reprinted, by permission, from the Miami Heat, 2002.

- *Ticket sales.* One of two types of sales within the organization, ticket sales people typically focus on selling season tickets, partial season tickets, and group tickets. These responsibilities force them to target not just individual ticket purchasers, but also groups and corporations that can buy either a larger number of tickets or more expensive season tickets. Ticket sales is a good first position in professional sport since there are a disproportionate number of openings because of the large number of tickets that need to be sold in order to maximize team revenues.

- *Corporate sales.* As opposed to ticket sales in which the emphasis is on the sales of individual tickets, corporate salespeople target corporations exclusively. Corporate salespeople may sell corporate sponsorships, luxury suites, or club seats.

- *Game experience.* Responsibilities for these positions focus on enhancing the experience of people attending games. Specific tasks may include overseeing the music, video boards, and public address messaging during a game. Opportunities in the area have increased as stadia and arenas have become more sophisticated and teams have increasingly focused on providing an entertaining experience both on and off the field, court, or ice.

- *Advertising.* Responsibilities in advertising include designing and writing advertising copy and identifying, securing, and placing advertisements in a variety of media. This responsibility may be handled by the sport organization or **outsourced** to an advertising agency that specializes in ad creation and placement.

- *Promotions.* Similar to the game experience area, the opportunities in this area have increased as organizations have focused on providing an optimal experience to spectators. Responsibilities in promotions typically include overseeing all promotional activity that occurs on the field of play or in the stands during the game.

- *Web site management.* As the importance of the Web site as a marketing communications tool has increased over the past 10 years, a need for people trained in Web site management has arisen. The responsibilities of the Web site manager include uploading and downloading content, working with the league offices to ensure conformity to appearance standards, working with corporate sponsors to place advertisements, and creating content that will increase traffic to the site.

- *Community relations.* This department may be part of the public relations or marketing department. The community relations staff is responsible for creating and administering grassroots functions, such as clinics and other charitable events that the team sponsors. They are also responsible for implementing leaguewide programs, such as the NBA Reads program.

- *Media relations.* This department is involved in assisting and working with the media by providing information necessary for game coverage and publicity. This includes ensuring that the needs of the media are met at every sporting event. People in media relations positions are also responsible for all publications, such as media guides, yearbooks, and game programs.

- *Customer relationship management.* People in this area focus on building databases of information about the team's customers so that the team can more effectively serve its customers and better meet their needs. This position may also include overseeing the marketing research efforts of the organization.

- *Hospitality coordinators.* Hospitality coordinators are responsible for the game-related needs of corporate clients, club seat holders, and luxury box owners. This would include coordinating the provision of food, beverages, and any other special needs (for example, computer/Internet connection) required by corporate clients.

- *Computer support staff.* The computer support staff are responsible for computer hardware and software used in all operations of the franchise. This department handles all purchasing, network maintenance, and report generation.

- *Ticketing.* This department may or may not include the ticket sales staff. Ticketing personnel are responsible for managing the ticket inventory. They are responsible for ticket distribution, printing, accounting, game day box office sales, complimentary tickets, and the financial settlement for the visiting team.

outsource—The process of hiring a company to perform an organizational function of the team or league. For example, professional teams often outsource their advertising to advertising agencies because of the expertise that these agencies possess.

Securing Employment and Working in Professional Sport

Without question, an internship is essential to securing a position in professional sport. You should begin to construct an informational file on the teams and organizations with whom you would like to intern and gain employment. This file should contain the names, phone numbers, and addresses of department heads within the organization. Supplement the file with information about the business activities of the franchise. Such information might include newspaper and journal articles, sales brochures, advertising examples, promotional schedules, and so on. It is essential to understand that the business area of the team is most likely where you will be working. Accordingly, you should be prepared to make a difference in that aspect of the organization. Although the box score is often interesting, knowing who hit .300 or the name of the leading rusher won't necessarily help your cause in gaining employment. In addition to knowing the business aspect of sport, you must understand the social role of sport and the place it occupies as a powerful cultural institution. It is only by understanding both sport business and sport's impact on a culture that you can truly comprehend the role and scope of sport.

In addition to developing and maintaining the file, supplement your experience while still in school. Obtaining a worthwhile internship with a solid organization is sometimes as difficult as finding employment. Part-time employment and volunteer experience in sales, game management, or customer service and hospitality are valuable assets on your résumé. You can obtain these experiences while still in school or during the summer. Whenever possible, meet and interview people in your chosen field. To effectively interview for internships and permanent positions, you should have a good understanding of the industry, its leaders, and its issues. You can develop this knowledge through the secondary sources in your file, personal interviews, and attending conferences and other presentations featuring industry leaders. Chapter 2 has some good ideas about informational interviewing.

Internship

Ideally, the internship should be a mutually beneficial relationship between you and the host orga-

nization. You should be able to develop a range of employment experience that translates into attractive job skills to a prospective employer. In exchange, the host organization should receive competent and reliable assistance in the performance of assigned tasks. Be aware that many pro sport organizations want interns to remain throughout the entire season, not just for a semester. This arrangement is beneficial for both parties. Organizations benefit because they do not have to recruit and train new people in the middle of the year. You benefit because you are able to be part of the entire cycle of franchise operations. Your goal as an intern should be to make yourself so indispensable that the team feels that they must hire you into a full-time position.

A Word of Advice

Although an internship is critical for employment in pro sport, successful completion of that internship does not guarantee you a job with that franchise. Other factors affect the ability of a professional sport franchise to offer part-time, contractual, or full-time employment to a deserving intern. These factors include employee turnover, the economic climate, organizational goals and objectives, and the hiring philosophy and financial stability of team ownership. Even so, as an intern working in professional sport you should strive to be an integral part of the organization and perform every assigned task to the best of your ability. In addition, you must demonstrate initiative.

LEARNING ACTIVITY

Identify the professional sport franchises, teams, or organizations in your area. Conduct an informational interview with an individual holding a position that interests you. What are the most attractive aspects of this job? What are the least attractive aspects?

SUMMARY

Professional sport is a large part of the entertainment, social, political, economic, legal, and cultural fabric of North America. The continued growth of the media and related technology, particularly television, ensures that professional sport is prevalent and highly accessible throughout North America regardless of the demographic characteristics of its audience. Because of this

accessibility and prevalence, the importance of the roles that labor, management, and government play often seem out of balance when compared with their roles in other forms of business. For the most part, reserve clauses, free agency, League Think, and antitrust exemptions exist only in the context of professional sport. These concepts are not essential in conducting the traditional activities of mainstream business operations, but appear to be essential to the survival of business as it relates to professional sport. Further, these concepts will be crucial for new professional sport leagues, such as the WNBA and WUSA, to understand if they are to be successful. By understanding the unique limitations and opportunities of professional sport as well as the revenue sources and the impact of the media, you can truly appreciate the career challenges and possibilities in the field.

REVIEW QUESTIONS

1. Briefly describe the historical evolution of major professional team sports.

2. Explain how the professional team sport product is different from a mainstream product.

3. What is "League Think" and why is it such an important concept for professional sport leagues?

4. Why have television ratings for professional sport leagues been decreasing lately?

5. What are the five most prevalent revenue sources for a professional sport team?

6. Describe the two different areas of opportunities within a professional sport organization.

7. Based on your reading, in what areas do you think there will be a growing number of jobs?

Job Opportunities

Promotions Coordinator

The Worcester Warthogs Baseball Club has an entry-level position in its promotions department available. The promotions coordinator will be responsible for the implementation of all in-game promotions that occur at Warthogs. Responsibilities will include scheduling promotions, working with sponsors to implement promotions, and actually implementing the promotions during games. The successful candidate will be a college graduate with some game promotion experience.

Director of Ticket Sales

The Peoria Predators of the Indoor Football League are seeking a person to oversee the sales of individual, group, and luxury suite tickets. This person will also oversee a staff of four other salespeople. The ability to work under pressure and meet sales objectives is a must. Additionally, the candidate should possess at least three to five years of ticket sales experience with a professional sport organization.

Media Relations Assistant

An individual with excellent writing skills is sought for a position with the Virginia Robins Basketball Team. This individual will be primarily responsible for the media guide and writing press releases. Some coordination with media, particularly during games, will be required as well. Bachelor's degree in journalism or sport management preferred. Some media relations experience is a plus.

Chief Marketing Officer

The Minnesota Lakes of the United Hockey League is seeking a person to coordinate and oversee the entire marketing operations for this highly competitive professional hockey club. Responsibilities include overseeing ticket sales, corporate sales, advertising, promotions, media relations, broadcasting, and community relations. The successful candidate will have at least 10 years of experience with professional sport organizations in various capacities. A proven track record generating revenue and increasing attendance is also important.

Video Coordinator

The Utah Coyotes Base Ball Club seeks a person to coordinate the videotaping of Coyotes games, opponents' games, and the games of potential draftees. The person should be well versed in various digital technology systems. Knowledge of the Pinnacle Systems video system is preferred. One to two years of video experience with another professional team is also preferred.

(continued)

(continued)

Web Site Manager

The El Paso Eels of the Women's Professional Basketball League is seeking a person to coordinate the design, layout, and content of its Web site. Because we are competing in a new league, this person will be responsible for overhauling the existing Web site and generating new ideas for attracting more visitors to the site. Additionally, the person will be responsible for coordinating the content with all other departments within the organization, including media relations, marketing, and broadcasting. Knowledge of HTML, Java, and additional Internet programming languages is important.

REFERENCES

Bernstein, A. (2000, January 17-23). Amex renews with WNBA and takes a local focus. *Street & Smith's SportsBusiness Journal*, p. 16.

Broadcast rights of major sports properties. (2000, October 2-8). *Street & Smith's SportsBusiness Journal*, p. 59.

Brockinton, L. (2000a, July 10-16). WNBA's global All-Star reach hits 154 countries. *Street & Smith's SportsBusiness Journal*, p. 14.

Brockinton, L. (2000b, December 25-31). TV ratings take a slide, many hit all-time lows. *Street & Smith's SportsBusiness Journal*, p. 23.

Browne, L. (1992). *Girls of summer*. Toronto: Harper Collins.

Federal Base Ball Club of Baltimore, Inc. v. National League of Professional Base Ball Clubs, 259 U.S. 200 (1922).

Frank, M. (2000, November 13-19). NBA cracks $50 barrier for average ticket price. *Street & Smith's SportsBusiness Journal*, p. 10.

Fraser et al v. Major League Soccer, 97 F. Supp. 2d 130 (2000).

Freedman, W. (1987). *Professional sports and antitrust.* New York: Quorum Books.

Gorman, J., & Calhoun, K. (1994). *The name of the game: The business of sports.* New York: Wiley.

Greenberg, M.J. (1993). *Sports law practice.* Charlottsville, VA: Michie.

Guterson, D. (1994, September). Moneyball: On the relentless promotion of pro sports. *Harper's Magazine*, p. 38.

Harris, D. (1986). *The league: The rise and decline of the NFL.* New York: Bantam Books, pp. 13-14.

A history of past women's professional basketball leagues. (1996). *ABL Courtside, 1,* 33.

Horovitz, B. (1996, October 18). A basketball league of their own: Women athletes leap through hoops to live their dreams. *USA Today*, p. 1B.

Howard, D.R., & Crompton, J.L. (1995). *Financing sport.* Morgantown, WV: Fitness Information Technology.

King, B. (2001, December 3-9). Selig delivers red-ink alert to owners. *Street & Smith's SportsBusiness Journal*, pp. 1, 10.

Lefton, T. (2001, December 10-16). MLB builds momentum with sponsors. *Street & Smith's SportsBusiness Journal*, p. 26.

Liberman, N. (2001, December 10-16). Baseball clicks on to profits. *Street & Smith's SportsBusiness Journal*, p. 25.

Minor league arena naming rights deals. (2001, August 13-19). *Street & Smith's SportsBusiness Journal*, pp. 16-17.

MLB attendance (final). (2001, October 15-21). *Street & Smith's SportsBusiness Journal*, p. 39.

MLS attendance (final). (2001, September 24-30). *Street & Smith's SportsBusiness Journal*, p. 41.

Mullin, B.J., Hardy, S., & Sutton, W.A. (2000). *Sport marketing.* Champaign, IL: Human Kinetics.

Naming rights deals at big-league facilities. (2001, August 13-19). *Street & Smith's SportsBusiness Journal*, pp. 18-19.

National Hockey League: Official Guide and Record Book, 1995-96 (1996). New York: Author.

NBA attendance (final). (2001, April 30 – May 6). *Street & Smith's SportsBusiness Journal*, p. 35.

NHL attendance (final). (2001, April 16-22). *Street & Smith's SportsBusiness Journal*, p. 31.

On the racks. (2000, September 4-10). *Street & Smith's SportsBusiness Journal*, p. 32.

Putting the past labor disputes in perspective. (2001, March 26-April 1). *Street & Smith's SportsBusiness Journal*, p. 30.

Rader, B.G. (1983). *American sports: From the age of folk games to the age of televised sports.* Englewood Cliffs, NJ: Prentice Hall.

Recent broadcast rights deals. (2000, October 2-8). *Street & Smith's SportsBusiness Journal*, p. 59.

Roberts, R. (1995, Spring). The salary cap in professional sports. *The Sports Lawyer*, p. 1.

Roberts, R., & Olson, J. (1995). *Winning is the only thing: Sports in America since 1945.* Baltimore: Johns Hopkins University Press.

Rofe, J. (2000a, December 25-31). Baseball's rich getting richer as economic ills go untreated. *Street & Smith's SportsBusiness Journal*, p. 23.

Rofe, J. (2000b, April 3-9). What new sponsorship can we sell? *Street & Smith's SportsBusiness Journal*, p. 24.

Salary growth since 1993 in the big four team sports. (2000, January 31-February 6). *Street & Smith's SportsBusiness Journal*, p. 29.

Sports Business Journal's NFL fan support rankings. (2001, January 22-28). *Street & Smith's SportsBusiness Journal*, p. 43.

Staudohar, P.D. (1989). *The sports industry and collective bargaining*. Cornell, NY: ILR Press.

Staudohar, P.D., & Mangan, J.A. (1991). *The business of professional sports*. Urbana, IL: University of Illinois Press.

Tannenbaum, M.B. (1994). An overview of the relationship between major and minor league baseball. *The Sports Lawyer, XI*, 1, 7-11.

Top web sites for U.S. leagues and governing bodies. (2001, March 19-25). *Street & Smith's SportsBusiness Journal*, p. 27.

White, G.E. (1996). *Creating the national pastime: Baseball transforms itself*. Princeton, NJ: Princeton University Press.

WNBA attendance (final). (2001, August 27-September 2, 2001). *Street & Smith's SportsBusiness Journal*, p. 22.

WUSA attendance final. (2001, August 20-26). *Street & Smith's SportsBusiness Journal*, p. 27.

Zimbalist, A. (1992). *Baseball and billions*. New York: Basic Books.

Chapter 16

Sport Management and Marketing Agencies

Mark A. McDonald, University of Massachusetts, Amherst
William A. Sutton, National Basketball Association

A sport management and marketing agency is a business that acts on behalf of a sport property. This sport property can be a person, a corporation, an event, a team, or even a place. The actions undertaken on behalf of the property may include one or more of the following: representation, negotiation, sales, licensing, marketing, or management. Given the scope of potential activities that encompass the arts, festivals, sport events, resorts, and music, a more appropriate term to describe these agencies is *sport and lifestyle management and marketing agencies.*

The first sport management and marketing agencies were formed primarily to represent athletes in contract negotiations and to seek endorsements and other revenue streams for these athletes. The International Management Group (IMG), established in 1960 by Mark H. McCormack in Cleveland, Ohio, was the first agency dedicated to representing professional athletes. In their own words, "IMG literally 'invented' sports management and marketing more than three decades ago" (International Management Group, 2000). As time has passed and the marketplace and opportunities have changed, sport marketing agencies have become diverse in their scope and focus. Today, sport marketing agencies are involved not only in contract negotiations but also in myriad other functions.

The purpose of this chapter is to provide an overview of sport management and marketing agencies and to introduce career opportunities within this rapidly growing segment of the sport industry. We will shed light on these unique and multifaceted companies by classifying the many agencies into four categories: full service, general, specialty, and in-house. Examples of each type of agency will help delineate the similarities and differences. Finally, this chapter will give basic

LEARNING OBJECTIVES

After studying this chapter, you will be able to do the following:

1. Explain the role, scope, and impact of sport management and marketing agencies as they relate to the business of sport.

2. Differentiate between the types of sport management and marketing agencies to determine which agencies are most appropriate for particular tasks and assignments.

3. Describe the evolution and growth of sport management and marketing agencies.

4. Define the functions performed by sport management and marketing agencies.

5. Appraise the career opportunities associated with sport management and marketing agencies.

information about career opportunities and challenges.

Creating a Sport Management and Marketing Agency Plan

It's a Tuesday morning at First National Bank in River City, USA. At a staff meeting, Ms. Smith, the regional president, states that First National is continuing to lose customers to Second City Federal—a bank that seems to appeal to younger and more upscale clients. Ms. Smith feels that First National's attempts to communicate with its market through traditional outlets such as advertising and direct mail have become too routine, and consequently the message is not being received. "It is for that reason," says Ms. Smith, "that I have asked Sport Properties Ltd., an international sport marketing agency, to assist us in developing a new communication strategy through sports and special events to help us retain our current customer base and, we hope, attract new customers."

The room begins to buzz with many questions: What is a sport marketing agency? What type of sport or special event is best associated with a bank? What services should we promote through the event? What exactly will the agency do?

At the same time, in the regional offices of Sport Properties Ltd., Mr. Brown, regional vice president, is meeting with his staff to discuss their upcoming presentation to First National Bank. "We have an excellent opportunity to use some of our existing properties, such as skiing, kayaking, and in-line skating, to create **grassroots** events that appeal to younger, more upscale individuals in each of First National Bank's primary markets." At that point, Ms. Perez, senior project director, asks about developing a tie-in with participants from each grassroots **venue** competing in a championship or finals at the headquarters of First National in River City. "Excellent concept, Ms. Perez!" says Mr. Brown. "Perhaps we should also consider finding other sponsors who might want to **co-op** this opportunity with First National. Let's begin preparing our agenda."

grassroots—A program targeted to individuals at the primary level of involvement. These programs are usually targeted to participants rather than spectators.

venue—A facility or site where a special event or sport activity takes place.

co-op—Involvement of many sponsors to share the costs and benefits associated with an event or sport activity.

The next section of this chapter reviews the diverse functions performed by agencies on behalf of sport properties.

Functions of Sport Management and Marketing Agencies

The scope of functions performed by sport management and marketing agencies is vast. As you read the following list, you can appreciate the degree of specialization necessary to discharge each duty. Although an agency might perform several or perhaps only one function, some agencies, such as IMG and Octagon, perform *all* of them.

- Client management and representation
- Client marketing and product endorsement
- Event creation and development
- Event management and marketing
- Property representation and licensing
- Television development and production
- Sponsorship solicitation and consulting
- Hospitality management services
- Grassroots and participatory programs
- Research and evaluation
- Financial planning and management

Client Management and Representation

Client management and representation involves representing a client in contract negotiations and making marketing decisions to manage the client's income potential and earnings. The contract negotiations could be between player and team, licensee and licensor, or product and endorser. The management function involves the agency in a strategic planning process for its client that may involve any of the following: financial planning, investment and management, marketing, personal appearances, and other forms of revenue production and management. For example, Michael Jordan's agent, David Falk of SFX Sports Group, not only negotiates Jordan's NBA player contracts, but also manages and advises Jordan on financial and marketing opportunities. SFX Sports Group is owned by Clear Channel, the largest operator of radio stations in the United States.

Client Marketing and Product Endorsement

Similar to the management function, client marketing involves the agency in the promotion and total marketing of the client. For a professional athlete, this may involve securing endorsement opportunities, product endorsements, personal appearances, book contracts, movie and television roles, interviews and feature stories, video games, and so on. SFX Sports Group, for example, secures Michael Jordan's endorsements for McDonald's and Hanes.

Event Creation and Development

The growth of sport television in the 1970s, the proliferation of sport networks in the 1990s, and the development of new satellite technology such as DirecTV have led to fiscally rewarding opportunities to create new sports and events (Crespo, 1995). Sports such as Arena Football and Major Indoor Lacrosse, increased numbers of college football bowl games, and a wider array of collegiate basketball doubleheaders have emerged to capitalize on this opportunity. Some television entities such as ESPN and Turner Broadcasting have created events to fill their **inventory**. (For example, ESPN created the Great Outdoor Games and the X-Games for this purpose.) Other events, such as the Quarterback Challenge, which was developed by Buffalo Bill's quarterback Jim Kelly through his agency Jim Kelly Enterprises, were created as primary revenue sources for their originators ("A New Era," 1995). IMG has either created or partially owns dozens of events ranging from the Target Stars on Ice figure skating tour to the Ericsson Open tennis tournament (Bernstein, 2000).

inventory—What a sport property has to sell. This refers not only to quantity but also to characteristics, traits, and other benefits.

LEARNING ACTIVITY

Select a sport event or activity (property). What criteria would you use in selecting an agency to represent that sport property? Construct a marketing inventory of the characteristics of that activity or event that you believe have value and are marketable.

Event Management and Marketing

Given the high cost of personnel (i.e., salaries and benefits), the need for specific expertise, the seasonality of some events, and the geographic scope of the activities, many sport organizations now hire outside agencies to manage and market their events. Event management and marketing agencies are involved in activities such as golf and tennis tournaments, festivals, bowl games, and other sport and lifestyle special events. This event management may involve any of the following areas: tournament operations, hospitality and entertainment, sponsorship and ticket sales, licensing and merchandising, television production, public relations, and promotion. PGI Inc., for example, is responsible for everything from light-

ing to buses of major sport events for clients such as Major League Baseball, the NFL, NBA, and PGA Tour. According to Wendy Nipper, director of marketing with PGI Inc., "As more and more people become involved in the sponsorship side of the sports industry, the leagues increasingly are outsourcing a lot of their event work" (Menninger, 2000). (For more information on outsourcing, see chapter 15.) Hyatt Hotels has a division called Regency Productions, which is an event management company specializing not only in hospitality, but also in event production and setup (Conklin, 1994). The National Basketball Association contracts Regency Productions for the NBA Jam Session held during the NBA All-Star Weekend.

Property Representation and Licensing

Sport management and marketing agencies often represent sport properties in promotional licensing and sponsor **solicitation** and **procurement**. A sport property can be defined as any sport or lifestyle entity that has name or event recognition, desirability, and perceived value, and that chooses to offer itself for some type of affiliation. Examples of sport and lifestyle properties include the Rose Bowl, the Rock and Roll Hall of Fame, the Houston Rockets, Camden Yard, the Rolling Stones, the U.S. Tennis Open, The Ohio State University, and the Taste of Cincinnati. The property can be a facility, an event, a team, an athletic program, a band or concert tour, and so on. Property representation can result in the sales of rights fees, promotional licensing opportunities, sponsorship sales, signage and advertising agreements, and endorsements.

solicitation—Requesting support or assistance on behalf of a sport property from a potential sponsor.

procurement—Successful solicitation of financial or other resources on behalf of the sport property.

Television Development and Production

The growth and proliferation of cable, satellite, and pay-per-view have created many opportunities and outlets for developing and producing programming for television. Host Communications, Creative Sports Marketing, and Raycom are agencies that have been involved in packaging rights fees for college football and basketball, and the subsequent sales of these rights to networks such as CBS, NBC, ABC, ESPN, and TBS.

The revenue potential of such television programming and the interest of the networks and their sponsors have had an impact on the traditional conference structure in collegiate sport, resulting in the emergence of 12 team conferences such as the Southeast Conference and the Big 12 Conference (the Big Eight plus Texas, Texas A&M, Texas Tech, and Baylor), which began play in 1996. For these new conferences, the result has been a lucrative market for a televised conference championship matching the winners of the two six-team divisions.

Traditional sport management and marketing agencies have recognized the opportunities that television presents and have aggressively moved to capitalize on them. IMG has long had its own television production division, Trans World International (TWI), so it could maximize the revenue derived from the properties it represents. Beginning more than 20 years ago with the made-for-TV competition among athletes from various sports, "The Superstars," IMG continues to add similar events such as the Lincoln Financial Group Battle at Bighorn featuring Tiger Woods and Jack Nicklaus versus Sergio Garcia and Lee Trevino played on July 29, 2002. TWI currently accounts for more than a third of all IMG profits (Bernstein, 2000).

Sponsorship Solicitation and Consulting

The most common functions of sport management and marketing agencies, regardless of the size or scope of the agency, are consulting about solicitation and securing corporate sponsorships. Corporations spent an estimated $8 billion on U.S. sports in 2000 (Mahony & Howard, 2001). Although many properties (e.g., teams, sport events, festivals) handle these functions in-house, most seek outside assistance in determining value and identifying and obtaining appropriate sponsors. Similarly, corporations and other potential sponsors often employ a sport management and marketing agency to identify properties that may assist them in achieving their corporate goals and objectives. Atlanta-based Bevilaqua International, a specialist in Olympic sport marketing, describes itself as a marketing consulting firm that specializes in working with corporations and major special events to enhance, protect, and **leverage** the marketing investment. "We work closely with our clients to develop cost-effective and results-oriented programs directed at corporate objectives such as improving brand sales, elevating awareness

and enhancing corporate image" (Bevilaqua International Inc., 1994).

leverage—To use a licensing agreement to create additional marketing opportunities that may or may not be directly related to the original agreement.

Some corporations, such as Gatorade, Coca-Cola, and Anheuser Busch, have in-house sport marketing departments that work directly with properties or through properties' agencies to reach an agreement.

Hospitality Management Services

A frequently overlooked function of a sport and marketing agency is that of creating, arranging, and managing hospitality management services. Hospitality management services include, but are not limited to, transportation and other logistical issues; menu and food service planning and management; corporate sponsor entertainment; special auxiliary event creation and management; housing; and awards, gifts, and recognition programs. As with most events and activities, the type and scope of these services vary greatly according to the event. In the United States, the Super Bowl is one of the most coveted destinations for hospitality packages in all of sport because of geographic location, appeal, and ticket demand. Corporations reward their best sales personnel, thank their highest-volume customers, and court new clients through invitations to this mega-event. The Super Bowl offers a prestigious opportunity to achieve these objectives. Agencies such as Party Planners West arrange transportation; accommodations; meals; auxiliary events such as cruises, golf tournaments, and postevent parties; gifts; and spouse programs (Conrad, 1995).

Grassroots and Participatory Programs

Grassroots programs are designed to build a following for a product, service, or organization. They may not pay immediate benefits, but they are essential to long-term growth by creating an interest among potential consumers. Most grassroots programs are aimed at children and adolescents who may or may not be consumers of the product, service, or organization in question but who possess the qualities, abilities, and potential to become consumers in the future. Grassroots programs are often designed to involve participants in activities and events that are held at local sites, which could be thousands of miles away from the headquarters of the sponsoring organization. These local events and activities are often targeted to certain demographic groups and ethnic markets. For example, Major League Baseball's RBI Program and the NHL's Street Skates programs are grassroots programs targeted to youth in the inner city.

Research and Evaluation

Evaluation and documentation are critical factors in determining the success of the various types of sport management and marketing programs discussed throughout this chapter. **Reengineering**, **downsizing**, **value added**, and measuring the impact are all concepts that stress a high degree of relevance and accountability, both in terms of the sport organization and the agency or program delivering the services. Research, through mail surveys, on-site surveys, personal interviews, pre- and **postevent impact analysis**, focus groups, and other methods, is essential to assist the decision maker in justifying a program's cost, value, and relevance to the client.

reengineering—Changing an organization's structure or philosophy to capitalize on existing opportunities or changing business environments.

downsizing—Becoming a smaller organization through reducing personnel or departments. This may result from a change in the organization's mission or direction.

value added—The perception, by the consumer, of added or augmented product or service benefits.

postevent impact analysis—Research conducted (usually by a third party but commissioned by a sponsor or the event itself) after the event has been completed to determine the effects that the event had on the sponsor's product (image, awareness, or sales) or on the community in general (economic growth through spending associated with the event).

Most corporations involved in sponsorship or licensing activities perform some type of assessment, either through an in-house department or by contracting with an agency that offers research and evaluation services. It would follow that the research agency selected would not be involved in the sponsorship and licensing sales process to ensure that it does not have a stake in the findings. Thus, the research agency selected should be a specialist in evaluating sponsorship and licensing programs or perhaps in sport consumer behavior.

Joyce Julius and Associates, Performance Research, and Audience Analysts are examples of research or consulting companies specializing in such services.

The services provided by Joyce Julius and Associates are among the most used and reputable in the industry (Cortez, 1992). In fact, through their primary products—*Sponsors Report* and the National Television Impression Value (NTIV) Analysis—Joyce Julius and Associates arguably set an industry standard. *Sponsors Report* is a publication that focuses on the value of the exposure received directly from national television broadcasts. This is done by calculating all clear, in-focus exposure time during the broadcast. Exposure time is the amount of time given to logos, signage, displays, and audio mentions during the broadcast. Clear, in-focus exposures refers to exposures that can be readily seen by the television viewers. These exposures are measured and converted to advertising costs per 30 seconds for the actual advertising costs on that specific broadcast. The NTIV Analysis determines the gross impressions from varied exposure sources and values these impressions using a single factor reflecting the comparative cost of national television media purchases (Schreiber, 1994).

The type of research most appropriate and the best agency to employ will vary with the scope and magnitude of the event, whether the event is televised, the types of sponsorship and licensing activities taking place at the event, the budget, and the commitment of the organization to undertake a sound research approach.

Financial Planning and Management

This is a highly specialized service involving accountants, financial planners and advisors, and investment specialists and portfolio managers. Few sport management and marketing agencies specialize in this type of work. IMG offers this service as part of its client management services and has assisted several of its clients in investing and planning well enough to start their own companies or to enter limited partnerships with IMG creating new ventures. The success of both Arnold Palmer and Jack Nicklaus in creating new companies and ventures is testament to the performance of IMG in discharging its fiscal planning duties. However, except for IMG and a few others, sport management and marketing agencies usually contract these services out to reputable financial planners and accountants whose primary function is not related to sport but to fiscal management and planning.

Types of Sport Management and Marketing Agencies

More than 1,000 agencies identify themselves as sport management and marketing agencies (Lipsey, 2001). This figure does not include city or state sport commissions, corporations such as Anheuser Busch and Gatorade, or divisions of leagues such as NBA Properties, Inc. If these quasi-agencies were included, the figure would exceed 3,500.

As we can expect, these agencies vary in size, budget, type of clientele, and scope of services. Some agencies perform a variety of services for one client, whereas others work for many clients but perform only one function. For example, ARL Proper-

Arnold Palmer on the links. The International Management Group was founded in 1960 to represent Palmer's marketing interests. Since then IMG has expanded to manage sport properties and events as well as athletes.

ties represents only pilots of the Unlimited Air Racing Series for licensing and merchandising opportunities. Examining the various types of agencies (full service, general, specialty, and in-house) will illustrate the variety and scope of sport and entertainment management and marketing agencies.

Full-Service Agencies

These agencies are exactly what the term implies; the full range of services, including client management, event creation, television development, sponsorship solicitation, hospitality services, research and evaluation, and financial planning, are performed by in-house personnel. Attorneys, accountants, sales personnel, public relations personnel, creative personnel, and management information services personnel are all contained in-house. Full-service agencies include the International Management Group (IMG), Octagon, and SFX Sports Group. Examining IMG provides an excellent overview of a full-service agency.

IMG, the first completely dedicated sport marketing agency, was initially created to represent the interests of golfer Arnold Palmer. As times changed and marketing forces such as television increased their impact on the sport scene, the roles of sport marketing agencies expanded to include managing not only athletes but other sport properties and events as well. IMG owes much of its early success to being visionary and recognizing the opportunities that the Golden Age of Sport Television (1958-1973) offered.

The diversity of IMG's endeavors reflects how successful the company has become. IMG represents athletes, performing artists, writers, fashion models, broadcasters, world-class events, corporations, resorts, and cultural institutions. IMG has evolved into the largest sport marketing agency in the world, with 85 offices employing more than 5,000 employees in 33 countries (IMG, 2000). IMG has four core businesses: client management, event management and marketing, television, and corporate marketing (see figure 16.1). Examining each core business is essential in comprehending the entire scope and magnitude of IMG.

Client Management

IMG's client management activities encompass contract negotiation, personalized strategic planning, endorsement marketing, corporate and resort affiliation, personal appearances, broadcasting, publishing, licensing, and merchandising (IMG, 2000). Due to the size and scope of IMG, as well as the many relationships it has constructed during

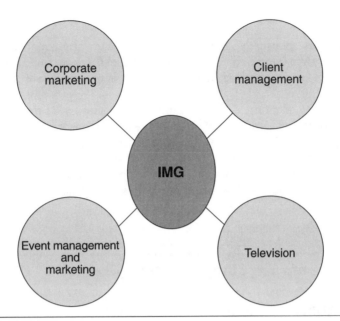

Figure 16.1 IMG's four core businesses.

Data from IMG Corporate Report (2001).

Scenario: Interning and Working for IMG

Ann Marie earned a BA degree in economics in 1987. Upon graduation, she worked for more than two years as a security analyst in New York, followed by two years in the product management department of a major commercial bank in the Boston area. After much reflection, she determined that her ultimate goal was to be involved with a sport-related product, and so she enrolled in a sport management graduate program.

After completing her course work at the master's level, Ann Marie accepted a year-long marketing internship with a college in Boston. Even though her goal was to obtain a job within the product management department of a sport-oriented company, she viewed this internship as an excellent learning opportunity. In this capacity she was involved in several activities with revenue-producing sports, including corporate sponsorship sales, organization of promotional activities, and collateral production and distribution. Through this internship, she learned that college athletics was not a good fit with her career goals.

Ann Marie's internship coordinator alerted her to another internship possibility with IMG in Boston assisting with two major Boston-area events (a men's professional tennis event and a women's professional golf event). In this capacity, she worked on group ticket sales, print advertising placements, hotel room barters, and gathering ad copy from tournament sponsors. Although not offered full-time employment at the completion of these two tournaments, Ann Marie was given a small stipend to continue with IMG working out of their Chicago office on a women's professional tennis tournament. Fortunately, Ann Marie had sufficient financial resources to allow her to accept this position. Finally, after the initial internship and an extended internship with IMG in Boston and Chicago, Ann Marie was offered a full-time position in the Boston office of IMG.

With IMG, Ann Marie has been involved with professional tennis, golf, and figure skating. Her typical day has varied dramatically, depending on whether events are 6 to 12 months or 6 to 12 weeks away. Her largest responsibility involves sponsorship sales. When dealing with companies new to sport sponsorship, she has to educate executives on how sport sponsorship can assist an organization in accomplishing goals such as increased visibility, enhanced corporate image, differentiation of products from competition, and client entertainment. According to Ann Marie, selling takes place 365 days a year; however, as an event draws near, other tasks become high priorities. Servicing event sponsors is obviously a top priority. It is crucial that all sponsor needs are

(continued)

(continued)

addressed and that every sponsorship benefit available to the organization is considered. Tickets, banners, program ads, television and radio spots, logo slicks, on-site promotions, merchandising booths, public address announcements, and on-site parties are all details that must be handled appropriately.

In addition to sponsor relations, Ann Marie has many other event responsibilities, including placement of print advertising, group ticket sales, player and sponsor hotel accommodations, and ordering printed materials (e.g., credentials, parking passes, and scorecards). For golf events, she also serves as the tournament coordinator, which involves many responsibilities such as serving as event liaison among the LPGA, tournament volunteers, pro-am participants, and neighborhood residents. Ann Marie says, "Stating that I wear many hats during the weeks before and during an event is an understatement!"

Table 16.1 Representative Sample of IMG Clients

Client	Sport or activity	Client	Sport or activity	Client	Sport or activity
Arnold Palmer	Golf	Martina Hingis	Tennis	Pete Sampras	Tennis
Brett Hull	Hockey	Tiger Woods	Golf	Itzhak Perlman	Music
Peyton Manning	Football	Kristi Yamaguchi	Figure skating	Jeff Gordon	Auto racing
Andre Agassi	Tennis	Bob Costas	Broadcasting	Anna Kournikova	Tennis
Annika Sorenstam	Golf	Chris Webber	Basketball	Pat Conroy	Author
Tommy Moe	Skiing	Lauren Hutton	Acting	Tyra Banks	Modeling
John Madden	Broadcasting				

the past four decades, IMG may enjoy a major advantage over competitors in attracting clients and providing services. Table 16.1 provides a partial listing of IMG clients.

One key to successful client management is to have satisfied, highly successful, and visible clients involved in a variety of sport and lifestyle activities. The success of the clients ensures successful negotiations and endorsements, while the visibility helps attract new clients who create a cyclical effect. Given the labor unrest in professional sport in the new millennium, the importance of having a client base that ensures income, stability, and diverse sports or activities cannot be overemphasized.

Event Management and Marketing

IMG is involved in creating, developing, and managing sport and lifestyle activities and events. The company also manages licensing, sponsorship, and broadcast rights for many of the oldest and most distinguished events on the international sport and event calendar. These events include Wimbledon, the America's Cup, the Australian Open, World Championship of Women's Golf,

Budweiser Grand Prix of Cleveland, and Ringling Brothers and Barnum & Bailey Circus. Given the diverse nature and varying levels and demands of these properties, as well as the combination of rights, duties, and obligations associated with these events, the complexity of the event management and marketing industry becomes clear.

Television

The television appendage of IMG is Trans World International (TWI), the largest independent source and distributor of sport programs in the world. The main function of TWI is to provide programming to major television networks around the world and to represent the entities owning the rights to those events (Parascenzo, 1993). TWI is able to accomplish this in three ways:

1. by serving as an advisor and consultant to rights holders,
2. by negotiating the sale of television rights, or
3. by creating and producing television series and events for sale or distribution.

Overall, TWI packages, produces, and distributes more than 4,000 hours of original programming per year (IMG, 2001).

Corporate Marketing

Much the same way that IMG capitalized on the opportunities afforded by television in the 1960s, it also recognized the clutter represented by television advertising in the 1980s and sought an effective strategy for assisting corporations in communicating to their target markets. IMG decided that the most effective way for corporations to communicate was through sport event and lifestyle marketing.

General Agencies

16W Marketing is a generalist type of agency that uses an integrated approach in the development of client programs. Led by partners Steve Rosner and Frank Vuono, 16W Marketing provides the following business components:

- *Athlete/coach/broadcaster marketing and representation:* Full-service representation for all off-field/court business and marketing endeavors, including licensing, endorsements, broadcaster contract negotiation, media placement, promotions, speaking engagements, and personal appearances. The company specializes in seeking "ownership" for athletes and celebrities, gaining equity positions with affiliated companies to provide mutual incentives to grow.

- *Team and venue services:* Helps professional teams, universities, and organizing bodies and sport authorities in franchise acquisition, management, marketing, and integrated sponsorship sales, including venue entitlement, stadium development, merchandising (including e-commerce), concessions, and retail sales.

- *Corporate consulting and property marketing:* Comprehensive strategic planning and implementation of integrated marketing programs for consumer products or service corporations, online/e-commerce fulfillment companies, manufacturers, retailers, and sport/entertainment management organizations. Services include sponsorship negotiations and evaluation, value-added media packages, licensing, merchandising, and cross-promotional ties.

- *Hospitality and event management:* Services include **turnkey** hospitality, event management, promotion coordination, and television packaging for top sport/entertainment events (including Su-

per Bowl, The Masters, U.S. Open, etc.), sponsorship sales, and licensing/merchandising, both on-site and at retail.

turnkey—A program or product that is fully executed by the vendor without further involvement from the client.

Specialty Agencies

A specialty agency specializes in the types of services it provides or in the scope of its clientele. For example, Bevilaqua International, based in Atlanta, specializes in Olympic marketing. All of its clients engage Bevilaqua International for the purpose of entering into contractual agreements with the U.S. Olympic Committee, the International Olympic Committee, or both. The contractual agreement may be endorsement, sponsorship, licensing, and so on, but it will be with an Olympic organizational unit. Thus, although Bevilaqua International performs a wide array of services, it offers these services only in conjunction with the Olympics (Smothers, 1992).

SportsMark Management Group Ltd. of Larkspur, California, is a specialty agency solely involved in event management and hospitality. SportsMark has entertained 27,000 guests at 50 Olympic hospitality events since the 1992 Winter Games in Albertville, France. Hospitality services provided include arranging hotel rooms and transportation, obtaining hard-to-get event tickets, and food and beverage services. Using the Olympics as a platform, the firm has been able to build strong business relationships with Fortune 500 corporations such as Xerox, Visa, General Motors, and AT&T (Schwartz, 2000).

In-House Agencies—Professional League Departments

In-house agencies are departments of companies (Anheuser Busch, Gatorade) that perform many sport marketing functions on behalf of the products and divisions of the parent company. These units are part of the corporation and are housed within that corporation to perform sport and lifestyle management and marketing functions for the corporation. In-house agencies have only one client—themselves—and function as **gatekeepers** in reviewing opportunities presented to them by other entities. In addition to this gatekeeping function, in-house agencies work with other units of the corporation, such as brand or product managers, advertising departments, public relations departments, and community affairs departments, to create or implement sport and lifestyle programming useful in achieving corporate objectives.

gatekeeper—The individual responsible for controlling the flow of proposals or solicitations to the decision maker.

One example of in-house agencies are professional league departments. Each professional sport league, and most sport organizations, have departments that focus their marketing and promoting efforts on the entire league or unit. For example, NBA Attractions and Entertainment, an NBA division, markets and promotes the NBA as a holistic product through special events and activities such as NBA Jam Session, the NBA Draft, and international tours and activities. NBA Attractions and Entertainment personnel work with the marketing departments of individual teams to promote the growth and development of the league itself. In order to do so, these personnel must understand the uniqueness and complexities of each team's market and must be prepared to assist teams in maintaining their identity while promoting the image of the whole league.

LEARNING ACTIVITY

Contact a sport management and marketing agency in your area. If there are no sport management and marketing agencies in your area, contact local advertising or public relations firms to determine if they have an appropriate client in the sport and lifestyle marketing area. Arrange an informational interview with someone in the agency who can provide you with an opportunity to learn more about the agency. In conjunction with your faculty advisor, structure a list of questions appropriate to ask during your informational interview. If feasible, attend a grassroots program or event managed or marketed by the agency. Observe signage, promotional activities, and agency employees during the activities. Write a critique based on your observations.

Careers Within Sport Management and Marketing Agencies

Careers in sport and lifestyle event management and marketing are challenging and varied. Many sport marketing agencies do not hire entry-level personnel. Instead, they bring in experienced people from other industry segments who have a network in place that they can use in generating new clients. A critical consideration in the hiring process, particularly in smaller agencies, is an assessment of a candidate's ability to get along, communicate, and be productive in a working environment with few staff members who must interact daily. In these smaller agencies, staff members must be compatible since they must act as a team. Sometimes this ability of a team to work together harmoniously is called chemistry.

In terms of educational background, a business degree with a marketing background is preferable. Sport management degrees, with several electives in business, are also desirable. Advanced degrees in business, law, or sport management are an advantage for the applicant.

LEARNING ACTIVITY

Using the same scenario outlined in the previous Learning Activity, interview an employee of a sport management and marketing agency to determine the steps in developing their career. What is their educational background? Did they do an internship? What is the scope of their duties on a day-to-day basis? Does the company offer internships or part-time employment? What do they look for in an entry-level person?

Clearly, the sport management and marketing agency segment of the sport economy is highly diverse and contains both generalists and specialists. While the personnel in larger sport management and marketing agencies are better able to function as specialists, those employed in smaller agencies must have a variety of skills and knowledge to perform their duties effectively. Skills essential to working in sport marketing and management agencies can be classified as organizational, technical, and people. Essential skills under each classification are provided in figure 16.2.

Challenges Facing Sport Management and Marketing Agencies

Although the sport management and marketing agency segment of the sport industry is growing in number of firms and job opportunities, agencies still face several difficult challenges in the years ahead. These challenges are similar to those encountered by advertising agencies, public relations firms, and similar enterprises. We can categorize them as follows.

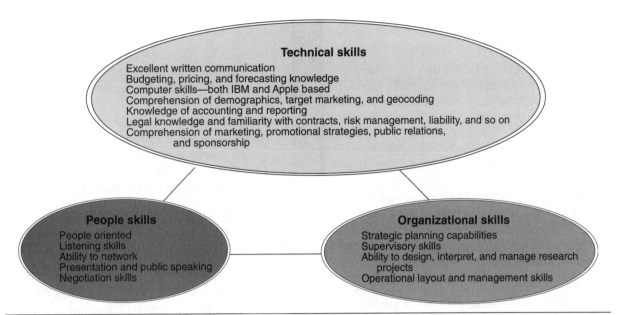

Excellent written communication
Budgeting, pricing, and forecasting knowledge
Computer skills—both IBM and Apple based
Comprehension of demographics, target marketing, and geocoding
Knowledge of accounting and reporting
Legal knowledge and familiarity with contracts, risk management, liability, and so on
Comprehension of marketing, promotional strategies, public relations,
     and sponsorship

People skills
People oriented
Listening skills
Ability to network
Presentation and public speaking
Negotiation skills

Organizational skills
Strategic planning capabilities
Supervisory skills
Ability to design, interpret, and manage research
     projects
Operational layout and management skills

Figure 16.2 Organizational, technical, and people skills essential for sport management and marketing agency personnel.

In-house Versus Outsourcing

Sometimes a sport management and marketing agency performs at a high level for a client for several years, at which time the client, feeling that he or she knows the functions that the agency performs, decides to dismiss the agency and bring that function in-house. This is a challenge for the agency because it might mean having to cut personnel and budgets as a result of losing the account. It might also mean losing a key staff member to the client who has hired that individual for his or her expertise and familiarity with the organization. This practice is becoming more prevalent in professional sport leagues, such as the NBA and NHL, and in collegiate athletics departments because of the need to maximize revenues. By bringing sponsorship, licensing, and broadcasting in-house instead of outsourcing them to agencies or hiring an outside agency to perform functions on their behalf, organizations feel that they will have more control and generate more income while cutting expenses (agency fees).

Labor Unrest

The recent labor strife in Major League Baseball, the National Hockey League, and the National Basketball Association created a situation in which sponsors and product manufacturers, two large revenue sources for agencies, have become reluctant to commit advertising dollars and resources to support broadcasts, special events, campaigns,

and endorsements to sports and players that could be on strike and thus out of the public's eye and interest. Agencies must therefore be prepared to develop contingency plans and show that these contingencies would be effective if implemented. Also, agencies may want to be prepared to help their clients become more diverse in their spending, thus averting dependence on one product or person.

Legislation and Judicial Review

In 1995 the Clinton administration worked with various federal agencies to eliminate tobacco and alcohol signage from sport stadia and arenas. This signage was commonplace in most professional athletics facilities throughout the United States, and agencies must determine a new course of action to provide exposure for their clients in these sports. They must also consider alternatives if such restrictions are broadened to include the auto racing industry, where tobacco and alcohol producers constitute a significant portion (if not the majority) of all sponsorship, **entitlement**, and signage at the facilities, on the cars, and on the drivers themselves. Could this situation be extended to beach volleyball and other sports that have significant ties with alcohol and tobacco?

entitlement—Associating the name of a sponsor with the name of an event or facility in exchange for cash or other considerations (e.g., the Mobil Cotton Bowl).

SUMMARY

A sport management and marketing agency is a business that acts on behalf of a sport property. Although these agencies were initially formed to represent athletes, they have evolved and now serve myriad functions, such as representation, negotiation, sales, licensing, marketing, and management. More than 1,000 companies are classified as sport management and marketing agencies. If quasi-agencies such as city and state sport commissions, divisions of leagues, and corporations such as Gatorade are included, the number of marketing and management firms exceeds 3,500. We can classify these agencies into the following four categories:

1. *Full-service agencies (e.g., the International Management Group)*—Provide a full range of services performed by in-house personnel.
2. *General agencies (e.g., 16W Marketing)*—Provide a variety of services to clients but are not involved in all potential agency functions.
3. *Specialty agencies (e.g., Bevilaqua International)*—Specialize in the type of services they provide or in the scope of clientele they serve.
4. *In-house agencies*—Departments of existing companies (e.g., Gatorade, NBA Attractions and Entertainment) that perform many sport marketing functions on behalf of the products or divisions of the parent company.

Personnel at larger sport marketing and management agencies tend to function as specialists, whereas those in smaller agencies need to have a greater variety of skills and knowledge. Degrees in business and sport management are preferred, with a background in marketing essential. Careers in sport and lifestyle management and marketing agencies are challenging and varied. Sport management and marketing agencies face several challenges in the coming years—in-house versus outsourcing, labor unrest, and legislative and judicial review.

REVIEW QUESTIONS

1. List and briefly describe the functions performed by sport management and marketing agencies.
2. Why is research and evaluation a crucial role performed by agencies?
3. How are specialty agencies different from full-service agencies?
4. What are some of the benefits of bringing functions such as sponsorship in-house instead of outsourcing to agencies?

Job Opportunities

Event Manager

Agency is looking for a well-qualified and experienced individual to be in charge of operational elements of a major professional golf tournament. Duties include logistics, designing and managing all corporate hospitality venues, planning and scheduling special events for sponsors and guests, scheduling and overseeing pre-event activities such as the Longest Drive competition and the Celebrity Pro-Am tournament.

Sponsorship Sales

West Coast agency is looking for experienced sales personnel to become members of a dynamic team-oriented sport marketing company. Client list includes several professional sport franchises, NASCAR, and professional golf. Successful candidates will have previous experience in sponsorship of media sales. Experience with Fortune 500 companies a plus.

Tournament Director

Aggressive East Coast sport marketing company is looking for an enthusiastic, outgoing individual with a strong tennis background to manage premier tennis events in Florida, Puerto Rico, and New York. Responsible for securing players, recruiting and training volunteers, scheduling officials, and working with broadcast and cable networks to ensure player availability. Fluency in Spanish, French, or German essential.

Agent

ProPlus, a 10-year-old firm specializing in representing and serving the needs of professional athletes, is searching for two new associates to join our team. Successful candidates will have advanced degrees in law, marketing, finance, or a combination thereof. Duties will include a combination of the following: contract negotiations, endorsements, financial management, appearances, and general consulting.

Product Placement

Large athletic footwear and apparel manufacturing company is seeking an individual to work with its agency of record to secure placement of athletic footwear and apparel products in major motion pictures and television programming. Individual should have a background in marketing or communications. Significant travel involved. Individual should have excellent communication skills and a familiarity with television and motion picture personalities and product use.

Market Research

Southwest sport marketing agency is looking for an individual with a background in marketing research to provide documentation to clients regarding the impact of sport and special events on product preference and use. Individual should have an advanced degree and training in both qualitative and quantitative research methods.

Sales Agent

NBA team searching for an individual to become part of an in-house agency to generate auxiliary income not directly related to the NBA franchise but using the assets of the franchise. Duties may include developing special events such as camps and clinics, and acquiring and marketing minor league franchises. Looking for experienced sales personnel—previous pro sport experience not essential but a plus. Looking for people who can think "outside the box."

REFERENCES

Bernstein, A. (2000, May 29-June 4). And the winner is . . . the top sports marketing agencies. *Street & Smith's SportsBusiness Journal*, 27, 37.

Bevilaqua International Inc. (1994). Corporate brochure and sales materials. Atlanta, GA: Author.

Conklin, M. (1994, January 25). Blackhawks' Chelios in spotlight as new ad rep for company. *The Chicago Tribune* (North Sports Final Edition), p. 7.

Conrad, E. (1995, January 10). NFL experience: Super Bowl-related bazaar will be running right next to JRS. *The Sun Sentinel* (Fort Lauderdale, Fla.), p. 10.

Cortez, J.P. (1992, June 1). Julius keeps the score for sports promotions: Leading marketers rely on consultancy's numbers. *Advertising Age*, 63(22), 10.

Crespo, M. (1995, February 14). You get more eyeballs: Satellite television sports. *Financial World*, 164(4), 94-98.

International Management Group. (2000). Corporate Report. Cleveland, OH: Author.

International Management Group. (2001). Corporate Report. Cleveland, OH: Author.

Lipsey, R.A. (Ed.). (2001). *Sports market place*. Princeton, NJ: Sportsguide.

Mahony, D., & Howard, D. (2001). Sport business in the next decade: A general overview of expected trends. *Journal of Sport Management, 15*, 275-296.

Menninger, B. (2000, May 29-June 4). Hidden hosts of big events. *Street & Smith's SportsBusiness Journal*, 32-33.

A new era in the NFL: Expansion '95. (1995). *Sport Magazine, 86*(9), 61.

Parascenzo, M. (1993, May 3). Prime time. *Business Week*, pp. 100-103.

Schreiber, A.L. (1994). *Lifestyle & event marketing*. New York: McGraw-Hill.

Schwartz, D. (2000, May 29-June 4). Super concierge to the Olympics, SportsMark claims its niche. *Street & Smith's SportsBusiness Journal*, p. 33.

Smothers, R. (1992, July 27). Barcelona Games start, and Atlanta is starting. *New York Times*, p. A13.

Chapter 17 _____

Sport Tourism

Heather Gibson, University of Florida

Since the mid-1990s there has been a growing emphasis on sport-related travel both in the sport and tourism industries and among academics as a topic for study. The Travel Industry Association of America (TIA), one of the foremost research agencies for tourism in the United States, conducted its first study specifically aimed at sport-related travel in 1999 (TIA, 1999). TIA estimated that between 1994 and 1999, 75.3 million U.S. adults traveled to take part in an organized sport event either as spectators or participants. Sport-related travel as a phenomenon stretches back over the centuries. The Greeks traveled to take part in the ancient Greek Games from as early as 900 B.C., and the Romans staged immensely popular sport competitions on a regular basis drawing large crowds of spectators (Coakley, 1990). However, in recent years, the term sport tourism has become more widely used to describe this type of tourism, and it has gradually become a specialized sector of the sport and tourism industries. Sport tourism as defined today encompasses three main types of travel and sport participation:

- *Active sport tourism*, a trip in which the tourist takes part in sport such as golf

- *Event sport tourism*, a trip in which the tourist watches a sport event such as the Super Bowl

- *Nostalgia sport tourism*, in which the tourist visits a sport-themed attraction such as the Baseball Hall of Fame in Cooperstown, New York (Gibson, 1998, a and b).

The purpose of this chapter is to explore the relationship between sport and tourism, to examine the three types of sport tourism, and to recognize some of the impacts of sport tourism such as environmental and sociocultural concerns. The intent is to provide future sport managers with an understanding of the symbiotic relationship between sport and tourism and to

LEARNING OBJECTIVES

After studying this chapter, you will be able to do the following:

1. Explain tourism and the tourism industry.
2. Describe the intersection between sport and tourism.
3. Distinguish among the three types of sport tourism: active, event, and nostalgia.
4. Discuss the sociocultural, economic, and environmental impacts of sport tourism.

present some of the issues related to this growing industry.

Tourism and the Tourism Industry

Tourism is the largest industry in the world. In 1998 it accounted for 8% of the world's gross domestic product and about 9% of the world's employment (World Tourism Organization, 1999). In the United States, tourism is the third largest retail industry behind automotive and food sales; in 1999 tourism was a $541.7 billion industry in the United States, generating about $82.6 billion in taxes. It is estimated that without the taxes generated from tourism each household would pay an additional $806 dollars in taxes per year (Travel Industry Association of America, 2000). The enormous size of the tourism industry is partly attributed to the range of services and products associated with it from airlines to rental cars, cruise ships to bus tours, campsites to five star resorts, and theme parks to national parks. Indeed, in one of the most widely used college textbooks on tourism, *Tourism: Principles, Practices, Philosophies,* Goeldner, Ritchie, and McIntosh (2000) proposed that any definition of tourism must include four components:

1. Tourists
2. Businesses providing goods and services for tourists
3. The government in a tourist destination
4. Host community, or the people who live in the tourist destination

The travel and tourism industry also encompasses a wide range of **traveler types**, from leisure travelers to business travelers to those visiting friends and relatives and a range of other reasons. In 1991 the World Tourism Organization (WTO), in an attempt to establish a standardized definition of tourism, proposed the following:

Tourism comprises the activities of persons traveling to and staying in places outside of their usual environment for not more than one consecutive year for leisure, business and other purposes.

If tourism constitutes the "*activities* of persons traveling," it would follow that a tourist is the individual who actually does the traveling outside of his or her home community. At the simple level this is correct; however, the defining characteristic of a tourist is not just the travel component. It also includes the reason or the motivation for the trip, the length of the trip, and even the distance traveled. One of the first organizations to define *tourist* was the United Nations Conference on International Travel and Tourism. In 1963 it defined international tourists as follows:

Temporary visitors staying at least 24 hours in the country visited and the purpose of whose journey can be classified under one of the following headings:

1. Leisure (recreation, holiday, health, study, religion, sport)

2. Business, family mission, meeting (IUTO, 1963)

traveler types—Different types of travelers from leisure tourists to business travelers or people visiting friends and family.

While the UN's definition of tourism appears to be consistent with the 1991 WTO definition, the two differ in breadth. Both encompass a wide range of travel possibilities, yet the question remains: Are all of them tourism? For many tourism scholars the answer is no. They would argue that tourists travel for leisure and that travel for business is a related but separate segment of the travel industry (Cohen, 1974; Pearce, 1985; Smith, 1989;

Yiannakis & Gibson, 1992). In the realm of sport tourism it would make sense to adopt the idea that a tourist is a leisure traveler because most sport-related trips constitute our everyday understanding of leisure as action that is intrinsically satisfying, noninstrumental in nature, and freely chosen within the constraints of an individual's everyday life (Kelly, 1999). Although most leisure scholars currently argue against thinking about leisure as totally separate from work (e.g., see Kelly & Freysinger, 2000), it might help us to think of sport tourism in terms of nonwork travel so as to be consistent with the definitions of tourism as leisure travel. Consequently, a sport tourist would be somebody who travels to play golf, to watch a favorite team play football, or to visit the newly renovated Basketball Hall of Fame in Springfield, Massachusetts, during a weekend or while on vacation or school break.

To help us further our understanding as to what constitutes a tourist, it is useful to look at Cohen's (1974) definition of tourist. Eric Cohen, one of the foremost sociologists studying tourism, proposed six characteristics of a trip associated with a tourist:

- *Temporary*—What length of trip constitutes "temporary"? Many definitions suggest that a person must be at least one night or 24 hours away from home to be defined as a tourist. Trips of less than 24 hours or day trips are usually referred to as excursions and the day-tripper as an excursionist (Goeldner et al., 2000).

- *Voluntary*—Here we get into the distinction between leisure travel and business travel. Are business travelers tourists? Those adopting a strict definition of the term would argue that they are not since tourism is leisure travel (Cohen, 1974; Yiannakis & Gibson, 1992). This line of thinking would fit with the voluntary nature of the trip as voluntary implies freedom of choice, which is a key element of leisure (Kelly, 1999).

- *Circular*—Complementing the idea of "temporariness," a tourist's journey encompasses a round-trip itinerary ending back home when the trip is over.

- *Distance*—Here we address the issue of how far a journey has to be in order to be classified as tourism. Some tourism agencies have specified distance; for example, the Canadian Travel Survey specifies that trips have to be at least 50 miles one way to be counted as tourism (Goeldner et al., 2000). In recent years many definitions of tourism now use such terminology as "traveling to and staying in places outside their usual environment"

(WTO, 1995) or home community instead of specifying a distance.

- *Nonrecurrent*—This characteristic addresses the ideas that tourism is viewed as "time out of the ordinary" (Graburn, 1989) and is a journey characterized by novelty and change (Cohen, 1974). So even though a person may drive to different locations every day for work, this is not considered a nonrecurrent trip since it isn't a novel experience.

- *Noninstrumental*—Cohen suggested that tourists are intrinsically motivated and they travel in search of novelty and change from their everyday routines. As such, tourism is pleasurable and not motivated by instrumental or external rewards such as money or prestige. Thus, according to Cohen, "a tourist is a voluntary, temporary traveler, traveling in the expectation of pleasure from the novelty and change experienced on a relatively long nonrecurrent round trip" (p. 533).

LEARNING ACTIVITY

Access an Internet search engine such as Yahoo or Google and type in the words *sport tourism* and see how many hits you find. Take a look at some of the Web sites, especially the ones linked to the national tourism organization for countries around the world. You will find that countries as diverse as Canada and Pakistan have sport tourism initiatives. You will also find universities around the world with specialist sport tourism degrees.

Defining Sport Tourism

Hinch and Higham (2001) wrote, "[l]ike most social science concepts, there are no universally accepted definitions of sport or tourism. . . . Each concept is rather amorphous and a variety of definitions have been developed to address a broad range of needs" (p. 46). Guided by Loy's (1968) definition of sport and Leiper's (1990) tourism attraction framework, the authors discuss some of the common themes among the existing definitions of sport tourism as follows:

- *Time dimension.* Sport tourism includes both the **sport excursionist** who travels away from home for less than 24 hours (e.g., on a day trip to go skiing) and the **sport tourist** who is away from home for more than 24 hours (e.g., on a weekend ski trip), where the time away is still temporary (Nogawa, Yamguchi, & Hagi, 1996).

- *Spatial dimension.* Travel takes participants outside of their home communities. This can involve travel to another town, state, or country (e.g., Gibson, 1998a; Hall, 1992; Hinch & Higham, 2001; Standeven & De Knop, 1999).

sport excursionist—Person who travels for sport and is away from home for less than 24 hours.

sport tourist—Person who travels for sport and is away from home for more than 24 hours.

- *Motivation.* The motivational debates concerning definitions of sport tourism center around the competitive nature of a sport and whether sport is the primary or secondary purpose of a trip. Taking a lead from Hall (1992) and later Hinch and Higham (2001), I would suggest that competition is best conceptualized on a continuum with minimal competition at one end and strong competition at the other. Does sport have to be the primary reason for the trip? I would concur with Gammon and Robinson (1997), who identify sport tourists as those whose primary motive for taking a trip is sport compared to what they call **tourism sport**, in which sport is a secondary motivation for taking the trip.

tourism sport—Persons participating in sport as a secondary activity. The trip is their prime motivation, not sport.

- *Form of the activity.* According to Hinch and Higham (2001), sport tourism is defined as "[s]port-based travel away from the home environment for a limited time, where sport is characterized by unique rule sets, competition related to physical prowess, and a playful nature" (p. 49). I have already suggested that competition is a motivation that can be placed on a continuum. Hinch and Higham suggested that physical prowess is another important characteristic used to define sport. I agree, since one of the major distinctions between sport and other activities is that sport requires physical movement in accordance with prescribed skills associated with a particular sport form. This leads us to a second characteristic of sport, what Loy (1968) called the **institutionalized rule set**. While the same sport can be played either in a formal setting with a referee and strict limitations on space and time or in an informal setting where space and time may be freely determined, the rules associated with that sport are consistent.

institutionalized rule set—Loy (1968) described this as the prescribed rules associated with a particular sport.

• *Behavior.* Most existing definitions of sport tourism distinguish between two types of behavior: *active,* in which an individual travels to take part in a sport, or *passive,* in which the individual travels to watch a sport (Hall, 1992; Hinch & Higham, 2001; Standeven & De Knop, 1999). Redmond (1991), in an innovative discussion about sport tourism, recognized the growing popularity of sport-themed destinations such as sport halls of fame, cruises in which tourists get to meet their favorite sport personalities, and sport stadia as tourist attractions. Like Redmond, I would argue that this type of sport tourism constitutes a third type of behavior motivated by nostalgia or a chance to worship a sport personality or stadium associated with a great team or event. I call this third type of behavior **nostalgia sport tourism**.

nostalgia sport tourism—Travel to visit sport halls of fame, sport-themed attractions such as cruises, or sport venues such as the Olympic Stadium in Sydney, Australia.

Thus, the working definition of sport tourism for this chapter will be one that has guided my work over the past five years. In 1998 I defined sport tourism as "leisure-based travel that takes individuals temporarily outside of their home communities to participate in physical activities [Active Sport Tourism], to watch physical activities [Event Sport Tourism], or to venerate attractions associated with physical activities [Nostalgia Sport Tourism]" (Gibson, 1998a, p. 49). Sport in this instance is characterized by differing degrees of competition, is associated with an institutionalized set of rules, and involves physical prowess associated with a specific sport form.

Active Sport Tourism

The first type of sport tourism is travel to take part in sport, or active sport tourism. De Knop (1987) suggested that tourism is changing. Tourists now want to be more active while on vacation. Part of this change can be attributed to the increasing sophistication of tourists and the response of the tourism industry in segmenting its product into specialized niche markets, one of which is sport tourism. Elliott-Spivak (1998), in writing about the growth of health spas in the United States, noted the "rapid expansion of health and fitness facilities connected to leisure travel experiences in the USA" (p. 68). In Aburdene and Naisbitt's (1992) book *Megatrends for Women,* Pat Halty, owner of an

Active sport vacations are increasing in popularity among tourists.

Courtesy of Susan J. Gavron, Bowling Green, OH

adventure travel company, said, "Baby boomers don't want to take a cruise and gain five pounds or 'veg out' on a beach. Lots of older people walk every day and like the idea of hiking instead of getting bussed from cathedral to cathedral" (p. 55). Writing in the travel pages of the *Hartford Courant*, Kathy Martin (1995) said "[i]n these fit times, you don't just stand around admiring exotic destinations; you hike, you float, climb, ski, trek, dive, sail, paddle, dogsled, horseback, mountain bike and sea kayak them" (p. 3). She went on to explain that you can now take an in-line skate tour around the foothills of the Rockies in Colorado.

De Knop (1987) suggested that sport participation on vacation is not a new trend. Taking a lead from his discussion about the growth of active sport tourism, a number of recent trends can be identified that might explain the increased popularity of active sport vacations.

• The range of sports offered to the tourist has increased from the more traditional sports of skiing, golf, and tennis to the newer offerings of mountain biking, snowboarding, organized cycling vacations, and learning how to drive a racing car. Even some of the national parks in the United States are using sport vacations to boost the number of visitors during their off-seasons. For example, Yellowstone National Park offers winter sport packages such as the "Experience Yellowstone: Yellowstone on Skis" package, which combines cross-country skiing with talks from naturalists about aspects of the park (Frommer, 2001).

• More individuals are choosing to take active sport vacations. We need to put this statement in context, however. The 1996 Surgeon General's Report on Physical Activity and Health (U.S. Dept. of HHS, 1996) lamented the lack of physical fitness among the general U.S. population. While people who are not regularly physically active at home may take part in sport on vacation (Standeven & De Knop, 1999), it is more likely that those who are active in sport in everyday life will be active sport tourists (Gibson, 1998b). Similarly, in a survey commissioned by Marriott International (Elrick & Lavidge, Inc., 1994), 22% of the respondents reported that opportunities to take part in sport are important when choosing a vacation. Standeven and De Knop estimated that sport tourism accounts for between 10 and 20 and 30% of the traveling public. This pattern was also noted in the United Kingdom by Mintel, who found that 10% of the domestic British special interest vacations taken in 2000 had sport as their primary purpose (Mintel, 2000).

• Around the world, awareness of sport vacations has grown. In Europe the term *activity holidays* (Foley & Reid, 1998) has been adopted to describe vacations encompassing activities Americans would associate with outdoor recreation such as hiking, sailing, and kayaking or resort-based sports such as scuba, tennis, and golf offered by specialist companies such as Mark Warner Holidays and Club Med. In the United States, companies such as Back Roads Active Vacations offer biking, walking, and hiking trips; ski resorts such as Stratton Mountain, Vermont, offer a summer golf school; and of course the warm weather resorts in Arizona, Florida, California, and so forth have long offered a range of sports from golf to tennis and various fitness activities. De Knop (1987) suggested that tourists are increasingly choosing particular resorts because of the sport facilities they offer. Redmond (1991) concurred with this and suggested that comprehensive sport and fitness facilities are becoming almost mandatory for any resort (p. 109). Since the 1980s hotel managers have increasingly realized that "fitness sells rooms" (Butwin, 1982, p. 115).

A review of some of the specific types of active sport tourism will illustrate the growth in opportunities for the active sport tourist. In addition, a look at some of the strategies being used by sectors of the tourism industry supports the idea that sport is increasingly being used to generate tourism.

Cruises

In recent years the cruise industry has begun to emphasize opportunities for both nostalgia sport tourism and **active sport tourism** through the use of themed cruises. Norwegian Cruise Lines launched its "Sports Afloat Program" in the late 1990s. Its promotion materials proclaim that "[w]e've got cruises for sports enthusiasts of all kinds: football, hockey, baseball, basketball, and volleyball." They even include motor sports (for more information, visit www.ncl.com). These cruises offer passengers the chance to take part in clinics, socialize with top athletes, and attend autograph sessions; as such, they fall into the realm of nostalgia sport tourism. Norwegian Cruise Lines also offers fitness cruises in which passengers can attend aerobics classes taught by top instructors, listen to health and fitness advice from top athletes and exercise experts, and use the extensive fitness and spa facilities on board the various ships.

The regular cruises also offer plenty of opportunities to take part in sport. For example, the *SS Norway* has four fitness directors on board who offer a program of team sports, aerobics, and nutrition classes. According to Cruise2.com, a Web site specializing in cruise travel planning and information, a typical day on board includes the opportunity to take part in 12 sport- and fitness-related activities including walking a mile on the Olympic track, aerobics classes, a table tennis tournament, and trap shooting (www.cruise2.com/SampleActivities). During ports of call most cruises offer passengers the chance to play golf. Indeed, on board Royal Caribbean Cruises' ship the *Legend of the Seas* there is even an 18-hole miniature golf course, and the *Voyager of the Seas* has a 40-by-60-foot ice rink. Even the prestigious *Queen Elizabeth 2* offers sport-themed cruises as part of its Spotlight Series on its transatlantic crossings. This series offers a range of programs targeted at special interests from sports to history and gardening.

active sport tourism—Travel to take part in sport, such as a golf vacation.

Amateur Sports

Amateur sport events have grown in recent years. These events are another of those crossover areas encompassing both active and event sport tourism. Amateur active sport events at the local, state, national, and even international levels are held throughout the year. Many community organizations host road races that attract not only local residents but also runners from outside of the community, both sport excursionists and active sport tourists (Nogawa et al., 1996). Of course, the major races such as the New York and Boston marathons are international events in which professional and amateur runners race side by side. However, lesser known races such as the Manchester Road Race in Connecticut held annually on Thanksgiving morning not only attract runners from local areas but often field people from all over the world including Europe and Africa.

Amateur sport events are held in a wide range of sports from archery to cycling, soccer to volleyball, swimming to rugby. Some of these events are multisport competitions and are targeted at various population segments. For example, the Junior Olympics holds regional and national events for young athletes, the Special Olympics has events for people with mental retardation, and the Transplant Games is for participants who have undergone transplant surgery. Since 1985 when the first Senior Games competition was held, over 250,000 athletes aged 50 and above have participated at the local, state, and national levels in a wide variety of sports (www.nsga.com). In a recent study conducted at the University of Florida (Gibson, Ashton-Shaeffer, Green, & Kessinger, 2002), "traveling to the different locations" and "meeting lots of new people" were cited by Senior Games participants as being important reasons for taking part in these events, as well as the chance to compete and participate in the various sports.

Another amateur sport event that draws participants from all over the world is the Gay Games. In an analysis of the lesbian and gay sport tourism industry, Pitts (1999) identified the Gay Games in particular as having "a positive impact on lesbian and gay sports participation travel" (p. 38) in terms of encouraging growth in the number of gay athletes traveling and the profusion of lesbian and gay sport events held each year.

Golf and Skiing

Over the past century two of the most popular forms of active sport tourism have been golf and snow sports, notably alpine or downhill skiing. Indeed, a representative for U.S. Airways explained that golf and skiing are the sport tourism foci for the airline. They fit their route structure to service these tourists during the appropriate seasons (Zachary, 1997). Interestingly, the growth in popularity of these two sports in the United States paralleled the development of transportation links, notably the railroad and building of resorts to accommodate the rail passengers.

In the 1890s and early 1900s when warm weather winter resorts began to grow in popularity first in California and then Florida, golf, the newly imported game from Scotland, found a home at some of these resorts. Khristine Januzik, of the Tufts Archives at Pinehurst in North Carolina, explained that "nobody put sports with resorts in those days" (cited in Ladd, 1995, p. 8) since the main attractions were the warm weather, eating, drinking, and socializing. However, two resort developers with considerable foresight, Henry Flagler and James Tufts Walker, commissioned golf courses for their two new resorts, the Breakers in Florida and Pinehurst in North Carolina, respectively. While both men faced much derision over their decisions to build 18-hole golf courses, just over a century later resort designer John Hill explained that "a resort hotel plus a good golf course adds a great deal of residual value to the property's land value" (Morse & Lanier, 1992, p. 46). Moreover, according to the North Carolina Travel Guide (NC Travel and Tourism Division, 1995), the Southern Pines-Pinehurst Area is now called the "golf capital of the world" (p. 105).

With the boom in golf through the late 1980s and 1990s (Aburdene & Naisbitt, 1992), Waters (1989) noted an increasing willingness of golfers to travel long distances to resorts with good golf courses. This also extends to international travel; many Japanese golfers come to the United States to play since their own courses are expensive (frequently costing several hundreds of U.S. dollars for one round) and the number of courses is limited due to a lack of space for building new facilities in the country (Pleumarom, 1992). Indeed, as Gee, Makens, and Choy (1989) pointed out, "[t]ravel for golf has spawned a major industry of hotels, resorts and even a golf museum.... Pinehurst, North Carolina; Palm Springs, California; and Myrtle Beach, South Carolina owe much of their success as visitor destinations to golf" (p. 372).

Today there are 26.7 million golfers (age 12 and over), including 6.3 million avid golfers (who play 25 or more rounds a year) in the United States and 17,108 golf courses, many of which are located in the southern United States in resort destinations (www.ngf.org). Not surprisingly, as Priestly (1995) pointed out, there is a correlation between the total number of golfers in a country and the number of golf tourists. The more golfers a country has, the more golf tourists it has. Moreover, when golfers live in areas with harsh winter climates or a lack of facilities, they are more likely to travel to pursue their sport, with many harboring a dream to play a round at the ultimate mecca of golf, the Old Course at St. Andrews in Scotland.

The development of downhill skiing in the United States shares many similarities with golf and golf tourism. In the 1930s the first cold weather resorts emerged as the popularity of alpine skiing grew. Sun Valley, Idaho, was the first all-inclusive ski resort in the United States and was designed as a way of increasing passenger numbers on the new westward expansion of the railroad. Subsequently, ski resorts in Aspen and Vail, Colorado; Park City, Utah; and Lake Tahoe, California, among others followed. Comparable to golf's geographical association with regions in the United States, these towns became synonymous with skiing.

However, unlike golf, which is slated to grow in popularity with the aging population (Aburdene & Naisbitt, 1992), participation in alpine skiing peaked during the 1970s, plateaued during the 1980s, and

began to decline in the 1990s (National Sporting Goods Association, 2000). Waters (1989) attributed the decline partly to the aging population and partly to the popularity of snowboarding among the younger generations. From 1992 to 1998 the number of snowboarders increased from 1.2 million to 3.6 million, while the number of skiers declined from 10.8 million to 7.7 million in the same period (National Sporting Goods Association, 2000). During the 1980s many ski resorts banned snowboarding, but as the number of skiers continued to decline, ski resorts began to actively court snowboarders by providing terrain parks and specialized lessons. In 2001 the famed Ajax Mountain in Aspen, Colorado, finally succumbed to the popularity of the snowboard and opened the mountain to both skiers and snowboarders (Kenworth, 2001).

Faced with stagnant growth, the ski industry has been engaged in an aggressive marketing campaign targeting families and the foreign skier over the past 10 years (Rowan & Sandberg, 1990). Like many other segments of the tourism industry, resort managers realized that in order to maintain profitability they had to combat **seasonality**. Seasonality refers to the variable patterns of visitation throughout the year at a destination. Most destinations have three seasons, a peak season, a shoulder season (which occurs just before and just after the peak), and an off-season. Ski resorts in particular have a definite season (winter), with fall and spring skiing on either side. With the decline in the number of skiers it became apparent at the start of the 1990s that there was an acute need to combat the effects of seasonality in order to remain profitable. Many ski areas added all-weather indoor and outdoor activities and facilities and actively targeted the convention market and nonskiing vacations (U.S. Travel Data Center, 1989). Thus, as Roger Cox noted in *Tennis Magazine*, Vermont is now the perfect summer tennis destination with many mountain resorts offering golf, tennis, and mountain biking facilities, among others (Cox, 1995).

seasonality—The variable patterns of tourist visitation throughout the year at a destination. Most destinations have three seasons: a peak season, a shoulder season (which occurs just before and just after the peak), and an off-season.

Becoming year-round destinations was not enough for many family-owned resorts, however. Faced with rising costs due to aging lift equipment, rising liability insurance rates, and the need for

343

snowmaking equipment, many independent resorts merged with or were acquired by one of four corporations: the American Skiing Company, Intrawest, Vail Resorts Inc., and Booth Creek, that emerged as the major players in the North American ski industry (Cohen, 1998). Cohen reported that 8% of the annual skier/snowboarder visits in North America now occur at Intrawest-owned ski resorts. Moreover, in partnering with the French Compagnie des Alpes (CDA), in 1998, Intrawest created an intercontinental ski conglomerate and actively targeted British skiers, enticing them to North America. In recent years, aided by a favorable currency exchange rate, North America now attracts 20% of the British ski market (Poon & Adams, 2000) and is the second most popular ski destination to France for Britons.

Thus, while the number of domestic skiers continues to decline, the ski industry has actively targeted the destination skier, the active sport tourist who spends more than a day at the resort, purchasing accommodation, food, and transportation as well as lift tickets in order to maintain its profitability in the 21st century. Moreover, golf and skiing continue to forge a closer relationship. Not only do ski resorts use golf to combat seasonality, but they also have begun to diversify their holdings. Intrawest, for example, now owns golf resorts in Florida and Arizona.

LEARNING ACTIVITY

Form a group of three or four students. Your group is on the planning and development committee of a new active sport tourism destination. This destination can be resort based such as a skiing or golf resort, a small-scale outfitter offering scuba or water-based trips, or any other fictitious active sport tourism company of your choice. Applying your knowledge of sport tourism, address the following issues:

1. Briefly describe your active sport tourism operation. Provide details about geographic location, climate, size, transportation, accommodations, and so on.

2. Who is likely to be your target market? Provide a demographic profile. Also include some information about the mode of participation that your destination or operation is likely to cater to (e.g., hard core, recreational/intermediate [i.e., not so committed to the activity], and beginners).

3. What might be some the potential barriers for tourists considering your destination or operation?

4. How might you encourage a wider participant base for your destination or operation than the typical profile you identified in question 2 (e.g., more diverse in race, age, gender, etc.)? This might include programming ideas.

5. How might your operation "give back" to the host community?

Once you have finished discussing each of these issues, write out your plan of action making sure that the proposed strategy is consistent with the type of operation and your potential client base. Present your plan of action to the class and be ready to defend and justify any ideas you have proposed.

Event Sport Tourism

The second type of sport tourism pertains to sport events as tourist attractions and the sport tourists who travel to watch them. In an attempt to combat seasonality and to create a **destination image**, towns and cities around the United States and the world are increasingly hosting sport events, from hallmark events such as the Olympics and World Cup Soccer to more regional events such as PGA golf tournaments or NCCA-sanctioned college sports to amateur events such as road races and the Senior Games, which draw spectators as well as active sport tourists. The competition among communities to host these events is intense as community leaders focus on the economic impact from event patrons, sponsorship deals, and television rights in the case of the major events (Ritchie, 1999). In recent years, as the **synergy** between sport and tourism has been recognized more readily (Standeven, 1998), community leaders are increasingly looking to generate tourism by developing a destination image through hosting sport events. In examining event sport tourism, it is useful to think about two levels: the **mega-event** or **hallmark event** that draws international attention and the **small-scale sport event** (Higham, 1999).

destination image—The impression people (especially potential tourists) hold of a certain location.

synergy—The interaction between two components, such as tourism and sport.

mega-event or hallmark event—A world-class event such as the Olympics or a world's fair.

small-scale sport event—A regular season sport event, such as amateur and youth tournaments and college sports.

Hallmark Events

Ritchie (1984) defined hallmark events as follows:

Major one-time or recurring events of limited duration, developed primarily to enhance the awareness, appeal and profitability of a tourism destination in the short and/or long term. Such events rely for their success on uniqueness, status, or timely significance to create interest and attract attention. (p. 2)

Hallmark events include world's fairs, carnivals and festivals such as Mardi Gras in New Orleans, important cultural or religious events such as a British royal wedding, and major sport events such as the Olympics or America's Cup sailing championship. Ritchie further added the criteria of "relative infrequency," "uniqueness" of the event, "aura of tradition," "excellence" in participants, and international attention (p. 3). For sport, the ultimate hallmark event is the Olympic Games, both summer and winter.

McFee (1990) observed, "the Olympic Games have become less and less a sporting event and more and more a tourist spectacle" (p. 147). He went on to explain that the idea of the Olympics as a tourist attraction is nothing new. Burton Holmes, an American in attendance at the first modern Olympics in Athens, Greece, commented, "the chief interest of the Olympic Games of 1896 lay in the splendid setting given them rather than in the Games themselves" (McFee, 1990, p. 147). When the United States held the FIFA World Cup Soccer Finals in 1994, the expressed intent was to bill them as a tourist event and not just a sport event (World Cup Soccer, 1993). Soon after FIFA announced that the United States would host the World Cup, the undersecretary of commerce for travel and tourism announced that "World Cup '94 [would] generate billions of dollars in tourism revenue and commercial activity, and is an opportunity for the world to experience the beauty and diversity of America" (World Cup Soccer, 1993, p. 4).

Similarly, at the U.S. Olympic Committee site visit to evaluate Tampa, Florida, as a potential host site for the 2012 Summer Olympics, the message put forth by the bid organizers was that central Florida's existing position as one of the world's top tourism destinations would be a major advantage in hosting the Olympics ("Tampa 2012," 2001). The region not only had the existing infrastructure in terms of hotels and airport facilities, but it already had an image around the world as a desirable tourism destination. Moreover, with 30,000 travel agents already marketing Florida, the 2012 Games had the potential to be the most heavily attended games ever.

The concept of destination image is one that drives many communities to invest so much in hosting one event. Crompton (1979) developed one of the most widely used definitions. He suggested that destination image is "the sum of beliefs, ideas and impressions that a person has of a destination" (p. 18). The image a destination has is important because it can influence whether tourists choose to visit a particular location (Crompton, 1979). If they do visit and there is a discrepancy between the images they hold and their actual experiences (Fakeye & Crompton, 1991), this may ultimately affect their feelings of satisfaction with their vacation. Tourist satisfaction is important since dissatisfied tourists may not only decide against future visits to a destination but may also influence family and friends against doing so. Word of mouth is an influential factor in vacation decision making as people listen to the opinions of people they know and trust. Dissatisfied tourists can persuade others not to choose a particular destination for a vacation (Goeldner et al., 2000).

Ritchie and Smith (1991) explained that many event planners work under the assumption that the increased awareness of a location following the hosting of an event will lead to increased tourism in the years following the event. The extent to which this occurs is open to debate. Ritchie (1999) suggested that many of the impressions people hold about a destination are tied to its level of competence in handling a major event and its perceived attractiveness. Transportation efficiency, environmental impacts, ticket distribution, and cost are all associated with this image. The extent to which event organizers can "react with competence and grace" to the unexpected problems is crucial (p. 12). For example, many people still remember the transportation difficulties associated with the 1996 Atlanta Olympic Games, a fact that was revisited by journalists in the opening days of the 2000 Sydney Olympic Games (NBC, 2000).

Much of Ritchie's research has been a longitudinal study of the tourism-related impacts of the 1988 Winter Games held in Calgary (e.g., Ritchie, 1999; Ritchie & Aitken, 1984; Ritchie & Lyons, 1990; Ritchie & Smith, 1991). In a study of the image of Canada and its cities and provinces among U.S. and European residents, Ritchie and Smith found that awareness of Calgary increased significantly during the Olympic year and the year following. In comparison, recognition of other Canadian cities such as Edmonton remained relatively stable over the four years of data collection. The authors concluded that hosting the Winter Games certainly raised the profile of Calgary among people around the world. However, only a year after the Games, this image was beginning to fade. The authors suggested that tourism officials in a region need to be aware of this decrease in image and take active measures with promotional campaigns.

Unfortunately, as Roche (1994) observed, "Mega-events (large scale leisure and tourism events such as Olympic Games and World Fairs) are short-term events with long-term consequences for cities that stage them" (p. 1). In a broadcast in conjunction with the 2002 Winter Olympics in Salt Lake City, ABC provided an update on the Nagano, Japan, site of the 1998 Winter Games (ABC, 2002). The games cost Nagano $10 billion, and the city was currently in debt. The facilities cost $1 million in operations and maintenance per year, and the revenue generated from renting them out for events had only brought in one-tenth of these costs. The bullet train built so that Olympic spectators could easily access the Games meant that skiers were now coming on day trips and not staying overnight in hotels, which resulted in a loss of revenue for the community. A Nagano resident said, "the Olympics made things great for a while, but it's been downhill since." Another said, "[our advice to Salt Lake is] enjoy it while you can."

Stories such as this are more common than not in the aftermath of mega-events. While communities continue to vie with one another to host them, there is a growing realization that hosting smaller-scale events might be more beneficial. Indeed, Ritchie (1999) raised the question as to whether recurring events such as the Boston Marathon or the Calgary Stampede are not more valuable to a community than one-time events such as the Olympics. Maybe the long-term impacts of hosting mega-events lies elsewhere in improved infrastructure and community pride rather than increased tourism visitation.

Small-Scale Event Sport Tourism

While mega-events such as the Olympics are regarded as the pinnacle for a community in terms of hosting a sport event, Higham (1999) suggested that we should pay more attention to what he calls "small-scale sports events" as they may provide communities with more benefits and fewer burdens than the short-lived hallmark events. He defined small-scale sport events as "regular season sporting competitions (ice hockey, basket-ball, soccer, rugby leagues), international sporting fixtures, domestic competitions, Masters or disabled sports, and the like" (p. 87). He suggested that small-scale sport events usually operate within a community's existing infrastructure, require minimal investment in terms of public money, are more manageable in terms of crowding and congestion, and may minimize the effects of seasonality for a destination. Indeed, following the Dallas/Fort Worth failed bid to host the 2012 Olympic Games, Sean Wood of the *Fort Worth Star-Telegram* suggested that the $8 billion generated from hosting amateur sport events each year might be more lucrative than the Olympics in the long run (Wood, 2001).

Many sport events around the United States fit the definition of small-scale, from professional and college-level sports to amateur sport events such as the Senior Games and Special Olympics, which represent that crossover between active and event sport tourism discussed earlier. One form of small-scale sport tourism event with much untapped potential is college sports. In an interview with the owner of a clothing and souvenir shop in Gainesville, Florida, home of the University of Florida Gators, Fisher (2000) found that the shop averaged 1,500 sales on a home football game day compared with 25 sales per day in the off-season. In a newspaper article preceding the University of Texas versus Oklahoma football game in October 2001, the game was seen as a relief for the Dallas area tourism industry following September 11, 2001. Dave Whitney, president of the Dallas Convention and Visitors Bureau, said the 100,000 visitors "will spend between $15 million and $17 million" in what "is always a big weekend for us" (Alm, 2001). Other communities around the United States also likely experience similar economic impacts from hosting college sport events.

Irwin and Sandler (1998) conducted one of the first academic studies on the tourism-related effects of college sport in the United States. They investigated the travel planning behaviors and expenditures of 1,646 fans attending 10 NCAA championships. As might be expected, fans spent most of their trip expenditures on accommodation and retail shopping. The authors also found that fans who were affiliated with a team participating in the championships (compared to unaffiliated spectators) spent an average of 6% more money per day and tended to stay longer at the destination. Irwin and Sandler recommended that community tourism agencies work closely with universities to market events actively and provide more information about the destination to potential event sport tourists.

One such community tourism agency that should work more closely with universities is the **convention and visitors bureau (CVB)** or the chamber of commerce. A CVB is a community agency funded by the "bed tax" or the local taxes you pay when you stay in a hotel or other commercial lodging facility. The responsibility of a CVB is to promote tourism in a community and to act as a centralized source of information about events, accommodations, and other visitor-related information.

Another local agency responsible for the development of small-scale event sport tourism is a **sports commission**. Some sports commissions are independent, nonprofit organizations, some are divisions of local convention and visitors bureaus, and others are government agencies at the city, county, or state level. In 1992, when the National Association of Sports Commissions (NASC) was established, there were 15 members; just 10 years later there are more than 280 members. This is not just a testament to the growth of the NASC, but to the realization among communities of the tourism potential associated with hosting sport events.

If we look at some of the events hosted by the Gainesville Sports Organizing Committee (GSOC) during 2000 we can see some of the potential that small-scale event sport tourism has for communities. To put these events in context, the city of Gainesville, Florida, has a population of 101,405 residents (North Central Florida Almanac, 2001) and approximately 4,500 hotel rooms available (Alachua County, 2002). The GSOC hosted 16 events in 2000, including the Gainesville Area Rowing Spring Regatta with 1,400 participants and 1,000 spectators over two days; the Florida High School Sports Association Track and Field Championships with 4,500 participants and 4,000 spectators over five days; and the Buy.com Florida Classic (professional golf), which attracted 5,000 spectators over five days. The crossover between active sport tourism and event sport tourism is evident in the numbers of participants and spectators at these events. High school sports, amateur sports, and regional professional events also fall under the umbrella of small-scale event sport tourism.

convention and visitors bureau (CVB)—A community agency funded by the "bed tax" or the local taxes paid from stays in commercial lodging facilities such as hotels. A CVB promotes tourism in a community and acts as a centralized source of information about events, accommodations, and other visitor-related information.

sports commission—Local or state agency responsible for attracting sport events to help communities capitalize on the potential benefits of sport tourism.

There is a growing recognition in communities around the United States and the world that, while hosting the Olympics may be out of the question, hosting small-scale sport events is a possibility. Even Walt Disney World in Florida recognized the value of the tourism potential associated with sport tourism by opening Disney's Wide World of Sports in 1997, which caters to both active and event sport tourism (see the sidebar on page 348).

For sport to become a successful strategy for tourism development, communities must learn to **leverage** the events. Leveraging entails using strategies to optimize the benefits or outcomes associated with an event. For example, in a study of the Honda Gold Coast Indy race in Australia, which is an annual event attracting 250,000 spectators over four days, Chalip and Leyns (2002) found that, out of the 22 business owners and managers they interviewed, only eight actively leveraged the event. The overwhelming attitude was that the "Indy promotes itself" (Chalip & Leyns, 2002). As more communities turn to event sport tourism as an economic and community development strategy, they replace the "if we build it, they will come" attitude with increased cooperation between sport and tourism agencies so that all of the potential benefits of an event are realized and the negatives are alleviated. (See chapters 10 on sport marketing and chapter 13 on event management for more details.) As Higham (1999) suggested, for event sport tourism to be successful, "it is important to recognize the need to attract or develop sporting events that complement the scale, infrastructure and resourcing capabilities of the host city" (p. 89). Getz (1997) suggested that perhaps "destinations should also think carefully about developing an appropriate and attractive *portfolio* of sport events in which the occasional mega-event . . . is balanced by bidding on lesser, occasional events and periodic local or regional-scale events" (p. 62).

leverage—Using strategies to optimize the benefits or outcomes associated with an event.

Nostalgia Sport Tourism

The third type of sport tourism is nostalgia sport tourism. Redmond (1991) identified a type of

Walt Disney World Florida: The Ultimate Sport Tourism Destination

Since 1997 Walt Disney World (WDW) in Orlando, Florida, has become an important venue for sport tourism in the state of Florida with the opening of its Disney's Wide World of Sports Complex. This venue contains world-class facilities for hosting a range of sport events from baseball and beach volleyball to basketball and gymnastics. The Milk House, the indoor venue, has over 30,000 square feet of space for competitions and seating for 5,000 spectators. Similarly, the tennis complex has 11 courts and room for 1,000 spectators with the capability of expanding seats to accommodate 7,500 people when hosting a professional event. The baseball stadium is the spring training venue for the Atlanta Braves and home of the minor league team the Orlando Rays. However, most of the sport events held at Disney's Wide World of Sport are youth and adult amateur competitions. These include the Pop Warner National Football Championships, high school field hockey championships, NCCA women's basketball, and the Transplant Games. The strategy behind Disney's Wide World of Sports is to use sport to promote its core product, the theme parks. Athletes and spectators are actively encouraged to visit the parks during their stay. In fact, theme park tickets are packaged with tournament fees and on-site hotel accommodation. Just as many communities in the United States have realized that youth and amateur sport events bring both athletes and families to their towns and cities, Disney uses the same strategy to attract more guests to their theme parks, thereby using sport tourism as a way of leveraging additional theme park tourism.

The Wide World of Sports Complex uses volunteer "sports enthusiasts" to help run the larger events. On event days, guests can participate in the NFL Experience, a simulated football training camp. Boston's Northeastern University even has a branch of its Center for the Study of Sport in Society housed within the complex, thereby providing research for use by the center and WDW. Moreover, on the WDW resort properties as a whole there are ample opportunities for guests to take part in sports whether playing a round of golf on one of the five championship courses, playing tennis on the 12 clay or 8 hard courts, or jet boating across the lagoon in the specially designed two-person water mouse boats. The Richard Petty Driving Experience helps guests realize their dreams of being a NASCAR driver. In September each year WDW even hosts the Danskin Triathlon for women, which entails swimming across the lagoon, running around the Magic Kingdom, and biking around Epcot. At the Disney Institute the auditorium has been used to host forums where fans get a chance to listen to and interact with their favorite athletes. There has even been talk of hosting sport-themed cruises on the Disney Cruise Lines. At the end of the day guests can watch their favorite athletes on the TV screens of ESPN Zone, which is part of the Board Walk shops and restaurants. Thus, in its diversity of sport tourism offerings, WDW provides opportunities for active, event, and nostalgia sport tourism in conjunction with visiting the four theme parks.

sport tourism that involves travel to visit sport halls of fame, taking sport-themed vacations on cruise ships or resorts, attending fantasy sport camps, and touring around famous sport stadia. In spring and summer 2001, the credit card company MasterCard had an advertising campaign showcasing the journey of two friends in a VW bus touring around the 30 major league baseball parks in the United States. This type of trip for a nostalgia sport tourist might be regarded as a dream vacation and a once-in-a-lifetime trip. Other nostalgia sport vacations might be more commonplace and involve such activities as visiting Cooperstown, home of the National Baseball Hall of Fame and Museum (www.baseballhalloffame.org), the LPGA Hall of Fame (www.worldgolf.com/wglibrary/history/lpgahoff.html), or the sport venues for the 2002 Salt Lake Winter Games (which incidentally were open to the public for over six years before the Games began).

Most Olympic and major sport stadia provide tours so that visitors can see behind the scenes from the locker rooms to the press boxes and the VIP seating. Somebody who can provide in-depth information about the venue and the history behind it generally guides these tours. On a tour of Stadium Australia, home of the 2000 Summer Games, visitors can even stand on a medal podium and pose for a photograph. In the United Kingdom, soccer fans of a particular team can not only visit the football grounds but also meet the players and relive significant events in the team's history. Manchester United, one of the perennial top teams in the English Football (soccer) League, pioneered these tours. In the United States, Sports Travel and Tours specializes in baseball tours. Their itineraries, usually include four or more major league games with the northeast itineraries including a side trip to Cooperstown, thereby combining both event and nostalgia sport tourism (www.sportstravelandtours.com).

Another trend over the past 10 years or so has been adult fantasy sport camps. Michael Jordan hosts a basketball fantasy camp in Las Vegas providing fans a chance to play basketball with him. Golf, baseball, football, and NASCAR all have fantasy sport camps where fans can spend a week or a weekend celebrating the sport of their choice. Walt Disney World in Florida has the Richard Petty Driving Experience, and in the lead-up to the 2002 Winter Games, the Salt Lake Ice Center even hosted a Zamboni driving fantasy camp.

Nostalgia sport tourism is a relatively underdeveloped area of study, yet the growing popularity of this type of tourism suggests that we need to pay more attention to it. Redmond and Snyder are two of the few scholars who have investigated sport tourism associated with sport museums and halls of fame (Lewis and Redmond, 1974; Redmond, 1973; Snyder, 1991). Redmond (1973) suggested that the "the ultimate *raison d'être* for a sports hall of fame, like the ancient Greek statuary, is the glorification of sporting heritage" (p. 42). Gammon (2001) explored the nostalgia sport tourism associated with the sport fantasy camp. He suggested that "fantasy camps provide both the opportunity to relive the past and the propensity to rewrite it" (Gammon, 2001, p. 6).

In agreement with these researchers, I would hypothesize that this form of tourism appears to be motivated by the need for nostalgia and heritage and may be related to a growing niche in tourism, that of heritage tourism. While heritage tourism is nothing new in itself, as Smith (1989) observed, many tourists engage in what she called "the museum and cathedral circuit" touring the "glories of the past." Just like sport tourism, heritage tourism emerged through the 1990s as a specialized niche market with regions of the world such as the United Kingdom specializing in this form of tourism (Watson & Kopachevsky, 1994). The question to be asked by researchers is, Why has nostalgia sport tourism become so popular in recent years? Is it because sport-themed vacations are more prevalent, or as a growing body of literature in tourism studies postulates, the need for nostalgia has become more important for people in the late 20th and early 21st centuries (Dann, 1994; Davis, 1979; Fowler, 1992). Wilson (1999) observed, "nostalgia oozes out of our popular culture. Even those of us who have not experienced a particular decade (e.g., the fabulous '50s or the turbulent '60s) find ourselves looking back to those eras with fondness" (p. 296).

Dann (1994) suggested: "[t]oday a great deal of time and energy is dedicated to looking backwards, toward capturing a past which, in many ways is considered superior to the chaotic present and the dreaded future" (p. 55). This raises the question, Why has the past become more highly valued than the future? Urry (1990) spoke of a "postmodern museum culture" (p. 107) in which almost anything can be found in a museum, from a Tupperware exhibit at the Smithsonian in Washington, D.C., to Jack Nicklaus's fly-fishing rod at the World Golf Hall of Fame in Florida. Dann postulated that due to the rapid changes brought about by technology in the mid- to late 20th century, nostalgia may help people deal with the uncertainty of postmodern life in which many things are unfamiliar. Heritage tourism sites provide us with familiarity and a sense "that we have seen it before" (p. 40).

Similarly, Bale (1988) discussed two concepts that are linked to identity: **place attachment** and **place pride**. In terms of place attachment, he postulated that in Western societies sport might have become a major forum for collective identity, especially as the increased pace of life prevents many people from being active in community life (Schor, 1991). Identifying with a sport team and attending games with thousands of other fans can be a major source of personal and collective identity. Place pride is generated by success in sport and the pride or psychic income a community has in its teams or athletes. Bale discussed the place pride evident in Clemson, South Carolina, home of the Clemson University Tigers, and the degree to which the town is decorated in the university colors, how sporting successes are documented on road signs as you enter the town, and the prevalence of tiger paw prints (the Clemson insignia) throughout the community.

place attachment—The sense of identity people develop with a location based on a sport team or figure.

place pride—The feelings of pride people have in their community arising out of the success of their local sport teams or athletes.

In our Gator football study, many of the fans referred to Gainesville as the mecca and described their journeys as pilgrimages (Gibson, Willming,

Courtesy of the Toledo Mud Hens Baseball Team

The home of the Toledo Mud Hens baseball team is Fifth Third Field in downtown Toledo, Ohio. Fans of a particular team can develop place attachment by identifying with that team and attending games with other fans.

The World Golf Hall of Fame: A Case Study in Nostalgia Sport Tourism

The World Golf Hall of Fame part of the World Golf Village is located 15 minutes from St Augustine, Florida. Since the World Golf Hall of Fame opened in 1998, more than one million visitors have walked through the 18 thematic areas that emulate an 18-hole golf course. Visitors are taken on a guided or self-guided tour through the history of golf from its beginnings in Scotland to its introduction and development in the United States to the technology now required to broadcast the top tournaments to viewers around the world. Each of the themed areas provides photos and narrative about historical developments in the game of golf. An 1880s style putting green complete with replica putters of the time allows visitors to try their hand at sinking a shot without the aid of today's high-tech equipment. A video golf swing analysis enables visitors to match their technique to the top player they most resemble. Tourists can have their photos taken atop a replica of the Swilkern Bridge on the 18th hole at St. Andrews or feel the pressure of television cameras and a crowd in the viewing gallery as they try to sink the championship putt. Shell Hall contains 84 crystal spheres commemorating the men and women who have been inducted into the hall of fame. Along the opposite wall are computer terminals where visitors can spend hours accessing databases documenting the career of each of the 84 inductees. Before leaving to try their hand at the 18-hole putting course or the 132-yard Challenge Hole, which offers the chance to experience hitting a shot to the Island Green hole number 17 at the famed Tournament Players Club, visitors can ascend the 190-foot memorial tower. The tower offers a panoramic view of the World Golf Village complete with shops, IMAX theater, resort hotels, golf courses, and homes for the golf enthusiast. While the hall of fame certainly provides for the nostalgia sport tourist, the golf courses and the PGA Tour Golf Academy provide opportunities for active sport tourism, and events such as the Senior Tour's Liberty Mutual Legends of Golf Tournament provide opportunities for event sport tourism. Thus, as a print advertisement for the World Golf Village says, "Built for those of you who think about golf morning, noon and night."

& Holdnak, 2002). Fans, many of whom have come from out of town, can be spotted throughout the year walking around the Swamp (Ben Hill Griffin Stadium) on the University of Florida campus. Bale argued that some sport facilities "can develop, over time, a sufficient mystique to become tourist attractions in their own right" (p. 120). As we noted earlier, tours of famous sport venues have been popular tourist attractions for years. Indeed, Hanis (2000) commented, "[w]ith several cities retiring classic stadiums and opening new ones, interest in baseball theme vacations is high" (p. 60). Even Fodor's, the tour book publisher, has a guide book titled *Baseball Vacations: Great Family Trips to Minor League and Classic Major League Ballparks Across America.* Perhaps Bales's thoughts about the mystique accompanying these "shrines" might help in our understanding of nostalgia sport tourism.

Understanding the Sport Tourist

In our look at the three types of sport tourism we have made some references to motivations and the preferences of certain age groups for different sports such as skiing and golf. For a researcher like myself who is interested in leisure behavior and the meanings associated with participating in sport and taking vacations, I tend to focus on the motivations of sport tourists and the influence of sociostructural characteristics such as gender and social class on their choice of behavior. In chapter 6, Sociological Aspects of Sport and Physical Activity, and chapter 7, Psychology of Sport Consumer Behavior, you have already read about many of the concepts we use to understand patterns of participation in sport. In understanding the sport tourist, we use many of the same concepts to understand behavior. For the future managers and marketers among you, this means understanding the needs and characteristics of your customers.

Sociodemographic Characteristics of Sport Tourists

A consistent finding in various studies over the years suggests that active sport tourists in particular tend to be relatively affluent, college educated, white, and male (Gibson, 1998b; Schreiber, 1976; Tabata, 1992). Indeed, Jo Gosline, sales manager of the National Golf Foundation, reported that "traveling golfers are relatively affluent; almost one third have annual household incomes greater than $50,000" (Morse & Lanier, 1992, p. 44). Likewise, in an early study of active sport tourists, Schreiber (1976) found that "the sports traveler is more affluent, better educated and more active than the traveler in general" (p. 86). While this may be good news for the upscale resorts and the sport and tourism industries in general, we may also need to question why women, minorities, and individuals from lower socioeconomic strata tend not to be active sport tourists. As Kidd (1996) argued, "despite the myth of sport as the great equalizer, participation is still heavily dependent upon the financial resources and cultural capital that class background

brings and this is structured by gender, ethnicity, and race" (p. 232).

From a social justice perspective, in line with the trends toward socially responsible marketing and business practices (Bright, 2001; Hoffman, 1999), future sport managers should work to increase the breadth of the participation profile of active sport tourists. The ski industry has sponsored several studies to understand why more women do not ski or tend to drop out of skiing (Hudson, 2000; Williams & Lattey, 1994) and, more recently, why nonskiers do not ski (Williams & Fidgeon, 2000). Cost was mentioned as a constraint in all of these studies, and for some, the images put forth by marketers of the lone skier jumping off a high cliff were more off-putting than encouraging for many nonskiers. Ultimately, by alleviating some of the constraints on participation, the sport and tourism industries would benefit by providing opportunities to previously excluded groups, thus increasing demand.

Getz (1997) and Nogawa and colleagues (1996) argued that more data are needed on the event sport tourist. Most studies on event sport tourism address the economic impact of the event (e.g., Carmichael & Murphy, 1996; Irwin, Wang, & Sutton, 1996) and as such generate profiles of event spectators, but few studies have conducted an in-depth look at the event sport tourist. In my studies of Gator fans, I found that two-thirds were male and that they came from a range of backgrounds in terms of education and income, from high school graduates to fans with advanced degrees, and were a range of ages (Gibson, Willming, & Holdnak, in press; Gibson, Willming, & Holdnak, 2002). From my studies of active sport tourists (Gibson, Attle, & Yiannakis, 1998) and event sport tourists, the latter are more diverse in terms of socioeconomic background, although not in terms of gender and race. The same conclusion can probably apply to nostalgia sport tourists, although in this realm we have less empirical evidence on which to draw. Snyder's (1991) observations at several halls of fame identify a prevalence of older people, especially males and fathers and sons. He suggested that fathers are socializing the next generation into the history and collective memories associated with a particular sport.

Motivations of Sport Tourists

We can draw upon work in tourism studies for some ideas regarding the issue of motivation and why people choose to be sport tourists. It is generally recognized that tourists are motivated by a desire for novelty and change (Cohen, 1974; Lee & Crompton, 1992). In relation to sport vacations, more specific sport-related motivations may also come into play. At the start of this chapter we discussed the idea that sport tourists are attracted to different levels of competition. Hudman (1980) also found that health was a motivator for sport tourists. Likewise, Nogawa and colleagues (1996) found that health, fitness, and challenge were primary motives among Japanese sport tourists. Additionally, these tourists loved taking part in their sports, a sentiment matched by the Senior Games participants we interviewed (Gibson et al., 2002). Learning new skills, competence mastery, or self-development might also be the prime **push factors** in selecting a particular vacation style (Ryan & Glendon, 1998). Spending time with family and friends is another often cited motivation among tourists (Crompton, 1979). Whether sport tourists are active, as in the case of Green and Chalip's (1998) flag football participants, or spectators, as in the case of our Gator fans (Gibson, Willming, & Holdnak, in press; Gibson, Willming, & Holdnak, 2002), the social aspect of a trip is often of prime importance to participants.

push factors—The motivations or personal reasons people choose certain types of vacations.

Some studies have explored the idea that sport tourists are not homogeneous in their motivations and expectations. Rice (1987) described three types of scuba divers: the hard core who are the highly committed participants, the tourists for whom diving is part of their vacation, and the potentials who are trying diving for the first time and may return again. Likewise, Richards (1996) used Gratton's (1990) concept of **skilled consumption** in his study of British skiers. The proposition here is that in leisure activities that require learning new skills and constant practice such as skiing, participants will constantly be searching for new challenges to further develop and test their skills. Richards found support for this proposition in that more advanced skiers were more concerned about the variety and degree of difficulty associated with a particular ski area than were beginners, who were more likely to be guided by price in their selection of a ski vacation.

skilled consumption—People will choose to take part in sport at certain destinations or in certain ways based on their level of skill in that sport (e.g., more highly skilled golfers will look for more challenging courses when they play).

Three Impacts of Sport Tourism: Sociocultural, Economic, and Environmental

As sport tourism continues to grow in popularity, we need to be aware of the potential negative impacts of this sector of the sport and tourism industries as well as the benefits that we have already discussed. In 1987 De Knop suggested that problems associated with sport tourism were already becoming apparent. He identified three particular problems:

1. Conflict of interest among different types of sport tourists—sociocultural impacts
2. Conflicts between sport tourists and host communities—sociocultural and economic impacts
3. Preservation of the environment—environmental impacts

We will take a look at each of these in turn.

Sociocultural Impacts of Sport Tourism

It is well documented in tourism studies that tourism can have both positive and negative effects on a host community. Some of the positive effects relate to economics, with tourism being a major source of income and employment for an area. Tourism may also lead to a renewed sense of pride among community members, whether it is in relation to showcasing their town or city to visitors or the heightened sense of excitement and community identity that frequently accompanies an event, especially if residents take an active role in it through volunteering (Garnham, 1996). This pride in community results in what Burgan and Mules (1992) called the **psychic income** associated with hosting an event. Tourism has also been shown to open up societies to new ideas and even bring about a liberalization of values in more rigid or closed cultures (Dogan, 1989). Tourism may provide the funding and the impetus to preserve historic buildings, traditional practices (dances, crafts, etc.), and natural settings.

psychic income—The pride people have in their community generated by hosting a sport event.

Hosting the America's Cup in 1987 has been credited as being the catalyst for the renovation of the downtown area in Freemantle, Australia

(ANZALS Opening Session, 2001). Indeed, in a longitudinal study of residents' perceptions of Freemantle toward hosting the America's Cup, Soutar and McCleod (1993) found that prior to the event residents in general feared the congestion and crowds that the event would bring. These problems never materialized to the extent residents were anticipating. In fact, with the infrastructural improvements and potential for increased tourism, residents felt that their quality of life would increase in the years to come.

Positive outcomes may not always result from sport events, however. Indeed, in another study of the 1987 America's Cup, Dovey (1989) found that in Perth (the city adjacent to Freemantle) the event was used as an excuse to manipulate the planning processes for new development, and residents had to live with the negative consequences of these decisions. In a study of the potential costs associated with the 2000 Sydney Olympics, Hall and Hodges (1996) pointed to the fact that different segments of a host community are unequally affected by a mega-event, with low-income residents suffering the most, as they are frequently displaced from their homes by plans to redevelop their neighborhoods with high-priced residences. This displacement of low-income residents has been a common practice in relation to the Olympics, as cities hosting the Games face decisions over where to build stadia, athletes' village, and so forth (Olds, 1998; Whitson & MacIntosh, 1993).

Event sport tourism is not the only type of tourism to have an impact on a host community. The crowding and congestion experienced by small ski towns or golf resort areas such as Myrtle Beach, South Carolina, also need attention. In most tourism regions, host communities experience a "love/hate" relationship with tourists. On the one hand residents realize that their economic well-being is often dependent on tourists, yet the high prices, traffic congestion, and sometimes increased crime that accompany living in a tourist destination may lead to resistance and even hostility among community members (Dogan, 1989). All of these impacts need to be carefully thought through in any proposed tourism development. However, as Burgan and Mules (1992), among others, argue, too frequently emphasis is placed on the potential economic benefits, and the voices of the community are often unheard or ignored.

Economic Impacts of Sport Tourism

As you read in chapter 12, when community leaders are trying to raise money to build a new sta-dium, host a professional franchise, or host a sport event, they often point to the projected economic benefits arising out of these projects. However, as studies have repeatedly shown over the years, particularly in relation to professional sport, as many as 70% of spectators come from within the metropolitan area (Crompton, 1995; Stevens & Wootton, 1997) and therefore are not event sport tourists according to any definition of a tourist. Thus, while using sport as a tourist attraction is a valuable strategy for economic and community development, we need to be sure when we read studies about the tourism-related impacts accruing from sport events that locals were not included in the people surveyed or the economic estimates generated. We also need to be clear about how economic impact is measured. As Crompton (1995) explained, at least 11 common mistakes can be identified when communities estimate economic impact, including using the wrong multiplier, measuring **time switchers** and **casuals,** and including people whose primary motivation was not to attend the event but who happened to be in the vicinity or switched the timing of their visit to coincide with the event. In their study of various aspects of the 2000 Sydney Olympic Games, the Cooperative Research Centre for Sustainable Tourism in Australia suggested that a cost-benefit analysis is more appropriate than emphasizing economic impact (Chalip & Green, 2001). Indeed, some of the preliminary lessons learned from the Olympics have been to focus not on the impacts of an event but to use strategic leveraging with the aim of maximizing the effects of the event (Chalip, 2001).

time switchers—Visitors who had been planning to visit the destination and then switched their visit to coincide with the event. Therefore, their spending cannot be attributed to the event.

casuals—People who happened to be visiting the destination and chose to attend the event instead of doing something else. Their attendance at the event is not their prime reason for visiting the destination.

Environmental Impacts of Sport Tourism

As the popularity of sport vacations increases, we must consider the impacts on the environment. Over the past 10 years, there has been a growing realization in the tourism industry that the environment is the core of the tourism product. Destroy the environment and you destroy the attractiveness of a destination and the reason tourists choose to visit. The growth in ecotourism has been one outcome of this environmental concern. More recently, however, there has been a push toward extending **sustainable development** practices to all segments of the tourism industry.

sustainable development—The protection of the social and environmental resources of a destination for the long term rather than emphasizing short-term gain (Goeldner et al., 2000).

Tabata (1992) wrote of the increasing pressure on the environment as the popularity of scuba diving grows. Pollution of the water, littering, anchor damage, trampling, and specimen collecting by the divers can destroy the natural resource base. Tensions between environmentalists and the alpine ski industry have been growing in recent years as well. In Vermont environmentalists have raised an alarm over the amount of water being taken from rivers for snowmaking. In Colorado an activist group called the Ski Area Citizen's Coalition produced a scorecard ranking resorts based on their environmental friendliness so that skiers could choose to ski at mountains employing sustainable practices if they so chose (Janofsky, 2000). Yellowstone National Park has banned snowmobiles because of the noise and air pollution they cause and the user conflict that has arisen between snowmobilers and cross-country skiers in the western part of the park.

Around the world, ski resort development is causing alarm among environmentalists (Hudson, 1996). As Buckley, Pickering, and Warnken (2000) explained, ski resorts are one of the most intensive forms of development in mountain regions, with tree clearing for ski runs and water usage for snowmaking and servicing the resorts. Moreover, lengthening seasons may combat the economic effects of seasonality, but it leaves little time for grass and plant regeneration and relief from the noise and air pollution from the sheer number of people using the mountain roads to access the resorts. Hudson suggested that there are ways to implement sustainable practices in ski resorts, but at present the commitment among resort developers and skiers and the awareness of the need for sustainability are lacking.

Some of the same concerns have been levied at the golf industry (Pleumarom, 1992). Golf courses are land intensive, and the use of chemicals on the greens and the water usage in desert areas have been of particular concern. Some golf courses have adopted strategies to protect the ecological balance of their courses with programs to protect wildlife sponsored by partnerships between the USGA and the Audubon Society among others (www.audubonintl.org/programs/acss/golf.htm). However, more still needs to be done in this area.

Over the past 10 years, the International Olympic Committee has charged host countries with implementing environmentally friendly practices in relation to the Olympic Games. The 1994 Winter Games in Lillehammer have been labeled the Green Games (Chernushenko, 1996). Project Environment Friendly Olympics was mandated by the Norwegian Parliament to protect the fragile ecology surrounding the small city of Lillehammer. Chernushenko argued that the 1994 Olympics provide a good example of event sport tourism and environmentalism that can be copied by future events to produce not only a better event but also satisfied tourists and a reputation as a clean and attractive destination. The organizing committee of the 2000 Sydney Games adopted policies established during the 1992 United Nations Earth Summit in developing their environmental guidelines. The United States Olympic Committee gave particular praise to the Tampa 2012 bid for its proposed environmental strategies. Thus, there is evidence of a growing realization of the need for sustainable development in tourism of all kinds. The question becomes, How do we balance the growing popularity of tourism in general and sport tourism in particular with the need to protect the natural and sociocultural environments and the impetus for greater economic profitability? A unified policy between sport and tourism agencies might be one way of balancing sustainability with profitability.

LEARNING ACTIVITY

Prepare a 15- to 20-minute presentation on a sport tourism enterprise, issue, or trend that you have read about in this chapter. Your presentation should make use of visual aids such as PowerPoint, video, and so on. Engage the class in discussion based on your presentation. Prepare a two-page handout to accompany your presentation. The first page should provide a detailed outline of the major points of your presentation, and the second page should list the major references for your topic. Some of the topics my class has presented include the Subway World Series (Mets vs. Yankees in 2001); Inside Cooperstown; Tourism Associated with the Field of Dreams; Golf Tourism in Korea; and Sport Tourism and Daytona Beach, Florida.

SUMMARY

You should now have a good overview of sport tourism both in terms of the academic knowledge and some practices around the world. We started the chapter by analyzing the sport and tourism connection. The focus was on understanding tourism and the tourism industry. Tourism is the world's largest industry and is composed of many segments, including transportation; accommodation; attractions; and the government and nongovernment agencies responsible for planning, setting policy, and marketing. A *tourist* is defined in this chapter as a leisure traveler on a voluntary, temporary, relatively long trip in pursuit of novelty and change. Sport tourism is defined as travel to participate in sport (active sport tourism), to watch sport (event sport tourism), or to venerate something or somebody associated with a sport (nostalgia sport tourism).

In reviewing the three types of sport tourism, we discussed some possible explanations as to why active sport tourism has become so popular over the past 10 years or so. Some of this popularity may be related to an increased awareness of the benefits of an active lifestyle coupled with increased opportunities to take part in sport on vacation at resorts, on cruises, and at amateur sport events. We took an in-depth look at golf and skiing as the most popular types of active sport tourism. Golf is increasing in popularity with the aging population, while the alpine ski industry has been struggling to sustain its market share. All sectors of event sport tourism, on the other hand, are increasing in popularity. There is intense competition among cities around the world to host the mega-events such as the Olympic Games and the World Cup Soccer Finals. However, there is also a growing realization among communities around the United States that small-scale sport tourism events may be more manageable and beneficial than mega-events. As a consequence, many communities now have sports commissions whose task is to attract sport events to their towns or cities. Sports commissions coupled with convention and visitors bureaus are helping many towns and cities throughout the United States develop sport tourism. The third type of sport tourism we discussed, nostalgia sport tourism, is the least well developed in terms of research and attention from tourism professionals. Nonetheless, around the United States and the world, sport halls of fame, museums, and sport-themed events are becoming more popular. Even the cruise industry has developed its own niche in the nostalgia sport tourism realm by offering cruises with various sport personalities.

Who is a sport tourist? This question was answered by drawing sociological and motivation theories. Sport tourists, especially active sport tourists, tend to be more affluent, college educated, and male. The task of future sport managers is to encourage more diversity in sport tourism participation. Sport tourists are motivated by an array of factors, from the need to experience competence and mastery, to spending time with family and friends, to the novelty and change associated with all forms of tourism.

We ended the chapter by looking at some of the impacts of the various types of sport tourism, from the effects on hosting communities, especially of mega-events, to the environmental impacts of these events. The last few Olympic Games, however, have paid particular attention to the environmental effects of their games. The economic impacts of sport always garner a lot of attention, and this is certainly a major reason so many communities have become involved in hosting sports events. Measuring economic impact, however, may not always be straightforward. Indeed, closer cooperation between sport and tourism agencies at all levels may be one way of reaping both the economic and social benefits of sport tourism while decreasing the negative impacts.

REVIEW QUESTIONS

1. Do you agree with the definition of sport tourism as set out in this chapter? Explain.

2. If sport tourism is leisure-based travel, is a professional athlete a sport tourist?

3. What strategies might you suggest to your community to better leverage the tourism associated with college sports?

4. What are the arguments for and against a city hosting the Olympic Games?

5. Why has nostalgia sport tourism become so popular in recent years?

6. How might you use the theories put forward in this chapter to segment the sport tourist market?

7. How might we encourage more women and minorities to take part in active sport tourism?

8. How might we alleviate some of the environmental impacts associated with sport tourism?

9. In what ways do you think sport tourism will continue to grow over the next 10 years?

10. What sorts of career opportunities are there in sport tourism for sport management majors?

11. Do we need to offer a separate degree in sport tourism at the university level? If yes, explain why a specialist sport tourism degree would be beneficial. If no, suggest how we might better prepare students for a career in sport tourism from within the existing degree programs.

Job Opportunities

Special Event Coordinator

Individual sought to plan citywide, year-round special events. Duties include coordination of booking entertainment and attraction, supervising setup crews, publicity and promotion, operation and maintenance of equipment. Must have public relations skills as well as excellent organizational abilities. Bachelor's degree in recreation preferred. Salary commensurate with experience.

Tour Guide

Energetic and enthusiastic person needed to conduct walking tours of the downtown sport, entertainment, and historical attractions. Individual must be bilingual in Spanish and English. Knowledge of city's rich culture and history required. Interested individual should apply to City Parks and Recreation Commission. Flexible hours. Excellent salary per hour.

Adventure Travel Leader and Coordinator

Adventures Are Yours now accepting applications for travel coordinators and leaders to plan and escort bicycling and hiking trips in the southwest United States. Trips range from two to four weeks for various age groups. Experience as a trip leader required as well as a strong desire to work with young people. Bachelor's degree required in sport management, recreation, tourism, or related area. Excellent benefits and salary.

Tournament Planner

Sponsoring corporation seeking individual to assist in the planning, development, and execution of international tennis tournament to be hosted in August. Candidate must have tournament planning experience to supervise committees that oversee a variety of events surrounding the four-day tournament. Bachelor's degree in sport management, recreation, leisure, tourism, or related area. Salary commensurate with experience.

Youth Activities Trip Leader

Community youth organization wishes to recruit responsible person to escort urban youth groups on adventure trips to include a variety of activities: skiing, hiking, horseback riding, climbing, and ropes courses. Applicants must have one year's experience working with behaviorally challenged youth. Bachelor's degree required.

Guest Relations Specialist

Major hotel corporation seeking energetic, motivated individual to run guest relations operations. Individual must plan activities and programs, escort small groups on the island, and assist in promoting special events hosted by hotel. Individual must have pleasing personality, love working with people, and be active. Bachelor's degree in sport management, hospitality management, recreation management, or tourism management required.

REFERENCES

ABC Evening News. (2002, February 10). Report on Nagano, Japan.

Aburdene, P., & Naisbitt, J. (1992). *Megatrends for women*. New York: Villard Books.

Alachua County (2002). Where nature meets culture. Retrieved February 20, 2002 from http://www.visitgainesville.net/

Alm, R. (2001, October 5). Area tourism industry hopes for a big score from Texas-OU game. *The Dallas Morning News*, p. D1.

ANZLS (2001). Opening session speaker, John Longley. Freemantle, Australia, July 2, 2002.

Bale, J. (1988). *Sports geography*. London: E and FN Spon.

Bright, A. (2001). The role of social marketing in leisure and recreation management. *Journal of Leisure Research, 32*, 12-17.

Buckley, R., Pickering, C., & Warnken, J. (2000). Environmental management for alpine tourism and resorts in Australia. In P. Godde, M. Price, & F. Zimmermann (Eds.), *Tourism and development in mountain regions* (pp. 27-45). Wallingford, UK: CAB International.

Burgan, B., & Mules, T. (1992). Economic impact of sporting events. *Annals of Tourism Research, 19*, 700-710.

Butwin, D. (1982). Hotel exercise facilities help travelers stay fit. *The Physician and Sports Medicine, 10*, 115-117.

Carmichael, B., & Murphy, P. (1996). Tourism economic impact of a rotating sports event: The case of the British Columbia Games. *Festival Management and Event Tourism, 4*, 127-138.

Chalip, L. (2001, February). *Leveraging the Sydney Olympics to optimize tourism benefits*. Paper presented at the International Conference on the Economic Impact of Sports, Athens, Greece.

Chalip, L., & Green, B.C. (2001, June 10-13). *Leveraging large sports events for tourism: Lessons learned from the Sydney Olympics*. Supplemental proceedings of the Travel and Tourism Research Association 32nd Annual Conference, Fort Myers, Florida.

Chalip, L., & Leyns, A. (2002). Local business leveraging of a sport event: Managing sport for economic benefit. *Journal of Sport Management, 16*, 132-158.

Chernushenko, D. (1996). Sports tourism goes sustainable: The Lillehammer experience. *Visions in Leisure and Business, 15*, 65-73.

Coakley, J. (2001). *Sport in society: Issues and controversies* (7th ed.). New York: McGraw-Hill.

Cohen, E. (1974). Who is a tourist? A conceptual clarification. *Sociological Review, 22*, 527-555.

Cohen, S. (1998, November). Transatlantic allies. *Continental Inflight Magazine*, 30-33.

Cox, R. (1995, July). Travel: Losing yourself in Vermont. *Tennis, 31*(3), 97.

Crompton, J. (1979). An assessment of the image of Mexico as a vacation destination and the influence of geographical location upon that image. *Journal of Travel Research, 17*(4), 18-23.

Crompton, J. (1995). Economic impact analysis of sports facilities and events: Eleven sources of misapplication. *Journal of Sport Management, 9*, 14-35.

Dann, G. (1994). Tourism: The nostalgia industry of the future. In W. Theobold (Ed.), *Global tourism: The next decade* (pp. 56-67). Oxford: Butterworth-Heinemenn.

Davis, F. (1979). *Yearning for yesterday: A sociology of nostalgia*. New York: Free Press.

De Knop, P. (1987). *Some thoughts on the influence of sport tourism*. In Proceedings of the International Seminar and Workshop on Outdoor Education, Recreation and Sport Tourism, pp. 38-45. Wingate Institute for Physical Education and Sport, Netanya, Israel.

Dogan, H. (1989). Forms of adjustment: Socio-cultural impacts of tourism. *Annals of Tourism Research, 16*, 216-236.

Dovey, K. (1989). Old scabs/new scars: The hallmark event and the everyday environment. In G. Syme, B. Shaw, D. Fenton, & W. Mueller (Eds.), *The planning and evaluation of hallmark events* (pp. 73-80). Aldershot, UK: Avebury.

Elliott-Spivak, S. (1998). Health spa development in the U.S.: A burgeoning component of sport tourism. *Journal of Vacation Marketing, 4*, 65-77.

Elrick & Lavidge, Inc. (1994). *Unmet vacation expectations*. Prepared for Marriott International, Washington D.C., April.

Fakeye, P., & Crompton, J. (1991). Image differences between prospective, first-time, and repeat visitors to the Lower Rio Grande Valley. *Journal of Travel Research, 30*(2), 10-16.

Fisher, J. (2000). The Gator Shop: In-person interview. Unpublished student paper, University of Florida, Gainesville, FL, Fall 2001.

Foley, M., & Reid, G. (1998). Activities, holidays and activity holidays in Scotland. In N. Ravenscroft, D. Phillips, & M. Bennett (Eds.), *Tourism and visitor attractions: Leisure, culture and commerce* (vol. 61, pp. 61-73). Eastbourne, UK: LSA Publications.

Fowler, P. (1992). *The past in contemporary society: Then and now*. London: Routledge.

Frommer, A. (2001, September 2). On a budget: Yellowstone's hot deals. *Los Angeles Times*, Part L, p. 2.

Gammon, S. (2001). Fantasy, nostalgia and the pursuit of what never was—but what should have been. In S. Gammon & J. Kurtzman (Eds.), *Sport tourism: Principles and practice* (pp. 61-71). LSA Publication #76. Eastbourne, UK.

Gammon, S., & Robinson, T. (1997). Sport and tourism: A conceptual framework. *Journal of Sports Tourism, 4*(3), 8-24.

Garnham, B. (1996). Ranfurly Shield Rugby: An investigation into the impacts of a sporting event on a provincial city, the case of New Plymouth, Taranaki, New Zealand. *Festival Management and Event Tourism, 4,* 145-149.

Gee, C., Makens, J., & Choy, D. (1989). *The travel industry* (2nd ed.). New York: Van Nostrand.

Getz, D. (1997). Trends and issues in sport event tourism. *Tourism Recreation Research, 22,* 61-74.

Gibson, H. (1998a). Sport tourism: A critical analysis of research. *Sport Management Review, 1,* 45-76.

Gibson, H. (1998b). Active sport tourism: Who participates? *Leisure Studies, 17,* 155-170.

Gibson, H., Ashton-Shaeffer, C., Green, J., & Kessinger, K. (2002, October 16-20). *"It wouldn't be long before I'd be friends with an undertaker": What it means to be a senior athlete.* Presented at the Leisure Research Symposium held in conjunction with the National Park and Recreation Association Congress, Tampa, FL.

Gibson, H., Attle, S., & Yiannakis, A. (1998). Segmenting the sport tourist market: A lifespan perspective. *Journal of Vacation Marketing, 4,* 52-64.

Gibson, H., Willming, C., & Holdnak, A.. (in press) "We're Gators . . . not just a Gator fan:" Serious leisure, social identity, and University of Florida football. *Journal of Leisure Research.*

Gibson, H., Willming, C., & Holdnak, A. (2002). *Small-scale event sport tourism: College sport as a tourist attraction.* In S. Gammon & J. Kurtzman (Eds.), *Sport tourism: Principles and practice* (pp. 3-18). Eastbourne, UK. LSA Publication #76.

Goeldner, C., Ritchie, J.R. Brent, & McIntosh, R. (2000). *Tourism: Practices, principles, philosophies.* New York: Wiley.

Graburn, N. (1989). Tourism: The sacred journey. In V. Smith (Ed.), *Hosts and guests: The anthropology of tourism* (2nd ed., pp. 21-36). Philadelphia: University of Pennsylvania Press.

Gratton, C. (1990, December). *Consumer behavior in tourism: A psycho-economic approach.* Paper presented at the Tourism Research into the 1990s Conference, Durham, UK.

Green, B., & Chalip. L. (1998). Sport tourism as the celebration of subculture. *Annals of Tourism Research, 25,* 275-292.

Hall, C. (1992). Adventure, sport and health tourism. In B. Weiler & C.M. Hall (Eds.), *Special interest tourism* (pp. 141-158). London: Bellhaven Press.

Hall, C., & Hodges, J. (1996). The party's great, but what about the hangover? The housing and social impacts of mega-events with special reference to the 2000 Sydney Olympics. *Festival Management and Event Tourism, 4,* 13-20.

Hanis, A. (2000, May 3). Take your home team on a baseball road trip. *Chicago Sun-Times,* p. 60.

Higham, J. (1999). Commentary—sport as an avenue of tourism development: An analysis of the positive and negative impacts of sport tourism. *Current Issues in Tourism, 2*(1), 82-90.

Hinch, T., & Higham, J. (2001). Sport tourism: A framework for research. *International Journal of Tourism Research, 3,* 45-58.

Hoffman, A. (1999). Environmental education in business school. *Environment, 41*(1), 4-6.

Hudson, S. (2000). The segmentation of potential tourists: Constraint differences between men and women. *Journal of Travel Research, 38,* 363-369.

Irwin, R., & Sandler, M. (1998). An analysis of travel behavior and event-induced expenditures among American collegiate championship patron groups. *Journal of Vacation Marketing, 4,* 78-90.

Irwin, R., Wang, P., & Sutton, W. (1996). Comparative analysis of diaries and projected spending to assess patron expenditure behavior at short-term sporting events. *Festival Management and Event Tourism, 4,* 29-37.

I.U.T.O. (1963). *The United Nations' conference on international travel and tourism.* Geneva, Switzerland: International Union of Official Travel Organizations.

Janofsky, M. (2000, December 3). Environmental groups' ratings rile ski industry. *New York Times,* p. 30.

Kelly, J. (1999). Leisure behaviors and styles: Social, economic, and cultural factors. In E. Jackson & T. Burton (Eds.), *Leisure studies: Prospects for the twenty-first century* (pp. 135-150). State College, PA: Venture.

Kelly, J., & Freysinger, V. (2000). *21st century leisure.* Boston: Allyn & Bacon.

Kenworth, T. (2001, April 6). Aspen takes snowbarding to new peak. *USA Today,* 3A.

Kidd, B. (1996). Inequality in sport, the corporation, and the state: An agenda for social scientists. *Journal of Sport & Social Issues, 19,* 232-248.

Ladd, S. (1995, July 7). Pinehurst: One man's vision. *Greensboro News and Record,* Weekend, pp. 8-10.

Lee, T. & Crompton, J. (1992). Measuring novelty seeking in tourism. *Annals of Tourism Research 19,* 732-751.

Leiper, N. (1990). Tourist attraction systems. *Annals of Tourism Research, 17,* 367-384.

Lewis, G. & Redmond, G. (1974). *Sporting heritage: A guide to halls of fame, special collections, and museums in the US and Canada.* New York: A.S. Barnes.

Loy, J. (1968). The nature of sport: A definitional effort. *Quest, 10,* 1-15.

Martin, K. (1995, December 13). The fit and adventuresome can now vacation by skate. *Hartford Courant,* Travel Section, p. 3.

McFee, G. (1990). *The Olympic Games as tourist event: An American in Athens, 1896.* Proceedings of the Leisure Studies Association Second International Conference, Leisure, Labour, and Lifestyles: International Comparisons (pp. 146-157), Conference Papers no. 43. Eastbourne, UK: LSA Publications.

Mintel, (2000, December). Special interest holidays. *Leisure Intelligence.* London, UK: Mintel International Group Ltd.

Morse, S., & Lanier, P. (1992). Golf resorts—Driving into the '90s. *The Cornell Hotel and Restaurant Administration Quarterly, 33,* 44-48.

National Sporting Goods Association. (2000). Ten year history of sports participation. Retrieved February 1, 2002, from www.nsga.org.

NBC. (2000, September 9). *Today Show* interview with John Coates, president of the Australian Olympic Committee.

Nogawa, H., Yamguchi, Y., & Hagi, Y. (1996). An empirical research study on Japanese sport tourism in Sport-for-All Events: Case studies of a single-night event and a multiple-night event. *Journal of Travel Research, 35,* 46-54.

North Carolina Travel and Tourism Division (1995). *North Carolina Travel Guide.* Raleigh, NC: NCTTD.

North Central Florida Almanac, March 25, 2001. *The Gainesville Sun.* (Insert with newspaper.)

Olds, K. (1998). Urban mega-events, evictions and housing rights: The Canadian case. *Current Issues in Tourism, 1*(1), 2-46.

Pearce, P. (1985). A systematic comparison of travel-related roles. *Human Relations, 38,* 1001-1011.

Pitts, B.G. (1999). Sports tourism and niche markets: Identification and analysis of the growing lesbian and gay sports tourism industry. *Journal of Vacation Marketing, 5*(1), 31-50.

Pleumarom, A. (1992). Course and effect: Golf tourism in Thailand. *The Ecologist, 22,* 104-110.

Priestley, G. (1995). Sports tourism: The case of golf. In G. J. Ashworth & A.G.J. Dietvorst (Eds.), *Tourism and spatial transformations: Implications for policy and planning* (pp. 205-223). Wallingford, UK: CAB International.

Poon, A., & Adams, E. (2000). *How the British will travel 2005.* Bielefeld, Germany: Tourism Intelligence International.

Redmond, G. (1973). A plethora of shrines: Sport in the museum and hall of fame. *Quest, 19,* 41-48.

Redmond, G. (1991). Changing styles of sports tourism: Industry/consumer interactions in Canada, the USA, and Europe. In M.T. Sinclair & M.J. Stabler (Eds.), *The tourism industry: An international analysis* (pp. 107-120). Wallingford, UK: CAB International.

Rice, K. (1987, February 9). Special report: Scuba diving—dive market requires specialized skill, information. *Tour Travel News,* 24-27.

Richards, G. (1996). Skilled consumption and UK ski holidays. *Tourism Management, 17,* 25-34.

Ritchie, J.R. Brent, (1984). Assessing the impact of hallmark events: Conceptual and research issues. *Journal of Travel Research, 23,* 2-11.

Ritchie, J.R. Brent, (1999). Lessons learned, lessons learning: Insights from the Calgary and Salt Lake Olympic Winter Games. *Visions in Leisure and Business, 18,* 4-13.

Ritchie, J.R. Brent, & Aitken, C. (1984). Assessing the impacts of the 1988 Olympic Winter Games: The research program and initial results. *Journal of Travel Research, 23,* 17-25.

Ritchie, J.R. Brent, & Lyons, M. (1990). OLYMPUS VI—A post event assessment of resident reaction to the XV Olympic Winter Games. *Journal of Travel Research, 29,* 14-23.

Ritchie, J.R. Brent, & Smith, B. (1991). The impact of a mega-event on host region awareness: A longitudinal study. *Journal of Travel Research, 30,* 3-10.

Roche, M. (1994). Mega-events and urban policy. *Annals of Tourism Research, 21,* 1-19.

Rowan, D. & Sandberg, D. (1990, January). The cosmopolitan future of America's ski resports. *Ski Area Management, 29,* 76-77.

Ryan, C., & Glendon, I. (1998). Application of leisure motivation scale to tourism. *Annals of Tourism Research, 25,* 169-184.

Schor, J. (1991). *The overworked American: The unexpected decline of leisure.* New York: Basic Books.

Schreiber, R. (1976, June 20-23). *Sports interest, A travel definition.* The Travel Research Association 7th Annual Conference Proceedings, 85-87, Boca Raton, Florida.

Smith, V. (1989). *Hosts and guests: The anthropology of tourism* (2nd ed). Philadelphia: University of Pennsylvania Press.

Snyder, E. (1991). Sociology of nostalgia: Sport halls of fame and museums in America. *Sociology of Sport Journal, 8,* 228-238.

Soutar, G., & McLeod, P. (1993). Residents' perceptions on impact of the America's Cup. *Annals of Tourism Research, 20,* 571-582.

Standeven, J. (1998). Sport tourism: Joint marketing—A starting point for beneficial synergies. *Journal of Vacation Marketing, 4,* 39-51.

Standeven, J. & De Knop, P. (1999). *Sport tourism.* Champaign, IL: Human Kinetics

Stevens, T., & Wootton, G. (1997). Sports stadia and arena: Realising their full potential. *Tourism Recreation Research, 22*(2), 49-56.

Tabata, R. (1992). Scuba diving holidays. In B. Weiler & C. Hall (Eds.), *Special interest tourism* (pp. 171-184). London, UK: Belhaven Press.

Tampa 2012. (2001). United States Olympic Committee site visit presentation, Tampa Convention Center, August 4.

TIA (1999). *Profiles of travelers who attend sports events.* Travel Industry Association of America. Washington, D.C.: Author.

Travel Industry Association of America. (2000). *Tourism works for America.* Washington DC: TIA Annual.

Urry, J. (1990). *The tourist gaze.* London: Sage.

U.S. Department of Health and Human Services (1996). *Physical activity and health: A report of the Surgeon General.* Atlanta: Author.

U.S. Travel Data Center (1989). *Discover America 2000: The implications of America's changing demographics and attitudes on the US travel industry.* Washington, DC: USTDC.

Waters, R. (1989). *Travel Industry World Yearbook: The big picture—1988-1989* (vol. 33). New York: Child & Waters.

Watson, G.L., & Kopachevsky, J. (1994). Interpretations of tourism as commodity. In Y. Apostolopoulos, S. Leivadi, & A. Yiannakis (Eds.), *Sociology of tourism* (pp. 281-300). London: Routledge.

Whitson, D., & Macintosh, D. (1993). Becoming a world-class city: Hallmark events and sport franchises in the growth strategies of western Canadian cities. *Sociology of Sport Journal, 10,* 221-240.

Williams, P., & Fidgeon, P. (2000). Addressing participation constraint: A case study of potential skiers. *Tourism Management, 21,* 379-393.

Williams, P., & Lattey, C. (1994). Skiing constraints for women. *Journal of Travel Research, 32,* 21-25.

Wilson, J. (1999). "Remember when . . ." A consideration of the concept of nostalgia. *ETC: A Review of General Semantics, 56,* 296-304.

Wood, S. (2001, November 4). Fort Worth, Texas, area aims for smaller sporting events after losing the Olympics. *Fort Worth Star-Telegram.*

World Cup soccer games finally come to America (1993, May 17). *Business America,* pp. 2-6.

World Tourism Organization (1995). *Concepts, definitions, and classification of tourism statistics.* Madrid, Spain: WTO.

World Tourism Organization (1999). *Tourism highlights 1999.* Madrid, Spain: WTO.

Yiannakis, A., & Gibson, H. (1992). Roles tourists play. *Annals of Tourism Research, 19,* 287-303.

Zachary, J. (1997). *Assembling the most attractive sport tourism packages.* Panel session at Teaming for Success: A Forum on Sport Tourism, Arlington, Virginia, March 6-8.

Chapter 18

International Sport

Ted G. Fay, SUNY Cortland

The purpose of this chapter is to delineate the principal structures and organizations that currently shape and define the international sport industry in the 21st century. A number of events, companies, teams, and sport personalities have transcended the isolation and limitations of parochial recognition to become ubiquitous international brands (e.g., Manchester United, the New York Yankees, the Dallas Cowboys, Wimbledon, the Super Bowl, the FIFA World Cup, the Tour de France, Jordan, Pele, Schumacher, Woods, Gretzky, Graf, Witt, and the Williams sisters). Due to space limitations, this chapter will not attempt to provide a comprehensive review by sport, organization, or industry type. Rather, it will provide snapshots of individuals, corporations, organizations, and events that are part of the international sport scene. This information should foster a better understanding of the ever-changing and expanding dimensions of international sport. This chapter will also emphasize the special skills, experiences, and competencies that will help a new sport management professional gain access to a career in international sport management.

LEARNING OBJECTIVES

After studying this chapter, you will be able to do the following:

1. Discuss the foundations on which the international sport industry has developed with respect to international sport federations, leagues, corporations, and events.

2. Describe the power structure and processes in which the international sport industry operates, including linkages within the industry.

3. Explain the import–export exchange process regarding sport products, services, and personnel throughout the world and its potential for expansion.

4. Identify the resources available and the knowledge and skills necessary to successfully compete for a job in the international sport marketplace.

5. Discuss trends in the field of international sport.

What Is International Sport?

We will consider at least two factors in determining whether a sport is international:

1. The degree or the regularity with which action by an organization or event within a sport is focused on international activity

2. The context in which an organization or event operates within the sport enterprise

For example, is a U.S. intercollegiate sport team that has one or more foreign players, travels overseas to play out-of-season exhibition games against foreign competition, or schedules preseason exhibition games against touring international teams involved in international sport? The number of foreign athletes on U.S. college sport teams at all levels (Divisions I through III) has risen sharply over the past 10 years. A quick survey of rosters in basketball, ice hockey, field hockey, soccer, skiing, track and field, tennis, and softball reveal an increased presence of male and female foreign players. Often, this talent makes the difference in terms of success and possibly national championships. An example of this strategy occurred at the University of Minnesota—Duluth (UMD) en route to winning the inaugural NCAA Division I Women's Ice Hockey Championship in 2001 and again in 2002. UMD employed Shannon Miller, the former coach of the 1998 Canadian Olympic Silver Medallist Team, who used her international connections to bring in players from six different foreign national teams to aid their championship effort.

But to answer the question of whether the intercollegiate team is involved in international sport—the answer is no. Despite the growing proliferation of international athletes on U.S. intercollegiate teams, these teams, their respective conferences, and the National Collegiate Athletic Association (NCAA) do not have international competition as their primary focus.

The context in which an organization operates within the sport enterprise is also an important factor in determining whether it can be characterized as being involved in international sport. Clearly, the Olympic Games, world championships in specific sports such as FIFA's World Cup in men's and women's soccer, major annual international events such as the Tour de France or Wimbledon, and multinational corporations such as International Management Group (IMG) or Nike are among the giants of international sport. It is more difficult, however, to assess whether an organization is engaged in international sport if it operates almost exclusively in one nation or is only occasionally involved with international athletes or clients such as intercollegiate sport in the United States or major U.S.-based professional sport leagues that regularly draft and use foreign players (e.g., the National Basketball Association, the National Hockey League, Major League Soccer, or Major League Baseball). This chapter will address only those governance structures, organizations, and events that are involved internationally on a regular basis or as one of their primary functions.

LEARNING ACTIVITY

Choose a country and research its most popular sport activities, sport facilities, and famous athletes to create a profile for a global sport atlas. Describe (if available) the prime sport exports and imports of this country, including the production of goods and services, the existence of prominent sport leagues and events, the development of players and coaches in particular sports, offices of international sport federations (IFs), and so on.

1972: A Snapshot of Key Historic Changes in International Sport

The year 1972 and those that followed witnessed historic geopolitical and global economic changes that have had a tremendous impact and ripple effect on international sport. Before the mid-1980s, international sport was defined primarily in terms of the quadrennial Olympic Games, the Davis Cup in men's tennis, or the FIFA World Cup in men's soccer, with nations and their respective political ideologies clamoring to stake their claims to being the world's best. During this period, the United States could be characterized as primarily an exporter of sport products and services, while being isolationist or unilateralist in its view that its men's professional teams were the world's best and their respective championships (e.g., the World Series, the Super Bowl) were the most important sport events. It should be noted that for the exception of the former East Bloc countries of the Soviet Union and East Germany, little focus in international sport was placed on women's sports.

One could argue that the Summer Olympics of 1972 held in Munich marked the birth of a new international sport revolution. Several benchmark events in this special year have had lasting effects on the international sport industry and marketplace. The tragic murder of nine Israeli Olympians by terrorists in the Olympic Village sent shock waves through the international sport establishment and changed forever the manner in which security would be dealt with at the Olympics and other major international sport events. Adidas, Puma, and other sporting goods manufacturers (Nike was not born yet!) were accused of intentionally contributing to the professionalization and commercialization of the 1972 Olympics through under-the-table payments to track and field athletes, swimmers, and alpine skiers (Guttman, 1994).

Controversy over the issue of whether professionals should be eligible to participate in the Olympic Games dramatically intensified after the Soviet Union's upset victory over the favored U.S. men's basketball team (72-71) in the Olympic basketball finals in Munich. The reaction of many in the United States and Western Europe to this shocking loss was to accuse the Soviet players of being professionals paid by their government, thereby openly challenging the equity of the contest. Many people believe that the idea of sending NBA all-stars instead of the best U.S. collegians (a.k.a. amateurs) gained serious momentum as a direct result of this bitterly contested loss.

Fuel was added to this debate when, one month after the 1972 Summer Olympics were over, a team of Canadian NHL all-stars (professionals) challenged the Olympic hockey champions (a.k.a. amateurs) from the Soviet Union for the first time. The Canadians barely emerged victorious in the so-called Series of the Century, which was ultimately decided by a single goal after eight games with the Soviets winning three games in the series (Terroux, 1972). None of these important sport moments, however, was as significant as U.S. president Nixon's decision to use sport as a diplomatic tool by sending a U.S. table tennis team to China in 1972. This historic event, sometimes referred to as "Ping-Pong diplomacy," is often cited as the beginning of the process of normalizing diplomatic and economic relations between the two superpowers.

Three subsequent boycotts of the Olympic Games—in 1976 by African nations over apartheid practices in South Africa, in 1980 by the United States and some Western allies over the Soviet invasion of Afghanistan, and in 1984 by the Soviet bloc in reprisal for U.S.-led action four years earlier—caused some within the International Olympic Committee (IOC) to believe that the Olympic movement was in serious jeopardy (Simson & Jennings, 1992). Faced with a potential political and financial disaster, the IOC reluctantly altered its rules governing corporate involvement for the 1984 Summer Olympic Games, thus allowing the Los Angeles Olympic Organizing Committee through its entrepreneurial CEO, Peter Ueberroth, to charge multimillion-dollar fees for Olympic corporate sponsorships. Prior to 1984, the IOC did not allow any company to use the five Olympic rings directly in its corporate advertising or be designated an official Olympic sponsor. The financial and marketing success of these Games despite the boycott by the Soviet Union and its allies touched off a sport marketing and event management revolution (Stotlar, 1993). In 1985 the International Olympic Committee completed its sport governance revolution under the leadership of its newly elected president Juan Antonio Samaranch when it eliminated all references to the term *amateur*, thus allowing each respective international sport federation to define its own eligibility rules. This landmark decision opened the door to the use of professional athletes and teams in Olympic sports and served to help level the playing field between the state-supported athletes of the Soviet bloc and their Western counterparts (Wilson, 1994).

Redefining International Sport

The changes in IOC eligibility criteria, coupled with the aftershocks of the fall of the Berlin Wall in 1989, had a profound impact on redefining the scope of international sport. The collapse of the Soviet Union and East Germany virtually eliminated some of the most powerful nations in Olympic history. This geopolitical shift inadvertently added a significant number of new nations to the Olympic family with the independence of the former Soviet republics (Powers, 1993). Over the past 30 years, the balance of power in international sport has shifted dramatically with each new breakthrough victory by an individual, team, or nation. Beginning with Australia's surprising win in the America's Cup in 1983, to the amazing feat of Americans Greg LeMond and Lance Armstrong in winning six Tour de France titles beginning in 1986, to Lu Chen of China being crowned the 1995 World Ladies Figure Skating Champion, to the U.S. women winning the FIFA World Cup in soccer in 1999, the previously predictable world of international sport has been forever changed. Swedes, Germans, Russians, and Czechs have taken turns dominating the professional women's and men's tennis tours while European, African, and Australian golfers regularly succeeded on the PGA and LPGA tours, thus demonstrating that single nations or regions can no longer dominate specific sports.

The so-called "Dream Team," made up of NBA All-Stars including Michael Jordan, Magic Johnson, and Larry Bird, debuted at the 1992 Summer Olympic Games in Barcelona. Ten years later, the sixth edition of Team USA, made up totally of NBA players, failed to make even the medal round at the 2002 FIBA Men's World Basketball Championships. Argentina ended a 58-game winning streak of Olympic and World Championship games by Team USA since the inception of the "Dream Team" with Yugoslavia then adding to U.S. woes by bouncing the Americans in the quarterfinals.

The decade of 1992 to 2002 witnessed a dramatic shift in power and dominance in the world of both men's and women's soccer (a.k.a. football) from being the entitlement of a few select European or South American teams to the emergence of teams from Africa, Asia, and the United States. In 1994 the United States successfully hosted soccer's men's FIFA World Cup to record crowds of spectators (3.58 million) and television viewers (2.1 billion worldwide). The U.S. men's team, typically unsuccessful in international play before 1994, produced both exciting and tragic results. Unfortunately, the ugly side effects of international sport were witnessed after the Colombian team returned home, having failed to qualify for the second round. A chilling example of nationalistic

Internation sport events such as the Tour de France are no longer dominated by single nations or regions.

soccer fever run amok was the revenge murder of the Colombian defensive player Andres Escobar, who had inadvertently scored on his own goal in Colombia's 2-1 loss to the United States allowing the U.S. team to advance out of the qualifying rounds. Eight years later, in 2002, the men's World Cup was cohosted spectacularly by Korea and Japan with the upstart Americans, Senegalese, and cohost Koreans crashing the final elite eight. The Korean team, led by a Dutch coach, became the first Asian team to qualify for the semifinals.

Soccer has continued to grow in its worldwide popularity with the formation of new professional leagues for men in Asia (Japan, Korea, China) and in the United States with the Major League Soccer league in 1996 and the new WUSA professional league for women in 2000 that features a collection of the world's top female talent. FIFA introduced the first soccer World Cup for women in 1991 in China, followed by Sweden in 1995 and the United States in 1999, where over 90,000 fans watched a scoreless final between China and the United States be settled by a shootout won by the United States (5 to 4) giving them their second World Cup title. The women's game has featured many nontraditional soccer nations with the United States, Norway, and China emerging as the dominant teams in both Olympic and World Cup competition and the traditional soccer powers such as Germany and Brazil ironically struggling to emerge as world powers. The successful hosting of the women's World Cup in 1999 has had a tremendous impact on the popularity of the game with young girls and women in both the United States and throughout the world. Players such as Mia Hamm, Brandi Chastain, Julie Foudy, and Tiffany Milbrett of the United States; Su Wen of China; and Sasi of Brazil are becoming well known throughout the soccer-playing world. Endorsements, professional league contracts, and television deals are now connected to the women's game. It should be noted that the ascent of the United States as a world power in women's soccer can be attributed in part to the role Title IX has played in supporting the development of women's sport.

Assessing the Expanding Market for International Sport

A trend in most professional sport leagues throughout the world has been the recruitment and development of top players from nontraditional sources of talent. Examples include European, African, and Chinese players in professional basketball (NBA in the United States); American, Asian, and African players in soccer (premier European leagues); Korean, Japanese, Caribbean, Latin American, and Australian players in baseball (MLB); Australians in women's softball (NCAA); plus an array of international stars from Europe, Asia, Australia, and South America in women's professional basketball (WNBA) and soccer (WUSA). The 1990s produced an unexpected star in the aftermath of the 1994 Major League Baseball strike in Hideo Nomo of the Los Angeles Dodgers. Nomo not only became the first Japanese player to play in the major leagues since 1965, but also was named to the 1995 National League All-Star team and named NL Rookie of the Year. Six years later his fellow countryman, Ichiro Suzuki, an outfielder, became an overnight phenomenon as the first Japanese nonpitcher in Major League Baseball when he won the American League's MVP, batting title, and Rookie of the Year awards in the same season.

The growing trend of international athletes competing overseas in elite U.S., European, or Asian-based professional sport leagues continues to transform and broaden the definition of what constitutes international sport. Successful and popular professional teams such as the New York Yankees (Major League Baseball) and Manchester United (English Premiership, Soccer) have created a unique business partnership to help each other create a unique worldwide brand. The leagues consciously use the fan impact of these players to market to a new ethnic audience within the United States (e.g., Japanese or Hispanic fans) and to expand their team brand through the sale of broadcast rights, team merchandise, and other product extensions overseas. This has been evidenced by a drop in fan attendance at Japanese professional baseball league games and an expanded interest among Japanese fans in watching Japanese players on television play for MLB teams in the United States.

These developments have forced men's major professional leagues in soccer, basketball, baseball, and hockey to form new working agreements with other professional leagues, individual franchises, and international sport federations. Leagues and franchises have struggled to create a new climate of cooperation and a more orderly international transfer of players, both of which have been confounded by court rulings in different countries such as the Bosman case. In what is viewed as a seminal case, the European Court of Justice ruled in 1996 that transfer fees for out-of-contract soccer players were illegal where players were being transferred between clubs in one EU nation and another. Bosman held that the quota systems for foreign-born players were also illegal (European Communities, 1995).

The international expansion of sport has also set off a flurry of activity in the sport marketplace. For example, more than 200 million people worldwide participate in basketball (Pitts & Stotlar, 2002). Recognizing the mature market in North America, the NBA launched a global marketing campaign in 1989 to expand the brand awareness of its teams, players, and league-licensed merchandise. This campaign was perfectly positioned to capitalize on the gold medal performance of the 1992 U.S. Olympic basketball team (a.k.a. Dream Team I) led by the NBA's best. It was as much by design as by happenstance that Michael Jordan and Magic Johnson became international sport icons, eclipsing the fame of even the most famous soccer players of that era. Now in the first decade of the 21st century, the NBA is arguably the most recognized sport brand in the world (Ukeman, 2000).

The end of the Cold War and the dissolution of the Soviet Union and East Germany helped spawn sport market economies in the new nation-states of Central and Eastern Europe. This was paralleled by a corresponding rise in sport market economies in emerging nations in South America and Asia in the 1990s. A vibrant global marketplace based on new sources and pathways in both the production and distribution of goods and services has stimulated a dynamic export–import exchange process among many nations and regions of the world (Klemm, 1994). Sport is often seen as a universal product that bridges cultural differences, customs, and belief systems and thus is a vital part of the growing international business exchange. The following case of the rise of China as a world force in sport illuminates the emergence of the ancient "Middle Kingdom" into the spotlight of the international sport enterprise.

LEARNING ACTIVITY

Deliver an oral presentation on a current critical issue or event in international sport. Familiarize yourself with a variety of sources that provide information relevant to international sport. At least half the sources you choose should be from non-U.S. periodicals or literature. We encourage you to use the Internet and electronic information sources. The presentation should explore critical issues as well as highlight important current events that are international in scope and focus.

China As an Awakening Sport Giant

International sport was controlled, organized, and dominated during the 20th century primarily by individuals and nations from the so-called developed world (e.g., United Kingdom, Western Europe, Russia, Japan, and the United States). The first decade of the 21st century will potentially radically change how the international sport industry is defined and who will continue to be or emerge as its prominent controlling agents. Business will no longer remain a cast of the usual suspects rooted in Anglo-Western power bases. Although the power language of sport business will remain English, a working grasp of Mandarin and possibly Cantonese will be necessary for corporations and organizations to be effective in their attempts to be players on this new dynamic stage.

Why China? In the words of James Carville, President Clinton's 1992 presidential campaign manager, "it's the economy, stupid." China is already the awakening giant of sport in the 21st century. It is no wonder that the International Olympic Committee and its corporate supporters along with the Barons of Football (a.k.a. FIFA World Cup soccer) have firmly tied their future growth to the economic reformists within the communist government in Beijing. Although risky, this strategic initiative could yield a tremendous economic windfall to the IOC and FIFA. China, with its burgeoning population of over 1.2 billion people or roughly 20% of the earth's total population, has emerged in the past decade as a very fertile ground for broad-based sport development (Ashton, 2001). Sheer population, however, does not necessarily provide the foundation for either elite sport development or a stable new frontier for sport investment. The necessary political, financial, and economic infrastructure also must be in place to foster a truly dynamic shift in the focus of the international sport enterprise toward Asia in general and toward China specifically.

Corporations must know how to navigate cautiously and patiently with the power brokers and hierarchies of Chinese business and sport, in which bribes and graft are expected and commonplace. The protection of brand and intellectual property is also constantly at risk. Relationships with ruling cells, cliques, or power elites must be built carefully and strategically since shifts in power are predictably unpredictable (Chu, 1991; Elashmawi & Harris, 1998).

Over the past decade China has emerged as a new Olympic power challenging the more traditional powers of the United States, Russia, Germany, and other Western countries. Following the blueprint of the former Soviet Union and the former East Germany, the Chinese have invested heavily in a government-run sport model that is designed to identify children at a very young age with potential and talent in specific sports and then to train and develop them intensively in residential training centers for elite and promising athletes. Similar also to its Soviet and East German predecessors, China also has focused on developing women's sports with a specific goal of rapidly boosting its Olympic medal haul in both the Summer and Winter Olympic Games. Although it has not forgotten to support its burgeoning men's program in gymnastics, basketball, and soccer, the Chinese government has invested millions of dollars in developing women's sports such as swimming and diving, track and field, basketball, volleyball, soccer, gymnastics, figure skating, and short-track speed skating where China has emerged as an Olympic power. These efforts have produced countless gold, silver, and bronze medals as evidenced by China's finishing third overall in total medals just behind the United States and Russia at the 2000 Sydney Olympic Games (Wallechinsky, 2001).

This strategy of developing winning international teams in a variety of high-profile sports has resulted in the development of a strong sense of national pride, while assisting the government in garnering increased international respect and legitimacy. The convergence of a number of critical geopolitical and economic forces from 1990 to 2002 have helped propel China into the elite power circle of international sport. An intentional strategic shift to a more market-based economy over the past 15 years along with the resultant development of a sizable middle class has critically aided in supporting a new and flourishing sport culture in China that is both participant and fan based. It is estimated that over 100 million Chinese are active in one or more sports ranging from the more traditional paddle or racket sports of table tennis and badminton to team sports such as basketball and soccer. In fact, soccer is king in terms of participation and fan and viewer interest in China

(Ashton, 2001). From a purely capitalist and entrepreneurial perspective, the numbers are simply staggering (see figure 18.1).

Primed for the 2008 Olympic Games

In 1993 the Chinese Olympic Committee was fully expecting a positive vote by the IOC membership on its bid to host the 2000 Summer Olympic Games. Five ballots later, China fell two votes short to Sydney, Australia. It was an open secret that the president of the International Olympic Committee (IOC), Juan Antonio Samaranch, wished to conclude his nearly 20 years in power by bringing the Games to China. Using the power and purse of the IOC, Samaranch actively courted the Chinese, whom he saw as an emerging Olympic power and a potential political and economic windfall for the IOC as a Summer Olympic host. It was also no secret that China was a source of sustained support for Samaranch's favorite initiatives throughout the 1990s (Jennings, 2001).

The Chinese bid was unsuccessful due to a variety of missteps leading up to the vote in 1993. These included China's bid committee members being somewhat naïve in how to play the game. The granting of payoffs and expensive gifts to, or in some cases the blatant attempts to bribe, individual IOC members has been incumbent with most Olympic bidding processes. The trick is to engage in the game while not getting caught. A gift of a priceless Ming vase to IOC president Samaranch for the International Olympic Museum was highly publicized in the U.S., European, and Australian press as being ill timed and suspicious at best (Jennings, 1996).

The early 1990s were also very sensitive times in East–West relations with regard to the Chinese government's hard-line policies on the reannexation of Taiwan, its bloody suppression of the prodemocracy protests in Tiananmen Square, and its

Quick Facts—China:

Area: 9,598,032 sq km (3,705,820 eq mi)
Population: 1.2 billion
Capital: Beijing (11,299,000 pop.)
Type of government: Communist
Famous leaders: Mao-Zedong, Chou En-Lai, Deng Xiaopeng
Major cities: Beijing, Guangzhou (Canton), Shanghai, Shenzhen, Macau, Nanjing, Hong Kong, Fuzhan, Wuhan
Tourism: 21 million visitors per year
Religion(s): Daoist, Buddhist, Muslim
Language(s): Mandarian, Cantonese, Shanghaiese, various regional dialects
Literacy: 82% of population
Life expectancy: 70 years of age
Climate: Northern and western regions have hot, dry summers and cold winters with the coastal areas milder and wetter. Southern regions have heavy rainfall between May and September.
Currency: Yuan (8.27 yuan equals $1.00 USD)
GDP per capita: $3,460 USD
Economy: Modified market-driven with strong government control; *Industrial*—iron and steel, coal, machine building, armaments, textiles, and apparel; *Agriculture*—rice, wheat, potatoes, sorghum; peanuts, tea, millet, cotton, pork, and fish; *Exports*—electrical machinery, clothing, footwear, toys, mineral fuels, leather, and plastics

Source: *Eartha*—International Atlas: DeLorme.

Quick Sport Facts—China:

Popular sports of interest: Soccer, basketball, table tennis, badminton, swimming, rugby, snooker, and tennis
Olympic/international sports (Winter): Short-track speedskating, women's figure skating, women's freestyle skiing
Olympic/international sports (Summer): Swimming and diving, gymnastics, track and field, table tennis, soccer, badminton, basketball, and volleyball
Major professional sport league: Soccer, basketball, volleyball, table tennis, and badminton
Famous athletes: Chen Liu (figure skating), Su Wen (women's soccer), Wang Zhi-Zhi, Yao Ming (basketball)
Leading sports manufacturer: Beijing Li Ning Sports Goods Company
Major international sport events—Host:
2001 World University Games
2002 Tennis Masters Cup
2003 FIFA Women's World Cup (soccer)
2004 Asian Football Cup (soccer)
2008 Summer Olympic Games (Beijing)
2008 Summer Paralympic Games (Beijing)
Popular TV/sports media: China Central Television (CCTV); ESPN Star TV (cable)
Homes with TV: 310 million
Homes with cable TV: 125 million

Source: *Sport Business International*: SBG London.

Figure 18.1   China by the numbers.

Source: Sport Business International: SBG London.

inability to stem the proliferation of counterfeiting and trademark abuses. Ironically, while governments argued over human rights and other issues, U.S. and European corporations were vying to greatly expand their business ventures in China. Among those who profited were sport apparel and footwear companies (e.g., Nike, Reebok, Adidas, Fila, and others), whose production relocations to Southeast Asia, including China, were based on the exploitation of workers in sweatshops (Roberts & Bernstein, 2000).

The bid for the 2000 Olympic Games was furthered compromised by the suspicions within various international sport federations and a number of Western nations regarding the rapid and accelerated rise of China as a power in two of the Olympics' marquee sports of track and field and swimming. Several factors intersected to fuel these suspicions. With the devolution of East Germany and the Soviet Union beginning with the fall of the Berlin Wall in 1989, a number of noted former East Bloc coaches and exercise scientists disappeared, only to reemerge in China. The hiring of many former East German coaches and sport scientists by China in the early 1990s also coincided with the surprise discovery of highly detailed documents in the former East Germany by German police. These documents revealed how the East German sports establishment systematically cheated for decades by using illegal drugs and blood doping techniques to help enhance the speed, strength, and stamina of its Olympic athletes in order to win medals. Many famous East German Olympic coaches and Olympic medal winners were identified through evidence provided by these socalled "doping documents" that were presented at trials conducted in both Germany and Canada organized to expose these unethical and illegal practices. Suspicions followed these coaches and sport scientists to China, in particular, as the Chinese women became dominant as a world power in swimming and track and field virtually overnight. Several well-publicized drug busts of Chinese swimmers and track athletes confirmed the widely-held suspicions that the Chinese athletes were "not clean" (Jennings, 1996).

So what happened to change things in favor of the Chinese being awarded the 2008 Summer Olympic Games when the IOC gathered in July of 2001 in Moscow? To begin with, the Chinese learned by hiring a major U.S. public relations and advertising firm, Hill and Knowlton, to manage its image and public relations campaign in advance of the vote. The Chinese Olympic Committee and its corre-

sponding national sport federations took a firm, if not controversial, stand against some of its own athletes in swimming and track and field by not sending some of their best athletes to Sydney for the Summer Olympics in 2000 in a effort to quell the rumors and suspicions of rampant state support for drug cheating. This action took place after the doping scandals in 1998 when Chinese swimmers were caught with vials of human growth hormone (HGH) in their luggage en route to Sydney for the 1998 world swimming championships (Ashton, 2001) .

The supporters of the official IOC position claimed that Beijing had the most compelling bid of all the cities vying for the 2008 Games and had seriously addressed the critical collective political, financial, human rights, and sport ethical issues (meaning doping scandals) since their near miss of 1993. The skeptics and cynics who follow the Olympic bidding process have described the vote that gave Beijing the 2008 Games on the second round as being a foregone conclusion based on a backroom deal. Many argued that this was essentially a parting gift to Samaranch on his retirement as Olympic chief and that little, if anything, had truly changed in China regarding critical issues prior to the vote (Jennings, 2001). The realities of the what, who, and why of the Olympic bidding process undoubtedly resided somewhere between these two conflicting viewpoints.

Nearly 20 years after the unexpected marketing success of the 1984 Olympic Games in Los Angeles, fueled by billions of dollars in television rights fees from NBC and others and additional tens of millions from 10 corporations for quadrennial worldwide sponsorship rights (the TOP group), the IOC has become an international sport marketing juggernaut. It is not a coincidence that many of these large multinational corporations already are present and doing business in China (Echikson & Webb, 2001, p. 48). The TOP group includes Coca-Cola, John Hancock, Kodak, McDonald's, Matsushita (Panasonic), Samsung, the SEMA Group, Sports Illustrated/Time, Visa, and Xerox. Millions, perhaps billions of advertising dollars are at stake as China prepares to host the 2008 Games (SBI, 2001, August). Many industry insiders have predicted that getting the 2008 Games for Beijing will trigger the largest stadium construction program the world has ever witnessed coupled with creating record-setting advertising revenues in the millions, perhaps billions. China expects to spend nearly 2.2 billion U.S. dollars or 18 billion yuan on new state-of-the art stadia and arenas in preparation for the Olympics and other major international events (Cronin, 2001). American stadium design companies HOK, Ellerbe Becket, and NTJJB are expected to be involved in the building of 18 new stadia and arenas and the renovation of 14 existing arenas in Beijing alone (Cronin, 2001).

The Chinese government also expects to spend the equivalent of $22 billion in its nonsport preparations that will include $10.8 billion on transport infrastructure, $5.4 billion on cleaning up the environment, $3.6 billion on information technology, and $1.8 billion on improved living conditions (SBI, 2001, August). This does not include the nearly $2 billion expected to be spent as part of the cost of managing and operating the 2008 Olympic and Paralympic Games or the costs associated with the marketing, management, and operation of a series of major international events leading up to the Games including the 2001 World University Games, the 2002 Tennis Masters Cup, the 2003 FIFA Women's World Cup (soccer), and the 2004 Asian Football Cup (soccer).

Based on past host city experiences, all will not be gold for the Chinese as they prepare the necessary infrastructure to host the world's largest sporting event in 2008. Lingering realities simply cannot be swept away overnight such as ongoing worldwide concerns of human rights abuses such as arbitrary detention and the executions of political dissidents. Global trade and resource production issues are expected to continue surrounding the existence of sweatshop labor that multinational corporations exploit for the production of apparel and athletic footwear at nearly slave wages in very oppressive working conditions (Engardio, & Belton, 2000). In addition, very serious environmental concerns could compromise the health of the athletes participating in the 2008 Games. Of particular concern for athletes is the air pollution found in Beijing and many of the other projected host cities, which is expected to be similar to the air quality in Los Angeles during the 1984 Olympic Games.

Other prime issues remain over the lack of a free press or the willingness of the Chinese government to grant unfettered access to the foreign press. Brand protection and intellectual property rights are very serious concerns for many Olympic sponsors as they wearily weigh the pros and cons of doing business on the mainland. Tensions over the status of Taiwan and its inclusion as a separate team recognized by the IOC also pose challenges to international diplomacy. The require-

ment of the host city to also host the Paralympic Games presents some very serious problems related to a cultural attitude in China toward people with disabilities in general and the lack of reasonable accommodations and accessibility specifically. It remains to be seen what the so-called Olympic legacy effect on China will be. Will it be similar to the social, political, and economic changes that occurred in South Korea following the 1988 Olympic Games (Pound, 1994)? One could argue that the 1988 Games in Korea created a momentum for the movement to a more open democratic society that was more willing to institute changes regarding some of its most isolationist trade practices. While the results will not be evident for some time, it is clear that the impact on the international sport enterprise will be enormous.

LEARNING ACTIVITY

Using basic demographic data, create a summary table showing the top Olympic nations through an analysis that compares the value of each medal won in the most recent Olympic and Paralympic Games as based on the relative cost per medal (i.e., rich countries spend more per capita than poor countries). This can be determined by using comparative data such as the number and type of medals won (e.g., gold, silver, bronze) with a nation's per capita income and their total overall population.

Effect of China on the International Sport Industry

China is likely to continue to liberalize its rules and its control over its prime athletic talent in order to export to professional leagues in North America and Europe, while growing a new generation of elite athletes, athletic participants, fans, and viewers. This was evidenced by Yao Ming (at seven feet, five inches tall) being selected as the first Asian number one overall draft pick in the 2002 NBA draft. Complicated negotiations facilitated by his American sports agent among the NBA, the Houston Rockets, the Chinese Basketball Federation, the Chinese Ministry of Sport, the Shanghai Sharks of the Chinese Basketball Association (CBA), and the NBA Players Association were necessary to gain Yao Ming's release to play in the United States.

Even without the successful Olympic bid, China has positioned itself to move into the mainstream in the world of soccer. Building on the international

China and its athletes, such as NBA player Yao Ming, are having an impact on the world of international sport.

success of its women's national team and the first qualifying success of its men's team for the 2002 FIFA World Cup held in Japan and Korea, China will define itself as a new epicenter of the world's most popular sport with the largest single boom in growth of fans, viewers, and participants that soccer has ever seen (Roberts, 2001, July 30).

The first two decades of the 21st century will witness a growing trend in China to privatize the professional side of its sport industry through aggressive stadium building and the rise of professional leagues such as the CBA in basketball and the C-League in soccer. The Chinese Football Association (CFA) has been able to garner more flexibility from the central government in Beijing, basing its operational strategy (e.g., merchandising, corporate sponsorships) more on a Western professional sport model than many experts thought possible. Whether it is Su Wen in women's professional soccer (WUSA), Yao Ming and Wang Zhizhi in men's professional basketball (NBA), or Peng Shuai and Li Na in women's professional tennis (WTA), China appears poised to evolve from merely exporting a few emerging sport heroes to developing a critical mass of elite male and female professional players who are able to perform at the highest level in the U.S.- and European-based professional leagues.

Chinese athletes are being represented by American-based sport marketing agencies and already have tie-ins to corporate sponsorship such as Nike and other footwear companies. Rights to represent elite Chinese players, lucrative exhibition tours and tournaments, and team and league sponsorships are up for grabs by overseas firms. Once again, however, these firms must carefully build alliances and partnerships within China or risk the loss of millions of dollars in investment similar to what happen to Lucent Technologies in its attempt to sponsor Chinese professional soccer in the late 1990s. Lucent thought it could use a U.S.-centric model of sport advertising and corporate sponsorship as a platform to sell its products to the Chinese market. It failed International Business 101 in that it did not understand well enough how to adapt to a more Chinese-centric model of establishing business relationships and networks. Money for billboards and TV advertisements alone was not enough.

Despite the ongoing protracted international debate over key geopolitical, environmental, and human rights issues prominent in the run-up to China's being voted into the World Trade Organization (WTO) as a full-fledged member in 2001 and Beijing being awarded the 2008 Olympic and Paralympic Summer Games, the ultimate winner in the emergence of China as a world player is the sport industry itself. The potential growth in real GDP for all segments of the international sport industry will come from new sport media and marketing opportunities, the rise of new professional leagues (soccer and basketball), the export of new elite athletic talent to professional leagues (e.g., basketball, tennis, and soccer), the incredible growth of new facilities of all types, and expanded sport manufacturing and product development. All of these will help fuel the continued growth of the sport enterprise well into the first two decades of the 21st century. With this ascendant boom in the development of a new sport infrastructure for China, other segments of the sport enterprise such as finance and licensing will continue to accelerate rapidly with the development of joint ventures and alliances between established U.S. and European sport firms and organizations and their Chinese partners. A review of the first decade of the 21st

Figure 18.2 Knowing where to begin learning how to break into the international sport industry can be confusing. Following these essential guidelines can help you get where you want to go.

Reprinted, by permission, from The Wilkinson Group.

century will show that power and profit in international sport will be counted in dollars, euros, *and* yuan.

Careers in International Sport

The nature and scope of the international sport industry is complex and continues to change so rapidly that you need an up-to-date road map to keep things straight (see figure 18.2). To work as an international sport manager, you must have a sound working knowledge of the processes of international business, local and regional culture, and sport with a clear recognition of who the key stakeholders are (e.g., organizations and people). From using sport teams and events to sell tobacco products, alcohol, Fords, and Hondas in Europe, to sponsoring Formula One car racing, to selling tourism in conjunction with the Olympics or a particular world championship, there is a definite relationship among events, products, and talent.

Nowhere is there such a direct relationship among sport, leisure, and business than in international sport.

What do you need to know as a prospective sport manager in preparation for a journey into international sport? Any corporation or sport organization choosing to do business in another country from a global rather than national perspective must understand the basics of finance, macroeconomics, manufacturing, distribution of products and services, retailing, and human resource management (Morrison, Conaway, & Douress, 2001). The first step in your journey, therefore, is developing an understanding of the primary trade treaties and agreements, such as the General Agreement on Tariffs and Trade (GATT), the North American Free Trade Agreement (NAFTA), and the rules and regulations affecting the European Union (EU). This knowledge will provide a rudimentary foundation from which you can research other important trade regulations, currency exchanges, and the legal issues revolving around brand protection and intellectual property. You must also know how free or restricted the movement of goods, services, persons, and capital is from nation to nation. Knowing your rights as a foreigner when doing business in another nation is also critical (Morrison, Conaway, & Douress, 2001). By gaining an in-depth awareness of how well you, your employees, and your investments will be protected by a given legal system, you will know what recourses you have if problems occur. The best protection, however, is to be culturally tuned in to the nation and region in which you are conducting business.

Many professional leagues and teams are concerned about whether intellectual property and copyright laws of a nation or regional economic group (e.g., China, Japan, Brazil, or the European Union) will protect their trademarks. They also need to know if other countries have laws or regulations that might inhibit the movement of players from one nation to another (e.g., Europe in soccer, Japan in baseball, or China in basketball), whether they have a system of binding contracts (e.g., the NBA and the NHL with the European leagues and MLB with its Latin American and Japanese counterparts), and in what currency to base the compensation for a given player (e.g., MLB and the NHL with Canadian and U.S teams).

Sport managers looking to become involved in international sport should be aware of these and other issues. In the following sections, we will explore two of the most pressing concerns in international sport today: relocating manufacturing companies and international sport governance.

Relocating Manufacturing Companies

Sporting goods manufacturing companies that have relocated most of the production of their footwear to China or Indonesia are faced with financial and ethical concerns (Bernstein, Shari, & Malkin, 2000). Does the attraction of a large, cheap labor force outweigh concerns over counterfeiting due to weak copyright laws, currency fluctuations and devaluations, and potentially new restrictive export and import laws? What are the ethical considerations when large multinational corporations such as Nike or Adidas profit from children and women toiling for pennies an hour in sweatshop conditions to produce name brand footwear (Jones, 1996; Robeson, 2001)? Is it exploitation to continuously move footwear production from one Third World country to another (e.g., from Korea and the Philippines to China and Indonesia) in search of the cheapest labor supply? What responsibility does a company have to the workers and countries it leaves behind? Ideally, these decisions are based on ethical value systems as well as on the stability of the political regimes where products are produced (e.g., Indonesia and Pakistan) and their respective diplomatic relations with the nations that host the corporate home offices such as the United States or the nations of Western Europe (Katz, 1994).

International Sport Governance

The next step on your journey into international sport is developing an understanding of international sport governance structure (see figure 18.3). Before 1985 international sport was defined by distinguishing amateur sport (IOC, NOC, LOOC, LOCs) from professional sport. International sport governance was focused on amateur sports that were included in the Olympic Games, Commonwealth Games, or hemispheric games (e.g., Asian, Pan-African, Pan-American Games), and among members of international sport federations (IFs) and their related national sport governing bodies (NSFs and NGBs).

As you can see in figure 18.3, however, several new entities have become involved in international sport governance over the past 20 years. The principal additions include professional sport organizations (PSOs), professional athlete unions and professional athlete representatives (PPUs and PARs), the Court of Arbitration for Sport (CAS), the World Anti-Doping Agency (WADA), and sport organization and event sponsors (SOs and ESs). The following two sections illustrate why these additional groups are included.

Corporate Sponsorship

One of the classic case studies that outlines the complexities of authority and control (i.e., governance) relative to the involvement of professional athletes on Olympic teams who have conflicting contractual endorsement contracts with Olympic

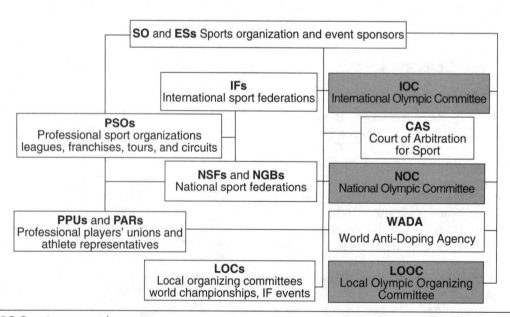

Figure 18.3 International sport governance.

Created by author, 2003.

sponsors involved the U.S. men's Olympic basketball team in 1992. The team included 11 NBA veterans who had been selected by a committee of NBA coaches and general managers. To obtain approval for each player to participate, the player, his agent, his sponsors, his team, his league, USA Basketball (NGB), and the U.S. Olympic Committee were involved in a series of negotiations to clarify the rules and regulations under which the athlete would be governed. The compensation rules, the playing rules, the dispute resolution rules, and the expectations of behavior and conduct were different from those outlined in the standard pro contracts.

Reebok was the 1992 official U.S. Olympic outerwear sponsor, providing warm-up jackets to all athletes. The agreements between the athletes and the U.S. Olympic Committee (USOC) were severely tested when some members of the team chose to cover the Reebok name with American flags as they stood on the victory podium to accept their gold medals. This action was initiated by Michael Jordan, who as a Nike-sponsored athlete, refused to be seen implicitly endorsing his company's competitor. This incident thrust the USOC, Nike, Reebok, and Jordan into a high-stakes public relations battle (Katz, 1994). After 1992, the USOC amended its athlete code of conduct to include language that requires all U.S. Olympic athletes to wear the official apparel provided by the Olympic sponsors of a given Olympics regardless of potential endorsement conflicts.

The IOC and its related NOC members have become very forceful in using all available legal means to limit, enforce, and counteract ambush advertising by corporations and organizations intent on circumventing the costs of sponsorship and official involvement in the Olympic Games. This is usually done by making references to the upcoming Olympic Games or events by linking an image of a sport or athletes with reference to the host city (e.g., "Good luck to our athletes in Salt Lake City") and by paying careful attention to not using the term "Olympic" or "Olympic Games" in an advertisement. The IOC, NOC, or LOOC cannot afford to be lax in their diligence to protect and support their corporate partners who have been granted a set of exclusive rights in exchange for tens of millions of dollars in sponsorships. To prevent future potential conflicts from happening between a team sponsor for an NGB (national governing body) (e.g., USA basketball) and a rival company that has an endorsement deal with Team USA's star players, the USOC has tightened its contracts and oversight. As part of its expanded role, the USOC has evolved a new partnership program called the Olympic Properties US or OPUS, in which it has maintained central control over its participating joint venture partners such as the Salt Lake City Olympic Committee (SLOC) for the 2002 Winter Olympic Games (USOC, 2001).

Arbitration

The second illustration regarding international sport governance, which also occurred in 1992, is related to U.S. track and field athlete Butch Reynolds' challenge of Olympic drug testing procedures. Reynolds failed an out-of-competition drug test and was disqualified from participating in the 1992 Olympic Games. He subsequently filed suit against the International Amateur Athletic Federation (IAAF), claiming that his urine specimens had been tampered with and that the analysis procedures had been flawed. This controversy highlighted the complex entanglements involving an athlete's right to sue an international sport federation over the right to compete in the Olympic Games.

A U.S. federal court held for Reynolds and threatened to freeze IAAF sponsorship money from U.S.-based corporations to force the IAAF to fulfill its obligations of a compensatory award (Weiler & Roberts, 1993). The problems caused by this situation and the implications of successful legal action pressured several international sport federations to join with the IOC in supporting the creation of the Court of Arbitration for Sport (CAS) to mediate sport-related disputes that cross national boundaries (Thoma & Chalip, 1996).

If this situation had happened 10 years later, the World Anti-Doping Agency (WADA), headed by ex-IOC vice president Dick Pound, would likely have assumed responsibility for and jurisdiction over for the Reynolds case. WADA was established in 2001 as a result of broad international public perception that many world records and gold medal results in the Olympic Games and many world championships in a variety of sports have been tainted by cheaters who have not been caught. As a result of the investigations into the Salt Lake City Olympic bid scandal, the IOC came under intense pressure to change its methods of operations including getting tough on drug enforcement (Jennings, 2001).

LEARNING ACTIVITY

Write a paper about a significant contemporary issue in international sport. Your topic should cut across the sport and international spectrum (for example, drug use, security, professionalization, commercialization, expansion, governance). This paper should not focus on any particular event per se (such as the Olympic Games); however, it could include the Olympic Games or some other event or league as a focal point. Use the "Final Word" column in *Street & Smith's SportsBusiness Journal* as an example for this project.

The Paralympic Games: A Special International Governance Concern

The Paralympic Games, which involve the world's elite athletes with physical and sensory disabilities, have emerged as one of the world's largest quadrennial sport events. The Winter and Summer Paralympic Games usually occur two weeks after the Olympic Games at the same location and in the same sport facilities requiring similar organizing capabilities and requirements as the Olympic Games. The LOOCs are now mandated by the IOC to organize and conduct the Paralympic events. Thus, when an Olympic bid is awarded to a city or region, it also brings with it a corresponding responsibility to organize the Paralympics Games as well. This has presented a set of new challenges for the IOC, its member NOCs, the LOOCs of Athens 2004, Turin 2006, and Beijing 2008, the international sport federations, and their corresponding national sport federations.

Under the leadership of the International Paralympic Committee (IPC), founded in 1992, and its corresponding National Paralympic Committees (NPCs), the Paralympics have emerged as a viable international sport movement. The separate but parallel structures that exist between the IOC and IPC, the NOCs and their corresponding NPCs, and the international sport federations and their national sport federation members will continue to be in the forefront of international and national debates in the first decades of the 21st century as these groups struggle over how to include athletes with disabilities into their organizations and events.

It is worth noting that the U.S. Olympic Committee has acted as its country's National Paralympic Committee (NPC) since 1995. At the time, this signaled a tremendous advance in the movement to integrate athletes with disabilities into the national and international sport mainstream. Under different leadership, the USOC executive board voted to spin off its NPC duties (read "segregate") into a new U.S. Paralympic Corporation (USPC). The United States Ski and Snowboard Association (USSA), which was the first national governing body in the world to integrate Paralympic athletes into its structure with the assimilation of the U.S. Disabled Ski Team (USDST) in 1986, also responded to changes in its leadership by reexamining its role and mission relative to Paralympic sport. The executive board of the USSA at first voted in 2000 to create a new segregated subsidiary similar to the proposed USPC and then reconsidered and voted to retain the USDST as a fully integrated part of its organization in 2001. It is predicted that governance challenges relating to the integration of athletes with disabilities into Olympic-related sport organizations will continue in the first decades of the 21st century. Some U.S. Olympic executives have begun to question whether these changes relative to disability sport will be viewed similarly to Title IX and gender equity issues as they have impacted intercollegiate athletics in the United States during the 1990s. In essence, will the national governing bodies of Olympic sports and the U.S. Olympic Committee be mandated by law to integrate their structures, teams, management, and governance regarding the needs of Paralympic athletes (Fay, 1999)?

Other important segments of the international sport industry that are not represented in figure 18.3 include arenas, stadia, sport products, ticketing, security, rehabilitation and sports medicine centers, accommodation, and travel. These elements are crucial to the conduct of any international sport event and are the areas in which most of the growth in the first decade of the 21st century will occur, thereby providing the most opportunities for entry-level sport managers.

Working Environments of International Sport Managers

If you are seeking a career in international sport, essential equipment will include a world atlas, a passport, visas (for some countries), bilingual dictionaries, a pocket guide to currency exchange rates, a credit card with a reasonable credit line, transportation tickets, a laptop computer with modem, a cellular phone, and two bags packed full of the most important items necessary to conduct business. You are embarking on an adventure that will test your wits with respect to your personal habits, eating preferences, language skills, cultural understanding, business etiquette, patience, and ability to develop a network of friendships. You will be told that your colleagues from other countries understand English more than they do or that you can obtain the services of an interpreter who, as it turns out, cannot or will not convey the nuances of the verbal exchange. In the highly personalized world of international business and sport, even a rudimentary understanding of the language you are engaged in can gain you an invaluable foothold over your competition (Barnett & Cavanagh, 1994; Morrison, Conaway, & Douress, 2001).

Computer skills and the ability to access the Internet to conduct online research are now often assumed as basic skills for entry-level sport management positions. International sport is a phone, fax, and e-mail culture based on strong oral and written communication skills, complemented by an understanding of electronic etiquette. A sales background and experience as an athlete are not requirements per se, but they are often perceived as a bonus in gaining and succeeding at a job. As an international sport manager, you must be willing and able to travel, necessitating an adequate level of fitness and health. In addition, there are long flights, long meetings compressed into schedules that are too short, and long periods away from home (Katz, 1994). You need to be patient, able to listen, and respectful of existing hierarchies as established by various cultures.

If you are involved in or interested in the international aspects of sport management, you should avail yourself of the wide range of publications in the field, including industry and trade publications, professional journals, newspapers, and magazines, in a effort to be up-to-date on international political, business, and sport trends. It is also wise to start a library of books and information that will augment off-the-shelf or library reference material. A daily or weekly regimen of reading key periodicals such as *Sport Business International, Street & Smith's SportsBusiness Journal,* the *Wall Street Journal, USA Today,* the *Economist,* or similar business and sport business periodicals is vital. Many of these periodicals also exist as Web-based resources as well. This practice will give you knowledge of general business practices in a given culture, keep you current on what is happening in the global economy, and give you an up-to-date understanding of world events. The Internet and a variety of online services provide easy access to key materials and daily periodicals that may not be available in hard copy at a library, bookstore, or newsstand (Brake, Walker, & Walker, 1995).

A basic knowledge of how an international sport operates, the specific rules of the game, how it is structured, and where the locus of power resides (politically and on the field of play) can enhance your marketability. Understanding growth and trends in licensing, marketing, promotion, event management, and contracts (player and event) is also helpful (Halbfinger, 1996). Familiarity with the shifting borders within geopolitical regions and the changing names of countries will prevent an inappropriate faux pas, such as forgetting that Czechoslovakia is now the separate nations of the Czech Republic and Slovakia; that Burma is now Myanmar; and that Croatia, Slovenia, Bosnia-Herzegovina, and Macedonia are no longer part of Yugoslavia (*Eartha,* 2001).

Success in the international sport and business sphere is predicated on personal contact and friendship. Attending meetings of national sport federations, professional associations, and other conferences and symposia will help you maintain and expand your network of professional contacts. Time availability, relevance to your professional interests, and financial resources are important factors to consider when choosing which associations, annual conferences, and trade shows to attend. Volunteering at a major international sport event, conference, or trade show is an effective way to gain access to the field and to demonstrate your capabilities as a potential employee.

An informational interview of professionals in the field can be valuable in learning more about the realities of working for U.S. sport organizations that do business with other cultures or of the effects of being relocated to a country in which you must speak a different language. There is no one pathway to a career in the expanding and shifting landscape of the international sport marketplace.

LEARNING ACTIVITY

In small groups, read and discuss the following books:

- Katz, D. (1994). *Just do it.* New York: Random House.
- Morrison, R., Conaway, W., & Borden, G. (1994). *Kiss, bow, or shake hands: How to do business in sixty countries.* Holbrook, MA: Bob Adams.
- Jennings, A. (2001). *The Great Olympic Swindle: When the world wanted its games back.* New York: Simon & Schuster.
- Whiting, R. (1990). *You gotta have wa.* New York: Vintage Books.

International Sport in the Next Decade

The international sport industry in the beginning of the 21st century has shifted from being perceived as a niche in the sport marketplace to representing the foundation of the sport enterprise. Market share and investment in a given sport product, service, or sport are now measured on a worldwide rather than national basis. New references are being made to aspects of the industry in economic terms and scales based on concepts such as the gross global sport product (GGSP). Although there will be attempts to restrict and protect segments of the industry based on national bias and policies, the future in the early decades of the 21st century portends an almost seamless integration and movement of goods, services, and personnel on a grand global scale. Major international trade agreements are beginning to have a direct impact on the industry, as most sports have escalated the export and import of international talent at all competitive levels. International exchanges in a broad cross section of sports at youth levels will continue to become more commonplace (Pitts & Stotlar, 2002). National and international sport federations will challenge professional leagues and franchises for global market share of trademark licensing and merchandise and in creating more global brand awareness (Barrand, 2001, pp 20-22). These federations and their key events will also profit from expanding television revenues made possible through worldwide cable deregulation, Internet agreements, and expanded access through satellite television. Name recognition and brand awareness of teams, athletes, and products will become global. These events will bring a host of new challenges to the sport industry, which will be compounded by cultural differences, national laws, and customs.

Concerns about gender equity, diversity, and equal access for athletes with disabilities will become prominent in the first decade of the 21st century. The growth and expansion of professional team sport leagues for women, particularly in North America in soccer (WUSA), basketball (WNBA), softball (WPSL), and perhaps ice hockey, will give rise to expanded marketing and management opportunities. The Paralympic Games will continue to push to achieve major event status through increased television, media, and spectator appeal. These trends will help provide more jobs in the international market-place in all sport-related areas for women, older people, and individuals with disabilities. Visionary and socially responsible consumer-oriented companies will stand to gain the most from these developments (Fay, Hums, & Wolff, 2000).

A new order of elite decision makers will assume command of the global sport industry based on pragmatic alliances among leagues, international federations, television networks, and corporate sponsors. Corporations will begin to seek brand identification with a particular sport, leading to the formation of corporate and national team alliances (Badenhausen, Nixolov, Alkin, & Ozanian, 1997). New sports such as in-line skating, triathlon, snowboarding, and mountain biking will emerge, and other sports, such as roller hockey, beach volleyball, endurance kayaking, and other adventure challenge events, will expand or be redefined. All of these sports will flourish due to broad, cross-generational participation and their appeal as televised events that garner the support of lifestyle-oriented corporations.

Expanded leisure time for members of elite and middle classes in South America, Asia, and parts of Africa will continue to fuel the expansion of golf, tennis, and other leisure and recreation sports worldwide. Expanded life expectancy will continue to support an international sport and leisure travel industry (see chapter 17), necessitating the expansion of facilities. These developments will plunge the international sport industry more deeply into debates related to the impact of sport and recreation on the environment (Muench & Armend, 1995). The International Olympic Committee has created a commission and a policy position addressing concerns about the enormity of the impact of the Olympic Games on local and regional environments. No less noteworthy have been the land use conflicts about building large-scale leisure and sport resorts in Third World countries, golf courses in sensitive mountain terrain or tropical rain forests, and stadia and arenas in environmentally or economically sensitive areas.

Career opportunities will expand in areas dealing with jurisdiction and dispute resolution related to international athletes' rights, doping and drug use and abuse (e.g., the World Anti-Doping Agency), the relocation of franchises from one nation to another, and other policy matters. By 2010 international and national sport federations, professional leagues, sport marketing agencies, cable and network television and radio, arenas and facilities, and sport product corporations will give hiring preference to individuals with backgrounds oriented to the global marketplace (Barrand, 2001, December).

So, what should an aspiring sport manager do to get a head start on the future? Those who have the courage to take reasonable risks based on sound research, knowledge, and experience will be rewarded. The road maps outlining the future of the internationalization of the sport industry are rapidly changing and continually being rewritten. Many clues, however, already exist in the allied fields of international business studies and multicultural management studies. Flexibility, cultural sensitivity, and understanding, coupled with communication and language skills, provide the foundation for entry into the international sport domain.

LEARNING ACTIVITY

The world championships might be coming to your city! Create a student group (of four or five) and select a sport that is on the program of events of the Olympic Games, Pan American Games, World University Games, or Paralympic Games. The international sport federation (IF) of your sport has awarded your country through its national governing body (NGB) the right to host the world championships in this sport three to four years from now. Your group has recently been formed to compete for the right to act as the organizing committee for this event in your city. Your group must prepare a preliminary report and presentation to submit to the executive committee of the NGB of your sport at its annual convention. The executive committee of the NGB will take a vote to determine which city will be awarded this bid. Keep in mind that recently this world championship was integrated to include Paralympic athletes and events in its official program.

SUMMARY

The two factors that determine whether a sport is international are (1) the degree or regularity to which an organization or governance structure is focused on international activity and (2) the context in which an organization or structure operates within the sport enterprise. Since 1972 several events (e.g., the growing commercialization of the Olympics, Nixon's Ping-Pong diplomacy, and several Olympic rule changes regarding eligibility of professional athletes) have had a profound effect on sport and the redefinition of international sport. Athletes are now recruited from all over the world by both professional and amateur teams, sport marketing and sport media have moved boldly into the international arena, and sport businesses have become an active part of the global economy. Professional sport leagues and franchises are forming global alliances (e.g., Yankees–Nets and Manchester United) as a means to develop cross-promotional and marketing platforms in emerging markets in Asia, South America, and Africa. Conscious strategic efforts by professional leagues (e.g., soccer, basketball, baseball, and ice hockey) have been used to export and expand global brand awareness. These efforts have included the promotion and distribution of league games through new cable and broadcast networks highlighting players from a particular country or region of the world (e.g., Nomo or Suzuki in Japan or Park in Korea). One particular strategy that has been effective is the allowance of top professionals in men's and women's basketball (NBA and WNBA), men's ice hockey (NHL), and women's soccer (WUSA) to participate on their respective national Olympic teams (Kaufmann, 2001). It is not by accident that Manchester United of the England Premiership League and arguably the most recognized worldwide brand in soccer is importing Asian and African players and exporting its team for international exhibition matches in those respective regions. These are natural extensions of the sport industry becoming more highly globalized in its focus and strategy.

Individuals who want to work in international sport should be familiar with geopolitical realities, cultural preferences and ways of being, treaties and trade agreements, the structure of international sport governance, the international working environment, modern communication technology, and corporate sponsorships. Reading relevant literature, attending professional meetings, volunteering at international sport events, and conducting informational interviews are wise strategies. The future of international sport promises continued expansion and should bring many opportunities for well-prepared sport managers.

Job Opportunities

Positions in International Sport Marketing Training Program

The world's number one international sports product corporation seeks qualified candidates for positions within the company's new international marketing and development division training program. B.S. in sport management or related field required. Two to four years' experience in international marketing and sales with knowledge of emerging economies a plus. Must be willing to complete a two-year training program.

Event Site Manager—International Mountain Biking Series

International event management company seeks candidates for this position for the company's new international mountain bike series. B.S. in sport management or related field required, with at least two years' experience in event management and international sport preferred. Successful candidate must be able to do extensive traveling and to relocate for periods of up to 45-60 days to race sites in the U.S., Canada, Japan, and Europe during late spring and summer. Prior mountain bike racing experience and a second language required.

Marketing Fulfillment Associate—FIFA '99 Women's World Cup Soccer

International sport marketing firm seeks applicants for this position to act as account representatives to major corporate clients in company's FIFA World Cup Soccer sponsor fulfillment program. B.S. in sport management or related field required, MBA or master's degree preferred. A background of at least two years of sport marketing and sales experience is a must. Candidate must demonstrate excellent oral and written communication skills. Fluency in a second language is a plus. Position requires extensive travel and on-site fulfillment support for clients.

Delegation Director—2004 Summer Paralympic Games

The U.S. Olympic Committee invites applications for qualified candidates for the position of delegation director for the U.S. Paralympic team selected to compete in the 2004 Summer Paralympic Games. M.S. in sport management or related field preferred with two to four years' experience in event management, international sport, and disabled sport preferred. Successful candidate must be able to do extensive traveling and to relocate for 45 days during the conduct of the Games. Prior Olympic/Paralympic experience a plus.

Regional Sales Manager—Latin America

A leading multinational sports product manufacturer seeks qualified candidates for this position. B.S. in sport management or a related field is required, with MBA or master's preferred. A background in sport and fitness is a must. Fluency in Spanish, plus three to five years' experience in international marketing and sales in developing markets is required. Applicant must be familiar with the cultures and economic strictures of Caribbean Rim countries. Must be willing to relocate to corporate divisional office in Mexico City.

Assistant Director of International Development

The National Hockey League seeks qualified applicants for this position. B.S. in sport management, business, or related field required, MBA in international business/marketing preferred. Fluency in German or Russian and two to four years of work experience in sales and marketing a must. Duties include overseeing and expanding NHL Enterprise merchandising, licensing, and television agreements with firms throughout Europe. Prior experience in hockey as a player or at a management level is a plus.

REFERENCES

Ashton, C. (2001. November). China comes out to play. *Sports Business International*, 28-31.

Badenhausen, K., Nixolov, C., Alkin, M. and Oazanian, K. (1997). More than a game: An in-depth look at the raging bull market in sport franchises. *Financial World, 166*, 6, 40-50.

Barrand, D. (2001, December). Building for a long-term future. *Sports Business International,* 20-22.

Barrand, D. (2001, October). Television captures the extremists. Sportel. London: Sports Business Group. 20-22.

Barrett, R., & Cavanagh, J. (1994). *Global Dreams: Imperial Corporations and the new world order.* New York: Simon & Schuster.

Bernstein, A., Shari, M. & Malkin E. (2000, November 6). The world of sweatshops. *Business Week,* 84-85.

Brake, T., Walker, D.M., & Walker, T. (1995). *Doing business internationally: The guide to cross-cultural success.* Boston, MA: McGraw-Hill.

Chu, Chin-Ning (1991). *The Asian mind game: Unlocking the hidden agenda of the Asian business culture—A Westerner's survival manual.* New York: Rawson Associates.

Cronin, S. (2001, July). China's Stadia revolution. Stadia business. *Sports Business International,* 9-11.

Eartha: World Travelog. (2000). Yarmouth, ME: DeLorme.

Echikson, W. & Webb, A. (2001, July 9). Guess who wants Bejing to get the games. *Business Week,* 48.

Elashmawi, F. & Harris, P.R. (1998). *Multicultural management 2000.* Houston, TX: Gulf Publishing Co.

Engardio, P. & Belton, C. (2000, November 6). Global capitalism: Can it be made to work better? *Business Week,* 72-75.

European Communities. (1995). Bosman Case.

Fay, T. (1999). *Race, gender, and disability: A new paradigm towards full participation and equal opportunity in sport.* Unpublished doctoral dissertation, University of Massachusetts, Amherst.

Fay, T. G., Hums, M. A. , & Wolff, E. A. (June 3, 2000*). Inclusion of sport for athletes with disabilities into nondisabled sport organizations.* North American Society for Sport Management Annual Conference, Colorado Springs, CO. May 3-June 4, 2000.

Guttman, A. (1994). *The Olympics: A history of the modern games.* Chicago: University of Illinois Press.

Halbfinger, D. M. (1996, January 14). Agent entrepreneur: Solomon pursues payoff in blending sports and entertainment in multimedia projects. *Boston Globe,* 45,51.

Jennings, A. (1996). *The new lords of the rings.* London: Pocket Books.

Jennings, A. (2001). *The great Olympic swindle: When the world wanted its games back.* New York: Simon & Schuster.

Jones, D. (1996, June 6). Critics tie sweatshop sneakers to 'Air' Jordan. *USA Today,* 1B.

Katz, D. (1994). *Just do it: The Nike spirit in the corporate world.* Holbrook, MA: Adams Media Corporation.

Kaufmann, M. (October 1-7, 2001). League tries to tap into Olympic spirit. *Street & Smith's SportsBusiness Journal,* 29.

Klemm, A. (1994, August). The export game. *Team Licensing Business,* 18-25.

Morrison, T., Conaway, W., & Douress, J.J. (2001). *Doing business around the world.* Paramus, NJ: Prentice Hall.

Muench, H., & Amend, P. (1995, January). International: Japan. *CBI, 16*(1), 20-23.

Pitts, B.G., & Stotlar, D.K. (2002). *Fundamentals of sport marketing* (2nd ed.). Morgantown, WV: Fitness Information Technology.

Pound, R.W. (1994). *Five rings over Korea: The secret negotiations behind the 1988 Olympic Games in Seoul.* New York: Little, Brown and Co.

Powers, J. (1993, February 21). New world borders. *Boston Globe Magazine,* 8-9.

Roberts, D. & Bernstein, A. (2000, October 2). 'A life of fines and beating'. *Business Week,* 22-128.

Roberts, R. (2001, July 30). For China's economic reformers, the 2008 Olympics are gold. *Business Week,* 49.

Robeson, D. (2001, July 2). The corporation: Just do something. *Business Week,* 70-71.

Simson, V., & Jennings, A. (1992). *Dishonored games: Corruption, money & greed at the Olympics.* New York: SPI Books.

Sport Business International. (2001, August). Sponsors licking their lips. 35.

Stotlar, D.K. (1993). *Successful sport marketing.* Brown & Benchmark, Dubuque, IA.

Terroux, G. (1972). *Face-off of the century: The new era Canada, USSR.* Montreal: Collier-Macmillan.

Thoma, J.E., & Chalip, L. (1996). *Sport governance in the global community.* Morgantown, WV: Fitness Information Technology.

Ukeman, L. (2000). *Sports Business International,* 35-37.

United States Olympic Committee. (2001). *2001 fact book.* Colorado Springs, CO: Author.

Wallechinsky, D. (2001). *The complete book of the winter Olympics.* Woodstock, NY: Overlook Press.

Weiler, P.C., & Roberts, G. R. (1993). *Sports and the law: Cases, materials, and problems.* St. Paul, MN: West Publishing, 699-705.

Wilson, J. (1994). *Sport, society, and the state: Playing by the rules.* Detroit: Wayne State University Press.

PART V

The Future
of Sport Management

As you progress through the curriculum at your college or university, some of your instructors will require you to write reports on research articles published in the sport management literature. Instructors assign these reports because they know that when you become a practicing professional, one of your obligations to your employer, to your employees, to the consumers of your products, and to the general public will involve being familiar with the research in your field. A problem with these assignments, however, is that students are seldom familiar with the reasons people conduct research, the ways in which they conduct it, or how to evaluate the published product. The two chapters in this section are designed to give you a basic understanding of these concepts.

Chapter 19 addresses the important issue of asking questions. Jacquelyn Cuneen and Bob Boucher explain why we ask questions in sport management, why accurate answers are so important, and why we should welcome others' scrutiny of the answers. Cuneen and Boucher also examine questions that have already been asked and answered in the sport management literature and identify additional questions that are awaiting consideration. After directing your attention to issues and concerns in specific segments of the sport management industry, the authors explain the role of commercial research companies in answering questions in the world of sport.

In chapter 20 Wendy Frisby tackles the assignment of explaining sport management research. She describes the research process and why research is important to sport managers. Frisby looks at different kinds of research (i.e., basic and applied) and provides examples of each. She then identifies different kinds of data (i.e., quantitative and qualitative) and explains how researchers decide which type of data they need and how they go about collecting both types. Frisby concludes by identifying and explaining the steps in the research process. These steps parallel the main sections of most published research articles, and they will provide a framework through which you can read and evaluate the articles your instructors will assign in subsequent courses.

The two chapters in this section have been included in this book because we know that in order to distinguish yourselves from "ordinary" sport managers, you will need excellent research evaluation skills. The better you can interpret and evaluate research, the less likely you will be to waste time and money on unsound suggestions. If you understand research, you will be able to make decisions grounded in the analysis of relevant data rather than depending on hunches or simply perpetuating tradition. The earlier you learn to evaluate research, the more meaningful those research article assignments will be later on. Moreover, the greater your skill in evaluating research, the more prepared you will be to make the difficult decisions that surely will come your way as a sport manager.

FOR MORE INFORMATION
Scholarly Associations

- North American Society for Sport Management (NASSM)
- European Association for Sport Management (EASM)
- Sport Management Association of Australia and New Zealand (SMAANZ)

Scholarly Publications

- *Academy of Management Review*
- *Administrative Science Quarterly*

- *Annuals of Tourism Research*
- *European Sport Management Quarterly*
- *Harvard Business Review*
- *Human Relations*
- *International Journal of Sport Management*
- *Journal of Business Research*
- *Journal of Park and Recreation Administration*

- *Journal of Sport Management*
- *International Journal of Sport Marketing and Sponsorship*
- *Management Review*
- *Sport Management Review*
- *Sport Marketing Quarterly*
- *Strategic Management Journal*

Chapter 19

Questions, Answers, and Sport Management Research

Jacquelyn Cuneen, Bowling Green State University
Robert Boucher, University of Windsor

Look-Look (2002), an American research firm specializing in youth trends, spends exorbitant amounts of time watching teens in malls, videotaping them at concerts, surveying them, talking to them in focus groups, and otherwise observing them in overt or covert ways to determine such things as what activities, clothing, or soft drinks they like now and what they might like next month. Why would the media, manufacturers, and retailers be so interested in what Look-Look finds out about teens? The answer: Those industries want access to some of the $150 billion a year the 33 million American teens spend and the additional $50 billion they influence their parents to spend on their behalf (*The Merchants of Cool*, 2002).

Thompson Tregear (2002), an Australian independent consulting company, works one on one addressing various aspects of managerial problems with numerous public- and private-sector sport and recreation clients. Why would companies such as Sydney International Aquatic Centre at Homebush, the Olympic Whitewater Canoe Slalom Complex at Penrith Lakes, and the Arena Sports Complex of Joondalup require Thompson Tregear's help when they all have their own strategies, plans, operational designs, and managerial systems? The answer: Those companies, while able to function steadfastly on a daily basis, have special questions about emerging issues such as strategic facility planning, policy evaluation and development, management restructuring, and a host of other matters that require a unique expertise.

Imagine that a university professor read Sutton and Watlington's (1994) report outlining Nike's concern that their aggressive pursuit of the growing women's market might adversely affect their image and relationship with their established men's

market. The professor designed a study to determine if Nike's "women's ads" significantly influenced men's loyalty to the Nike brand. Why would a teacher care about Nike's bottom line? The answer: This information would be useful to the professor's sport marketing students and thus, eventually, to any brand or retailer for whom they might work. Further, regardless of whether the information is useful "on the street," it is interesting from a sociological point of view, extends the body of knowledge in sport management, and leads scholars to a better understanding of sport as an institution.

Asking suitable questions and getting accurate answers is critical to every sport management sector in the current Information Age. Every organization has myriad questions that arise constantly both during and outside of working hours. You can answer all of your questions by the end of one business day, then come in the next day to a new set of questions that emerged overnight, some even related to yesterday's answers. Questions are important because their answers set the stage for decision, action, profit, satisfaction, and success. If you know how to ask the right questions, can answer questions for your company, or know how to get the answers from available sources or databases, your organization will value your contributions highly. Information of the kind presented in the Q & A elements interspersed throughout this chapter and the kind of information collected by Look-Look, Thompson Tregear, and sport scholars is vital for amateur and professional sport, manufacturers and brands, and innumerable other sport management enterprises whose personnel work in all sectors of the fields of sports information, marketing, promotions, operations, management, and media.

Wendy Frisby's overview of sport management research (see chapter 20) no doubt will convince you that the products (i.e., results) of the various research processes enable managers to improve their supervisory and decision-making practices in our knowledge-based economy. This chapter relates to Frisby's chapter by addressing the crucial role of questions and, more important, answers in the function and conduct of sport management.

Q & A

Question: Do Clothing Companies Benefit From Paying Athletes to Wear Their Gear?

Answer: It appears to be a good strategy for companies. CBS TV's Saturday night (September 8) prime-time coverage of Venus and Serena Williams' 2001 U.S. Open tennis final was very beneficial for each player's clothing-endorsement company. Cameras showed Venus' Reebok-logoed clothing on screen for a total of 5 minutes and 9 seconds and Serena's Puma-logoed clothing for 5 minutes and 24 seconds. Minutes translated to dollars means that Reebok had $1.2 million and Puma $1.3 million in **exposure** value (Joyce Julius Company, 2001).

exposure—The amount of time, in seconds or minutes, that a company (advertiser) potentially has the viewer's or listener's attention.

Companies gain valuable exposure when professional athletes such as Venus Williams wear their logoed clothing.

© Human Kinetics

Why Understanding Research Is Important to Sport Managers

Research is often unpopular with undergraduate students who aspire to exciting careers in the world of sport and physical activity. The current generation of students, like others who have gone before it, appears to get satisfaction out of the more practical, hands-on elements of undergraduate preparation and is less enamored with theory and research. In truth, only individuals who have served in a management position will fully appreciate the role of research in assisting with the managerial role.

Stop and think for a minute: If your family doctor graduated from a prestigious medical school in 1990, wouldn't you expect this physician to be up-to-date with the medical developments in the 2000s? Similarly, it never bothers us that the pilot of our 747 from New York to Paris is approximately 55 years of age and received a pilot's license perhaps 30 years ago. We assume that this pilot has kept up-to-date with the latest developments in aviation including safety procedures and technology. The developments since our doctors, pilots, and countless other professionals received their initial certifications and credentials have come about largely as the result of research. Being able to read, understand, and apply scientific findings leads to progress; the world would be quite a different place without the contributions of millions of scientific studies. The area of sport management is certainly no different from other professional areas. With access to current research in human resources, leadership, marketing, organizational development, and so many other areas, the practicing sport manager has a much better chance of choosing sensible alternatives to everyday managerial problems. Computer software, diversity training, and improvements in human rights legislation are but three of the more positive developments that have tended to humanize the art and science of management.

Q & A

Question: Is There One Single Best Time to Assess Workers' Performances in a Sport Organization?

Answer: While there is no cut-and-dried time line, frequent evaluations using uniform protocols do seem to constitute the best method (Chelladurai, 1999).

Addressing Questions and Gathering Information Without Bias

Sport's 21st-century managers need to understand the importance of questions, know how and why questions emerge (i.e., know the path of a question), and must be able to formulate and pose original and clear-cut questions of their own. Questions in any industry, but particularly in sport, emerge as a result of changes in the economy, law, culture, technology, and other sectors that affect sport's operations and bottom lines. Thus, sport companies should not make bottom-line decisions without reliable data. While many methods exist for obtaining reliable data (see chapter 20), the starting point for any path leading to dependable information is a good question. Questions and their subsequent answers enable sport managers to know their environment, personnel, industry, market, customers, and trends.

According to Pearse's classic theory (cited in Kerlinger, 1986), there are four ways of knowing (i.e., acquiring knowledge or information or fixing one's beliefs):

1. Through *tenacity*. One knows that a fact is the truth because people have always clung to the fact and believe it to be the truth even though evidence may exist to the contrary. For instance, many people subscribe to the theory that sport participation builds character even though much empirical evidence exists to show that there is no relationship whatsoever between sport and moral development, good citizenship, and other valued traits (Eitzen, 1999). In fact, some evidence shows that sport might bring out the worst of character traits in athletes. Yet many still hold firmly to the belief that sport builds character because this notion has been firmly ingrained in their consciousness and they believe it to be so in spite of reasonable contradictions.

2. Through *authority*. One knows that something is right because someone with obvious expertise has said so. For instance, if ABC's Robin Roberts explains that the WNBA primarily plays the game of basketball on a horizontal plane (i.e., back and forth) while the NBA plays on a vertical plane (i.e., up and down) and that each level requires a unique but equivalent level of proficiency, one accepts her thesis because of her specific talent in sport analysis.

3. Through *intuition*. One knows that something is true through a sense of reason that is so strong that it might even override experience. The case that sport builds character is a good example of intuition (also called the a priori method).

4. Through *science*. One knows that something is rational because information has been collected absent of biases and precise conclusions can be supported with empirical evidence. For instance,

Armstrong (2001) found that among 26,537 fans whose estimated median expenditure was $227 per day while attending Cincinnati's 2000 River Front Classic (a sport and entertainment event whose highlight was a championship football game between Howard University and Bethune Cookman College), Ohio residents contributed to 53% of total spending, Cincinnati-area residents added 33%, and 12% came from out-of-state residents. These facts are accepted as accurate because they are empirical and the researcher collected data under controlled conditions with as few outside factors as possible swaying the outcome.

Of course, the scientific method provides the most accurate and correct information route that sport managers should use to answer their questions unless they are fortunate to work in an environment replete with firmly established procedures, have impeccable instincts or access to someone else's impeccable instincts, or have contacts whose knowledge will not be questioned. In fact, even in the presence of tenacity, authority, and intuition, sport managers must answer questions without biases. Science, through the data it yields, provides the firmest basis for obtaining answers; it is systematic, controlled, empirical, and self-critical. There can be no better means to arrive at accurate, useful, productive answers.

Q & A

Question: How Will the U.S. Government Monitor Internet Gambling and Address Any Problems That Arise From It?

Answer: The U.S. government may not monitor it at all. Federal laws related to anti-gambling most often defer to states' Tenth Amendment rights to govern according to the people's will (Claussen & Miller, 2001).

The Folly of Trial-and-Error Management

Would any of us drive a car or take a medicine that wasn't thoroughly tested by the appropriate agencies? Probably not. In similar fashion, we are well aware of the extensive research conducted on hockey sticks, baseballs, hardwood floors, bobsleds, athletic apparel, and virtually every tangible piece of equipment remotely related to the "wide world of sport." We take for granted that conducting experimental studies to improve ath-

letic performance by increments as small as minutes is progress.

When it comes to the management of sport enterprise, however, sometimes the standards are not as exacting. It's easy to become enthralled by someone's "neat idea" or what is being done at another university or in a similar sport in another country. In real terms, trial and error often seems to be the watchword in the everyday management practices of sport. Hundreds of promotions are conducted, marketing plans formulated, and strategic plans developed *all without research*. Even with a great deal of thought, many of these ventures are doomed to failure. Having sound intuition and a wealth of experience is fortunate, but trial and error can be expensive. Successful marketing strategies, comprehensive human resources strategies, and so many other aspects of the sport management domain are based on sound theories derived from research. Admittedly, we are all students of the trial-and-error process in that we make decisions without all the possible information or sometimes when we don't have the time or resources to explore all the options. However, why do this on purpose? Why not gather information about your question(s) and make your decisions based on sound information?

A Question's Path: The Need for Information

Questions sometimes emerge merely as a result of curiosity. The sport management professor described earlier was curious about Nike's advertising effects and set out to answer questions about Nike's ads so the results could be used in the classroom to train new marketers, shared with the professoriate so others could use it in class, or published in trade journals so marketers and brands could benefit from the new knowledge. However, in sport management practice and all professional settings, questions are most often crucial elements that materialize frequently as business strategies are designed or revised.

If you live in Toronto and want to open a new sporting goods store in your city, you should have many questions about the feasibility of such a venture. What questions would you have, and what answers might you need? Would you find it useful to know that sales of sporting goods in Canada increased nearly 16% between 1997 ($5,145,000 total sales) and 2000 ($5,964,000 total sales)? What questions would you have about those increases? Would the answers influence what you stock in your store? Should you designate more display space for equipment, clothing, or shoes? It would be valuable for you to know that 53% of the increased sales were related to equipment purchases while 25% were related to footwear. What stores would be your main competitors? It would be essential for you to know that Canadian Tire is the number one overall retail outlet in both units and dollars; however, Sears leads all Canadian retailers in sport apparel sales, while Sport Chek leads in sales of athletic footwear (Sporting Goods Manufacturers Association, 2000a). What else would you need to know before you invest in your new venture? Would it help to know how many Canadian Tire or Sears retail stores are located within an hour's driving radius of Toronto? Do you want to know the Canadian retail category profiles for merchandise, equipment, and apparel for golf, biking, hockey, camping, fishing, or curling? What sports are popular with kids? Here are some hints for you: According to canadianinfolink (2001), the most popular sports for 6- to 10-year-old Canadian children are swimming, soccer, and baseball. Do their preferences change as they get older? Somewhat, in that baseball, swimming, and hockey are most popular among 11- to 14-year-olds. How many Toronto-area consumers between the ages of 5 and 60 buy sporting goods? What sporting goods do they buy most frequently? Do most customers buy the goods for themselves, or do they purchase them for others? As you can see, questions and unbiased answers are vital to sport managers' success. In other words, you have to know your market. The best way to do that is to ask questions and obtain information through research.

Questions are useful only when they are constructed well and thus elicit appropriate answers. They must address the exact topics you are interested in, and the answers must relate explicitly to your information needs.

LEARNING ACTIVITY

Find the answers to the questions posed earlier regarding the Toronto sporting goods market. Find the same answers regarding the sporting goods market in your hometown. Find the same answers for the sporting goods market in the city closest to your college or university. Compare all the findings and draw conclusions about the markets.

Question Construction: Careful Planning and Useful Results

Some of sport's most pressing current questions relate to its own financial strategies and worth, but recent concerns with questioning methods have prompted mainstream business to view sport's data-collection processes with skepticism. For example, **economic impact analyses,** a long-standing tool for assessing the net monetary influence of an event on its community's economy, are being scrutinized in the 21st century for their fundamental biases. The goal of an economic impact analysis is to determine tangible net income change as a result of staging an event in a community. However, because of owners' and sponsors' vested interests, exaggerated claims about an event's impact can be purposely supported by an economic analysis. Crompton (1995) reported that sport facilities, city officials, and other related beneficiaries may go so far as to sponsor studies with the actual intent of showing a positive impact. Regrettably, some of the economic impact studies are neither objective nor impartial and therefore are biased in painting a bright picture for the study's sponsors. In other words, impact analyses are often used by sport organizations to justify their own pet positions (Howard & Crompton, 1995). The questions used in the analyses and the ways the questions are posed are often designed to influence respondents to answer in certain ways.

economic impact analysis—An analysis used to determine tangible net income change as a result of staging an event in a community.

Further, even when a study is designed without bias, a poorly written question can yield inaccurate information. Imagine that an arena management company wants to convince a local chamber of commerce that basketball games at their site infuse significant amounts of money into the local economy. Suppose the company asks 10,000 fans at each of 20 basketball games during the season, How much money did you spend on food in our city as a result of attending this basketball game? All of the 10,000 fans at each game respond that they spent no less than $18 on food. The arena company might then rush to tell restaurant owners that at least $180,000 is added to their collective bottom line every time there is a home game for a total of at least $3,600,000 across a 20-game season. However, examine the question and the way it was asked. The question merely addressed food purchases; questions did not address food purchases specifically in local restaurants. Thus, from the way the question was posed, fans may have assumed that they were being asked to state how much they spent at arena concessions. They may have even responded with the amount they spent at local fast-food franchises as well as at the arena. In other words, unless a question is asked with precision and absent of bias, answers cannot be specific and resulting information can be interpreted with varied meanings. When meanings vary, then conclusions are incomplete.

Fortunately, several companies specialize in asking questions properly and assist many sport organizations when those organizations lack the know-how to craft questions or are otherwise unable to obtain the answers on their own. While it may seem inconvenient or impractical to outsource information collection, commercial firms and independent research houses do an outstanding job of collecting useful data and, further, are often able to provide sport organizations with more precise answers to their questions since the commercial firms have no stake in the outcome.

LEARNING ACTIVITY

Construct at least 20 questions that will address the economic impact of an event in your community. Be sure to ask the questions properly in order to yield accurate data for the event and its sponsors.

The Question and Answer Industry: Commercial Research in Sport Management

According to CASRO, the Council of American Survey Research Organizations (2002), there are over 2,000 research companies in the United States alone with the mission of answering questions on behalf of other companies that lack the resources to conduct their own important business research. Any company might need help in answering questions because their regular personnel lack expertise in a newly developing area or because it would be economically infeasible for the company to employ full-time personnel to address questions that need to be answered only

periodically. When companies have questions that they are unable to answer themselves, they often hire the services of a research house.

CASRO identified two types of research houses: (1) interviewing companies that specialize in questioning people either by a structured or openended method and (2) full-service companies that act as independent consultants by designing questionnaire(s), coding participants' responses, analyzing data, and reporting and interpreting results. Taylor Nelson Sofres Intersearch (2001) of Horsham, Pennsylvania, and NFO World Group (2002) of Greenwich, Connecticut, are two companies offering full-service custom research services. Generally, the firms address emerging questions regarding market and brand evaluation and management; product development; pricing, distribution, and advertising; customer satisfaction; and advertising effectiveness.

Several research companies specialize in providing expert research services exclusively to sport organizations. Often, teams', manufacturers', and retailers' most pressing questions relate to consumers and marketing, and thus many of the commercial companies address marketing and promotional issues on behalf of sport. NASCAR, Nike, and other large and small sport organizations have used the services of commercial research companies in their market and management planning. Table 19.1 lists five of the most visible sport research companies and describes their services.

Q & A

Question: Do Companies Get Good Exposure From Their Stadium Naming Rights?

Answer: You decide! ABC announcer Al Michaels made 12 verbal references to Invesco Field at Mile High Stadium during the 2001 *Monday Night Football* season opener. Joyce Julius Company (2001) estimates Michaels's references to be worth $1.6 million in exposure value.

Action Research and Problem Solving

Because sport management is such an applied field, research questions posed in sport management are less theoretical than those posed in some other fields. Research questions in sport management are usually related to solving real management problems as opposed to more esoteric con-

Table 19.1 List of Consultants Specializing in Sport Business Research

Consultant	Specialty
American Sports Data, Inc. Hartsdale, NY	Specializes in consumer survey research for sport, fitness, and health industries. Provides major research for Sporting Goods Manufacturers Association and International Health & Racquet Sportsclub Association. Purveyors of the Superstudy® of Sports Participation.
ESPN Chilton (ESPN Sports Poll) White Plains, NY www.sportspoll.com/	Analyzes American adults and teens in order to monitor TV viewing, sport and event attendance, and sport industry trends. Their ESPN-Chilton Sports Poll is quoted frequently by scholars as well as by various professional literature and the popular press.
Joyce Julius & Associates, Inc. Ann Arbor, MI www.joycejulius.com/	Evaluates independent sports and special events programs through a "Sponsors Report" that documents in-broadcast television exposure or their National Television Impression Value Analysis (NITV) that contains full-program sponsorship analysis.
Performance Research Newport, RI and Performance Research Europe Ltd. Oxfordshire, UK www.performanceresearch.com/	Evaluates sponsorship effectiveness for sports, music, theme parks, arts, and other entertainment industries. Specializes in on-site data collection and research.
Sports Business Research Network Princeton, NJ	Provides continuously updated market research and industry news on sports participation equipment sales, broadcasting, sponsorships, and marketing.

cerns that dominate other areas of inquiry. Much like engineering and even medicine, research in the sport management field is often judged by its utility. Does it contribute to the building of a stronger bridge? or Will it cure an infectious disease? are measures of the research in engineering and medicine. Markers in the sport management area are equally measurable. Solving a labor dispute with umpires, determining the appeal of a new sport in the Midwest of the United States, and making an ailing franchise profitable are problems that are just as meaningful in the world of sport as are structural and medical problems to engineers and doctors.

As a consequence of being a practically oriented area of study the sport management field is an ideal forum for what is commonly known as **action research**. World-renowned sociologist Kurt Lewin (1946) is often given credit for coining the term, which referred to generating knowledge about a social system while at the same time attempting to change it. In sport management circles, this would involve solving problems that come directly from the sport enterprise. In short, action research says, *identify the problem* and *fix it!*

A relatively new area of action research is called **participatory action research** (Argyris & Schon,

1991); it involves the subjects of the research being full partners in the process of solving the problem. They provide feedback, help with the research design, and become active contributors to the process. An example of this might be the citizens of a midsize town being involved in a sport/recreation study to determine the facility needs of the town in the next decade. Surveys need to be distributed, interviews must be conducted, and a variety of interest groups must be contacted. While professional researchers are often hired to do such a study, the chances of a successful outcome usually rest on the cooperation and candor of civic leaders and townspeople. By going through a systematic process in which everyone with a stake is engaged, participatory action research contributes to solving the problem—in this case, creating a comprehensive facility plan for the town for the next decade.

Critics of action research say that it does not compare to valid scientific experimentation, and it does not contribute to theory (Tinning, 1992). However, given the dynamic nature of the sport management field and the constantly shifting consumer base, action research appears to be an extremely viable option. Some possible research questions that could be addressed by this approach are as follows:

1. What crowd control measures would be effective for European soccer games?

2. How can the public sector and private enterprises share in the building and use of major sport venues?

3. How can golf courses be designed to be more accessible to be people with disabilities?

4. What new sports should be added to college athletic programs to reflect the changing cultural and ethnic makeup of the student body?

action research—Generating knowledge about a social system while at the same time attempting to change it.

participatory action research—A type of action research in which the subjects of the research are full partners in the process of solving the problem.

Q & A

Question: When Are Group Decisions Better Than Unilateral Decisions on Behalf of an Organization?

Answer: You should consider three factors when deciding to use the input of a group: (1) the importance of the actual quality of the decision, (2) the degree to which others must commit to the decision in order for it to be successfully implemented, and (3) the reasonable length of time you have to make the decision (Chalip, 2001).

How Statistics Can Lie

You don't have to go very far to find evidence that the use of statistical information inundates our daily lives. The television commercials tell us that "Four out of five dentists surveyed recommend toothpaste Brand X." The nightly news broadcast mentions that our chances of getting the flu this winter are one in a hundred without a flu shot and one in twenty with the shot. On a daily basis professional and amateur sport stars break records at what appears to be a "record-breaking pace." Goals, home runs, number of coaching victories, and the youngest player to ever score 10,000 points are all examples of what we seem to want to count, put in some kind of chronology, and have at the ready in case we

need to compare, contrast, or provide information.

North America has clearly demonstrated a preoccupation with sport statistics. While statistics can be very useful, those aspiring to be sport managers should beware of the indiscriminate and in some cases intentional misuse of statistical information. Often, we tend to make decisions on the basis of the "stats" that have been presented to us. In 1954 Darrell Huff wrote a delightful little book titled *How to Lie With Statistics*. The book was reprinted in 1982 and most recently in 1993 and has become a best-seller in a number of countries. In a lighthearted way, Huff described how we are all fooled by the presentation of statistical data and given a sense of false confidence because the "numbers back it up." We have adapted two of Huff's examples in the following sections to illustrate how sport managers are influenced by statistics, and how they must be careful in using them. Used correctly, statistical information complements the research process. Without proper care, however, statistics can be misleading at best, and unethical at worst.

Example 1: The Well-Chosen Average

The *Windsor Star* (Dec. 13, 2001) sport section contained an article with the following headline: "Salaries Up 18 Percent." The article was reporting Major League Baseball salary information from the 2001 season. The most dramatic information provided in the article was that Major League Baseball's average salary "broke the 2 million dollar barrier for the first time in 2001 at $2,138,896 ("Salaries Up," 2001). The mean (or average) reported is a measure of central tendency and does provide some information to be sure. However, we must be careful how this average is used and what it hides! The two million does *not* reflect that the New York Yankees paid 31 players an average of $3,930,334, which represented the largest payroll in Major League Baseball. Nor does the league average indicate that the Montreal Expos had the lowest payroll, which averaged out to $926,333 per player. While these figures were reported in the same article, the two million plus figure was likely the most quoted and no doubt most used in the salary negotiation and arbitration cases over the following season.

Intuitively, we also would want to question the impact that the "huge salaries" have on this reported average. With several players making over 100 million dollars, the average may not be the most representative figure in Major League Baseball salaries. Of all the measures of central tendency, the mean is most affected by extreme measures (either low or high). Perhaps the arithmetic average could be replaced by the median (the middle salary) or the mode (the salary most commonly earned). Some other "well-chosen averages" to be wary of might be (1) the average income of the spectators at the professional sport event, (2) the average age of joggers, (3) the average amount spent on sport equipment in a year, or (4) the average length of employment for service employees at the stadium. In short, be careful! These data are useful but only with a great deal of other information. As Huff suggested, "An unqualified average is virtually meaningless" (1982, p. 29).

Example 2: Built-In Bias

Huff says, "To be worth much, a report based on sampling must use a representative sample, which is one from which every source of bias has been removed" (1993, p. 18).

Sometimes when we do research in sport management, we have a strong desire to get a pleasing answer. Surveys are used to gauge customer satisfaction, to determine fan allegiance, and a host of other factors. Because we can rarely survey the entire population, samples are drawn to represent the much larger number of people. If the sample is representative of the larger population, we can draw inferences and be more assured that our conclusions are sound. However, in a number of instances the sample is not representative. Analyze the following hypothetical situations to see if you can spot the problem:

1. The Detroit Red Wings survey spectators at a game to determine fan allegiance.
2. The city council of Edmonton stalls on plans for a new stadium because of an outcry of opposition in the letters to the editor section of the local newspaper.
3. The cost of playing Little League Baseball in a midwestern town was increased to $100 per season on the basis of a survey conducted that determined the average income of the players' parents.
4. A survey of spectators at a local automobile racetrack revealed that 60% would be receptive to having junk food replaced by more nutritious offerings.

On the surface, each of the scenarios is a legitimate way to use information to improve decision making in the sport management environment. However, we must be very careful what we ask; whom we ask; how we ask; and, most important, what we conclude. Take, for example, the previous hypothetical situations:

1. The information derived from the Red Wing survey will be biased by the fact that the fan allegiance of spectators would be presumed to be quite high. To get better information, comparisons between casual fans and regular fans would be more useful. However, the best information might come from the people who don't attend the games.

2. People who write letters to the editor are not necessarily representative of the population of a given city. The overwhelming majority may be in favor of a new stadium but don't feel it necessary to have their thoughts appear in print. Also, the letter writers were not preselected by any sampling process—they volunteered to write and thus create an imbalance of opinion about which the newspaper readers must be alert.

3. If the average income survey was self-reported, then the Little League Baseball officials should be careful in using the results. On the one hand, people tend to inflate their earnings when asked, and because we already know about the "well-chosen average," this may not be a representative figure for the parents of a large number of young players.

4. Surveys that ask people about habits and practices that are "good for them" are almost always supported. Reporting differences between attitudes and actual behavior in survey research is well established (Singleton & Straits, 1999). In short, people may say they would like to see more nutritious food at the concession stands—yet junk food will continue to be the biggest seller.

To summarize, it is fair to say that statistics can provide precise and needed information that will assist in making sport management decisions. However, one must be extremely careful in drawing conclusions from the numbers alone. They provide only part of the picture!

Will It Work in Peoria?

Sport managers face a variety of complicated problems on a daily basis. It would not be uncommon for the general manager of a hypothetical sport organization to handle the following situations in a typical morning at the office: (1) read over and

Profile: Tracy L. Schoenadel, Executive Director, ESPN Sports Poll

Remember when you read in the ESPN Sports Poll that the NFL, MLB, NBA, college football, and figure skating lead the sport world in fan bases? Or, do you recall when the ESPN Sports Poll showed us that the Dallas Cowboys are the number one favorite football team among fans, the L.A. Lakers are the number one favorite basketball team, the New York Yankees are the number one favorite baseball team, and the Detroit Red Wings are the number one favorite hockey team? That, and all other information you read in any ESPN Sports Poll, was presented to you largely through the efforts of Tracy L. Schoenadel, EdD, the poll's executive director. Dr. Schoenadel asks questions and obtains answers for a living.

The ESPN Sports Poll (2002), the industry standard for sport-related measurement, is a syndicated survey service providing information about fans, media viewing and listening habits, event attendance, and sport industry trends to major league teams, broadcast networks, manufacturers' brands, sponsorship agencies, and media such as *Street & Smith's SportsBusiness Journal*. The ESPN poll's information helps corporations evaluate their sponsorship, marketing, and promotional strategies; enables teachers and researchers to have access to clear-cut, cutting-edge information; and provides fans with fun facts to discuss with friends.

Since the poll's data collection team interviews 2,000 participants for about a half-hour via telephone each month, Dr. Schoenadel's days begin early and end late in cities all across North America. She is on the road at least two times per week and travels to such places as the Super Bowl, Daytona 500, various conventions in Las Vegas, and the NCAA women's and men's Final Four tournaments. During the first quarter of 2002 alone, she logged nearly 20,000 miles in air travel since on any given day she might supervise a survey of NFL, WUSA, NASCAR, Extreme Games, and LPGA fans or ask questions of followers of 30 other sport and event franchises. She supervises a large and diverse staff of professional "question askers" who contact people to inquire about such things as endorsements, TV viewership, game attendance patterns, spending, online purchasing, sport or leisure activities, products usage, or myriad other important points of interest to the poll's clients. The poll monitors event interest, sponsor and advertiser awareness, and other important aspects of over 50 events (e.g., All-American Soap Box Derby, Little League World Series, Olympics, British Open, Nabisco Championships, Kentucky Derby, Tour de France).

Over 400 people work daily for the ESPN Sports Poll conducting telephone interviews, processing and analyzing data, coding interview data, and producing data files. Dr. Schoenadel supervises 10 project directors who write monthly reports, identify trends in data, respond to ad hoc requests, and develop custom questions for clients such as leagues, media, sponsors, advertising agencies, and sport marketing agencies. Her project directors, most of whom hold baccalaureate or master's degrees, have strong backgrounds in research and sport, and they travel once or twice a month to collect data at sport events or to make presentations to clients.

Dr. Schoenadel recommends that anyone interested in pursuing a career in sport market data collection should major in sport management or business as an undergraduate, then obtain a master's degree in sport management with a specialization in research and statistics. However, a doctorate is necessary to work in an executive director capacity. Experience in working with people is essential, as well. She states that "the best experience for my current job was probably teaching sport management classes at the University of Richmond and the University of Connecticut. This experience helped me learn to present to a small audience of 10, and that prepared me for an audience of 500, which I often address at conferences. Teaching helped me understand the client better by understanding the students and their individuality. Plus, teaching is the best preparation for moderating focus groups, too."

Once you are working in the information industry, it is crucial to keep up on news and other issues by reading trade journals and papers such as *USA Today* in order to remain informed of current topics in sport and mainstream business and culture. Dr. Schoenadel believes that sport pollsters and information analysts "really have to stay on top of the industry with regard to sponsorship deals, marketing, promotions, etcetera. My staff must have an eye for the data because even the slightest change is worth reporting, but it makes little difference to highlight this change if they are not aware of the cause such as a labor strike, the return of Michael Jordan, the September 11 terror attacks, and so forth."

What are the most important skills and aptitudes for a job such as Dr. Schoenadel's? Writing skills are critically important, of course. So is a penchant for accuracy and detail. However, the ability to keep a secret is vital. Through the ESPN Poll's research, Dr. Schoenadel and her staff often know about key announcements, sport news events, league business, and sponsorship deals well in advance of general release. If they shared secrets even with close friends and family, sport commerce deals could change drastically.

approve preliminary budget requests, (2) meet with a small group of disgruntled employees who are not happy with a reorganization of their department, (3) participate in a conference call with league officials to resolve a disciplinary case, (4) chair a marketing committee meeting that finalizes a sponsorship agreement with a "blue chip" donor, and (5) view a rehearsal of a halftime show for an upcoming play-off game. In reality no morning could be considered "typical" in the life of a practicing sport manager.

How the manager reacts to these situations and the decisions that are rendered are the result of many influences. Background, education, values, motives, and numerous other factors blend together and provide the impetus for the manager's decisions. Referring to the original list, consider the following questions: (1) What budget items were approved? Why these and not others? (2) How did the manager placate the disgruntled employees? (3) What factors were considered important, and what sanctions were imposed in the discipline case? (4) What approach was taken with the "blue chip" donor? (5) How did the manager judge the halftime rehearsal? What do the spectators want, and how do you know this is what they want? It is easy to see that a variety of alternatives are readily available. We would all like to think that the final decisions would be well thought out based on the best possible information. No one wants sport managers to rely on intuition alone or "fly by the seat of their pants." Notwithstanding the effects of education, background, and the other previously mentioned factors—there must be a better way! Wouldn't it be more efficient to rule out some alternatives to simplify the decision-making process?

When a sport manager hears of a "neat marketing idea" that is all the rage of Triple A baseball in the southern United States, the manager has to ask, Will it work in Peoria? What this means is that the astute sport manager is concerned that there may be some geographical, cultural, or economic factors that contributed to the success of the marketing idea in the southern states but that wouldn't be the case in "Peoria" or other parts of North America. From experience we know that the

central portion of the United States (represented by Peoria, Illinois) is generally more conservative than other parts of the continent. An old adage states if something works in Peoria, it will probably work anywhere. This may be because of the perception that the population of this area is less prone to gimmicks, quick fixes, and slick marketing ideas. Or it may just be promoters' perceptions that midwestern Peoria is a prototype of typical America, and if something works there, it will work anywhere.

In any case, deciding whether something will work in Peoria is basically guesswork. How can we really know if it will work in Peoria or for any other part of the world for that matter? The answer is research! Carefully conducted research studies can provide very important answers to serious questions. As mentioned earlier, trial-and-error approaches can be expensive.

LEARNING ACTIVITY

Interview one of the organizational strategists or market analysts in a sport organization of your choice. Ask to observe the next data collection series. (*Note:* Results of program or market analyses are often confidential, and your request may be reasonably refused.)

Important Research Questions Addressed

While some authors note that sport management has been around since at least as long ago as 11 B.C. when Herod, king of Judea, staged very elaborate athletic spectacles (Frank, 1984; see also chapter 1), the study and documentation of research in this area is a much more contemporary occurrence. Since the mid-1980s a number of academic and professional associations have been formed that have stimulated research and scholarly activity in sport management. The North American Society for Sport Management (NASSM), the European Association for Sport Management

(EASM), and the Sport Management Association of Australia and New Zealand (SMAANZ) are among the more notable associations that foster research as part of their mandates. Each association hosts an annual conference at which sport management research is shared in the form of presentations, roundtable discussions, and keynote addresses. In addition, each association publishes a journal. As a result of hundreds of presentations and countless publications, the body of knowledge is growing. The following listing will give you an overview of the important issues over the past several years:

• *Journal of Sport Management.* The original scholarly journal in the field has been published since 1987. It is the official publication of the North American Society for Sport Management. Following are some research questions posed in this journal:

1. What constitutes sexual harassment in sport, and what coach behaviors may now be the basis of a lawsuit? (Wolohan & Mathes, 1996)

2. What is the relationship between broadcasting and attendance at minor league hockey games? (Zhang, Pease, & Smith, 1998)

3. What are the causes of stress for NCAA athletics directors? (Copeland & Kirsch, 1995)

4. What personal characteristics are important in those holding high-level positions in professional baseball? (Hofacre & Branvold, 1995)

5. What can be done to harmonize international antidoping policies? (Houlihan, 1999)

• *Sport Marketing Quarterly.* Published by Fitness Information Technology Inc. since 1992, this journal is designed to serve both the academician and the practicing sport marketer. Following are some research questions posed in this journal:

1. What is the level of consumer knowledge regarding "ambush marketing"? (Lyberger & McCarthy, 2001)

2. How does promotion timing influence Major League Baseball attendance? (Boyd & Krehbiel, 1999)

3. What factors cause spectators to keep coming to games? (Quick, 2000)

4. What are the service quality expectations of consumers of sport and fitness centers? (Papadimitriou & Karteroliotis, 2000)

• *European Sport Management Quarterly.* This journal was first distributed in 1994 as the *European Journal for Sport Management* (1994-2000). It is the official publication of the European Association for Sport Management. Following are some research questions posed in this journal:

1. How is service quality in sport-related businesses measured? (Woratschek, 2000)

2. How important is the concept of organizational culture to sport organizations? (Westerbeek, 1999)

3. How can sport management education meet the demands of the new global economy? (Pike, 1994)

4. How can we be sure that we don't overestimate the economic impact of sport events? (Késenne, 1998)

5. What does sport really cost? (Taks & Renson, 1994)

• *Sport Management Review.* The Sport Management Association of Australia and New Zealand has published this journal since 1998. It is distributed as a service to sport industries worldwide and encourages collaboration between scholars and practitioners. Following are some research questions posed in this journal:

1. How do organizations change when they move from amateur to professional? (Skinner, Stewart, & Edwards, 1999)

2. What role do attitudes have in a fan's intention to watch professional basketball teams? (Mahony & Moorman, 1999)

3. Should taxpayers' money be used to subsidize major sporting events? (Mules, 1998)

4. How does a sport organization that relies on volunteers ensure their ongoing commitment? (Cuskelly & Boag, 2001)

5. What can be learned from a collective bargaining simulation? (Gahan & Macdonald, 2001)

• *International Journal of Sport Management.* This journal was first published in January 2000 and is geared to sport management and athletics administration professionals at the national and international levels. Following are some research questions posed in this journal:

1. How do international student-athletes adjust to life on American college campuses? (Ridinger & Pastore, 2000)

2. Does a transformational leadership style make athletics directors more effective? (London & Boucher, 2000)

3. What motivates fans to attend professional basketball games? (Pease & Zhang, 2001)

4. How will a 10-step "crisis management model" help sport managers? (Stoldt, Miller, Agres, & Comfort, 2000)

5. Why do North American companies sponsor sport? (Lough, Irwin, & Short, 2000)

6. What factors influence the personal sport expenditures of the citizens of Norway? (Thrane, 2001)

• *Journal of Sport & Social Issues.* This journal publishes the ideas and manuscripts of sport scholars who are interested in understanding the relationship between sport and society as a whole. Many diverse theoretical and disciplinary perspectives are reflected in this journal, including those of interest to sport management students. Following are some research questions posed in this journal:

1. What happens to fans when teams relocate to another city? (Lewis, 2001)

2. Is there gender parity at the Olympics? (Eastman & Billings, 1999)

3. Is it possible to determine when an economic impact analysis is misused? (Hudson, 2001)

4. How does transnational advertising of sport affect reimaging of national culture? (Silk and Andrews, 2001)

5. Is it possible to classify the various kinds of spectators who support world-class soccer? (Giulianotti, 2002)

• *Journal of Sports Economics.* This journal first appeared in February 2000 and is published by Sage Publications. The journal editorial board has forged an affiliation with the International Association of Sports Economists. The journal appeals to an eclectic audience including people from the fields of business, finance, law, and economics. Following are some research questions posed in this journal:

1. What is the value of public goods generated by a professional ice hockey team? (Johnson, Groothuis, & Whitehead, 2001)

2. What factors enter into final-offer arbitration in salary bargaining in Major League Baseball? (Faurot, 2001)

3. How does past performance influence the guarantee in professional boxing contracts? (Tenorio, 2000)

4. Is there an earnings gap between male and female National Collegiate Athletic Association (NCAA) head basketball coaches? (Humphreys, 2000)

5. What factors determine the "ability to find talent" in the annual Major League Baseball draft? (Spurr, 2000)

As you can see, much has been accomplished in the research area since the mid-1980s. However, in comparison to the more established disciplines such as psychology, education, and business, the amount of research completed is still relatively limited. Only with systematic and diligent inquiry will the field of sport management progress and flourish. The prospects are excellent, however, as the amount of sound research has increased significantly in the past two decades.

After you have examined some of sport management's burning issues over the last several years, you may want to read the entire text of the research articles in the journals so you can learn more about the full question-and-answer process. Check the reference listing for the full citation of the articles if you want to find them in your library.

Q & A

Question: Do Internet Listeners Represent a Desirable Sport Market?

Answer: Yes! Thirty-one percent of 2001 World Series listeners on MLB.com had incomes exceeding $100,000, 82% had college or postgraduate degrees, and 43% spend more than $500 on Internet purchases per year. Most listeners (83%) were between 25 and 54 years of age, 89% were males, and listeners accessed the games from home 60% of the time and from work 33% of the time (Arbitron, 2001).

Caution! Pothole on the Road to Progress

Frisby (see chapter 20) will identify several sources of sport management research (e.g., trade journals, the World Wide Web, academic journals, government documents, consulting reports), and she will introduce you to what has been previously researched and how important it is for a discipline to gain acceptance and recognition in our society. At the present time an increasing amount of research is being completed as sport management spreads to all parts of the globe. With increased rapidity, the body of knowledge will continue to grow, thus providing a solid base for the study and application of sound managerial practices in the sport environment.

Yet while the field is indeed growing and the research proliferating at a rapid rate, an area of concern has become apparent. Parks (1992) outlined the difficulty quite clearly when she noted the struggle between those doing the research and those who must apply the knowledge. As stated earlier, the applied nature of sport management makes it doubly important that a strong link exist between what researchers choose to investigate and the actual needs of those in the field. As Parks communicated it, "Questions still remain how best to translate sport management theory into practice" (p. 221). The key word is *translate,* and that leads to a very important observation. Over the past decade or even longer, a number of journals have appeared that are dedicated to specific audiences in the larger sport management/administration field. Some journals are very specifically geared to the administration of athletics departments or to sport tourism. Others are global in orientation and contain articles of broad generic interest. Put on a continuum with theoretical and practical as polar opposites, the various journals show an interesting and obvious gap (see figure 19.1). There doesn't seem to be any journals that translate research findings to the practitioner. Porter and McKibbon (1988) observed that published research is geared toward the academic community and is written in such a way that other researchers understand the terminology, methods, and results, but almost no one else can! In fact the readership of the more theoretical journals is almost exclusively professors and graduate students in institutions of higher learning. The more practical journals, on the other hand, cater to a membership that is involved in the ongoing administration and management of sport venues, athletics departments, marketing firms, health clubs, and professional teams.

Compare the editorial boards of the *Journal of Sport Management* and *SportsTravel Magazine.* A listing of a journal's board members usually appears somewhere inside an issue or on the back cover. What conclusions can you make about the two boards? Notice that the gap between these two groups is magnified by the fact that there don't seem to be any journals devoted to a common ground, where both researchers and practitioners can contribute. Such a journal might be called *Interface* and would solicit articles with the following characteristics: (1) research explained to the practitioner with emphasis placed on relevance and application, (2) practitioners writing about problems they have faced and how research might help, (3) researchers and practitioners writing about collaborative efforts that used research to solve real problems.

The perceived gap between theory and practice in this field may be narrowed by how we report our research findings. Academics cannot assume that the results of their well-conceived and eloquently written studies will reach or have an impact on the field. Similarly, practitioners should not assume that research is too esoteric to be of practical use. Some effort must be made to answer the questions, What does this really mean? and How can it be of use to me? Perhaps the establishment of journals and even conferences designed

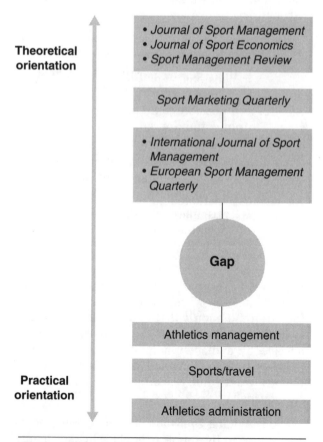

Figure 19.1 A hole in the literature!

to "bridge the gap" would contribute to this end. Research questions generated from this kind of collaboration would get higher marks for relevance than is perhaps the case today.

Q & A

Question: What Are the Top-Selling Licensed Goods?

Answer: The top sellers are T-shirts ($4,827,189), knit shirts ($2,162,661), fleece-wear tops ($1,770,250), jackets ($1,137,087), shorts ($724,555), swimsuits ($370,801), warm-ups ($268,138), fleece-wear bottoms ($268,077), and athletic socks ($186,244) (SBRnet, 2002).

Emerging Questions in Sport Management

What kinds of events have happened in the world over the past few years that would prompt sport managers to have new questions? What kinds of questions would you have about the various issues if you were a sport manager dealing with change in your management and leadership as it intersects with public, community, media, financial and legal issues, your facilities and the events that are staged in them, ethics, and various sociocultural dimensions? Several major issues will impact sport in this new millennium. A few of the most urgent are addressed in the following sections.

The Changing Consumer

While North American sport organizations have for decades marketed to the 18- to 34-year-old male, a late 20th century Sporting Goods Manufacturers Association (1998) *State of the Industry Report* indicated that actually 84% percent of women and 93% of men are sport fans. In fact, 89% of all Americans 12 years and older are sport fans. Their favorite sports are the National Football League (NFL), followed by Major League Baseball (MLB) and the National Basketball Association (NBA). Further, people who participate in sport activities are fans of about eight sports, while nonparticipants are fans of about four sports (Sporting Goods Manufacturers Association, 1998). Knowing this, what questions do you have about the sport consumer of the future? Should sport be promoted via the same print and electronic media? What specific questions would you have about the fans of pro sport franchises and sport's other customers? Examine figure 19.2. What questions come to mind about the future of sport consumption when you see how the population, and by default sport fans and consumers, may change in the 21st century?

Let's consider the age factor. Baby boomers, a much-sought-after North American market since the 1950s, will continue to have disposable income and surplus leisure time as they ease into retirement. Does that make you want to rethink any promotional strategies in order to include this affluent group in your marketing plan? More questions may help you decide whether to market exclusively to baby boomers, however. The SGMA (2001b) monitored over one hundred sport and fitness activities and found that many Americans participated at least once during 1999 in one or more extreme activities (see table 19.2). Does this make you consider targeting Generation X, Generation Y, and echo boomers (see figure 19.3)? Nike, Warner Brothers, and Frito-Lay have no questions about that; those companies are already courting the younger market and hope to tie up brand loyalty by distributing free textbook covers in 35,000 schools across the United States (Sporting Goods Manufacturers Association, 1998).

Notice the trends for women who consume sport (see figure 19.4). Do you have any ideas on how to reach them? Should advertising to women aged 18 to 34 be different from advertising to men aged 18 to 34? Do women respond to celebrity endorsements by purchasing the endorsed products? Sutton and Watlington (1994) found that women are more likely to research a product and make informed purchases than to be motivated by the hero worship associated with responses to endorsements. Will this affect endorsement trends for athletes and other celebrities? How will you advertise to men as well as to the female and male youth sport markets without alienating the increasingly important women's market? Will women respond to cause marketing? As you can see, many issues arise regarding the new sport consumer; sport marketers will need data-based, scientific information in order to answer their questions and react to consumer needs in a way that builds brand loyalty.

You should have an infinite number of questions about the 21st century sport consumer. Answers to your questions will be even more critical as the century progresses because all economic indicators from the U.S. Department of Commerce

Changing Demographics: Age

- 5 million fewer adults under the age of 35 than in early 90s
- Adults, aged 30-44, will decrease 7 million
- Adult, aged 45-70, will increase in excess of 20 million

Changing Demographics: Baby Boomers

- 81 million "baby boomers" (born 1945-1960)
- Discretionary purchase power
- Recreational lifestyles
- Buy lots of athletic footwear and active sports apparel

Changing Demographics: Ethnicity Hispanic

- Hispanic Americans = 29.3 million
- 42 million (14% of the U.S. population) by 2010
- 75% increase from 1990
- Buying power $356 million ($24 billion in clothing and shoes)
- Forecasts: $72 billion by 2010 (Buy soccer and baseball equipment and footwear and apparel)

Changing Demographics: Ethnicity Asian

- 10 million Asian Americans (3% of American population)
- Spending power $225 billion
- America's fastest growing ethnic segment (set to double by 2025)
- Well educated and not homogeneous
- Adjust strategy to reach this market that is "diverse within diverse"

Figure 19.2 The changing American consumer.

Source: Sporting Goods Manufacturers Association (1998).

Table 19.2 The SGMA Baker's Dozen: List of 13 Most Frequent Sport and Fitness Activities Among Americans Aged 6 and Over

Activity	Number of Participants
1. In-line skating	29,024,000
2. Skateboarding	11,649,000
3. Mountain biking	7,854,000
4. Snowboarding	7,151,000
5. Paintball	7,121,000
6. Artificial wall climbing	6,117,000
7. Trail running	5,232,000
8. BMX bicycling	3,977,000
9. Wakeboarding	3,581,000
10. Roller hockey	3,287,000
11. Street hockey	2,448,000
12. Mountain/rock climbing	1,947,000
13. Boardsailing/windsurfing	655,000

Source: Sporting Goods Manufacturers Association (2001b).

Changing Demographics: Generation X (Baby Busters) and Gen Y

- 44 million "busters" (Generation X)
- Market patterns difficult to trace
- 62 million "echo boomers" or "Generation Y" (born between 1980-95)
- Small segment
- Single parent or blended parent families
- Unpredictable BUT seem to like: cable TV, interactive media (influences purchases), team sports and individual lifetime sports (tennis, golf, bowling)

Specifics on Gen Y

- Tail end of this group (current teens)
- N = 30 million by 2006
- Annual buying power $100 billion plus

Figure 19.3 Generation X and Generation Y.

Source: Sporting Goods Manufacturers Association (1998; 2001a).

Women's Market Data

- Women spent slightly more ($5.4 billion: 5.2 billion) than men on goods
  - Women control up to 80% of the sporting goods/apparel market
  - 86% of sports apparel sales are to females
- 38 million females age 6 and up participate frequently in sport
  - *1987-1997 increases:*
    - 20% in outdoor activity
    - 23% in fitness activity
    - 21% in team sports
    - 22% in individual sports

Current/Future Consumption: Female Market

- 10.6 million females regularly walk for fitness
  - 6 million ride stationary bicycles
  - 4 million exercise on treadmills
  - 3.6 million use free weights
  - 56.2% of the "core" market for fitness activities
- 38% of all college athletes are women
- 41% of all high school athletes are girls
- Increases since 1992: Soccer = 55%; Fast-pitch softball = 37%; Volleyball = 22%

Figure 19.4 Growth segment: Women sport consumers.

Source: Sporting Goods Manufacturers Association (1998) and Mallory, McGraw, Sieder, & Fischer, 1995.

forecast a decline in retail purchasing by 2003. Sales, which typically rose 4% per annum in the early 1990s, will level off to 2%, and discretionary spending on services and entertainment such as sport will fall (Sporting Goods Manufacturers Association, 1998). What responses will you make? What questions will you ask about the falloff, and whom will you ask? What sources will you consider reliable?

Appropriate questions and information-based answers will be fundamentally important in solving sport's emerging problems and vital issues. Questions, answers, and reliable information will be the salvation in the face of dwindling attendance figures and may mean the difference between failure and solid sales, profitable bottom lines, and contented personnel.

Competencies Sport Managers Will Require in the Next Decade

Chelladurai (1999) identified several key issues associated with sport and recreational management (see table 19.3). As new information constantly changes the way we interact with each other and evolving electronic sources yield updated information almost hourly, it is reasonable to presume that sport and leisure managers will need different competencies as we make our way through the new millennium. Many trend analysts see a drastic change in the 21st century workplace as technology allows us to complete almost any of our work from home. Cohen and colleagues (1993) reported that Faith Wohl, human resources director for DuPont, believes that workplaces will be obsolete by the middle of the 21st century. How will managers' concerns change as a result? Will managers need to be concerned with personalities when the varied personalities within an organization will be working at home instead of interacting on site? How will managers complete job appraisals when all they have to judge is the final product since the process itself will be hidden at home?

Spectator Services in the 21st Century

Neil Postman of New York University's Department of Culture and Communications (cited in Cohen et al., 1993) believes that technology will privatize even social activities. In other words, we will all shop, vote, and seek entertainment through our own home electronics. Will this extension of the "**cocooning**" phenomenon as described by Popcorn (1992) and Popcorn and Marigold (1998) affect sport's delivery? How will we use sport as a spectator event? Will we attend sport events or watch and listen primarily from home? Will stadia and arenas be smaller as a result of our tendency to stay home? Will stadia and arenas eventually be obsolete like the workplace? Will new 21st century security measures prompt us to upgrade our home technology so we can view safely and cheaply from home? How will escalated 21st century security measures affect sport ticketing? What forms of identification may be required to purchase or reserve tickets? Will fans still flock to games? If so, how long before game time should fans arrive to stand in security lines? How will you get answers to these questions if your employer asks you to find this information?

cocooning—The tendency of consumers to stay home and order-in all forms of entertainment such as movies and videos as well as food and other provisions.

As you can see, one question brings about several more. Getting precise answers in an efficient manner becomes more imperative as questions multiply.

Q & A

Question: Are Oral Contracts Really Legally Binding?

Answer: Oral contracts, as long as there is evidence to show the agreed terms, are generally enforceable (Sharp, 2001).

Table 19.3 Chelladurai's Major Sport and Recreation Managerial Issues

Major managerial issue	Associated categorical issues
Managing human resources	Volunteers, professionalism, clients
Managing individual differences	Abilities, values, personality, motivation
Human resource practices	Job design, performance appraisal, staffing, reward systems, leadership, organizational justice
Attitudinal outcomes	Job satisfaction, job commitment

Dealing With Volunteers

Managing "the human resource" generally entails training, motivating, supervising, and evaluating regular paid employees. How people behave in a sport organization reflects how they view their jobs, their career paths, and other factors related to the exchange of wages for work. However, in the sport world, many of our events rely on volunteers to make them successful. From experience we know that virtually all sport events, from the Olympics to soap box derbies, use unpaid individuals in a variety of capacities. An example of this would be the 10,000 volunteers that made the 1995 World University Games in Fukuoka, Japan, an unprecedented success ("A 3 Billion Dollar Passion," 1994).

From a research standpoint, sport managers should know the motivations behind volunteerism, the characteristics of individual volunteers, and various other important factors. From limited research to date we know the following about volunteers at sport events: (1) Volunteers are enthusiastic about the event and less enthusiastic about the organization that puts it on (Getz, 1997), (2) recognition is an important element in motivating and retaining volunteers (Wilkinson, 1988), (3) volunteerism increases after retirement (Tedrick, 1990), and (4) volunteers prefer short-term responsibilities (Getz, 1997).

Perhaps the most important question to answer through research is, Why do people volunteer? Clearly, people volunteer for very personal and specific reasons, but evidence suggests that there is usually "something in it for them." Whether for prestige, friendship, self-fulfillment, or altruism, people are "there" because it is better than "not being there." Research at the Calgary Winter Olympics revealed that "personal enrichment" and "helping others" were the two most powerful motivations of the almost 1,000 volunteers who were surveyed (Gibbins, 1986). Evidence also suggests that volunteers will become more prominent in sport events in the future. With individuals retiring at a younger age and sport organizations being reluctant to hire full-time employees, reliance on the volunteer sector will probably increase. While many questions need to be answered regarding the management of volunteers, the following seem to be most appropriate:

1. What are the needs of genders, visible minorities, and handicapped populations when they volunteer?

2. What are some effective recruiting strategies?

3. How do you avoid overcommitting volunteers?

4. How can you effectively integrate volunteers with paid employees?

5. How can you overcome boredom related to mundane volunteer tasks?

6. Is your reward system consistent with volunteer needs?

7. How are training requirements different for a volunteer staff?

These and other questions must be addressed to ensure that the volunteer workforce is managed as effectively as the paid staff. Howell (1986) identified the following leading factors related to volunteer frustration:

1. Disagreement about how to reach goals

2. Lack of training

3. Lack of communication

4. Conflict with paid staff

5. The feeling of "being useless"

6. Lack of influence

7. Too much bureaucracy

LEARNING ACTIVITY

After reading the section on research questions, formulate your own questions about something you would like to know in one of the following areas: (1) the pay structure for professional athletes, (2) the popularity of sports by geographic region, or (3) ethical behavior in the administration of sport for youth.

What Else Do You Need to Ask?

Many more sport managerial issues will arise as the field grows and the century progresses. Changing technologies, workforces, spectators, venues, security measures, and a plethora of other factors will influence the sport product and the ways in which it is managed. Many scholars and practicing sport managers foresee changes in media delivery, Internet developments, game management, and fan services to be at the forefront of managers' questions. What issues and problems do you foresee? How will you solve them to the satisfaction of upper management, fans, and shareholders? Do you have the answers?

If you do not, then you can find them by designing and asking good questions.

Q & A

Question: Do Winning Teams Generate Higher Revenues Than Losing Teams?

Answer: While data vary on this question, there appears to be a relationship between regular season wins and higher gate/stadium revenues with NFL teams (Reese & Nagel, 2001).

SUMMARY

Questions and their subsequent answers are critical to sport managers in our information-based economy. Questions emerge continuously in any venture, and all decisions associated with a venture should be surrounded by well-constructed questions and reliable answers. Sport's most successful 21st century managers will be the ones who understand the importance of questions and information in their decision making. While there are numerous ways of obtaining answers, data-based information provides the most accurate road map for decision making. Questions must be designed to yield unbiased answers, and the resulting information must be used appropriately.

When companies ask good questions and obtain precise answers, their planning is enhanced and their bottom lines are healthier. Commercial research firms are often the most suitable sources of questions and answers for any sport agency, regardless of size and resources. However, scholarly, professional, and focus literature constitute excellent sources of information and often lead readers to ask additional questions of their own. Changing political, economical, and consumer issues affecting sport's finances, management, and delivery make questions, answers, and information crucial as the 21st century progresses.

REVIEW QUESTIONS

1. Why will 21st century sport managers need to know how to ask good questions and obtain accurate answers?

2. Explain the importance of scientific data in sport management decision making.

3. Under what circumstances would a commercial research firm be able to make invaluable contributions to a sport organization? What might make a commercial firm a better question-and-answer source than a sport organization's regular employees?

4. What value is brought to a sport organization by the answers provided within academic and professional literature?

5. Which area of future concern do you feel is most important for sport managers to address: the changing consumer, managerial competencies, spectator service delivery, volunteer management, or other issues related to sport delivery and fan enjoyment?

6. What other issues do you see affecting sport's management? How will you identify these major issues? What questions do you have about the issues and their resolution?

7. Under what circumstances would you recommend that your company employ the services of companies such as Look-Look, Thompson Tregear, Joyce Julius, Performance Research, or any of the other commercial research houses? What questions or issues do you think these companies will be addressing in the future?

REFERENCES

Arbitron. (2001). *Arbitron study reveals that listeners to World Series games on mlb.com were well-educated, affluent and active online consumers.* Retrieved November 19, 2002 from www.arbitron.com/home/content.stm.

Argyris, C., & Schon, D. (1991). Participatory action research and action science compared: A commen-tary. In W.F. Whyte (Ed.), *Participatory action research.* Newbury Park, CA: Sage.

Armstrong, K.L. (2001). Black consumers' spending and historically black college sport events: The marketing implications. *Sport Marketing Quarterly, 10,* 102-111.

Boyd, T.C., & Krehbiel, T.C. (1999). The effect of promotion timing on Major League Baseball attendance. *Sport Marketing Quarterly 8*, 23-34.

A 3 billion dollar passion! (1994). *FISU Magazine 29*, 12-13.

canadainfolink. (2001). *Teaching & learning about the provinces & territories of Canada*. Retrieved November 10, 2002, from www.canadainfolink.ca/canmap.htm# sports.

Chalip, L. (2001). Group decision making and problem solving. In B.L. Parkhouse (Ed.), *The management of sport* (pp. 93-110). New York: McGraw-Hill.

Chelladurai, P. (1999). *Human resource management in sport and recreation*. Champaign, IL: Human Kinetics.

Claussen, C.L., & Miller, L.K. (2001). The gambling industry and sports gambling: A stake in the game? *Journal of Sport Management, 15*, 350-363.

Cohen, W., Cook, G.G., Daniel, M., Friedman, D., Gest, T., Goode, E.E., Grant, L., Guttman, M., Hardigg, V., Hawkins, D., Lief, L., Mingerbrook, S., Saltzman, A., Toch, T., Whitman, D., & Zimmerman, T. (1993, October 25). Beyond 1993: From dream swapping to virtual shopping, the way it will be in 2053. *U.S. News & World Report, 115*, 70-80.

Copeland, B.W., & Kirsch, S. (1995). Perceived occupational stress among NCAA Division I, II, and III athletic directors. *Journal of Sport Management 9*, 70-77.

Council of American Survey Research Organizations. (2001). *Taking responsibility for the future*. Retrieved September 6, 2002, from www.casro.org.

Crompton, J.L. (1995). Economic impact analysis of sports facilities and events: Eleven sources of misapplication. *Journal of Sport Management 9*, 14-35.

Cuskelly, G., & Boag, A. (2001). Organizational commitment as a predictor of committee member turnover among volunteer sport administrators: Results of a time-lagged study. *Sport Management Review 4*, 65-86.

Eastman, S.T., & Billings, A.C. (1999). Gender parity in the Olympics: Hyping women athletes, favoring men athletes. *Journal of Sport & Social Issues, 23*(2), 140-170.

Eitzen, D.S. (1999). *Fair and foul: Beyond the myths and paradoxes of sport*. New York: Rowman & Littlefield.

ESPN Sports Poll. (2002) *Welcome to the ESPN Sports Poll Website*. Retrieved September 6, 2002, from www.sportspoll.com.

Faurot, D.J. (2001). Equilibrium explanation of bargaining and arbitration in Major League Baseball. *Journal of Sports Economics, 2*, 22-34.

Frank, R. (1984). Olympic myths and realities. *Arete: The Journal of Sport Literature 1*(2), 155-161.

Gahan, P.G., & Macdonald, R.D. (2001). Collective bargaining simulation: The Federal Football League versus the National Association of Professional Footballers. *Sport Management Review 4*, 89-114.

Getz, D. (1997). *Event management & event tourism*. Elmsford, NY: Cognizant Communication Corporation.

Gibbins, R. (1986). Volunteers and volunteerism in Calgary: A methodological overview. *Volunteers and Volunteerism in Calgary Series No. 1*, Research Unit for Public Policy Studies, University of Calgary.

Giulianotti, R. (2002). Supporters, followers, fans, and flâneurs: A taxonomy of spectator identities in football. *Journal of Sport & Social Issues, 26*, 25-46.

Hofacre, S., & Branvold, S. (1995). Baseball front office careers: Expectations and realities. *Journal of Sport Management 9*, 173-181.

Houlihan, B. (1999). Policy harmonization: The example of global antidoping policy. *Journal of Sport Management 13*, 197-215.

Howard, D.R., & Crompton, J.L. (1995). *Financing sport*. Morgantown, WV: Fitness Information Technology.

Howell, A. (1986). Why do volunteers burn out and drop out? *Volunteers and volunteerism in Calgary series, No. 8*, Research Unit for Public Policy Studies, University of Calgary.

Hudson, I. (2001). The use and misuse of economic impact analysis: The case of professional sport. *Journal of Sport & Social Issues, 25*, 20-39.

Huff, D. (1982). *How to lie with statistics*. New York: W.W. Norton.

Huff, D. (1993). *How to lie with statistics*. New York: W.W. Norton.

Humphreys, B.R. (2000). Equal pay on the hardwood: The earnings gap between male and female NCAA Division I basketball coaches. *Journal of Sports Economics, 1*, 299-307.

Johnson, B.K., Groothuis, P.A., & Whitehead, J.C. (2001). The value of public goods generated by a major league sports team. *Journal of Sports Economics 2*, 6-21.

Joyce Julius Company. (2001). *A second look*. Retrieved November 10, 2001, from: www. joycejulius.com/home.htm.

Kerlinger, F.N. (1986). *Foundations of behavioral research* (3rd. ed.). Fort Worth, TX: Holt, Rinehart, and Winston.

Késenne, S. (1998). Cost-benefit-analysis of sport events. *European Journal for Sport Management 5*(2), 44-49.

Lewin, K. (1946). Action research and minority problems. *Journal of Social Issues 2*, 34-36.

Lewis, M. (2001). Franchise relocation and fan allegiance. *Journal of Sport & Social Issues 25*, 6-19.

London, C., & Boucher, R. (2000). Leadership and organizational effectiveness in Canadian university athletics. *International Journal of Sport Management 1*, 70-87.

Look-Look. (2002). *Information and research connecting you to youth culture*. Retrieved September 6, 2002, from www.look-look.com/looklook/html/index_.html.

Lough, N.L., Irwin, R.L., & Short, G. (2000). Corporate sponsorship motives among North American companies: A contemporary analysis. *International Journal of Sport Management 1,* 283-295.

Lyberger, M.R., & McCarthy, L. (2001). An assessment of consumer knowledge of interest in and perceptions of ambush marketing strategies. *Sport Marketing Quarterly 10,* 130-137.

Mahony, D.F., & Moorman, A.M. (1999). The impact of fan attitudes on intentions to watch professional basketball teams on television. *Sport Management Review 2,* 43-66.

Mallory, M., McGraw, D., Sieder, J. J., & Fischer, D. (1995, November 6). Women on a fast track. *U.S. News and World Report,* 199, 60-72.

The merchants of cool. (2002). Retrieved September 6, 2002, from www.pbs.org/wgbh/pages/frontline/shows/cool/.

Mules, T. (1998). Taxpayer subsidies for major sporting events. *Sport Management Review 1,* 25-43.

NFO World Group. (2002). *Marketing minds who specialize in research.* Retrieved September 6, 2002, from www.nfow.com/.

Papadimitriou, D.A., & Karteroliotis, K. (2000). The service quality expectations in private sport and fitness centers: A reexamination of the factor structure. *Sport Marketing Quarterly 9,* 157-164.

Parks, J.B. (1992). Scholarship: The other "bottom line" in sport management. *Journal of Sport Management 6,* 220-229.

Pease, D.G., & Zhang, J.T. (2001). Socio-motivational factors affecting spectator attendance at professional basketball games. *International Journal of Sport Management 2,* 31-59.

Pike, L.L. (1994). Business education and executive development implications for sport management programs. *European Journal for Sport Management 1*(2), 76-89.

Popcorn, F. (1992). *The Popcorn report: Faith Popcorn on the future of your company, your world, your life.* New York: Harperbusiness.

Popcorn, F., & Marigold, L. (1998). *Clicking: 17 trends that drive your business—and your life.* New York: Harperbusiness.

Porter, L.W., & McKibbon, L.E. (1988). *Management education and development: Drift or thrust into the 21st century?* New York: McGraw-Hill.

Quick, S. (2000). Contemporary sort consumers: Some implications of linking fan typology with key spectator variables. *Sport Marketing Quarterly 9,* 149-156.

Reese, J.T., & Nagel, M.S. (2001). The relationship between revenues and winning in the National Football League. *International Journal of Sport Management, 2,* 125-133.

Ridinger, L.L., & Pastore, D.L. (2000). A proposed framework to identify factors associated with international student-athlete adjustment to college. *International Journal of Sport Management 1,* 4-24.

Salaries up 18 percent. (2001, December 13), *The Windsor Star,* p. F4.

SBRnet. (2002). *Sports Business Research Network.* Retrieved September 6, 2002, from www.sgrnet.com/.

Sharp, L.A. (2001). Contract law and sport applications. In B. Parkhouse (Ed.), *The management of sport* (pp. 199-212). New York: McGraw-Hill.

Silk, M., & Andrews, D.L. (2001). Beyond the boundary? Sport, transnational advertising, and the reimaging of national culture. *Journal of Sport & Social Issues, 25,* 180-201.

Singleton, R.A., & Straits, B.C. (1999). *Approaches to social research.* New York: Oxford University Press.

Skinner, J., Stewart, B., & Edwards, A. (1999). Amateurism to professionalism: Modeling organizational change in sporting organizations. *Sport Management Review 2,* 173-192.

Sporting Goods Manufacturers Association. (1998). *State of the Industry Report. Technical Report-Financial Day International* (The Super Show), Atlanta, Georgia. Retrieved February 4, 1998, from www.sportlink.com/research/1998_ research /industry/98soti.html.

Sporting Goods Manufacturers Association. (2001a). *Market reports and studies.* Retrieved November 10, 2002, from www.sgma.com/index.html.

Sporting Goods Manufacturer's Association. (2001b). *A baker's dozen report on extreme sports.* Retrieved November 10, 2002, from www.sgma.com/index.html.

Spurr, S.J. (2000). The baseball draft: A study of the ability to find talent. *Journal of Sports Economics, 1,* 66-85.

Stoldt, G.C., Miller, L.K., Agres, T.D., & Comfort, P.G. (2000). Crisis management planning: A necessity for sport managers. *International Journal of Sport Management 1,* 253-266.

Sutton, W.A., & Watlington, R. (1994). Communicating with women in the 1990s: The role of sport marketing. *Sport Marketing Quarterly, 3*(2), 9-14.

Taks, M., & Renson, R. (1994). What does sport really cost? A micro-economic study of the consumer cost of golf and soccer. *European Journal for Sport Management 1,* (i)22-34.

Taylor Nelson Sofres Intersearch. (2001). *Market information for leadership.* Retrieved November 4, 2002 from www.intersearch.tnsofres.com.

Tedrick, T. (1990). How to have the help you need. *Parks and Recreation 25,* 64.

Tenorio, R. (2000). The economics of professional boxing contracts. *Journal of Sports Economics, 1,* 363-383.

Thompson Tregear. (2002). *Quality solutions provided by specialist management consultants to the sport and recreation industry.* Retrieved September 6, 2002, from www.thompsontregear.com.au/home_page.htm.

Thrane, C. (2001). The differentiation of personal sport expenditures: The Norwegian case. *International Journal of Sport Management 2*, 237-251.

Tinning, R. (1992). Action research as epistemology and practice: Towards transformative educational practice in physical education. In A.C. Sparke (Ed.), *Research in physical education and sport: Exploring alternative visions.* London: The Falmer Press.

Westerbeek, H. (1999). A research model and some [marketing oriented] reasons for studying the culture of organizations. *European Journal for Sport Management, 6*(2), 69-87.

Wilkinson, D.G. (1988). *The event management and marketing institute.* Willowdale, Ontario: The Event Management and Marketing Institute.

Wolohan, J.T., & Mathes, S. (1996). Title IX and sexual harassment of student athletes: A look back and to the future. *Journal of Sport Management 10*, 65-75.

Woratschek, H. (2000). Measuring service quality in s ports. *European Journal for Sport Management 7*(2), 22-43.

Zhang, J.J., Pease, D.G., & Smith, D.W. (1998). Relationship between broadcasting media and minor hockey game attendance. *Journal of Sport Management 12*, 103-122.

Chapter 20

Understanding Sport Management Research

Wendy Frisby, University of British Columbia

Regardless of the area that you are studying, an understanding of the research process is important for a number of reasons. Research is a systematic way of examining the hunches, assumptions, and questions we have about a wide range of sport-related phenomena. Exercise scientists are interested in questions related to biomechanics, exercise physiology, and motor learning, while sport management researchers are interested in questions related to marketing, finance, policy, and a number of other topics highlighted in this book. While exercise scientists often conduct research in different settings from those used by sport management researchers (e.g., laboratories instead of sport organizations) using very different approaches (e.g., experiments rather than surveys, interviews, and observations), both groups are concerned with generating findings that are reliable and credible. These findings can then be used to make decisions to inform managerial practice, to build knowledge in a subject area, or both.

Sometimes research findings will support our initial hunches and assumptions, while at other times the findings will contradict and challenge them. Research that challenges our intuition or commonsense way of thinking can encourage us to consider new and improved ways of managing sport. For example, we may assume that everyone in our community has equal access to the sporting opportunities available, but research may reveal that there are considerable disparities in participation based on income, gender, race and ethnicity, age, sexuality, and other factors. If we pay close attention to this evidence, it will encourage us to consider new ways of marketing and delivering sport programs so that more people can enjoy the many health benefits of participation.

This chapter will introduce some key concepts and different types of research conducted in the

LEARNING OBJECTIVES
After studying this chapter, you will be able to do the following: 1. Explain what research is and why it is important to sport managers. 2. Differentiate between science and pseudo-science. 3. Distinguish between basic and applied research and provide examples of each. 4. Differentiate between quantitative and qualitative data. 5. Describe common approaches used to collect quantitative and qualitative data. 6. Explain the components of the research process.

sport management field. It will provide an overview of the research process to serve as a foundation for developing your knowledge and skills in this area. Some of the challenges encountered when conducting research will also be discussed. The overall purpose of the chapter is to provide you with a basis for becoming both a good producer and a good consumer of research so that you can become a more informed decision maker.

Making Informed Decisions

Regardless of whether the findings obtained from research confirm or challenge our hunches and assumptions, they will help us make better decisions. This is why sport managers are increasingly relying on research before investing financial, human, and other types of resources into new or ongoing projects. They want to avoid the costly

407

errors that can occur when decisions are based on false or unfounded assumptions. For example, successful athletic apparel companies conduct extensive research on their customers and competitors before investing in new products and bringing them to market. A failure to do so could result in major financial losses. Sport managers want assurances that their decisions will help them achieve desired goals based on evidence that has been carefully collected, analyzed, and interpreted.

Judging the Quality of Research

Sport managers face considerable challenges interpreting research if they lack adequate training. Due to the information explosion that has accompanied the emergence of a knowledge-based economy, individuals are being bombarded with research from a variety of sources including the media, the Internet, trade journals, academic journals, consulting and governmental reports, workshops and conference presentations, as well as research done for their own organizations. Because research varies considerably in quality, sport managers must be able to critically evaluate the research methods used and the data analysis techniques employed in order to judge whether the conclusions drawn and the recommendations made are reliable and credible.

Considering the Source

The source of the research is one consideration to take into account, but you cannot assume that because findings are reported in an academic journal, the research is necessarily of high quality. Even though most academic journals use a rigorous review process to ensure the high quality of published material, the research design may still be problematic. Many people are suspicious of research reported over the Internet and with good reason. While some Web sites contain research information that has been carefully monitored or reviewed, many do not. Readers often have difficulty determining whether information on the Internet is credible because few details regarding the research design or the qualifications of the researcher may be made available.

Questions to Ask

Many questions must be asked when judging the quality of research, including the following:

1. Are the purpose, research questions, and hypotheses of the research clearly stated?
2. Is a strong rationale for conducting the study provided?
3. Who conducted the research, and what are their credentials?
4. Who sponsored the research, and how will they benefit from it?
5. What is the source of the research, and is there a rigorous review process in place for ensuring quality?
6. Are the key concepts or variables under investigation clearly defined?
7. If applicable, was relevant literature or background information drawn upon?
8. Were ethical considerations taken into account when conducting the research?
9. Were the methods used to collect the data appropriate?
10. What sampling techniques were used, and were they appropriate?
11. Are the measures or indicators of key concepts valid and reliable?
12. How were the data recorded and analyzed?
13. What are the limitations of the study design?
14. Were explanations for the findings provided, and are they justified?
15. Are conclusions and recommendations provided, and are they supported by the findings?

While this chapter cannot provide all the information you need to thoroughly address the previous questions, it will provide an overview of key concepts and the research process plus a number of additional resources. Taking additional courses in research methods and data analysis will increase your knowledge and skills in this area.

Challenges Encountered

In addition to being able to judge the quality of research conducted by others, sport managers may sometimes want to conduct research firsthand by either evaluating programs, conducting market research to retain or attract customers, comparing financial costs and expenditures over time, or designing feasibility studies prior to building new sport facilities or starting new sport-related businesses. If sport managers do not know how to properly design and carry out research, they will encounter considerable difficulty and are unlikely to obtain the information required. For example, inexperienced researchers often underestimate the time, money, and skills that are required to conduct research properly. They may design a survey, send it out, and obtain a reasonable response rate only to discover that they do not know how to enter and analyze the results using a spreadsheet or statistical computer program. As a result, the data contained in the survey may never be used in helping to inform decision making.

Challenges can arise even when sport managers recognize their lack of knowledge in research and hire outside research consultants. Sport managers will still require knowledge and skills in order to assess the quality of proposals tendered by different consultants bidding on research projects.

As a sport management student, you will encounter challenges as you progress through your postsecondary degree program because you will be attempting to locate and evaluate research information available from a wide variety of sources. You may also have the opportunity to conduct research, either for a course project or through a field placement with a sport organization. If you are planning to pursue a graduate degree or a position in government or industry requiring research skills, you will need a strong foundation. Even if you do not anticipate that research will be a major component of your future career, you will need to be able to understand, evaluate, and use research when problem solving and making professional decisions.

LEARNING ACTIVITY

Ask one of your sport management professors to describe his or her research interests. How did he or she become interested in sport management research, and what challenges have arisen while conducting it? Write a brief report comparing the research interests of your sport management professor with the types of research that you might expect to do when you graduate given your career goals.

Key Concepts

There are a number of different ways of approaching **sport management research;** the choice of approach will depend on the purpose of the study. Some studies are done to improve the effectiveness and efficiency of operations, while others are conducted to solicit the opinions of employees, volunteers, or customers. Other studies are designed to critique the way sport organizations are currently managed as a starting point for determining how organizational policies, structures, and practices can be made more inclusive. Familiarity with the following key research concepts will be useful: (1) science and pseudoscience, (2) basic and applied research, (3) quantitative and qualitative data, and (4) validity and reliability.

sport management research—A systematic way of examining the hunches, assumptions, and questions about a wide range of sport-related phenomena.

Science and Pseudoscience

When we hear the word *science*, we might associate it with experiments done in high school or with exercise physiology laboratories in which subjects' heart rates are monitored at conditions of rest and maximum output to determine fitness levels. This type of laboratory and experiment-based science is known as natural science, and it has a long historical tradition in physical education and kinesiology programs in colleges and universities. Social science is another type of science that includes areas such as sport sociology, sport psychology, and sport management. In general, a social science approach to sport is concerned with individuals, groups, and organizations as they interact in a complex social, cultural, economic, political, and technological environment (Slack, 1997). Several examples of the types of research questions of interest to social science researchers in sport management were provided in chapter 19.

Even though the natural and social sciences use very different research techniques and methods, the goal of both is to systematically collect and analyze data to produce knowledge. A systematic approach to research entails the following:

- Clearly stating the purpose of the research
- Developing measures or indicators of key concepts under investigation
- Deciding on the appropriate research methods
- Considering the ethical dimensions involved
- Carefully collecting and analyzing the data
- Drawing on or developing theories to explain the findings
- Making well-founded recommendations

Sport managers who understand the research process are in the best position to judge whether a systematic approach has been used in order to determine whether to base their decisions on the information generated.

A growing body of research appears to have a scientific basis when in fact it does not. Theories promoting the latest managerial or marketing techniques that are not based on systematic research are known as **pseudoscience.** Numerous examples of pseudoscience can be found in popular press books, in infomercials on television, in newspapers or magazines articles, and on the Internet. "Get rich quick" schemes that provide unsubstantiated evidence to support the claims being made are another example of pseudoscience. While the person espousing the latest scheme or trend may appear to be an expert, technical language may be used, and promises of dramatic outcomes may be made, sport managers must be skeptical of pseudoscience that is masquerading as science. Although several well-known "management gurus" have made personal fortunes by speaking at various engagements and selling popular "how to do it" books, not all of their theories and recommendations are supported by the systematic collection, analysis, and interpretation of data. To sort out what types of research information are credible and to avoid basing decisions on information that is biased, misleading, or faulty, an understanding of sport management research is essential.

pseudoscience—Information that appears to be based on systematic research when it is not.

One way to determine whether a piece of research qualifies as science or pseudoscience is to analyze it using the 15 questions for judging the quality of research listed earlier. If it is not clear who conducted the research or what their credentials are, if few details are provided about the sample or research methods, and if no mention is made of the validity and reliability of the measures or indicators used, you should be highly suspicious of the claims being made. It is possible that a systematic approach to research was used, but until that can be verified, you should critically question whether the conclusions and recommendations are justified and be hesitant about relying on the information when making decisions.

LEARNING ACTIVITY

Find an example of pseudoscience by locating a popular press book or information on the Internet that espouses a management theory or trend that does not appear to be backed up through the systematic collection and analysis of data. Based on the 15 questions used to judge the quality of research, what features of the article appeared to be trustworthy, and what features made you cautious about accepting the claims being made?

Basic and Applied Research

The social sciences use two general types of research: basic and applied. While there are not always clear distinctions between these two types of research and they can be highly interrelated, it is helpful to understand some of the differences in their goals and approaches. **Basic research** is usually done in universities or research institutes with the goal of advancing a body of knowledge in a subject area. It focuses on developing theories or explanations for why things operate in certain ways. When conducting basic research, direct practical outcomes are not always immediately apparent even though questions often arise from practical problems, and the findings can often provide a foundation for developing new managerial systems and approaches.

basic research—Research designed to test or develop theories to add to the body of knowledge.

In the sport management field, basic research has been done on topics such as leadership, organizational change, and organizational structure. For example, in my own doctoral research (Frisby, 1986), I was interested in determining whether elements of Max Weber's theory of bureaucracy existed in volunteer Canadian national sport organizations (NSOs) that manage various Olympic and non-Olympic amateur sports. In the 1800s Weber predicted that bureaucracy would become dominant in business, government, education, religion, and other institutions because it provided structure and stability, even though we often associate bureaucracy with "red tape" and inefficiency. I was interested in determining whether this theory held up in a volunteer sport context and whether sport organizations that were more bureaucratic in structure were also more effective in achieving their goals. I then set out to determine how to measure the various features of bureaucracy and organizational effectiveness in the NSOs. To do this, I developed items for a survey that was sent to the managers of all of these organizations. After conducting a statistical analysis of the survey data, I was able to conclude that the more bureaucratic the structure was in these volunteer sport organizations, the more likely they were to achieve their goals of generating revenues and placing teams or athletes highly in international competition. However, I further hypothesized that if these organizations were to become too bureaucratic, effectiveness could eventually decline. In the end, I provided the managers of the sport organizations who participated in my study with recommendations on their organization's structure because my data were collected and analyzed in a systematic way. However, my main motivation at the time was to add to the sport management literature by drawing on, testing, and advancing an existing managerial theory through the study of sport organizations.

Most sport managers will be interested in **applied research** because it is designed to help answer practical questions such as how to increase market share and customer satisfaction. While the purpose of applied sport management studies is often more narrowly defined and the aim is to produce practical results that are of immediate use, a systematic approach to research is still required.

applied research—Research designed to answer practical sport management questions.

Some common types of applied research in sport management include marketing research, feasibility studies, and evaluation research. Marketing research covers a broad range of topics including testing spectator or client preferences, analyzing the impact of promotional strategies, and determining the effect of pricing strategies used by competitors. Feasibility studies focus on the costs and benefits of launching new initiatives and determining whether there is sufficient demand, appropriate locations, enough trained staff, and so on to justify proceeding.

There are many different types of evaluation research, but all of them address the fundamental question, How are we doing? This may include an assessment of how well existing policies, programs, and strategies are working or of improvements required to increase customer satisfaction levels. Needs assessments, program evaluations, and employee performance appraisals are all examples of applied evaluation research (Chelladurai, 1999).

Action research is another type of applied research, and, although it is less commonly used in the sport management field, it is a way of bringing study participants, practitioners, and researchers together to tackle problems of mutual concern (Frisby, Crawford & Dorer, 1997; Greenwood & Levin, 1998). For example, it is well known that those living below the poverty line are much less likely to participate in sport because of the high costs of programs, apparel, and equipment. By collaborating on all phases of the research process with those living in poverty, community sport managers can identify their barriers to participation and develop action strategies for overcoming them.

Quantitative and Qualitative Data

One way to determine whether a systematic approach to research has been undertaken is to examine the information source to ascertain whether empirical data have been collected. We usually associate data with numbers or statistics, but sport managers rely on many different types of data. Data in the form of numbers are known as **quantitative data**, while data in the form of words, pictures, or actions are known as **qualitative data**. The choice of data depends on the research question, and sometimes both types of data are required to fully address our research questions. For example, a program evaluation might entail tracking the number of new and repeat participants as well as conducting interviews with them to determine if any changes to the program are desired. Common methods of collecting quantitative and qualitative data will be discussed later in this chapter.

quantitative data—Data in the form of numbers.

qualitative data—Data in the form of words, pictures, or actions.

Validity and Reliability

Prior to determining whether to collect quantitative, qualitative data, or both, researchers must determine how they are going to measure the various managerial concepts under investigation. Since many concepts are abstract (we cannot touch them or observe them directly), it is rarely possible to come up with perfect measures or indicators of them. For example, managerial concepts such as bureaucracy, organizational effectiveness, and customer satisfaction are abstract and multifaceted and therefore difficult to define and measure. One way to measure abstract concepts is to create appropriate survey questions or other data collection techniques.

For example, centralized decision making is a key feature of a bureaucratic structure. In order to measure this abstract concept, I asked the NSO managers to indicate who usually made decisions in their organizations. If the managers indicated that they usually made decisions, this would mean that decision making was centralized or concentrated at the top levels of the organization. If the managers indicated that various volunteer committees made the decisions, then I could surmise that a decentralized or less bureaucratic structure was operating because persons in other levels of the organization had decision-making power. Observing how decisions were actually made at NSO meetings would be another way of operationalizing or measuring the decision-making structure. This example illustrates how different research methods can be used to translate abstract concepts of interest to sport managers into quantitative or qualitative data that can be analyzed and interpreted. It is important to note, however, that our measures are rarely perfect indicators of the abstract concept under investigation.

To determine how well our quantitative and qualitative data collection techniques measure abstract concepts of interest, **validity** and **reliability** are important considerations. Validity assesses how well our measures capture the meaning of abstract concepts, while reliability refers to how consistent or dependable our measures are (Neuman, 2000). A sport manager can have more faith in research if the measures used capture the meaning of the abstract managerial concept and hold up over time and across different groups.

validity—The degree to which measures capture the meaning of abstract concepts.

reliability—The consistency or dependability of measures of abstract concepts.

To illustrate, a manager of a fitness facility can assume that low prices, cleanliness, and qualified instructors contribute to customer satisfaction. If customers confirm that only these three factors contribute to their satisfaction, then the measures devised by the manager would have high validity because they fully capture the meaning of the concept. However, if customers reveal that other factors such as variety in program offerings and having the latest weight training equipment also contribute to their satisfaction, then these additional measures should be incorporated into survey or interview questions.

Using this same example, the fitness facility manager should also consider whether the measures of customer satisfaction are reliable by testing whether they are consistent over time and across different groups when all other conditions remain constant. If customers were asked to fill out a customer satisfaction survey twice and similar results are found both times, then the measures are dependable over time. If different subgroups (e.g., men and women) answer survey questions accurately (e.g., by not differentially overstating or understating their age and education), then the indicator is reliable across subgroups.

While quantitative and qualitative researchers often use different terminology and techniques for assessing validity and reliability, both groups are interested in producing results that are credible, dependable, and believable (Marshall & Rossman, 1999). Some of the strategies they use to achieve these goals are carefully defining abstract concepts, examining results over time and across subgroups, and using multiple sources of data.

In addition to understanding key concepts, sport managers must also have an understanding of what a systematic approach to research entails. The next section offers further information on the various components of the research process.

The Research Process

A number of steps should be followed when conducting research. As decisions are made at each step, adjustments in the other steps are usually required. Therefore, it is not appropriate to view the research process in a linear fashion. As figure 20.1 reveals, considering each step helps to clarify the purpose of the study as well as the other steps that make up the process. An example of each step is provided in "Scenario: An Example to Illustrate the Research Process" on page 418.

Clarifying the Purpose of the Study

Writing a clear purpose statement that is not too broad or vague is the first step of the research process. Sport managers often have specific topics or issues in mind, but they must focus the purpose of the study in order to make decisions about the other steps in the research process. If the purpose of the study is vague or too broad, researchers will have considerable difficulty determining what research methods are most appropriate. Talking with other members of the organi-

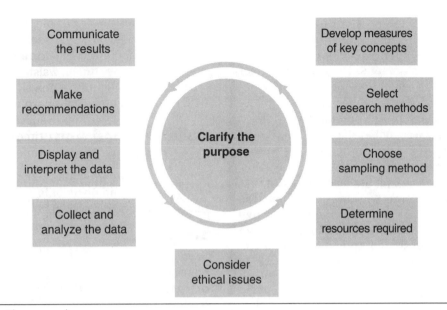

Figure 20.1 The research process.

zation to clarify the intent of the study, identifying specific information gaps, and determining how the information will be used will help to clarify the purpose.

Developing Measures of Key Concepts

In addition to clarifying the purpose, researchers usually pose research questions or hypotheses to guide their research. All key concepts contained in these statements must be clearly defined. Referring to definitions provided in up-to-date management textbooks, journal articles, or research reports is often helpful. Once key concepts are clearly defined, researchers can rely on existing survey scales or develop their own questions to measure them.

Selecting Research Methods

Having determined the purpose and the research questions or hypotheses of the study, researchers must then decide what research methods to use. As discussed in more detail later, surveys, secondary data analyses, document analyses, interviews, focus groups, and observations are commonly used research methods in the sport management field.

Choosing a Sampling Method

Sampling is a strategy used by researchers when it is impossible or impractical to include all members of the study population. When polls are conducted to predict voting patterns in political elections, the time and cost involved in polling all citizens in a nation is prohibitive. By sampling carefully, researchers can often predict with a high degree of accuracy what the outcome of the vote would be if it were held at a particular point in time. However, since it is never possible to predict results for a population with 100% accuracy when sampling, researchers must report the degree of accuracy and margins of error that can be expected.

Researchers approach sampling differently depending on whether they are collecting quantitative or qualitative data. When the aim is to collect quantitative data, the overall goal of sampling is usually to generalize the findings from a smaller sample to a larger population. In this instance, probability sampling methods are employed. Randomness, the key principle underlying probability sampling methods, ensures that each person in the study population has an equal chance of being selected. For example, the manager of a ski resort might be interested in polling snowboarders to determine what new jumps should be added to the ski hill. He or she could then put existing names on the membership list in a hat and draw them at random before soliciting opinions. Using this method, each snowboarder who is a current member (i.e., the population) has an equal chance of being selected to participate in the study.

Researchers collecting qualitative data are more interested in obtaining in-depth understandings of topics or issues and are usually not interested in generalizing their findings from a sample to a population. Therefore, they usually use nonprobability sampling techniques to study people, events, or situations. The goal is to select study participants who represent the study population even though it may not be possible to select them randomly. Using the previous example, if membership lists were not available, the ski resort manager could approach snowboarders on the hill on a particular day and ask them to name other snowboarders who frequently use the hill so that he or she can ask them the same questions. This type of nonprobability sampling is known as snowball sampling, and it is an appropriate choice if the researcher is interested in finding out about the social networks of people or organizations. A weakness of this approach is that the views of those selected may not adequately represent the views of the larger study population.

Determining the Resources Required

Undertaking research requires time, expertise, finances, equipment, and supplies. After calculating the resources required, researchers sometimes have to adjust the purpose, sampling technique, or other dimensions of the study. For example, it may be necessary to select a smaller sample when conducting survey research if, after developing the budget, the mailing costs are found to be prohibitive.

Considering Ethical Issues

Researchers must carefully consider a number of ethical issues before undertaking their research. Sport management faculty members often obtain ethical approval from their colleges or universities before conducting research. While sport managers normally do not require this type of formal ethical approval, taking ethics into account will ensure a professional approach to research and will help maintain good public relations.

In terms of ethical issues, study participants have the right to know what the purpose of the study is, who is sponsoring the research, and how the research will be used before deciding whether to participate. Participation in research should be voluntary, and study participants should have the right to decide whether their names or their organizations will be identified in the research. Because sport management research focuses on the practices and policies of sport organizations, the possible repercussions of the research should be anticipated. For example, it would be unethical for a sport manager to ask a field placement student to pose as a potential customer in order to obtain information about a competitor. If the competitor found out that the student was not really a potential customer, the student's reputation and that of the field placement organization would be tarnished.

Collecting and Analyzing Quantitative Data

Surveys, secondary data analyses, and content analyses are common techniques used in the sport management field to collect quantitative data.

Surveys

Surveys can be mailed, posted on the Internet, conducted over the telephone or through e-mail, or used when intercepting people at different types of sport events. Surveys are used when researchers are interested in hearing from a sample of persons about a particular topic. Those who agree to participate are asked a series of questions, and their responses are usually recorded in a numerical format. For example, in a survey designed to gauge purchasing patterns, spectators may be intercepted and asked if they purchased merchandise available at a sport event. If a respondent says yes, the response could be assigned a value of 1, and if the respondent says no, the response could be given a value of 2. The researcher can then enter the values reported from all respondents into a spreadsheet to determine the percentage of spectators who purchased merchandise at the event.

Other common ways of converting responses on surveys into quantitative data include providing a five-point scale for questions soliciting opinions or asking persons to rank-order their preferences. Open-ended questions can be used on surveys, but responses are often difficult to code numerically. When researchers want to ask a number of open-ended questions, interviews or focus groups are a more appropriate choice of methodology (Neuman, 2000). Depending on the type of numerical data collected, researchers can compute a number of different statistics on spreadsheets or with computer software programs to reveal patterns in the data that they can then display in tables, graphs, or charts.

LEARNING ACTIVITY

As a class project, develop a one-page survey to determine the career aspirations of sport management students. Develop five or six survey questions that measure different aspects of the abstract concept "career aspirations." Ensure that responses provided for each question can be assigned a numerical value. Have each student fill out the survey and enter his or her responses onto one computer spreadsheet. Calculate the percentage of students who responded to the different values for each question and compare the findings. Discuss the possible explanations for the similarities and differences observed.

Secondary Data Analysis

Obtaining existing statistics that were collected previously for another reason, perhaps by a government agency or a research firm, and reanalyzing them to address a research question of interest is called secondary data analysis. To illustrate, entrepreneurs interested in starting new sport-related businesses will commonly examine demographic data available through government sources on populations residing in a specific geographic area as one strategy for determining if there will be sufficient demand for their business. Secondary data analysis refers to the fact that a researcher collected the data previously for another purpose, while primary data analysis means that the researcher collected the data firsthand.

Content Analysis

Conducting a content analysis is a third common way of collecting numerical data. This involves examining the content of written materials (e.g., budget statements or newspaper articles) and recording certain information or features about them. For example, a newly hired sport manager who is preparing for an upcoming budget meeting may want to conduct a content analysis of previous financial statements to determine what the major expenditures and revenues have been in the

past. Table 20.1 summarizes some of the major advantages and disadvantages of the common methods used to collect quantitative data.

Collecting and Analyzing Qualitative Data

Interviews, focus groups, observations, and content analyses are common techniques for collecting qualitative data to shed light on the meanings that people associate with various sport-related activities. Usually the goal of collecting qualitative research is to obtain a better understanding of how people are thinking or feeling about an issue or situation. For example, a professor can review a sport management student's résumé and academic transcripts in order to locate a suitable field placement for that student (e.g., a content analysis), but interviews with the student will reveal more in-depth information about his or her career goals and interests. Qualitative data are often displayed as direct word-for-word quotes made by respondents; these quotes can also be used as testimonials to promote key attributes or benefits of products, services, or programs. Using the previous example, the professor could conduct follow-up interviews with students upon completion of their field placements to determine if the program was successful and then use their direct comments when developing promotional material to advertise the benefits of the program to future applicants (e.g., "This internship was a terrific learning experience that helped me clarify my career goals"). With the student's permission, the professor could use this type of qualitative data to promote the program to new students the following year. Qualitative data can also be displayed in the form of photographs or video clips. Computer

Table 20.1 Common Methods of Collecting Quantitative Data

Method	Main advantage	Main disadvantage
Mailed surveys	Can be used on larger samples	Low response rate
Internet or e-mail surveys	Quick response is possible	Only those with computers can participate
Telephone surveys	Immediate response	Respondents may feel their privacy is invaded
Intercept surveys	Immediate response	Ensuring sample is representative
Secondary data analysis	Avoid costs of primary research	Not all data required may be available
Content analysis	Budgets, marketing material, planning documents, and media broadcasts are usually available	Not all data required may be available in these documents

software programs are available to help manage and analyze large qualitative data sets.

Interviews

Face-to-face or telephone interviews are commonly used in sport management research because they often have a higher response rate than mail-in surveys. Researchers are able to clarify any confusion resulting from the questions asked, and more in-depth responses can usually be obtained (Palys, 1997). While making direct contact with people through interviews is thought to humanize the research process, the amount of time required to conduct one-on-one interviews is a major disadvantage of this data collection method. Careful consideration must be given to the interview questions asked, and it is advisable to seek permission from respondents to tape-record interviews so that an accurate recording of responses can be obtained. Interviews can be used in combination with written surveys to provide information on how to properly word survey questions, and following surveys to help uncover possible explanations for the results.

LEARNING ACTIVITY

After developing the survey to examine the career aspirations of sport management students in the previous learning activity, work with your classmates to develop five or six interview questions that would reveal additional information on this topic. Working in pairs, conduct interviews with your classmates and use tape recorders to record the responses. Avoid questions with yes or no answers, and use follow-up questions to probe for in-depth responses. Transcribe the taped responses into a word processing file and compare the responses. How did the interview data augment the survey data collected previously? Compare the advantages and disadvantages of using surveys and interviews to examine student career aspirations.

Focus Groups

Focus groups are another method used to solicit qualitative data. A major advantage of this technique is that researchers can interview 8 to 10 people at the same time (Inglis, 1992). Focus groups are often used in marketing research when researchers want to test new products or promotional strategies on a specific target group. Similar to interviews, care must be taken when developing questions, and tape-recording sessions will help ensure the accurate recording of the data. However, researchers must be trained to manage group dynamics when conducting focus groups because some participants may dominate discussions so that the full range of views on the topic are not revealed.

Observations

While researchers can often quantify observations of different types of behavior or sport settings, they can also record them in written field

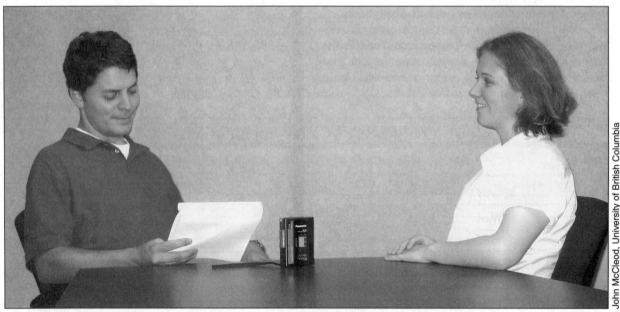

Sport management students practicing interviews.

John McCleod, University of British Columbia

notes. To illustrate, the problem of parental violence at children's sport events has been receiving considerable media attention. If you were the manager of a sport program or facility in which there were a growing number of complaints about parental behavior, you could conduct an observational study to determine if the complaints were accurate. You may decide to attend games randomly and develop an observation checklist to record the numbers and types of inappropriate parental behavior. You could also write your thoughts about what is causing or escalating the problems and possible strategies for reducing it. By doing so, you would have developed a systematic way of collecting data that will likely help you arrive at a better solution than if you had failed to conduct research systematically. Conducting interviews and focus groups with parents, players, coaches, and referees and finding out how other sport managers have attempted to handle this problem would be other valuable sources of information.

Content Analysis

A content analysis of documents, media broadcasts, and other types of communications can be used to collect both quantitative and qualitative data. To illustrate, a sport management student might be interested in determining whether female and male athletes receive equal television coverage and treatment during the Olympic Games. A content analysis that would generate quantitative data related to this question would entail recording on-air coverage over a designated time frame and totaling the number of hours devoted to the coverage of each gender. In terms of qualitative data, the content of the comments made by Olympic sportscasters could be analyzed to determine whether common stereotypes about male and female athletic performances are still being perpetuated (Kane & Greendorfer, 1994). If an emphasis is placed on the physical appearance rather than the athletic accomplishments of female athletes in comparison to male athletes, this would indicate differential treatment by the media based on the gender of the athlete.

Table 20.2 summarizes some of the main advantages and disadvantages of methods commonly used by sport management researchers to collect qualitative data.

LEARNING ACTIVITY

Locate a recent issue of a sport management journal and determine how many articles contained quantitative data, qualitative data, or a combination of both types of data. Choose one article and determine whether surveys, secondary data analysis, content analysis, interviews, focus groups, observations, or other techniques were used to collect the data.

Displaying and Interpreting the Data

As mentioned previously, quantitative data are usually displayed in graphs, tables, and charts, while qualitative data are usually displayed as direct quotes, pictures, or other types of visuals. When interpreting the data, researchers should provide alternative explanations for the results. Sometimes these alternative explanations contradict one another and further research is required to determine which competing explanation has more merit.

Making Recommendations

When making practical recommendations, researchers must be sure they are well founded given the results. Sport managers should be suspicious of recommendations that do not deal directly with the purpose of the study or that generalize the findings improperly. For example, the researchers of a study referred to in chapter 17 that is also discussed in the following scenario (Chalip & Leyns, 2002) took care not to generalize their findings beyond the 22 businesses examined

Table 20.2 Common Methods of Collecting Qualitative Data

Method	Main advantage	Main disadvantage
Interviews	In-depth responses are possible	Time intensive
Focus groups	Less time intensive than interviews	Managing group dynamics
Observations	Can confirm or refute other types of data	Actions are often open to multiple interpretations
Content analysis	Data can be collected without talking to people directly	Data obtained are often open to multiple interpretations

because they used a nonprobability sampling technique. The recommendations they made pertained directly to the businesses studied and provided managers with important information.

Communicating the Results

The final step in the research process is determining how best to communicate the results. A variety of formats can be used such as final reports, journal articles, and verbal presentations. Researchers should tailor their communication strategies by carefully considering the intended audience. For example, sport managers might be more interested in the findings and recommendations, while academicians might be more interested in hearing about the research methods employed.

Scenario: An Example to Illustrate the Research Process

Laurence Chalip, a professor from the University of Texas, and Anna Leyns, a marketing executive for PRISM, a sport marketing firm in the United Kingdom, published an article titled "Local Business Leveraging of a Sport Event: Managing an Event for Economic Benefit" in the *Journal of Sport Management* in 2002. The article contained information on four qualitative studies conducted to examine the tactics used by local businesses to leverage visitor spending during a major sport event. The researchers argued that while a growing body of literature touts the economic benefits of hosting sport events, there is little evidence about whether local business managers know how to effectively leverage sales during an event.

Purpose of the Study

The purpose of the study was to determine whether small local businesses on the Gold Coast of Australia attempted to leverage sales when the city hosted the Honda Indy car race. A clear and specific focus is apparent in the purpose statement because leveraging tactics were specified as the abstract managerial concept under investigation, small local businesses in one geographic area were sampled, and one specific sport event served as the case study.

Measures of Key Concepts

The researchers defined leveraging tactics as "the means by which local businesses cultivate spending by event visitors, particularly impulse spending" (Chalip, 2001). Leveraging tactics were measured by asking managers of small local businesses whether their businesses attempted to capitalize on the Indy. If managers identified leveraging tactics, the researchers asked whether they had been effective. If they had not used leveraging tactics, the researchers asked why they had not implemented promotional activities during the Indy.

Research Methods

Given the purpose of the study, interviews with managers of small local businesses were an appropriate choice of methodology. The interviews allowed the researchers to obtain an in-depth understanding of managers' reasons for choosing to leverage the event or not and provided insights into their business practices.

Sampling Method

Because the goal of this study was to understand managerial practices of a select group rather than to generalize the findings to a larger population, the researchers used a nonprobability sampling technique known as quota sampling. Quota sampling helped to ensure that there were differences in the sample to represent the characteristics of local businesses on the Gold Coast. In this case, the researchers wanted to ensure representation from different types of small businesses based on their proximity to the event site. As a result, a total of 22 managers were interviewed, including 8 restaurant managers, 7 retail store managers, and 7 hoteliers. For each industry, the researchers chose businesses that were inside the event venue, adjacent to the event venue, and one to three kilometers away from the event venue.

Resources Required

The budget required to conduct the study was minimal because the researchers, who have considerable research experience and expertise, conducted the interviews themselves and inputted and analyzed the data. The equipment and supplies required included tape recorders, audiotapes, and a computer. The researchers did invest a considerable amount of time traveling to the businesses for the interviews, conducting the 22 interviews, transcribing them, participating in a task force, and writing the journal article.

Ethical Issues

Anonymity was one ethical issue that the researchers had to consider because most managers do not want details about their business operations made public. In particular, obtaining financial statements before and after the event would have allowed the researchers to determine whether sales increased during the event, but understandably, the managers were reluctant to release this information. The researchers assured the managers that their names, the names of their businesses, and their financial information would not be identified in the reporting of the research.

Collecting and Analyzing the Data

The researchers contacted the managers in person by visiting the businesses to arrange interview times. Interviews were tape-recorded and transcribed word for word into a word processing file. The researchers used Strauss's (1987) open coding technique to generate themes (e.g., efforts to promote businesses during the Indy) and subthemes (e.g., creating displays that captured the atmosphere of the Indy) identified in the interview data.

Displaying and Interpreting the Data

Because they collected qualitative data, the researchers displayed the results in the form of direct quotes. For example, the following response was typical of the rationale used by managers for not using leveraging tactics during the event: "It sells itself, basically. We get a lot of repeat business. That's about how it works" (Chalip & Leyns, 2002, p. 139).

The researchers found that only 8 of the 22 businesses employed tactics to leverage the Indy. They provided a number of possible explanations for this finding. Businesses close to the event felt that promotions were unnecessary because they assumed business would automatically increase during the event, while businesses located away from the event felt they were too far away to be attractive to Indy visitors.

Making Recommendations

Chalip and Leyns (2002) used an innovative approach to provide managers with recommendations on how to encourage visitor spending at future events. They formed a task force of nine experts (representing the areas of tourism, event management, marketing, hotel management, and small business) to consider the challenges of and prospects for leveraging the Indy. One of the task force's recommendations was that neighborhood businesses should band together to implement a coordinated strategy rather than initiating independent efforts on their own.

Communicating the Results

Chalip and Leyns shared their findings with a larger Gold Coast Visioning Project that involved a partnership with the city and local businesses to reposition the Gold Coast within the tourism industry. In addition, because leveraging tactics are of interest to sport management researchers, educators, and students, the researchers communicated their findings in the *Journal of Sport Management*.

SUMMARY

Sport management research is available in a variety of sources, and managers are increasingly relying on it to make informed decisions. In order to assess what types of sport management research are reliable and credible, a sound foundation in research is required. Understanding key concepts such as science and pseudoscience, basic and applied research, qualitative and quantitative data, and reliability and validity, as well as the research process, can help sport managers judge the quality of research so they can make sound decisions.

Engaging in the research process can be highly stimulating and rewarding. Clarifying the purpose

419

of the study is an important first step. Developing measures that adequately represent the abstract concepts of interest; selecting the research methods and sample; ensuring that research is conducted in an ethical way; and collecting, analyzing, and interpreting the results are other interrelated steps in the research process. Effectively communicating the results and making well-founded recommendations can help sport managers improve

their practices and may advance the body of knowledge in the sport management field.

In addition to incorporating research into their course work, sport management students can attend conferences, join associations that promote sport management research such as the North American Society for Sport Management, and refer to publications within the sport management and business fields.

REVIEW QUESTIONS

1. Discuss five key ways that pseudoscience differs from science, and then explain why a scientific approach can provide sport managers with more trustworthy information on which to base decisions.

2. Differentiate between basic and applied research and provide an example of each in the sport management field.

3. Differentiate between quantitative and qualitative data and describe one common data

collection technique for each. In your answer, provide one main advantage and one main disadvantage of each data collection technique discussed.

4. Once the purpose of a study has been determined, what are the other nine steps in the research process? Choose one of these steps and discuss how the purpose of the study might be refined after taking this step into account.

REFERENCES

Chalip, L. (2001). Sport and tourism: Capitalizing on the linkage. In D. Kluka & G. Schilling (Eds.), *The business of sport* (pp. 78-89). Oxford, UK: Meyer & Meyer.

Chalip, L., & Leyns, A. (2002). Local business leveraging of a sport event: Managing an event for economic benefit. *Journal of Sport Management, 16*, 132-158.

Chelladurai, P. (1999). *Human resource management in sport and recreation.* Champaign, IL: Human Kinetics.

Frisby, W. (1986). The organizational structure and effectiveness of voluntary organizations: The case of Canadian national sport governing bodies. *Journal of Park and Recreation Administration, 4*, 61-74.

Frisby, W., Crawford, S., & Dorer, T. (1997). Reflections on participatory action research: The case of low-income women accessing local physical activity services. *Journal of Sport Management, 11*, 8-28.

Greenwood, D.J., & Levin, M. (1998). *Introduction to action research: Social research for social change.* Thousand Oaks, CA: Sage.

Inglis, S. (1992). Focus groups as a useful qualitative methodology in sport management. *Journal of Sport Management, 16*, 173-178.

Kane, M.J., & Greendorfer, S. (1994). The media's role in accommodating and resisting stereotyped images of women in sport. In P. Creedon (Ed.), *Women, media and sport: Challenging gender values* (pp. 28-44). Thousand Oaks, CA: Sage.

Marshall, C., & Rossman, G.B. (1999). *Designing qualitative research* (3rd ed.). Thousand Oaks, CA: Sage.

Neuman, W.L. (2000). *Social research methods: Qualitative and quantitative approaches* (4th ed.). Boston: Allyn and Bacon.

Palys, T. (1997). *Research decisions: Quantitative and qualitative perspectives* (2nd ed.). Toronto: Harcourt Brace Canada.

Slack, T. (1997). *Understanding sport organizations: The application of organization theory.* Champaign, IL: Human Kinetics.

Strauss, A.L. (1987). *Qualitative analysis for social scientists.* New York: Cambridge University Press.

Index _____

About the Editors

Janet B. Parks, DA, is a distinguished teaching professor, former graduate studies coordinator, and former sport management division chair for the School of Human Movement, Sport, and Leisure Studies at Bowling Green State University in Ohio.

She was a founding member of the North American Society for Sport Management (NASSM), which has honored her with the Earle F. Zeigler Award for professional achievement (1992) and the Distinguished Service Award (2001). She is a NASSM research fellow; a fellow in the Research Consortium of the American Alliance for Health, Physical Education, Recreation and Dance; and the recipient of the Outstanding Achievement Award from the Sport Management Council of the National Association for Sport and Physical Education. In 1994-1995 and 2002-2003 she was an honorary fellow in the Women's Studies Research Center at the University of Wisconsin at Madison.

Janet B. Parks

Her published works include textbooks, book chapters, journal articles, and research reports. Sport management career development, sexist language, and gender issues in sport are among her research interests.

She was the first editor in chief for the Sport Management Library and was one of the founding co-editors of the *Journal of Sport Management*. Widely respected in the field, Dr. Parks makes frequent presentations to professional societies and serves as a consultant to several university sport management programs.

Dr. Parks received her doctor of arts in physical education from Middle Tennessee State University and completed postdoctoral study at the University of Wisconsin at Madison. She makes her home in Bowling Green, Ohio, where she enjoys biking and working out in her free time.

Jerome Quarterman, PhD, is an associate professor and member of the graduate faculty in sport management at Florida State University. He teaches a wide range of graduate courses, including Organizational Theory; Research Methods; Organizational Behavior; Human Resource Management; Intercollegiate Athletics Administration; Race and Sport in Society; and Ethics in Sport Management. He has also taught students in both the undergraduate and graduate degree programs at Bowling Green State University.

Dr. Quarterman's prior work experiences include teaching at Hampton University, Alabama State University, Kentucky State University, and Southern University and serving as intercollegiate athletics director at Central State University and Alabama State University.

He has been published in the *Journal of Sport Management,* the *Physical Educator,* and the *International Journal of Sport Psychology.* His current research interest is applying organizational behavior research to sport industry management.

Jerome Quarterman

Dr. Quarterman received his bachelor of science degree from Savannah State University, a master of education degree from Kent State University, and a doctorate of philosophy from Ohio State University. Dr. Quarterman is the proud parent of two grown children, Terrance and Michele.

About the Contributors

Robertha Abney, PhD, is the associate athletic director and an associate professor at Slippery Rock University. She has distinguished herself as an authority in minorities in leadership roles in sport. She currently serves on the National Collegiate Athletic Association (NCAA) Division II Management Council and Committee on Infractions. She served on the NCAA Division II Nominating Committee from 1997 to 2001 and was president of the National Association for Girls and Women in Sport (NAGWS). Dr. Abney was selected to represent the International Council for Health, Physical Education, Recreation, Dance and Sport in Beijing, China. She continues to give presentations and to publish.

Robin Ammon Jr. is the sport management program coordinator at Slippery Rock University, Pennsylvania. He earned a doctor of education degree in sport administration from the University of Northern Colorado in 1993. His areas of research include legal liabilities in sport, risk management in sport and athletics, and management and marketing components for special events. He has written more than a dozen articles in refereed journals, five chapters in sport management books, and two textbooks. He has presented several times at local, regional, national, and international conferences on a variety of topics about facilities including legal, security, and crowd management issues. In 2002 he was elected president of the North American Society for Sport Management (NASSM). Dr. Ammon is the coauthor of *Sport Facility and Event Management,* a comprehensive text for anyone with an interest in or association with the sport management industry.

Ketra L. Armstrong, PhD, is an assistant professor of sport management at Ohio State University. Her teaching and research specialization is sport marketing and sport consumer behavior. Her research—which has appeared in the *Journal of Sport Management, Sport Marketing Quarterly, Journal of Sport and Social Issues, Journal of Sport Behavior, Women in Sport and Physical Activities Journal,* and *International Journal of Sport Management*—focuses on marketing sport to consumers and women of African descent. Dr. Armstrong is a former conference sport administrator, assistant athletics director, college basketball coach, and student-athlete (basketball player). Over the years Dr. Armstrong has had integral roles in the management and marketing of numerous national and

international sport events. She is also a lecturer and consultant to universities and sport organizations in Africa and the Caribbean. Dr. Armstrong is the former vice president for marketing for the National Association of Girls and Women in Sport, and she is a board member for the National Women's Hall of Fame. Dr. Armstrong is also a freelance sport broadcaster.

F. Wayne Blann, EdD, earned his doctorate degree from Boston University and is a professor of sport management at Ithaca College. In 1986, he developed the sport marketing course in sport management curriculum at Ithaca College and continues to teach this course. Dr. Blann pioneered research on American collegiate and professional athletes' and coaches' career transitions. He has served as consultant to the NBA, the NFL, the NHL Players' Association, and Major League Baseball Players' Association. Since 1996, the Professional Athletes Career Transition Program (PACTP) developed by Dr. Blann has served as the model for athlete career education programs. He has given several presentations at national and international conferences and has published articles in sport management, applied sport psychology, sport sociology, and applied research in coaching and athletics journals and newsletters.

Robert Boucher, PhD, professor and chair of the department of kinesiology at the University of Windsor, Ontario, has extensive experience as a leader in the academic and applied areas of sport management. He has served as president of the North American Society for Sport Management (NASSM) and the Canadian Intramural Recreation Association (CIRA). He was the head of the department of athletics and recreational services at the University of Windsor from 1987 to 1996. He served as the chef de maison for the 1997 World University Games in Sicily, Italy, and as the assistant chef for the 1995 World University Games in Fukoka, Japan. Dr. Boucher has published an edited book with Dr. W. James Weese and has written articles that appear in a variety of academic and professional journals. Dr. Boucher received the Dr. Earle F. Zeigler Lecture Award for contributions to sport management by NASSM in 1996 and the Distinguished Service Award in 2002.

Jacquelyn Cuneen, EdD, is a professor in Bowling Green State University's internationally renowned sport management program. Her main teaching areas are sport and event promotion and sport management field experiences. Dr. Cuneen is an established scholar whose research focuses on sport-related advertising and professional preparation of sport managers. She has authored or coauthored more than 30 scholarly and research articles. She is coauthor of *Sport Management Field Experiences,* the first textbook written specifically for sport management experiential education and the first publication in Fitness Information Technology (FIT), Inc.'s Sport Management Library Series. Dr. Cuneen is a charter research fellow in the North American Society for Sport Management. Prior to her academic career, Dr. Cuneen was account executive, director of women's programming, and educational correspondent for two New York State-based ABC radio affiliates. She is a former president of the North American Society for Sport Management, is currently Ohio's representative to the National Association for Girls and Women in Sport, and was the 2001 West Virginia University Sport Management Distinguished Alumna of the Year. She was coeditor of the *Journal of Sport Management* 2001 special issue, *Sport in the New Millennium.*

Timothy D. DeSchriver, PhD, is an assistant professor in the department of sport management at the University of Massachusetts at Amherst. He earned his doctor of education degree in physical education with an emphasis in sport administration from the University of Northern Colorado. He has worked as a field economist for the U.S. Department of Labor, served as interim associate athletic director at the University of Northern Colorado, and spent four years as an assistant professor at Western Carolina University. He currently teaches classes on sport finance and sport economics at both the undergraduate and graduate levels. Dr. DeSchriver's research interests are sport consumer demand, pro sport ownership incentives, and sport facility financing. He has published articles in the *Journal of Sport Management, Eastern Economic Journal, Sport Marketing Quarterly, International Sports Journal,* and *Street & Smith's SportsBusiness Journal.* He has been involved in research projects for the NCAA, the Major Indoor Soccer League, and the National Steeplechase Association. He was also coauthor of the textbook *Sport Finance.*

Joy T. DeSensi, EdD, is currently professor and head of the sport and leisure studies department at the University of Tennessee. She earned her doctoral degree from the University of North Carolina at Greensboro. Her research interests include ethics in sport management; women in sport; and gender, race, and ethnicity in sport. She is coauthor of *Ethics and Morality in Sport Management* and has authored numerous book chapters and articles. She has served on the editorial boards of scholarly journals, was editor of the *Journal of Sport Management,* and is the current associate editor of *Quest.* She is a founding member of the North American Society for Sport Management; has served as the president of the Southern Academy of Women in Physical Activity, Sport, and Health; the Philosophic Society for the study of Sport;

and the National Association for Physical Education in Higher Education. Her professional achievements include Distinguished Alumna awards from the University of Memphis and the University of North Carolina at Greensboro, service awards, and recognitions for teaching and research.

Ted G. Fay, Phd, is associate professor and coordinator of the sport management program at SUNY Cortland in Cortland, New York. He earned his doctoral degree from the University of Massachusetts at Amherst. He serves as a research fellow at the Center of the Study of Sport at Northeastern University related to the Disability Sport Initiative. His research interests include international sport management; the Paralympic and Olympic movements; and comparative policy studies examining equity in management with respect to race, gender, and disability. Dr. Fay has worked in administrative positions with a variety of national sport governing bodies and remains actively involved in the international Paralympic movement. He was a member of the 1988 Winter Olympic team as a cross-country ski coach.

Lawrence W. Fielding, PhD, is a full professor and coordinator of the sport management program in the department of kinesiology at Indiana University. He earned his doctoral degree in sport history from the University of Maryland. He has published more than 50 articles in sport history and sport management and has conducted sport research for the past 30 years. He is a member of the North American Society for Sport History (NASSH) and presented the Stewart E. Staley Address in 1985. Dr. Fielding is also a member of the North American Society for Sport Management (NASSM) and was named an NASSM research fellow in 2002.

Wendy Frisby, PhD, is an associate professor at the University of British Columbia, where she teaches the third-year research methods course. She earned her doctoral degree in kinesiology (sociology of sport) from the University of Waterloo, Canada. Dr. Frisby was the editor of the *Journal of Sport Management* from 2000 to 2003. She is a member of the North American Society for Sport Management (NASSM) and the International Institute for the Study of Sport Management. She has published more than 30 articles in refereed journals and conference proceedings and has written several book chapters and government reports. Dr. Frisby participated in a collaborative research effort with several public sector partners and women living below the poverty line. The study identified community organizing practices that include women living in poverty in local physical activity and recreation programs as a health promotion strategy.

Heather Gibson, PhD, is an assistant professor in the department of recreation, parks, and tourism at the University of Florida at Gainesville. She has an international reputation as a scholar in sport tourism and has presented keynote addresses at international conferences in Finland and the United Kingdom. She earned her doctoral degree in sport, leisure, and exercise science from the University of Connecticut; her educational background encompasses both sport and tourism studies. She has published both conceptual and empirical work on sport tourism and is the author of one of the most widely cited articles in sport tourism, "Sport Tourism: A Critical Analysis of Research," which was published in *Sport Management Review* in 1998. Dr. Gibson, together with Laurence Chalip of the University of Texas, has been instrumental in bringing sport tourism to the attention of sport management professionals in the North American Society for Sport Management (NASSM).

James M. Gladden, PhD, is an assistant professor of sport management at the University of Massachusetts. Dr. Gladden has more than 10 years of sport marketing research and consulting experience and is an expert in brand management as applied to sport. He has published articles in academic journals and in sport industry publications. He coauthored the article "Managing

North American Major Professional Sport Teams in the New Millennium: Building, Sharing, and Maintaining Equity," which was published in the *Journal of Sport Management* in 2001. The article emphasizes the importance of generating assets through strategic alliances and the importance of focusing on and serving consumer needs. Dr. Gladden has also provided brand management consulting to several organizations, including the National Basketball Association and the Ladies Professional Golf Association. He earned his doctoral degree from the University of Massachusetts at Amherst.

B. Christine Green, PhD, is an active researcher studying consumer behavior of sport event volunteers, active sport participants, and fans in a variety of sport settings. An assistant professor at the University of Texas at Austin, Dr. Green earned her doctoral degree in sport management from the University of Maryland. She designed and implemented the volunteer management system for the British Olympic Association's pre-Games training camp and participated in the strategic planning efforts to redesign the Australian university sport system. Dr. Green was the head of the research team that studied the motivation and commitment of the Sydney 20000 Olympic volunteers. She is a member of the American Marketing Association and the North American Society of Sport Management.

Kathryn S. Hoff is an assistant professor of human resource development in the College of Technology at Bowling Green State University, where she earned her PhD in higher education administration and MEd in career and technology education. She spent more than 20 years as a human resource development practitioner responsible for internship and cooperative educa-

tion programs, college relations and recruiting, career development and management for employees, organiza-

tional change management, and training and development. Dr. Hoff currently serves as the managing director of the Academy of Human Resource Development, an international association of scholars and practitioners whose mission is research to advance human resource development.

Jason Jackson is the chairman of the EyeJax Foundation and has served on the foundation's board since its inception in July 2001. In May 2002, Jackson concluded a seven-year stay at ESPN. He was most recently the host of ESPN2's *NBA 2Night,* ESPN's *NBA Matchup,* and ESPN's *SportsCenter* and ESPN.com's NBA page. Jackson served as host for ESPN's coverage of the NBA All-Star Game and NBA Finals from 1997 to 2002. Before joining ESPN, Jackson worked at WSVN-TV in Miami as a reporter and anchor. Jackson is a graduate of Bowling Green State University with a bachelor of arts degree in communications.

Mary Jo Kane, PhD, is a full professor in the school of kinesiology and the director of the Tucker Center for Research on Girls and Women in Sport at the University of Minnesota. In 1996, Dr. Kane was awarded the first distinguished professorship related to women in sport and physical activity— the Dorothy McNeill Tucker Distinguished Chair for Women in Sport and Exercise Science. Professor Kane was elected by her peers as a fellow in the American Academy of Kinesiology and Physical Education, the highest honor in her field. Dr. Kane is an internationally recognized scholar on sport and gender. She is particularly interested in the media's treatment of female athletes. Her most recent research examines representations of adolescent female athletes in young adult sports fiction.

Stuart M. Keeley, PhD, is a professor at Bowling Green State University. He was designated Distinguished Teaching Professor of Psychology by the BGSU Board of Trustees in 1999, primarily on the basis of his commitment to the teaching of critical thinking to undergraduates both in a stand-alone course and as a component of all the courses he teaches. Dr. Keeley is coauthor of the textbook *Asking the Right Questions: A Guide to Critical Thinking,* which is now in its sixth edition. He is also the author of *Asking the Right Questions in Abnormal Psychology.* He has presented numerous workshops on various topics related to critical thinking at the International Conference on Critical Thinking and Educational Reform; his workshops emphasized tips for teaching critical thinking and designing assignments for critical thinking courses.

JoAnn Kroll is the director of career services at Bowling Green State University. Her department is responsible for career planning, student employment, cooperative education and internships, job placement, and alumni career management services for a student population of 18,000. She earned her MEd in higher education administration from Kent State University. The National Association of Colleges and Employers has twice honored her department with its prestigious Award of Excellence for Educational Programming. She served as a consultant in Russia, helping to establish the first career services center and a national network of career services professionals. She has written several book chapters and is a frequent speaker at professional conferences.

Ming Li is the director of the School of Recreation and Sport Sciences and an associate professor in sports administration at Ohio University. He received his doctor of education degree in sport administration from the University of Kansas. Dr. Li's interests include international sport management and the financial and economic aspects of sport. Before joining Ohio University, he taught at Georgia Southern University, where he coordinated the graduate and undergraduate sport management programs. He was the recipient of the 2000-2001 Award for Excellence in Service by Georgia Southern University for his contributions to his profession, the school, and the community. Dr. Li holds memberships on the editorial boards of *Journal of Sport Management, International Sports Journal,* and *International Journal of Sport Management.* He has published more than 20 articles in refereed journals, two books (*Economics of Sport* and *Badminton Everyone*), and two book chapters. He has made numerous refereed presentations at state, national, and international conferences.

Daniel F. Mahony is an associate professor and chair of the department of health promotion, physical education, and sport studies at the University of Louisville. He earned his doctoral degree in sport management from Ohio State University. He has worked for the accounting firm of Peat Marwick Main & Co., the North Hunterdon High School athletic department, the West Virginia University athletic department, the University of Cincinnati athletic department, and the Cincinnati Reds. Dr. Mahony currently teaches classes on sport finance and athletics in higher education. He is an active researcher in sport consumer behavior and intercollegiate athletics and has had articles published in *Journal of Sport Management, Sport Management Review, Sport Marketing Quarterly, International Sports Journal, International Journal of Sport Marketing and Sponsorship, International Journal of Sport Management, Professional Ethics, European Journal of Sport Management,* and *Journal of Sport and Social Issues*. He was a coauthor of the textbook *Economics of Sport.*

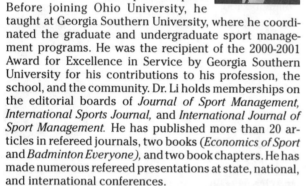

Mark A. McDonald is an associate professor of sport management at the University of Massachusetts at Amherst, where he received a PhD in 1996. Dr. McDonald has published in the *Journal of Sport Management, Sport Marketing Quarterly, International Journal of Sports Marketing & Sponsorship,* and *Journal of Sport and Social Issues.* He served as coeditor for the special *Sport Marketing*

Quarterly issue on relationship marketing in sport and is on the editorial boards for the *European Sport Management Quarterly, Sport Management Review,* and the *International Journal of Sports Marketing & Sponsorship.* He has given more than 30 presentations in the United States and abroad, and his research interests include sport sponsorship, relationship marketing, and measuring service quality for sport organizations. He has coauthored two books, *Cases in Sport Marketing* and *Sport Marketing: Managing the Exchange Process.*

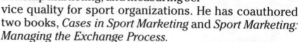

Lori Miller, EdD, is the chair of the department of kinesiology and sport studies and a professor in sport administration at Wichita State University. She has published more than 40 publications on legal issues, including "The Non-Lawyer Educator Teaching Legal Issues in Higher Education: Legally and Educationally Defensible?" in the *Journal of Legal Aspects of Sport* in 2002 and

"Online Sports Gambling: Regulation or Prohibition?" in *Journal of Legal Aspects of Sport* in 2001. She has made numerous presentations on sport and legal issues at international, national, and local conferences. Dr. Miller is a member of the Society for the Study of Legal Issues, which awarded her the 2000 Leadership Award. She also belongs to the North American Society for Sport Management, which recognized her as a research fellow in 2001.

Brenda Pitts is professor in sport marketing and the program director of sport management at Georgia State University at Atlanta, after having spent 6 years at Florida State University and 12 years at the University of Louisville. Dr. Pitts' research interests are in sport marketing, historical analysis of sport business, sport management programs and curriculum, and lesbian and gay sport business. She is author or coauthor of three sport marketing textbooks and numerous publications and presentations; she also is the author of numerous papers published in several scholarly journals such as the *Journal of Sport Management, Sport Marketing Quarterly, Journal of Vacation Marketing,* and *International Journal of Sport Management.* She has consulted in sport marketing for various sport businesses, served as a curriculum consultant in sport management, and spoken at many conferences. Dr. Pitts was the recipient of the Dr. Earle F. Zeigler Scholar Award in 2000 and became one of the first research fellows of the North American Society for Sport Management in 2001.

Catherine Pratt, PhD, is assistant to the dean for college relations at Bowling Green State University. Dr. Pratt's extensive experience in marketing and public relations includes working for Carl Buyoir and Associates in New York City, where she provided media training for professional athletes, wrote and edited radio documentaries, wrote and produced TV news video and films, and

appeared as on-air talent in news and corporate videos and films for clients such as Hallmark, Post Cereals,

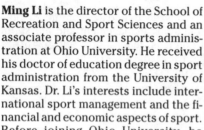

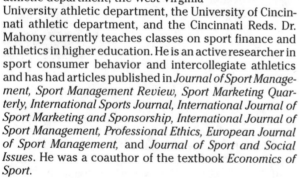

Johnson Wax, Borg-Warner, and RCA. She received her doctoral degree in mass communication from Bowling Green State University.

Ellen J. Staurowsky is professor and chair of the department of sport studies at Ithaca College. She received her doctoral degree in sport management and psychosocial aspects of sport from Temple University. On 75 occasions Dr. Staurowsky has presented to learned societies, professional associations, and conferences on gender equity and Title IX, pay equity and equal employ-ment opportunity, the exploitation of athletes, the faculty role in reforming college sport, representation of women in sport media, and the misappropriation of American Indian imagery in sport. She has published numerous articles in scholarly and professional journals. In 1998, she coauthored the book *College Athletes for Hire: The Evolution and Legacy of the NCAA Amateur Myth.* Dr. Staurowsky is a member of the editorial board for the *Journal of Sport Management, Women in Sport and Physical Activity Journal,* and *Athletic Management.* In the fall of 2002, she assumed responsibilities as president-elect of the North American Society of Sport Sociology.

G. Clayton (Clay) Stoldt is an assistant professor and serves as coordinator of the graduate sport administration program at Wichita State University. He teaches classes in sport public relations, sport marketing, and sociology of sport. Dr. Stoldt's research activities have focused on sport public relations issues. As graduate coordinator, he oversees a program that includes more than 125 graduate students. Dr. Stoldt received his doctor of education from the University of Oklahoma. Before working at Wichita State, Dr. Stoldt worked in the athletics department at Oklahoma City University where he served as sports information director, radio play-by-play broadcaster, and development officer. He also served as an adjunct instructor at both Oklahoma City University and the University of Oklahoma, where he taught courses in sport management and mass communication.

David K. Stotlar, EdD, is a professor of sport management in the areas of sport marketing and sport law at the University of Northern Colorado. He has had more than 50 articles published in professional journals and has written several book chapters in sport marketing, fitness risk management, and sport law. He is the author of several textbooks, including *Developing Successful Sport Sponsorship Plans,* which was published in 2001. He has made numerous presentations at international and national professional conferences and has conducted international seminars in sport management and marketing for various sport councils, federations, and institutes. Dr. Stotlar served as the media sub-center supervisor for the Soldier's Hollow venue at the 2002 Winter Olympic Games in Salt Lake City. He received the Earle F. Zeigler Award from the North American Society for Sport Management in 1999 and was named an NASSM research fellow in 2001.

William A. Sutton serves as vice president of team marketing services for the National Basketball Association (NBA) and holds an appointment as professor in the sports studies department at the University of Massachusetts at Amherst. Before assuming his present positions, Dr. Sutton was a principal in the consulting firm Audience Analysts and had worked for such clients as the NBA, NFL, NHS, Major League Baseball Properties, LPGA, NCAA, Hoop-It-Up, IBM, Mazda, and Sprint. A former president of the North American Society for Sport Management (NASSM), Dr. Sutton has also served as coeditor of *Sport Marketing Quarterly* and serves on the editorial board of the *Journal of Sports Marketing & Sponsorship.* Dr. Sutton is widely published in sport marketing and has made more than 100 national and international presentations. He is coauthor of the texts *Sport Marketing,* published in 2000, and *Sport Promotion and Sales Management,* published in 2002.